에듀윌 토익

단기완성 850+

LC & RC

에듀윌이
너를
지지할게

ENERGY

세상을 움직이려면

먼저 나 자신을 움직여야 한다.

– 소크라테스(Socrates)

머리말

토익 700~850점대의 학습자에 최적화된 구성

이 책은 토익 700점과 850점 사이의 정체기에 빠져 있는 학생들의 고민을 해결하는 데 목표를 두고 기획되었습니다. 그래서 그 구간의 학생들을 테스트 그룹으로 조직하여, 그들이 LC와 RC의 각 파트에서 겪는 학습상의 어려움과 자주 틀리는 문제들을 분석한 다음, 그 결과를 바탕으로 각 파트의 특성에 맞게 학습 플로우를 설계했습니다. 따라서 어떤 유형은 가볍게, 어떤 유형은 상당히 많은 분량을 할애하여 심도 있게 다루었습니다. 예를 들어, 파트 3, 4의 그래픽 유형은 LC에서 고정적으로 출제되지만 700~850점 구간의 학생들이 늘 고전을 면치 못합니다. 그래서 최근 3년간의 기출 문제를 빠짐없이 분석하여 개발한 다양한 실전 문제를 통해 해당 유형을 완벽하게 대비할 수 있게 했습니다. 파트 5의 문법 영역에서도 테스트 그룹이 자주 틀리는 문제들만을 선별하여 별도의 고난도 PRACTICE 문제로 구성했습니다.

고득점의 비결은 탄탄한 기본기와 충분한 빈출 유형 연습

고득점을 얻으려면 어려운 문제를 많이 풀어봐야 한다고 생각하기 쉽습니다. 하지만 고득점의 비결은 오히려 빈출 유형 훈련으로 다져진 탄탄한 기본기에 있습니다. 예를 들어, LC의 경우 대화에서 걸핏하면 사용되는 일상적인 패턴이 자연스럽게 귀에 들려야 중간 중간 튀어나오는 어려운 단어들을 포착해낼 여유가 생깁니다. RC에서도 빈출 어휘들의 의미와 다양한 쓰임을 정확히 알고 기본적인 문장 구조 파악 능력을 갖추고 있다면, 낯선 단어가 나와도 당황하지 않고 문맥을 통해 그 의미를 유추해낼 수 있습니다. 기본적인 패턴과 문장 구조, 어휘들을 처리하는 데 잦은 버퍼링이 생기는 상태라면, 출제 빈도가 낮은 어휘나 문제에 노력을 투자하는 것은 그야말로 시간 낭비일 뿐입니다.

토익에 등장하는 대부분의 대화나 지문은 일반인들이 직장에서 흔히 겪는 상황들을 바탕으로 만들어집니다. 그렇기에 토익 문제의 85% 이상은 기존에 반복 출제되었던 대화 상황, 지문, 어휘들을 바탕으로 한 빈출 유형들로 구성되며, 이 빈출 문제들만 실수 없이 맞힐 수 있다면 850점은 어렵지 않게 넘을 수 있습니다. 이 책은 방대한 토익 기출 문제 분석을 토대로 빈출 유형들을 빠짐없이 정리했으며, 다양한 변형 문제들을 통해 어떤 유사 문제가 나와도 빠르게, 실수 없이 풀 수 있는 실력을 갖추게 하는 데 역점을 두었습니다.

[에듀윌 토익 단기완성 850+ LC&RC]와 함께 하루 빨리 원하는 토익 목표를 달성하고, 더 원대한 목표를 향해 정진하기를 바라겠습니다.

에듀윌 어학연구소

목차

LC

PART 1

PART 2

PART 3

PART 4

RC

PART 5

PART 6

PART 7

이 책의 **특장점**

PART 2 출제 경향 및 전략

질문과 3개의 응답을 듣고, 질문에 가장 적절한 응답을 고르는 파트로 총 25문항이 출제된다. 성우는 대부분 남녀로 이루어지지만 간혹 다른 국적의 동성 성우로 이루어지는 경우도 있다.

문제 유형

WH의문문과 의문사가 없는 일반 의문문, 그리고 평서문으로 구분할 수 있으며, 각각 평균 13문제씩 비슷한 비율로 출제된다.

1. **WH의문문: Who/What/Which/When/Where/Why/How...?**

Q Who's in charge of the conference this year? 누가 올해 콘퍼런스 담당인가요?
Q What's the size of this apartment unit? 이 아파트 한 가구의 면적이 어떻게 되나요?
Q When does the shop close? 그 상점은 언제 닫나요?
Q Where is the career workshop being held? 커리어 워크숍은 어디에서 열리고 있나요?
Q How was your vacation? 휴가는 어땠어요?
Q Why did William move to Boston? William은 왜 보스턴으로 이사했나요?
▸ WH의문문은 Do you know when the library opens? 와 같이 간접의문문으로 출제되기도 한다.

출제 경향 및 전략

PART별 특징과 출제 경향, 문제 유형, 단계별 듣기 전략, 자주 사용되는 오답 트릭 등을 철저히 분석하여, 이를 토대로 학습 방향을 정확히 잡고 시작할 수 있게 했다.

UNIT 01 화자의 직업 및 대화 장소

빈출 문제 유형

화자의 직업 및 신분
- **What industry (field)** do the speakers work in? 화자들은 어느 산업[분야]에서 일하고 있는가?
- **What kind of business** do the speakers work for? 화자들은 어떤 업종에 종사하는가?
- **What type of business** is the woman calling? 여자는 어떤 종류의 회사에 전화하고 있는가?
- **Where** does the woman most likely work? 여자는 어디에서 일할 것 같은가?
- **Who** most likely is the man? 남자의 직업은 무엇일 것 같은가?
- **What service** does the man's company provide? 남자의 회사는 어떤 서비스를 제공하는가?

장소 관련 질문: 주로 상점, 식당, 병원, 박물관, 공장, 박람회장, 비행기, 기차 등이 출제된다.
- Where are the speakers? 화자들은 어디에 있는가?
- Where is the conversation most likely taking place? 대화는 어디에서 일어나고 있는 것 같은가?

UNIT

각 UNIT에는 PART 1 고득점 핵심 포인트, PART 2 고난도 문제 유형, PART 3, 4 빈출 문제 유형, 대표 유형 맛보기 등의 코너를 마련하여 기본을 탄탄히 다지는 동시에 고득점 획득에 꼭 필요한 실력을 기를 수 있도록 했다.

PRACTICE 고난도(의도 파악, 그래픽)

1. Where does the speaker most likely work?
(A) At a car wash
(B) At a moving company
(C) At a car rental service
(D) At an auto mechanic shop

2. What does the speaker imply when he says, "which will be a major job"?
(A) A deposit must be paid.
(B) The work will take him some time.
(C) He needs to hire more people.
(D) He is about to go on vacation.

3. What does the speaker say about this evening?
(A) An employee will be present.

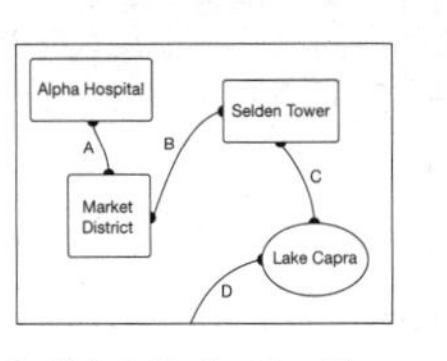

7. What project does the speaker mainly discuss?
(A) A city hall
(B) A walkway
(C) A riverside park

PRACTICE & PART TEST

쉬운 유형은 PRACTICE로, 어려운 유형은 고난도 PRACTICE로 실전 연습을 한 다음, PART TEST로 최종 실력 점검을 할 수 있게 하였다.

PART 5 출제 경향 및 전략

PART 5는 품사 및 동사의 올바른 활용 형태(시제, 태, 분사, 수 일치)를 묻는 문법 문제와, 문맥에 알맞은 단어 및 관용 표현을 고르는 어휘 문제로 이루어진다. 문법 문제와 어휘 문제는 거의 비슷한 비중으로 출제된다. 문법 문제 중에서도 명사, 동사, 형용사, 부사 중에서 빈칸에 알맞은 품사를 고르는 문제는 매회 가장 큰 비중으로 출제되므로 고득점 획득을 위해 놓쳐서는 안 된다. 어휘는 동사, 명사, 형용사, 부사, 전치사로 이루어진 문제들이 2~3문제씩 출제되며, 접속사 및 관용어구로 이루어진 문제들은 평균 1~3문제가 출제되나 빈도가 불규칙한 편이다.
PART 5는 시간 단축을 위해 선택지를 먼저 보고 문제의 유형을 파악한 후 해당 문제의 풀이 전략에 따라 문제를 푸는 것이 일반적이다. 아래의 네 가지 대표 유형을 통해 문법과 어휘 문제의 기본적인 접근 방식을 익혀보자.

[문법]

알맞은 품사/어형 고르기

Mr. Wood's ------- to the Paris branch was postponed until next year.
(A) transfer 명사, 동사
(B) to transfer to부정사
(C) transferred 과거분사

❶ 선택지 확인
선택지가 transfer라는 동일한 어근에서 파생된 다른 품사의 어휘들이므로 자리 문제.
❷ 빈칸 앞뒤 확인
빈칸 앞의 Mr. Wood's는 명사를 수식하는 한정사이므로 빈칸에는 명사가 온다.

출제 경향 및 전략

PART별 특징과 출제 경향, 문제 유형, 문제 풀이 전략 등을 철저히 분석하여 정확한 학습 방향을 잡을 수 있게 했다.

UNIT 01 명사

1 관사/소유격+명사

빈칸 앞에 관사(a, an, the), 소유격(her, Mr. Wood's) 등의 한정사가 있으면 빈칸에는 명사가 온다.

관사+명사 Because of unexpected competition, the store still had **an** excess / excessive of one hundred televisions left in stock.
예상치 못한 경쟁으로 인해 그 가게에는 텔레비전이 아직도 100대가 재고로 남아 있었다.

소유격+명사 Nicholas & Son and Johnston Co. have formed a mutually beneficial partnership to increase **their** profits / profitable.
Nicholas & Son과 Johnston 사는 그들의 이익을 증대시키기 위해 상호 이득이 되는 제휴 관계를 맺었다.

2 형용사/분사+명사

형용사+명사 The restaurant on Mesa Street is having a **large** celebration / celebrate to mark its tenth anniversary. 메사 스트리트에 있는 그 식당은 10주년을 축하하기 위해 대규모 축하 행사를 하고 있다.

UNIT

PART 5는 문법 사항별 핵심 문법과 빈출 유형을 한 페이지나 두 페이지로 압축해서 정리했다. 문법 학습이 끝난 뒤 PRACTICE를 통해 바로 실력을 점검하고, 고득점 도전 코너를 통해 고난도 문제에 대비할 수 있게 했다.

UNIT 01 주제/목적

문제 풀이 전략

주제/목적을 묻는 문제는 첫 번째 문제로 자주 출제된다. 질문을 통해 주제/목적 문제라는 것을 확인했다면 지문을 보고 글의 주제/목적을 파악한다. 주제/목적 문제는 대부분의 경우 제목이나 지문의 앞부분에 단서가 나오는데, 그 내용을 정확히 파악한 후 가장 적절한 선택지를 선택한다.

질문 유형

What is the article **mainly about**? 기사는 주로 무엇에 관한 것인가? [주제]
What is being **advertised**? 무엇이 광고되고 있는가? [주제]
What is the **purpose** of the e-mail? 이메일의 목적은 무엇인가? [목적]

대표 유형 맛보기

PART 6, 7은 문제 유형별로 UNIT을 구성했다. PART 7은 문제 풀이 전략, 질문 유형, 대표 유형 맛보기로 UNIT별 핵심만을 파악한 후 바로 PRACTICE를 학습하도록 구성하여 학습 부담을 크게 줄였다.

학습 일정표

2주 완성 코스

	DAY 1	DAY 2	DAY 3	DAY 4	DAY 5	DAY 6	DAY 7
1주	**PART 1** UNIT 01~02 PRACTICE PART TEST 1, 2 월 일	**PART 2** UNIT 01~06 PRACTICE PART TEST 월 일	**PART 3** UNIT 01~06 PRACTICE 월 일	**PART 3** UNIT 07~09 PART TEST 월 일	**PART 4** UNIT 01~04 월 일	**PART 4** UNIT 05~06 PRACTICE PART TEST 월 일	**PART 5** UNIT 01~05 월 일

	DAY 8	DAY 9	DAY 10	DAY 11	DAY 12	DAY 13	DAY 14
2주	**PART 5** UNIT 06~10 월 일	**PART 5** UNIT 11~14 PRACTICE PART TEST 월 일	**PART 6** UNIT 01~05 PART TEST 월 일	**PART 7** UNIT 01~05 월 일	**PART 7** UNIT 06~08 PART TEST 월 일	실전 모의고사 월 일	오답 위주 복습 월 일

4주 완성 코스

	DAY 1	DAY 2	DAY 3	DAY 4	DAY 5
1주	**PART 1** UNIT 01~02 PRACTICE PART TEST 1, 2 월 일	**PART 2** UNIT 01~06 PRACTICE PART TEST 월 일	**PART 3** UNIT 01~03 월 일	**PART 3** UNIT 04~06 PRACTICE 월 일	**PART 3** UNIT 07~09 PRACTICE PART TEST 월 일

	DAY 6	DAY 7	DAY 8	DAY 9	DAY 10
2주	**PART 4** UNIT 01~04 월 일	**PART 4** UNIT 05~06 PRACTICE PART TEST 월 일	**실전 모의고사** LISTENING TEST 월 일	**PART 5** UNIT 01~03 월 일	**PART 5** UNIT 04~06 월 일

	DAY 11	DAY 12	DAY 13	DAY 14	DAY 15
3주	**PART 5** UNIT 07~09 월 일	**PART 5** UNIT 10~12 월 일	**PART 5** UNIT 13~14 PRACTICE PART TEST 월 일	**PART 6** UNIT 01~03 월 일	**PART 6** UNIT 04~05 PART TEST 월 일

	DAY 16	DAY 17	DAY 18	DAY 19	DAY 20
4주	**PART 7** UNIT 01~03 월 일	**PART 7** UNIT 04~06 월 일	**PART 7** UNIT 07~08 PART TEST 월 일	**실전 모의고사** READING TEST 월 일	오답 위주 복습 월 일

TOEIC 소개

토익이란?

TOEIC은 Test of English for International Communication(국제적인 의사소통을 위한 영어 시험)의 약자로, 영어가 모국어가 아닌 사람들이 비즈니스 현장 및 일상생활에서 필요한 실용 영어 능력을 갖추었는가를 평가하는 시험이다.

시험 구성

<table>
<tr><th>구성</th><th colspan="3">파트</th><th colspan="2">문항 수</th><th>시간</th><th>배점</th></tr>
<tr><td rowspan="4">Listening Comprehension</td><td>Part 1</td><td colspan="2">사진 묘사</td><td>6</td><td rowspan="4">100</td><td rowspan="4">45분</td><td rowspan="4">495점</td></tr>
<tr><td>Part 2</td><td colspan="2">질의 응답</td><td>25</td></tr>
<tr><td>Part 3</td><td colspan="2">짧은 대화</td><td>39</td></tr>
<tr><td>Part 4</td><td colspan="2">짧은 담화</td><td>30</td></tr>
<tr><td rowspan="5">Reading Comprehension</td><td>Part 5</td><td colspan="2">단문 빈칸 채우기</td><td>30</td><td rowspan="5">100</td><td rowspan="5">75분</td><td rowspan="5">495점</td></tr>
<tr><td>Part 6</td><td colspan="2">장문 빈칸 채우기</td><td>16</td></tr>
<tr><td rowspan="3">Part 7</td><td rowspan="3">독해</td><td>단일 지문</td><td>29</td></tr>
<tr><td>이중 지문</td><td>10</td></tr>
<tr><td>삼중 지문</td><td>15</td></tr>
<tr><td>합계</td><td colspan="3">7 Parts</td><td colspan="2">200문항</td><td>120분</td><td>990점</td></tr>
</table>

출제 범위 및 주제

업무 및 일상생활에서 쓰이는 실용적인 주제들이 출제된다. 특정 문화나 특정 직업 분야에만 해당되는 주제는 출제하지 않으며, 듣기 평가의 경우 미국, 영국, 호주 등 다양한 국가의 발음이 섞여 출제된다.

분야	주제
일반 업무	계약, 협상, 영업, 홍보, 마케팅, 사업 계획
금융/재무	예산, 투자, 세금, 청구, 회계
개발	연구, 제품 개발
제조	공장 경영, 생산 조립 라인, 품질 관리
인사	채용, 승진, 퇴직, 직원 교육, 입사 지원
사무실	회의, 메모/전화/팩스/이메일, 사무 장비 및 가구
행사	학회, 연회, 회식, 시상식, 박람회, 제품 시연회
부동산	건축, 부동산 매매/임대, 기업 부지, 전기/수도/가스 설비
여행/여가	교통수단, 공항/역, 여행 일정, 호텔 및 자동차 예약/연기/취소, 영화, 전시, 공연

접수 방법

- 한국 TOEIC 위원회 사이트(www.toeic.co.kr)에서 인터넷 접수 기간을 확인하고 접수한다.
- 시험 접수 시 최근 6개월 이내에 촬영한 jpg 형식의 사진 파일이 필요하므로 미리 준비한다.
- 시험 10~12일 전부터는 특별 추가 접수 기간에 해당하여 추가 비용이 발생하므로, 접수 일정을 미리 확인하여 정기 접수 기간 내에 접수하도록 한다.

시험 당일 준비물

신분증	주민등록증, 운전면허증, 기간 만료 전 여권, 공무원증 등 규정 신분증만 인정 (중·고등학생에 한하여 학생증, 청소년증도 인정)
필기구	연필, 지우개 (볼펜, 사인펜은 사용 불가)

시험 진행

오전 시험	오후 시험	진행 내용
09:30 – 09:45	02:30 – 02:45	답안지 작성 오리엔테이션
09:45 – 09:50	02:45 – 02:50	쉬는 시간
09:50 – 10:05	02:50 – 03:05	신분증 확인
10:05 – 10:10	03:05 – 03:10	문제지 배부 및 파본 확인
10:10 – 10:55	03:10 – 03:55	듣기 평가 (LC)
10:55 – 12:10	03:55 – 05:10	독해 평가 (RC)

성적 확인

성적 발표	미리 안내된 성적 발표일에 한국 TOEIC 위원회 사이트(www.toeic.co.kr) 및 공식 애플리케이션을 통해 확인 가능하다.
성적표 수령	온라인 출력 또는 우편 수령 중에서 선택할 수 있고, 온라인 출력과 우편 수령 모두 1회 발급만 무료이며, 그 이후에는 유료로 발급된다.

LC

PART 1 사진 묘사 (6문항)

문제지

1. 

음성

Number 1. Look at the picture marked number 1 in your test book.

(A) He's staring at a vase.
(B) He's pouring a beverage.
(C) He's spreading out a tablecloth.
(D) He's sipping from a coffee cup.

PART 2 질의 응답 (25문항)

문제지

7. Mark your answer on your answer sheet.

음성

Number 7.
When will the landlord inspect the property?

(A) No, it failed the inspection.
(B) I'll e-mail him about it.
(C) Do you like the apartment?

PART 3 짧은 대화 (39문항) & PART 4 짧은 담화 (30문항)

문제지 (PART 3)

32. What is the conversation mainly about?
(A) A boat ride
(B) A history lecture
(C) A nature hike
(D) A bicycle tour

33. What does the woman ask the man to do?
(A) Select a size
(B) Show a receipt
(C) Provide a phone number
(D) Show an ID card

34. What does the woman suggest purchasing?
(A) A map
(B) A beverage
(C) A gift card
(D) A parking pass

음성

Questions 32 through 34 refer to the following conversation.

M Hello. I'd like to sign up for the historic district bike tour. When does the next one depart?
W At eleven o'clock... um... about twenty minutes from now. And there are still a few spots left.
M Oh, that's great. I'd like one ticket, please.
W All right. And we provide all participants with a helmet and a safety vest. Please choose which size would be best for you.
M Sure. I'll take a medium.
W You might also want to buy something to drink to take with you. There's a convenience store right across the street.

Number 32. What is the conversation mainly about?

Number 33. What does the woman ask the man to do?

Number 34. What does the woman suggest purchasing?

PART 5 단문 빈칸 채우기 (30문항)

101. If the parade goes ------- as planned, the planning committee members will be pleased.

(A) preciseness
(B) precisely
(C) precise
(D) precision

PART 6 장문 빈칸 채우기 (16문항)

Questions 131-134 refer to the following article.

BALTIMORE (April 9)—The fitness club chain Power Gym -------(**131.**) changes to its membership options. A spokesperson from the company's head office, Frank Jacobs, said they are adjusting their policies based on customer feedback.

-------(**132.**). The new policy will allow people to purchase one-day, one-week, or one-month passes, depending on their needs. This will support the company's commitment to making the gym convenient and -------(**133.**). A parking garage will also be added to the gym's main site downtown. -------(**134.**) will begin on that project sometime in June.

PART 7 독해 (54문항)

Questions 153-154 refer to the following article.

Recall of Bratton Smartwatches

September 3—Smartwatch manufacturer Bratton has announced the recall of its Dola-9 line of smartwatches after being on the market for only 2 weeks. No serious injuries have been reported, but the product presents a risk of burns to the user, as the battery in the device may get too hot. Customers with a faulty device are eligible for a replacement or a full refund. Those who own a Dola-9 smartwatch are asked to contact the company at 1-800-555-7932. Once connected, you can input the serial number and automatically be informed of what steps to take next. Those with further inquiries can also leave a message for the customer service team.

153. What is indicated about the Dola-9 smartwatch?

(A) Its battery can overheat.
(B) It takes two weeks to be replaced.
(C) Its mileage is not recorded correctly.
(D) It has caused severe injuries.

154. What does the article recommend that Dola-9 owners do first?

(A) Visit a store
(B) Reset the device
(C) Call a helpline
(D) E-mail customer service

LC

PART 1

PART 1 출제 경향 및 전략

제시된 사진을 보고 4개의 문장을 들은 뒤 그중 사진을 가장 적절하게 묘사한 선택지를 고르는 파트이다.
LC 전체 100문항 중 6문항이 출제된다. 선택지 (A), (B), (C), (D)는 문제지에 표기되지 않는다.

사진 유형

인물이 나오는 사진과 사물이나 풍경만 나오는 사진으로 분류할 수 있다. 인물 사진은 1인 사진이 보통 2~3문제씩 가장 많이 등장한다. 사물 또는 풍경만 나오는 사진은 보통 한 문제씩 고정적으로 출제되며, 간혹 두 문제가 출제되기도 한다. 사진의 상황은 대부분 일 또는 일터와 관련되어 있으며, 종종 일상생활을 묘사하는 사진도 출제된다.

P1_출제 경향 및 전략 해석 p.2

1인 사진

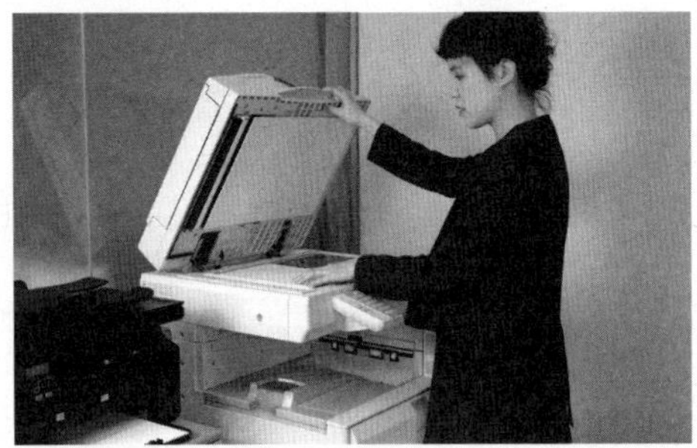

음성

(A) She's fixing a printer.
(B) She's putting on a jacket.
(C) She's examining some papers.
(D) She's photocopying a document.

2인 사진

음성

(A) They're removing their helmets.
(B) They're folding some paper.
(C) One of the men is marking a drawing.
(D) One of the men is measuring a windowpane.

3인 이상 사진

음성

(A) Customers are picking out some groceries.
(B) Customers are waiting in a line.
(C) A cashier is taking out some cash.
(D) A cashier is opening a cash register.

사물 또는 풍경 사진

음성

(A) Some pictures are hanging on a wall.
(B) Some artwork is propped against a sofa.
(C) A light fixture is mounted on a wall.
(D) A potted plant is positioned on a table.

단계별 듣기 전략

STEP 1 | 사진의 포커스 부분을 보며 음성 듣기

각 문제는 "Look at the picture marked number (번호) in your test book."이라는 음성 지시에 이어 바로 4개의 선택지가 음성으로 제시된다. 이때 항상 해당 문제의 사진을 보고 있어야 하며, 사진에서 가장 중심이 되는 피사체에 포커스를 둬야 한다. 특히 인물 사진은 항상 가장 도드라진 인물의 동작과 복장, 인물이 들고 있는 사물에 초점을 맞추고 음성을 들어야 하며, 사진의 배경이나 가장자리에 있는 불분명한 인물이나 사물은 무시해도 좋다.

Examples

1.

2.

STEP 2 | 오답 소거하기

파트1에서 선택지 (A), (B), (C), (D) 음성 간의 간격은 1초밖에 되지 않는다. (A)를 듣고 정답인지 아닌지 고민하다가 (B)를 못 듣게 되면 안 된다. 각 선택지를 듣자마자 음성에 언급된 사물이 사진에 있는지, 그 사물의 상태가 올바로 묘사되어 있는지, 인물의 복장이나 동작이 올바로 묘사되어 있는지 즉각적으로 판단하고 오답을 소거해 가야 한다.

Look at the picture marked number 1 in your test book.

(A) She's putting items in a basket. (×)	(A) 여자가 상품들을 바구니에 담고 있다.
(B) She's holding a vegetable in each hand. (○)	(B) 여자가 양손에 채소를 들고 있다.
(C) She's displaying some products. (×)	(C) 여자가 상품을 전시하고 있다.
(D) She's slicing some cabbages. (×)	(D) 여자가 양배추를 썰고 있다.

STEP 3 | 지난 문제에 미련 갖지 않기

파트1의 각 문제 사이의 간격은 5초다. 5초 사이에 정답을 체크하고 바로 다음 사진을 보고 있어야 한다. 이전 문제에 미련을 못 버리고 갈팡질팡하다 보면 다음 사진을 제대로 못 보게 되고 결국 허둥지둥하다가 다음 문제도 놓치고 만다.

빈출되는 사물 명칭과 인물의 동작 표현 숙지

파트1에서 고득점을 얻기 위해서는 결국 토익에 등장하는 다양한 사물들의 명칭과 사람의 동작을 나타내는 표현들을 정확히 알고 그 발음들을 정확히 구분해 들을 수 있어야 한다. 850점 이상을 목표로 한다면 본 책에 정리되어 있는 빈출 사물과 동작 표현들을 완벽히 외워둬야 하며, 900점 이상을 노린다면 추가적으로 온라인에서 제공하는 사진과 표현들을 숙지하기 바란다.

▶ 파트1 사진 표현 모음: 에듀윌 도서몰 (book.eduwill.net) 로그인〉도서 자료실〉부가학습 자료실

UNIT 01 인물 사진 묘사

P1_U1

고득점 핵심 POINT

1. 오답은 주로 사진 속에 있는 사물들을 사용하되 엉뚱한 동사를 쓰거나, 사진 속에 없는 사물을 언급한다.

(A) He is pushing a wheelbarrow. → 동사 (×)
(B) He is trimming some branches. → 동사 (×)
(C) He is raking some leaves.
(D) He is clearing up some debris. → 사물 (×)

(A) 남자가 손수레를 밀고 있다.
(B) 남자가 나뭇가지를 다듬고 있다.
(C) 남자가 나뭇잎을 갈퀴로 긁어모으고 있다.
(D) 남자가 잔해를 치우고 있다.

정답 (C)

2. 상태를 나타내는 동사와 동작을 나타내는 동사를 혼동해서는 안 된다.

(A) The man is organizing a toolbox.
(B) The man is lifting some furniture.
(C) The man is carrying a wooden plank.
(D) The man is putting on a helmet. → 동작 (×)

(A) 남자가 공구함을 정리하고 있다.
(B) 남자가 가구를 들어올리고 있다.
(C) 남자가 널빤지를 나르고 있다.
(D) 남자가 헬멧을 쓰고 있다.

정답 (C)

▶ is putting on은 착용하는 동작, is wearing은 착용하고 있는 상태를 묘사한다. 따라서 (D)는 The man is wearing a helmet.이 되어야 한다. 공사장에서 쓰는 안전모는 hard hat이라고도 한다.

동작 VS. 상태

He **is putting on** a jacket.
(×) is wearing
남자가 재킷을 입고 있다.

He **is wearing** a helmet.
(×) is putting on
남자가 헬멧을 쓰고 있다.

She**'s wearing** glasses.
(×) is putting on
여자가 안경을 쓰고 있다.

She**'s riding** a bicycle.
(×) is getting on
여자가 자전거를 타고 있다.

▶ 옷, 신발, 넥타이, 안경, 모자, 장갑, 스카프 등을 몸에 착용하고 있을 때 is wearing을 쓴다.
▶ 벗는 동작을 나타낼 때는 is taking off 또는 is removing을 쓴다.

3. **사람과 사물이 함께 묘사될 수 있다. 그럴 경우 보통 두 개 선택지는 사물 주어, 나머지 두 개는 사람 주어로 구성된다.**

(A) **Some papers** have been stacked on the floor.
(B) **Some binders** have been lined up on a shelf.
(C) **A woman** is photocopying some documents.
(D) **A woman** is adjusting a computer monitor.

(A) 종이들이 바닥에 쌓여 있다.
(B) 바인더들이 선반에 일렬로 세워져 있다.
(C) 여자가 서류들을 복사하고 있다.
(D) 여자가 컴퓨터 모니터 위치를 조정하고 있다.

정답 (B)

4. **사람의 행동을 사물을 주어로 사용하여 수동 진행형(is / are being p.p.)으로 묘사할 수 있다.**

(A) A tree **is being planted**.
(B) A shovel is leaning against a fence.
(C) A woman is filling up a watering can.
(D) A man is emptying out a bucket.

(A) 나무가 심어지고 있다.
(B) 삽이 담장에 기대어져 있다.
(C) 여자가 물뿌리개에 물을 채우고 있다.
(D) 남자가 양동이를 비우고 있다.

정답 (A)

▶ (A)는 They're planting a tree.를 수동 진행형으로 바꾼 것이다.

Examples

She **is painting** a wall.
여자가 벽에 페인트를 칠하고 있다.

⬇

A wall **is being painted**.
벽에 페인트가 칠해지고 있다.

He **is repairing** a roof.
남자가 지붕을 수리하고 있다.

⬇

A roof **is being repaired**.
지붕이 수리되고 있다.

CHECK-UP

 P1_U1_Check-up 정답 및 해설 p.2

1.

(A) (B) (C) (D)

2.

(A) (B) (C) (D)

UNIT 02 사물 및 풍경 사진 묘사

P1_U2

고득점 핵심 POINT

1. 사물 및 풍경은 주로 [have/has been p.p.] 또는 [are/is p.p.] 형태로 묘사된다. 오답은 주로 사진 속의 사물을 이용하되 위치나 상태가 잘못 묘사된다.

(A) A lamp has been mounted on a wall.
(B) Some cushions have been set on an armchair.
(C) Some curtains have been laid out on the floor.
(D) A potted plant has been placed on a windowsill.

(A) 램프가 벽에 설치되어 있다.
(B) 쿠션 몇 개가 팔걸이의자에 놓여 있다.
(C) 바닥에 커튼이 펼쳐져 있다.
(D) 화분이 창턱에 놓여 있다.

정답 (B)

2. 사물 묘사에서도 [be -ing]가 쓰일 수 있으며, 시험에 자주 나오는 표현들을 꼭 암기해 두도록 한다.

hang 걸리다, 걸다	Clothing **is hanging** on racks. 옷들이 옷걸이에 걸려 있다. Some pictures **are hanging** on a wall. 사진들이 벽에 걸려 있다.
face 마주보다	Some chairs **are facing** each other. 의자들이 서로 마주보고 있다. Some chairs **are facing** the sea. 의자들이 바다를 향해 있다.
lean ~에 기대다	A ladder **is leaning** against a fence. 사다리가 울타리에 기대어 있다. A bike **is leaning** against a building. 자전거가 건물에 기대어 있다.
line ~을 따라 늘어서다	Some trees **are lining** a walkway. 나무들이 보도를 따라 늘어서 있다. Some vehicles **are lining** both sides of a street. 차량들이 거리 양쪽으로 늘어서 있다.

Clothing **is hanging** on racks.

Some chairs **are facing** the sea.

A ladder **is leaning** against a fence.

3. **[There is/are] 또는 [be 전치사구]로 묘사할 수도 있다.**

There are some vehicles lining the side of a street.
길가에 차량이 늘어서 있다.

Some shoes **are on display** on a shelf.
신발 몇 켤레가 선반에 진열되어 있다.

Some floor tiles **are in a pattern**.
바닥 타일에 무늬가 있다.

4. **사람이 없는데 [사물 is/are being p.p.]로 묘사되고 있다면 오답일 확률이 높다.**

(A) A rear door of a van has been left open.
(B) Some boxes are being carried out of a building. → 진행 (×)
(C) Some crates are being unloaded from a truck. → 진행 (×)
(D) A vehicle is stopped at a traffic signal.

(A) 밴의 뒷문이 열려 있다.
(B) 몇 개의 상자들이 건물 밖으로 운반되고 있다.
(C) 트럭에서 운반 상자 몇 개를 내리고 있다.
(D) 차량이 교통 신호에 멈춰 있다.

정답 (A)

▶ 아래와 같이 특정한 경우 사진에 사람이 없을 때에도 수동 진행형이 쓰일 수 있으므로 주의해야 한다.

Merchandise **is being displayed** in a case.
상품이 케이스에 진열되어 있다.
→ is on display와 같은 의미.

Some grass **is being watered**.
잔디밭에 물이 뿌려지고 있다.
→ 기계에 의해 물이 뿌려지고 있는 상황.

CHECK-UP

P1_U2_Check-up 정답 및 해설 p.2

1.

(A) (B) (C) (D)

2.

(A) (B) (C) (D)

빈출 표현 모음

1 동작 묘사

arranging some chairs 의자를 정돈하고 있다
writing on a document 서류에 적고 있다
taking some notes 메모를 하고 있다
talking on a phone 전화 통화하고 있다
packing some luggage 짐을 싸고 있다
watering some flowers 꽃에 물을 주고 있다
cutting the grass 잔디를 깎고 있다
tying his shoe 신발 끈을 매고 있다
facing a screen 스크린을 향해 있다
standing in line 줄지어 서 있다
photocopying a document 서류를 복사하고 있다
operating some machinery 기계를 조작하고 있다
looking through her handbag 핸드백을 뒤지고 있다
loading some bricks onto a cart 카트에 벽돌을 싣고 있다
examining a flyer 전단지를 살펴보고 있다
studying a drawing 설계도를 살펴보고 있다
lifting some furniture 가구를 들어올리고 있다
carrying a shopping bag 쇼핑백을 들고 있다
exiting through a door 문을 통과해 나가고 있다
handing out some flyers 전단지를 나눠주고 있다
resting against a railing 난간에 기대어 있다
sweeping a walkway 보도를 쓸고 있다
washing a window 창을 닦고 있다
wiping down a countertop 조리대를 닦고 있다
removing his gloves 장갑을 벗고 있다
clearing snow from a car 차의 눈을 치우고 있다
crouching to grab an item 물건을 집으려 웅크리고 있다
bending down to use a saw 허리를 숙여 톱질하고 있다

2 사물 묘사

자주 쓰이는 동사들

Some pillows have been **placed** on a bed. 베개들이 침대에 놓여 있다.

Sets of utensils have been **arranged** on napkins. 식기 세트들이 냅킨 위에 놓여 있다.

Some bags have been **set** on the floor. 가방들이 바닥에 놓여 있다.
A tent has been **set up** near some cars. 텐트가 차들 옆에 설치되어 있다.
Food has been **set out** for an event. 음식이 행사를 위해 마련되어 있다.

A drawer has been **left** open. 서랍이 열려 있다.

Some boxes are **stacked** in a warehouse. 몇몇 상자가 창고에 쌓여 있다.

자주 쓰이는 전치사구

Some bricks are stacked **in a pile.** 벽돌들이 **무더기로** 쌓여 있다.
Some vehicles have been parked **in a row**. 차량들이 **일렬로** 주차되어 있다.
The audience is seated **in a circle**. 청중이 **동그랗게** 앉아 있다.
A potted plant has been set **on top of** a desk. 화분이 책상 **위에** 놓여 있다.
Some chairs have been placed **by** a fountain. 의자 몇 개가 분수 **옆에** 놓여 있다.
A toolbox has been set down **next to** some tires. 도구상자가 타이어 **옆에** 놓여 있다.
Buildings are located **along** the shoreline. 건물들이 해안선**을 따라** 위치해 있다.
Two monitors are being positioned **side by side**. 두 개의 모니터가 **나란히** 위치해 있다.
A garden has been planted **outside of** a building. 정원이 건물 **밖에** 가꿔져 있다.

PRACTICE 고난도

P1_Practice 정답 및 해설 p.3

1.

2.

3.

4.

5.

6.

1.

2.

3.

4.

5.

6.

1.

2.

3.

4.

5.

6.

LC

PART 2

출제 경향 및 전략

PART 2 출제 경향 및 전략

질문과 3개의 응답을 듣고, 질문에 가장 적절한 응답을 고르는 파트로 총 25문항이 출제된다. 성우는 대부분 남녀로 이루어지지만 간혹 다른 국적의 동성 성우로 이루어지는 경우도 있다.

문제 유형

WH의문문과 의문사가 없는 일반 의문문, 그리고 평서문으로 구분할 수 있으며, 각각 평균 11·11·3문항의 비율로 출제된다.

1. WH의문문: Who / What / Which / When / Where / Why / How...?

Q Who's in charge of the conference this year? 누가 올해 콘퍼런스 담당인가요?

Q What's the size of this apartment unit? 이 아파트 한 가구의 면적이 어떻게 되나요?

Q When does the shop close? 그 상점은 언제 닫나요?

Q Where is the career workshop being held? 커리어 워크숍은 어디에서 열리고 있나요?

Q How was your vacation? 휴가는 어땠어요?

Q Why did William move to Boston? William은 왜 보스턴으로 이사했나요?

▶ WH의문문은 Do you know when the library opens? 와 같이 간접의문문으로 출제되기도 한다.

2. 일반 의문문 + 평서문

조동사 **Q** Did you finish preparing your presentation? 발표 준비를 끝냈나요?

조동사 **Q** Will you be at the meeting this afternoon? 오늘 오후 회의에 참가하시나요?

Be동사 **Q** Is there a café on this level of the hotel? 호텔의 제가 있는 층에 카페가 있나요?

▶ 조동사와 Be동사로 이루어진 질문은 부정 의문문과 부가 의문문으로도 출제된다.
ex) Didn't you...? (부정 의문문) You finished..., didn't you? (부가 의문문)

제안 **Q** Why don't we hold a fund-raiser? 모금 행사를 여는 게 어때요?

선택 **Q** Do you prefer to take the bus or the train? 버스 타길 선호하세요, 아니면 기차를 선호하세요?

평서문 **Q** I haven't received the updated employee list yet. 업데이트된 직원 명단을 아직 받지 못했어요.

단계별 듣기 전략

Example

Who's picking up the clients at the airport?
(A) In Terminal 2.
(B) Martin is. (○)
(C) She's my new client.

STEP 1 | 질문의 첫 부분을 놓치지 말고 들어야 한다. 특히 의문사로 물어보는 경우, 의문사만 듣고도 어느 정도 답을 고를 수 있는 경우가 많으므로 어떤 의문사로 물어보는지 유의해서 들어야 한다.

STEP 2 | 오답을 소거해 가며 정답을 고른다. (A)는 질문의 특정 단어(airport)와 관련된 연상어(terminal)를 사용하였고, (C)는 질문에 언급된 단어(client)를 그대로 사용하여 오답을 만들었다.

자주 사용되는 오답 트릭

1. 유사한 발음을 이용한 오답 트릭

Q Who gave the presentation on the launch event? 출시 행사에서 누가 발표를 했나요?

A (×) I already ate lunch. 저는 이미 점심을 먹었어요. → launch ≠ lunch

A (○) The project manager, I believe. 프로젝트 책임자였을 거예요.

2. 유사 의미 또는 연상 관계의 단어들을 이용한 오답 트릭

Q You transferred to this branch recently, didn't you? 최근에 이 지점으로 옮기셨죠, 그렇지 않나요?

A (×) No, we used a moving company. 아니요, 우리는 이사 업체를 이용했어요. → transfer와 유사한 의미의 move

A (○) Yes, just last week. 네, 지난주에 왔어요.

3. 질문 속 의문사가 아닌 다른 의문사에 맞게 답변한 오답 트릭

Q When will the printer be repaired? 프린터는 언제 고쳐지나요?

A (×) On my desk. 제 책상 위에요. → Where

A (○) Probably this afternoon. 아마도 오늘 오후에요.

4. 질문 속 어휘를 반복한 오답 트릭

Q Do you think our customers will like our new logo? 고객들이 우리의 새로운 로고를 좋아할 거라고 생각하나요?

A (×) I stayed late to help a customer. 저는 고객을 돕기 위해 늦게까지 있었어요. → 질문의 customer 반복

A (○) Yes, it's very attractive. 네, 그건 굉장히 멋져요.

여러 종류의 질문에서 두루 쓰일 수 있는 답변

몇몇 답변들은 다양한 종류의 의문문에서 두루 정답으로 사용될 수 있으며, 이런 표현들은 한꺼번에 외워두는 것이 유용하다.

Question		Answer
Q Who's going to select a candidate for the position? 누가 그 자리의 후보자를 뽑을 거죠?		I'm not sure. 잘 모르겠어요.
Q When are you going to interview the candidates? 그 후보자들을 언제 면접 볼 건가요?	➡	Brian will know. Brian이 알 거예요.
Q Did you select a candidate for the position? 그 자리의 후보자를 뽑았나요?		You'll have to ask Sam. Sam에게 물어보셔야 할 거예요.
Q Was it James or Chris who interviewed the candidates? 그 지원자들을 면접 본 게 James인가요 Chris인가요?		You'd better ask Sam. Sam에게 물어보는 게 좋을 거예요.

UNIT 01 Who/What/Which 의문문

Who

어떤 일의 담당자가 누구인지를 물어보는 질문이 가장 많으며, 사람 이름이나 직책명으로 답하는 경우가 가장 흔하다.

1. 사람 이름이나 직책명으로 답변하는 경우

Example 01 P2_U1_Ex01

Who's designing our new logo?
(A) Terry is working on it.
(B) Yes, the cover design is great.
(C) In about two weeks.

누가 새 로고를 디자인하고 있죠?
(A) Terry가 작업하고 있어요. (○)
(B) 네, 표지 디자인이 훌륭해요. (×)
(C) 약 2주 후요. (×)

빈출 답변
A1 Paul takes care of that. Paul이 맡아 하고 있어요.
A2 Paul, as far as I know. 제가 알기로는 Paul이요.
A3 Paul said he would. Paul이 하겠다고 했어요.
A4 Paul's in charge. Paul이 담당하고 있어요.
A5 The chief designer. 수석 디자이너요.

2. 회사명으로 답변하는 경우

Q Who's going to sponsor this year's fund-raiser? 올해 모금 행사는 누가 후원할 예정이죠?
A A new hotel called Paradise View. Paradise View라는 새로운 호텔에서요.

3. 자주 쓰이는 제3의 답변

Q Who's leading the focus group meeting next week? 누가 다음 주에 포커스 그룹 회의를 이끌죠?
A1 It's been delayed until July. 그건 7월로 연기되었어요.
A2 It hasn't been decided yet. 아직 결정되지 않았어요.
A3 We're still deciding. 아직 결정하는 중이에요.
A4 I'll have to check my notes. 메모한 걸 확인해 봐야겠어요.
A5 That will be announced later today. 그건 오늘 오후에 공지될 거예요.
A6 Didn't you get the e-mail this morning? 오늘 아침에 이메일 못 받으셨어요?

4. 고난도 Who로 물어보는 질문이지만 의도적으로 난이도를 높이기 위해 시간이나 일정, 즉 When에 관련된 내용을 정답으로 만들기도 한다.

Example 02 P2_U1_Ex02

Who's going to submit the budget report today?
(A) I thought it's due tomorrow.
(B) Donna should be in the office.
(C) The quarterly report.

오늘 누가 예산안을 제출할 거죠?
(A) 기한이 내일까지라고 생각했어요. (○)
(B) Donna는 사무실에 있을 거예요. (×)
(C) 분기 보고서요. (×)

What, Which

What/Which 의문문은 의문사 바로 뒤에 나오는 명사에 의해 답변이 결정되는 경우가 많으므로, 특히 앞부분을 집중해 들어야 한다.

1. What kind/type of...? What 명사...? What is/조동사...?

Q **What kind of food** does your restaurant serve? 당신의 식당은 어떤 종류의 음식을 제공하나요?
A Italian, mostly. 주로 이탈리아 음식이요.

Q **What flight** should I book for our business trip to Boston? 보스턴 출장에 어떤 비행기를 예약해야 할까요?
A The earlier we arrive, the better. 빨리 도착할수록 좋아요.

Q **What is** the marketing department's phone number? 마케팅 부서의 전화번호가 어떻게 되죠?
A All the information is available online. 모든 정보는 온라인에 있어요.

2. What do you think about...? ~에 대해 어떻게 생각하세요?

Q **What do you think about** our new company brochure? 새로운 회사 안내책자에 대해 어떻게 생각하세요?
A We'd better reduce the size of the title. 제목 크기를 좀 줄이는 게 좋겠어요.

3. Which 질문에 대한 대답에서는 주로 one/ones를 사용하여 질문에 나온 명사의 반복을 피한다. 하지만 one이 사용되지 않는 답변도 얼마든지 가능하다.

Q Which bus stop is closest to your workplace? 직장에서 가장 가까운 버스 정류장은 어디에요?
A **The one** on Maple Street. Maple Street에 있는 거요.

Q Which training session are you going to attend tomorrow? 내일 어떤 교육 훈련에 참석할 거예요?
A Well, **the ones** in the morning filled up quickly. 음, 오전 교육은 금세 다 찼어요.

Q Which restaurant do you usually go to? 주로 어느 식당에 가세요?
A I always eat at the company cafeteria. 저는 항상 회사 구내식당에서 먹어요.

4. 고난도 Which로 물어볼 경우 무조건 one이 쓰인 것을 정답으로 골라서는 안 된다.

Example 03 P2_U1_Ex03

Which company was hired to renovate the building?
(A) That project has been postponed.
(B) One of our most popular designs.
(C) A 7-story building.

건물 개조를 위해 어떤 회사가 고용됐나요?
(A) 그 프로젝트는 연기되었어요. (○)
(B) 우리의 가장 인기 있는 디자인 중 하나요. (×)
(C) 7층 건물이에요. (×)

CHECK-UP P2_U1_Check-up 정답 및 해설 p.7

1.	(A)	(B)	(C)	**4.**	(A)	(B)	(C)
2.	(A)	(B)	(C)	**5.**	(A)	(B)	(C)
3.	(A)	(B)	(C)	**6.**	(A)	(B)	(C)

UNIT 02 When/Where 의문문

When

When과 Where는 집중해서 듣지 않으면 헷갈리기 쉬우며, 그래서 When/Where 질문에서는 장소와 시간 관련 선택지가 함정으로 함께 나오는 경우가 많다.

1. When과 Where 관련 선택지가 함께 나오는 경우

Example 01 P2_U2_Ex01

When will the prototype be ready for testing?
(A) On the third floor.
(B) By Thursday morning.
(C) Just a few components.

견본이 언제 테스트를 위해 준비될까요?
(A) 3층에서요. (×) → Where에 관한 답변
(B) 목요일 아침까지요. (○)
(C) 그저 몇 가지 부품입니다. (×)

2. 시제별 질문과 답변

과거	**Q** When did we last conduct a safety inspection? 우리가 마지막으로 안전 검사를 한 게 언제죠? **A1** About two months ago. 두 달 전쯤에요. **A2** Sometime last week. 지난주쯤에요.
현재	**Q** When does the museum open? 박물관은 언제 문을 열죠? **A** Not until 10:00 in the morning. 아침 10시 넘어야 해요.
미래	**Q** When are they going to replace the copy machine? 언제 그들이 복사기를 교체할 건가요? **A** Before the end of the month. 이달 말 이전에요.

3. 제3의 답변

Q When will our pasta be ready? 저희 파스타는 언제 나오나요?
A I'll check with our chef. 주방장에게 물어볼게요.

Q When are the new employees starting? 신입사원들은 언제부터 출근하죠?
A There are two people left to interview. 두 명 더 면접을 봐야 해요.

4. 고난도 시간에 관련된 내용이 선택지 문장의 끝에 나올 수도 있으므로 항상 문장을 끝까지 들어야 한다.

Example 02 P2_U2_Ex02

When will the new partnership be announced?
(A) She's a partner in a law firm.
(B) At the board meeting next week.
(C) I'm happy to work with you.

새로운 파트너십은 언제 발표될까요?
(A) 그녀는 법률회사의 파트너입니다. (×)
(B) 다음 주 이사회에서요. (○)
(C) 당신과 함께 일하게 돼서 기쁩니다. (×)

Where

전치사를 사용한 정답이 가장 많으며, 오답으로 When에 관련된 답변이 자주 사용된다.

1. 장소 / 위치로 답변

Q Where is the investment seminar being held this year? 투자 세미나가 이번 해에는 어디에서 열리나요?
A The same hotel as last year. 작년과 같은 호텔에서요.

Q Where can I find an extra stapler? 여분의 스테이플러를 어디에서 찾을 수 있나요?
A In the bottom desk drawer. 책상 서랍 맨 아래 칸에서요.

2. 반문으로 답변

Q Where is the presentation remote clicker? 프레젠테이션용 리모컨이 어디에 있죠?
A Didn't Helen use it at the meeting yesterday? Helen이 어제 회의할 때 쓰지 않았나요?

3. 제3의 답변

Q Where are the keys to the storeroom? 창고 열쇠는 어디에 있나요?
A Helen had them last. 마지막으로 Helen이 그것들을 가지고 있었어요.

Q Where did you buy this coffee machine? 이 커피 머신 어디에서 샀어요?
A It was a gift. 선물로 받았어요.

Q Where should I park when I go to the conference? 컨퍼런스에 가면 어디에 주차해야 하죠?
A It's better to take a taxi. 택시를 타는 게 나을 거예요.

Q Where should we examine these product samples? 이 제품 샘플들을 어디에서 검사해야 할까요?
A No one is in the conference room. 회의실에 아무도 없어요. (회의실에서 검사하는 게 좋겠다는 뜻)

4. 고난도 단순히 장소 / 위치 관련 전치사(in, on, at, by 등)만 듣고 정답을 선택해서는 안 된다.

Example 03 P2_U2_Ex03

Where's the nearest pharmacy?
(A) In the first drawer.
(B) The closest one is on Hewes Street.
(C) Dr. Martin is not available today.

가장 가까운 약국은 어디에 있나요?
(A) 첫 번째 서랍에요. (×)
(B) 가장 가까운 곳은 Hewes Street에 있어요. (○)
(C) Martin 선생님은 오늘 진료 불가능하세요. (×)

CHECK-UP P2_U2_Check-up 정답 및 해설 p.8

1.	(A)	(B)	(C)	**4.**	(A)	(B)	(C)
2.	(A)	(B)	(C)	**5.**	(A)	(B)	(C)
3.	(A)	(B)	(C)	**6.**	(A)	(B)	(C)

UNIT 03 How/Why 의문문

How

주로 How 다음에 오는 단어에 따라 답변 유형이 결정되므로 질문의 앞부분을 유의해서 들어야 한다.

1. 수량, 빈도, 기간 등: How many/much/long/often/soon...?

Q **How many** chairs need to be set up for the seminar? 세미나에 얼마나 많은 의자가 설치돼야 하죠?
A At least twenty. 적어도 스무 개요.

Q **How much** does this toaster oven cost? 이 오븐 토스터는 얼마인가요?
A It's on sale for 450 dollars. 세일해서 450달러예요.

Q **How long** have you worked with John? John과 함께 일을 한 지 얼마나 됐나요?
A About four years. 4년쯤이요.

Q **How often** does the tennis club meet? 테니스 클럽은 얼마나 자주 모이나요?
A Once every two weeks. 2주에 한 번이요.

Q **How soon** will the company brochure be ready? 회사 소개 브로셔가 얼마나 빨리 준비될까요?
A Not until next week. 다음 주나 되어야 해요.

2. 의견: How was...?/How did you like...?

Q **How was** the trade show yesterday? 어제 열렸던 무역박람회는 어땠나요?
A It was very successful! 굉장히 성공적이었어요!

Q **How did you like** the café? 그 카페는 마음에 들었나요?
A It was great. Well worth the drive. 훌륭했어요. 운전해서 찾아간 보람이 있었어요.

3. 방법: How do I...?

Q **How do I** sign up for the seminar? 그 세미나에 어떻게 등록하죠?
A You need to fill out a form online. 온라인에서 양식을 작성하셔야 돼요.

4. 고난도 "How did ~ go?"는 "~은 잘됐나요?, ~은 어떻게 됐어요?"라는 뜻의 패턴으로 자주 출제된다.

Q **How did** the product demonstration **go**? 제품 시연은 잘됐나요?
Q **How did** the sales presentation **go**? 영업 프레젠테이션은 잘됐나요?
Q **How did** your interview **go** yesterday? 어제 면접은 잘됐나요?

Example 01 P2_U3_Ex01

How did yesterday's meeting with the clients go?
(A) Our biggest customer.
(B) It went well. Thanks.
(C) I go to Amsterdam every year.

어제 고객들과의 미팅은 잘됐나요?
(A) 우리의 가장 큰 고객이에요. (×)
(B) 잘됐어요. 고마워요. (○)
(C) 전 암스테르담에 해마다 가요. (×)

Why

Why 의문문에 대한 답변은 because/for 또는 to부정사로 시작하는 경우가 많다. 특히, Why 질문에 Because가 선택지로 쓰였다면 거의 어김없이 정답이다.

1. 이유/원인으로 답변

Example 02 P2_U3_Ex02

Why will the museum be closed tomorrow?	왜 박물관이 내일 문을 닫죠?
(A) It's a week from tomorrow.	(A) 내일부터 일주일이에요. (×)
(B) It was an exhibit on ancient Egypt.	(B) 고대 이집트 관련 전시회였어요. (×)
(C) Because it's a national holiday.	(C) 공휴일이라서요. (○)

▶ Because가 생략된 상태로 답변할 수도 있다.

A1 It's closed on Mondays. 월요일마다 문을 닫아요.
A2 It will be renovated. 보수 공사를 할 거예요.

2. 목적으로 답변

Q Why did Mitchell leave early today? Mitchell은 왜 오늘 일찍 떠났죠?
A1 To pick Mr. Torres up from the train station. 기차역으로 Mr. Torres를 모시러 가기 위해서요.
A2 For a client meeting. 고객과의 미팅을 위해서요.

3. 고난도 반문으로 답변

Q Why do we have another meeting about the budget? 왜 또 예산안에 대해 회의하는 거죠?
A Have you seen last quarter's sales figures? 지난 분기 매출액 보셨어요?

Q Why haven't the tables been set up in the garden? 테이블이 왜 정원에 설치되지 않았죠?
A Have you seen the weather forecast? 일기예보 보셨어요?

Q Why aren't the trainees in the conference room now? 왜 교육생들이 지금 회의실에 없는 거죠?
A Didn't you get an e-mail with the updated schedule? 수정된 일정을 이메일로 못 받으셨어요?

Q Why are they moving the bookshelves now? 그들이 왜 지금 책장을 옮기고 있는 거죠?
A Is the noise bothering you? 소음이 거슬리세요?

CHECK-UP

P2_U3_Check-up 정답 및 해설 p.9

1.	(A)	(B)	(C)	**4.**	(A)	(B)	(C)
2.	(A)	(B)	(C)	**5.**	(A)	(B)	(C)
3.	(A)	(B)	(C)	**6.**	(A)	(B)	(C)

UNIT 04 Yes/No 의문문

일반 의문문 (조동사/Be동사)

조동사/Be동사로 시작하는 일반 의문문 모두 Yes/No로 답변할 수 있지만 종종 Yes/No가 생략된 형태의 정답도 등장한다.

1. Do/Have...?

Q Did you take the bus to get here? 버스 타고 여기에 오셨어요?
A1 Yes, it took longer than I thought. 네, 생각보다 오래 걸렸어요.
A2 No, I drove. 아니요, 운전해서 왔어요.

Q Have you met Mr. Lee, the new HR director? 새 인사부장으로 온 Mr. Lee를 만나봤어요?
A1 Yes, I just met in the meeting. 네, 방금 회의에서 만났어요.
A2 No, I just got back from vacation. 아뇨, 제가 방금 휴가에서 돌아왔어요.
A3 I've been in meetings all day. 전 하루 종일 회의에 참석했어요.

2. Will/Should...?

Q Will you be at the staff meeting in the afternoon? 오후에 직원 회의에 참석하시나요?
A1 Yes, I'll be there. 네, 참석할 거예요.
A2 I have a dentist appointment. 치과 예약이 있어요.

Q Should we reserve a conference room for the interview? 면접을 위해 회의실을 예약해야 할까요?
A1 Yes, could you do that now? 네, 지금 해 주실 수 있어요?
A2 I heard it was canceled. 그건 취소됐다고 들었어요.

3. Be동사 의문문

Q Is Jamie Lopez attending today's seminar? Jamie Lopez가 오늘 세미나에 참석하나요?
A Alex has the guest list. Alex가 손님 명단을 가지고 있어요.

Q Are these bookmarks for sale? 이 책갈피들은 판매하는 건가요?
A Feel free to take one. 무료로 하나 가져가세요.

4. 고난도 **Yes/No로 답변 후 엉뚱한 내용이 이어지거나 연상 어휘를 이용한 오답에 주의한다.**

Example 01 P2_U4_Ex01

Do you have Paul's e-mail address?	Paul의 이메일 주소를 아세요?
(A) He moved to Miami last year.	(A) 그는 작년에 마이애미로 이사했어요. (×)
(B) Sure, I'll text it to you.	(B) 물론요, 문자로 보내드릴게요. (○)
(C) Yes, by mail will be better.	(C) 네, 우편이 나을 거예요. (×)

▶ (C)는 Yes로 답변했지만 e-mail과 mail의 혼동을 이용한 오답이다.

부정/부가 의문문

부정 의문문이나 부가 의문문 모두 Yes/No로 답할 수 있다.

1. 부정/부가 의문문은 일반 의문문과 마찬가지로 묻는 내용에 긍정이면 Yes, 부정이면 No로 응답한다.

일반 **Q** Are you organizing our launch party? 당신이 출시 파티를 기획하고 있나요?
부정 **Q** Aren't you organizing our launch party? 당신이 출시 파티를 기획하고 있지 않나요?
부가 **Q** You are organizing our launch party, aren't you? 당신이 출시 파티를 기획하고 있죠, 그렇지 않나요?
A1 Yes, with Harry in Human Resources. 네, 인사부서의 Harry와 함께요.
A2 No, Ms. Derby is handling it. 아뇨, Ms. Derby가 맡고 있어요.

2. 부가 의문문은 긍정/부정 모두 "..., right?" 형태로 대체될 수 있다.

Q The last train to Boston hasn't departed yet, has it? 보스턴행 막차가 출발 안 했죠, 그렇죠?
Q The last train to Boston has departed, hasn't it? 보스턴행 막차가 출발했죠, 그렇지 않나요?
⇨ The last train to Boston has/hasn't departed yet, right? 보스턴행 막차가 출발 했죠/안 했죠, 그렇죠?
A1 Yes, it just left. 네, 방금 떠났어요.
A2 No, you've got 10 minutes. 아뇨, 10분 남았어요.

3. 고난도 Don't/Didn't you...?와 같이 you를 주어로 물어본다고 해서 'I'로 시작하는 답변에 현혹되어서는 안 된다.

Example 02 P2_U4_Ex02

Don't you need to order a flowerpot for the lobby?
(A) Linda took care of it last week.
(B) I water the plant once a week.
(C) In numerical order, please.

로비에 놓을 화분을 주문해야 하지 않나요?
(A) Linda가 지난주에 처리했어요. (○)
(B) 그 식물에 일주일에 한 번씩 물을 주고 있어요. (×)
(C) 번호순으로 부탁합니다. (×)

▶ (B)는 Don't you...?에 대한 질문에 주어를 "I"로 사용하는 동시에 flowerpot과 연상되는 plant를 사용하여 오답을 만들었다.

4. 고난도 부정/부가 의문문에 의문문이나 반문으로 답하는 경우도 정답이 될 수 있다.

Q Can't you reschedule the interview? 면접 일정을 다시 잡을 수는 없나요?
A Can I get back to you later? 나중에 다시 연락드려도 될까요?

Q You're going to attend the training session tomorrow, right? 내일 교육에 참석할 거죠, 그렇죠?
A Do you think that's necessary? 그 교육이 필요할까요?

CHECK-UP

P2_U4_Check-up 정답 및 해설 p.9

1.	(A)	(B)	(C)	**4.**	(A)	(B)	(C)
2.	(A)	(B)	(C)	**5.**	(A)	(B)	(C)
3.	(A)	(B)	(C)	**6.**	(A)	(B)	(C)

UNIT 05 제안/요청 및 선택 의문문

제안/요청 의문문

제안/요청 의문문에는 Sure, OK, Sorry 등으로 시작하여 동의나 거절을 나타내는 답변이 일반적이지만, 그러한 표현 없이 바로 구체적인 내용을 언급하는 답변도 빈번하게 출제된다.

1. 제안 의문문: Why don't/How about/Would you like to/Can I...?

Q **Why don't** we interview the two candidates at the same time? 두 후보를 동시에 면접 보면 어때요?
A OK, that sounds good. 네, 좋은 생각이에요.

Q **How about** hiring more temporary workers? 임시직을 더 고용하는 건 어때요?
A There's not much money in the budget. 예산이 넉넉하지 않아요.

Q **Would you like to** come on a hike with us this Sunday? 이번 일요일에 우리와 함께 하이킹 갈래요?
A There's a lot of rain in the forecast. 일기예보에 비가 많이 온다는데요.

Q **Can I** help you move your desk? 책상 옮기는 거 도와드릴까요?
A I think I can manage on my own. 저 혼자 할 수 있을 것 같아요.

2. 요청 의문문: Could/Can/Would you...?

Q **Could/Can you** give me a ride to work tomorrow? 내일 회사까지 좀 태워줄 수 있어요?
A Sure, I'd be happy to. 물론이죠.

Q **Would you** please take notes at the meeting? 회의 시간에 회의록 좀 작성해 주실래요?
A OK, I'll take care of that. 네, 제가 맡아 할게요.

Q **Would you** be willing to give a speech at the ceremony? 기념식에서 연설하실 의향 있으세요?
= Would you be interested in giving a speech at the ceremony?
A I'm leaving on an urgent business trip tomorrow. 전 내일 급하게 출장을 떠나요.

3. 고난도 Would you mind...?는 정중하게 부탁할 때 쓰이며, 직역하면 '~를 꺼리시나요?'라는 뜻이기 때문에 No 또는 Not at all로 답하면 수락을 뜻한다.

Example 01 P2_U5_Ex01

Would you mind looking for cheaper venues?
(A) I found it very useful.
(B) Not at all.
(C) Yes, that's the cheapest one.

더 저렴한 장소를 찾아봐 주시겠어요?
(A) 그건 매우 유용했어요. (×)
(B) 물론이죠. (○)
(C) 네, 그게 가장 저렴한 거예요. (×)

4. 고난도 질문으로 답할 경우

Q Would you mind forwarding those e-mails to Mr. Ruskin in Human Resources?
그 이메일들을 인사팀의 Mr. Ruskin에게 전달해 주시겠어요?
A What's his e-mail address? 그분 이메일 주소가 어떻게 되죠?

선택 의문문

선택 의문문은 항상 A or B...?의 형태로 끝나며, 둘 중 하나를 선택하는 답변이 가장 많이 출제된다.

1. 둘 중 하나를 선택할 경우

Q Would you like a refund or an exchange? **A** A refund, please.	환불을 원하세요, 교환을 원하세요? 환불이요.
Q Would you like to see the doctor on Monday or Thursday? **A** Thursday works better.	월요일에 진찰을 받으시겠어요, 목요일에 받으시겠어요? 목요일이 더 나아요.
Q Do you want your commercial to run at eight or nine P.M.? **A** I'd prefer nine.	저녁 8시에 광고가 나가길 원하세요, 9시에 나가길 원하세요? 9시요.

2. 아무거나 / 제3의 답변

Q Would you prefer to fly in the morning or the afternoon? **A** Whichever one is cheaper.	아침 항공편이 좋으세요, 저녁 항공편이 좋으세요? 아무거나 더 싼 거요.
Q Have you finished reviewing the report or do you need more time? **A** I'm finishing it now.	보고서 검토는 끝났나요, 아니면 시간이 더 필요한가요? 지금 마무리하고 있어요.

3. 고난도 질문에 언급된 단어를 사용하지 않고도 둘 중 하나를 선택하는 정답도 가능하다.

Example 02 P2_U5_Ex02

Have you moved or are you at the same address?
(A) The same time next week.
(B) I still live at Greenwood Street.
(C) They're a great moving company.

당신은 이사를 갔나요, 아니면 주소가 그대로인가요?
(A) 다음 주 같은 시간요. (×)
(B) 저는 아직 Greenwood Street에 살아요. (○)
(C) 그 회사는 정말 좋은 이사 업체예요. (×)

CHECK-UP

P2_U5_Check-up 정답 및 해설 p.10

1.	(A)	(B)	(C)	**4.**	(A)	(B)	(C)
2.	(A)	(B)	(C)	**5.**	(A)	(B)	(C)
3.	(A)	(B)	(C)	**6.**	(A)	(B)	(C)

UNIT 06 평서문

평균 세 문제가 출제된다. 평서문에는 뚜렷한 패턴이 없기 때문에 답변 또한 다양할 수밖에 없으며, 따라서 파트2에서 가장 어려운 난이도에 속한다. A-B 형태의 대화에서 A는 항상 평서문이며, 선택지에 해당하는 B는 평서문 또는 의문문이 될 수 있다.

1. 평서문 - 의문문: 평서문에 질문으로 답할 경우

Example 01 P2_U6_Ex01

We need a project assistant by the end of this month.	이달 말까지는 프로젝트 보조가 필요해요.
(A) Thanks for your assistance.	(A) 도와주셔서 고마워요. (×)
(B) Have you considered Ella Morita?	(B) Ella Morita를 고려해 보셨나요? (○)
(C) It's next to the projector screen.	(C) 그건 프로젝터 스크린 옆에 있어요. (×)

More examples

A I'm going to try to fix this copy machine. 이 복사기를 고쳐 보려고요.
B Are you sure it can be repaired? 정말 고칠 수 있겠어요?

A This month's training schedule has been revised. 이번 달 교육 일정이 수정되었습니다.
B Which dates have been changed? 어떤 날짜가 바뀌었죠?

2. 평서문 - 평서문: 특정 문제를 언급하거나 제안 또는 요청을 하는 경우가 많다.

Example 02 P2_U6_Ex02

I tried turning the projector on, but it didn't work.	프로젝터를 켜려고 했는데 안 돼요.
(A) Why is it being moved?	(A) 왜 옮겨지고 있는 거죠? (×)
(B) That place isn't far from here.	(B) 그 장소는 여기서 멀지 않아요. (×)
(C) The sales department used it yesterday.	(C) 영업부에서 어제 그걸 사용했었어요. (○)

More examples

A I'm having trouble finding a carpenter to renovate the roof. 지붕을 개조하려고 목수를 찾고 있는데 쉽지 않네요.
B Marty's had a lot of work done to his home. Marty가 자기 집 수리를 많이 했었어요.

A I can help set up the tables if you'd like. 원하시면 테이블 설치하는 걸 도와드릴게요.
B Thanks, but you don't have to do that. 고맙습니다만 그러실 필요는 없어요.

CHECK-UP P2_U6_Check-up 정답 및 해설 p.11

1.	(A)	(B)	(C)	**4.**	(A)	(B)	(C)
2.	(A)	(B)	(C)	**5.**	(A)	(B)	(C)
3.	(A)	(B)	(C)	**6.**	(A)	(B)	(C)

PRACTICE 고난도

P2_Practice 정답 및 해설 p.12

UNIT 01~03

Mark your answer on your answer sheet.

1. (A) (B) (C)

2. (A) (B) (C)

3. (A) (B) (C)

4. (A) (B) (C)

5. (A) (B) (C)

6. (A) (B) (C)

7. (A) (B) (C)

8. (A) (B) (C)

9. (A) (B) (C)

10. (A) (B) (C)

11. (A) (B) (C)

12. (A) (B) (C)

13. (A) (B) (C)

14. (A) (B) (C)

15. (A) (B) (C)

UNIT 04~06

Mark your answer on your answer sheet.

16. (A) (B) (C)

17. (A) (B) (C)

18. (A) (B) (C)

19. (A) (B) (C)

20. (A) (B) (C)

21. (A) (B) (C)

22. (A) (B) (C)

23. (A) (B) (C)

24. (A) (B) (C)

25. (A) (B) (C)

26. (A) (B) (C)

27. (A) (B) (C)

28. (A) (B) (C)

29. (A) (B) (C)

30. (A) (B) (C)

PART TEST

P2_PT 정답 및 해설 p.15

1. Mark your answer on your answer sheet.

2. Mark your answer on your answer sheet.

3. Mark your answer on your answer sheet.

4. Mark your answer on your answer sheet.

5. Mark your answer on your answer sheet.

6. Mark your answer on your answer sheet.

7. Mark your answer on your answer sheet.

8. Mark your answer on your answer sheet.

9. Mark your answer on your answer sheet.

10. Mark your answer on your answer sheet.

11. Mark your answer on your answer sheet.

12. Mark your answer on your answer sheet.

13. Mark your answer on your answer sheet.

14. Mark your answer on your answer sheet.

15. Mark your answer on your answer sheet.

16. Mark your answer on your answer sheet.

17. Mark your answer on your answer sheet.

18. Mark your answer on your answer sheet.

19. Mark your answer on your answer sheet.

20. Mark your answer on your answer sheet.

21. Mark your answer on your answer sheet.

22. Mark your answer on your answer sheet.

23. Mark your answer on your answer sheet.

24. Mark your answer on your answer sheet.

25. Mark your answer on your answer sheet.

LC

PART 3

PART 3 출제 경향 및 전략

두 명 또는 세 명의 대화를 듣고, 이와 관련된 3개의 문항에 알맞은 답을 고르는 파트이며 총 13개 대화문으로 구성된다. 3인 대화문은 13개 대화문 중 고정적으로 2개가 출제된다.

대화의 종류

파트3에서는 주로 사내 업무, 인사, 행사, 사무기기 및 시설 등 회사에서 일어날 수 있는 다양한 주제의 대화가 출제된다. 대화는 대개 남녀 성우로 구성되지만 간혹 동성 간의 대화로도 구성된다.

문제 유형

기본적으로 대화의 장소나 주제, 화자의 신분, 화자가 제안하거나 요청하는 것, 화자가 다음에 할 일, 논의해야 할 이슈 등을 묻는 유형이 꾸준히 출제되고 있다. 고난도 유형으로는, 화자의 말 중 특정 대사를 지목하여 그 대사의 의도가 무엇인지를 묻는 의도 파악 문제(2문항), 시각 자료와 연계하여 푸는 문제(3문항)가 매회 고정적으로 출제되고 있으며, 고득점을 위해서는 이러한 빈출 유형들을 충분히 연습할 필요가 있다.

단계별 듣기 전략

STEP 1 | 질문만 빠르게 훑고 키워드에 표시한다.

각 대화를 듣기 전에 세 문항의 질문들만 재빠르게 훑어보고 질문의 키워드에 표시해 놓는다. 키워드만으로 대화의 어떤 부분을 주의 깊게 들어야 할지 빠르게 판단해야 한다. 아래의 예시들의 경우에는 대화가 진행되는 흐름에 따라 '대화의 장소 〉 남자가 사고자 하는 것 〉 여자가 남자에게 요청하는 것' 순서로 꼭 들어야 할 내용들을 놓치지 말아야 한다.

32. **Where** is the conversation taking place? → 앞부분에서는 대화 장소를 파악해야겠군!

33. What will the man most likely **purchase**? → 다음으로 남자가 뭘 사고자 하는지 들어야겠군!

34. What does the woman **ask** the man to do? → 마지막 부분에서 여자가 남자에게 뭘 하라고 요청하겠군!

종종 세 문제 중 첫 번째 질문은 대화의 전반적인 상황과 화자들의 관계를 파악할 수 있게 해 준다.

ex What type of business is the woman calling? 여자는 어떤 종류의 회사에 전화하고 있는가?

▶ 대화를 듣기 전에 calling을 통해서 여자가 어떤 업체에 전화를 하는 상황이라는 것을 미리 알 수 있다. 이를 염두에 두고 들으면 대화를 이해하기가 훨씬 수월해진다.

STEP 2 | 지시문을 듣고 2인 대화인지 3인 대화인지 파악한다.

문제지 상에서는 2인 대화인지 3인 대화인지 쓰여 있지 않다. 대화가 시작되기 전에 나오는 지시문에서 three speakers라고 한다면 3인 대화라는 것을 미리 염두에 두고 들어야 당황하지 않는다.

Questions 47-49 refer to the following conversation **with three speakers**.

STEP 3 | 대화의 순서와 문제의 순서는 대부분 일치한다.

거의 대부분 첫 번째 문제는 대화의 초반에, 두 번째 문제는 대화의 중반에, 마지막 문제는 대화의 후반부에 단서가 놓여 있다. 따라서 대화의 초반부를 들을 때는 첫 번째 문제의 선택지들을 보고 있어야 하며, 대화가 전개됨에 따라 두 번째, 세 번째 문제의 선택지로 차례로 시선을 옮겨 가야 한다.

Example

P3_U0_Ex 정답 및 해설 p.009

W [32]Thank you for visiting the Kaysville Aquarium. How may I help you?

M I'd like admission tickets for two adults, please.

W The regular ticket is 22 dollars. However, [33]you can get a season ticket for just 75 dollars. That allows you to visit our site as many times as you want for one year.

M Hmm... Since we live locally, we'll probably come back many times. I guess I'll take that.

W Great! [34]All I need is for you to fill out this application form.

32. Where is the conversation taking place?
(A) At a movie theater
(B) At an aquarium
(C) At an art museum
(D) At a stadium

33. What will the man most likely purchase?
(A) A group ticket
(B) A half-day ticket
(C) A season ticket
(D) A student ticket

34. What does the woman ask the man to do?
(A) Complete a form
(B) Call another branch
(C) Show an ID card
(D) Make a phone call

정답의 단서를 알리는 큐(Cue)를 놓치지 말고 들어야 한다

대화에는 정답의 결정적 단서가 나오기 전에 그 단서가 곧 등장할 것이라는 것을 미리 알려주는 일종의 큐(Cue) 역할을 하는 표현들이 종종 쓰인다. 예를 들어 Thank you for visiting... 다음에는 Kaysville Aquarium처럼 회사나 가게 이름이 나온다. 그리고 회사나 가게 이름은 위의 경우 대화 장소를 묻는 문제의 단서가 된다. 또, 마지막 여자 대사의 All I need is...는 34번 요청 문제의 단서가 나올 것이라는 것을 알리는 큐(Cue)가 된다. 이 밖에도 토익에 빈출되는 특정 문제 유형들의 단서를 알리는 패턴화된 큐들을 알아두면 모든 대화를 듣지 못했더라도 어렵지 않게 정답을 찾을 수 있다. 이 책에서는 그런 큐들을 문제 유형별로 일목요연하게 정리해 두었다.

선택지는 종종 패러프레이즈 된다

대화 속 단어는 선택지에서 유사 의미의 다른 단어로, 또는 상위 카테고리의 단어로 패러프레이즈 되는 경우가 많다. 위의 Example에서는 여자 대사의 fill out this application form이 34번의 (A) Complete a form으로 패러프레이즈 됐다.

fill out this application form ➡ complete a form

동일한 의미는 아니더라도 구체적 단어들을 포괄하는 상위 개념의 단어로 교체되기도 하는데, 예를 들어 party는 event로, shirt는 clothes로, name and phone number는 contact information으로 교체되는 경우들이다.

UNIT 01 화자의 직업 및 대화 장소

빈출 문제 유형

화자의 직업 및 신분

- **What industry [field]** do the speakers work in? 화자들은 어느 산업[분야]에서 일하고 있는가?
- **What kind of business** do the speakers work for? 화자들은 어떤 업종에 종사하는가?
- **What type of business** is the woman calling? 여자는 어떤 종류의 회사에 전화하고 있는가?
- **Where** does the woman most likely work? 여자는 어디에서 일할 것 같은가?
- **Who** most likely is the man? 남자의 직업은 무엇일 것 같은가?
- **What service** does the man's company provide? 남자의 회사는 어떤 서비스를 제공하는가?

장소 관련 질문: 주로 상점, 식당, 병원, 박물관, 공장, 박람회장, 비행기, 기차 등이 출제된다.

- Where are the speakers? 화자들은 어디에 있는가?
- Where is the conversation most likely taking place? 대화는 어디에서 일어나고 있는 것 같은가?

대표 유형 맛보기

1. 화자의 직업 및 신분

Example 01 미남/영녀 P3_U1_Ex01

M Susan, have you finished **the cover design for the March issue** yet?
W I didn't get the portrait for the main image yet. Without it, I can't start working on fonts and colors.
M The shooting was supposed to be finished yesterday, but the model's flight was delayed. I'll call the photographer to try and hurry him up.

남 Susan, 3월호 표지 디자인 끝났나요?
여 메인 이미지로 쓸 인물 사진을 아직 못 받았어요. 메인 이미지 없이는 폰트하고 컬러 작업을 시작할 수 없어요.
남 촬영이 어제 끝나기로 되어 있었는데 모델이 탄 비행기가 연착됐어요. 제가 사진작가한테 전화해서 서둘러달라고 재촉해 볼게요.

What industry do the speakers most likely work in?
(A) Magazine publishing
(B) Interior design
(C) Advertising
(D) Aviation

화자들은 어느 산업 분야에서 일할 것 같은가?
(A) 잡지 출판
(B) 실내 디자인
(C) 광고
(D) 항공

정답 (A)

▶ 화자의 신분 및 화자의 회사에서 제공하는 서비스 및 상품 등을 물어볼 수도 있다.
Who most likely is the woman? → A designer (여자는 누구일 것 같은가? → 디자이너)
What does the speakers' company sell? → Magazine (화자들의 회사는 무엇을 파는가? → 잡지)

2. 대화 장소

Example 02

미남/영녀 P3_U1_Ex02

M Hi, Ruth. How's **the order of cakes** for the Riverside Hotel coming along? They have to be ready by noon. **W** I'm a little behind. It's a little more complex than I thought it would be. **M** Hmm... Then, why don't you ask Tom for help?	남 안녕하세요, Ruth. Riverside Hotel에서 주문한 케이크는 어떻게 돼 가나요? 정오까지는 준비되어야 해요. 여 조금 늦어졌어요. 생각했던 것보다 좀 더 복잡해요. 남 흠... 그럼, Tom한테 도와달라고 하면 어때요?
Where most likely are the speakers? → At a bakery	화자들은 어디에 있을 것 같은가? → 제과점

▶ the order of cakes → 케이크를 주문받았다는 것을 통해 제과점에서 대화가 진행되고 있음을 알 수 있다.

PART 3

놓치지 말아야 할 큐(Cue)

전화 상황에서는 아래의 표현들 뒤에 자신의 소속이나 신분을 밝히므로 절대 놓치지 말고 들어야 한다.

- Hello, **thank you for calling** Quint Computers Customer Service. ~에 전화 주셔서 감사합니다
- Hello, **you've reached** IT department. 당신은 ~에 전화 주셨습니다
- Hi, **this is** Killian Scott, hiring manager from WeSoftware. 저는 ~입니다

Example 03

미녀/호남 P3_U1_Ex03

W **Thanks for calling** Appleyard Flowers. How may I help you? **M** I just ordered flowers online to be delivered today. **W** Oh, yes. Was that the rose bouquet for the retirement party?	여 Appleyard Flowers에 전화 주셔서 감사합니다. 어떻게 도와드릴까요? 남 방금 온라인으로 오늘 배송되는 꽃배달 주문을 했는데요. 여 아, 네. 은퇴 파티용 장미 부케 주문이었죠?
What type of business is the man calling? → A flower shop	남자는 어떤 종류의 업체에 전화하고 있는가? → 꽃집

▶ 남자의 전화를 받는 상대방, 즉 여자가 일하는 회사를 묻고 있으므로 여자의 대화에 큐(Cue)가 있을 가능성이 높다. Thanks for calling 다음에 바로 업체 이름이 나오므로 쉽게 정답을 찾을 수 있다.

CHECK-UP

P3_U1_Check-up 정답 및 해설 p.19

1. What industry do the speakers work in?
(A) Publishing
(B) Transportation
(C) Construction
(D) Finance

2. Who most likely is the man?
(A) An interior designer
(B) A real estate agent
(C) A safety inspector
(D) An apartment manager

UNIT 02 대화 목적 및 주제

빈출 문제 유형

전화, 방문, 여행 등의 목적

- What is the **purpose** of the telephone call? 전화의 목적은 무엇인가?
- **Why** is the woman calling? 여자가 전화하는 이유는 무엇인가?
- What is the **purpose** of the **man's visit**? 남자의 방문 목적은 무엇인가?
- What is the **purpose** of the **man's trip**? 남자의 여행 목적은 무엇인가?

대화의 주제: 논의되고 있는 이슈, 제품, 행사 등을 묻는 경우

- What are the speakers mainly **discussing**? 화자들은 주로 무엇에 대해 논의하고 있는가?
- What does the woman want to **discuss**? 여자는 무엇을 논의하고 싶어 하는가?
- **What type of product** are the speakers discussing? 화자들은 어떤 종류의 제품을 논의하는가?
- **What problem** is being discussed? 무슨 문제가 논의되고 있는가?
- **What kind of event** is taking place? 어떤 행사가 개최되고 있는가?

대표 유형 맛보기

1. 전화 목적

Example 01 미남/영녀 P3_U2_Ex01

M Thank you for calling the Westfield Museum. How may I help you?
W Hi, **I'm calling to** find out if the museum has any guided tour programs specifically for students.
M Yes, we're running *Great Paintings* programs every Friday and Saturday. I can e-mail you an information packet, if you'd like.
W That would be wonderful.

남 Westfield Museum에 전화주셔서 감사합니다. 무엇을 도와드릴까요?
여 안녕하세요. 박물관에 특별히 학생들을 위한 가이드 동반 프로그램이 있는지 알아보고 싶어 전화드립니다.
남 네, Great Paintings라는 프로그램을 매주 금요일과 토요일에 운영하고 있습니다. 원하신다면, 이메일로 관련 정보를 보내드릴 수 있습니다.
여 그래 주시면 정말 감사하겠습니다.

Why is the woman calling?
(A) To ask about a guided tour
(B) To confirm a schedule
(C) To sign up for a seminar
(D) To book a consultation

여자는 왜 전화를 하는가?
(A) 가이드 동반 투어에 대해 문의하기 위해
(B) 일정 확정을 위해
(C) 세미나에 등록하기 위해
(D) 상담을 예약하기 위해

정답 (A)

▶ 전화 통화의 경우 흔히 I'm calling to..., I'm calling because... 뒤에 전화를 건 목적이 나온다.
ex) **I'm calling because** I haven't received my order yet. ➜ 정답: To make a complaint
아직 주문한 물건을 받지 못해 전화드립니다. ➜ 정답: 불만을 표하기 위해

2. 방문 목적

Example 02 영녀/미남 P3_U2_Ex02

W Hi, I'm Elaine Clifford. **I'm here for** an interview for a position as a sales manager.
M Good morning. May I see your identification? I'll need it to make a visitor's badge for you. All visitors must wear a badge while they're in the building.

여 안녕하세요, 저는 Elaine Clifford인데요, 영업 관리자 직에 면접을 보러 왔습니다.
남 안녕하세요. 신분증 좀 볼 수 있을까요? 손님의 방문자 명찰을 만들어 드려야 해서요. 모든 방문객들은 건물에 있는 동안 명찰을 착용하셔야 합니다.

What is **the purpose** of the woman's visit?
➜ To have an interview

여자의 방문 목적은 무엇인가?
➜ 면접을 보기 위해

▶ I'm here to (동사) / for (명사)... 뒤에 방문 목적이 나오는 경우가 많다.
ex) Hi, **I'm here to fix** some damaged floor tiles. ➜ 정답: To repair tiles
안녕하세요. 파손된 바닥 타일을 고치기 위해 왔습니다. ➜ 정답: 타일을 수리하기 위해

PART 3

3. 주제

Example 03 호남/미녀 P3_U2_Ex03

M Hi. I'm going to **rent a kayak** for my family. Do you have it available now?
W Yes, and if you rent it for more than two hours, we'll give you a 20% discount.
M That sounds great.
W Please wait over there for 10 minutes while I'm getting a kayak ready for you. And if you'd like to get some snacks to take along, we have a refreshment stand inside.

남 안녕하세요. 제 가족과 탈 카약을 대여하려고 하는데. 지금 탈 수 있나요?
여 네, 두 시간 이상 대여하시면 20% 할인을 해 드리고 있습니다.
남 그거 좋네요.
여 제가 카약을 준비해 놓는 동안 저쪽에서 10분만 기다려 주세요. 그리고 배에 가지고 탈 간식거리가 필요하시면 안에 매점이 있습니다.

What are the speakers mainly **discussing**?
➜ Boat rental

화자들은 주로 무엇에 대해 논의하고 있는가?
➜ 배 대여

▶ kayak을 상위 개념의 단어인 boat로 바꾸어 표현한 boat rental이 정답이다.

CHECK-UP

P3_U2_Check-up 정답 및 해설 p.20

1. What is the purpose of the telephone call?
(A) To place an order
(B) To arrange an interview
(C) To confirm a contract
(D) To cancel an appointment

2. What problem is being discussed?
(A) An electric outage
(B) A road closure
(C) Bad weather
(D) A broken vehicle

UNIT 03 요청, 제안

빈출 문제 유형

상대방에게 무엇을 하라고 요청하거나 해 보자고 제안하는 경우

- What does the man **ask** the woman to do? 남자는 여자에게 무엇을 하라고 요청하는가?
- What does the man **tell** the woman to do? 남자는 여자에게 무엇을 하라고 말하는가?
- What does the man **want** the woman to do? 남자는 여자가 무엇을 하기를 원하는가?
- What does the man **say** the woman should do? 남자는 여자에게 무엇을 해야 한다고 말하는가?
- What does the man **suggest** the woman do? 남자는 여자에게 무엇을 할 것을 제안하는가?
- What does the man **suggest** doing? 남자는 무엇을 할 것을 제안하는가?

상대방에게 무엇을 해 주겠다고 제안하는 경우

- What does the man **offer** to do? 남자는 무엇을 하겠다고 제안하는가?

대표 유형 맛보기

Example 미남 / 영녀 P3_U3_Ex

M You wanted to speak with me, Carol?
W Yes. I wanted to run something by you since you're the manager here. It seems like we don't get a lot of customers in the morning, but a lot of people want to go furniture shopping after they get off of work.
M What do you mean?
W I think it makes more sense for us to push back our starting time and stay open later. That way more people can shop here after work.
M Aah, I see. That's a good idea. **Can you set up an employee meeting today**? I need to discuss this with everyone else.

남 Carol, 할 말이 있다고 했죠?
여 네, 여기 점장님이시니까 같이 의논하고 싶은 게 있었어요. 우리 매장에 오전에는 손님이 많지 않은데, 많은 사람들이 퇴근하고 가구 쇼핑하기를 원하거든요.
남 무슨 뜻이죠?
여 매장 오픈 시간을 뒤로 미루고 좀 더 늦게까지 영업하는 게 좋을 것 같아요. 그러면 퇴근 후에 더 많은 사람들이 우리 매장에서 쇼핑할 수 있을 거예요.
남 그렇겠군요. 좋은 생각입니다. 오늘 직원 회의를 잡아주시겠어요? 다른 직원들과 논의해 봐야겠어요.

[어휘] run A by B B에게 A에 대한 의견을 묻다

What does the man **ask** the woman to do?
(A) Organize a meeting
(B) Contact a customer
(C) Set up a display
(D) Give a presentation

남자는 여자에게 무엇을 하라고 요청하는가?
(A) 회의 잡기
(B) 고객에게 연락하기
(C) 디스플레이 설치하기
(D) 발표하기

정답 (A)

▶ 보통 이 유형의 문제는 세 문항 중 마지막 문항으로 출제된다. 문제에서 ask... to do?를 보자마자 대화의 후반부에 요청에 관련된 표현(Cue)이 나올 거라고 예측해야 한다. 남자가 여자에게 요청하는 것이므로 남자 대사를 주의 깊게 들어야 하며, Can you....?가 단서를 알리는 큐(Cue)가 된다.

▶ 정답 선택지에서는 대화의 set up a meeting을 organize a meeting으로 바꿔 표현했다.

놓치지 말아야 할 큐(Cue)

상대에게 요청/제안	**Can/Could you** send me his e-mail address? 그의 이메일 주소를 저에게 보내줄 수 있나요? **Will you** provide me with your account number? 계정 번호를 알려주시겠어요? **Would you** consider promoting him to Susan's old position? 그를 Susan이 맡던 직책으로 승진시키는 것에 대해 고려해 주시겠어요? **Would it be possible** for you to give us a demonstration? 저희에게 시연해 주시는 게 가능할까요? **Why don't you** do some research about that? 그것에 대해 조사를 해 보시는 게 어때요?
	I'd suggest that you check it again before submitting it. 그걸 제출하기 전에 다시 검토해 보세요. **I'd highly recommend** you contact them right away. 그들에게 바로 연락해 보세요. **I'd appreciate it if** you'd fill out this form. 이 양식을 작성해 주시면 감사하겠습니다. **I'd really like you to** tell me about your new book. 당신의 새 책에 대해 말씀해 주시겠어요? **Please** inform HR of which days you'd like to use for your vacation. 언제 휴가를 쓰고 싶은지를 인사팀에 알려주세요.
	You'll have to fill out this form. 이 양식을 작성해 주셔야 합니다. **You'll need to** fill out an online request form from our Web site. 저희 웹사이트에서 온라인 요청서를 작성하셔야 해요. **I need you to** submit the request in advance. 기안서를 미리 제출해 주셔야 해요.
	Why don't we draw a blueprint for the plan? 그 계획에 대한 청사진을 그려볼까요? **How about** reaching out to tour guides? 여행 가이드들에게 연락해보는 건 어때요? **Let's** switch to my laptop. 내 노트북으로 바꿔봅시다.
상대에게 무엇을 해 주겠다고 제안	**Why don't I** run a test first? 제가 먼저 검사를 해 보면 어떨까요? **I can** refund the amount to your credit card. **Would you like me to** do that? 귀하의 신용카드로 그 금액을 환불해 드릴 수 있습니다. 그렇게 해드릴까요? **How about I** find out what events are coming up in our area? 제가 우리 지역에서 어떤 행사들이 열릴 예정인지 알아볼까요?

CHECK-UP

P3_U3_Check-up 정답 및 해설 p.20

1. What does the woman ask the man to do?

(A) Modify a contract
(B) Finalize a payment
(C) Extend the deadline
(D) Obtain a supervisor's approval

2. What does the woman suggest doing?

(A) Conducting market research
(B) Hiring more staff
(C) Offering a rewards program
(D) Finding a consultant

UNIT 04 문제, 걱정

빈출 문제 유형

- **What problem** do the women mention? 여자들은 무슨 문제를 언급하는가?
- According to the woman, what might cause a **problem**? 여자에 따르면, 무엇이 문제를 일으킬 수 있는가?
- What does the man say he is **concerned** about? 남자는 무엇에 대해 걱정된다고 말하는가?
- What is the woman **concerned** about? 여자는 무엇에 대해 걱정하는가?
- What is causing a **delay**? 무엇이 지연을 일으키고 있는가?
- Why does the man **apologize**? 남자는 왜 사과하고 있는가?
- **What complaint** did customers have about the product? 고객들은 그 상품에 대해 어떤 불만을 가졌는가?

대표 유형 맛보기

Example 미남/영녀 P3_U4_Ex

M Excuse me, wasn't the train to Crayford supposed to leave at 11:00?

W Right, but the Bexley Transportation authority has suspended all rail service due to emergency railroad repair.

M I see. Then, is every train canceled all day?

W The repair is expected to end in about 2 hours, and after that operations should return to normal.

M Okay, then I guess I'll grab a bite to eat nearby.

W There are some good cafés near the Bexley Hotel across the street. And we'll be posting updates on our mobile app, so be sure to check it regularly.

M Thanks.

남 죄송하지만 Crayford로 가는 기차가 11시에 떠나지 않나요?

여 맞아요, 하지만 Bexley 교통 당국에서 긴급 철로 수리 때문에 모든 철도 운행을 중단했어요.

남 그렇군요. 그럼 오늘 모든 기차가 취소된 건가요?

여 수리는 약 2시간 후면 끝날 거로 예상되는데, 그 후엔 운행이 정상화될 거예요.

남 알겠습니다. 근처에서 간단하게 요기라도 해야겠네요.

여 길 건너 Bexley Hotel 근처에 괜찮은 카페들이 좀 있어요. 그리고 모바일 앱에 공지가 올라가니까 수시로 확인해 보셔야 해요.

남 감사합니다.

What problem does the woman mention?

(A) The weather is bad.
(B) Some tickets are sold out.
(C) The railroad is under repair.
(D) Her car is not working.

여자는 어떤 문제를 언급하는가?

(A) 날씨가 안 좋다.
(B) 표가 매진되었다.
(C) 철로가 수리중이다.
(D) 여자의 차가 고장났다.

정답 (C)

▶ 질문의 What problem...?을 보자마자 대화에 특정 문제 상황이 언급될 것임을 예측하고 들어야 한다.

▶ 질문에서 "여자가 언급하는 문제"가 무엇이냐고 물어봤으므로 여자의 대사에 단서가 들어 있다.

▶ but이나 unfortunately 뒤에는 거의 어김없이 문제 상황이 언급되므로 그 뒷부분을 집중해서 들어야 한다. 여자 대사의 but 뒤에 긴급 철로 수리 때문에(due to emergency railroad repair) 철도 운행이 중단되었다고 했으므로, 정답은 (C)가 된다.

놓치지 말아야 할 큐(Cue)

The customers liked the fact that the new headphone is wireless. **But** there were complaints about the battery life. ➜ [정답] The battery life was short.	고객들은 새 헤드폰이 무선이라는 사실을 좋아했어요. 하지만 배터리의 수명에 대한 불만이 있었습니다. ➜ [정답] 배터리 수명이 짧았다.
I called the supplier this morning but **unfortunately**, the bricks we wanted are sold out. ➜ [정답] Some materials are not available.	오늘 아침에 공급업체에 전화했는데 아쉽게도 우리가 원하는 벽돌은 품절이에요. ➜ [정답] 일부 재료를 이용할 수 없다.

빈출 문제 상황

I didn't use any hotel breakfast, but there's a charge for it here. ➜ [정답] A bill is not correct.	저는 호텔 조식을 이용하지 않았는데 여기 그에 대한 비용이 청구되었네요. ➜ [정답] 청구서가 잘못됐다.
I'm stuck in traffic on the Johnson Highway. It looks like I'm going to be about 30 minutes late. ➜ [정답] Traffic is heavy.	존슨 고속도로에서 빠져 나오질 못하고 있어요. 30분 정도 늦을 것 같아요. ➜ [정답] 차가 많이 막힌다.
Well, I just finished setting up the tables outside, but the Browns Seafood is running late on their deliveries. ➜ [정답] A delivery has been delayed.	방금 야외 테이블 준비를 마쳤는데, Browns Seafood에서 배송이 늦어지고 있어요. ➜ [정답] 배송이 지연되었다.
The cost to install the solar panels is almost double what we anticipated. We don't have enough money for that. ➜ [정답] A project is too expensive.	태양 전지판 설치비가 우리가 예상했던 것의 거의 두 배예요. 우리는 그만한 돈이 없어요. ➜ [정답] 프로젝트 비용이 너무 많이 든다.
Oh, unfortunately, I'll be attending a conference then. Could I reschedule for next week? ➜ [정답] She has a prior commitment.	오 이런, 그때는 제가 컨퍼런스에 참석해야 해요. 다음 주로 일정을 바꿀 수 있을까요? ➜ [정답] 그녀는 선약이 있다.

PART 3

CHECK-UP

P3_U4_Check-up 정답 및 해설 p.21

1. What problem does the man mention?

(A) A deadline was missed.
(B) A product is out of stock.
(C) An order was not delivered.
(D) Some staff members are unavailable.

2. What does the man say he is concerned about?

(A) Location
(B) Available dates
(C) Cost
(D) Size

UNIT 05 특정 시간

빈출 문제 유형

질문 속에 구체적인 시간 및 날짜가 언급되는 유형으로 대화 속에 해당 시간 및 날짜가 그대로 언급된다.

- What does the woman say she is going to do **tomorrow**? 여자는 내일 무엇을 할 것이라고 말하는가?
- What has Reed Birney been working on **recently**? Reed Birney는 최근에 어떤 일을 하고 있는가?
- What will the speakers do **this afternoon**? 화자들은 오늘 오후에 무엇을 할 것인가?
- What does the woman want to do on **Friday morning**? 여자는 금요일 오전에 무엇을 하고 싶어 하는가?
- What will happen **at the end of November**? 11월 말에 무슨 일이 일어날 것인가?

대표 유형 맛보기

Example 01

미남/영녀 P3_U5_Ex01

M Thanks for calling Alabama Moving Services. What can I do for you?

W Hi, I'm moving out of the neighborhood early next month. I have a lot of things I want to take with me, including furniture and some fragile items. I want them all to be taken care of at the same time.

M That won't be a problem. You can take a picture of all the items you want moved, send them to our e-mail, and we'll show up on the designated day with moving vans to help you.

W Will you be able to wrap my fragile items for me?

M Yes, but that comes at an additional fee. And you need to **send us pictures of those items by the end of the week.**

W No problem.

남 Alabama 이삿짐센터에 전화해 주셔서 감사합니다. 뭘 도와 드릴까요?

여 안녕하세요. 저는 다음 달 초에 이사를 갑니다. 가구와 깨지기 쉬운 물건들을 포함해서 가지고 가고 싶은 것들이 많아요. 모든 것들이 한꺼번에 잘 처리되었으면 해요.

남 그건 문제되지 않을 거예요. 옮기려는 모든 품목을 사진으로 찍어서 저희 이메일로 보내주시면 지정된 날짜에 이삿짐 트럭을 가지고 댁에 방문할 겁니다.

여 깨지기 쉬운 물건들을 포장해 주실 수 있을까요?

남 네, 하지만 추가 요금이 부과됩니다. 그리고 이번 주말까지 그 물건들의 사진을 우리에게 보내주셔야 합니다.

여 문제없습니다.

What will the woman be doing this week?

(A) Renovating her home
(B) Sending some pictures
(C) Moving to a new place
(D) Starting a new job

여자는 이번 주에 무엇을 할 것인가?

(A) 집을 개조하는 것
(B) 사진을 보내는 것
(C) 새로운 곳으로 이사하는 것
(D) 새로운 일을 시작하는 것

정답 (B)

▶ 문제에서 여자가 할 일을 묻고 있지만 정답의 단서는 남자의 대사에 들어 있을 수도 있으므로 두 사람의 대사를 모두 집중해서 들어야 한다.

▶ 문제의 this week가 대화에 그대로 언급되는 경우가 많지만, 위의 대화에서처럼 by the end of the week와 같이 변형되어 나타날 수도 있다. 또한, 대화에 언급된 다른 시간 정보(early next month)와 헷갈려서는 안 된다.

Example 02

미남/영녀 P3_U5_Ex02

M Good morning, Ms. Sheldon. Is it possible to put some more money into the magazine's guest article budget?
W As you know, the budget has been the same for a while now.
M Yes, but this quarter is our 10 year anniversary special. I wanted to have a special guest author write an article praising the magazine. But I'm concerned if we get someone famous, they're going to ask for more money.
W Oh, I forgot about the anniversary special.
M We could try to find someone cheaper, but **Paul Adelstein is one of the most famous critics** these days.
W You're right. I have a management meeting to attend now, so **I'll try to get in contact with him in the afternoon**. I'm glad I have his number I got at the conference this spring.

남 안녕하세요 Ms. Sheldon. 잡지의 초청 기사 예산에 돈을 좀 더 쓸 수 있을까요?
여 아시겠지만 예산은 한동안 동결돼 왔어요.
남 네, 하지만 이번 분기는 10주년 기념 특집이에요. 저는 특별 초청 작가에게 저희 잡지를 호평하는 기사를 쓰게 하고 싶어요. 하지만 유명한 사람을 쓰면 돈을 더 달라고 할 테니까 그게 걱정이에요.
여 아, 기념일 특집을 깜빡했네요.
남 더 싼 사람을 찾아볼 수도 있지만, Paul Adelstein은 요즘 가장 유명한 비평가들 중 한 명입니다.
여 당신 말이 맞아요. 지금은 참석해야 할 경영진 회의가 있어서 오후에 그에게 연락해 볼게요. 다행히 올봄 컨퍼런스에서 받은 그의 번호를 가지고 있습니다.

What will the woman do **in the afternoon**?

(A) Contact a critic
(B) Review a report
(C) Host a meeting
(D) Consult with a supervisor

여자는 오후에 무엇을 할 것인가?

(A) 비평가에게 연락하기
(B) 보고서 검토하기
(C) 회의 주최하기
(D) 상사와 의논하기

정답 (A)

▶ 문제에서 여자가 할 일을 묻고 있지만 여자뿐만 아니라 남자의 대사에도 정답의 단서가 들어 있다. 여자가 "I'll try to get in contact with him in the afternoon"이라고 했고, him은 바로 앞 남자의 대사에서 Paul Adelstein이라는 비평가(critic)를 말하므로 정답은 (A) Contact a critic이 된다.

▶ (C) Host a meeting은 마지막 여자의 대사에 언급된 have a management meeting to attend를 사용한 함정이다.

PART 3

CHECK-UP

P3_U5_Check-up 정답 및 해설 p.22

1. According to the woman, what will happen in three weeks?

(A) An inventory count
(B) An annual clearance sale
(C) An anniversary party
(D) A grand opening

2. What does the man say he will do later today?

(A) Give a presentation
(B) Fill out an online survey
(C) Reserve a vehicle
(D) Visit a community center

UNIT 06 다음에 할 일

빈출 문제 유형

파트3에서 가장 많이 나오는 유형 중 하나이며, 대개 3문제 중 마지막 문제로 출제된다.

- What will the man do **next**? 남자는 다음에 무엇을 할 것인가?
- What will the man most likely do **next**? 남자는 다음에 무엇을 할 것 같은가?
- What are the women most likely planning to do **next**? 여자들은 다음에 무엇을 할 계획인 것 같은가?
- What does the woman say she **will do**? 여자는 무엇을 할 것이라고 말하는가?

대표 유형 맛보기

Example 01

영녀 / 미남 P3_U6_Ex01

W Hello, West Square Apartments leasing office. How can I help you?

M Hi, I currently live in unit 305, but I'm wondering if there are any larger units available to rent in the building.

W Yes, we have one apartment which has three rooms and two bathrooms. Perfect timing, as the lease on it ends at the end of the month.

M Sounds great. And is that facing south? I'm growing a garden on a balcony.

W Yes, it gets sunlight for most of the day. **I'll call the current tenant** to figure out a time for a viewing.

여 안녕하세요, West Square Apartments 임대 사무실입니다. 무엇을 도와드릴까요?

남 안녕하세요, 저는 현재 305호에 살고 있는데, 건물 내에 더 큰 아파트가 임대로 나와 있는지 궁금합니다.

여 네, 방 3개와 화장실 2개가 딸린 아파트가 하나 있어요. 때마침 전화 주셨네요. 이번 달 말에 임대가 끝나거든요.

남 좋아요. 남향인가요? 제가 발코니에 정원을 가꾸고 있거든요.

여 네, 거의 하루 종일 햇빛이 들어요. 제가 현 세입자에게 전화해서 방을 구경할 수 있는 시간을 알아볼게요.

What will the woman **do next**?

(A) Visit a client
(B) E-mail a contract
(C) Make a phone call
(D) Go on a tour

여자는 다음에 무엇을 할 것인가?

(A) 고객 방문하기
(B) 메일로 계약서 보내기
(C) 전화하기
(D) 견학하기

정답 (C)

▶ "... do next?"로 끝나는 유형은 대개 대화의 끝부분에 단서가 있으므로 항상 끝부분을 집중해서 들어야 한다.

▶ 여자가 다음에 할 일을 묻고 있으므로 여자의 대사를 집중해서 들어야 한다.

▶ 여자가 I'll call the current tenant...라고 했으므로 (C) Make a phone call이 정답이다.

▶ **I'll..., Let me..., I'm going to..., I'm planning..., Let's... I can..., I have to..., I'd better...** 등은 "do next" 문제의 큐가 되며, 그 뒤에 정답의 단서가 나온다.

Example 02

미남/영녀 P3_U6_Ex02

M Hello, I'm Leo from the IT department. I was told you need assistance setting up a video conference. I can help you with anything you need.
W Thank you so much. This meeting is very important to our team. We're looking to get funding from the government for our new project, so we have to speak with state officials.
M No problem. I can help with that.
W I can control the microphone to mute people if they make too much background noise, right?
M Of course.
W I also want to be able to share my computer screen with the participants. Can I do that?
M Sure, you can do all of that quite easily. **Let me use the manual to show you how.**

남 안녕하세요, 저는 IT부서의 Leo입니다. 화상 회의를 설정하는 것에 도움이 필요하시다고 들었습니다. 필요하신 게 있으면 뭐든 도와드릴게요.
여 정말 감사드립니다. 이 회의는 저희 팀에 매우 중요합니다. 새로운 프로젝트를 위해 정부로부터 자금을 받으려 하는데, 그 때문에 주 공무원들과 얘기를 나눠야 해요.
남 문제없습니다. 도와드릴 수 있어요.
여 사람들이 너무 많은 배경 소음을 일으키면 마이크를 제어해서 사람들의 음성을 안 들리게 할 수 있죠?
남 물론이죠.
여 그리고 제 컴퓨터 화면을 참가자들과 공유할 수 있으면 좋겠어요. 그렇게 할 수 있나요?
남 그럼요, 어렵지 않습니다. 설명서를 보면서 어떻게 하는지 알려 드릴게요.

What will the man **do next**?

(A) Consult a manual
(B) Speak with his supervisor
(C) Install a projector
(D) Arrange a meeting

남자는 다음에 무엇을 할 것인가?

(A) 설명서 참고하기
(B) 상사와 이야기하기
(C) 프로젝터 설치하기
(D) 회의 잡기

정답 (A)

▶ 남자가 다음에 할 일을 묻고 있으므로 마지막 부분에 나오는 남자의 대사를 집중해서 들어야 한다.

▶ 남자가 "Let me use the manual..."이라고 했으므로 (A) Consult a manual이 정답이다. consult는 '상담하다, 상의하다'라는 뜻 이외에도 정보를 얻기 위해 책이나 자료 등을 '참고하다'라는 뜻이 있다.
(ex. consult a map 지도를 참고하다/살펴보다)

CHECK-UP

P3_U6_Check-up 정답 및 해설 p.22

1. What will the man most likely do next?

(A) Make a phone call
(B) Prepare for a meeting
(C) Go to lunch
(D) Send out an announcement

2. What will the woman most likely do next?

(A) Inspect some equipment
(B) Speak with her colleagues
(C) Pick up clients
(D) Reschedule a demonstration

PRACTICE UNIT 01~06

1. Who most likely is the man?
(A) A marketing consultant
(B) A news reporter
(C) A construction manager
(D) A web developer

2. What problem does the man mention?
(A) Some materials are missing.
(B) The project is too expensive.
(C) The weather is bad.
(D) A crew member quit.

3. What will the man do next?
(A) Send an e-mail
(B) Make a phone call
(C) Write a report
(D) Visit a government office

---

4. Who most likely is the woman?
(A) A physician
(B) A film director
(C) An architect
(D) An interior designer

5. What does the man say happened this morning?
(A) He received an e-mail message.
(B) He discovered a problem.
(C) He met with a contractor.
(D) He was late to work.

6. What does the man offer to do?
(A) Conduct an interview
(B) Submit a report
(C) Arrange a conversation
(D) Share some data

---

7. What does the woman's company sell?
(A) Hiking gear
(B) Mobile applications
(C) Health food
(D) Children's clothing

8. What point does the man emphasize?
(A) A Web site has changed.
(B) A customer is unhappy.
(C) A product is reliable.
(D) A price has increased.

9. What is the woman pleased about?
(A) An advertising campaign
(B) A delivery service
(C) A skilled employee
(D) A new supplier

---

10. Where does the woman work?
(A) At a retirement community
(B) At a university
(C) At a recruitment agency
(D) At a hospital

11. What is the purpose of the man's visit?
(A) He is meeting a relative.
(B) He is inquiring about a job.
(C) He is delivering a product.
(D) He is making a payment.

12. What will the man probably do next?
(A) Watch a short film
(B) Tour the facilities
(C) Fill out an application
(D) Write an e-mail

---

13. Who is the woman?
(A) A clothing salesperson
(B) A grocer
(C) A travel agent
(D) A tailor

14. What does the man say will happen next week?
(A) He will take a vacation.
(B) He will host a meeting.
(C) He will sign a contract.
(D) He will attend an event.

15. What will the man probably do next?
(A) Make a payment
(B) Complete a form
(C) Collect a receipt
(D) Write a review

---

16. According to the woman, what recently happened at her business?
(A) An investor was found.
(B) Employees asked for higher pay.
(C) The customer base grew.
(D) The location was changed.

17. What can the man's company do?
(A) Provide the wait staff
(B) Arrange the dining room
(C) Prepare quality meals
(D) Make food deliveries

18. What does the woman say she could do to announce the partnership?
(A) Plan a special event
(B) Create commercials
(C) Start a social media campaign
(D) Publish a newspaper advertisement

---

19. Where is the conversation most likely taking place?
(A) At an office building
(B) At a fitness center
(C) At a ski resort
(D) At a sporting goods store

20. What does the man give to the woman?
(A) A phone number
(B) A receipt
(C) A form
(D) A Web site link

21. What will the woman most likely do next?
(A) Make a phone call
(B) Go to a waiting area
(C) Submit a job application
(D) Talk to a staff member

---

22. What problem does the man mention?
(A) He injured himself.
(B) He got a flat tire.
(C) His engine malfunctioned.
(D) His gas tank was leaking.

23. What does the woman suggest doing?
(A) Going to a specific repair shop
(B) Checking warranty information
(C) Purchasing new insurance
(D) Asking for a refund

24. What does the man say he will look for?
(A) An invoice
(B) A manual
(C) A business card
(D) A police report

UNIT 07 의도 파악

빈출 문제 유형

이 유형은 항상 다음의 세 가지 형태 중 하나로만 출제되며, 파트3에서는 39문항 중 2문항으로 고정되어 있다.

What does the man imply when he says, "that happens all the time"?
남자가 "걸핏하면 그래요"라고 말할 때 무엇을 의미하는가?

What does the man mean when he says, "I ran out of handouts"?
남자가 "유인물이 다 떨어졌어요"라고 말할 때 무엇을 의미하는가?

Why does the woman say, "It won't take that long"?
여자는 왜 "그건 그렇게 오래 걸리지 않을 거예요."라고 말하는가?

대표 유형 맛보기

Example

미남/영녀 🎧 P3_U7_Ex 정답 및 해설 p.27

M Heather, we haven't planned anything for the Sheffield Summer Music Festival taking place next weekend. But it would be a good publicity opportunity.
W There will definitely be a lot of people there.
M Exactly. I thought that we could give out free cans of our line of sodas. And we could get limited edition cans printed with the festival's logo.
W **That could take up to two weeks.**
M That's true. Maybe we could think of another way to stand out.

1. What event will take place next weekend?
(A) A music festival
(B) A charity fund-raiser
(C) An anniversary party
(D) A company picnic

2. What does the speakers' company produce?
(A) Athletic gear
(B) Clothing
(C) Beverages
(D) Outdoor furniture

3. Why does the woman say, "**That could take up to two weeks**"?
(A) To offer an apology for an error
(B) To suggest extending a deadline
(C) To complain about a service
(D) To express concern about a plan

▶ 이 유형은 한 세트에서 두세 번째 문항으로 자주 출제된다. 위 문제에서는 의도 파악 문제가 제일 마지막에 있으므로 대화의 마지막 부분을 집중해서 들어야 한다. 정해진 큐(Cue)가 없으므로 앞뒤 맥락을 잘 파악해서 들어야 하는 고난이도 유형이다.

▶ 여자의 대사는 남자의 말에 대한 대답이므로 결국 남자의 대사에 근거해 의도를 파악해야 한다. 남자가 제품 홍보 방법으로 한정판 음료 캔에 페스티벌 로고를 찍어서 나눠주자고 제안했고, 여자는 그렇게 하려면 2주가 걸린다고 했으므로, 결국 여자의 말에는 '그 방법은 너무 오래 걸려서 어려울 것이다'라는 염려가 담겨 있다.

※ UNIT 07~09는 고난도 유형으로, 실제 문제처럼 풀어볼 수 있도록 Check-up 대신 온전한 세트로 구성된 PRACTICE를 제공합니다.

PRACTICE 고난도

P3_U7_Practice 정답 및 해설 p.27

1. What type of business does the woman work for?
(A) A marketing firm
(B) A travel agency
(C) A publishing company
(D) A law firm

2. What does the woman mean when she says, "we're looking to hire as soon as possible"?
(A) She will retire soon.
(B) The timeline will be modified.
(C) Additional funding is required.
(D) The man should make a quick decision.

3. According to the woman, what does the company offer?
(A) Free meals
(B) A travel stipend
(C) A company credit card
(D) An employee discount

4. What industry do the speakers most likely work in?
(A) Furniture
(B) Fitness
(C) Cosmetics
(D) Clothing

5. What is the woman annoyed by?
(A) Some materials are low quality.
(B) Some equipment is broken.
(C) Some designs are unusable.
(D) Some decisions haven't been made.

6. Why does the man say, "Summer is coming in a few months"?
(A) To stress the need for urgency
(B) To remind the woman of a deadline
(C) To fix a scheduling error
(D) To express eagerness for a vacation

7. What problem does the woman mention?
(A) Sales are down.
(B) A delivery is late.
(C) Data is missing.
(D) A product is flawed.

8. What does the woman imply when she says "The project has already been a long haul"?
(A) Employees have been working hard.
(B) The company has hired new people.
(C) The project should be stopped.
(D) The game is for advanced players.

9. What will the man do next?
(A) Do some online research
(B) Write a formal complaint
(C) Send an e-mail
(D) Have a meeting

10. What field do the speakers work in?
(A) Manufacturing
(B) Finance
(C) Architecture
(D) Agriculture

11. Why does the man say, "I've narrowed everything down to two designs"?
(A) To assure the woman that the meeting won't take long
(B) To ask the woman for permission
(C) To show surprise about blueprints
(D) To express disappointment about a plan

12. What does the woman say she will do after work?
(A) Attend an anniversary dinner
(B) Grab a meal to take home
(C) Go to a doctor's appointment
(D) Plan for a vacation

UNIT 08 3인 대화

• 총 13세트 중 2세트는 항상 세 사람과의 대화로 구성된다.

• 3인 대화에서는 대화에 앞서 항상 음성으로 "Questions 00~00 refer to the following conversation **with three speakers.**"라고 제시된다.

• 3인 대화에서는 의도 파악 문제와 그래픽 문제가 출제되지 않는다.

대표 유형 맛보기

Example

미남/영녀/미녀 P3_U8_Ex 정답 및 해설 p.29

Questions 1-3 refer to the following conversation with three speakers.

M Thankfully, Ms. Washington, it looks like your arm is all healed. We'll get you started on physical therapy during your next visit.

W1 Oh, but I thought my physical therapy appointment was also today.

M I'm so sorry about that. There must have been a mistake when setting up your appointment. We only have you scheduled for an x-ray.

W1 Ahh, I see.

M Ms. Rislov, could you please schedule a physical therapy appointment for Ms. Washington?

W2 Sure. But I should update your contact information. We normally send out reminders for appointments, but it seems we don't have your cell phone number on file. Do you mind filling out this contact form?

W1 No problem.

1. Where most likely are the speakers?
   (A) At a community center
   (B) At a fitness club
   (C) At a legal firm
   (D) At a hospital

2. Why does the man apologize?
   (A) Some equipment is not working.
   (B) A coworker arrived late.
   (C) A scheduling error was made.
   (D) A bill is not correct.

3. What will Ms. Washington do next?
   (A) Make an appointment
   (B) Fill out a form
   (C) Stop at a pharmacy
   (D) Contact an insurance company

▶ 2번과 같이 남자 또는 여자가 사과하는 이유를 묻는 문제는 파트 3과 4에서 자주 등장하는 유형이며, 대화의 sorry 또는 apologize라는 표현 뒤에 바로 단서가 나오는 경우가 대부분이다.

▶ 3명의 대화에서는 3번 문제처럼 종종 문제에 사람의 이름이 직접 언급된다. 위의 경우, 대화에 여자가 두 명이기 때문에 What will the woman do next?로 쓰게 되면 the woman이 두 여자 중 누구를 가리키는지 알 수 없어 Ms. Washington이라고 대화 속의 이름을 직접 언급하고 있다. 따라서 세 명의 대화일 경우 **문제에 사람의 이름이 있다면 대화를 들을 때 그 이름을 절대 놓쳐서는 안 된다.**

PRACTICE 고난도

P3_U8_Practice 정답 및 해설 p.30

1. Where do the women work?
(A) At a chemical plant
(B) At a construction company
(C) At an interior design firm
(D) At a conference center

2. What is the man's job?
(A) Sales representative
(B) Building manager
(C) Software engineer
(D) Restaurant chef

3. What does Jolene plan to do in the afternoon?
(A) Visit a property
(B) Give a demonstration
(C) Return to her office
(D) Watch a presentation

---

4. What will be constructed near a factory?
(A) A parking lot
(B) A gas station
(C) A storage facility
(D) A waste site

5. What is the residents' biggest concern?
(A) Safety
(B) Noise
(C) Funds
(D) Traffic

6. Why has a new meeting location been chosen?
(A) It provides more space.
(B) The original venue was booked.
(C) It is easier to travel to.
(D) The residents preferred the new location.

---

7. What industry do the men most likely work in?
(A) Hospitality
(B) Media
(C) Electronics
(D) Architecture

8. What is the purpose of the telephone call?
(A) To inquire about a field trip
(B) To place an order
(C) To set up an interview
(D) To return some merchandise

9. What will be sent to the woman?
(A) A warranty
(B) Directions to a location
(C) A copy of a contract
(D) Some safety instructions

---

10. What kind of product are the speakers discussing?
(A) Furniture
(B) Office supplies
(C) Kitchenware
(D) Home appliances

11. What problem does the woman mention?
(A) An item is out of stock.
(B) A sale price has not been posted.
(C) An item is damaged.
(D) A bill is not correct.

12. What does the manager offer the woman?
(A) A warranty
(B) Express shipping
(C) A store membership
(D) A full refund

UNIT 09 그래픽

- 파트3에서 그래픽 문제는 항상 3세트가 출제된다. 대화에 딸린 3문제 중 한 문제는 제시된 시각자료와 관련되어 있으며, 목록, 표, 지도, 평면도, 그래프, 쿠폰 등 다양한 시각자료들이 사용될 수 있다.
- 세 문항의 키워드를 파악하는 동시에 주어진 그래픽의 핵심 정보까지 한꺼번에 고려해야 하는 문제로 가장 까다로운 문제 유형에 속한다. 그래픽 유형은 항상 2인 대화로만 출제된다.

대표 유형 맛보기

Example

미남/영녀/미녀 P3_U9_Ex 정답 및 해설 p.32

Questions 1-3 refer to the following conversation and menu.

W Hey, Marcus. Our new employees are coming in for orientation next week, and we have to decide the menu for their welcome lunch. Which of these dishes looks the best to you?

M Hmm. Last time we had new employee training, we got the steak and potatoes. It was a big hit.

W I remember that. Our budget is a little smaller this year, so I think we'll have to get something different.

M Well, then how about the pasta?

W I think that's a good idea. Chicken and curry sound good options too, but their restaurants are a little far from here.

M Right, and before you call the restaurant to book a table, we still need to prepare the exact schedule for orientation, so I think we'd better get started on that right away.

Menu Option	Price
Indian Curry	$7 per person
Pasta	$10 per person
Fried Chicken	$11 per person
Steak and Potatoes	$16 per person

1. What are the speakers preparing for?
(A) A retirement dinner
(B) A county fair
(C) An orientation
(D) A client visit

2. **Look at the graphic. How much will the speakers most likely spend per person?**
(A) $7
(B) $10
(C) $11
(D) $16

3. What will the speakers do next?
(A) Speak to their superiors
(B) Ask guests to take a survey
(C) Make a reservation
(D) Prepare a schedule

▶ 2번 문제와 그래픽을 파악하는 데에만 집중한 나머지 1번과 3번을 대충 들어서는 안 된다. 한 문제를 맞히려다가 쉬운 두 문제를 놓치는 건 오히려 손해다.

▶ "Look at the graphic."이라고 되어 있는 문제를 읽고 문제의 포인트에 따라 그래픽의 핵심 정보를 빠르게 파악해야 한다. 문제에서 한 사람당 얼마를 쓸 것인가를 묻고 있으므로, 대화에서는 제시된 표의 메뉴 이름이 언급될 것이라는 걸 예측해야 한다.

▶ 남자가 오리엔테이션 메뉴로 파스타를 제시했고, 여자가 "That's a good idea."라고 했으므로 정답은 파스타의 가격인 (B) $10가 된다.

PRACTICE 고난도

🎧 P3_U9_Practice 정답 및 해설 p.32

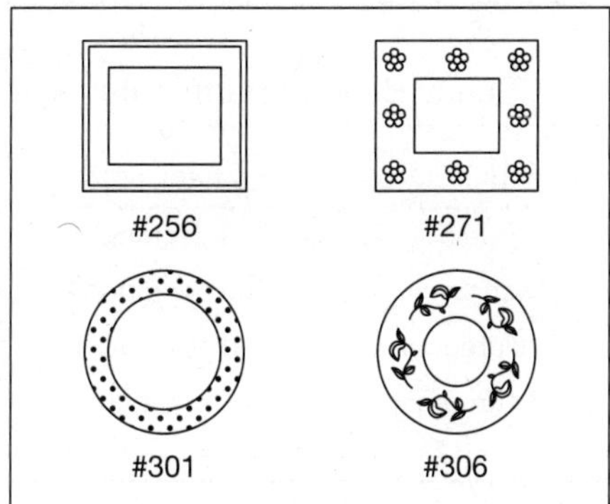

1. Look at the graphic. Which dish pattern is the man interested in?
   (A) Pattern #256
   (B) Pattern #271
   (C) Pattern #301
   (D) Pattern #306

2. What problem does the woman mention?
   (A) Some items are out of stock.
   (B) Catalogues are outdated.
   (C) Some items are limited edition.
   (D) Shipping fees will increase.

3. According to the man, what will happen in September?
   (A) A new employee will join his business.
   (B) A new product will launch.
   (C) A restaurant will have a re-opening.
   (D) A mall will open downtown.

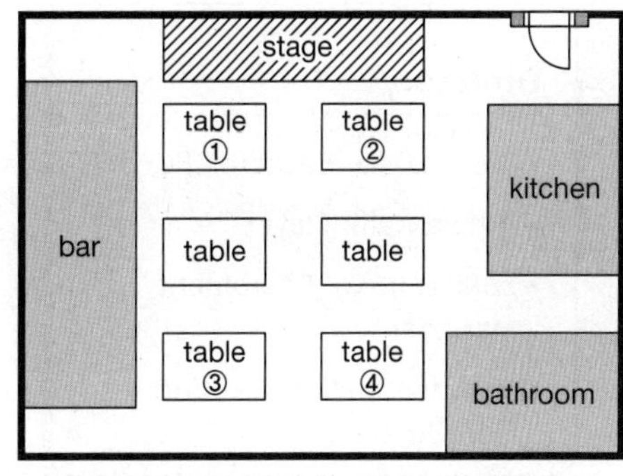

4. According to the man, what has caused the delay?
   (A) The roads are slippery.
   (B) Parking is unavailable.
   (C) Rush hour traffic is bad.
   (D) A location was changed.

5. Why is the man meeting with his business partner?
   (A) To discuss a potential merger
   (B) To talk about a job candidate
   (C) To analyze a product's sales
   (D) To prepare for a company launch

6. Look at the graphic. Where will the man sit?
   (A) Table 1
   (B) Table 2
   (C) Table 3
   (D) Table 4

뒤에 PRACTICE 계속

Directory

- Inez Garcia: Basketball Coach
- Amala Kalil: Player
- Suki Tanoko: Equipment Manager
- Jennifer Snell: Marketing Coordinator

Sunny Beach Apartments

Unit	Rent
Studio	$1,000 per month
1 bedroom	$1,500 per month
2 bedrooms	$1,750 per month
3 bedrooms	$2,000 per month

7. Look at the graphic. Who is the woman?

(A) Inez Garcia
(B) Amala Kalil
(C) Suki Tanoko
(D) Jennifer Snell

8. What problem do the speakers discuss?

(A) A game has been delayed.
(B) The fans are angry.
(C) The players are tired.
(D) The team was sold.

9. What will the man most likely do next?

(A) Post an advertisement
(B) Purchase new uniforms
(C) Upgrade flight tickets
(D) Search for accommodations

10. Why does the woman want to move soon?

(A) She got a new job.
(B) She is pregnant.
(C) Her building is unsafe.
(D) Her rent is too high.

11. What does the man like about the bigger unit?

(A) The interior design
(B) The scenic view
(C) The modern appliances
(D) The large bathrooms

12. Look at the graphic. What is the price of the unit the woman wants to rent?

(A) $1,000 per month
(B) $1,500 per month
(C) $1,750 per month
(D) $2,000 per month

Schedule

Emilio Lopez	9 am
Kate Marrone	11 am
Yeonsu Lee	2 pm
Leopold Fritz	4 pm

13. What kind of event is taking place?

(A) A business seminar
(B) A film festival
(C) An award ceremony
(D) A charity fund-raiser

14. Look at the graphic. When will the man call a client?

(A) 9 am
(B) 11 am
(C) 2 pm
(D) 4 pm

15. What problem does the woman mention?

(A) A lecturer might be late.
(B) A conference room is closed.
(C) The caterer missed a delivery.
(D) The audience is too small.

Flight #	Departing From	Arriving At
156	Detroit	New York City
205	Atlanta	Miami
310	Honolulu	Los Angeles
644	San Francisco	Seattle

16. Look at the graphic. Where is the woman departing from?

(A) Detroit
(B) Atlanta
(C) Honolulu
(D) San Francisco

17. How will the man help the woman?

(A) By providing a refund
(B) By checking an extra bag
(C) By putting her in first class
(D) By talking to airport security

18. What will the woman most likely give the man next?

(A) Her flight ticket
(B) Her credit card
(C) Her voucher
(D) Her e-mail address

PART TEST

1. What change is the company making?
(A) It is offering flexible scheduling.
(B) It is opening a new office location.
(C) It is providing discounted meals.
(D) It is reimbursing travel expenses.

2. What does the woman suggest doing?
(A) Raising a concern to management
(B) Submitting a preference quickly
(C) Researching some products
(D) Participating in a job interview

3. What will the man most likely do next?
(A) Speak with a coworker
(B) Call a customer
(C) Ask for a refund
(D) Conduct a training session

---

4. What kind of business do the speakers most likely have?
(A) A convenience store
(B) A landscaping company
(C) A hardware store
(D) A farm

5. What does the man suggest doing?
(A) Purchasing more land
(B) Offering a new product
(C) Adding more plants
(D) Building a new structure

6. What does the woman say she will do?
(A) Check their inventory
(B) Purchase materials
(C) Hire a professional
(D) Renew a contract

---

7. Why is the woman calling?
(A) To discuss a property listing
(B) To reserve a hotel room
(C) To check on an application status
(D) To submit a payment

8. According to the man, what affects the price?
(A) The number of parking spaces
(B) The usage of a shared room
(C) The amount of customers
(D) The presence of advertising

9. What does the man recommend bringing tomorrow evening?
(A) A recommendation letter
(B) A form of ID
(C) A down payment
(D) Proof of income

---

10. Why does the man need help?
(A) An office has been moved.
(B) A machine is malfunctioning.
(C) A train route has changed.
(D) An item is missing.

11. What does the man say he is frustrated about?
(A) Spending too much money
(B) Running late for an appointment
(C) Receiving false information
(D) Waiting in a long line

12. What will the man most likely do next?
(A) Use an app
(B) Take a taxi
(C) Call a manager
(D) Ride a bus

---

13. Where do the speakers most likely work?

(A) A concert hall
(B) A grocery store
(C) A restaurant
(D) A delivery service

14. What is the woman doing?

(A) Cleaning some equipment
(B) Talking to a supplier
(C) Preparing special orders
(D) Training new staff

15. What does Gerald suggest doing?

(A) Expanding their offerings
(B) Replenishing inventory
(C) Starting a marketing campaign
(D) Opening a second location

---

16. What are the speakers preparing for?

(A) A standardized test
(B) A game show
(C) A sporting event
(D) A public lecture

17. What problem does the woman mention?

(A) Some advertisements were wrong.
(B) A script is flawed.
(C) The participants are unprepared.
(D) A camera is broken.

18. Who is José Carrasco?

(A) An engineer
(B) A temporary worker
(C) A manager
(D) A screenwriter

---

19. What does the woman thank the man for?

(A) Submitting a proposal
(B) Closing a sale
(C) Recommending a vendor
(D) Leading a meeting

20. Why is the gathering being planned?

(A) The company had record sales.
(B) An employee is retiring.
(C) A manager is having a birthday.
(D) Some workers need a break.

21. What does the woman imply when she says, "I would be happy to prepare some homemade dishes"?

(A) A caterer is an unnecessary expense.
(B) The restaurant has bad reviews.
(C) The company will refuse to pay for catering.
(D) Everyone should bring their own dishes.

---

22. Where do the speakers work?

(A) At a bank
(B) At a sporting goods store
(C) At a health club
(D) At a credit card company

23. What does the man recommend doing?

(A) Changing opening hours
(B) Lowering the prices
(C) Creating new advertisements
(D) Selling unused equipment

24. What does the man predict?

(A) The company will reduce wages.
(B) A new facility will keep its members.
(C) A location's rent will increase.
(D) Customers will post positive reviews.

---

25. What area do the speakers most likely work in?

(A) Marketing
(B) Information technology
(C) Research
(D) Human resources

26. What happened recently?

(A) New employees were hired.
(B) A department was moved.
(C) The company building was renovated.
(D) A computer was updated.

27. What does Mei Ling offer to do?

(A) Post a job listing
(B) Create some instructions
(C) Call some customers
(D) Host a meeting

---

28. Who is the man?

(A) A musician
(B) A photographer
(C) A film reviewer
(D) An actor

29. What does the man imply when he says, "taking it could help me gain some traction in the industry"?

(A) He does not have much experience.
(B) He is still earning a degree.
(C) He was given bad advice by his agent.
(D) He wants to switch careers.

30. What does the woman say she will do?

(A) Provide some contact information
(B) Attend an event
(C) Write a recommendation letter
(D) Read a contract

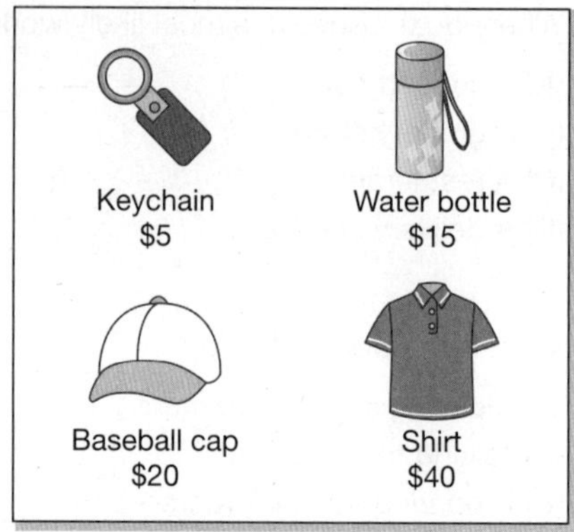

31. Who will the woman give the gift to?

(A) Facility residents
(B) Upper management
(C) Family members
(D) Business partners

32. Look at the graphic. How much is the item that the man recommends?

(A) $5
(B) $15
(C) $20
(D) $40

33. What does the man say he will do?

(A) Contact a manager
(B) Do an inventory check
(C) Provide an extra item
(D) Offer a payment plan

Sales prices	
Plastic bag (4)	$3
Small basket (6)	$4
Large basket (9)	$6
Bucket (12)	$8

34. What do the speakers sell?

(A) Coffee beans
(B) Fruit
(C) Nuts
(D) Dairy products

35. Look at the graphic. How much will the speakers charge for each sale?

(A) $3
(B) $4
(C) $6
(D) $8

36. What does the woman want help with?

(A) Loading the truck
(B) Setting up the booth
(C) Transporting the product
(D) Advertising the event

Underwater Diver

Level Name	Level Number
Coral Adventure	1
Swimming with Whales	2
Deep Ocean	3
Buried Treasure	4

37. What are the speakers mainly discussing?

(A) A research project
(B) A product release
(C) An advertising campaign
(D) A supplier change

38. Look at the graphic. Which level is having issues?

(A) Coral Adventure
(B) Swimming with Whales
(C) Deep Ocean
(D) Buried Treasure

39. What does the woman offer to do?

(A) Contact the sales team
(B) Postpone an event
(C) Request more funding
(D) Create a job posting

LC

PART 4

PART 4 출제 경향 및 전략

파트4는 한 사람의 음성으로 이루어진 담화(talk)를 듣게 된다. 71번부터 100번까지 총 10개의 담화가 출제되며, 파트3과 마찬가지로 한 담화당 세 개의 문제로 구성되어 총 30개 문제로 구성된다.

담화의 종류

크게 아래의 5가지로 분류할 수 있으며, 회의 발췌와 전화 메시지, 안내방송, TV/라디오 방송 등은 매회 빠지지 않고 출제된다.

회의 발췌	업무 관련 안건에 대해 논의하는 회의의 일부 내용
전화 메시지	- 전화 건 사람이 자동 응답기에 남긴 음성 메시지 - 회사나 관공서에서 미리 녹음해 둔 부재중 자동 응답 메시지
안내방송 및 공지	공항, 기내, 상점, 공연장 등 공공장소에서 이루어지는 안내방송 및 사내 공지
TV/라디오 방송	- 지역 뉴스, 일기예보, 교통 안내방송 및 팟캐스트 교양 프로그램 - 제품이나 서비스, 업체, 행사, 이벤트 등을 홍보하기 위한 광고
연설, 소개, 견학/관광 안내	- 컨퍼런스나 개관식 같은 각종 행사에서의 모두발언이나 기조연설 - 강연 및 인물 소개, 관광이나 견학을 이끄는 가이드의 안내, 작업현장 지침 등

문제 유형

파트3의 문제 유형과 크게 다르지 않다. 다만 담화의 종류에 따라 특정 유형이 좀 더 자주 출제되는 경향이 있다. 예를 들어 전화 메시지에서는 화자가 전화를 건 이유가 자주 출제되고, 회의에서는 논의되고 있는 문제점에 대해, 공공장소 안내 방송에서는 담화가 일어나고 있는 장소, 강연이나 방송은 담화의 주제, 광고에서는 광고의 대상을 묻는 문제가 자주 등장하는 편이다. 파트4에서는 의도 파악 유형이 3문항, 그래픽 관련 문항이 2문항 출제된다.

PART 3과 다른 점

1. 파트4에서는 새로운 담화가 시작되기 앞서 각 담화의 유형을 미리 음성으로 알려준다.

• Questions 71 through 73 refer to the following **announcement**.

이때 the following 이후에 나오는 단어를 정확히 들어야 담화의 상황을 이해하기 쉽다.
▶ announcement (공지), telephone message (전화 메시지), recorded message (자동 응답 메시지), excerpt from a meeting (회의 발췌), broadcast (방송), speech (연설), advertisement (광고), tour information (관광) 등

2. 파트3에서는 화자가 두 명이었기 때문에 문제에 the man, the woman, 또는 the speakers가 쓰였다면, 파트4에서는 화자가 한 명이기 때문에 the speaker와 the listener(s)가 쓰인다.

• Who is the speaker?
• What are the listeners asked to do next?

단계별 듣기 전략

문제의 키워드를 파악한 다음 담화의 흐름에 따라 차례로 문제를 풀어나가야 한다. 들을 때는 아래의 빨간색으로 표시해 놓은 표현들처럼 문제의 단서들이 나올 것이라는 것을 미리 알려주는 큐(Cue)들을 인지하고 있어야 그 다음에 나오는 단서들을 놓치지 않고 들을 수 있다.

Example

P4_U0_Ex 정답 및 해설 p.43

Questions 71-73 refer to the following field trip information.

I'm glad you all could join me on this tour of our rare books collection. [71] **Here at the Jonestown Library**, we believe in the value of preserving literature from the past. That's why we have this unique collection of books that requires special care and handling. [72] **Please make sure to avoid touching anything** here because all the materials are very sensitive. [73] **First, let's take a look at our medieval archives** on the basement floor. Follow me, please.

71. **Where** is the tour taking place?
    정답 At a library

72. What does the speaker **remind** the listeners to do?
    정답 Avoid touching anything

73. What will listeners **see first** on the tour?
    정답 Some old archives

PART 4

놓치지 말고 들어야 할 큐(Cue)

문제의 특정 키워드들은 담화에서도 그대로 쓰여 뒤에 나올 단서를 제시하는 큐(Cue)의 역할을 하는 경우가 많다.

1. **문제에 특정 사람 이름, 시간, 날짜가 언급되는 경우**
   Q What did **Tom Clancy** start doing last December? → [담화] Joining us today to walk you through the process is **Tom Clancy**, who started teaching coding at the public library in December.

2. **문제에 give, offer, send, receive, recommend, apologize 등의 동사가 있는 경우**
   Q Why does the speaker **apologize**? → [담화] We **apologize** for the inconvenience the construction noise may cause.

3. **문제에 impressed with, pleased/excited/concerned about, proud of가 있는 경우**
   Q What does the speaker say he is **pleased about**? → [담화] I was really **pleased** by how much sales of the new wireless mouse have increased as well.

4. **문젯거리나 걱정거리를 묻는 경우, but, unfortunately 등이 큐로 제시된다.**
   Q What **problem** does the speaker mention? → [담화] I recently ordered a chair from your Web site. I chose white one, **but** I received black one.

5. **문제에 remind가 있는 경우, remind, remember, please 등이 큐로 제시된다.**
   Q What does the speaker **remind** the listener about? → [담화] And **remember** there are only a few openings left for the training, so be sure to sign up soon if you're interested.

UNIT 01 회의 발췌

회의에서 한 화자의 담화를 발췌한 형태로, 업무 관련 내용을 논의하거나 사내 새로운 소식, 정책의 변화 등을 공지하는 내용이 주를 이룬다. 평균 2세트가 출제된다.

대표 유형 맛보기

Example

미남 🎧 P4_U1_Ex

Questions 1-3 refer to the following excerpt from a meeting.

I'd like to talk about a new initiative at our company. Reaching a larger audience has become **the number one priority** for us. The executives have decided we need to be more innovative when it comes to advertising our products. That's why we hired **Susan Hoover**, a digital marketing expert, to join our team. She is here to help us reevaluate our current marketing strategy and make useful changes going forward. Right now, she is asking everyone to use their social media presence to gather data on our company. Instructions on how to do so will be sent out later today. I know we all have a lot of work already, but **this affects us all**.

1. What does the speaker say is **a top priority**?
   (A) Improving worker efficiency
   (B) Lowering manufacturing costs
   (C) Retaining quality employees
   (D) Advertising to more people

2. Who is **Susan Hoover**?
   (A) A marketing specialist
   (B) A course instructor
   (C) A renowned doctor
   (D) A human resources expert

3. Why does the speaker say, "**this affects us all**"?
   (A) To prevent future mistakes
   (B) To encourage participation
   (C) To apologize for a delay
   (D) To express opposition

저는 우리 회사의 새로운 계획에 대해 이야기하고 싶습니다. 더 많은 청중에게 다가가는 것이 우리에게 최우선 과제가 되었습니다. 임원들은 우리가 제품 광고에 있어서 좀 더 혁신적일 필요가 있다고 결정했습니다. 그래서 디지털 마케팅 전문가인 Susan Hoover를 팀에 영입했습니다. 그녀는 우리가 현재의 마케팅 전략을 재평가하고 앞으로 유용한 변화를 꾀하는 것을 돕기 위해 여기에 왔습니다. 지금, 그녀는 여러분 모두 자신의 소셜 미디어를 활용하여 우리 회사에 대한 데이터를 수집할 것을 요청하고 있습니다. 구체적인 지침은 오늘 오후 보내드릴 것입니다. 여러분 모두 일이 많은 것은 알지만, 이것은 우리 모두에게 영향을 미칩니다.

EXPRESSIONS

initiative 계획
executive 간부, 중역
when it comes to ~에 관하여
reevaluate 재평가하다
go forward 일이 진척되다
instructions 지침

1. 화자는 무엇이 가장 최우선 순위라고 말하는가?
   (A) 직원 효율성을 향상하는 것
   (B) 제조원가를 낮추는 것
   (C) 우수한 직원을 유지하는 것
   (D) 더 많은 사람들에게 광고하는 것

2. Susan Hoover는 누구인가?
   (A) 마케팅 전문가
   (B) 과목 담당 강사
   (C) 저명한 의사
   (D) 인사 전문가

3. 화자는 왜 "이것은 우리 모두에게 영향을 미칩니다"라고 말하는가?
   (A) 앞으로의 실수를 막기 위해
   (B) 참여를 권장하기 위해
   (C) 지연에 대해 사과하기 위해
   (D) 반대를 표하기 위해

정답 **1.** (D) **2.** (A) **3.** (B)

빈출 표현

소식 공지	I'm happy to announce that... ~을 발표하게 되어 기쁩니다. I want to update you on... ~에 대한 최근 소식을 알려드리겠습니다. Before we end our meeting, I'd like to share... 회의를 마치기 전에 ~을 공유하고 싶습니다.
안건 제시	To get started, I want to discuss... 우선, ~에 대해 논의하고 싶습니다. The last thing I want to discuss at today's meeting is... 오늘 회의에서 마지막으로 논의하고 싶은 것은...
문제	But due to yesterday's equipment failure, we're behind on filling the orders. 하지만 어제 기계 결함으로 인해, 주문량을 소화하지 못하고 있습니다. Unfortunately we are more than two months past the scheduled completion date. 유감스럽게도 예정된 완료일이 2개월 이상 지났습니다.
전환	Moving on, this quarter our sales are... 계속해서, 이번 분기 저희 매출이... Okay, next on the agenda... 그럼 다음 안건은... Now on to the next item on the agenda for this board meeting. 이제 이사회 회의 안건의 다음 항목으로 넘어가겠습니다.

PART 4

CHECK-UP

P4_U1_Check-up 정답 및 해설 p.43

1. Who most likely are the listeners?
(A) Investors
(B) Marketing specialists
(C) Executives
(D) Product designers

2. According to the speaker, what is the company going to change?
(A) The type of car it makes
(B) The location of the headquarters
(C) The publisher for its catalog
(D) The way it collects customer feedback

3. Why does the speaker say, "you'll probably change your mind if you look at this"?
(A) To correct a mistake
(B) To express doubt
(C) To reject a suggestion
(D) To offer reassurance

4. What industry do the speakers work in?
(A) Advertising
(B) Construction
(C) Software
(D) Shipping

5. What does the speaker thank the listeners for?
(A) Filling out a survey
(B) Meeting sales goals
(C) Finalizing a contract
(D) Creating a new device

6. Why does the speaker say, "we do have a limited hiring budget"?
(A) To encourage the listeners to make more sales
(B) To remind the listeners about losses
(C) To tell the listeners that she will not hire more staff
(D) To suggest that the listeners buy new software

UNIT 02 전화 메시지

전화를 건 사람이 수신자에게 남기는 메시지가 주를 이루며, 종종 회사나 공공기관의 자동 응답 메시지도 출제된다. 평균 2세트가 출제된다.

대표 유형 맛보기

Example

영녀 P4_U2_Ex

Questions 1-3 refer to the following telephone message.

인사 및 자기소개 Hello, I'm Dorothy Miller

용건 and I'm looking for someone to build a Web site for a new online clothing store **I'll be opening** in May. I saw the Web site you made for my friend, **Maria Thompson**, the other day. I was very impressed by how intuitive and sophisticated its design is, and Maria couldn't speak more highly of you. I'd like to meet you in person and discuss the project if you're available early next week. I'll have had a storyboard for the Web site ready to **show you** by then.

회신 요청 Please call me at 525-9526 at your earliest convenience.

1. What type of business is the speaker planning to **start**?
   (A) A beauty salon
   (B) A bookstore
   (C) An online shop
   (D) A web magazine

2. What did **Maria Thompson** do for the speaker?
   (A) Repair an office
   (B) Design a dress
   (C) Develop a Web site
   (D) Recommend a business

3. What does the speaker want to **show the listener** next week?
   (A) An itinerary
   (B) A storyboard
   (C) A logo
   (D) A floor plan

인사 및 자기소개 안녕하세요, 저는 Dorothy Miller라고 합니다.

용건 저는 5월에 오픈할 새로운 온라인 쇼핑몰의 웹사이트를 만들 사람을 찾고 있습니다. 며칠 전 당신이 내 친구 Maria Thompson을 위해 만든 웹사이트를 봤어요. 정말 직관적이고 세련된 사이트 디자인에 감명을 받았고, Maria는 당신을 칭찬하는 데 여념이 없었죠. 당신이 다음 주 초에 시간이 된다면 직접 만나서 프로젝트에 대해 논의하고 싶습니다. 그때쯤이면 웹사이트용 스토리보드를 보여 드릴 준비가 되어 있을 거예요.

회신 요청 가능한 한 빨리 525-9526으로 전화 주십시오.

EXPRESSIONS

look for ~을 찾다
intuitive 직관적인
sophisticated 세밀한, 세련된
can't speak more highly of ~를 더없이 칭찬하다
meet someone in person ~을 직접 만나다

1. 화자는 어떤 사업을 시작하려고 계획 중인가?
   (A) 미장원
   (B) 서점
   (C) 온라인 상점
   (D) 웹 잡지

2. Maria Thompson은 화자를 위해 무엇을 했나?
   (A) 사무실 수리
   (B) 드레스 디자인
   (C) 웹사이트 개발
   (D) 거래처 추천

3. 화자는 다음 주에 청자에게 무엇을 보여주기를 원하는가?
   (A) 여행 일정
   (B) 스토리보드
   (C) 로고
   (D) 평면도

정답 **1.** (C) **2.** (D) **3.** (B)

빈출 표현

인사	Hi, **this message is for** Brian. This is Selena from human resources. 안녕하세요. 이 메시지는 Brian에게 보내는 겁니다. 저는 인사팀의 Selena입니다. **You've reached** the desk of Erika Watts. 당신은 Erika Watts 자리에 전화 주셨습니다. (자동 응답 메시지)
용건	**I'm returning your call regarding** the seminar I'll be giving at your company. 귀사에서 개최할 세미나 관련하여 회신 전화드립니다. **I'm following up about** the hotel you asked me to book for next month's conference. 안녕하세요. 다음 달 있을 컨퍼런스를 위해 예약하라고 하셨던 호텔에 관련해서 전화드립니다. **I'm calling because** my computer suddenly went down. 제 컴퓨터가 갑자기 먹통이 돼서 전화드립니다. Hi, it's Susan, your travel agent. **I'm calling about** the updated itinerary. 안녕하세요. 당신의 여행 에이전트 Susan입니다. 변경된 여행 일정 관련해 전화드려요. Hey, it's Jeff. **I'm calling to see if** you're free on Thursday. 안녕하세요, Jeff입니다. 목요일에 시간 되는지 확인차 전화드립니다.
맺음말	Please call me back at extension 618. 내선 618번으로 전화 부탁드려요. Call me and let me know what you think. 어떻게 생각하시는지 전화로 알려주세요. Please call me at your earliest convenience. 시간 되시는 대로 바로 전화 부탁드려요.

CHECK-UP

P4_U2_Check-up 정답 및 해설 p.44

1. Why is the speaker calling?
(A) To correct a mistake
(B) To plan an upcoming trip
(C) To ask for advice
(D) To request a schedule change

2. What does the speaker say about a job candidate?
(A) She has good references.
(B) She speaks several languages.
(C) She decided to work somewhere else.
(D) She does not live in the area.

3. What did the speaker send in an e-mail?
(A) A schedule
(B) A cost estimate
(C) A contract
(D) A résumé

4. Why is the speaker currently unavailable?
(A) He is attending an industry event.
(B) He is taking time off.
(C) His team is undergoing training.
(D) His office equipment is malfunctioning.

5. What kind of business does the speaker most likely work for?
(A) A computer software distributor
(B) A magazine publisher
(C) An electronics manufacturer
(D) A recording studio

6. According to the speaker, what can be found on the Web site?
(A) A job description
(B) An event calendar
(C) A photo gallery
(D) An entry form

UNIT 03 안내방송 및 공지

공항, 기차역, 선착장, 기내, 상점, 공연장, 도서관 등 공공장소에서 이루어지는 안내방송이 주로 출제되며, 기업에서 직원들에게 공지 사항을 알리는 내용도 빈번하게 출제된다. 평균 1~2세트가 출제되며, 출제되지 않는 경우도 있다.

대표 유형 맛보기

Example

미남 P4_U3_Ex

Questions 1-3 refer to the following announcement.

Flyers, may I please have your attention? Starting next week, Terminal B will be out of operation, so no planes will be departing from there. All flights will either depart from Terminal A or Terminal C while **Terminal B is being renovated**. We expect renovations to take a few months, so we appreciate your patience until they are complete. Since Terminal A and Terminal C are on the far ends of the airport, **we recommend allocating extra travel time** to reach your gate before it closes.

1. **Where** is the announcement most likely being made?
   (A) At a ferry terminal
   (B) At a subway station
   (C) At a bus terminal
   (D) At an airport

2. **Why** is a change being made?
   (A) To renovate some facilities
   (B) To improve traffic flow
   (C) To save customers money
   (D) To increase energy efficiency

3. What does the speaker **recommend**?
   (A) Arriving earlier than usual
   (B) Postponing any travel plans
   (C) Reserving tickets online
   (D) Contact customer service

여행객 여러분은 주목해 주시기 바랍니다. 다음 주부터 B 터미널은 이용할 수 없게 되어 그곳에서 이륙하는 비행기는 없을 것입니다. B 터미널이 보수되는 동안엔 모든 항공편이 A 터미널이나 C 터미널에서 출발하게 됩니다. 보수는 몇 달 정도 걸릴 것으로 예상하며, 따라서 완료될 때까지 승객 여러분들의 양해를 부탁드립니다. A 터미널과 C 터미널이 공항 양쪽 끝에 위치하기 때문에, 게이트가 닫히기 전에 도착할 수 있도록 이동 시간을 충분히 할당할 것을 권해 드립니다.

EXPRESSIONS

flyer 비행기 승객
out of operation 운영하지 않는
we appreciate your patience until... ~때까지 기다려 주시면 감사하겠습니다
allocate (시간이나 돈 등을) 할당하다

1. 안내방송은 어디에서 이루어지는 것 같은가?
   (A) 연락선 터미널에서
   (B) 지하철역에서
   (C) 버스 터미널에서
   (D) 공항에서

2. 변경은 왜 이루어지고 있는가?
   (A) 일부 시설 보수를 위해
   (B) 통행 흐름을 개선하기 위해
   (C) 고객들의 비용 절감을 위해
   (D) 에너지 효율 향상을 위해

3. 화자는 무엇을 추천하는가?
   (A) 평소보다 일찍 도착하는 것
   (B) 여행 일정을 보류하는 것
   (C) 표를 온라인으로 예매하는 것
   (D) 고객 서비스 센터에 전화하는 것

정답 **1.** (D) **2.** (A) **3.** (A)

빈출 표현

공공 시설	Attention, passengers. Renovation work to upgrade our train station is underway. 승객 여러분, 주목해 주세요. 우리 기차역을 업그레이드하기 위한 개조 공사가 진행 중입니다. Attention for all passengers waiting for the 5 P.M. ferry to Jekyll Island. Due to a storm along the coast, this ferry has been canceled. Jekyll Island로 가는 오후 5시 페리를 기다리는 승객 여러분께 안내 말씀드립니다. 이 여객선은 해안가 폭풍으로 인해 결항되었습니다. Attention travelers. The 7 P.M. Bluestar Airlines flight to Sydney has been canceled. We regret the inconvenience this may cause you. 여행객 여러분께 안내 말씀드립니다. 시드니행 Bluestar Airlines 오후 7시 항공편이 취소되었습니다. 이로 인해 불편을 끼쳐 죄송합니다. Attention shoppers! Today is the first day of our summer sales event. All seafood is now on sale. Don't miss out. 고객 여러분, 주목해 주세요! 오늘은 여름 할인 행사 첫날입니다. 모든 해산물이 지금 할인 중입니다. 놓치지 마세요.
기업	Attention employees, a reminder that starting June 1st, the main entrance to the office building will be inaccessible while the road is repaved. 직원 여러분, 주목하세요. 6월 1일부터 도로 보수 공사가 진행되는 동안 사무실 건물 정문에 출입할 수 없게 됨을 다시 한번 알려드립니다. I have an announcement for the production line staff. As you've noticed, the main conveyor belt is temporarily out of order. 생산라인 직원 여러분께 공지 사항이 있습니다. 아시다시피 메인 컨베이어 벨트가 일시적으로 고장났습니다.

PART 4

CHECK-UP

P4_U3_Check-up 정답 및 해설 p.44

1. What does the speaker say will happen this evening?
(A) New books will be added.
(B) The shelves will be rearranged.
(C) The online catalog will be updated.
(D) The reference desk will be moved.

2. According to the speaker, how can listeners get more information?
(A) By speaking to a librarian
(B) By checking the Web site
(C) By picking up a handout
(D) By calling the front desk

3. What is taking place tomorrow?
(A) A group discussion
(B) A book signing
(C) An academic talk
(D) A film showing

4. Where does the announcement most likely take place?
(A) At a hair salon
(B) At a grocery store
(C) At a convention center
(D) At a farmer's market

5. What is mentioned about Joe's Pickles?
(A) It has a discount event.
(B) It only accepts cash.
(C) It is not present.
(D) It went bankrupt.

6. What does the speaker encourage the listeners to do?
(A) Arrive early
(B) Greet people nicely
(C) Work overtime
(D) Ask for help

UNIT 04 TV/라디오 방송 및 팟캐스트

지역 뉴스, 일기예보, 교통 안내 등의 방송 및 팟캐스트 교양 프로그램이 주로 출제되며, 평균 1~2세트가 출제된다.

대표 유형 맛보기

Example

미남 P4_U4_Ex

Questions 1-3 refer to the following broadcast.

You're listening to *Business Today* on 167 F.M. Radio. For today's episode, we'll be **focusing on** promoting your business through social media. Getting enough engagement online is crucial to having a successful business. It's **important** to separate yourself from your competition. This involves creating a distinct social media presence that is associated with your company alone. For more advice on how to do this, we have **Stacy Lee**, founder of Sell-it, a popular marketing consulting firm. Welcome, Stacy.

1. What is the **focus** of the episode?

(A) Promoting technological innovation
(B) Offering training programs
(C) Improving employee satisfaction
(D) Using social media

2. What does the speaker say is **important**?

(A) Creating a distinct presence
(B) Attending networking events
(C) Developing new products
(D) Following industry standards

3. Who is **Stacy Lee**?

(A) An office worker
(B) A news reporter
(C) A financial analyst
(D) A marketing expert

여러분은 지금 167 F.M. 라디오의 〈비즈니스 투데이〉를 듣고 계십니다. 오늘 에피소드에서는 소셜 미디어를 통해 여러분의 사업을 홍보하는 것에 초점을 맞추겠습니다. 온라인상에서의 활발한 참여는 성공적인 영업에 매우 중요합니다. 여러분의 회사를 경쟁사와 차별화하는 것이 중요합니다. 여기에는 당신의 회사만이 가질 수 있는 뚜렷한 소셜 미디어 존재감을 창출하는 것이 포함됩니다. 이 방법에 대한 추가 조언을 위해 인기 있는 마케팅 컨설팅 회사인 Sell-it의 설립자인 Stacy Lee를 모셨습니다. 환영합니다, Stacy.

EXPRESSIONS

focus on ~에 초점을 맞추다
promote 홍보하다
engagement 참여
crucial 중대한
distinct 뚜렷한, 특유의
be associated with ~과 연관되다

1. 이번 회차의 초점은 무엇인가?

(A) 기술 혁신 촉진
(B) 연수 프로그램 제공
(C) 직원 만족도 향상
(D) 소셜 미디어 활용

2. 화자는 무엇이 중요하다고 하는가?

(A) 뚜렷한 존재감 만들기
(B) 네트워킹 이벤트 참석하기
(C) 신제품 개발하기
(D) 산업 표준 따르기

3. Stacy Lee는 누구인가?

(A) 사무직원
(B) 취재 기자
(C) 금융 분석가
(D) 마케팅 전문가

정답 **1.** (D) **2.** (A) **3.** (D)

빈출 표현

행사	In local news, here's a reminder from the Bayland Community Center about their fund-raising event this Saturday evening. 지역 뉴스입니다. 베이랜드 지역 문화 센터에서 이번 주 토요일 저녁에 열릴 모금행사에 대해 다시 한번 전해 드립니다. You're listening to *Culture Hour* with Benjamin Feldom. First up in culture news is the Alvarado Art Museum's upcoming gala. 여러분께서는 Benjamin Feldom의 〈컬처 아워〉를 듣고 계십니다. 첫 번째 문화계 소식은 곧 있을 알바라도 미술관의 경축 행사입니다.
교통	As of today, Hamilton Street between 3rd and 5th Avenues will be closed to traffic for emergency repair work. 오늘부로 3번가와 5번가 사이의 해밀턴 거리는 긴급 수리 작업을 위해 교통이 통제될 것입니다. It's 10 o'clock, time for the traffic update on Radio 105. A work crew is painting lines on Austin Street, so there have been reports of some delays in the area. 10시 정각, 라디오 105 교통 정보 업데이트 시간입니다. 오스틴 가에서 차선 페인트 작업이 진행 중이며, 이로 인해 그 지역에 일부 정체가 있다는 보도입니다.
착공	The city broke ground on the new Houston Central Museum this morning. 시 당국은 오늘 아침 새로운 휴스턴 중앙 박물관을 착공했습니다. The city's public transit agency has announced that construction has begun on the new Grantson train station. 시 교통 당국은 새로운 Grantson 기차역 공사를 시작했다고 발표했습니다.

PART 4

CHECK-UP

P4_U4_Check-up 정답 및 해설 p.45

1. What does Discover Works fund?
(A) Park renovations
(B) Music groups
(C) Stage performances
(D) Short films

2. According to the speaker, why should listeners arrive early?
(A) To get a good seat
(B) To save money
(C) To meet the performers
(D) To avoid heavy traffic

3. What is available on the town park Web site?
(A) A discussion board
(B) A series of videos
(C) Membership information
(D) A list of events

4. What is the podcast mainly about?
(A) Chemistry
(B) Video games
(C) Travel
(D) Astronomy

5. What did Kiran Buttar recently do?
(A) She hosted a public fund-raiser.
(B) She started a business.
(C) She created innovative technology.
(D) She earned a scholarship.

6. According to the speaker, why should listeners subscribe to the annual plan?
(A) To learn about private events
(B) To download the transcript
(C) To meet other members
(D) To access the full episode

UNIT 05 광고

제품, 서비스, 업체, 행사 등을 홍보하기 위한 광고가 주로 출제된다. 평균 1세트가 출제되며, 출제되지 않는 경우도 있다.

대표 유형 맛보기

Example

미남 🎧 P4_U5_Ex

Questions 1-3 refer to the following advertisement.

Looking for the perfect place to hold your next conference? Look no further than the Maple Square Convention Center. With our spacious auditoriums, extensive parking facilities, and easy access to public transportation, Maple Square Convention Center is the ideal location for both small and large gatherings. But there's another reason why you should hold your next convention here. **We're famous for** our incredibly low prices. If you are interested in booking with us, **please call** our friendly staff at 555-0138 for pricing and available dates.

1. What is being **advertised**?
   (A) A grocery store
   (B) A convention center
   (C) A restaurant
   (D) A travel destination

2. What is the business **famous** for?
   (A) Its amenities
   (B) Its modern design
   (C) Its prices
   (D) Its food

3. What does the speaker **suggest** listeners do?
   (A) Make a phone call
   (B) Visit a Web site
   (C) Schedule a tour
   (D) Place an order

다음 콘퍼런스를 주최할 완벽한 장소를 찾고 계신가요? 메이플 광장 컨벤션 센터 외에는 더 찾아볼 것도 없습니다. 넓은 강당, 대규모의 주차 시설, 그리고 대중교통으로의 접근이 용이한 메이플 광장 컨벤션 센터는 작고 큰 모임 모두를 위한 이상적인 장소입니다. 하지만 여러분이 다음 컨벤션을 이곳에서 열어야 하는 또 다른 이유가 있습니다. 우리는 굉장히 저렴한 가격으로 유명합니다. 예약에 관심 있으시다면, 555-0138로 친절한 저희 직원에게 전화하셔서 가격 및 이용 가능한 날짜를 문의해주세요.

EXPRESSIONS

look no further than ~보다 나은 곳을 찾을 수 없다
spacious 넓은
auditorium 강당, 회관
access to ~에의 접근
gathering 모임, 회합
incredibly 믿을 수 없을 정도로, 엄청나게

1. 광고되는 것은 무엇인가?
   (A) 식품점
   (B) 컨벤션 센터
   (C) 식당
   (D) 여행 관광지

2. 업체는 무엇으로 유명한가?
   (A) 편의 시설
   (B) 현대적 디자인
   (C) 가격
   (D) 음식

3. 화자는 청자들에게 무엇을 하도록 제안하는가?
   (A) 전화하기
   (B) 웹사이트 방문하기
   (C) 투어 예약하기
   (D) 주문하기

정답 **1.** (B) **2.** (C) **3.** (A)

빈출 표현

상품 및 서비스	**Rest assured we guarantee that** our work will be done by fully trained expert technicians. 모든 작업이 완전히 훈련된 전문 기술자들에 의해 이루어질 것을 보장합니다. Our hotel venue **features** several halls that can accommodate any event. 저희 호텔 행사장은 어떠한 이벤트도 수용할 수 있는 여러 홀을 특징으로 합니다. **What sets us apart from our competitors**? You don't owe one penny until all pests on your premises have been eradicated. 우리가 경쟁사와 무엇이 다르냐구요? 저희는 해충이 박멸되지 않는다면 단 한 푼도 청구하지 않습니다. **In celebration of** our 5th anniversary, we're offering 10% off all your purchases in July. 창립 5주년을 기념하여 7월에 구매하시는 모든 상품을 10% 할인해 드립니다.
방문 유도	To get this deal, you must **schedule an appointment** either by phone or online. 이 혜택을 얻으시려면, 전화나 온라인으로 예약을 하셔야 합니다. For more information, **go online** and schedule a complimentary consultation with one of our representatives. 더 많은 정보를 원하신다면 온라인으로 저희 직원과의 무료 상담을 예약해 주세요. For a list of all our locations, **visit our Web site** at www.alphachair.com. 모든 지점의 목록을 찾으시려면 저희 웹사이트 www.alphachair.com에 방문해 주세요.

CHECK-UP

P4_U5_Check-up 정답 및 해설 p.46

1. What is being advertised?
   (A) An exterminator
   (B) A housecleaner
   (C) A pet care service
   (D) An interior designer

2. What is available for free?
   (A) A cleaning product
   (B) A home inspection
   (C) An hour of work
   (D) A membership card

3. How can listeners receive a discount?
   (A) By referring a friend
   (B) By creating a social media post
   (C) By using a promo code
   (D) By booking multiple appointments

4. How does each tour begin?
   (A) Refreshments are served.
   (B) A video is shown.
   (C) A lecture is given.
   (D) Safety gear is distributed.

5. What kind of gift do participants receive at the end of the tour?
   (A) A poster
   (B) A discount coupon
   (C) A bag of coffee
   (D) A postcard

6. What does the speaker warn the listeners about?
   (A) A health risk
   (B) An age restriction
   (C) Potential closures
   (D) Limited parking

UNIT 06 연설, 소개, 견학/관광 안내

• 컨퍼런스, 개관식 등 각종 행사에서의 모두발언이나 기조연설, 강연, 연사 소개 등이 주로 출제된다.
• 견학이나 관람, 관광을 이끄는 가이드의 안내, 업무 및 작업 지침 등이 출제된다.

대표 유형 맛보기

Example 미남 🎧 P4_U6_Ex

Questions 1-3 refer to the following introduction.

Thank you for coming to our ceremony today. We are pleased to host the ninth annual Art Awards **here at Grayson Academy**. I'm very excited to welcome our guest speaker, artist **Howard Penn**. He recently wrote a book called *How to Paint Anything*, which has topped several bestseller lists. During his talk tonight, he will explain how he became both a renowned painter and bestselling author. **After his speech**, we will announce the winners of this year's competition and then offer some free drinks and snacks in the lobby.

1. Where is the talk **taking place**?
   (A) At a museum
   (B) At an academy
   (C) At a club meeting
   (D) At a bookstore

2. According to the introduction, what did **Howard Penn** recently do?
   (A) He received an award.
   (B) He made a famous artwork.
   (C) He conducted some research.
   (D) He wrote a popular book.

3. What are the listeners invited to do **after the event**?
   (A) Buy some artwork
   (B) Enjoy some refreshments
   (C) Learn more about the venue
   (D) Take home a free gift

오늘 기념 행사에 와 주셔서 감사드립니다. 이곳 그레이슨 아카데미에서 아홉 번째 연례 예술 시상식을 개최하게 되어 기쁩니다. 저희의 초청 연사인, 예술가 Howard Penn을 들뜬 마음으로 모시겠습니다. 그는 최근에 〈How to Paint Anything(무엇이든 그리는 방법)〉이라는 책을 썼고, 그것은 여러 개의 베스트셀러 목록의 정상을 차지했습니다. 오늘 밤 그의 연설 중에, 그가 어떻게 유명한 화가와 베스트셀러 작가가 되었는지에 대해 설명할 것입니다. 그의 연설 뒤에, 올해 대회 수상자를 발표하겠으며 그 후엔 무료 음료와 간식을 로비에서 제공할 것입니다.

EXPRESSIONS

be pleased to do ~하게 되어 기쁩니다
host 개최하다
academy 학교, 예술원, 학술원
top ~의 위에 놓이다, 능가하다
renowned 저명한
competition 대회

1. 담화는 어디에서 이루어지는가?
   (A) 박물관에서
   (B) 예술원에서
   (C) 동호회 모임에서
   (D) 서점에서

2. 소개에 따르면, Howard Penn은 최근에 무엇을 하였는가?
   (A) 그는 상을 탔다.
   (B) 그는 유명한 미술품을 만들었다.
   (C) 그는 연구를 하였다.
   (D 그는 인기 있는 책을 썼다.

3. 청자들은 행사 뒤에 무엇을 하도록 초대받는가?
   (A) 미술품 사기
   (B) 다과 즐기기
   (C) 장소에 대해 더 알아보기
   (D) 무료 선물을 집에 가져가기

정답 **1.** (B) **2.** (D) **3.** (B)

빈출 표현

연설 강연	Thank you all for being here for this workshop for salespeople. 판매원들을 위한 워크숍에 와 주신 모든 분께 감사드립니다. I'd like to welcome you all to the grand opening of Newbury Park. 뉴베리 공원의 개막식에 오신 여러분 모두를 환영합니다. Welcome to Harper Company's third annual conference on international business. Harper Company의 제3회 국제 비즈니스에 관한 연례 회의에 오신 걸 환영합니다. It's wonderful to see such a great turnout for this year's conference on hotel management. 올해 호텔 경영 학회에 이렇게 많은 인원이 참가하다니 정말 기쁩니다.
견학 관람 여행	Thank you for joining this tour of our electric car manufacturing plant. Today, I'll be showing you how we produce our range of cars. 이번 저희 전기차 제조 공장 견학에 함께해 주셔서 감사합니다. 저는 오늘 우리가 어떻게 다양한 자동차를 생산하는지 보여 드리겠습니다. As we tour the Crescent Museum today, you'll see a wide rage of artifacts from the Middle Ages. 오늘 Crescent Museum을 견학하는 동안, 여러분은 중세 시대의 다양한 유물들을 보게 될 것입니다. During today's bus tour, you will have a chance to see the city's legendary architecture. 오늘 버스 투어 동안, 여러분은 도시의 전설적인 건축물을 볼 기회를 가질 것입니다.

PART 4

CHECK-UP

P4_U6_Check-up 정답 및 해설 p.47

[Tour information]

1. What is made at the farm?

(A) Organic milk
(B) Cotton
(C) Beef jerky
(D) Fresh fruit

2. What will listeners have the chance to do?

(A) Take a walk with the animals
(B) Taste the products
(C) Provide food for the animals
(D) Meet the owners

3. What will listeners receive?

(A) A video link
(B) Sauces for snacks
(C) A leaflet
(D) A brush

[Speech]

4. What location is the speaker discussing?

(A) An art museum
(B) An amusement park
(C) A petting zoo
(D) An athletic field

5. What special offer does the speaker mention?

(A) A complimentary meal
(B) A voucher for a friend
(C) A discount for large groups
(D) An annual membership plan

6. What will take place on Friday?

(A) An art workshop
(B) A guided tour
(C) A live concert
(D) A movie screening

PRACTICE 고난도(의도 파악, 그래픽)

1. Where does the speaker most likely work?
   (A) At a car wash
   (B) At a moving company
   (C) At a car rental service
   (D) At an auto mechanic shop

2. What does the speaker imply when he says, "which will be a major job"?
   (A) A deposit must be paid.
   (B) The work will take him some time.
   (C) He needs to hire more people.
   (D) He is about to go on vacation.

3. What does the speaker say about this evening?
   (A) An employee will be present.
   (B) A part will arrive.
   (C) The business will be closed.
   (D) A payment system will be updated.

---

4. What is the purpose of the talk?
   (A) To tell the listeners about a lawsuit
   (B) To announce a new return policy
   (C) To prepare the listeners for complaints
   (D) To propose a team expansion

5. What does the speaker imply when he says, "We've radically changed our production process"?
   (A) The company once used dangerous chemicals.
   (B) Products are selling at a higher margin.
   (C) Productivity has increased dramatically.
   (D) A news report was wrong.

6. What are the listeners asked to do?
   (A) Read a handout
   (B) Take a short break
   (C) Write a report
   (D) Respond to some e-mails

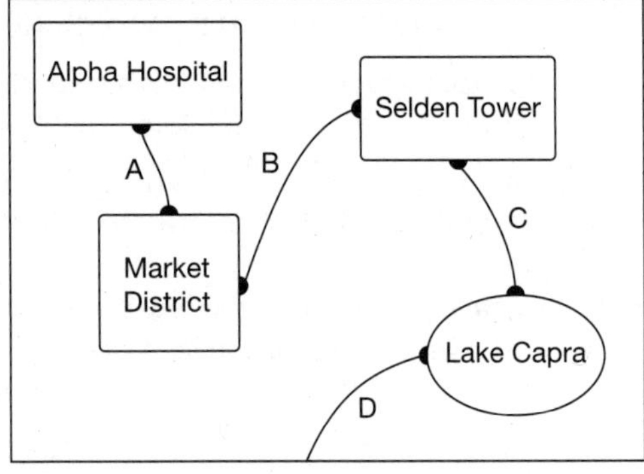

7. What project does the speaker mainly discuss?
   (A) A city hall
   (B) A walkway
   (C) A riverside park
   (D) A sports arena

8. Why was the project initiated?
   (A) A company offered to pay for it.
   (B) It was decided by the taxpayers.
   (C) The city mayor said it was necessary.
   (D) It was prompted by a research report.

9. Look at the graphic. According to the speaker, which segment of the project has been completed?
   (A) Segment A
   (B) Segment B
   (C) Segment C
   (D) Segment D

Unit Features	Unit Type			
	A	B	C	D
Two bedrooms	✓			✓
Ocean view		✓		✓
Massage chair	✓		✓	

10. Look at the graphic. Which type of unit does the speaker mention?

(A) Type A
(B) Type B
(C) Type C
(D) Type D

11. What does the speaker emphasize about the hotel?

(A) Its family-friendly atmosphere
(B) Its low prices
(C) Its high-quality food
(D) Its cleanliness

12. What will happen tomorrow?

(A) The speaker will take a day off.
(B) The hotel will be closed.
(C) The speaker will visit a client.
(D) The hotel will be fully booked.

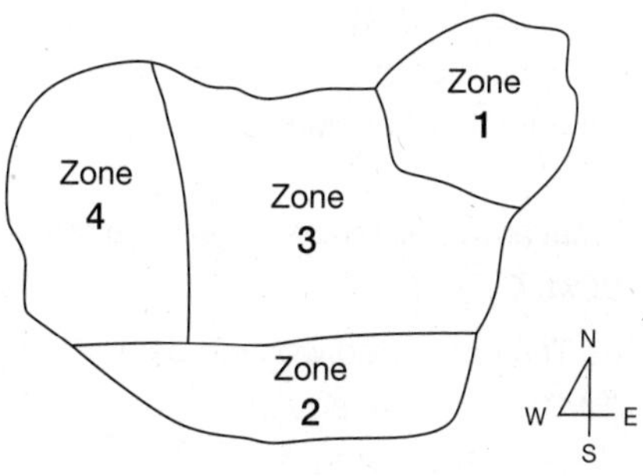

13. What does the speaker's company sell?

(A) Stationery
(B) Beauty products
(C) Auto parts
(D) Pharmaceuticals

14. Look at the graphic. Which region provided the least amount of sales last quarter?

(A) Zone 1
(B) Zone 2
(C) Zone 3
(D) Zone 4

15. According to the speaker, what will be launched at the end of the year?

(A) A research project
(B) Digital appliances
(C) A new product line
(D) Online advertisements

1. What position have the listeners been hired for?
(A) Tour guide
(B) Housekeeping staff
(C) Receptionist
(D) Supermarket clerk

2. What are the listeners asked to write down?
(A) Their preferred working days
(B) Their uniform size
(C) A contact number
(D) A password

3. What does the speaker say about a system?
(A) It has recently been upgraded.
(B) It is for managers only.
(C) It takes a while to restart.
(D) It does not get used very often.

---

4. What department does the speaker work in?
(A) Purchasing
(B) Marketing
(C) Data management
(D) Product development

5. What problem does the speaker mention?
(A) He had to work overtime.
(B) A conference room is locked.
(C) Some lights are not working.
(D) Some files were temporarily lost.

6. Where will the speaker most likely go at 2:00 P.M.?
(A) To a department store
(B) To a lecture hall
(C) To a bank
(D) To a train station

---

7. What does the speaker's company sell?
(A) Paint
(B) Pottery
(C) Furniture
(D) Jewelry

8. What does the speaker imply when she says, "those won't go on the Web site until April"?
(A) She is experiencing some technical difficulties.
(B) She thinks another task is more important.
(C) She found an error in the schedule.
(D) She wants to apologize for a delay.

9. What mistake does the speaker think the company made?
(A) It set its prices too low.
(B) It spent too much money on advertising.
(C) It changed to an unreliable supplier.
(D) It offered a fast delivery option.

---

10. Where does the announcement most likely take place?
(A) On a ferry
(B) On a train
(C) On an airplane
(D) On a bus

11. What are the listeners encouraged to do?
(A) Refrain from eating
(B) Fasten their seat belts
(C) Move to another level
(D) Stop using their phones

12. What will most likely happen next?
(A) More information will be given.
(B) The route will be changed.
(C) More passengers will be picked up.
(D) Luggage will be collected.

13. What is being advertised?
(A) A concert hall
(B) A tour company
(C) A hotel
(D) An airline

14. What benefit of the business does the speaker mention?
(A) It offers full refunds on cancellations.
(B) It can accommodate last-minute requests.
(C) It uses environmentally friendly materials.
(D) It provides customizable options.

15. What is being offered in March?
(A) A meal voucher
(B) A group discount
(C) A free clothing item
(D) An insurance policy

---

16. Who most likely is the speaker?
(A) A fitness instructor
(B) A park ranger
(C) A bus driver
(D) A research scientist

17. What does the speaker apologize for?
(A) A fee increase
(B) An unexpected closure
(C) A delayed start
(D) A printing error

18. What will some of the listeners most likely do next?
(A) Fill a container
(B) Watch a demonstration
(C) Select some snacks
(D) Put on name tags

---

19. Who is Terrance Hickman?
(A) A potential investor
(B) A new staff member
(C) A university professor
(D) A board member

20. Which department do the listeners most likely work in?
(A) Graphic design
(B) Technical support
(C) Advertising
(D) Legal

21. Why does the speaker say, "you all had the same opportunity"?
(A) To give a warning about deadlines
(B) To acknowledge the top employees
(C) To encourage listeners to help
(D) To explain a misunderstanding

---

22. Who is the speaker most likely calling?
(A) A translator
(B) An architect
(C) An accountant
(D) A financial advisor

23. What does the speaker mean when she says, "the board meeting is tomorrow"?
(A) She cannot reserve the room she wanted.
(B) She needs to reschedule an appointment with the listener.
(C) She will have some information soon.
(D) She would like the listener to give a presentation.

24. What does the speaker plan to do this afternoon?
(A) Attend a conference
(B) Train a colleague
(C) Sign a contract
(D) Visit a family member

Test Results	
Test #	Distance
1	95 miles
2	121 miles
3	103 miles
4	99 miles

25. Where are the listeners?

(A) At a staff orientation
(B) At a job interview
(C) At a press conference
(D) At an awards banquet

26. According to the speaker, what happened in February?

(A) An invention's patent was approved.
(B) A safety report was publicized.
(C) A department head was changed.
(D) A company acquisition was finalized.

27. Look at the graphic. Which test run did the speaker participate in?

(A) Test 1
(B) Test 2
(C) Test 3
(D) Test 4

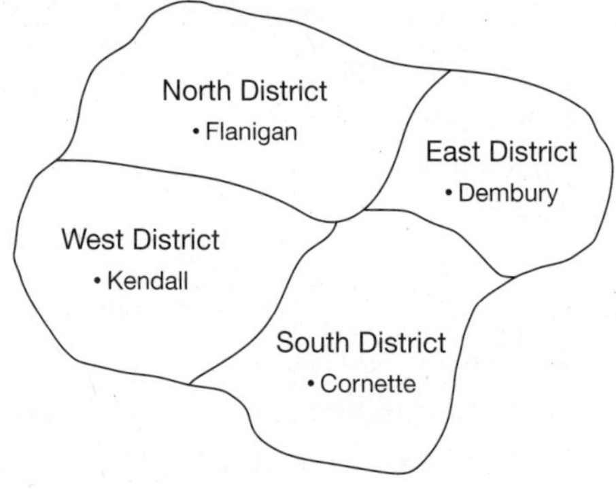

28. Who did the speaker talk to in the morning?

(A) Utility company employees
(B) Department store managers
(C) Emergency workers
(D) Factory supervisors

29. Look at the graphic. Which district experienced storm damage?

(A) The East District
(B) The West District
(C) The North District
(D) The South District

30. What does the speaker ask Annabelle's team to do?

(A) Review a document
(B) Call some clients
(C) Clear an area
(D) Repair a vehicle

비가 와야 무지개가 뜨고
밤이 깊어야 새벽이 오고
산고를 겪어야 아기가 태어납니다.
감동은 고난의 열매입니다.

– 조정민, 『인생은 선물이다』, 두란노

RC

PART 5

PART 5 출제 경향 및 전략

PART 5는 품사 및 동사의 올바른 활용 형태(시제, 태, 분사, 수 일치)를 묻는 문법 문제와, 문맥에 알맞은 단어 및 관용 표현을 고르는 어휘 문제로 이루어진다. 문법 문제와 어휘 문제는 거의 비슷한 비중으로 출제된다. 문법 문제 중에서도 명사, 동사, 형용사, 부사 중에서 빈칸에 알맞은 품사를 고르는 문제는 매회 가장 큰 비중으로 출제되므로 고득점 획득을 위해 놓쳐서는 안 된다. 어휘는 동사, 명사, 형용사, 부사, 전치사로 이루어진 문제들이 2~3문제씩 출제되며, 접속사 및 관용어구로 이루어진 문제들은 평균 1~3문제가 출제되나 빈도가 불규칙한 편이다.
PART 5는 시간 단축을 위해 선택지를 먼저 보고 문제의 유형을 파악한 후 해당 문제의 풀이 전략에 따라 문제를 푸는 것이 일반적이다. 아래의 네 가지 대표 유형을 통해 문법과 어휘 문제의 기본적인 접근 방식을 익혀보자.

[문법]

알맞은 품사/어형 고르기

Mr. Wood's ------- to the Paris branch was postponed until next year.

(A) transfer 명사, 동사
(B) to transfer to부정사
(C) transferred 과거분사
(D) transferable 형용사

해석 Mr. Wood의 파리 지사로의 전근이 내년으로 연기되었다.

❶ **선택지 확인**
선택지가 transfer라는 동일한 어근에서 파생된 다른 품사의 어휘들이므로 자리 문제.

❷ **빈칸 앞뒤 확인**
빈칸 앞의 Mr. Wood's는 명사를 수식하는 한정사이므로 빈칸에는 명사가 온다.

❸ **정답 선택**
명사인 (A) transfer가 정답이다.

알맞은 동사 형태 고르기

A retirement party will be held next week for Mr. Schmidt, who ------- for Melon Technologies for over 30 years.

(A) works 단수 주어 현재 시제
(B) was worked 단수 주어 과거 시제
(C) have worked 복수 주어 현재완료 시제
(D) has been working 단수 주어 현재완료진행 시제

해석 Mr. Schmidt의 은퇴 파티가 다음 주에 열리는데, 그는 Melon Technologies에서 30년 넘게 일해 왔다.

❶ **선택지 확인**
선택지가 work라는 동일한 어근에서 파생된 다양한 형태의 동사들이므로 동사 문제.

❷ **문법 사항 확인 및 오답 소거**
빈칸은 Mr. Schmidt를 수식하는 주격 관계절의 동사 자리이다. 주격 관계절의 동사는 선행사에 수 일치한다. 선행사인 Mr. Schmidt가 단수 명사이므로 단수 동사가 정답이 되므로 (C)를 오답으로 소거한다.

❸ **정답 선택**
뒤에 현재완료 시제와 어울려 쓰이는 부사구(for over 30 years)가 있으므로 (D)가 정답이다.

[어휘]

알맞은 전치사 고르기

------- coming to work early, Mr. Earl sometimes works on weekends to make sure he meets deadlines.

(A) As long as 접속사: ~하는 한
(B) After 접속사, 전치사: ~한 후에
(C) In addition to 전치사: ~뿐만 아니라
(D) However 접속 부사: 하지만, 아무튼

해석 Mr. Earl은 일찍 출근하는 데다가 마감일을 맞추기 위해 가끔 주말에 일을 하기도 한다.

❶ 선택지 확인
선택지가 접속사, 전치사, 접속 부사 등으로 이루어져 있으므로 접속사 또는 전치사를 찾는 문제.

❷ 빈칸 앞뒤 〈주어+동사〉 확인
빈칸 뒤에 주어 없이 coming이 이어지므로 빈칸은 전치사 자리. 따라서 접속사 (A)와 접속 부사 (D)를 소거할 수 있다.

❸ 정답 선택
문맥상 일찍 출근하는 것 외에 주말 근무도 한다는 내용이 되는 게 자연스러우므로 (C) In addition to가 정답이다.

알맞은 어휘 고르기

During the interview, each candidate was asked to describe their previous work -------.

(A) experience 경험
(B) consumption 소비
(C) drop 하락
(D) occasion 경우, 행사

해석 면접 도중 각 지원자는 자신의 예전 경력에 대해 말할 것을 요청받았다.

❶ 선택지 확인
선택지가 다양한 의미의 명사들로 구성되어 있으므로 명사 어휘 문제.

❷ 빈칸 앞뒤 해석
선택지를 빈칸에 넣어 빈칸 앞뒤의 단어들과 연결하여 해석한다.
(A) work experience 업무 경험
(B) work consumption 업무 소비
(C) work drop 업무 하락
(D) work occasion 업무 경우

❸ 정답 선택
해석이 가장 자연스러운 (A)가 정답이다. 빈칸 바로 앞뒤 단어의 연결만으로 단서가 불충분하다면 previous work experience(예전 업무 경험), describe their previous work experience(그들의 예전 업무 경험을 말하다)와 같이 해석의 범위를 확장한다.

UNIT 01 명사

1 관사/소유격+명사

빈칸 앞에 관사(a, an, the), 소유격(her, Mr. Wood's) 등의 한정사가 있으면 빈칸에는 명사가 온다.

관사+명사 Because of unexpected competition, the store still had **an** **excess** / excessive of one hundred televisions left in stock.
예상치 못한 경쟁으로 인해 그 가게에는 텔레비전이 아직도 100대가 재고로 남아 있었다.

소유격+명사 Nicholas & Son and Johnston Co. have formed a mutually beneficial partnership to increase **their** **profits** / profitable.
Nicholas & Son과 Johnston 사는 그들의 이익을 증대시키기 위해 상호 이득이 되는 제휴 관계를 맺었다.

2 형용사/분사+명사

형용사+명사 The restaurant on Mesa Street is having a **large** **celebration** / celebrate to mark its tenth anniversary. 메사 스트리트에 있는 그 식당은 10주년을 축하하기 위해 대규모 축하 행사를 하고 있다.

분사+명사 The **written** **agreement** / agreeable between HC Media and the band clearly outlined the terms for licensing the music.
HC Media와 그 밴드 사이의 서면 합의에는 음반 판권 조건들이 명확하게 서술되어 있었다.

3 주어/목적어/보어 자리

주어 **Acceptance** / Accept to the law firm's internship program **depends** on university transcripts and recommendations. 그 로펌의 인턴십 프로그램 합격 여부는 대학교 성적 증명서와 추천서에 달려 있다.
→ 주어는 Acceptance, 동사는 depends이고, to the law firm's internship program은 주어를 수식하는 전치사구이다.

동사의 목적어 New employees should **obtain** **approval** / approved from their assigned mentors before leaving the office. 신입 직원들은 퇴근하기 전에 자신들에게 배정된 멘토에게서 승인을 얻어야 한다.

전치사의 목적어 Restaurant owners should make sure their kitchens are ready **for** **inspection** / inspect at all times. 식당 주인들은 주방이 언제든 점검받을 수 있도록 준비해 놓아야 한다.
→ 명사는 전치사 뒤에 위치하여 전치사의 목적어 역할을 할 수 있다.

주격 보어 The store's holiday season sales event **was** an unprecedented **success** / successful.
그 상점의 연휴 세일 행사가 전례 없는 성공을 거두었다.
→ 빈칸 앞에 be동사 was가 있으므로 빈칸은 주격 보어 자리이자 관사 an과 형용사 unprecedented의 수식을 받는 명사 자리이다.

고득점 도전 목적격 보어

The department head **called Mr. Reuben** a great **leader** / leadership for finishing the project ahead of schedule. 부서장은 프로젝트를 예정보다 빨리 끝냈다는 이유로 Mr. Reuben을 훌륭한 리더라고 불렀다.
→ 동사 call의 목적격 보어 자리이자 관사 a와 형용사 great의 수식을 받는 자리이다. leadership은 명사이지만 목적어인 Mr. Reuben과 동격의 관계가 성립하지 않기 때문에 오답이다.

4 복합 명사

〈명사+명사〉로 이루어진 복합 명사의 첫 번째나 두 번째 자리에 오는 단어의 품사를 묻는 문제가 출제된다.

road repair 도로 수리	delivery receipt 배송 영수증
repair service 수리 서비스	keynote speech 기조 연설
product line 제품(군)	expiration date 유효 기간, 만기일
meeting agenda 회의 안건	contract negotiation 계약 협상
work site 작업장	travel budget 출장 예산
hiring process 채용 과정	quality standards 품질 기준
baggage allowance 수하물 중량 제한	e-mail reminder 이메일 알림

고득점 도전

The botanical garden is the most popular tourist / touristic **attraction** in Cincinnati.
그 식물원은 신시내티에서 가장 인기 있는 관광지이다.
→ tourist attraction은 '관광 명소'라는 뜻의 복합 명사이다. 빈칸이 명사 앞에 있을 경우 명사를 수식하는 형용사 또는 분사 자리로 착각하기 쉬우므로 주의해야 한다.

5 사람 명사 VS. 사물/추상 명사

선택지에 사람 명사와 사물 명사가 있으면 해석을 통해 문제를 풀어야 한다.

Despite being **the largest** producer / production of textiles in the country, Grenadine's Fabrics has seen a steady decline in profits.
Grenadine's Fabrics는 국내 최대의 직물 생산업체임에도 불구하고 수익이 지속적으로 감소하고 있다.
→ 문맥상 빈칸은 주절의 주어인 Grenadine's Fabrics를 가리키므로 '생산'이 아니라 '생산업체'가 되어야 한다.

6 단수 명사 VS. 복수 명사

선택지에 명사가 두 개 있으면 가산/불가산 여부와 관사의 유무, 그리고 동사의 수 일치를 살펴야 한다.

가산 VS. 불가산 If your copier is **in need of** repair / repairs, you're advised to select a certified technician.
복사기를 수리해야 할 경우, 공인된 기사를 선택하는 것이 좋습니다.
→ repair는 가산 명사와 불가산 명사로 모두 쓰일 수 있으나, in need of와 함께 쓰일 때에는 항상 불가산 명사로만 쓰인다.

관사의 유무 The event organizer called the management office to ask **for** permission / permit to use the event hall. 행사 기획자는 행사장을 사용하기 위한 허가를 요청하기 위해 관리실에 전화했다.
→ 빈칸은 전치사 for의 목적어 자리이므로 명사가 와야 한다. 빈칸 앞에 부정 관사 a/an이 없으므로 빈칸은 불가산 명사 또는 복수 명사가 되어야 하는데, permit(허가증)은 가산 명사이므로 부정 관사 없이 쓰려면 복수형인 permits가 되어야 한다. 따라서 '허가'를 뜻하는 불가산 명사인 permission이 정답이다.

수 일치 The museum cannot be opened to the public until structural defects / defect **are** repaired.
그 박물관은 구조적 결함이 수리될 때까지 대중에게 개방될 수 없다.

7 명사 VS. 동명사

Construction / Constructing **of** the Lowell Bridge has been postponed due to inclement weather.
Lowell Bridge의 건설은 악천후 때문에 연기되었다.
→ 동명사도 명사 역할을 할 수 있지만 뒤에 오는 전치사 of의 수식을 받을 수 있는 것은 명사 construction이다. 동명사(constructing)는 명사의 역할을 하는 동시에 동사의 속성을 지니고 있기 때문에 바로 뒤에 목적어가 와야 한다.

PRACTICE

1. According to the company newsletter, the vice president will hold a ------- on the firm's progress this Thursday.
   (A) discussing
   (B) discussed
   (C) discussion
   (D) will discuss

2. Speak with a supervisor if any safety ------- occur near the assembly line.
   (A) violated
   (B) violations
   (C) violate
   (D) violates

3. The lawyers carefully review negotiated ------- to check for any problems.
   (A) agree
   (B) agreements
   (C) agreed
   (D) agreeing

4. Irene Krakow intends to meet a ------- from her gym tomorrow morning.
   (A) train
   (B) trainer
   (C) trained
   (D) training

5. There is ------- among the bank tellers to accept the contract proposal put forth by management.
   (A) hesitate
   (B) hesitated
   (C) hesitation
   (D) hesitating

6. Mr. Cromwell was given a choice of ------- after he completed the Maxell Project successfully.
   (A) assigning
   (B) assigns
   (C) assigned
   (D) assignments

7. Dover Sporting Goods has a long-term ------- with several baseball teams in the local area.
   (A) affiliate
   (B) affiliated
   (C) affiliation
   (D) affiliating

8. ------- will be advised to avoid the roads in the mountains on account of the expected heavy snowfall.
   (A) Travel
   (B) Travelers
   (C) Traveled
   (D) Traveling

9. In ------- with the CEO's decision, all employees were given an extra day of paid leave.
   (A) accord
   (B) according
   (C) accordance
   (D) accords

10. During the holiday season, all hotel ------- made online will be completely nonrefundable.
    (A) booked
    (B) book
    (C) booking
    (D) bookings

11. Mr. Hightower expressed ------- that his bridge design was selected by the mayor of the city.

(A) satisfy
(B) satisfaction
(C) satisfying
(D) satisfyingly

12. Mr. Burbank will establish a group of ------- to handle the new clients the company has obtained.

(A) consultant
(B) consultants
(C) consulting
(D) consulted

13. Pianist Judy Watson's ------- the past three days have been widely praised by audience members.

(A) perform
(B) performed
(C) performance
(D) performances

14. In Piedmont, the ------- of some new buildings resembles that used in ancient Rome.

(A) styling
(B) stylist
(C) styled
(D) style

15. According to government -------, homes should use energy-efficient insulation materials.

(A) recommendations
(B) recommends
(C) to recommend
(D) will recommend

16. Despite his continual ------- at Weyland Aerospace for thirty years, Dan Jenkins resigned to work at another company.

(A) employee
(B) employing
(C) employed
(D) employment

17. Employees are supposed to report any ------- on business trips no matter how small.

(A) expensive
(B) expensively
(C) expenses
(D) expensed

18. Mr. Klein was asked to make a ------- regarding how to enter the South American market.

(A) propose
(B) proposer
(C) proposing
(D) proposal

고득점 도전

19. Stores were informed that ------- of the new product line would be limited for the next two months.

(A) distribution
(B) distributing
(C) distribute
(D) distributed

고득점 도전

20. Dr. Audrey is always eager to give her scientists ------- that they need for their experiments.

(A) materially
(B) materials
(C) materialize
(D) materialization

UNIT 02 대명사

1 인칭대명사

주어가 되는 주격 인칭대명사와 명사(구)를 수식하는 소유격 인칭대명사를 묻는 문제가 많이 출제된다.

주격 **The Web site** is now unavailable as **it** / he is undergoing routine maintenance.
그 웹사이트는 정기 유지 보수를 받고 있기 때문에 현재 이용할 수 없다.

목적격 The department manager will **give us** / ourselves **the new schedule** for the summer season.
부장님이 새로운 하계 스케줄을 우리에게 주실 겁니다.
→ 동사 give는 〈give+간접목적어+직접목적어〉 구조로 목적어를 두 개 취하는 동사이다.

소유격 Ms. Duda is persuading the executives to postpone the product launch until **her** / hers **team** is ready. Ms. Duda는 자신의 팀이 준비될 때까지 제품 출시를 미뤄 달라고 경영진을 설득하고 있다.

소유대명사 A coworker of **mine** / me will be taking a business trip to Ulaanbaatar in a few weeks.
제 동료 중 한 명이 몇 주 후에 울란바토르로 출장을 갑니다.

2 부정대명사

anyone, everyone **Anyone** / Those **who has been** working with the company for over six months **is** eligible for a holiday bonus. 회사에서 6개월 이상 근무한 사람은 누구나 상여금을 받을 자격이 있다.
→ anyone, everyone은 뒤에 단수 동사가 이어지고, those (who)는 뒤에 복수 동사가 이어진다.

one, ones **The tire** was replaced with a new **one** / ones because it was flat.
그 타이어는 펑크가 나서 새 타이어로 교체되었다.
→ one은 앞에 언급된 명사(tire)를 대신하여 사용되며 앞에 반드시 한정사가 온다.

3 지시대명사

The commercial real estate prices in Southfield are significantly lower than **those** / that in Sherwood.
사우스필드의 상업용 부동산 가격은 셔우드의 그것보다 현저히 낮다.
→ 앞에 나온 복수 명사(The commercial real estate prices)를 대신할 수 있는 말이 들어가야 하므로 복수형 지시대명사인 those가 적절하다.

4 재귀대명사

재귀용법 For the team-building exercises, **workers** were asked to organize **themselves** / them into groups of four. 팀 단합 활동을 위해 직원들은 4인 1조를 편성할 것을 요구받았다.
→ 동사 organize의 목적어는 주어인 workers와 동일하므로 재귀대명사인 themselves가 적절하다. 재귀용법으로 쓰인 재귀대명사는 생략할 수 없다.

고득점 도전 **강조용법**

The CEO of Stockton Tech usually gives new employees a building tour **himself** / him.
Stockton Tech의 대표이사는 보통 신규 입사자들에게 자신이 직접 건물 견학을 시켜 준다.
→ 〈주어+동사+목적어〉가 갖추어진 완전한 문장에서는 강조용법의 재귀대명사를 생략할 수 있다.

PRACTICE

정답 및 해설 p.56

1. Ms. Toole is flying to Memphis tomorrow because ------- has to meet a potential client there.
   (A) her
   (B) hers
   (C) she
   (D) herself

2. ------- who is interested in a career in robotics is welcome to apply for the position.
   (A) All
   (B) Anyone
   (C) Whatever
   (D) Whomever

3. The staff meeting is mandatory, so ------- must cancel conflicting appointments and attend it tomorrow.
   (A) another
   (B) everybody
   (C) which
   (D) every

4. After reading a section of the novel, Jules Desmond ------- will autograph copies of it.
   (A) him
   (B) he
   (C) his
   (D) himself

5. Please use the training manuals in the back of the room rather than ------- sitting on the table.
   (A) anyone
   (B) those
   (C) other
   (D) each

6. Whenever a project is complete, please contact ------- manager to receive a new assignment.
   (A) your
   (B) yours
   (C) yourself
   (D) you

7. Even though the tires are only two years old, Ms. Vernon decided to replace ------- with a new set.
   (A) them
   (B) they
   (C) their
   (D) themselves

8. The best ------- who applied for the engineering position was Rita Kraus, to whom we should offer the job.
   (A) each
   (B) one
   (C) what
   (D) another

고득점 도전

9. The tour bus we rode in is painted red, so it was easy to locate ------- even in a full parking lot.
   (A) us
   (B) our
   (C) ours
   (D) ourselves

고득점 도전

10. Ms. Atkins has turned ------- into a highly competent computer programmer thanks to hard work and dedication.
   (A) her
   (B) hers
   (C) herself
   (D) her own

UNIT 03 형용사와 한정사

1 형용사

형용사 VS. 분사

New employees will watch an instructional / instructing **video** about how to assemble the device. 신입 직원들은 그 장치를 조립하는 방법에 관한 교육용 동영상을 시청할 것이다.
→ 빈칸이 형용사 자리이고, 선택지에 형용사와 분사가 있으면 형용사가 우선한다.

주격 보어

The recruits **seem** eager / eagerly to start their first day on the job.
신입 사원들은 하루 빨리 업무 첫날을 시작하기를 바라는 것 같다.

목적격 보어

Attention to detail **makes Ms. Rose** reliable / reliably and easy to work with.
꼼꼼한 성격 덕분에 Ms. Rose는 믿을 만하고 함께 일하기 편한 사람이다.
→ 〈주어(Attention to detail)+동사(makes)+목적어(Ms. Rose)+목적격 보어〉의 문장 구조이다. 등위접속사 and 뒤에 나오는 easy의 품사가 형용사라는 것도 정답의 단서가 된다.

고득점 도전 형용사 VS. 형용사

Without reliable / reliant **information**, stock traders would not be able to handle their clients' investments in a responsible manner.
신뢰할 수 있는 정보가 없다면 증권 거래인들은 고객의 투자금을 책임감 있게 처리할 수 없을 것이다.
→ reliable(믿을 수 있는)과 reliant(의존적인) 중에서 의미상 information을 수식하기에 적절한 것은 reliable이다.

부사 형태의 형용사

Ms. Jenkins instructed her workers to respond to every e-mail in a timely / timer **manner**.
Ms. Jenkins는 그녀의 직원들에게 모든 이메일에 제때에 응답하도록 지시했다.
→ timely는 -ly 형태지만 부사가 아니라 형용사이다. 비슷한 형태의 단어로는 costly(비싼), lively(활발한), elderly(나이가 든) 등이 있다.

비교급

The latest SUV by Eighto Motors is more spacious / spaciously **than** it looks.
Eighto Motors의 신형 SUV는 보이는 것보다 공간이 넓다.

최상급

The Mumbai branch had **the** highest / higher sales numbers out of the whole global sales team. 뭄바이 지점은 모든 글로벌 영업 팀 중에서 매출액이 가장 높았다.

2 한정사

한정사는 뒤에 나오는 명사의 의미를 한정하는 일종의 형용사로서, 단수 명사를 수식하는 한정사와 복수 명사를 수식하는 한정사를 구분해야 한다.

each/every +단수 명사

Our managers ensure that every / all **product** is of the highest quality.
우리 관리자들은 모든 제품이 최고의 품질을 갖추도록 합니다.

all+복수 명사 /불가산 명사

Mr. Lambert was surprised that all / every **his coworkers** wrote him a letter for his retirement party. Mr. Lambert는 모든 동료가 그의 은퇴식을 위해 편지를 쓴 것에 놀랐다.

any+단복수 명사 /불가산 명사

A safety label is attached to the product to prevent any / each **accidents** with children.
그 제품에는 어린이 사고를 예방하기 위해 안전 라벨이 부착되어 있다.

both A and B

Both / Either **the design team and the marketing team** work together to make the most eye-catching book covers. 디자인 팀과 마케팅 팀 모두 가장 눈길을 끄는 책 표지를 만들기 위해 협업한다.
→ either는 〈either A or B〉의 형태로 쓰인다.

PRACTICE

정답 및 해설 p.57

1. Ms. Howell has a comprehensive understanding of even the ------- developments in technology these days.
(A) late
(B) lateness
(C) lately
(D) latest

2. After attending the workshop, ------- person has to do some hands-on training in the lab.
(A) every
(B) which
(C) because
(D) many

3. It is ------- to create an agenda before a meeting so that all important points are covered.
(A) benefit
(B) benefiting
(C) beneficial
(D) beneficially

4. Destiny Media only hires ------- applicants willing to work hard to achieve their goals.
(A) ambition
(B) ambitions
(C) ambitious
(D) ambitiously

5. It is vital that items be shipped to customers in a ------- manner.
(A) timely
(B) time
(C) times
(D) timing

6. ------- technicians are required to wear safety gear in the laboratory during the workday.
(A) Each
(B) All
(C) Either
(D) None

7. Attendees said the dance performances were the most ------- part of the festival.
(A) impress
(B) impression
(C) impressive
(D) impressively

8. After he gets promoted, Horace Powers intends to take ------- days of vacation with his family.
(A) several
(B) either
(C) whatever
(D) another

고득점 도전

9. Ms. Cunningham has worked on multiple ------- projects during the past few years.
(A) extensive
(B) extend
(C) extending
(D) extends

고득점 도전

10. Luxor Furniture designs ------- office chairs for individuals who remain seated most of the day.
(A) comfort
(B) comfortable
(C) comforting
(D) comfortably

UNIT 04 부사

1 동사/분사 앞뒤에 나오는 부사

부사+동사

The food critic **favorably** / favored **reviewed** the chef's special dishes.
음식 평론가는 그 요리사의 특선 요리들을 호의적으로 평가했다.

동사+부사

BT News gets a lot of traffic to its Web site because it **advertises** **heavily** / heavy on social media. BT News는 소셜 미디어에 엄청나게 광고를 하기 때문에 웹사이트 트래픽이 많다.

동사+명사+부사

The factory inspector **examined** each of the manufactured items **carefully** / careful.
공장 검사관은 제조된 제품들 각각을 주의 깊게 살펴보았다.
→ carefully는 명사 items 뒤에 있지만, 실제로는 앞에 나온 동사 examined를 수식한다.

be동사+부사+분사

The store's refund policy **is** **clearly** / clear **stated** on its Web site.
그 가게의 환불 정책은 웹사이트에 분명하게 명시되어 있다.

be동사+분사+부사

All elevators in the building **are inspected** **regularly** / regular by Mr. Jones.
건물 내의 모든 엘리베이터는 Mr. Jones에 의해 주기적으로 점검을 받는다.

2 조동사 뒤에 나오는 부사

have+부사+과거분사

The sales manager **has** **successfully** / success **negotiated** contracts with a variety of corporate clients. 영업 담당자는 다양한 기업 고객들과 성공적으로 계약을 협상해 왔다.
→ 동사에 따라 〈have+과거분사+부사〉의 형태로 나오기도 한다.

조동사+부사+동사원형

After the reading, the author **will** **personally** / personal **sign** copies of his new novel for fans.
낭독이 끝나고 나서 작가는 팬들을 위해 자신의 신작 소설에 직접 사인해 줄 것이다.

3 형용사와 부사 앞에 나오는 부사

부사+형용사

The local bookstore has a **surprisingly** / surprising **large** selection of children's books.
그 지역 서점에는 놀라울 정도로 많은 아동 도서가 있다.

부사+부사

To the average buyer, the mini tablet is **considerably** / considerable **more** attractive than the extra-large one. 보통의 구매자에게 미니 태블릿은 특대형 태블릿보다 훨씬 더 매력적이다.
→ considerably는 a lot의 의미로서, 부사 more 앞에서 more의 의미를 강조한다.

4 전치사, 부사절 접속사 앞에 나오는 부사

Gilmore Manufacturing announced a new round of hiring **shortly** **after** reporting earnings that were higher than expected. Gilmore Manufacturing은 예상보다 높은 실적을 발표한 직후 또 다른 신규 채용을 발표했다.

PRACTICE

정답 및 해설 p.58

1. The improvements to the Web site were ------- made by the director of the IT Department.
   (A) personal
   (B) personals
   (C) personality
   (D) personally

2. The audience was impressed by the ------- realistic special effects in the film.
   (A) high
   (B) higher
   (C) highest
   (D) highly

3. The sign indicates that the room is ------- off limits to unauthorized personnel.
   (A) clear
   (B) clearly
   (C) clearer
   (D) clearest

4. Mr. Olson, the office manager, ------- instructed his employees to arrive on time for special events.
   (A) repeat
   (B) repeating
   (C) repeated
   (D) repeatedly

5. Tour participants must be on time because the boat departs ------- at 7:00 A.M.
   (A) prompt
   (B) promptly
   (C) prompted
   (D) promptness

6. Since she started working at Meridian Inc., Julie Sharpe has ------- received recognition for her accomplishments.
   (A) regular
   (B) more regular
   (C) regulars
   (D) regularly

7. The waiter asked the diners ------- if they had enjoyed their meal at the restaurant.
   (A) polite
   (B) politeness
   (C) politely
   (D) most polite

8. Customer service representatives were instructed to solve all complaints more -------.
   (A) prompt
   (B) prompts
   (C) promptness
   (D) promptly

고득점 도전

9. The warehouse supervisor had the boxes of electronics ------- removed to make space for the new shipment.
   (A) haste
   (B) hasten
   (C) hastened
   (D) hastily

고득점 도전

10. The winner of the raffle at the county fair will be determined by a ------- selected number this evening.
   (A) randomly
   (B) randomize
   (C) to randomize
   (D) random

UNIT 05 동사, 수 일치, 태, 시제

1 동사 자리와 형태

동사 자리

The Trimble Gallery celebrated / celebrating its twenty-fifth anniversary with a large reception. Trimble 미술관은 성대한 연회로 25주년을 축하했다.
→ 동사는 주어 뒤에 오며, 동명사, to부정사 등은 문장의 동사 자리에 올 수 없다.

동사 자리+태

The electronics company has sold / was sold **more than one million copies** of its new game console. 그 전자 회사는 자사의 새로운 게임기를 백만 대 넘게 팔았다.
→ 빈칸 뒤에 목적어인 more than one million copies가 있으므로 능동태가 와야 한다.

조동사 +동사원형

Residents **must** separate / separates their household trash from their recyclable items.
주민들은 가정용 쓰레기와 재활용 가능한 품목을 분리해야 한다.

명령문

Please confirm / confirmed that all of the items you have ordered are in the box.
주문하신 모든 물품이 상자 안에 있는지 확인하시기 바랍니다.
→ 명령문은 주어 없이 동사원형 혹은 〈Please+동사원형〉으로 문장이 시작된다.

고득점 도전 특정 동사 뒤 동사원형

The landlord **demanded that** tenants give / gave one month's notice before leaving.
집주인은 임차인이 나가기 한 달 전에 통보해 줄 것을 요구했다.
→ 제안, 요구, 명령을 의미하는 ask, request, require, demand, suggest, propose, recommend, advise 등의 동사가 쓰이면 목적어인 that절에서는 〈should+동사원형〉을 쓰는데, 이때 should는 생략되는 경우가 많다.

2 수 일치

수식어가 긴 주어의 수 일치

A new company policy that affords workers more rights was enacted / have been enacted last week. 직원들에게 더 많은 권리를 주는 회사의 새 정책이 지난주에 제정되었다.
→ 단수 주어인 A new company policy가 주격 관계절(that ~ rights)의 수식을 받는 구조이므로 단수 동사인 was enacted가 와야 한다.

복수 형태의 단수 명사

Humax Electronics has / have been our most reliable supplier for the past 20 years.
Humax Electronics는 지난 20년간 우리의 가장 믿음직스러운 공급업체였다.
→ 회사명과 같은 고유명사는 이름에 -s가 붙어도 단수로 취급한다.

수 일치+태

An increase in profits has allowed / was allowed / allow **Warren Industries** to hire more employees. 수익 증가로 Warren Industries는 더 많은 직원을 고용할 수 있게 되었다.
→ 단수 주어(An increase)가 전치사구(in profits)의 수식을 받는 구조이다. 따라서 빈칸에는 단수 동사가 들어가야 하므로 복수 형태의 allow는 맞지 않다. 빈칸 뒤에 목적어(Warren Industries)가 있으므로 능동태인 has allowed가 적절하다.

고득점 도전 수 일치+시제

Since Henry's Café built a drive-through window, **the number** of visitors to the coffee shop has increased / increases / have been increasing.
Henry's Café가 드라이브스루 창구를 만든 이후 커피숍을 찾는 방문객 수가 증가했다.
→ 단수 주어(the number)가 전치사구(of visitors ~ shop)의 수식을 받는 구조이다. 따라서 빈칸에는 단수 동사가 들어가야 하므로 복수 형태의 have been increasing은 적절하지 않다. 앞에 현재완료 시제와 어울려 쓰이는 부사절(Since ~ window)이 있으므로 현재완료 시제인 has increased가 적절하다.

3 능동태와 수동태

빈칸 뒤에 목적어가 있으면 능동태를, 목적어가 없으면 수동태를 쓴다.

능동태 VS. 수동태 — Mongoose LTC **established** / was established **a new branch** in Bangkok to cover the Southeast Asian market.
Mongoose LTC는 동남아시아 시장을 담당하도록 방콕에 지점을 신설했다.

고득점 도전 태+시제

For the past few weeks, sales of high heels **have been outperforming** / will be outperforming / are outperformed **sneakers** at Shoe Emporium.
지난 몇 주 동안 Shoe Emporium에서 하이힐의 판매가 운동화를 능가하고 있다.
→ 빈칸 뒤에 목적어 sneakers가 있으므로 빈칸에는 능동태가 적절하다. 그리고 빈칸 앞에 현재완료 시제와 어울려 쓰이는 부사구(For the past few weeks)가 있으므로 능동태 현재완료진행 시제인 have been outperforming이 적절하다.

4 시제

시제 문제는 자주 어울려 쓰이는 부사나 시간의 부사구가 시제 판별의 단서가 된다.

단순 시제 — Diesel Motors **expected** / expects to open a new factory in Colorado **last month** but faced a labor shortage. Diesel Motors는 지난달 콜로라도에 새 공장을 열 것으로 예상했으나 인력난에 직면했다.
→ 과거의 시점을 나타내는 last month라는 부사구가 있으므로 단순 과거 시제를 사용한다.

진행 시제 — The ingredients **are being shipped** / are shipped to the restaurant **later this afternoon**.
재료들은 오늘 오후 늦게 식당에 배송될 것이다.
→ 현재진행 시제가 가까운 미래를 나타내는 표현과 함께 쓰이면 예정된 미래의 일을 나타낼 수 있다.

완료 시제 — VitaMint **has made** / will make some major improvements in its new supplement formula **in recent weeks**. VitaMint는 최근 몇 주간 그들의 새로운 보충제 제조법을 크게 개선했다.
→ 현재완료 시제와 어울려 쓰이는 표현에는 for(~ 동안), since(~ 이래로), already(이미), just(막, 방금), yet(아직), so far(지금까지), over(~에 걸쳐), in recent weeks(최근 몇 주간), in just one year(1년 만에) 등이 있다.

주절-종속절의 시제 — After Mr. Han **gave** / has been giving his presentation, the staff **understood** the new software more clearly. Mr. Han이 발표를 하고 나서 직원들은 새로운 소프트웨어를 더 명확하게 이해했다.
→ 주절의 시제가 과거(understood)이고 문맥적으로도 주절과 종속절의 상황이 모두 과거에 일어난 일이므로 종속절도 과거 시제로 써야 한다.

고득점 도전 시간/조건 부사절의 시제

Mr. Grantham will announce the good news to his employees **when** they **return** / will return from winter break next week. Mr. Grantham은 직원들이 다음 주에 겨울 휴가에서 돌아오면 좋은 소식을 발표할 예정이다.
→ when, before, until, once, as soon as, if, in case 등이 이끄는 시간 및 조건 부사절에서는 현재 시제가 미래 시제를 대신한다. (단, if절은 문맥에 따라 예외 허용)

PRACTICE

1. Danzig Office Supplies ------- cash payments for large purchases by domestic buyers.
   (A) preference
   (B) preferable
   (C) preferring
   (D) prefers

2. Many technology companies ------- new employees in spring after they graduate from college.
   (A) hirer
   (B) hiring
   (C) hires
   (D) hire

3. Daylight Media ------- news shows on the Internet and consider doing television as well.
   (A) has broadcast
   (B) is broadcasting
   (C) will broadcast
   (D) was broadcasting

4. The bid submitted by Eagle Builders ------- the requirements listed by the city government.
   (A) fulfill
   (B) fulfilling
   (C) fulfills
   (D) to fulfill

5. The work on the project will be complete as soon as David Simpson -------.
   (A) finishes
   (B) will finish
   (C) was finishing
   (D) finished

6. It is believed that Mr. Reynolds ------- several contracts with overseas corporations.
   (A) negotiating
   (B) to negotiate
   (C) is negotiated
   (D) has negotiated

7. The store's hours of operation ------- throughout the year depending on the season.
   (A) differ
   (B) differs
   (C) difference
   (D) different

8. The software from Star Technology ------- immediately after the company purchased it.
   (A) downloaded
   (B) had downloaded
   (C) was downloaded
   (D) download

9. ------- the contract if you feel that the terms in it are agreeable to you.
   (A) Signing
   (B) Signed
   (C) Signs
   (D) Sign

10. Ms. Alderson proposed that all full-time employees ------- present for the speech by the outgoing CEO.
    (A) being
    (B) had been
    (C) were
    (D) be

정답 및 해설 p.59

11. Please complete the insurance paperwork you received while the orientation stage ------- set up.

(A) is being
(B) was
(C) being
(D) has been

12. The office manager ------- more desks and chairs to accommodate the newest employees.

(A) will be ordered
(B) ordering
(C) will be ordering
(D) to order

13. Applicants with strong work ethics can ------- interviewers to hire them.

(A) convince
(B) to convince
(C) be convinced
(D) convincing

14. Do not submit the request for a grant to local authorities until it ------- by Ms. Parker.

(A) is reviewing
(B) reviews
(C) is reviewed
(D) will be reviewed

15. The number of computer chips ordered by foreign manufacturers ------- by thirty percent.

(A) has been reduced
(B) have been reduced
(C) is reducing
(D) were reduced

16. Dr. Morelli, the company's head scientist, ------- a large team of medical researchers.

(A) to supervise
(B) supervises
(C) supervision
(D) supervising

17. The meeting ------- because several expected attendees could not attend due to conflicting schedules.

(A) to cancel
(B) is canceling
(C) was canceled
(D) will cancel

18. Be sure to review the user's manual because ------- the precise method for installing the appliance.

(A) to explain
(B) it explains
(C) an explanation of
(D) one explaining

고득점 도전

19. By the end of this month, Caldwell International ------- seven employees to its Singapore branch.

(A) transfers
(B) will have transferred
(C) is transferring
(D) had transferred

고득점 도전

20. Refunds given to customers are considered valid when ------- by the store manager.

(A) processing
(B) processed
(C) process
(D) processes

UNIT 06 to부정사와 동명사

1 to부정사

to부정사는 문장에서 명사(~하는 것), 형용사(~하려는, ~하기 위한), 부사(~하기 위해, ~하기에, ~하는 데)의 역할을 하며, 명사 역할을 할 때는 주어, 목적어, 보어 등으로 쓰일 수 있다. 토익에서는 부사 역할을 하는 to부정사를 묻는 문제의 출제 비중이 높다. to부정사와 동명사는 모두 동사 자리에 올 수 없다는 것도 기억해 두자.

명사 The objective for this month is **to sell** / sell 5% more than we did last month.
이번 달 목표는 우리가 지난달에 판매했던 것보다 5% 더 많이 판매하는 것이다.

형용사 Executives at Franklin Auto agreed that it was time **to manufacture** / manufactures electric vehicles. Franklin Auto의 임원들은 전기 차를 생산해야 할 시기라는 데 동의했다.

부사 The CEO does everything she can **to support** / supporting her employees.
대표 이사는 직원들을 지원하기 위해 그녀가 할 수 있는 모든 것을 한다.

관용표현 The CEO does everything she can **in order to support** her employees.
대표 이사는 직원들을 지원하기 위해 그녀가 할 수 있는 모든 것을 한다.

2 동명사

동명사는 동사원형에 -ing가 붙은 형태로 '~하는 것, ~하기'로 해석한다. 명사의 성질을 가지고 있기에 주어, 보어, 목적어의 역할을 하며, 또한 동사의 성질을 가지고 있기에 목적어를 취하거나 부사의 수식을 받을 수 있다. 그리고 전치사 뒤에서 전치사의 목적어로 쓰일 수 있다. 토익에서는 전치사의 목적어를 묻는 문제의 출제 비중이 높다.

주어 **Creating** / Create **an impressive portfolio** will help you get jobs in graphic design.
인상적인 포트폴리오를 만드는 것은 그래픽 디자인 분야에서 일자리를 얻는 데 도움이 될 것이다.

보어 One of the receptionist's duties **is answering** / answer every incoming call.
접수원의 업무 중 하나는 걸려 오는 전화를 모두 받는 것이다.

전치사의 목적어 Ms. Kirk is in charge **of overseeing** / overseen everything that happens on the assembly line.
Ms. Kirk는 조립 라인에서 일어나는 모든 것을 감독하는 일을 맡고 있다.

고득점 도전 **동명사를 목적어로 취하는 동사**

The board of trustees will **consider expanding** / to expand the business into other ventures.
이사회는 그 사업을 다른 모험적인 사업으로 확장하는 것을 고려할 것이다.
→ consider는 to부정사가 아닌 동명사를 목적어로 취한다. 이러한 동사에는 suggest(제안하다), finish(끝마치다), enjoy(즐기다), recommend(추천하다), avoid(피하다) 등이 있다.

PRACTICE

정답 및 해설 p.61

1. Ken Richards is the top candidate ------- the new team being formed in the R&D Department.

(A) be leading
(B) was led
(C) will lead
(D) to lead

2. In July, Alps Airlines will start ------- its newest routes to cities throughout Asia.

(A) promoting
(B) promoted
(C) promotes
(D) promote

3. The company's CEO plans to permit workers ------- for promotions twice a year.

(A) applies
(B) to apply
(C) applying
(D) applied

4. Mr. Solomon stated that he considers ------- the Auckland branch a mistake due to its profitability.

(A) close
(B) closing
(C) to close
(D) has closed

5. ------- guarantee faster delivery times, the company exclusively uses local courier Mercury Delivery.

(A) In spite of
(B) As soon as
(C) In order to
(D) With regard to

6. We must arrive at the airport within the next twenty minutes if we are ------- our flight to Moscow.

(A) to make
(B) make
(C) made
(D) being made

7. Since ------- a new air conditioner in the office, management has noticed a significant improvement in productivity.

(A) installers
(B) installation
(C) installment
(D) installing

8. Mr. Edwards utilized a professional architect ------- what would become the company's new research center.

(A) designed
(B) is designing
(C) designs
(D) to design

고득점 도전

9. The marketing team's goal is to advertise more online yet ------- its expenditures.

(A) reduce
(B) reducing
(C) reduces
(D) reduced

고득점 도전

10. In the past five years, Amanda Watson has gone from sweeping the floors in the store to ------ it.

(A) owner
(B) owning
(C) be owning
(D) owned

UNIT 07 분사

1 현재분사와 과거분사

현재분사는 동사원형에 -ing가 붙어 능동의 의미를 나타내고, 과거분사는 동사원형에 -ed가 붙어 수동의 의미를 나타낸다. 분사는 형용사처럼 명사를 수식할 수 있으며, to부정사, 동명사와 마찬가지로 동사 자리에 올 수 없다.

명사 앞에서 수식

Please contact Mr. Jones immediately and e-mail him the **corrected** / correcting **agreement**.
즉시 Mr. Jones에게 연락해서 수정된 동의서를 이메일로 보내 주십시오.
→ (○) corrected agreement 수정된 동의서 / (×) correcting agreement 수정하는 동의서

Departing / Departed **passengers** must complete a security check in order to fly.
출발하는 승객들은 비행을 하기 위해 보안 검사를 완료해야 한다.
→ (○) departing passenger 출발하는 승객 / (×) departed passenger 출발한 승객

명사 뒤에서 수식

There are many **factors contributing** / contributed to the decrease in interest in print newspapers.
종이 신문에 대한 관심 감소에 기여하는 많은 요인이 있다.
→ (○) contributing factor 기여하는 요인 / (×) contributed factor 기여된 요인
명사 뒤에 오는 현재분사는 〈관계대명사+동사〉를 축약한 형태로서 contributing은 which contribute로 바꿔 쓸 수 있다.

Enjoy your stay at the Bizmark Hotel and be sure to try the delicious **cookies offered** / offering in the executive lounge.
Bizmark Hotel에서 즐거운 시간을 보내시고 특별 라운지에서 제공되는 맛있는 쿠키를 꼭 드셔 보세요.
→ (○) offered cookies 제공되는 쿠키 / (×) offering cookies (스스로) 제공하는 쿠키
명사 뒤에 오는 과거분사는 수동의 의미를 지니며, 명사와 과거분사 사이에는 〈관계대명사+be동사〉가 생략되어 있다. 이 문장에서는 cookies 뒤에 〈which are〉가 생략되었다고 볼 수 있다.

2 분사구문

부사절이 시간, 조건, 이유, 동시 상황 등을 나타낼 때, 주절의 주어와 부사절의 주어가 동일하면 부사절은 분사절로 축약되기도 한다.

시간

Arriving / Arrive at the airport, Mr. Smith called the client to postpone the meeting.
Mr. Smith는 공항에 도착했을 때[도착하자마자] 고객에게 전화해 회의를 연기했다.
→ Arriving = When[As soon as] Mr. Smith arrived

조건

Stored / Storing in a cool place, these foods will last for weeks.
이 식품들은 서늘한 곳에 보관되면 몇 주 동안 유지된다.
→ Stored = If these foods are stored

결과

Our startup business's stock value was up again, **marking** / mark another company record.
우리 스타트업 사업의 주식 가치가 다시 오르면서 회사의 또 다른 기록을 세웠다.
→ marking = and marked
현재분사가 이끄는 절은 연속된 일이나 결과를 나타낼 수 있다.

고득점 도전 **부사절이 과거완료 시제일 때는 〈having+과거분사〉로 전환한다.**

Having / Had retired, Mr. Dornan decided to travel to Europe.
Mr. Dornan은 퇴직 후 유럽으로 여행을 가기로 결심했다.
→ Having retired = After Mr. Dornan had retired

PRACTICE

정답 및 해설 p.62

1. Ms. Long examined the ------- progress report that was submitted by the team leader.
(A) revised
(B) revising
(C) revises
(D) revise

2. Using professional accountants is highly recommended for ------- businesses.
(A) expansion
(B) expansions
(C) expanding
(D) expanded

3. ------- meetings should be rescheduled for mutually convenient times.
(A) Postponed
(B) Postpone
(C) Postpones
(D) Postponing

4. Any customer ------- with a product is entitled to return it within seven days of purchase.
(A) displeases
(B) displeased
(C) displease
(D) displeasing

5. Eric Murphy remained at his home during his entire vacation, ------- rest rather than travel.
(A) prefers
(B) had preferred
(C) preferring
(D) was preferred

6. Mr. Roberts has some ------- remarks he would like to share with the audience.
(A) preparing
(B) prepared
(C) preparation
(D) prepare

7. To use the electric saw properly, you need to read the instructions ------- in the manual.
(A) include
(B) included
(C) inclusion
(D) to include

8. Any employees ------- to attend the upcoming workshop on accounting must speak with Ms. Taylor.
(A) had hoped
(B) hoped
(C) would hope
(D) hoping

고득점 도전
9. The new kiosks are expected to significantly reduce the amount of time ------- in line.
(A) spend
(B) spending
(C) to spend
(D) spent

고득점 도전
10. ------- this Saturday, the Hamilton Department Store will offer discounts on every item in the store.
(A) Began
(B) Beginning
(C) Begins
(D) Begin

UNIT 08 전치사

1 다의어로 쓰이는 빈출 전치사

for	~ 동안 (기간)	Alex's Diamonds will be shut down **for** two months. Alex's Diamonds는 두 달 동안 문을 닫을 것이다.
	~을 위해, ~에	Mr. Liu writes a weekly column **for** a local newspaper. Mr. Liu는 지역 신문에 주간 칼럼을 연재한다.
from	~으로부터	Roughly 40% of KLP & Co.'s business comes **from** overseas clients. KLP & Co의 사업 실적 중 대략 40%는 해외 고객으로부터 나온다.
	from A to B	Highway 11 will soon be widened **from** two lanes **to** four. 11번 고속도로는 곧 2개 차선에서 4개 차선으로 확대될 것이다.
within	~ 이내에 (기간)	You can expect your package **within** 3–4 business days. 영업일로부터 3~4일 이내에 물품을 받으실 수 있을 것입니다.
	~ 이내에 (거리, 범위)	This apartment is **within** walking distance of many popular attractions. 이 아파트는 많은 인기 명소를 도보로 갈 수 있는 거리에 있다. → within walking distance of: ~에서 도보 거리에 있는
by	~까지 (기간)	These are the mid-year goals that we need to reach **by** the end of the quarter. 이것들은 우리가 분기 말까지 달성해야 하는 올 중반 목표들이다.
	~을 함으로써	Ms. Vowsky contributed to the project **by** taking and organizing all of the meeting notes. Ms. Vowsky는 모든 회의 메모를 기록하고 정리함으로써 프로젝트에 기여했다.
of	~의	Employees **of** the factory are asked to wear a safety helmet at all times. 공장 직원들은 항상 안전모를 쓸 것이 요구된다.
	~ 중에	**Of** the four new turtleneck designs, the one with white polka dots is the most popular. 새로운 네 개의 터틀넥 디자인 중에서 하얀 물방울무늬가 있는 것이 가장 인기 있다.
	as of ~ 일자로, ~부터	**As of** Monday, January 19, the company's name will be changed to Data Xpress. 1월 19일 월요일부터 회사명이 Data Xpress로 변경될 것이다.
with	~와 함께	Watches from Walencia come **with** a quality guarantee that lasts for five years. Walencia의 시계는 5년 품질 보증서가 딸려 나온다. → come with: (상품에) ~이 딸려 있다
	~을 가지고	**With** its new logo and marketing strategy, Sistema Inc. is headed in the direction of success. 새로운 로고와 마케팅 전략을 가지고 Sistema 사는 성공을 향해 나아가고 있다.
	provide/replace A with B	Plymouth Supplies can **provide** your staff **with** stylish uniforms in a wide range of colors. Plymouth Supplies는 귀사의 직원들에게 다양한 색상의 세련된 유니폼을 제공할 수 있습니다. → provide A with B A에게 B를 제공하다 / replace A with B A를 B로 대체하다

2 빈출 전치사구

because of	~ 때문에	**Because of** transportation delays, some conference participants arrived late. 교통편의 지연으로 인해 학회 참석자 몇 명이 늦게 도착했다.
due to	~ 때문에	The database is temporarily unavailable **due to** the routine maintenance of the system. 시스템 정기 유지 보수 때문에 데이터베이스를 일시적으로 사용할 수 없다.
owing to	~ 때문에	**Owing to** a shortage of materials, the renovations will not be finished by the original completion date. 자재 부족 때문에 보수 공사는 원래 완공 일자까지 끝나지 못할 것이다.
prior to	~ 전에, ~에 앞서	The last person to leave the office must make sure the security alarm is set **prior to** locking the door. 마지막으로 퇴근하는 사람은 문을 잠그기 전에 보안 경보 장치가 설정되어 있는지 확인해야 한다.
according to	~에 따르면	**According to** recent surveys, most guests' favorite part of the resort is the rooftop lounge. 최근 조사에 따르면 그 리조트에서 투숙객 대부분이 좋아하는 부분은 옥상 휴게실이다.
in addition to	~뿐만 아니라	**In addition to** coming to work early, Mr. Earl sometimes works on weekends to make sure he meets deadlines. Mr. Earl은 일찍 출근하는 것 외에 마감일을 맞추기 위해 가끔 주말에 일을 하기도 한다.
instead of	~ 대신에	On weekends during the winter months, the store closes at 5:30 P.M. **instead of** 7:00 P.M. 가게는 겨울 주말에 오후 7시 대신 오후 5시 30분에 문을 닫는다.
rather than	~보다는	The hotel collects payment when the guests check in **rather than** at booking. 그 호텔은 예약할 때보다는 투숙객이 체크인할 때 요금을 받는다.

3 -ing형 전치사

including	~을 포함하여	It seems like Krazy Kola can be found everywhere, **including** remote parts of the world. Krazy Kola는 오지를 포함하여 세계 어디서나 볼 수 있는 것 같다.
following	~에 따라, ~ 후에	**Following** the release of the movie, Anne Stanton became famous. 그 영화의 개봉 후에 Anne Stanton은 유명해졌다.
concerning	~에 관한	She plans to inform us of issues **concerning** client confidentiality. 그녀는 우리에게 고객 비밀 유지에 관한 쟁점들을 알려줄 계획이다.
regarding	~에 관해	Mr. Diaz noted that it is important to establish safety policies **regarding** the use of company vehicles. Mr. Diaz는 회사 차량 사용에 관한 안전 정책을 수립하는 것이 중요하다고 언급했다.

PART 5

PRACTICE

1. All interns must arrive by 7:30 A.M. on Monday ------ an orientation event.
(A) for
(B) with
(C) as
(D) over

2. Any returns of products sold online by Blaine Toys must be made within two weeks ------- delivery.
(A) before
(B) on
(C) of
(D) since

3. ------- serving as the firm's accountant, Melissa Standish is employed as the office manager.
(A) As a result
(B) Because of
(C) With regard to
(D) In addition to

4. ------- each performance at the county fair, a team of volunteers cleans the entire theater.
(A) Following
(B) Through
(C) Around
(D) Within

5. ------- reporting breaking news stories accurately, Melinda Carter was able to improve her reputation as a journalist.
(A) By
(B) On
(C) With
(D) About

6. Hudson Mining has seen the value of its stock double ------- its discovery of gold three months ago.
(A) before
(B) since
(C) unless
(D) therefore

7. ------- the many people on the Hardaway Textiles salesforce, Ms. Montague is the most productive.
(A) Into
(B) Above
(C) For
(D) Of

8. ------- the advice of several experts in the industry, Mr. Harrison managed to start his own business.
(A) For
(B) With
(C) Along
(D) Over

9. ------- her desire to live in Europe, Ms. Hooper volunteered for a transfer to her firm's Milan office.
(A) Because of
(B) During
(C) Consequently
(D) As well

10. Mr. Abernathy will attend graduate school on weeknights ------- his interest in furthering his education.
(A) for
(B) due to
(C) since
(D) regarding

11. ------- government regulations, hard hats must be worn on the premises by everyone at all times.

(A) According to
(B) Instead of
(C) As a result
(D) However

12. Mr. Dearborn resigned his position ------- the busy holiday season.

(A) prior to
(B) except
(C) in accordance with
(D) instead of

13. The five individuals scheduled for interviews were selected ------- a pool of seventy-eight applicants.

(A) with
(B) for
(C) out
(D) from

14. Nelson Technology has a tradition of providing workers and their families ------- tickets to local cultural events.

(A) for
(B) with
(C) at
(D) on

15. ------- the popularity of its newest sneakers, Paladin Shoes increased production of them.

(A) Everything
(B) Perhaps
(C) Owing to
(D) In all

16. Kathy Ibsen expects to be named assistant manager in her department ------- the next few months.

(A) since
(B) within
(C) approximately
(D) at

17. All individuals should clean their workspaces and turn off their computers ------- departing the office.

(A) before
(B) until
(C) over
(D) beyond

18. Marconi Textiles manufactures women's clothing from a variety of fabrics, ------- cotton and silk.

(A) including
(B) meanwhile
(C) as soon as
(D) throughout

고득점 도전

19. A decision ------- performance bonuses will be made by the end of the month.

(A) with
(B) among
(C) concerning
(D) for

고득점 도전

20. ------- taking on temporary staff, Mr. Flint asked his team to work overtime in March.

(A) Apparently
(B) Rather than
(C) According to
(D) Over

UNIT 09 접속사

1 빈출 부사절 접속사

등위 접속사, 상관 접속사, 명사절 접속사에 비해 부사절 접속사를 묻는 문제의 출제 비율이 압도적으로 높다.

시간	when	~할 때	The mobile application will notify you **when** the delivery driver is at your doorstep. 그 휴대 전화 애플리케이션은 배달 기사가 문 앞에 오면 당신에게 알려 줍니다.
	while	~하는 동안	The bank will be closed tomorrow **while** the vault is being repaired. 은행은 내일 금고가 수리되는 동안 문을 닫을 것이다.
	whenever	~할 때마다	**Whenever** the printer is out of ink, please report it to the maintenance department. 프린터의 잉크가 부족할 때마다 관리 부서에 그 사실을 보고해 주세요.
	as soon as	~하자마자	Intercity bus services will resume **as soon as** the snow is cleared. 눈이 치워지는 대로 시외버스 운행을 재개할 예정이다.
	since	~한 이후로	He has worked for himself **since** he graduated from university. 그는 대학을 졸업한 이후로 1인 기업으로 일해 왔다.
이유	as	~이므로	Please wrap these vases in additional packaging material **as** they are extremely fragile. 이 꽃병들은 매우 깨지기 쉬우니 추가 포장재로 포장해 주세요.
	since	~이기 때문에	I am interested in hiring your company **since** you have been in business for a long time. 귀사가 오랫동안 사업을 해왔기 때문에 저는 귀사를 고용하는 것에 관심이 있습니다.
	now that	~이기 때문에	**Now that** I live close to my office, I walk to work. 사무실 근처에 살기 때문에 나는 걸어서 출근한다.
양보, 대조	although	~이기는 하지만	**Although** the weather was rainy, a record number of people attended the parade. 비가 내리기는 했지만 기록적인 숫자의 사람들이 퍼레이드에 참여했다.
	even though	비록 ~이지만	**Even though** it was only 10 A.M., Hardy Bakery had already sold out of bread for the day. 비록 오전 10시밖에 안 되었지만, Hardy Bakery는 이미 그날 판매할 빵이 다 팔려 나갔다.
	while	~한 반면에	**While** other companies tend to follow trends, the handbags at LACY are always classic styles. 다른 회사들은 유행을 따르는 경향이 있는 반면에, LACY의 핸드백은 항상 고전적인 스타일을 고수한다.
조건	if	~이라면	Orders may be delayed **if** the item is temporarily out of stock. 일시적으로 재고가 없을 경우 주문이 지연될 수 있습니다.
	once	일단 ~하면	They will make an announcement **once** the date of the event is scheduled. 일단 행사 날짜가 정해지면 그들이 공지할 겁니다.
	unless	~하지 않는 한	Visitors should not leave the lobby **unless** they are given permission. 방문객들은 허가를 받지 않은 이상 로비를 떠나서는 안 됩니다.
목적, 결과	so that	~하도록	Ms. Denton postponed her trip to France **so that** she could attend Dr. Pollard's speech. Ms. Denton은 Pollard 박사의 연설에 참석할 수 있도록 프랑스 여행을 연기했다.

2 등위 접속사

등위 접속사에는 and(그리고), but(그러나), or(또는), so(그래서), yet(그렇지만) 등이 있다.

or	또는	Tickets can be purchased **at the ticket booth or through our Web site.** 티켓은 매표소에서 또는 우리의 웹사이트를 통해서 구입할 수 있습니다. → 등위 접속사는 단어와 단어, 구와 구, 절과 절을 대등하게 연결한다.
so	그래서	Mr. Juan was not available to work last week, **so** Mr. Vettel filled in for him. Mr. Juan은 지난주에 근무를 할 수 없어서 Mr. Vettel이 그를 대신하여 근무했다.
yet	그렇지만	Negotiating is a critical skill, **yet** many people find it a difficult one to master. 협상은 중요한 기술이지만 많은 사람들은 그것을 숙달하기 어려운 기술로 여긴다.

3 상관 접속사

either A or B	A 또는 B	Suggestions can be **either sent** to the company e-mail **or placed** in the feedback box. 제안서는 회사 이메일로 보내거나 건의함에 넣을 수 있습니다.
neither A nor B	A와 B 둘 다 아닌	**Neither Mr. Herbert nor his employees** were aware of the safety issues at the amusement park. Mr. Herbert와 그의 직원들 모두 놀이공원의 안전 문제를 인지하지 못했다.

4 명사절 접속사

주로 동사 뒤 목적어 자리에 나오는 명사절 접속사가 무엇인지를 묻는 문제가 출제된다.

whether	~인지 아닌지	Ms. Chomley was not sure **whether** the CFO position would be right for her. Ms. Chomley는 최고재무책임자 직책이 자신에게 맞을지 확신할 수 없었다.
that		Most retailers have reported **that** the new A5 smartphone is already sold out. 대부분의 소매점은 새로 나온 A5 스마트폰이 이미 품절되었다고 알렸다.

5 전치사로도 쓰이는 접속사

before, after, since 등의 뒤에서 주어가 생략된 채 동명사가 이어지기도 한다.

before	~ 전에	**Before leaving** the office, please make sure all the lights and computers have been shut off. 사무실을 떠나기 전에 모든 전등과 컴퓨터가 꺼져 있는지 확인해 주세요.
since	~ 이후로	Investgain's new CEO has made noticeable improvements **since taking** on her current role. Investgain의 새로운 최고경영자는 현재의 역할을 맡은 이후로 눈에 띄는 발전을 이루어 냈다.

PART 5

PRACTICE

1. During inclement weather, staff members should consider ------- working from home or taking public transportation to the office.
   (A) and
   (B) either
   (C) since
   (D) if

2. Jasmine Cartier worked on her presentation skills ------- is now an accomplished public speaker.
   (A) and
   (B) for
   (C) however
   (D) or

3. ------- Mr. Hamilton spent half of July on vacation, he recorded the highest number of sales on his team.
   (A) In order that
   (B) Although
   (C) Furthermore
   (D) In spite of

4. More library books are being returned on time ------- the checkout system was computerized.
   (A) around
   (B) apparently
   (C) so
   (D) since

5. ------- Emerson Inc. releases a new product, it markets the item heavily.
   (A) Because
   (B) During
   (C) Whenever
   (D) Such

6. Remember to sign up for a membership at Aubrey's Bookstore ------- you can be eligible for special offers.
   (A) so
   (B) for
   (C) or
   (D) still

7. Famed chef Andrew Hutchins states that ------- fresh ingredients are used, dishes taste much better.
   (A) when
   (B) despite
   (C) for
   (D) how

8. The board of directors must determine ------- the business climate in Canada is ideal for opening a new facility there.
   (A) around
   (B) whether
   (C) whereas
   (D) although

9. Ms. Grayson drove to the seminar in St. Louis ------- the other members of her group chose to fly there.
   (A) in spite of
   (B) such as
   (C) as well as
   (D) even though

10. ------- a customer specifies express delivery, all orders are mailed one day after being received.
    (A) Except
    (B) Because
    (C) Unless
    (D) Even

11. Kevin Watts decided to remain at Nottingham Securities ------- he received a substantial pay raise.

(A) as a result
(B) because
(C) not only
(D) or

12. First-time buyers at Jupiter Groceries can receive free delivery ------- request a sample food platter at no extra cost.

(A) or
(B) so
(C) both
(D) even

13. ------- she accepted a position at Dubois Bank, Ms. Harrison studied finance at a school in Lisbon.

(A) How
(B) Before
(C) Which
(D) Rather

14. ------- Raymond Mercer runs his own restaurant, he is responsible for acquiring ingredients daily.

(A) As if
(B) Moreover
(C) That
(D) Now that

15. ------- a location for the annual shareholders' meeting is determined, an announcement will be made.

(A) In order that
(B) As of
(C) Instead
(D) Once

16. ------- interest rates are increasing, fewer people are getting mortgages on new homes.

(A) Except
(B) Since
(C) However
(D) Why

17. By the end of the day, neither Stella Reynolds ------- Jeffery Harper had submitted their proposals for the Edmund Project.

(A) nor
(B) and
(C) if
(D) so

18. Please explain the malfunction precisely with your new device ------- our technician can tell you how to repair it.

(A) so that
(B) since
(C) nor
(D) if

고득점 도전

19. ------- Harris Manufacturing delivered the products to its client in Memphis, full payment was not made until two weeks later.

(A) In order to
(B) While
(C) Thereby
(D) Supposedly

고득점 도전

20. Anyone is welcome to speak during the meeting but ------- they have something positive to contribute.

(A) when
(B) only if
(C) even so
(D) rather than

UNIT 10 관계사

1 관계대명사

관계대명사는 두 문장을 하나로 연결하는 접속사 역할을 하는 동시에 대명사 역할을 하며, 주격 관계대명사의 출제 빈도가 높다.

주격

Library patrons **who** / which fail to return a book by the due date will be charged a fee.
반납 기한을 어기는 도서관 이용자에게는 수수료가 부과됩니다.
→ 선행사가 사람 명사인 patrons이므로 사람을 가리키는 주격 관계대명사 who나 that이 적절하고 사물이나 동물을 가리키는 which는 적절하지 않다.

목적격

Mr. Brown carefully examined **the estimate** **which** / whom Millbrook Furniture **provided**.
Mr. Brown은 Millbrook Furniture에서 제공한 견적서를 꼼꼼히 검토했다.
→ which의 선행사는 the estimate이며, provided의 목적어가 된다. 선행사가 사물이므로 사람을 가리키는 목적격 관계사인 whom은 적절하지 않다. 목적격 관계대명사는 생략할 수 있다는 것도 알아 두자.

소유격

Ms. Hayes booked the restaurant **whose** / which menu contains vegetarian dishes.
Ms. Hayes는 채식 메뉴가 있는 식당을 예약했다.
→ Ms. Hayes booked the restaurant. The restaurant's menu contains vegetarian dishes.

what

Excellent customer service is **what** / that sets us apart from our competitors.
훌륭한 고객 서비스가 우리를 경쟁사와 차별화하는 것이다.
→ 관계대명사 what은 '~ 것'이라고 해석하며, 선행사를 이미 포함하고 있기 때문에 what 앞에는 선행사가 올 수 없다.

2 관계부사

관계부사에는 when, where, why, how 등이 있으며, 뒤에 문법적으로 완전한 절이 이어진다.

Mr. Wilson runs several businesses in London, **where** / which he grew up.
Mr. Wilson은 런던에서 사업체 몇 개를 운영하고 있는데, 그곳은 그가 성장기를 보낸 곳이다.
→ 관계부사는 〈전치사+관계대명사〉로 바꿔 쓸 수 있는데, 이 문장에서 where는 in which로 바꿔 쓸 수 있다.

3 복합관계사

복합관계사는 〈관계대명사+ever〉, 〈관계부사+ever〉의 형태이며, 〈관계대명사+ever〉 뒤에는 불완전한 절이, 〈관계부사+ever〉 뒤에는 완전한 절이 이어진다.

whoever ~하는 사람은 누구나	whichever 어느 ~이든	whatever ~하는 것은 무엇이나
whenever ~할 때마다	wherever ~하는 곳은 어디서나	however 아무리 ~해도

고득점 도전

Shoppers can enjoy a strong Wi-Fi signal **wherever** / however they go in the mall.
쇼핑객들은 쇼핑몰에서 어디를 가든 강력한 와이파이 신호를 즐길 수 있다.
→ '쇼핑몰에서 어디를 가든'이라는 내용이 되는 게 자연스러우므로 wherever가 적절하다. wherever는 〈where(관계부사)+ever〉의 형태이므로 뒤에 완전한 절이 이어진다.

PRACTICE

정답 및 해설 p.67

1. Mr. Cross stated that ------- recruits the highest number of new clients this month will receive a cash bonus.
   (A) whose
   (B) when
   (C) whoever
   (D) whom

2. Nantucket Construction is owned by Peter Carroll, ------- has lived in the local area since his childhood.
   (A) so
   (B) which
   (C) who
   (D) and

3. Logistics companies ------- deliver goods on time are in high demand in most parts of the country.
   (A) whom
   (B) that
   (C) what
   (D) they

4. Jessica Yeltsin established a charitable foundation ------- she attempted to use to end the local homeless crisis.
   (A) there
   (B) what
   (C) that
   (D) how

5. Jacobson Financial clients ------- make new investments in January are eligible for a free consultation.
   (A) whose
   (B) who
   (C) what
   (D) which

6. The conference will be held at the Piedmont Hotel, ------- there are modern facilities capable of supporting large crowds.
   (A) except
   (B) including
   (C) where
   (D) which

7. The government ordered an investigation into the building collapse, the cause of ------- will require some time to determine.
   (A) that
   (B) who
   (C) it
   (D) which

8. Ms. Matthews decided to hire Ryan Varnum, ------- expertise in the field of corporate law was well known.
   (A) whose
   (B) himself
   (C) which
   (D) whom

고득점 도전

9. The orientation speaker explained ------- it takes to be a success at Hollmann International.
   (A) what
   (B) that
   (C) those
   (D) their

고득점 도전

10. Mr. Acuna teaches a training course ------- participants learn to use the firm's computer system.
   (A) who
   (B) in which
   (C) as well as
   (D) in order to

UNIT 11 고득점 획득을 위한 명사 어휘

associate 동료
sales **associate** 영업 사원

occasion 때, 경우
for any **occasion** 어떤 경우에도
관련어 occasionally 때때로

durability 내구성
have a unique design and excellent **durability**
독특한 디자인과 뛰어난 내구성을 가지고 있다
관련어 durable 내구성이 있는

delegation 대표단
a member of a **delegation** 대표단의 일원

defect 결함
be inspected for possible **defects**
혹시 있을지도 모를 결함을 검사 받다

estimate 견적(서); 추정하다
provide free cost **estimates** 무료 비용 견적을 제공하다

approval 승인
get **approval** from the CEO 사장의 승인을 얻다
관련어 approve 승인하다

benefit 혜택, 이익; 도움이 되다; 이익을 얻다
benefit from ~로부터 혜택을 얻다
generous employee **benefits** plan
넉넉한 직원 복지 제도

issue 문제; (출판물의) 호; 발급하다
resolve technological **issues** 기술적인 문제를 해결하다
this month's **issue** of the magazine 잡지의 이달 호

capacity 능력, 자격
make a decision in her **capacity** as president of the company 회사의 사장 자격으로 결정을 내리다

agenda 의제, 안건
meeting **agenda** 회의 안건

site 장소, 현장
work **sites** 작업장, 일터
oil-drilling **site** 석유 시추 현장

addition 추가된 것, 부가물
the newest **addition** to the sales force
영업 인력에 새로 추가된 인원
관련어 additional 추가의, 부가적인

priority 우선권, 우선 사항
highest **priority** 최우선 사항

venue 장소, 현장
a popular **venue** for athletic competitions
인기 있는 운동 경기 장소

recipient 수상자, 수령인
recipient of a customer service award
고객 서비스 상의 수상자

initiative 주도권; 계획
take the **initiative** 주도하다, 주도권을 쥐다
관련어 initiate 시작하다

range 범위
a **range** of 다양한
offer a broad **range** of medical services
광범위한 의료 서비스를 제공하다

warranty 보증(서)
one-year **warranty** that covers major repairs
주요 수리를 포함하는 1년짜리 보증

alert 경보; 경고하다
serve as an **alert** 경보의 역할을 하다

location 위치, 장소
have offices in more than thirty **locations**
30개소 이상에 사무실을 두다
관련어 locate 위치하다, 위치를 찾다

profitability 수익성
the potential **profitability** of expanding its overseas market 해외 시장 확대의 잠재적인 수익성
관련어 profitable 수익성이 있는

budget 예산; 저가의, 저렴한
budget surplus 예산 흑자
offer **budget** flights to Mexico
멕시코로 가는 저가 항공편을 제공하다

confirmation 확인, 확정
receive an e-mail **confirmation** of his hotel booking 호텔 예약 확정 이메일을 받다
관련어 confirm 확인하다, 확정하다

revision 수정, 변경
make a **revision** to the agreement 계약서를 수정하다
관련어 revise 수정하다, 변경하다

dimension 크기, 규모
the **dimensions** of a swimming pool 수영장의 크기

aspect 측면, 양상
the most challenging **aspect** of managing a hotel 호텔을 운영하는 데 있어서 가장 도전적인 측면

audit 회계 감사
conduct an **audit** 회계 감사를 실시하다

availability 이용 가능성
the limited **availability** of land 토지의 제한된 이용 가능성
관련어 available 이용 가능한

notice 공지; 알아차리다
give 24 hours' **notice** 24시간 전에 공지하다
관련어 noticeably 현저하게, 눈에 띌 정도로

subsidy 보조금, 장려금
government **subsidy** 정부 보조금
관련어 subsidize 보조금을 주다

application 지원(서); 앱
accept **applications** for entry-level positions
신입직에 대한 지원서를 받다
관련어 apply 지원하다, 신청하다

reminder 알림, 상기시키는 것
send patients an e-mail **reminder**
환자들에게 이메일 알림을 보내다
관련어 remind 상기시키다

exception 예외
make an **exception** 예외를 두다
with the **exception** of ~을 제외하고
관련어 exceptional 예외적인, 특별한

distribution 분배, 배포
fast **distribution** of goods to the stores
매장으로의 신속한 물품 배포
관련어 distribute 분배하다

renovation 보수, 수리
undergo **renovations** 보수를 받다
관련어 renovate 보수하다, 수리하다

inventory 재고, 물품 목록
inventory management software 재고 관리 소프트웨어

presence 존재
increase their **presence** on social media
SNS에서 그들의 존재감을 높이다

overview 개요, 개관
overview of a camera's primary features
카메라의 주요 기능에 대한 개요

panel (토론회의) 패널; 판
a **panel** of university professors
대학교 교수로 이루어진 패널
install solar **panels** 태양 전지판을 설치하다

emphasis 강조, 중점
place an **emphasis** on ~에 중점을 두다
관련어 emphasize 강조하다

appraisal 평가
performance **appraisal** 성과 평가

PRACTICE

1. Several local companies do not permit telecommuting because they prefer their employees have a physical ------- in the office.
(A) appearance
(B) method
(C) work
(D) presence

2. A ------- of long-term customers was responsible for rating the supermarket's newest products.
(A) system
(B) version
(C) survey
(D) panel

3. The latest ------- to the company's fleet of vehicles is an SUV made by Cobra Motors.
(A) addition
(B) device
(C) object
(D) program

4. Redecorating the employee lounge is considered a low ------- at this time.
(A) priority
(B) venture
(C) attempt
(D) consequence

5. Mr. Peterson has not needed to repair his lawnmower once since buying it thanks to its -------.
(A) measurement
(B) variety
(C) consideration
(D) durability

6. Interested customers can acquire a 3-year ------- that covers all necessary repairs.
(A) service
(B) warranty
(C) budget
(D) promise

7. Edmund Blair was named the ------- of a scholarship allowing him to study in England for one year.
(A) recipient
(B) reward
(C) applicant
(D) attendee

8. Adelaide Park is a regular ------- for events such as company get-togethers and charity fundraisers.
(A) venue
(B) port
(C) edition
(D) case

9. A notable ------- of the architect's style is her reliance on the natural environment for some features.
(A) design
(B) aspect
(C) relief
(D) tradition

10. Should there be any ------- during the hiring process, Ms. Bradley needs to be consulted at once.
(A) possibilities
(B) faults
(C) bargains
(D) issues

정답 및 해설 p.68

11. A financial expert questioned the ------- of Douglas Aerospace since it has been in debt for the past several years.

(A) recurrence
(B) profitability
(C) issue
(D) acceptance

12. A government ------- will be conducted next week to confirm no laws have been broken.

(A) method
(B) purpose
(C) audit
(D) inspector

13. One ------- of working at Devlin Inc. is that the company allows its employees to work from home.

(A) benefit
(B) variation
(C) impact
(D) reminder

14. All tours of the company are suspended due to a lack of guides until further -------.

(A) awareness
(B) reception
(C) provision
(D) notice

15. All customers will receive an e-mail ------- of their orders within five minutes of placing them.

(A) confirmation
(B) evaluation
(C) contribution
(D) reception

16. Mr. Hamilton was asked to make several ------- to the grant request he submitted to the Chamberlain Group.

(A) revisions
(B) decisions
(C) specifications
(D) productions

17. ------- levels at the store have decreased on account of the shipping problems happening nationwide.

(A) Personnel
(B) Inventory
(C) Management
(D) Replacement

18. The vice president requested a rough ------- of the time required to complete the work on the new advertising campaign.

(A) persuasion
(B) requirement
(C) estimate
(D) strategy

고득점 도전

19. Ms. Scott contacted the airline and inquired about the ------- of seats on Friday's late-night flight to Berlin.

(A) assurance
(B) availability
(C) application
(D) appearance

고득점 도전

20. The fundraising ------- led by Denice Burns will last two months and should raise one million dollars.

(A) league
(B) initiative
(C) imperative
(D) symbol

UNIT 12 고득점 획득을 위한 형용사 어휘

utmost 극도의, 최대한의
be of **utmost** importance 극도로 중요하다

eligible 자격이 있는
be **eligible** to receive an annual bonus
연간 보너스를 받을 자격이 있다
관련어 eligibility 적격, 적임

substantial 상당한
earn a **substantial** amount of money
상당한 액수의 돈을 벌다

complimentary 무료의
a **complimentary** bottle of shampoo 무료 샴푸 한 통

appropriate 적절한, 적당한
programs **appropriate** for all ages
모든 연령대에 적절한 프로그램들

stuck 움직일 수 없는, 갇힌
be **stuck** in traffic 교통 혼잡에 갇히다

primary 주된, 주요한
the **primary** concern of the company
회사의 주된 관심사

anticipated 기대하던, 대망의
a highly **anticipated** exhibit 매우 기대되는 전시회
관련어 anticipate 예상하다, 기대하다

skeptical 회의적인
be **skeptical** of[about] ~에 대해 회의적이다

upcoming 다가오는, 곧 있을
the **upcoming** holiday sale 곧 있을 휴일 세일

exclusive 독점적인
have an **exclusive** interview with
~와 독점 인터뷰를 하다

mandatory 의무적인
take a **mandatory** training program
의무적인 교육을 받다
관련어 mandate 명령하다

tentative 잠정적인
tentative schedule for next year's conference
잠정적인 내년도 학회 일정

consecutive 연속적인
for the third **consecutive** year 3년 연속으로

affordable 가격이 알맞은, 저렴한
affordable price 저렴한 가격

likely 유망한; ~할 것 같은
the **likely** winner of the election 선거의 유력한 승자

extensive 광범위한, 방대한
extensive knowledge of Asian history
아시아 역사에 대한 방대한 지식

competitive 경쟁력이 있는
provide a **competitive** salary in the industry
업계에서 경쟁력 있는 급여를 지급하다
관련어 competition 경쟁

prestigious 권위 있는, 일류의
receive a **prestigious** award 권위 있는 상을 받다

rapid 빠른, 급속한
make a **rapid** change 빠른 변화를 이루다

preliminary 예비의
the **preliminary** results from consumer survey
소비자 설문 조사의 예비 결과

prompt 즉각적인
receive a **prompt** reply 즉각적인 답변을 받다

reassuring 안심시키는, 걱정을 없애 주는
see some **reassuring** developments
일부 고무적인 진전을 보다

nutritious 영양가가 높은
nutritious vegetables 영양가가 높은 채소
관련어 nutrition 영양분

overdue 연체된, 지체된
settle an **overdue** account 연체된 계정을 정리하다

superior 우수한, 뛰어난
superior organizational skills 뛰어난 조직력

qualifying 자격을 주는
pass a **qualifying** exam 자격 시험을 통과하다
관련어 qualify 자격을 갖추다, 자격을 주다

former 예전의, 전임의
former vice president 전임 부사장

strategic 전략적인
strategic move to attract more customers
더 많은 고객을 유치하기 위한 전략적 움직임
관련어 strategy 전략

incremental 서서히 증가하는
incremental improvements rather than radical changes 급진적인 변화가 아닌 점진적인 개선

intense 강렬한, 열렬한
under **intense** pressure 극심한 압박을 받는

frequent 잦은, 빈번한; 자주 가다
frequent visitors 단골 손님들
관련어 frequency 빈도

routine 정기적인, 일상적인; 일상적인 일
undergo **routine** maintenance 정기적인 유지 보수를 받다

ingenious 독창적인, 재치 있는
ingenious design 독창적인 디자인

discontinued 단종된
discontinued printer model 단종된 프린터 기종
관련어 discontinue 단종하다

supplemental 보충의, 추가의
supplemental information 추가 정보

functional 작동하는, 기능을 다하는
be fully **functional** 완전히 정상적으로 작동하다

immense 엄청난, 거대한
immense lobby with a café in the middle
중앙에 카페가 있는 엄청난 규모의 로비

verifiable 증명할 수 있는
verifiable facts 입증 가능한 사실

disposable 쓰고 버릴 수 있는
disposable umbrella covers 일회용 우산 커버
관련어 dispose 버리다, 폐기하다

dependent 의존적인
be highly **dependent** on seasonal sales
계절적인 판매에 크게 의존하다

overwhelming 압도적인, 엄청난
overwhelming victory 압도적인 승리
관련어 overwhelm 압도하다

PRACTICE

1. Jessica Roth, a reporter with the *Hampton Times*, had an ------- interview with Emerson Howell, the state governor.
   (A) intermittent
   (B) alternate
   (C) exclusive
   (D) imperative

2. The training program for the new marketing software is not -------, but employees are advised to take it.
   (A) mandatory
   (B) exposed
   (C) practiced
   (D) replaced

3. All customer complaints should be handled in a ------- manner by store representatives.
   (A) relative
   (B) close
   (C) prompt
   (D) various

4. Interns at Milton Technology are assigned ------- tasks to go along with the mentoring they receive.
   (A) opposing
   (B) routine
   (C) proficient
   (D) accessible

5. The CEO was satisfied with the ------- results from the customer survey conducted at the end of the year.
   (A) practical
   (B) remote
   (C) reassuring
   (D) exterior

6. One of the most highly ------- movies of the summer is the thriller directed by Martin Lincoln.
   (A) anticipated
   (B) proposed
   (C) revolutionary
   (D) revised

7. Thanks to his ------- list of contacts, Mr. Rumsfeld was able to secure several new clients for his firm.
   (A) abundant
   (B) extensive
   (C) refuted
   (D) qualified

8. Ms. Cartwright requested a ------- increase in her salary as a reward for her recent performance.
   (A) confident
   (B) costly
   (C) substantial
   (D) beneficial

9. The ------- duties of the office manager will be to supervise employees while resolving any issues between them.
   (A) eligible
   (B) comparative
   (C) primary
   (D) flexible

10. Mr. Dunlop's mechanic informed him that his truck was ------- for an oil change.
    (A) concerned
    (B) overdue
    (C) reported
    (D) clear

정답 및 해설 p.69

11. Several parts of the city still have ------- housing despite being close to the financial district.
(A) possible
(B) timely
(C) coordinated
(D) affordable

12. To become an engineer, a person must pass the ------- exam that is held twice a year.
(A) qualifying
(B) repeated
(C) accomplished
(D) diverse

13. Employees at Verducci Consulting receive ------- raises depending upon their annual performance.
(A) severe
(B) advanced
(C) incremental
(D) decisive

14. Jackson Auction House requests that potential buyers make ------- offers on items they are bidding on.
(A) competitive
(B) relaxed
(C) advanced
(D) everyday

15. Those who are ------- for paid time off must receive written permission from a supervisor.
(A) revealed
(B) permitted
(C) eligible
(D) assorted

16. The programmer encountered ------- problems when trying to download the software to her computer.
(A) frequent
(B) generous
(C) alternative
(D) essential

17. Most evaluators mention the ------- performance of the new sedan manufactured by Meridian Motors.
(A) absolute
(B) integrated
(C) superior
(D) discreet

18. Several roads downtown have been closed in preparation for the ------- parade through the city.
(A) reported
(B) upcoming
(C) temporary
(D) identified

고득점 도전
19. The appliance remains ------- despite its heavy usage over the years.
(A) specific
(B) functional
(C) obvious
(D) enterprising

고득점 도전
20. The new line of cosmetics by Bakersfield was ------- on account of several users suffering allergic reactions.
(A) promoted
(B) exported
(C) convinced
(D) discontinued

UNIT 13 고득점 획득을 위한 부사 어휘

adequately 충분히; 적절히
adequately test the product 제품을 충분히 테스트하다

remotely 원격으로, 멀리서
work **remotely** 원격 근무를 하다

frequently 자주, 빈번히
one of the most **frequently** visited places
사람들이 가장 자주 방문하는 장소 중 하나

thoroughly 완전히, 철저히
be reviewed **thoroughly** 철저히 검토되다

shortly 곧, 얼마 안 있어
shortly after the meeting 회의 직후에

closely 면밀히, 자세히
work **closely** with marketing on the project
그 프로젝트에 대해 마케팅과 긴밀히 협력하다

seldom 거의 ~ 않다
be **seldom** late to a meeting 회의에 좀처럼 늦지 않다

dramatically 극적으로, 크게
dramatically affect traffic in the area
지역의 교통에 크게 영향을 미치다

highly 매우, 대단히
a **highly** respected research organization
매우 존경 받는 연구 기관

electronically 전자적으로, 온라인으로
be distributed **electronically** 전자적으로 배포되다, 이메일을 통해 배포되다

unexpectedly 뜻밖에, 예상치 못하게
draw an **unexpectedly** large audience
예상 외로 많은 관중을 끌어 모으다

directly 직접, 곧바로
respond **directly** to an e-mail 이메일에 곧바로 답하다

freshly 새롭게, 최근에
the **freshly** repainted wall 최근에 다시 칠한 벽

mostly 주로
customers who are **mostly** interested in science fiction novels 주로 공상 과학 소설에 관심 있는 고객들

definitely 분명히, 확실히
definitely agree 전적으로 동의하다

strictly 엄격히
be **strictly** prohibited by law
법으로 엄격히 금지되어 있다

gradually 점점
gradually expand vegetarian menu options
채식주의자용 메뉴 선택권을 점점 늘리다

unanimously 만장일치로
vote **unanimously** 만장일치로 투표하다

initially 처음에
cost more than **initially** estimated
당초 예상보다 비용이 많이 들다

temporarily 임시로, 일시적으로
be **temporarily** closed 일시적으로 폐쇄되다

entirely 전적으로
be **entirely** the fault of 전적으로 ~의 잘못이다

currently 현재, 지금
be **currently** seeking a full-time employee
현재 정규직 직원을 찾고 있다

beforehand 사전에, 미리
be notified two days **beforehand**
이틀 전에 미리 통지를 받다

previously 전에, 이전에
artists who have not **previously** made a film
전에 영화를 만들어본 적이 없는 예술가들

instead 대신에
move the meeting to 1 P.M. **instead**
회의를 대신 오후 1시로 옮기다

rapidly 빠르게, 급속히
rapidly growing demand for IT specialists
IT 전문가에 대한 급증하는 수요

extremely 매우, 아주
be **extremely** pleased 매우 기쁘다

considerably 상당히, 많이
vary **considerably** 상당히 다르다

promptly 정각에; 즉시
arrive **promptly** at 7:00 P.M. 오후 7시 정각에 도착하다

far 훨씬, 아주
reserve train tickets **far** in advance
기차표를 한참 전에 예매하다

momentarily 잠시, 잠깐 (동안)
She was **momentarily** surprised when her boss offered her a promotion.
상사가 승진을 제안했을 때 그녀는 잠시 놀랐다.

randomly 무작위로
be **randomly** chosen 무작위로 뽑히다

eventually 결국, 마침내
be **eventually** finished on schedule
마침내 예정대로 끝나다

elsewhere 다른 곳에서, 다른 곳으로
items that are not available **elsewhere**
다른 곳에서는 구입할 수 없는 물품들

accordingly 그에 따라, 그에 맞춰
The proposals must be submitted in writing and will be responded to **accordingly.** 제안서는 반드시 서면으로 제출되어야 하며 마찬가지의 방법으로 답변될 것이다.

alike 똑같이, 비슷하게
children and adults **alike** 아이와 어른 모두

indeed 정말로, 사실은
be **indeed** an error in the calculation
사실은 계산상의 실수이다

overly 너무, 지나치게
be **overly** complicated 지나치게 복잡하다

eagerly 간절히, 열렬히
eagerly await the results of ~의 결과를 간절히 기다리다

properly 제대로
work **properly** 제대로 작동하다

significantly 상당히, 현저히
significantly increase the productivity of the staff 직원들의 생산성을 현저히 증가시키다

apparently 보아하니
Apparently, heavy rains are expected this weekend. 보아하니 이번 주말에 폭우가 예상된다.

PRACTICE

1. Mary Hartford plans to skip the opening day of the conference and will ------- appear on the second day.
(A) instead
(B) variously
(C) literally
(D) similarly

2. Employees should submit all documents requesting the reimbursement of expenditures -------.
(A) fortunately
(B) gracefully
(C) electronically
(D) revealingly

3. Mr. Burns was ------- offered a low salary, but the company increased the amount when he rejected it.
(A) pleasantly
(B) entirely
(C) initially
(D) particularly

4. Denton Office Supplies makes sure to package and deliver all online orders -------.
(A) seriously
(B) promptly
(C) hardly
(D) really

5. The board of directors voted ------- to offer Reid Harmon the position of CEO at Watergate Industries.
(A) enormously
(B) possibly
(C) unanimously
(D) regularly

6. Please read the instructions ------- prior to attempting to install the appliance in your kitchen.
(A) happily
(B) almost
(C) justly
(D) thoroughly

7. Perkins Electronics ------- closed its factory in Mexico by order of its new president.
(A) convincingly
(B) accidentally
(C) unexpectedly
(D) preferably

8. Only those individuals ------- subscribing to the *Daily Times* are eligible for a special discount offer.
(A) precisely
(B) currently
(C) merely
(D) coincidentally

9. Ms. Galbraith ------- improved office efficiency by implementing a new filing system.
(A) ever
(B) significantly
(C) shortly
(D) exactly

10. Mr. Edwards ------- flies late at night, but he needed to arrive in Tokyo by this morning.
(A) seldom
(B) then
(C) however
(D) who

정답 및 해설 p.70

11. Regular library patrons and visitors ------- are invited to see Janet Evans read from her latest novel this Friday evening.
(A) meanwhile
(B) alike
(C) quite
(D) truly

12. While he had lunch at a café with a client yesterday, Mr. Orbison ------- eats at the company cafeteria.
(A) mostly
(B) only
(C) powerfully
(D) swiftly

13. The restaurant run by chef Otto von Steuben offers dishes not available -------.
(A) elsewhere
(B) beyond
(C) around
(D) approximately

14. Since it has secured outside funding, Nano Technologies is ------- hiring more employees for its new facility.
(A) overly
(B) rarely
(C) rapidly
(D) uniquely

15. No time off will be granted in December, so make your vacation plans -------.
(A) properly
(B) cleanly
(C) definitely
(D) accordingly

16. Despite always working in Newport, Ken Dayton was concerned that he would ------- be transferred abroad.
(A) frequently
(B) eventually
(C) nearly
(D) obviously

17. The package left our warehouse two days ago and will be delivered to your office -------.
(A) lately
(B) fairly
(C) shortly
(D) formerly

18. The community parking lot was closed ------- while the surface was repaved.
(A) finally
(B) temporarily
(C) cautiously
(D) narrowly

고득점 도전
19. After checking the budget, Ms. Jenkins determined that there is ------- enough money left for an employee gathering.
(A) neither
(B) else
(C) more
(D) indeed

고득점 도전
20. To ensure that the application process goes smoothly, prepare all of your documents -------.
(A) freely
(B) beforehand
(C) anywhere
(D) likewise

UNIT 14 고득점 획득을 위한 동사 어휘

comply with ~에 따르다
comply with quality standards 품질 기준에 따르다
관련어 compliance 준수, 따름

equip (장비를) 갖추다
be **equipped** with a refrigerator
냉장고가 갖추어져 있다
관련어 equipment 장비

lack 부족하다, 없다
lack the communication skills
의사소통의 기술이 부족하다

handle 다루다, 처리하다
handle client information 고객 정보를 다루다

address 다루다, 처리하다; 보내다; 연설하다
address employee concerns 직원들의 우려를 처리하다

obtain 얻다, 획득하다
obtain a free quote 무료 견적을 받다

outline 요점을 말하다, 개요를 서술하다
outline the strengths and weaknesses of
~의 장점과 약점을 서술하다

specify 명시하다
specify the time of day 하루 중 시간을 지정하다
관련어 specification 사양, 명세

extract 이끌어내다, 추출하다
extract insights from a research report
연구 보고서에서 통찰력을 이끌어내다

direct 향하게 하다; 직접적인
direct questions to the department manager
부서장에게 문의하다

waive (권리를) 포기하다, 적용하지 않다
waive registration fee 등록비를 면제하다

secure 확보하다; 안전한
secure funding from foreign investors
외국인 투자자들로부터 자금을 확보하다
관련어 security 보안

grant 승인하다; 부여하다
grant employees more paid leave
직원들에게 보다 많은 유급 휴가를 부여하다

admit 입장시키다; 인정하다
be **admitted** to a building 건물 안으로 입장하다

facilitate 촉진하다, 활성화하다
facilitate team-building workshops
팀워크 향상 워크숍을 활성화하다

ensure 확실하게 하다, 보장하다
ensure exceptional quality 뛰어난 품질을 보장하다

assign 배정하다, 할당하다
be **assigned** to a task 과제를 배정 받다
관련어 assignment 과제, 임무

encourage 격려하다, 장려하다
encourage clients to report errors
고객들에게 오류 사항을 알리라고 장려하다

undergo 받다, 겪다
undergo corporate restructuring
기업 구조조정을 겪다

double 두 배로 하다
double the size of the staff
직원의 규모를 두 배로 늘리다

bring up 제기하다, (화제를) 꺼내다
bring up a subject at a meeting
회의에서 주제를 꺼내다

implement 시행하다
implement an extensive recycling program
광범위한 재활용 프로그램을 시행하다

demonstrate 시연하다, 설명하다; 증명하다
demonstrate how to operate a camera
카메라를 조작하는 방법을 시연하다
관련어 demonstration 시연

establish 설립하다, 확립하다
establish guidelines regarding the handling of confidential information
기밀 정보 취급에 관한 지침을 수립하다
관련어 establishment 설립, 확립; 시설

manage 관리하다; 어렵사리 해내다
manage social media content SNS 컨텐츠를 관리하다
관련어 management 경영, 경영진

evolve 발전하다
evolve from a local supplier to a national distributor 지역 공급업체에서 전국적인 유통업체로 발전하다

limit 제한하다; 제한
limit passengers to one carry-on bag
승객들의 수하물 가방을 하나로 제한하다

post 게시하다
be **posted** online 온라인에 게시되다

enforce 실시하다, 시행하다
enforce a new regulation 새로운 규정을 시행하다

analyze 분석하다
analyze project details carefully
프로젝트의 세부 사항을 신중히 분석하다
관련어 analysis 분석

feature 특징을 이루다
feature live jazz music 라이브 재즈 음악이 특징이다

authenticate 진짜임을 증명하다
authenticate the message 메시지가 진짜임을 증명하다

expand 확장하다
expand the international foods section
해외 식품 코너를 확장하다
관련어 expansion 확장

clarify 명확하게 하다
clarify the new policy on vacation days
휴가일에 관한 새로운 방침을 명확하게 하다
관련어 clarification 해명, 설명

perform 행하다, 실시하다; 공연하다, 연주하다
perform well in his job interview
취업 면접을 잘 해내다
관련어 performance 실적, 성과; 공연

lease 임대하다, 빌리다; 임대
lease a rental car 렌터카를 빌리다

coincide with ~와 동시에 일어나다; ~와 일치하다
coincide with a conference 회의와 시간이 겹치다

redeem (현금이나 상품으로) 교환하다
redeem a coupon 쿠폰을 교환하다

explore 개척하다
explore the region for investment opportunities
투자 기회를 찾아 지역을 개척하다

submit 제출하다, 내다
submit expense reports 지출 보고서를 제출하다
관련어 submission 제출

PRACTICE

1. Mr. Washington ------- a strict policy of not allowing workers to arrive at meetings late.
(A) disturbs
(B) minimizes
(C) enforces
(D) reveals

2. To ------- that all individuals are treated fairly, rules must apply equally to everyone.
(A) bargain
(B) appoint
(C) integrate
(D) ensure

3. The date of the seminar will be changed so that it does not ------- with the company picnic.
(A) collaborate
(B) coincide
(C) report
(D) assign

4. Greg's Shopping Club ------- the shipping fee for all purchases of $100 or more.
(A) clears
(B) waives
(C) explores
(D) automates

5. Be sure to ------- the size and the color of each article of clothing you order.
(A) balance
(B) multiply
(C) specify
(D) reconcile

6. Discount coupons must be ------- prior to the expiration date listed on the back.
(A) portrayed
(B) determined
(C) advanced
(D) redeemed

7. Please ------- your username on the company's intranet system no later than Friday afternoon.
(A) transform
(B) authenticate
(C) develop
(D) import

8. Individuals applying for the position must ------- a complete physical checkup.
(A) approve
(B) examine
(C) undergo
(D) attempt

9. Despite being highly educated, Mr. Bevers ------- the necessary leadership skills to take on an executive position.
(A) replaces
(B) reveals
(C) portrays
(D) lacks

10. Ms. Jansen ------- to contact her assistant despite having left her phone at her home.
(A) failed
(B) considered
(C) managed
(D) projected

11. The facility ------- state-of-the-art workout equipment that is also easy to use.
(A) features
(B) removes
(C) reports
(D) disrupts

12. Members of the museum tour can ------- their questions to the guide at any time.
(A) oppose
(B) direct
(C) allow
(D) prioritize

13. Brian Harper ------- the documents necessary for him to receive his accounting license.
(A) submitted
(B) invited
(C) proposed
(D) inquired

14. The user's manuals ------- the necessary steps people must take to utilize the equipment.
(A) consider
(B) submit
(C) outline
(D) attempt

15. Staff members traveling abroad can ------- company credit cards by speaking with a supervisor.
(A) promote
(B) obtain
(C) apply
(D) remain

16. Everyone who visits the factory should ------- with any instructions provided by employees there.
(A) comply
(B) conclude
(C) appear
(D) practice

17. The airline stated that it would ------- its regulations regarding carry-on baggage.
(A) clarify
(B) hinder
(C) expose
(D) participate

18. The new CEO, Deborah Burgess, promised to ------- concerns about possible layoffs at the Toronto facility.
(A) offer
(B) restructure
(C) advertise
(D) address

고득점 도전
19. The customer was ------- compensation for his loss when the shipment was damaged during delivery.
(A) enhanced
(B) granted
(C) regarded
(D) detected

고득점 도전
20. Fairmont Cab ------- a new policy requiring its drivers to have comprehensive insurance covering themselves and their passengers.
(A) implemented
(B) associated
(C) instructed
(D) transported

PRACTICE 고난도

1. To ensure the final draft of the magazine is printed on time, reporters should make all ------- to their texts prior to June 8.
   (A) revisions
   (B) essays
   (C) recommendations
   (D) proposals

2. Agriculture experts recommend providing the ------- environment possible for plants in order that they have a good chance of thriving.
   (A) most stable
   (B) more stably
   (C) stabilizing
   (D) stability

3. Mr. Kamal will examine the incoming résumés to determine ------- reflect the necessary qualifications for the management position.
   (A) now that
   (B) even though
   (C) some such
   (D) which ones

4. Following the investigation, it was determined that the delay at the warehouse was caused by a few ------- boxes.
   (A) mislabeled
   (B) mislabeling
   (C) mislabel
   (D) mislabels

5. Nelson Recruitment insists that job applicants ------- with the recruiter to create clear employment goals.
   (A) cooperating
   (B) cooperate
   (C) cooperation
   (D) cooperated

6. Ms. Maddock's ------- for the event venue include ample parking and a state-of-the-art sound system.
   (A) preferably
   (B) preferences
   (C) preferable
   (D) preference

7. Sales of Newton Footwear increased online and in stores ------- after the launch of an ad campaign featuring professional athletes.
   (A) promptly
   (B) prompt
   (C) prompted
   (D) promptness

8. Any losses ------- the failure to correctly analyze the level of risk may be the responsibility of the investment firm.
   (A) whereabouts
   (B) apart
   (C) resulting from
   (D) in compliance with

9. ------- with a complaint regarding the effectiveness of the laundry detergent will be promptly directed to a customer service agent.
   (A) One another
   (B) Whoever
   (C) Anyone
   (D) Theirs

10. Mr. Conway was able to begin the keynote address on time ------- there were technical difficulties with the sound equipment earlier in the day.
   (A) even though
   (B) not only
   (C) owing to
   (D) while

11. The controversial nature of the infrastructure project on municipal land provoked a ------- discussion at yesterday's public forum.
(A) resistant
(B) lively
(C) perishable
(D) current

12. ------- the training objectives of the session have already been met, we should use the remaining time for more casual team-building activities.
(A) Since
(B) Until
(C) Whenever
(D) Unless

13. The lifetime warranty on all washing machines from Larkin Appliances is not surprising, given the company's products are known for -------.
(A) modification
(B) durability
(C) proximity
(D) accomplishment

14. How ------- the bus fares will increase depends on the average number of passengers and the expected fuel expenditures.
(A) substantiality
(B) substantially
(C) substance
(D) more substantial

15. All budget decisions must be approved by Tony Calderon, the ------- of the annual music festival, in advance.
(A) organizing
(B) organization
(C) organizer
(D) organize

16. Multiple rejections of the building permit forced the construction company ------- its development of the vacant plot into a tower of luxury apartments.
(A) abandoned
(B) abandonment
(C) to abandon
(D) abandons

17. ------- the severe weather predicted for this Saturday, the event planners for the International Food Festival have postponed the event.
(A) By means of
(B) Ever since
(C) In light of
(D) Considering that

18. Elkview Engineering has established ------- an excellent reputation that it no longer needs to allocate funds for marketing and advertising.
(A) even
(B) such
(C) yet
(D) more

19. Everyone on the product development team agrees that ------- is the most impressive prototype submitted to the national design competition.
(A) us
(B) ours
(C) we
(D) ourselves

20. ------- the international transfer request is submitted by 3 P.M., Henley Bank will finalize the transaction on the same day.
(A) Until
(B) Provided
(C) As soon as
(D) Just as

21. The attractive interest rate offered by Lapointe Bank ------- customers to open new accounts and move surplus funds into them.
(A) motivate
(B) has motivated
(C) is being motivated
(D) have been motivating

22. VT Logistics plans to terminate the contract with Camden Couriers because the firm has been ------- unable to meet delivery deadlines.
(A) intensely
(B) steadily
(C) consistently
(D) tentatively

23. The department head anticipates ------- more on travel expenses next year to improve the relationships with clients through face-to-face meetings.
(A) to spend
(B) spend
(C) has spent
(D) spending

24. The majority of first-class travelers are willing to pay extra for a direct flight ------- spend additional time dealing with a layover.
(A) in fact
(B) as a result of
(C) in case of
(D) rather than

25. Murillo Incorporated's overseas expansion plan involves hiring an accounting firm ------- employees have experience with overseas tax regulations.
(A) what
(B) how
(C) which
(D) whose

26. The purchase of more equipment to enable automation has ------- the size of the workforce needed at the manufacturing facility.
(A) gathered
(B) regarded
(C) monitored
(D) decreased

27. The new policy on unpaid medical leave will go into effect immediately ------- the details are posted on the company Web site.
(A) until
(B) after
(C) any
(D) that

28. A review of the user information revealed that approximately forty-five percent of employees ------- the database that was announced in the e-mail.
(A) calculated
(B) introduced
(C) accessed
(D) inquired

29. Supervisors should take the time to listen to concerns from members of their team, ------- busy they may be.
(A) rather than
(B) indeed
(C) however
(D) as well

30. ------- Mr. Zhang not missed reaching his sales quota for the quarter, he might have been considered for the promotion.
(A) Having
(B) Has
(C) Had
(D) Have

정답 및 해설 p.76

1. Mr. Cross assisted in the kitchen since ------- of his chefs arrived at the restaurant on time.
   (A) nothing
   (B) nobody
   (C) neither
   (D) anyone

2. According to financial experts, manufacturing companies should expect to make record ------- this year.
   (A) profitable
   (B) profitability
   (C) profiting
   (D) profits

3. It is expected that the automated system will make the factory workers ------- at their jobs.
   (A) product
   (B) production
   (C) productive
   (D) producer

4. The R&D team at Dayton Tech ------- a second chance to find a solution to the manufacturing problem.
   (A) gave
   (B) will give
   (C) is giving
   (D) has been given

5. The customer was fairly ------- for her loss when several items were broken during delivery.
   (A) approved
   (B) appreciated
   (C) compensated
   (D) rewarded

6. ------- members of the team felt that their ideas should be implemented at once.
   (A) Every
   (B) One
   (C) Both
   (D) Neither

7. The background noise continued ------- the speech, making it difficult for some audience members to hear anything.
   (A) throughout
   (B) around
   (C) at
   (D) since

8. Mr. Greg believes March is an appropriate time ------- the new line of products coming out in spring.
   (A) advertising
   (B) advertisement
   (C) to advertise
   (D) will advertise

9. At first glance, the design of the building seems ------- and makes good use of available space.
   (A) efficient
   (B) efficiency
   (C) efficiently
   (D) efficiencies

10. Harrison Shipbuilding saw orders increase last quarter, ------- its rival, Baden Inc., reported a record loss.
   (A) thanks to
   (B) despite
   (C) consequently
   (D) whereas

11. The process of ------- at Stanton Bank requires proof of residency and two forms of picture identification.
(A) verification
(B) withdrawal
(C) imposition
(D) adjustment

12. Most analysts considered Edward Hope's greatest accomplishment to be ------- his company out of bankruptcy.
(A) get
(B) getting
(C) had gotten
(D) did get

13. The Spruce Corporation agreed to work in ------- with Magpie Inc. to develop low-cost housing in Richmond.
(A) reflection
(B) deduction
(C) conjunction
(D) accumulation

14. All employees are asked to be ------- at the seminar in order to learn as much as possible.
(A) optional
(B) impulsive
(C) attentive
(D) collaborative

15. Dr. Hatfield instructed ------- who had been working nonstop since the morning to take a break.
(A) those
(B) one
(C) themselves
(D) each

16. While the seminar was considered -------, nearly everyone in the Accounting Department registered for it.
(A) optional
(B) concluded
(C) progressive
(D) responsible

17. Ms. Jacobs, one of Failsafe's top managers, ------- a class on leadership at the local university.
(A) teach
(B) teaches
(C) teacher
(D) is taught

18. The machinery must be operated ------- to prevent it from suffering a malfunction.
(A) fairly
(B) properly
(C) surely
(D) creatively

19. Ms. Oxford closely ------- random items in an effort to find flaws with the manufacturing process.
(A) concentrates
(B) purchases
(C) examines
(D) develops

20. The images captured by the magazine's new photographer are quite visually -------.
(A) to appeal
(B) appealed
(C) appeals
(D) appealing

21. Please ------- to put on your safety gear properly to avoid potential injuries.

(A) remember
(B) to remember
(C) will remember
(D) remembering

22. Mr. Hollander is the person responsible ------- confirming that proper procedures are being followed.

(A) to
(B) with
(C) for
(D) on

23. The bridge was only ------- complete when construction was halted due to the discovery of a design flaw.

(A) partial
(B) partially
(C) partiality
(D) partialness

24. Megan Reyna's major -------- to the charity was recruiting several wealthy donors.

(A) bonus
(B) support
(C) contribution
(D) variation

25. An item is considered ------- by Grossman Shipping when it is signed for by the recipient.

(A) delivery
(B) delivered
(C) to deliver
(D) was delivered

26. Jeremy Tyler's next project will be a ------- with two members of the Marketing Department.

(A) collaborate
(B) collaborator
(C) collaborating
(D) collaboration

27. All full-time employees at Focal Inc. ------- its major clients are invited to its celebration being held on December 29.

(A) as well as
(B) meanwhile
(C) so that
(D) in order to

28. We were instructed to do ------- was necessary to ensure that the festival was held successfully.

(A) whatever
(B) which
(C) that
(D) who

29. The Sales Department plans on ------- at least six members of the staff to focus on sales in North America.

(A) commit
(B) committed
(C) to commit
(D) committing

30. Mr. Davis strongly believes that ------- should be offered an executive position at Leeway's.

(A) he
(B) his
(C) him
(D) himself

RC

PART 6

PART 6 출제 경향 및 전략

문제 유형과 출제 경향

PART 6는 하나의 지문에 4개의 빈칸 채우기 문제로 구성되어 있어 PART 5와 PART 7의 중간적 성격을 띤다. 한 지문에 할당된 4문제 중 3문제는 문법(시제, 태, 대명사 등), 품사, 어휘, 접속 부사 문제 등으로 이루어져 있고, 나머지 한 문제는 문맥에 맞는 문장 고르기 문제로 구성된다.

Questions 131-134 refer to the following e-mail.

해석 및 해설 p.79

To: All Blacktail Logistics Employees <stafflist@blacktaillogistics.com>
From: Alfred Orozco <a.orozco@blacktaillogistics.com>
Date: November 12
Subject: Performance reviews

Dear Blacktail Logistics Staff:

Throughout next week, the managers will be conducting performance evaluations for all staff members. We carry out this task -------(**131.**) to ensure that you understand your role. -------(**132.**), we want to make sure you are well supported in operating at your peak level. You will meet with your immediate supervisor to discuss your strengths as well as areas that need -------(**133.**). Following the evaluation, you will have the opportunity to complete a comment card. This can be submitted directly to the HR department, and the comments will remain anonymous. -------(**134.**). Your supervisor will inform you of the time your evaluation is scheduled.

Thank you for your cooperation,

Alfred Orozco
Office Manager, Blacktail Logistics

131. (A) occasionally
(B) occasional
(C) occasion
(D) occasions

132. (A) In contrast
(B) As a result
(C) However
(D) In addition

133. (A) proficiency
(B) improvement
(C) configuration
(D) permission

134. (A) So, please share your honest opinions.
(B) We believe you will excel in your new role.
(C) Fortunately, leadership skills can be developed over time.
(D) Policy updates are always posted online promptly.

문제 풀이 전략

PART 6는 하나의 글을 읽고 문제를 풀어야 하는 파트이긴 하지만 상당수의 문제들은 PART 5와 마찬가지로 빈칸이 놓여 있는 문장만으로 답을 찾을 수 있다. 예를 들어, 품사 문제는 빈칸 앞뒤에 있는 단어들의 품사나 문장 성분, 또는 빈칸이 속한 문장의 구조만 파악해도 답을 찾을 수 있다. 하지만 시제와 어휘 문제는 두 개 이상의 선택지가 정답 후보로 남을 경우 반드시 앞뒤 문맥을 고려해야만 정답을 찾을 수 있다. 특히 문장과 문장을 연결하는 접속 부사나 문맥에 맞는 문장 고르기 문제는 예외 없이 문맥을 통해 해결해야 한다. 그러므로 고득점을 목표로 PART 6의 모든 문제를 맞추고자 한다면, 지문을 처음부터 읽어 내려가며 순차적으로 문제를 푸는 것이 좋다.

131. (A) occasionally
(B) occasional
(C) occasion
(D) occasions

품사
품사 문제는 같은 어휘에서 파생된 다른 품사의 어휘들로 선택지가 구성된다. 빈칸이 속해 있는 구나 절을 이루는 어휘들의 품사를 파악하는 것만으로도 문제를 풀 수 있다.

132. (A) In contrast
(B) As a result
(C) However
(D) In addition

접속 부사
접속 부사는 항상 문장 앞에 놓이며, 빈칸이 속한 문장과 바로 앞 문장의 논리적 연결 관계(인과, 역접, 예시 등)가 판단의 기준이 된다.

133. (A) proficiency
(B) improvement
(C) configuration
(D) permission

어휘
서로 다른 의미의 어휘들로 선택지가 구성되며, 빈칸이 속한 문장을 해석하는 것만으로 문제를 풀 수 없다면 보다 넓은 문맥을 따져 판단해야 한다.

134. (A) So, please share your honest opinions.
(B) We believe you will excel in your new role.
(C) Fortunately, leadership skills can be developed over time.
(D) Policy updates are always posted online promptly.

문맥에 맞는 문장 고르기
문단의 시작 부분에 빈칸이 있는 경우를 제외하고는 대부분의 빈칸은 바로 앞 문장과 얼마나 잘 연결되느냐가 우선적인 판단의 근거가 되므로, 빈칸 뒤에 오는 문장보다는 앞에 오는 문장을 항상 먼저 확인해야 한다.

UNIT 01 문법

해석 p.79

1. **e-mail (이메일)**

Dear Ms. Lampron,

Thank you for becoming a member of the Victoria City Bookstore. -------(1.) membership helps support small businesses and ensures that physical books remain in print. Though our storefront is modest, we offer a wide array of titles and express shipping for most books not currently on our shelves.

(A) Her (B) His (C) Your (D) Their

→ Victoria City Bookstore의 회원이 된 것은 이메일의 수신인인 Ms. Lampron이고, 빈칸이 있는 문장에서는 Ms. Lampron에게 회원 자격의 혜택을 설명하고 있으므로, '당신의'라는 의미의 소유격 인칭대명사인 (C) Your가 적절하다.

2. **memo (회람)**

Hogan Insurance's annual banquet will take place on Friday, December 17, at 7 P.M. All Hogan Insurance employees and their families are invited, so please RSVP to the administrative office. The top-performing employees at the company -------(2.) at the end of the dinner. We hope to see you all there!

(A) will be recognized (B) have been recognized
(C) were recognized (D) will recognize

→ 빈칸 뒤에 목적어 없이 전치사구가 이어지므로 수동태가 나와야 한다. (A), (B), (C)가 정답 후보가 되는데, 첫 번째 문장에서 annual banquet은 12월 17일이라는 미래의 시점에 열린다고 했으므로 미래 시제인 (A) will be recognized가 정답이다.

3. **notice (공지)**

Notice to Staff Members

Please do not turn off your computers before leaving work on Friday, as the IT team is scheduled to update the software. We -------(3.) a software update every month in order to ensure the security of our system. Should you have any questions, please direct them to Sean Hendrix, the IT manager, at extension 18.

(A) were carrying out (B) will be carried out (C) are carried out (D) carry out

→ 빈칸 뒤에 목적어인 a software update가 있으므로 빈칸에는 능동태가 들어가야 한다. (A)와 (D)가 정답 후보가 되는데, every month라는 시간의 부사구가 있으므로 현재 시제인 (D) carry out이 정답이다. 이처럼 현재 시제는 반복되는 행위를 나타낼 수 있다.

PRACTICE

정답 및 해설 p.80

Questions 1-4 refer to the following article.

NAPLES, Italy—Romulus Construction is a highly respected company in the region of Naples. -------(1.) acquires and develops land and then sells complete homes in Naples and the surrounding area. These units are known for the quality of their construction -------(2.) their affordability.

Romulus Construction just announced that it -------(3.) to acquire a large stretch of land along the coast. "We're going to construct private residences there while also maintaining the beauty of the natural environment," said Ernesto Humbert, the CEO of Romulus. "-------(4.). We will be releasing more details in the coming weeks."

The company added that it hopes to purchase more land in the near future.

1. (A) They
(B) It
(C) He
(D) There

2. (A) as well as
(B) except for
(C) in order to
(D) in the meantime

3. (A) plan
(B) is planning
(C) will be planned
(D) have been planned

4. (A) The buildings being constructed are nearly complete.
(B) A decision on purchasing the land must be made soon.
(C) One family has already moved into its new home.
(D) We believe the homes we build will be popular with buyers.

UNIT 02 품사

해석 p.80

1. **e-mail (이메일)**

Your subscription to *World Travel Magazine* is due to expire on August 31. To continue ------- issues of this publication, please follow the link below and complete the online form as soon as possible. That way, you can be sure that you will not miss any of our helpful articles about the best vacation destinations around the globe.
1.

(A) receipt (B) received (C) receive (D) receiving

→ 빈칸 앞에 동사 continue가 있고 뒤에 목적어인 issues가 있으므로, 빈칸은 continue의 목적어인 동시에 issues를 목적어로 취할 수 있는 동명사가 와야 한다. 따라서 (D) receiving이 정답이다.

2. **announcement (발표)**

The city of Branchburg has approved the construction of a new apartment complex in the northern neighborhood of Rockwell. The building will contain forty-five one-bedroom units and on-site laundry facilities. The aim is to supply affordable housing for the workers of Skye Amusement Park, a popular ------- for tourists, as well as commuters who use the express bus route.
2.

(A) attract (B) attraction (C) attractive (D) attracts

→ 빈칸 앞에 관사 a와 형용사 popular가 있으므로 빈칸은 명사 자리이다. 따라서 (B) attraction이 정답이다.

3. **article (기사)**

The R&D team at Sampson Foods has developed a new packing procedure for its line of healthy snacks. The items will now be packaged with an additional layer of plastic to maintain an airtight environment. The change is expected to provide more consistent and ------- results in the texture and taste of the food, even over a long storage period.
3.

(A) predictable (B) prediction (C) predict (D) predictably

→ 빈칸 뒤에 명사가 있고 등위 접속사 and 앞에 형용사 consistent가 있으므로, 빈칸에는 consistent와 함께 results를 수식하는 형용사가 와야 한다. 따라서 (A) predictable이 정답이다.

PRACTICE

정답 및 해설 p.81

Questions 1-4 refer to the following memo.

To: Senior Staff
From: Helen Schnell
Subject: Oxford Plant Update
Date: August 10

For three months, we've advertised heavily for the positions that must be filled at our new plant in Oxford. -------(1.). We are currently ahead of schedule and should have every position fully staffed by the end of August. We are also interested in -------(2.) the plant with experienced workers. Anyone interested in transferring to Oxford should contact -------(3.). Preference in the hiring process will be given to current employees. We'll be conducting a tour of the site next week. To see it in person, reply to this e-mail, and I'll make the necessary -------(4.).

1. (A) Bids for the design of the facility are being accepted now.
(B) We decided to close it down after getting negative reviews.
(C) Our CEO will make an important announcement this afternoon.
(D) I'm pleased to announce that half of those positions have been filled.

2. (A) replacing
(B) designing
(C) employing
(D) staffing

3. (A) me
(B) I
(C) mine
(D) my

4. (A) arrange
(B) arranging
(C) arrangements
(D) arranged

1. **advertisement (광고)**

The National History Museum offers visitors a fascinating glimpse into the lives of people from long ago. Our exhibits feature clothing items, pottery, art, and more. Admission is just $7.50 per person. The museum is easily -------- (1.) by public transportation using bus 104 or 1288. For more information, visit our Web site at www.nationalhm.org.

(A) reliable (B) detectable (C) favorable (D) accessible

→ (A) 신뢰할 수 있는 (B) 찾아낼 수 있는 (C) 호의적인 (D) 접근 가능한, 이용 가능한
빈칸 뒤에 by public transportation(대중교통으로)이라는 전치사구가 있으므로, '접근할 수 있는, 갈 수 있는'이라는 의미의 (D) accessible이 적절하다.

2. **letter (편지)**

Dear Ms. Burnett,

We are pleased to inform you that your application for a small business loan from Arlington Bank has been approved. The funds will be credited to your business account within 5 working days. Please retain the enclosed loan -------- (2.) for your records. Should you have any questions or concerns, feel free to contact our customer service team.

(A) institution (B) retrieval (C) agreement (D) excerpt

→ (A) 기관 (B) 회수 (C) 계약(서) (D) 발췌
'enclosed loan --------'의 빈칸에 선택지들을 넣어 보면 '동봉된 대출 계약서'가 문맥상 가장 자연스러우므로 (C) agreement가 정답이다.

3. **notice (공지)**

NOTICE TO SALISBURY SUITES TENANTS

We have scheduled an electrician to visit our site on January 19 in order to have the corridor lights rewired. While the work is taking place, there will be no electricity to the building. The power will be shut off at 9 A.M. and then will be -------- (3.) no later than 2 P.M. We apologize for any inconvenience this may cause.

(A) restored (B) shifted (C) enforced (D) surpassed

→ (A) 복구하다 (B) 이동하다 (C) 시행하다 (D) 능가하다
주어인 The power(전기, 전력) 및 앞서 나온 동사구인 be shut off(차단되다)와 관련이 있는 (A) restored가 정답이다.

PRACTICE

정답 및 해설 p.82

Questions 1-4 refer to the following article.

HARTFORD (May 19)—Hartford-based charity Peterson House announced its annual fundraiser will be on July 1. Peterson House was -------(1.) in 2001 and has focused on providing food, clothes, and educational supplies for children in the Hartford area.

Peterson House President Jenny Blair said, "We're going to be holding a silent auction for the first time ever. We -------(2.) by the opportunity that this presents for us."

Ms. Blair added that the charity has -------(3.) completed construction on its new office following several delays. --------(4.). She also stated that the charity has some big plans for summer and fall and that she will discuss them at a later date.

1. (A) founded
(B) donated
(C) appealed
(D) constructed

2. (A) excite
(B) are exciting
(C) are excited
(D) excitement

3. (A) always
(B) finally
(C) instead
(D) specially

4. (A) The work was heavily affected by poor weather this spring.
(B) She expects to raise a million dollars at the auction.
(C) Ms. Blair has worked at the charity since 2001.
(D) The charity is pleased with the support it has received locally.

UNIT 04 접속 부사

해석 p.82

1. **e-mail (이메일)**

Hi, Ashley.

Thanks for volunteering to lead the training workshop for new employees next week. I just found out that we will have employees from both our branch and the Wooddale branch. This brings the total of participants to 25, up from 13. -------, we are moving the workshop to the main conference room, as it is larger. Please let me know if you have any questions.
1.

(A) Even so (B) Therefore (C) For example (D) Otherwise

→ (A) 그렇다 하더라도 (B) 그러므로, 따라서 (C) 예를 들어 (D) 그렇지 않으면
빈칸 앞의 내용은 원인, 뒤의 내용은 그로 인한 결과이므로 인과 관계를 나타내는 접속 부사인 (B) Therefore가 정답이다.

2. **information (안내문)**

Brisbane Hotel is having the elevators in the main lobby replaced on Thursday, August 8. Guests are asked to use the stairwell, located directly to the right of the front desk, to get to their rooms. -------, guests may use the elevators near the Jacobs Street entrance. Thank you for your patience.
2.

(A) Initially (B) Alternatively (C) Unfortunately (D) Even if

→ (A) 처음에, 원래 (B) 그렇지 않으면 (C) 불행히도 (D) 설령 ~라고 할지라도
빈칸 앞의 내용은 객실로 갈 수 있는 첫 번째 방법이고, 빈칸 뒤는 첫 번째 방법을 사용하지 않을 경우 이용할 수 있는 두 번째 방법이므로 대안을 나타내는 접속 부사인 (B) Alternatively가 정답이다.

3. **e-mail (이메일)**

Dear Mr. Bradley,

I would like to recommend Blake Patterson for promotion to team leader. Mr. Patterson has been working for the company for five years, and he is well respected within our department. He has excellent written communication skills. -------, he can express himself well in conversations. I believe Mr. Patterson would thrive in this role.
3.

(A) Namely (B) On the other hand (C) Nonetheless (D) Likewise

→ (A) 즉 (B) 반면에 (C) 그럼에도 불구하고 (D) 마찬가지로, 역시
빈칸 앞의 문장은 Blake Patterson이 서면 의사소통 기술이 뛰어나다고 했고, 빈칸이 있는 문장은 그가 대화를 할 때도 의사소통 기술이 뛰어나다는 정보를 전달하고 있으므로, 앞선 내용과 대등하게 연결하는 접속 부사인 (D) Likewise가 정답이다.

PRACTICE

정답 및 해설 p.82

Questions 1-4 refer to the following e-mail.

To: Carl Lambert <carl_lambert@safehold.com>
From: Harold Beemer <hbeemer@safehold.com>
Date: October 3
Subject: Scheduling

Dear Mr. Lambert,

This is in regard to next week's schedule. -------, I am unable to work next Monday. My supervisor, Brenda Malone, approved my request for time off on Monday, October 10, last week, as I ------- my parents, who live out of town then. I am departing this Friday and returning on Monday night. I assume Ms. Malone did not inform you of this matter.
(1. and 2. mark the blanks)

-------. I would gladly exchange shifts with someone who can work in my place on Monday.
3.

Please let me know how we can rectify this situation. I can meet you anytime to discuss our -------.
4.

Regards,

Harold Beemer

1. (A) Unfortunately
(B) Sincerely
(C) Apparently
(D) Possibly

2. (A) have visited
(B) visit
(C) to visit
(D) will be visiting

3. (A) It has been a pleasure working here for you.
(B) Thank you for understanding my situation.
(C) I noticed I am not scheduled to work on Tuesday.
(D) This was the first vacation of the year for me.

4. (A) options
(B) selections
(C) conditions
(D) devices

PART 6

UNIT 05 문맥에 맞는 문장 고르기

해석 p.83

1. article (기사)

Hilltop Rentals has procured new investment funds to expand its fleet of rental cars. A spokesperson for Hilltop Rentals said that eighty small, fuel-efficient cars will be purchased. -------(1.). The changes are in response to customer feedback indicating that a wider selection was needed. Details about rental options can be found at www.hilltop-rentals.com.

(A) They vary in price depending on the parking time.
(B) Employees are pleased with the better working hours.
(C) The company will also buy ten moving vans.
(D) He has received several complaints about the cost of renting.

→ 빈칸 앞에서 연비가 좋은 소형 차량을 구입한다고 했고, 빈칸 뒤에서는 복수 명사인 the changes를 써서 그런 변화들은 고객의 의견에 따른 것이라고 했으므로, 빈칸에는 고객의 의견에 따라 실시되는 또다른 변화에 관한 정보가 나오는 것이 자연스럽다. 따라서 "회사는 10대의 이삿짐 트럭도 구입할 것이다."라는 의미의 (C)가 정답이다.

2. e-mail (이메일)

Dear Ms. Milton,

I would like to propose moving one of the copy machines from the 5th-floor employee lounge to the 3rd-floor offices. This would help to save time, as many employees have to go up several flights of stairs just to copy documents. -------(2.). It would solve the problem of the lounge being too crowded, which I have had numerous complaints about.

Sincerely,

Keisha

(A) In addition, we could free up some space.
(B) The machines with the best reviews are usually more expensive.
(C) Many people find the instruction manual confusing.
(D) We can save paper by printing on both sides.

→ 빈칸 바로 뒤의 대명사 It이 가리키는 것을 찾아야 한다. 휴게실이 너무 붐비는 문제를 해결할 수 있다고 했으므로, 빈칸에는 직원 휴게실에 있는 복사기를 치우는 것의 이점에 관한 내용이 나오는 것이 적절하다. 따라서 "또한, 우리는 일부 공간을 비울 수 있습니다."라는 의미의 (A)가 정답이다.

PRACTICE

정답 및 해설 p.83

Questions 1-4 refer to the following advertisement.

Daniels Landscaping

Daniels Landscaping -------(1.) care of properties for more than two decades. We provide a variety of landscaping services to make your home or place of business look as nice as possible. This includes cutting grass, trimming bushes, planting trees and flowers, and watering yards. -------(2.), we can provide other services related to caring for outdoor areas.

Our landscapers are all highly qualified with several years of experience each. -------(3.). The prices at Daniels Landscaping cannot be beat. Our work is -------(4.) to please, or you will get your money back. Call 555-9845 for more information.

1. (A) takes
(B) has been taking
(C) was taken
(D) took

2. (A) However
(B) In addition
(C) As a result
(D) For instance

3. (A) Fortunately, we have a large team of workers.
(B) Don't forget to check out our Web site.
(C) Thank you for your interest in us.
(D) They also work efficiently and cheerfully.

4. (A) guaranteed
(B) apparent
(C) promised
(D) surprised

Questions 131-134 refer to the following advertisement.

International Business News Report is the best source of information on business. Find out all the latest news from around the globe and be aware of various -------(131.) in the world of business. Our reporters are some of the top names in the industry. They write articles -------(132.) and provide updates whenever new information becomes available. To subscribe, visit our Web site at www.ibnr.com/subscriptions. Joining the site gets you access to our -------(133.) archives and allows you to take part in online chats with some of the leading individuals in various fields. Why wait? -------(134.).

131. (A) appeals
(B) trends
(C) subscriptions
(D) versions

132. (A) comparatively
(B) seriously
(C) progressively
(D) daily

133. (A) complete
(B) completion
(C) to complete
(D) completing

134. (A) We appreciate your continued dedication to our magazine.
(B) Let us tell you about the special sale that we are having.
(C) Your first issue will arrive in the mail by Monday morning.
(D) Subscribe today and start learning more about business.

Questions 135-138 refer to the following advertisement.

First Avenue Mechanics

Is your car's engine making strange noises? Would you like your car to run better? -------. (**135.**) Take your vehicle to First Avenue Mechanics. Our licensed mechanics will get your car running ------- (**136.**) in no time. They can also repair both minor and major problems to the body of your vehicle. You don't need to make an appointment. We're open twenty-four hours a day. So just come on down to 85 First Avenue and drop off your vehicle. We'll fix it the same day in ------- (**137.**) cases. Visit our Web site at www.firstavenuemechanics.com to see our ------- (**138.**) price list.

135. (A) Then it's time to take a closer look into your car.
(B) Each vehicle is inspected with great care.
(C) Our new cars are offered at reasonable prices.
(D) Some parts may need to be specially ordered.

136. (A) apparently
(B) fairly
(C) conveniently
(D) smoothly

137. (A) every
(B) much
(C) most
(D) their

138. (A) comprehension
(B) comprehended
(C) comprehending
(D) comprehensive

Questions 139-142 refer to the following Web site.

Nantucket Seafood: Delivery Policy

Nantucket Seafood is able to ship everywhere in the country within 48 hours. -------. **139.** Those individuals ------- **140.** live within 3 hours of our factory in Nantucket can opt for same-day courier delivery. Prices vary ------- **141.** upon the weight of the package and the distance it is traveling. All deliveries must be signed for by the recipient unless we are notified at the time the order is placed. We are not ------- **142.** for deliveries delayed due to bad weather or other unavoidable problems. For more information, please contact a customer service representative.

139. (A) All orders are packed in dry ice and shipped by express mail.
(B) More seafood options will be available in the coming weeks.
(C) Our prices are guaranteed to be the lowest in the country.
(D) That means your order should have already arrived.

140. (A) which
(B) what
(C) who
(D) they

141. (A) considering
(B) depending
(C) waiting
(D) reporting

142. (A) responding
(B) responsive
(C) responsible
(D) responsibly

Questions 143-146 refer to the following e-mail.

To: Alexandria Houston
From: Winston Pierce
Subject: Wallpaper
Date: July 5

Dear Ms. Houston,

The wallpaper your company provided for my store has been selling very well. My customers like the designs and ------- **143.** with how the wallpaper looks in their homes. ------- **144.**. As such, I would like a regular ------- **145.** of wallpaper each month.

I would also like to increase the number of designs. Currently, I have seven of your designs available, but I think fifteen would be better. Would you please send me some samples of your most popular designs? ------- **146.** I see them, I will be able to determine which ones I should carry.

Regards,

Winston Pierce

Pierce Home Furnishings

143. (A) please
(B) are pleased
(C) will please
(D) are pleasing

144. (A) My store recently added a new department.
(B) Customers are trying to buy items online.
(C) Many want me to install the wallpaper for them.
(D) They also love the low prices we charge.

145. (A) ship
(B) to ship
(C) shipment
(D) shipments

146. (A) Still
(B) Before
(C) Once
(D) However

RC

PART 7

PART 7 출제 경향 및 전략

문제 유형과 출제 경향

PART 7은 총 54문제가 출제되며, 10개의 단일 지문, 2개의 이중 지문, 3개의 삼중 지문으로 구성된다. 최근 3년간의 출제 경향을 분석해 보면, 단일 지문에서는 e-mail(이메일)의 출제 비율이 18% 정도로 가장 높고, article(기사), notice(공지), advertisement(광고) 등이 그 뒤를 잇는다. text-message chain(문자 메시지)과 online chat discussion(온라인 채팅)도 매회 1개씩 출제된다. 이중 지문과 삼중 지문에서도 e-mail(이메일)의 출제 비율이 40% 이상으로 압도적으로 높으며, Web page(웹페이지), form(양식), article(기사), advertisement(광고) 등이 그 뒤를 잇는다.

Questions 164-167 refer to the following e-mail.

정답 및 해설 p.86

To: Allison Holder
From: Clarissa Simpson
Date: March 16
Subject: Important Message

Dear Allison,

As of November 1, our company will no longer provide health insurance for any of our employees, both full time and part time. Instead, employees will be given small increases in their salaries that will enable them to acquire private health insurance of their own.

The cost of running a group policy like we currently do here at Newport Technology has increased too much in recent times and is making us lose money. The board of directors has therefore decided to make this change as a cost-cutting measure. We are planning to provide consulting services for our employees to assist them in selecting the insurance provider that will be best for them and their families.

David Schuler will be in charge of the transition. He will be providing you with weekly updates until the first of November. We plan to make an announcement regarding this change in June, so we anticipate receiving many questions from employees around that time.

Regards,

Clarissa Simpson
Newport Technology

문제 풀이 전략

보통 PART 7 단일 지문의 경우 문제를 먼저 확인한 후 지문을 읽는 것이 효과적이다. 문제에 나온 질문을 염두에 두고 읽으면 질문과 관련된 부분에 보다 집중해서 지문을 읽어내려갈 수 있으며, 따라서 지문을 읽는 시간을 단축할 수 있기 때문이다. 또한 대부분의 PART 7 문제의 단서는 지문에 순차적으로 제시되기 때문에 문제의 순서에 따라 답을 찾기 위한 단서의 위치도 짐작할 수 있다. 첫 번째 문제를 풀었다면, 두 번째 문제를 풀 때는 지문을 처음부터 검색할 필요 없이 첫 번째 문제의 단서가 나온 뒷부분만 검색해도 문제의 단서를 찾을 수 있다.

164. What is the purpose of the e-mail?

(A) To provide information
(B) To request assistance
(C) To schedule a meeting
(D) To ask for advice

주제/목적
주제, 목적을 묻는 문제는 거의 모든 지문에서 첫 번째 문제로 자주 출제되며, 주로 지문의 앞부분에서 단서를 찾을 수 있다.

165. What is suggested about Newport Technology?

(A) It plans to hire new workers in the summer.
(B) It is in the healthcare industry.
(C) It has branches in other countries.
(D) It is not currently making a profit.

추론/암시
지문에 언급된 내용에 근거하여 추론했을 때 사실과 가장 부합하는 것을 고르는 문제이다. 선택지의 내용들이 지문의 특정 부분에 국한되지 않고 여러 부분에 분산된 경우가 있으므로, 애매한 경우 선택지의 키워드를 중심으로 해당 부분을 찾아 정확히 확인해야 한다.

166. According to Ms. Simpson, what will Mr. Schuler do?

(A) Determine employees' salary increases
(B) Work together with the board of directors
(C) Provide Ms. Holder with updates
(D) Find new insurance providers for employees

세부 사항
PART 7에서 가장 많이 출제되는 질문 유형으로서, Who(누가), What(무엇을), Where(어디서), When(언제), How(어떻게), Why(왜)로 시작하여 세부적인 내용을 묻는다.

167. The word "transition" in paragraph 3, line 1, is closest in meaning to

(A) development
(B) approach
(C) change
(D) revision

동의어 찾기
지문에 나온 특정 단어와 의미상 가장 유사한 단어를 찾는 질문 유형으로서, 단어의 사전적인 의미를 묻는 것이 아니라 문맥상 의미를 묻는다.

UNIT 01 주제/목적

문제 풀이 전략

주제/목적을 묻는 문제는 첫 번째 문제로 자주 출제된다. 질문을 통해 주제/목적 문제라는 것을 확인했다면 지문을 보고 글의 주제/목적을 파악한다. 주제/목적 문제는 대부분의 경우 제목이나 지문의 앞부분에 단서가 나오는데, 그 내용을 정확히 파악한 후 가장 적절한 선택지를 선택한다.

질문 유형

What is the article **mainly about**? 기사는 주로 무엇에 관한 것인가? [주제]

What is being **advertised**? 무엇이 광고되고 있는가? [주제]

What is the **purpose** of the e-mail? 이메일의 목적은 무엇인가? [목적]

대표 유형 맛보기

e-mail (이메일)

해석 p.86

Dear Mr. Douglas,

It has been more than six months since you have visited us for a routine checkup. You can make an appointment to have your teeth cleaned and checked for cavities by clicking here. We have five dentists on staff, and all of them are ready to assist you. Should you have a particular dentist you prefer, you can indicate that when you make your appointment.

Sincerely,

Tina Gooden
White Teeth Clinic

이메일을 보낸 목적을 묻는 문제이며, 이메일이나 편지를 보낸 목적은 보통은 문두에 드러난다. Mr. Douglas가 정기 검진을 받은 지 6개월 이상의 시간이 지났다는 것을 알리는 이메일 내용이다.

Q What is the main purpose of the e-mail?

(A) To recommend a new location
(B) To provide a reminder
(C) To promote a new service
(D) To confirm a booking

검진을 받아야 한다는 것을 상기시켜 주고 있으므로 (B)가 정답이다. 토익에서 reminder는 주로 어떤 내용을 상기시켜 주는 것 또는 그 내용을 의미한다.

PRACTICE

정답 및 해설 p.86

Questions 1-3 refer to the following press release.

FOR IMMEDIATE RELEASE

Porterhouse Manufacturing to Conduct Product Demonstration

Porterhouse Manufacturing is one of the world's leading manufacturers of advanced machinery. Today, the company announced that it will be holding a product demonstration for a machine that its engineers have just completed and that the company intends to market in winter. The event will take place at the company's headquarters in Atlanta at 3:00 P.M. on Monday, October 3. The product being demonstrated is the newest automobile engine by the company. This engine is set to revolutionize the automobile industry as it is 35% more efficient than any other engine currently available.

Reporters and news broadcasters interested in attending the event in person must register in advance. To do so, contact company public relations employee Gregory Frye at 555-2871 during regular business hours. Individuals with podcasts and blogs and an interest in automobile technology are invited to attend as well. Jeremy Smith, the lead engineer for the project, will be available to answer questions following the demonstration. Attendees will be permitted to take pictures and videos.

1. What is the purpose of the press release?

(A) To inform investors of a product release
(B) To publicize a company's updated service
(C) To give details on how to acquire a company's product
(D) To provide information about a product demonstration

2. How can people register for the event?

(A) By visiting a blog that reports on technology
(B) By calling an employee of Porterhouse Manufacturing
(C) By signing up on the Porterhouse Manufacturing Web page
(D) By speaking with a reporter who will cover the event

3. What is indicated about the upcoming event?

(A) It requires the payment of a fee to attend.
(B) It will take place on a weekend.
(C) Attendees will be allowed to ask questions.
(D) A video will be shown to the attendees.

UNIT 02 NOT / True

문제 풀이 전략

지문의 내용과 일치하거나 일치하지 않는 선택지를 찾는 문제로서, 문제를 풀기 위해 지문을 전반적으로 검색하여 선택지와 대조해야 하며, 단서가 순차적으로 제시되지 않는 경우가 종종 있기 때문에 난이도가 가장 높은 편이다. NOT / True 문제는 '선택지 (A) → 지문 확인, 선택지 (B) → 지문 확인, 선택지 (C)..., 선택지 (D)...'와 같은 과정을 거쳐 각각의 선택지에 해당하는 부분을 지문에서 찾아 대조해가며 답을 찾아야 한다.

질문 유형

What is **NOT mentioned** as a feature of the program? 프로그램의 특징으로 언급되지 않은 것은 무엇인가?

What is **true** about the job? 일자리에 대해 사실인 것은 무엇인가?

What is **indicated** about the contest? 대회에 대해 언급된 것은 무엇인가?

대표 유형 맛보기

advertisement (광고)

해석 p.87

Greenbrier Writing Workshop, Meeting 1
1:00–3:00 P.M.
Greenbrier Public Library
April 11

Would you like to write like a professional? Do you have great ideas for stories but don't know how to put them into words? Then the upcoming workshop hosted by Allison Herbst is for you. Ms. Herbst has published more than ten novels and also teaches at Greenbrier Community College.

To register and to see the complete schedule for the entire series, go to www.greenbrierlibrary.org. All workshops are free, but advance registration is a must. Ms. Herbst will answer questions after the workshop concludes.

> 워크숍을 알리는 광고 지문이며, 시간, 날짜, 사람, 대학교 등의 여러 정보가 나온다. 선택지 (A)는 지문의 All workshops are free와 내용상 상충되므로 소거하고, (B)는 Greenbrier Public Library라는 구체적 장소가 등장하므로 소거한다. (D)는 지문에 나오는 Greenbrier Community College가 워크숍을 주관한다는 내용이 없으므로 소거한다.

Q What is indicated about the workshop?

(A) People must pay to attend it.
(B) It will take place online.
(C) It will be led by an author.
(D) A college is hosting it.

> 워크숍은 Allison Herbst가 주관하는데, Allison Herbst는 여러 권의 소설책을 출간한 작가이므로, 작가가 워크숍을 이끌 것이라는 (C)가 정답이다.

PRACTICE

정답 및 해설 p.87

Questions 1-3 refer to the following information.

Silverwood Botanical Garden Pass

Silverwood Botanical Garden is the largest in the entire state. Covering more than 200 acres, the garden features not only trees, flowers, and plants native to the Southeast but also a wide variety of nonnative species, including those from the tropics. Visitors to the garden can enjoy hiking through the wooded areas, picnicking by our five ponds, and seeing some of the wildlife that inhabits the area.

A Silverwood Botanical Garden pass costs only $50 per year and covers an entire family of four. It permits daily access to the garden as well as free parking. Your contribution will allow us to maintain the plants in the garden and to acquire new ones.

A pass may be purchased at the ticket office or online at www.silverwoodbg.org. Please note that special discounts on food or other products sold at the stores near the ticket office are not available.

1. Which activity is mentioned in the information?

(A) Hiking
(B) Swimming
(C) Hunting
(D) Camping

2. What is indicated about the Silverwood Botanical Garden?

(A) It only has plants from the local area.
(B) It relies solely on donations from its members.
(C) It allows guests to go fishing in the ponds.
(D) It is larger than other nearby botanical gardens.

3. What is a benefit of a Silverwood Botanical Garden pass?

(A) Lower prices on food
(B) Guided tours of the garden
(C) Discounts on souvenirs
(D) Complimentary parking

UNIT 03 추론/암시

문제 풀이 전략

지문에 언급된 내용을 바탕으로 그 안에 숨겨진 의미를 파악하여 이를 가장 잘 표현한 선택지를 고르는 문제이다. 선택지는 지문에 나온 표현이 다시 나오거나 유사한 표현으로 패러프레이징되어 제시되는데, 패러프레이징의 난이도가 높은 경우에는 오답을 하나씩 소거해 가면서 정답을 찾는 것이 효율적이다. 질문에 키워드가 있다면 지문에서 키워드를 검색하면 되지만, 그렇지 않은 경우 지문을 읽어 내려가며 선택지 내용을 하나하나 대조해야 한다. 지문이 길고 복잡한 경우 NOT/True 문제처럼 '선택지 (A) 확인 → 지문 확인 → 선택지 (B) 확인 → 지문 확인'과 같은 과정으로 문제를 푸는 것이 시간 절약에 효과적이다.

질문 유형

Who **mostly likely** is Mr. Martin? Mr. Martin은 누구이겠는가?

What is **suggested** about Ms. Barrett? Ms. Barrett에 대해 암시된 것은 무엇인가?

Where would the notice **most likely** appear? 공지는 어디에 나타나겠는가?

대표 유형 맛보기

text-message chain (문자 메시지)

해석 p.88

Emily Hudson (2:24 P.M.)
David, the budget reports for September were due yesterday. I'm still waiting for yours, though.

David Weber (2:25 P.M.)
I'm sorry. I just returned from a trip to Helsinki. I'm working on it now.

Emily Hudson (2:26 P.M.)
I didn't know you were traveling abroad. I hope your trip was successful. Do you think your department went over budget?

David Weber (2:27 P.M.)
I'll let you know by the end of the day.

Emily Hudson (2:28 P.M.)
Thanks. I need to finish my final report by Friday, but I can't do that until I get your numbers.

질문의 키워드인 Ms. Hudson으로 지문을 검색한다. Ms. Hudson은 Emily Hudson이며, 따라서 Emily Hudson이 한 말에서 I(나)로 시작하는 문장에서 정답의 단서가 나오거나, 문자 메시지의 상대방인 David Weber가 한 말에서 you(당신)로 시작하는 문장에 단서가 나올 수 있다.

Q What can be inferred about Ms. Hudson?

(A) She will take a business trip to Helsinki.
(B) She knew Mr. Weber was away from the office.
(C) She has not completed her own report yet.
(D) She will meet her supervisor on Friday.

Emily Hudson이 마지막으로 한 말을 보면 금요일까지 자신의 최종 보고서를 끝내야 한다고 했으므로 아직 보고서를 끝마치지 못한 것을 알 수 있다. 문두에 나오는 budget reports는 각 부서에서 Emily Hudson에게 제출한 것이므로 질문과 관련이 없다.

PRACTICE

정답 및 해설 p.88

Questions 1-3 refer to the following online chat discussion.

Bill Hagler (2:03 P.M.)	Hello, everyone. How is the work on the property going? Are we going to finish on time? I'd really like to be able to open on March 1.
Susan Denton (2:06 P.M.)	Everything is looking good, Bill. The kitchen is almost entirely installed. The tables and chairs are going to arrive tomorrow. We'll need someone to help set them up.
Dallas Blair (2:08 P.M.)	Chris and I can do that, Susan. Just let me know what time I should be there.
Susan Denton (2:09 P.M.)	Thanks, Dallas. I really appreciate your being willing to work on your day off.
Dallas Blair (2:10 P.M.)	Oh, I spoke with the owner of the shop right next to ours. He said that he's planning to retire in the next couple of months.
Bill Hagler (2:11 P.M.)	Is his shop going to be available for rent?
Dallas Blair (2:12 P.M.)	That's what he said. We should probably check into it. It might be possible to connect the two places. That would give us more space, so we could expand the dining room.
Susan Denton (2:13 P.M.)	I'll get in touch with a real estate agent.
Bill Hagler (2:14 P.M.)	Sounds great, Susan.

1. Where do the writers most likely work?

(A) At a restaurant
(B) At a real estate agency
(C) At a supermarket
(D) At a bakery

2. What is Mr. Hagler concerned about?

(A) Paying for the installation of some equipment
(B) Opening an establishment by a certain date
(C) Finding workers willing to set up some tables
(D) Getting along with the shopkeeper next door

3. At 2:13 P.M., why does Ms. Denton write, "I'll get in touch with a real estate agent"?

(A) To say she will ask about lowering the monthly rent
(B) To indicate she can sign a rental agreement
(C) To state she needs to find a new apartment
(D) To offer to check on an available property

UNIT 04 세부 사항

문제 풀이 전략

PART 7에서 가장 많이 출제되는 질문 유형으로서, Who(누가), What(무엇을), Where(어디서), When(언제), How(어떻게), Why(왜)로 시작하여 세부적인 내용을 묻는다. 세부 사항 문제는 질문의 키워드로 지문을 검색해야 하는데, 주로 사람 이름이나 업체명과 같은 명사가 키워드가 되지만, 동사(구)도 키워드가 될 수 있다. 지문에서 키워드와 관련 있는 부분을 찾았다면 해당 문장이나 바로 앞뒤의 내용을 확인한 후 선택지를 확인한다.

질문 유형

Who is Mr. McClellan? Mr. McClellan은 누구인가?

What does Cregar sell? Cregar는 무엇을 판매하는가?

Why did Ms. Cairns send the memo? Ms. Cairns는 왜 회람을 보냈는가?

How should Mr. Thurman respond to the request? Mr. Thurman은 어떻게 요청에 답해야 하는가?

대표 유형 맛보기

article (기사)

해석 p.89

Stamford Daily

June 28—The city of Stamford has declared that the house located at 86 Bellevue Drive is a historical structure. The home, currently owned by Mark Whitman, was constructed in 1772. It has been the ancestral home of the Whitman family since that time. Mayor Thomas Whittaker stated the home is now protected and cannot be torn down. Mr. Whitman no longer lives in the house but intends to refurbish it and will provide tours for those interested in learning about life in colonial times. According to Mr. Whitman, many furnishings are from the time when the house was built.

문제의 키워드는 Whitman, house on Bellevue Drive 등이며, 키워드를 확인했다면 지문에서 키워드를 빠르게 검색하여 정답의 단서를 찾는다.

Q What does Mr. Whitman plan to do with the house on Bellevue Drive?

(A) Renovate it so that he can live in it
(B) Sell it to the city of Stamford
(C) Let people visit it to look at it
(D) Transform it into a furniture museum

Mr. Whitman은 더 이상 the house on Bellevue Drive에 살고 있지 않지만, 그곳을 새로 단장해 사람들에게 투어를 제공할 것이라고 했으므로 (C)가 정답이다.

PRACTICE

정답 및 해설 p.89

Questions 1-3 refer to the following e-mail.

To:	All Dearborn Finance Employees
From:	Jefferson Grant, CEO
Date:	July 27
Subject:	David Stillman

To all Dearborn Finance employees,

I regret to inform you that David Stillman has informed me he is stepping down from his position here at Dearborn Finance. Mr. Stillman has worked as our chief researcher for more than twelve years. He has decided to take a position near his hometown so that he can help care for his elderly parents. Please be sure to let David know how much you valued his time here and wish him good luck.

Due to David's departure, we need to fill his job as soon as possible. Anyone interested in the research position should send an e-mail to Susan Westmoreland at susan@dearbornfinance.com. Be sure to explain why you are qualified for the position and attach a copy of your résumé as well.

David has agreed to help train his replacement, so we are hoping to fill the position within the next three weeks so that he can work with the new employee for a few weeks after that.

Sincerely,

Jefferson Grant
CEO
Dearborn Finance

1. What is one purpose of the e-mail?

(A) To announce a job opportunity
(B) To request volunteers
(C) To schedule a company outing
(D) To describe a change in the company's structure

2. What is Mr. Stillman doing?

(A) Getting transferred to the company's head office
(B) Returning to school to get a degree
(C) Retiring to spend time with his family
(D) Resigning to take another position

3. What is NOT indicated about Mr. Stillman?

(A) He will leave Dearborn Finance in three weeks.
(B) He is a lead researcher of the company.
(C) He has worked at Dearborn Finance for more than a decade.
(D) He is willing to train another employee.

UNIT 05 문장 삽입

문제 풀이 전략

주어진 문장이 들어가기에 가장 적절한 위치를 찾는 문제로서, 해당 지문의 마지막 문제로 출제된다. 먼저 질문에서 따옴표로 묶인 문장을 정확히 해석한 후 문맥에 맞는 위치를 찾아야 하며, 주어진 문장에 it, this와 같은 대명사가 있다면 그것이 가리키는 것이 나온 문장의 뒤가 적절한 위치가 된다. additionally(또한), alternatively(그 대신에)와 같은 접속 부사가 있다면 앞 문장과의 맥락을 파악하여 문제를 푼다.

질문 유형

In which of the positions marked [1], [2], [3], and [4] does the following sentence best belong?
"It took a while for the concept to catch on."

[1], [2], [3], [4]로 표시된 위치 중 다음 문장이 들어가기에 가장 적절한 곳은?
"그 개념이 인기를 얻는 데는 다소의 시간이 걸렸다."

대표 유형 맛보기

article (기사)

해석 p.89

PENSACOLA (April 19)—Atlantic Shipping made a shocking announcement last night. —[1]—. The company stated that CEO Kevin Davenport would be stepping down immediately. Mr. Davenport had just started working at Atlantic in March, so his sudden decision to resign has left everyone surprised. —[2]—. Melissa Samuels, a company spokesperson, said that Bradley Wellman, the company's vice president of operations, would act as the interim CEO until a permanent replacement could be found. —[3]—. She did not provide a timeline for when the company expects to have a new leader. —[4]—.

주어진 문장을 해석하면 "그가 떠나는 이유에 대해서는 아무런 발표도 없었다."이며, 따라서 누군가가 떠나기로 했다는 내용 뒤에 주어진 문장이 들어갈 수 있다.

Q In which of the positions marked [1], [2], [3], and [4] does the following sentence best belong?
"No announcement regarding the reason for his departure was given."

(A) [1]
(B) [2]
(C) [3]
(D) [4]

주어진 문장의 키워드를 먼저 파악해야 한다. 키워드는 his departure(그의 사임)이며, 지문에 그와 관련된 내용이 있는지 빠르게 탐색한다. resign이 departure와 같은 의미이므로, resign이 있는 문장의 주변에 있는 [2]부터 주어진 문장을 대입해 본다.

PRACTICE

정답 및 해설 p.90

Questions 1-3 refer to the following article.

NORFOLK (September 4)—A new restaurant has just opened in Norfolk, and it is rapidly becoming one of the city's most popular eateries. The name of the establishment is Kirk's Diner. Owned by Stephanie Kirk, the restaurant specializes in Italian and Spanish food. —[1]—.

Almost all of the food served at the restaurant comes from local farmers, something which Ms. Kirk is very proud of. —[2]—. "The Norfolk area produces lots of great food, and I'm pleased that my restaurant can serve it to our customers," she said.

Ms. Kirk is not only the owner but also the head chef. She studied culinary arts at the Milan Cooking School in Italy. Later, she worked as a chef in Europe in London, Paris, and Athens. —[3]—. She came back home to Norfolk last year, where she worked at Italian Delights. Now, she has her own restaurant. —[4]—. Judging from the long waits for tables, it is going to be a successful place.

1. What is the purpose of the article?

(A) To review a meal at a restaurant
(B) To describe a business's grand opening
(C) To promote a new product
(D) To introduce a dining establishment

2. What is stated about Ms. Kirk?

(A) She is the owner of a restaurant.
(B) She speaks Italian and Spanish.
(C) She has a farm in Norfolk.
(D) She studied cooking in London.

3. In which of the positions marked [1], [2], [3], and [4] does the following sentence best belong?
"She spent more than twenty years living abroad."

(A) [1]
(B) [2]
(C) [3]
(D) [4]

UNIT 06 동의어 찾기

문제 풀이 전략

먼저 질문에서 따옴표로 묶인 단어를 지문에서 찾는다. 이메일의 수신인/발신인/날짜/제목과 기사나 광고의 제목 등은 단락(paragraph)으로 간주하지 않으므로 주의한다. 해당 단어가 지문에서 구동사나 콜로케이션의 일부라면 바로 앞뒤 단어만 확인해도 답을 찾을 수 있지만, 그렇지 않다면 단어가 속한 문장이나 절을 해석한 후 선택지를 확인하거나, 그마저도 어렵다면 선택지들을 문장에 하나씩 대입하여 해석해 본다.

질문 유형

질문 뒤에 물음표가 없는 것이 특징이며, 다중 지문의 경우 앞에 해당 지문의 종류가 명시된다.

[단일 지문] The word "measure" in paragraph 1, line 4, is closest in meaning to
첫 번째 단락 네 번째 줄의 "measure"와 의미상 가장 가까운 것은?

[다중 지문] **In the memo**, the word "courtesy" in paragraph 2, line 3, is closest in meaning to
회람에서 두 번째 단락 세 번째 줄의 "courtesy"와 의미상 가장 가까운 것은?

대표 유형 맛보기

Web page (웹페이지)

해석 p.90

Thank you for registering to become a member of the online shopping club at Lux Warehouse. All of our members receive automatic 10% discounts on all purchases as well as free express shipping. For a complete list of benefits, click here. Be sure to check your e-mail every Sunday night, as you will receive a members-only special offer then. Members are also frequently asked to grade new products and may receive requests to complete customer satisfaction surveys. We want to ensure our most loyal customers are happy with our service.

grade의 앞뒤를 확인하면, new products를 목적어로 취하는 동사라는 것을 알 수 있다. 같은 문장 내의 또다른 동사구인 complete customer satisfaction surveys (고객 만족도 설문 조사를 하다)를 통해 유추해 보면, grade new products는 '신제품을 평가하거나 등급을 매기다'라는 의미임을 유추할 수 있다.

Q The word "grade" in line 7 is closest in meaning to

(A) purchase
(B) sample
(C) rate
(D) consider

grade와 의미가 가장 비슷한 (C) rate를 정답으로 선택한다.

PRACTICE

정답 및 해설 p.90

Questions 1-3 refer to the following advertisement.

CHAMBERLIN MARKETING

Many small businesses have outstanding products and services they would like to sell. However, their owners have neither the time nor the ability to market these goods and services. Fortunately, Chamberlin Marketing can handle all of their needs.

Chamberlin Marketing has been in business for thirty-five years. We have provided assistance to more than 500 small businesses during that time. We have assisted companies in marketing themselves locally, nationwide, and internationally. Our employees have experience in numerous markets, and each of them is familiar with at least one foreign language.

If you would like a one-hour consultation, please call us at 555-0271 during regular business hours. Tell us about your company, and we'll come up with a preliminary marketing plan at no cost to you. There's no obligation to use our services. But if you do, you won't regret it.

1. The word "handle" in paragraph 1, line 3, is closest in meaning to

(A) take care of
(B) think about
(C) promote
(D) reveal

2. What is indicated about Chamberlin Marketing?

(A) It focuses on marketing products online.
(B) It can promote goods in foreign countries.
(C) It was established in the past decade.
(D) It has more than 500 employees.

3. What is Chamberlin Marketing offering to small business owners?

(A) A discount on making a Web page
(B) Reduced rates
(C) A free consultation
(D) A cash refund

UNIT 07 이중 지문

문제 풀이 전략

176~185번까지 10문제가 출제되며, 지문당 5문제가 출제된다. 5문제 중 4문제는 주제/목적, NOT/True, 추론/암시, 세부 사항, 동의어 찾기 문제 등으로 구성되며, 1문제는 두 지문 모두에서 정답의 단서를 찾아야 하는 연계 문제로 구성된다. 문장 삽입 문제는 출제되지 않는다. 주제/목적 문제는 지문의 앞부분을 확인하면 정답의 단서를 찾을 가능성이 높고, 동의어 찾기 문제 또한 해당 문장만 정확히 해석하면 정답을 찾을 가능성이 높다. 그러므로 문제 풀이 시간이 부족하다면 이 두 가지 유형의 문제만이라도 반드시 맞춘다는 각오로 임해야 한다. 두 개의 지문 모두에서 단서를 찾아야 하는 연계 문제를 가장 손쉽게 해결할 수 있는 방법은 숫자에 집중하는 것이다. 한 지문에서 가격, 수량, 시간, 날짜 등을 나타내는 숫자가 나온다면 다른 지문에서 그 숫자와 관련된 단서를 찾을 가능성이 높다.

대표 유형 맛보기

Questions 1-5 refer to the following article and label.

해석 p.91

Calico Crackers to Change Labels

LOS ANGELES (September 5)—Calico Crackers, the popular whole-wheat snack food, has announced plans to change its product labels. The packaging will now provide pairing suggestions, such as which variety of cheese goes best with each Calico Crackers flavor. The company's aim is to get customers to try the crackers with other foods instead of just on their own.

The move is intended to help Calico Crackers regain market share after Crispy Dreams overtook the company as the top snack cracker on the market. The heavy competition has prompted Calico Crackers officials to look for new ways to promote the product.

"Calico Crackers are a great snack when you're on the go," said company spokesperson Jocelyn Watkins. "But when you're at home, you can create more elaborate recipes and food combinations with our crackers. All the labels we make after September 25 will have these added ideas, and we would love to hear about our customers' own creations on our social media platforms."

CALICO CRACKERS

Herb and Garlic Flavor

100g

Packaged in Toronto, Canada

Pairing Suggestion: Why not try these crackers with cream cheese or topped with sun-dried tomatoes?

Visit www.calicocrackers.com to find step-by-step video recipes of more dishes you can make with Calico Crackers!

1. According to the article, what does Calico Crackers hope to do for customers?
(A) Reduce the amount of packaging in their purchases
(B) Make it easier for those with allergies to check the ingredients
(C) Inspire them to try their product with new foods
(D) Quickly determine which cracker flavor they may like

첫 번째 문제는 주로 첫 번째 지문의 앞부분에서 단서를 찾을 수 있으며, 질문에서 'According to the article'과 같이 지문이 지정되었다면 해당 지문을 검색하면 된다. "The company's aim is to get customers to try the crackers with other foods"에 정답의 단서가 나온다.

2. What does the article suggest about Crispy Dreams?
(A) It has recently started producing snacks.
(B) It sells more goods than Calico Crackers.
(C) It is currently based in Los Angeles.
(D) It is the cheapest brand on the market.

Crispy Dreams를 키워드로 기사 지문을 검색하면 "Crispy Dreams overtook the company as the top snack cracker on the market."이라는 단서를 찾을 수 있다.

3. In the article, the word "prompted" in paragraph 2, line 2, is closest in meaning to
(A) assisted
(B) caused
(C) rushed
(D) reminded

"The heavy competition has prompted Calico Crackers officials to look for new ways to promote the product."에서 동사 prompted는 Calico Crackers officials로 하여금 어떤 행동을 하도록 촉발했다는 의미이다.

4. What is suggested about the package's label?
(A) It was made in a new food factory.
(B) Its weight was listed incorrectly.
(C) It is for a newly released product.
(D) It was printed after September 25.

연계 문제로서, 질문의 label을 키워드로 지문을 검색하되 숫자에 집중한다. 첫 번째 지문에서 9월 25일 이후에는 라벨에 음식 페어링 정보가 추가된다고 했는데, 두 번째 지문에서 페어링 제안을 찾을 수 있다.

5. According to the label, what can customers do on a Web site?
(A) Suggest new cracker flavors
(B) Write product recipe reviews
(C) Watch instructional videos
(D) Download a coupon

마지막 문제는 주로 마지막 지문의 뒷부분에서 단서를 찾을 수 있다. 두 번째 지문의 "Visit ~ with Calico Crackers!"에서 웹사이트에서 단계별 동영상 레시피를 찾을 수 있다고 했다.

PRACTICE

Questions 1-5 refer to the following e-mail and report.

E-Mail

To: information@jasperrealty.com
From: samjackson@hoffmanassociates.com
Date: August 18
Subject: Office Space

To Whom It May Concern,

My firm has plans to open a small branch office in Lincoln. One of my colleagues suggested that I contact your agency to assist in the process of finding an acceptable office.

The branch office will have ten people working there. The space needs a minimum of six individual offices as well as an open workspace that can accommodate the other employees. The building needs to be within a couple of blocks of a bus stop since that is how many of the employees commute to work. It would be ideal if there's a parking lot for clients to park in, but it's not a must. Being close to local restaurants and coffee shops would be ideal as well.

Please let me know what properties are available that fit my criteria. I would also like to know roughly how much the utilities will cost on a monthly basis. We would like to open the office within two months, so we need to find a place soon. We can sign a two-year lease as well.

Sam Jackson
Hoffman Associates

Possible Office Spaces for Hoffman Associates

Prepared by Alice Moreno

88 Rhubarb Avenue
Four individual offices and a large open space for six people. Free parking in the basement. Right in front of a bus stop.

192 Catfish Lane
Seven individual offices and one open space for five people. Electricity provided by solar power. One block away from a bus stop and the train station.

27 Hamilton Boulevard
Two open spaces for twelve people. No individual offices. Daycare center located in the same building. Four blocks away from a bus stop. Public parking lot nearby.

64 Maple Street
Brand-new building. Twelve individual offices. Restaurants located in the basement. Great view of the seafront. Near a bus stop.

1. In the e-mail, the word "accommodate" in paragraph 2, line 2, is closest in meaning to
   (A) locate
   (B) approve
   (C) fit
   (D) satisfy

2. What does Mr. Jackson request?
   (A) The prices of utilities
   (B) A sample contract
   (C) A map of the local region
   (D) Telephone numbers of office owners

3. What information about the office spaces is NOT provided?
   (A) The nearby facilities
   (B) The number of individual offices
   (C) The location of public transportation
   (D) The monthly rent

4. According to the report, what is true about the office space located on Hamilton Boulevard?
   (A) It has twelve individual offices.
   (B) There is enough room for twelve people.
   (C) It is close to the bus station.
   (D) There is no parking lot close to it.

5. Which office space would Mr. Jackson most likely be interested in?
   (A) 88 Rhubarb Avenue
   (B) 192 Catfish Lane
   (C) 27 Hamilton Boulevard
   (D) 64 Maple Street

UNIT 08 삼중 지문

문제 풀이 전략

186~200번까지 15문제가 출제되며, 지문당 5문제가 출제된다. 이중 지문에서는 5문제 중 1문제가 연계 문제로 출제되지만, 삼중 지문에서는 5문제 중 2문제가 연계 문제로 출제된다. 문장 삽입 문제와 동의어 찾기 문제는 출제되지 않는다. 이중 지문의 문제 풀이 전략과 마찬가지로, 삼중 지문에서도 주제/목적 문제는 놓치지 말아야 한다.

대표 유형 맛보기

Questions 1-5 refer to the following Web page, form, and e-mail.

해석 p.93

International Association of Biomedical Engineers (IABE)

Fifteenth Annual Conference

Location: Bayside Hotel, Athens, Greece
Date: September 22—25
Theme: New Trends in Biomedical Engineering

Please note the following important dates:
* Proposal submissions – March 1
* Proposal acceptance – May 1
* Complete paper submissions – June 30

All proposals should be between 400 and 500 words and should be submitted online at our Web site at www.iabe.org/proposals. Please follow the instructions on the Web site regarding how to write the proposal.

Registration for the conference begins on June 1. The fee includes a conference T-shirt, refreshments, the luncheon, attendance at all sessions, and a copy of all papers. Please register at www.iabe.org/registration.

Attendee — $500 / early registration before June 20
Attendee — $600 / registration after June 20
Presenter — $400
Student — $300

https://www.iabe.org/registration

International Association of Biomedical Engineers
Fifteenth Annual Conference Registration

Name: Susanna Madsen
Company: Klein Pharmaceuticals
Area of Interest: Pharmaceutical Development
Telephone Number: 805-555-8573
E-mail: smadsen@klein.com
Registration Fee: $500

To: Susanna Madsen
From: Sunshine Hotel
Date: August 14
Subject: RE: Questions

Dear Ms. Madsen,

We are looking forward to having you as a guest here next month. To respond to your questions, the hotel is a five-minute walk from the sea. You will find all kinds of places to shop and to eat near the hotel. We are also located right across the street from the conference you are attending. You can therefore walk there with ease. If you have any other questions, please let me know.

Sincerely,

Ioannis Papadopoulos
Customer Service Representative
Sunshine Hotel

1. According to the Web page, what is true about the conference?

(A) A lunch event will be held during it.
(B) It is open only to IABE members.
(C) Some people can attend it for free.
(D) It will last for one week.

NOT/True 문제는 단서가 순차적으로 제시되지 않는 경우가 종종 있다. 첫 번째 지문 중반부의 "The fee includes ~ all papers."에서 정답의 단서를 찾을 수 있다.

2. When will individuals most likely be notified whether their proposals have been accepted?

(A) On March 1
(B) On May 1
(C) On June 1
(D) On June 30

지문에서 여러 개의 날짜가 제시된 부분을 집중적으로 검색한다.

3. What is suggested about Ms. Madsen?

(A) She is not a member of the IABE.
(B) She is attending the conference for a second time.
(C) She signed up for the conference before June 20.
(D) She is going to present a paper at the conference.

연계 문제로서 Madsen을 키워드로 지문을 검색하면 두 번째 지문에서 Susanna Madsen의 등록비가 500달러라는 것을 알 수 있다. 다시 $500을 키워드로 다른 지문을 검색하면 정답의 단서를 찾을 수 있다.

4. Why did Mr. Papadopoulos send the e-mail?

(A) To confirm a room reservation
(B) To offer a special discount
(C) To respond to some inquiries
(D) To change the date of a booking

Papadopoulos를 키워드로 지문을 검색하면 Ioannis Papadopoulos는 세 번째 지문의 발신인으로서 Susanna Madsen의 질문에 답하기 위해 이메일을 썼다는 것을 알 수 있다.

5. What is indicated about the Sunshine Hotel?

(A) It is located close to the Bayside Hotel.
(B) It recently underwent renovations.
(C) It offers a discount to conference attendees.
(D) It does not have any vacancies in September.

연계 문제로서 먼저 Sunshine Hotel을 키워드로 지문을 검색하여 단서를 확인하고, 다시 그 단서를 키워드로 다른 지문을 검색하는 방법으로 문제를 푼다.

PART 7

PRACTICE

Questions 1-5 refer to the following Web page and e-mails.

https://www.bostontours.com/tours

Boston Tours has over thirty-three years of experience providing tours of the city and the surrounding area. Every tour is led by a guide who is a native of the area and has a strong familiarity with all of the most notable places to see in Boston. We offer four tours for people to choose from.

Package 1 A half-day tour of downtown Boston and an aquarium visit - $50/person
Package 2 A half-day tour of Boston with a focus on shopping downtown - $40/person
Package 3 A one-day tour of Boston and Cambridge with visits to Harvard, MIT, the aquarium, and Beacon Hill - $80/person
Package 4 A one-day tour of Boston and the surrounding area that includes visits to historical sites related to the American Revolution $100/person

For more information or to arrange a booking, send an e-mail to information@bostontours.com.

To: information@bostontours.com
From: Marcus Cartwright <marcus_c@prometheus.com>
Date: June 11
Subject: Tour

Hello,

I'm planning a family trip to New England this summer, and your company was recommended by a friend who has used your services before. She said your guides are knowledgeable and the tour she went on was entertaining and educational.

We're going to be in the Boston area from June 28 to July 1. I'd prefer to take a tour on the first day we're there. But if there are no available spots on that day, the next day is fine with us. There are five of us in my family. My wife and three children will be accompanying me. The children love history, so we hope you have a tour that can accommodate us.

Regards,

Marcus Cartwright

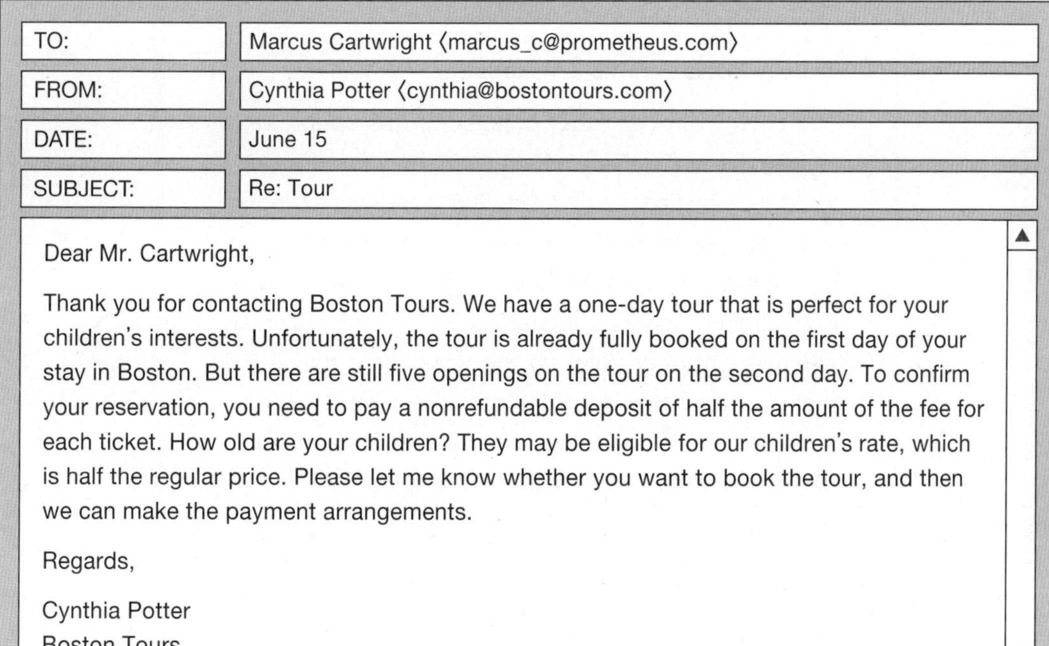

TO:	Marcus Cartwright 〈marcus_c@prometheus.com〉
FROM:	Cynthia Potter 〈cynthia@bostontours.com〉
DATE:	June 15
SUBJECT:	Re: Tour

Dear Mr. Cartwright,

Thank you for contacting Boston Tours. We have a one-day tour that is perfect for your children's interests. Unfortunately, the tour is already fully booked on the first day of your stay in Boston. But there are still five openings on the tour on the second day. To confirm your reservation, you need to pay a nonrefundable deposit of half the amount of the fee for each ticket. How old are your children? They may be eligible for our children's rate, which is half the regular price. Please let me know whether you want to book the tour, and then we can make the payment arrangements.

Regards,

Cynthia Potter
Boston Tours

1. What does the Web page indicate about Boston Tours?

(A) It hires guides that can speak foreign languages.
(B) It recently started giving tours of Boston.
(C) It accepts both cash and credit card payments.
(D) It has been in business for more than three decades.

2. What is indicated about Mr. Cartwright?

(A) He grew up in the Boston area.
(B) He will be traveling with his family.
(C) He is visiting Boston for the first time.
(D) He will spend one week in Boston.

3. Which package will Mr. Cartwright most likely select?

(A) Package 1
(B) Package 2
(C) Package 3
(D) Package 4

4. When most likely will Mr. Cartwright go on a tour?

(A) On June 15
(B) On June 28
(C) On June 29
(D) On July 1

5. What does Ms. Potter request from Mr. Cartwright?

(A) His credit card information
(B) The names of his family members
(C) The place where he should be picked up
(D) The ages of his children

Questions 147-148 refer to the following notice.

Asbury Road Parking Lot Update

The recent poor weather conditions this spring have caused the renovation work on the Asbury Road parking lot to be significantly delayed. The work was expected to be completed by May 1. However, construction crews were unable to access the site during the snowy weather. Furthermore, some structural issues were identified by engineers, further delaying the work. As a result, the project is now scheduled for completion by August 15. Anyone who has questions is welcome to contact Russell Mayer at Vanderbilt Construction at 802-555-9361.

147. What is the purpose of the notice?

(A) To report on recent weather conditions
(B) To explain a change in some plans
(C) To apologize for missing a deadline
(D) To provide details on work to be done

148. What is indicated about the Asbury Road parking lot project?

(A) It is not going to be finished on time.
(B) It will expand the size of the parking lot.
(C) It will be complete in May.
(D) It is expected to go over its budget.

Questions 149-151 refer to the following form.

Purchase Request Form

Employee Name: Kenneth Dumont
Request Date: November 11
Department: IT
E-mail: kdumont@dmr.com

Item	Vendor	Quantity
Syntax 4000 Digital Camera	MTR Technology	1
Xtreme 1000G Laptop Computer	CompuServe	1
4TB External Hard Drive	CompuServe	2
Steady Sound Headphones	Techno Sound	1

- When submitting this form, please attach other relevant information that will enable the items to be purchased. This includes the addresses of the Web pages where the items can be acquired and captured images of the items.
- No requests will be approved without the signature of your immediate supervisor.
- The items purchased are for work use only and not for personal use.

Employee Signature: Kenneth Dumont

Department Head Signature: Leslie Wheeler

149. Which item does Mr. Dumont request more than one of?

(A) The digital camera
(B) The laptop computer
(C) The external hard drive
(D) The headphones

150. What did Mr. Dumont most likely submit along with the form?

(A) A cash payment
(B) Receipts
(C) Images of the items
(D) A credit card number

151. Who most likely is Ms. Wheeler?

(A) An employee at MRT Technology
(B) A client of Mr. Dumont's
(C) A member of the Purchasing Department
(D) The IT Department supervisor

Questions 152-155 refer to the following article.

Brentwood News

February 26

Grant Autos, one of the country's biggest vehicle manufacturers, will be opening a manufacturing facility in Brentwood. The facility will be where Roth Textiles was once located. The existing buildings are in the process of being demolished, and three new manufacturing centers will be erected in their place. The first center will be operational within eighteen months while the other two will take up to two years before they are complete.

Jefferson Trent, a senior vice president at Grant Autos, stated, "We hope to produce up to 300 vehicles a day when all three facilities are operational. We're making a big investment in Brentwood, and we expect it to pay off for us."

Grant Autos will hire more than 2,500 full-time employees to work at the complex. Most of them will work on the manufacturing line. However, over the next two years, the company will also be seeking designers, engineers, executives, and others to employ.

152. What is the purpose of the article?

(A) To report on a business merger
(B) To describe a problem in Brentwood
(C) To announce the opening of a factory
(D) To promote some Grant Autos vehicles

153. Who is Mr. Trent?

(A) A factory manager
(B) A Grant Autos executive
(C) An automobile maker spokesperson
(D) A Brentwood government official

154. The phrase "pay off" in paragraph 2, line 6, is closest in meaning to

(A) reimburse
(B) develop
(C) recall
(D) succeed

155. According to the article, what will Grant Autos do?

(A) Hire a variety of workers
(B) Renovate an existing facility
(C) Request a loan from the city
(D) Design a new line of vehicles

Questions 156-159 refer to the following e-mail.

To: Tim Chapman <timchapman@chapmandesigns.com>
From: Dustin Peters <d_peters@beaumontconsulting.com>
Date: Design Decision
Subject: August 19

Dear Mr. Chapman,

I want to thank you and your team for the five options you presented to us for the redesign of the interior of our office. In addition, I appreciate your being patient and waiting for our response. I'm very sorry that happened. Several individuals involved in the decision-making process were on vacation and only returned to the office this week. Still, we have made our decision and hope you can begin working on the project before the end of the month. – [1] –.

We have decided to go with the third option, entitled "Futuristic Design." – [2] –. We love the unique appearance of this design and think that it will go well with our company's image. It also has plenty of open space, which makes the office look bigger than it is in reality. – [3] –.

Before the work begins, we need to discuss a few aspects of the design. I wonder if you and your team are available to come here to meet us in person this week. – [4] –. Please let me know if you have time for that.

Sincerely,

Dustin Peters

156. Who most likely is Mr. Chapman?

(A) A financial consultant
(B) An interior designer
(C) A property agent
(D) A residential architect

157. Why does Mr. Peters apologize to Mr. Chapman?

(A) He made a mistake in a previous e-mail.
(B) He forgot to attend a scheduled meeting.
(C) He failed to submit a payment on time.
(D) He did not respond for a long time.

158. What is indicated about "Futuristic Design"?

(A) It was favored by everyone at the company.
(B) It will take a short time to implement.
(C) It matches the image that the company has.
(D) It can be done within the company's budget.

159. In which of the positions marked [1], [2], [3], and [4] does the following sentence best belong?
"That will give us the opportunity to go over the design in detail."

(A) [1]
(B) [2]
(C) [3]
(D) [4]

Questions 160-164 refer to the following advertisement and e-mail.

Sanderson Home Improvement

Sanderson Home Improvement has been helping homeowners in the Sturbridge area for more than twelve years. We provide a wide variety of services on both a regular and one-time basis.

Some of the services we provide are:

- Air conditioning installation and maintenance
- Roof installation and repairs
- Chimney cleaning
- Swimming pool construction
- Home expansion and repairs

Contact Information

General Information: Cody Wilde, cwilde@sandersonhomes.com
Air Conditioning: Julius Clover, jclover@sandersonhomes.com
Roof and Chimney: Eric Blaine, eblaine@sandersonhomes.com
Swimming Pools: Carla Crow, ccrow@sandersonhomes.com
Home Renovations: Douglas Montana, dmontana@sandersonhomes.com

E-Mail

To: Carla Crow <ccrow@sandersonhomes.com>
From: Alyson Roswell <a_roswell@moderntimes.com>
Date: April 11
Subject: Tomorrow

Good afternoon, Carla.

I'm afraid I need to delay tomorrow's visit by Jack Haley's work crew. I have to take a trip out of town. I'm leaving tonight and won't return until late tomorrow, so there won't be anyone home to let the workers in tomorrow. I'm terribly sorry about that.

I know there are only two more days to go until the project is complete. That's what Mr. Haley told me this morning. I'll be home the rest of the week, so I think the crew can finish up everything by the weekend.

Once the work is complete, I'll make the final payment.

Regards,

Alyson Roswell

160. What is suggested about Sanderson Home Improvement?

(A) It is located in Sturbridge.
(B) It offers discounts to customers.
(C) It offers a chimney design service.
(D) It installs heaters in homes.

161. According to the advertisement, who should be contacted about cooling systems?

(A) Julius Clover
(B) Douglas Montana
(C) Cody Wilde
(D) Eric Blaine

162. What is the main purpose of Ms. Roswell's e-mail?

(A) To postpone some work
(B) To schedule a meeting
(C) To arrange a payment
(D) To discuss a job opportunity

163. What is Ms. Roswell most likely having done at her house?

(A) Air conditioning installation
(B) Chimney cleaning
(C) Home expansion
(D) Swimming pool construction

164. Who most likely is Mr. Haley?

(A) A construction supervisor
(B) A roof installer
(C) The CEO of Sanderson Home Improvement
(D) A customer of Sanderson Home Improvement

Questions 165-169 refer to the following e-mail, invoice, and memo.

E-Mail

TO: Preston Peterson ⟨ppeterson@tristatemedia.com⟩

FROM: Curtis Harrier ⟨curtis_harrier@vanguardautos.com⟩

DATE: October 11

SUBJECT: Notes

ATTACHMENT: @comments

Dear Mr. Peterson,

My team and I watched the initial version of the video your team at Tristate Media made for Vanguard Auto's newest vehicle. We were impressed with your work. The video clearly shows how well the Stallion handles, especially in off-road situations. There are a few issues in the video I would like for you to address.

* At 10 seconds: Please include the company name and logo in large print at the bottom of the screen.
* At 25 seconds: The shots of the vehicle's interior are not clear. We want viewers to see how comfortable the interior is. Could you please reshoot that part?
* At 1 minute: There is too much dust in the off-road scene. It makes the car difficult to see.

I've outlined these issues further in the attached document. I'm looking forward to seeing the final version of the video by October 19. We're sending it to all our dealers around the country as well as some top clients. Please get in touch with me if you have any questions regarding my suggested changes.

Regards,

Curtis Harrier
Media Department
Vanguard Autos

Vanguard Autos

Invoice 5433
Billing Date: November 15
Delivery Date: November 19

Bill To: Silverado Ranch
45 Buffalo Lane
Billings, Montana

Quantity	Item Number	Description	Unit Price	Total
5	57231	Stallion SUV	$53,000	$265,000
			Tax	$10,600
			Total	$275,600

MEMO

To: All Employees
From: Christina Wilson, Vice President of Sales
Date: November 20
Re: Congratulations

I'd like to thank everyone for the work you did in creating the recent informational video for the Stallion. Our national dealers love it, and so do the clients to whom we sent it. I'd especially like to thank Mr. Harrier for the work he did in getting the video done.

The Stallion doesn't officially go on sale until December 1, but we have already sold some units. They were delivered yesterday to a long-term customer. Ben Freeman, who made the purchase, told us the video was instrumental in getting him to buy the vehicles without even test-driving them. We're going to need some commercials for the Stallion done soon, so I'm expecting great things from you in December.

165. What is attached to the e-mail?
(A) An invoice
(B) A description of a new vehicle
(C) A review of a video production
(D) A copy of a receipt

166. Why does Mr. Harrier want to reshoot the scene at 25 seconds?
(A) The vehicle is moving too fast.
(B) The image in the video is unclear.
(C) There is too much dust in the scene.
(D) The company logo does not appear.

167. What does the invoice indicate about the Stallion?
(A) The purchaser ordered five of them.
(B) A discount was provided.
(C) There was a fee for delivery.
(D) They were delivered on November 15.

168. Whom does Ms. Wilson specifically praise?
(A) A member of the Media Department
(B) A long-term client
(C) A video producer
(D) A national salesperson

169. Where does Mr. Freeman most likely work?
(A) At Vanguard Autos
(B) At Silverado Ranch
(C) At Tristate Media
(D) At a test-driving center

LC+RC

실전 모의고사

정답 및 해설 p.99

실전 모의고사 LC+RC

LISTENING TEST

In the Listening test, you will be asked to demonstrate how well you understand spoken English. The entire Listening test will last approximately 45 minutes. There are four parts, and directions are given for each part. You must mark your answers on the separate answer sheet. Do not write your answers in your test book.

PART 1

Directions: For each question in this part, you will hear four statements about a picture in your test book. When you hear the statements, you must select the one statement that best describes what you see in the picture. Then find the number of the question on your answer sheet and mark your answer. The statements will not be printed in your test book and will be spoken only one time.

Statement (C), "He's making a phone call," is the best description of the picture, so you should select answer (C) and mark it on your answer sheet.

1.

2.

GO ON TO THE NEXT PAGE

3.

4.

5.

6.

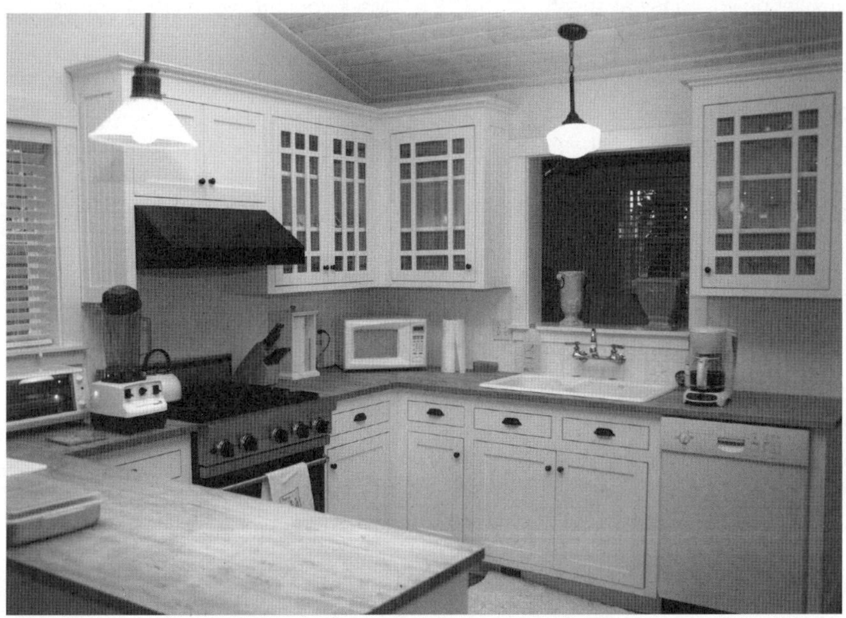

GO ON TO THE NEXT PAGE

PART 2

Directions: You will hear a question or statement and three responses spoken in English. They will not be printed in your test book and will be spoken only one time. Select the best response to the question or statement and mark the letter (A), (B), or (C) on your answer sheet.

7. Mark your answer on your answer sheet.

8. Mark your answer on your answer sheet.

9. Mark your answer on your answer sheet.

10. Mark your answer on your answer sheet.

11. Mark your answer on your answer sheet.

12. Mark your answer on your answer sheet.

13. Mark your answer on your answer sheet.

14. Mark your answer on your answer sheet.

15. Mark your answer on your answer sheet.

16. Mark your answer on your answer sheet.

17. Mark your answer on your answer sheet.

18. Mark your answer on your answer sheet.

19. Mark your answer on your answer sheet.

20. Mark your answer on your answer sheet.

21. Mark your answer on your answer sheet.

22. Mark your answer on your answer sheet.

23. Mark your answer on your answer sheet.

24. Mark your answer on your answer sheet.

25. Mark your answer on your answer sheet.

26. Mark your answer on your answer sheet.

27. Mark your answer on your answer sheet.

28. Mark your answer on your answer sheet.

29. Mark your answer on your answer sheet.

30. Mark your answer on your answer sheet.

31. Mark your answer on your answer sheet.

PART 3

Directions: You will hear some conversations between two or more people. You will be asked to answer three questions about what the speakers say in each conversation. Select the best response to each question and mark the letter (A), (B), (C), or (D) on your answer sheet. The conversations will not be printed in your test book and will be spoken only one time.

32. Where most likely are the speakers?
(A) At a shipping company
(B) At a national park
(C) At a hardware store
(D) At a cleaning service

33. According to the man, what has caused a problem?
(A) A staff shortage
(B) A scheduling conflict
(C) Some poor reviews
(D) Some broken equipment

34. What does the woman say she will do?
(A) Print a document
(B) Hire a specialist
(C) Check a manual
(D) Process a payment

---

35. Who most likely is the man?
(A) A building owner
(B) An art instructor
(C) An interior designer
(D) A journalist

36. What is the woman concerned about?
(A) Increased costs
(B) Safety issues
(C) Unavailable materials
(D) A missed deadline

37. What does the woman suggest doing?
(A) Taking a training session
(B) Looking at some images
(C) Contacting a manufacturer
(D) Placing a rush order

---

38. Who are the men meeting with?
(A) A real estate agent
(B) A mechanic
(C) A safety inspector
(D) An accountant

39. What are the men concerned about?
(A) A location is difficult to find.
(B) A site is not large enough.
(C) A form is missing information.
(D) A parking fee is too high.

40. What will the speakers most likely do next?
(A) Enter a building
(B) View a document
(C) Go to another site
(D) Take some measurements

---

41. Why is the woman calling?
(A) To request a discount
(B) To reschedule a delivery
(C) To make a payment
(D) To inquire about returns

42. Why did the woman order some items?
(A) She plans to transport some items.
(B) She must repair some machinery.
(C) She will give gifts to employees.
(D) She is redecorating her office.

43. What will the man do next?
(A) Drive to the woman's business
(B) Update a company Web site
(C) Speak to the woman's manager
(D) Check an employee's availability

GO ON TO THE NEXT PAGE →

44. Where does the man work?

(A) At a computer repair shop
(B) At a medical clinic
(C) At a bank
(D) At an employment agency

45. Why does the woman need to make a change?

(A) She is having car problems.
(B) She will take a business trip.
(C) She must lead a class.
(D) She is not feeling well.

46. What will the woman most likely do next?

(A) Make a formal complaint
(B) Provide new contact information
(C) Confirm an expiration date
(D) Contact another branch

---

47. Where do the speakers most likely work?

(A) At a farm
(B) At a warehouse
(C) At a café
(D) At an appliance store

48. Why does the woman say, "the training period is already quite long"?

(A) To reject a suggestion
(B) To reassure the man
(C) To offer her assistance
(D) To suggest changing a schedule

49. What does the man mention about Steven?

(A) He has a lot of experience.
(B) He is dissatisfied with the work conditions.
(C) He can recommend a supplier.
(D) He may have trouble with a workload.

---

50. Where are the speakers?

(A) At a movie theater
(B) At a library
(C) At a restaurant
(D) At a gym

51. What does Joseph give the woman information about?

(A) Meeting staff members
(B) Participating in group classes
(C) Accessing an account
(D) Touring a facility

52. What does the woman say she did last month?

(A) She moved to a different city.
(B) She started a new job.
(C) She received a certification.
(D) She began studying online.

---

53. What industry do the speakers most likely work in?

(A) Advertising
(B) Technology
(C) Energy
(D) Pharmaceuticals

54. What change are the speakers discussing?

(A) Relocating to another site
(B) Purchasing some machinery
(C) Extending the hours of operation
(D) Raising salaries for employees

55. What does the woman offer to do?

(A) Set up some sale items
(B) Contact a specialist
(C) Review some financial data
(D) Gather feedback from the staff

---

56. What problem is the man calling about?

(A) He has forgotten a password.
(B) He provided some incorrect information.
(C) He lost his most recent bill.
(D) He has been overcharged.

57. Where does the woman work?

(A) At a shipping service
(B) At a moving company
(C) At an Internet provider
(D) At an accounting firm

58. What did the man do last month?

(A) He moved to a new address.
(B) He upgraded a service package.
(C) He launched his own business.
(D) He visited the woman's company.

---

59. What are the speakers discussing?

(A) A job opening
(B) A product release
(C) A company relocation
(D) An annual event

60. What department does the woman most likely work in?

(A) Finance
(B) Marketing
(C) Information technology
(D) Operations management

61. Why does the woman say, "The project manager has already moved up our deadline"?

(A) To demonstrate urgency
(B) To show appreciation
(C) To propose a compromise
(D) To express confusion

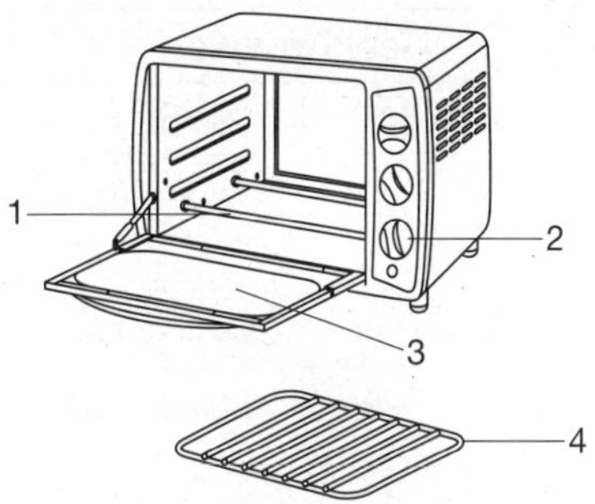

62. Where does the man work?

(A) At a research institute
(B) At a restaurant
(C) At a department store
(D) At a law firm

63. Look at the graphic. Which part has been damaged?

(A) Part 1
(B) Part 2
(C) Part 3
(D) Part 4

64. What will the woman probably do next?

(A) Look for a product manual
(B) Order replacement parts
(C) Send a list of locations
(D) Check an item's availability

GO ON TO THE NEXT PAGE

New Arrivals!	
Circles: code G33 Colors: blue, green	**Stripe:** code H18 Colors: brown, blue
Waves: code N29 Colors: blue, gray	**Stars:** code P77 Colors: red, gray

65. What will Tahoka Manufacturing change?

(A) A shipping schedule
(B) A warranty period
(C) An office location
(D) A storage fee

66. What does the woman like about Tahoka Manufacturing?

(A) The speed of deliveries
(B) The wide selection of patterns
(C) The friendliness of the staff
(D) The quality of its materials

67. Look at the graphic. Which design do the speakers agree to order?

(A) G33
(B) H18
(C) N29
(D) P77

Performance Schedule	
7:00 P.M.	Tango Treats
7:30 P.M.	Marlana Music
8:00 P.M.	BC Dance Troupe
8:30 P.M.	The Chapmans

68. Why does the man want to have a party?

(A) A team has completed a project.
(B) A colleague received a promotion.
(C) A company was nominated for an award.
(D) A sales goal was exceeded.

69. Look at the graphic. Which group is Libby a member of?

(A) Tango Treats
(B) Marlana Music
(C) BC Dance Troupe
(D) The Chapmans

70. What problem does the man mention?

(A) A venue is in a remote area.
(B) A transportation service is unavailable.
(C) The price of admission is high.
(D) Some team members will be absent.

PART 4

Directions: You will hear some talks given by a single speaker. You will be asked to answer three questions about what the speaker says in each talk. Select the best response to each question and mark the letter (A), (B), (C), or (D) on your answer sheet. The talks will not be printed in your test book and will be spoken only one time.

71. What type of business is being advertised?
(A) A catering service
(B) An event space
(C) A rental home
(D) A movie theater

72. What does the speaker say the business is most known for?
(A) Its talented staff
(B) Its convenient location
(C) Its lengthy history
(D) Its original architecture

73. What can listeners do on a Web site?
(A) Look at pictures
(B) Read reviews
(C) Find a discount code
(D) Make a booking

---

74. What is the podcast episode about?
(A) Online advertising
(B) Computer programming
(C) Starting a business
(D) Expanding overseas

75. What does the speaker say Ms. Dambe is good at?
(A) Solving technical glitches
(B) Getting funding
(C) Understanding customers
(D) Negotiating with suppliers

76. What will the speaker discuss next?
(A) A subscription service
(B) A research project
(C) A listener question
(D) A news report

---

77. What will happen next Monday?
(A) A presentation will be delivered.
(B) A product will be purchased.
(C) A new location will be opened.
(D) An office space will be redesigned.

78. What inspired the speaker?
(A) An advertisement
(B) A famous book
(C) An employee suggestion
(D) A media report

79. How can listeners learn about the benefits of the new lights?
(A) By reading an email
(B) By visiting a Web site
(C) By looking at a handout
(D) By watching a video

---

80. What type of business is the listener calling?
(A) A cable provider
(B) A consulting company
(C) An energy company
(D) An automobile manufacturer

81. What does the speaker imply when she says, "We thank you for your patience"?
(A) The responders are untrained.
(B) The company is closing soon.
(C) Many people are complaining.
(D) The repairs are not yet complete.

82. How can the listener stay updated?
(A) By getting automated e-mails
(B) By calling again later
(C) By receiving text alerts
(D) By checking a Web site

GO ON TO THE NEXT PAGE

83. Why have some citizens complained?

(A) Street parking is unavailable.
(B) The roads are damaged.
(C) Street cleaning is too infrequent.
(D) Parking garages are too expensive.

84. What is John Daly concerned about?

(A) Higher taxes
(B) Environmental damage
(C) Increased traffic
(D) Construction noise

85. What will certain residents receive?

(A) Parking passes
(B) Hotel booking fees
(C) Event tickets
(D) Transportation services

---

86. What is the topic of the seminar?

(A) Manufacturing
(B) Shipping
(C) Publishing
(D) Journalism

87. Why does the speaker thank some of the listeners?

(A) They raised questions.
(B) They shared their experience.
(C) They attended previous talks.
(D) They gave feedback on the slides.

88. Why does the speaker mention the back of the room?

(A) Refreshments are available there.
(B) A worker is sitting there.
(C) Informational materials are there.
(D) A book is on sale there.

---

89. Why is Matteo away from his business?

(A) He is meeting a supplier.
(B) He is delivering a lecture.
(C) He is at a job interview.
(D) He is viewing real estate.

90. Why does the speaker say, "Fettuccini alfredo has always been a hit with our regulars"?

(A) To make a suggestion
(B) To provide a compliment
(C) To demonstrate a problem
(D) To congratulate an achievement

91. What good news does the speaker share about the restaurant?

(A) It won an annual award.
(B) It had an influx of customers.
(C) It received attention online.
(D) It appeared in a television show.

---

92. What type of business does the speaker most likely work at?

(A) A hardware store
(B) A construction company
(C) A furniture store
(D) A delivery service

93. What does the speaker imply when he says, "I have experience in sales"?

(A) He will mentor some employees.
(B) He will take over for some shifts.
(C) He will interview candidates soon.
(D) He will offer extra pay for overtime work.

94. What does the speaker expect the listeners to do?

(A) Reorganize the store layout
(B) Clean an area
(C) Organize a luncheon
(D) Plan a hiring event

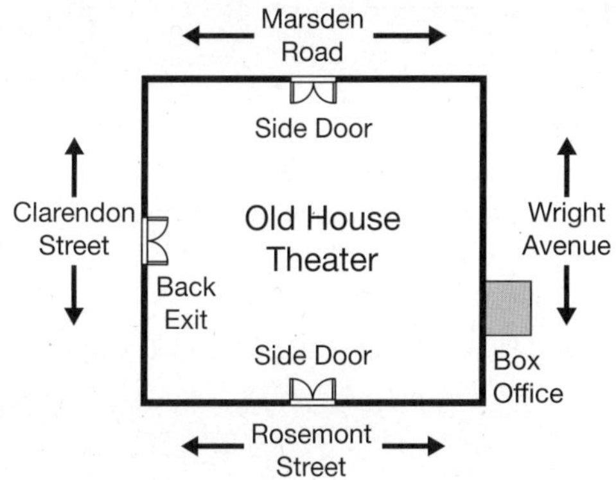

95. Who most likely is the speaker?
(A) A bus operator
(B) A tour guide
(C) A rideshare driver
(D) A train conductor

96. Look at the graphic. Where does the speaker want to meet?
(A) On Clarendon Street
(B) On Wright Avenue
(C) On Rosemont Street
(D) On Marsden Road

97. How can the listener confirm the change?
(A) By calling the company
(B) By sending a message
(C) By using an app
(D) By standing outside

Innersville Bus Station	
Terminal A	Fulton Bus Lines
Terminal B	Kiwi Bird Bus Travel
Terminal C	Speedy Friends Buses
Terminal D	Clockwork Bus Company

98. Who is the audience for the talk?
(A) Travel agents
(B) Employees
(C) Town residents
(D) Investors

99. According to the speaker, why was the facility needed?
(A) The government wants to reduce car traffic.
(B) The old bus station was in bad condition.
(C) The town lacks public transportation options.
(D) The local airport recently closed.

100. Look at the graphic. Which terminal will have the first departure?
(A) Terminal A
(B) Terminal B
(C) Terminal C
(D) Terminal D

GO ON TO THE NEXT PAGE

READING TEST

In the Reading test, you will read a variety of texts and answer several different types of reading comprehension questions. The entire Reading test will last 75 minutes. There are three parts, and directions are given for each part. You are encouraged to answer as many questions as possible within the time allowed.

You must mark your answers on the separate answer sheet. Do not write your answers in your test book.

PART 5

Directions: A word or phrase is missing in each of the sentences below. Four answer choices are given below each sentence. Select the best answer to complete the sentence. Then mark the letter (A), (B), (C), or (D) on your answer sheet.

101. The consulting firm intends to hold a training ------- for its newest employees next week.

(A) session
(B) method
(C) approach
(D) way

102. The order coming from Europe is ------- going to arrive no later than tomorrow evening.

(A) fairly
(B) severely
(C) accurately
(D) supposedly

103. Ms. Patterson ------- her desire to attend the marketing seminar in Dallas to her supervisor.

(A) asked
(B) submitted
(C) expressed
(D) alerted

104. Sylvester Deli's selection of meats is ------- than all other stores in the city.

(A) greatly
(B) greater
(C) greatest
(D) great

105. We regret to announce Mr. Carpenter's ------- from his position in the R&D Department.

(A) resign
(B) to resign
(C) resignation
(D) will resign

106. Nearly ------- individual at the logistics conference is directly involved in the industry.

(A) almost
(B) all
(C) those
(D) every

107. All transactions with clients are ------- both on paper and electronically.

(A) record
(B) recorded
(C) recording
(D) records

108. Mr. Anderson scheduled a staff meeting for the ------- of discussing this month's budget.

(A) purpose
(B) view
(C) opinion
(D) appointment

109. As soon as the seminar attendees arrive, ------- will be divided into groups for a role-playing activity.

(A) they
(B) them
(C) their
(D) themselves

110. A government inspection must be conducted ------- new regulations have just been enacted.

(A) however
(B) in spite of
(C) because
(D) as soon as

111. The new law resulted in increased ------- in the financial industry by foreigners.

(A) supply
(B) method
(C) possession
(D) investment

112. It is well known that Mr. Jackson, one of the newest managers, ------- to work evening shifts at the restaurant.

(A) prefer
(B) prefers
(C) is preferred
(D) is being preferred

113. Ms. Chamberlain will be absent ------- roughly one week while she travels to Madrid on business.

(A) within
(B) on
(C) during
(D) for

114. The engineer must determine the precise ------- of the crack in the pipe.

(A) location
(B) locate
(C) locating
(D) located

115. Ms. Lopez described the new product ------- when asked about it by the board of directors.

(A) tremendously
(B) certainly
(C) thoughtfully
(D) ultimately

116. Those part-timers ------- work contracts expire next month should speak with Ms. Matisse by this Thursday.

(A) which
(B) whose
(C) when
(D) that

117. Executives who transfer to foreign branches receive higher salaries ------- are responsible for their own housing.

(A) but
(B) since
(C) as well
(D) in order to

118. Each bolt must be attached ------- to ensure that the shelf stays together.

(A) tights
(B) tightness
(C) tightly
(D) tighten

119. The cargo cannot be unloaded from the ship ------- permission from local authorities.

(A) without
(B) between
(C) instead of
(D) except

120. Since no funding is currently available, the bridge is only ------- constructed.

(A) partial
(B) partially
(C) partials
(D) partialness

GO ON TO THE NEXT PAGE →

121. ------- the latest information from the sales team, the new cosmetics line is selling better than anticipated.

(A) Because
(B) Consequently
(C) In spite of
(D) According to

122. Domestic ------- in the computer industry has been increasing over the past four months.

(A) employable
(B) employment
(C) employee
(D) employer

123. After considering the formal request, management ------- agreed to provide its employees with extra paid vacation.

(A) eventual
(B) eventuality
(C) eventually
(D) event

124. Industry experts believe exports ------- in the coming months due to issues with the supply chain.

(A) decline
(B) declined
(C) will decline
(D) have been declining

125. Local farmers reported ------- high crop yields despite the relatively cool summer weather.

(A) surprisingly
(B) imperatively
(C) annually
(D) gradually

126. Despite market research indicating that customers were ------- about the item, Gladden Technology halted production of it.

(A) impressed
(B) fantastic
(C) determined
(D) enthusiastic

127. Skylar Electronics plans to manufacture more computers locally yet ------- them to countries in Europe.

(A) distribute
(B) distributing
(C) distributes
(D) distributed

128. Concert attendees were ------- with the performances of both bands.

(A) maintained
(B) expected
(C) admired
(D) satisfied

129. To organize the maintenance request forms, Mr. Gibson created a ------- folder for storing the documents.

(A) designate
(B) designated
(C) designating
(D) designates

130. When Ms. Sulla received her monthly electric bill, she ------- her power usage had declined from the previous month.

(A) noticed
(B) glanced
(C) appeared
(D) repeated

PART 6

Directions: Read the texts that follow. A word, phrase, or sentence is missing in parts of each text. Four answer choices for each question are given below the text. Select the best answer to complete the text. Then mark the letter (A), (B), (C), or (D) on your answer sheet.

Questions 131-134 refer to the following notice.

To All Customers,

We regret ------- **131.** you that the Kensington branch of Marigold Bakery will be closed as of March 31. We will no longer be able to provide pastries, cakes, and ------- **132.** items to our customers there. The building in which the bakery is located is being renovated, so we have no choice in this matter.

------- **133.**. They are in Mayfield, Westside, and Haywood. You can also order online and have your items delivered for free. Thank you again for your ------- **134.** support during the past seventeen years.

131. (A) inform
(B) will inform
(C) have informed
(D) to inform

132. (A) all
(B) other
(C) another
(D) every

133. (A) Please be aware that we have three other locations nearby.
(B) We have decided to expand the store to let more customers dine in.
(C) The cost of doing business in Kensington has increased greatly.
(D) It is no longer possible to remain in the food-supply business.

134. (A) continue
(B) continues
(C) continual
(D) continually

GO ON TO THE NEXT PAGE

Questions 135-138 refer to the following memo.

To: All Employees

From: Eric Horner

Date: February 11

Subject: Gym Membership

I am pleased to announce that management has agreed to sponsor gym memberships for full-time employees. This perk ------- (**135.**) by a number of you in the January employee satisfaction survey. Starting on March 1, employees can receive a voucher for a free membership at Westfield Gym. Please request one only if you ------- (**136.**) to work out regularly. The voucher is good for a half-year membership. When the ------- (**137.**) ends, you can ask for an additional one. It does not include working out with a personal trainer. ------- (**138.**).

135. (A) is requested
(B) requested
(C) was requested
(D) has been requested

136. (A) anticipate
(B) appear
(C) intend
(D) approve

137. (A) period
(B) coupon
(C) training
(D) tour

138. (A) We hope you all use the facility here.
(B) Thank you for your support.
(C) A voucher has been sent to each of you.
(D) You must pay for that yourself.

Questions 139-142 refer to the following notice.

It is time once again to submit nominations for end-of-the-year awards. This year, two awards -------. **139.**

The first is the employee of the year. The second is the newcomer of the year. All nominations must be received by Maryanne Carter by November 30. Please include a brief statement explaining ------- **140.** the person you nominate should receive the award.

The winners will be announced at our annual get-together on December 29. -------. **141.** Each winner will receive a cash ------- **142.** and several other prizes.

139. (A) were presented
(B) are presenting
(C) present
(D) will be presented

140. (A) why
(B) how
(C) where
(D) when

141. (A) Mr. Anderson, our CEO, hosted the ceremony.
(B) We had nearly perfect attendance at last year's party.
(C) This year's event will be at the Hillsdale Restaurant.
(D) Invitations will be sent to all of the winners.

142. (A) salary
(B) trophy
(C) medal
(D) reward

GO ON TO THE NEXT PAGE →

Questions 143-146 refer to the following information.

Thank you for purchasing an appliance from Madison Electronics. We take -------(143.) in the quality of our products. Should you experience any problems with your appliance, please contact us at 1-888-555-8473. Our toll-free hotline is open twenty-four hours a day. Our customer service representatives -------(144.) to assist you anytime.

Your appliance comes with a full two-year warranty. However, if an unauthorized person works on the item, the warranty will -------(145.) be in effect.

For more information, visit our Web site at www.madisonelectronics.com. -------(146.).

143. (A) proud
(B) proudness
(C) prided
(D) pride

144. (A) have stood by
(B) stood by
(C) are standing by
(D) will stand by

145. (A) never
(B) such
(C) no longer
(D) still

146. (A) Refunds must be requested within 10 days of purchase.
(B) You can also e-mail us at info@madisonelectronics.com.
(C) Please be sure to keep your receipt.
(D) You must send the item in its original packaging.

PART 7

Directions: In this part, you will read a selection of texts, such as magazine and newspaper articles, e-mails, and instant messages. Each text or set of texts is followed by several questions. Select the best answer for each question and mark the letter (A), (B), (C), or (D) on your answer sheet.

Questions 147-148 refer to the following notice.

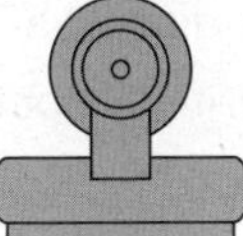

Attention: All City Lifeguards

Your work schedules will be sent to your phones by text message starting on April 30. Schedules will arrive every Sunday night no later than 6:00 P.M. Should you have any scheduling conflicts or issues, please respond to the message within an hour. In case of inclement weather, text messages indicating that pools or beaches are closed may be sent at any time.

Please contact Wendy Sullivan in the City Parks and Recreation office to make sure that your phone number currently on file is accurate.

147. What is one thing that lifeguards will be notified about by text message?

(A) Overtime opportunities
(B) Staff meetings
(C) Schedules
(D) Government inspections

148. Why should lifeguards contact the office?

(A) To request time off work
(B) To confirm certain information
(C) To inquire about weather conditions
(D) To request assistance

GO ON TO THE NEXT PAGE

Questions 149-150 refer to the following article.

Bradenton Times

October 11—Local businessman Harold Grimes has just announced that he intends to establish another business in Bradenton. Mr. Grimes owns four restaurants in town as well as two supermarkets. His new venture, however, will not be in the food industry. Instead, he is opening a medical clinic. Grimes Medical Care will be located at 67 Easton Drive across from the Bradenton Library. While Mr. Grimes himself has no medical background, he stated a need to have quality, affordable medical care for the people of the city. The clinic will employ five full-time doctors and have state-of-the-art medical equipment.

Mr. Grimes said he expects the clinic to open in November. Interested individuals can call 539-9573 for more information about the specialties of the doctors and making appointments.

149. What is indicated about Mr. Grimes?

(A) He studied medicine at university.
(B) He will replace some doctors at a clinic.
(C) He has several business establishments.
(D) He is involved in local politics.

150. Why is Grimes Medical Care being opened?

(A) To give local residents good health care
(B) To replace a hospital that is closing
(C) To provide specialized surgical options
(D) To fulfill a request from Bradenton residents

Questions 151-154 refer to the following article.

TORONTO (April 23)—In an effort to break into the European market, Canadian electronics manufacturer Galleon, Inc. has signed an agreement with Baldrick to examine the markets in several countries.

Baldrick is a consulting firm headquartered in London, England, and has offices in Madrid, Rome, Paris, and several other major European cities. —[1]—. "We feel like we understand what Europeans want," said CEO Ian Smythe. "We've assisted numerous other North American firms in their efforts to succeed in Europe, and we're positive we can assist Galleon as well."

Baldrick has been in business for more than three decades and is the largest family-owned consulting company in England. —[2]—.

"It's not easy to switch from one market to another," said Mr. Smythe. "For instance, American consumers may expect certain functions from their electronic devices whereas European customers have no interest in those at all. —[3]—. We'll identify how Galleon can adapt its products in order to be successful."

Galleon anticipates having a report from Baldrick by December of this year. —[4]—. Once it analyzes the data, it will begin efforts to produce products tailor-made for export next year.

151. How is Baldrick helping Galleon, Inc.?

(A) By analyzing production trends
(B) By recruiting new employees
(C) By determining consumer preferences
(D) By improving its computer database

152. What does the article mention about Baldrick?

(A) Its main office is located in Toronto.
(B) It manufactures electric appliances.
(C) It is owned by another company.
(D) It opened over thirty years ago.

153. According to Mr. Smythe, how are consumers different from one another?

(A) What brand names they buy
(B) What functions they want in devices
(C) What detail of instruction they need
(D) What prices they want to pay

154. In which of the positions marked [1], [2], [3], and [4] does the following sentence best belong?
"It also has branches in Asia and North America."

(A) [1]
(B) [2]
(C) [3]
(D) [4]

GO ON TO THE NEXT PAGE

Questions 155-156 refer to the following text-message chain.

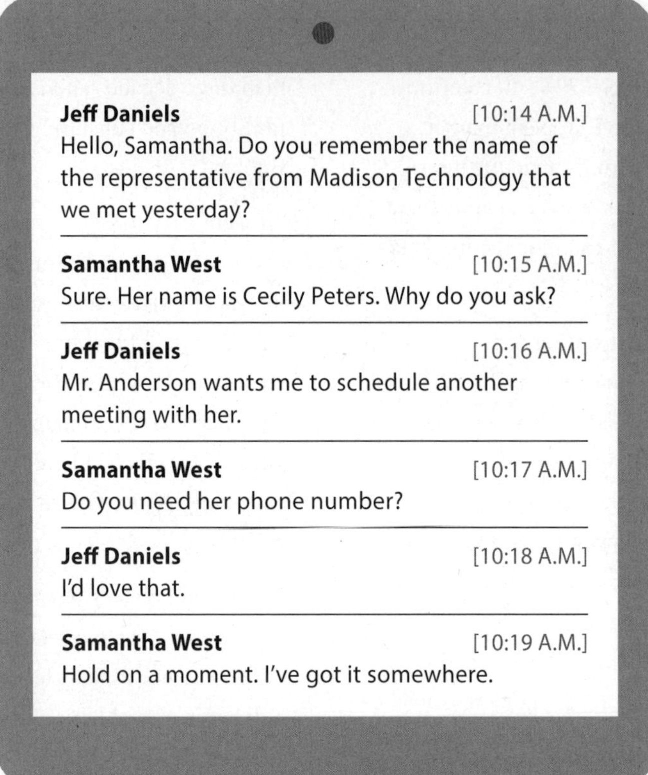

Jeff Daniels [10:14 A.M.]
Hello, Samantha. Do you remember the name of the representative from Madison Technology that we met yesterday?

Samantha West [10:15 A.M.]
Sure. Her name is Cecily Peters. Why do you ask?

Jeff Daniels [10:16 A.M.]
Mr. Anderson wants me to schedule another meeting with her.

Samantha West [10:17 A.M.]
Do you need her phone number?

Jeff Daniels [10:18 A.M.]
I'd love that.

Samantha West [10:19 A.M.]
Hold on a moment. I've got it somewhere.

155. What is suggested about the writers?

(A) They work for Madison Technology.
(B) They have to submit a report to Mr. Anderson.
(C) They attended a meeting together the previous day.
(D) They will give Ms. Peters a product demonstration.

156. At 10:18 A.M., what does Mr. Daniels most likely mean when he writes, "I'd love that"?

(A) He wants a person's contact information.
(B) He is willing to meet Ms. West sometime today.
(C) He is happy Ms. West will schedule a meeting.
(D) He is eager to purchase a new phone.

Questions 157-159 refer to the following advertisement.

Graham's Custom Shoes

Graham's Custom Shoes are the ideal gift for someone special in your life. They are made with soft leather in a variety of colors. The shoes are sized perfectly for each customer's feet. —[1]—. They are guaranteed to last for at least three years. —[2]—. Since the shoes are custom made, customers must either visit the store in person or send precise measurements of their feet to us online. —[3]—. To learn more about the styles available, visit us at 58 Rochester Road or go to www.grahamscustomshoes.com. —[4]—. Try us once, and you'll never purchase shoes from anyone else again.

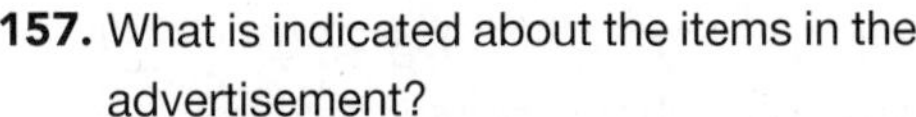

157. What is indicated about the items in the advertisement?

(A) They are made from the same type of material.
(B) They all have the same price.
(C) They require around two weeks to be made.
(D) They can be mailed to international addresses.

158. What does the advertisement recommend that some customers do?

(A) Call for more information
(B) Submit pictures of their preferred style
(C) Ask about the product guarantee
(D) Provide accurate information

159. In which of the positions marked [1], [2], [3], and [4] does the following sentence best belong?
"Be sure to check each foot since individual feet are slightly different in size."

(A) [1]
(B) [2]
(C) [3]
(D) [4]

GO ON TO THE NEXT PAGE

Questions 160-163 refer to the following letter.

March 11

Patrick Peterson
546 Mercer Avenue
Sacramento, CA 94258

Dear Mr. Peterson,

As a long-time shopper at Daniel's Green Grocer, you must be aware that we sell a variety of domestic and international foods. You should also know that we have a deli and a bakery, where we create many foods.

We would like to receive your input regarding the foods we make. We are therefore extending an opportunity to you to become a food taster.

Simply show up here on your designated weekend. You'll be given samples of between five and ten different foods to try. The foods you'll be sampling will include baked goods, pastries, cheeses, meats, and cooked foods such as lasagna and ziti. Then, you provide your frank opinion of each item by completing a short survey. The entire process should take ten minutes.

To sign up for this opportunity, drop by Daniel's anytime within the next two weeks and speak with Marjorie Benson, the store manager. In return for your assistance, you'll receive a $10 store coupon as well as free samples you can take home.

We hope to receive a positive response soon.

Regards,

Eric Quinn
CEO, Daniel's Green Grocer

160. What is the purpose of the letter?
(A) To announce a special sale
(B) To advertise some new products
(C) To discuss an employment opportunity
(D) To request participation in an activity

161. What is indicated about Daniel's Green Grocer?
(A) It has multiple branches in the city.
(B) It is the city's largest grocery store.
(C) It sells food from other countries.
(D) It will construct a new bakery soon.

162. The word "sampling" in paragraph 3, line 2, is closest in meaning to
(A) tasting
(B) providing
(C) attending
(D) reporting

163. What can Mr. Peterson receive from Daniel's Green Grocer?
(A) An express delivery service
(B) Monthly coupons
(C) Free food
(D) Membership in a shopper's club

Questions 164-165 refer to the following Web page.

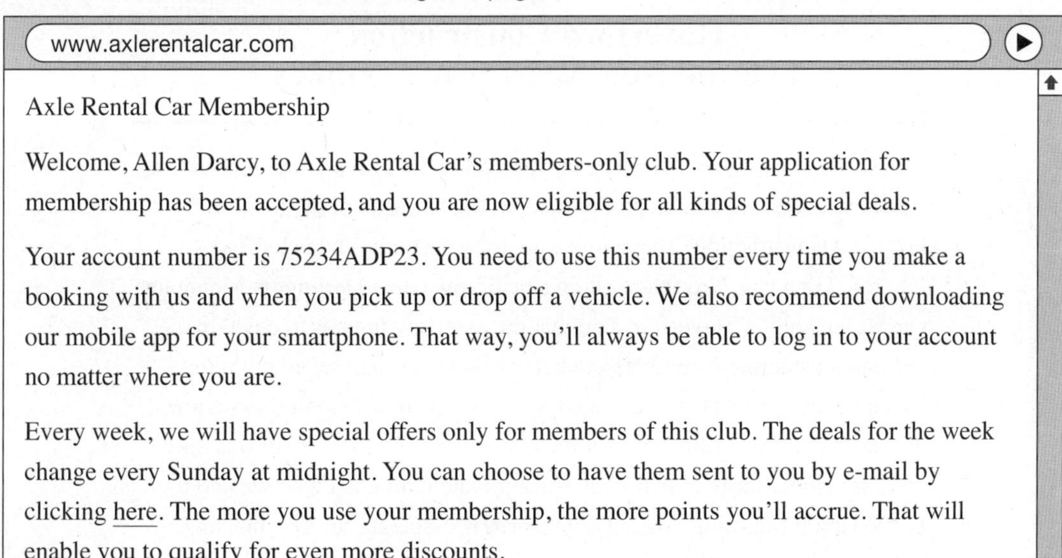

www.axlerentalcar.com

Axle Rental Car Membership

Welcome, Allen Darcy, to Axle Rental Car's members-only club. Your application for membership has been accepted, and you are now eligible for all kinds of special deals.

Your account number is 75234ADP23. You need to use this number every time you make a booking with us and when you pick up or drop off a vehicle. We also recommend downloading our mobile app for your smartphone. That way, you'll always be able to log in to your account no matter where you are.

Every week, we will have special offers only for members of this club. The deals for the week change every Sunday at midnight. You can choose to have them sent to you by e-mail by clicking here. The more you use your membership, the more points you'll accrue. That will enable you to qualify for even more discounts.

164. What must Mr. Darcy do when getting a vehicle?

(A) Present his account number
(B) Show a valid driver's license
(C) Pay with a credit card
(D) Prove that he has insurance

165. What is indicated about the Axle Rental Car's members-only club?

(A) It lets members rent vehicles for free.
(B) It is open only to long-term customers.
(C) It requires payment of an annual fee.
(D) It offers multiple deals each week.

GO ON TO THE NEXT PAGE

Questions 166-168 refer to the following article.

Haverford Construction to Build New Apartment Complex

SUDBURY (November 12)—The mayor's office in Sudbury announced last night that it had sold a large plot of land on the outskirts of the town to Haverford Construction. The land covers fourteen acres and is located alongside Highway 32 on the eastern side of town near Darlington Mountain. A spokesperson for Haverford said that the company intends to develop the land into an apartment complex containing no fewer than seven buildings. The company expects to release its designs for the new complex sometime early next year. According to a source in the mayor's office, there was only one other bidder for the land. That was a private individual who wanted to use the land for farming. The city, however, is desperate for new housing. With several companies announcing plans to construct facilities near town, the local population is expected to increase greatly soon. Thus, securing more housing is of the utmost importance to the mayor's office.

166. Where is the land that was acquired located?

(A) On Darlington Mountain
(B) Opposite the mayor's office
(C) Near a farm
(D) On the eastern side of Sudbury

167. According to the article, why is there a need for housing in Sudbury?

(A) Many homes in the town are in poor condition.
(B) Some apartment complexes burned down recently.
(C) Housing prices in the local area are rising too fast.
(D) Many people will move there in the near future.

168. The word "securing" in line 12 is closest in meaning to

(A) preserving
(B) obtaining
(C) inspecting
(D) guarding

Questions 169-171 refer to the following information.

E-Z Wash Laundry

E-Z Wash Laundry is proud to announce it is no longer necessary for customers to carry coins to use our washers and dryers. Instead, customers can purchase cards and put money on them. Then, these cards can be used to operate the machines.

To use our new system, simply do the following:

1. Go to one of the machines at the back of the store. Select the amount of money you want to put on a card and then insert the necessary cash.
2. You will then receive a card with credit on it.
3. Put your laundry in a washer or dryer and select the setting you would like.
4. Insert your card in the slot and press the "Use" button. The machine will begin running, and the fee will be deducted from your card.

You can use the machines to receive a refund for any funds on your card that you do not use.

169. What is the purpose of the information?

(A) To apologize for a mistake
(B) To explain the results of a survey
(C) To announce a new service
(D) To promote a branch opening

170. What should a person do after choosing the cycle for their clothing?

(A) Put money in a slot
(B) Insert a card
(C) Speak with an employee
(D) Add laundry detergent

171. What is indicated about the cards?

(A) They can be used only one time.
(B) Users can get their money back from them.
(C) They have an expiration date.
(D) Credit cards can be used to put money on them.

GO ON TO THE NEXT PAGE

Questions 172-175 refer to the following online chat discussion.

Dieter Kimball [1:12 P.M.] Hi, everyone. I just got back to the office and noticed someone left some folders on my desk. Who was that?

Sally Beecher [1:15 P.M.] George and I did that, Mr. Kimball. We need your approval for some expenditures. As you know, the company picnic is fast approaching, and we were chosen to organize it.

George White [1:16 P.M.] Do you have time to look at everything today? We could be in your office in five minutes.

Dieter Kimball [1:17 P.M.] I'm meeting Sylvester Mann at 1:30.

George White [1:18 P.M.] Do you know how long that's going to take?

Dieter Kimball [1:19 P.M.] It's hard to say. We have a lot to go over. Is there anything I should know about in the folder you gave me?

Sally Beecher [1:20 P.M.] The only issue is that we're going to exceed our budget a bit. More people than usual have committed to attending with their families. So we had to purchase more food and other supplies than normal.

George White [1:21 P.M.] That's our primary concern, but there are a couple of other minor issues we'd like to discuss, too.

Dieter Kimball [1:22 P.M.] Drop by my office at four thirty. We can go over everything then.

SEND

172. Who most likely is Mr. Kimball?

(A) A job applicant
(B) A supervisor
(C) An event planner
(D) A client

173. What does Mr. White want to do?

(A) Change the date of an event
(B) Receive extra funding
(C) Meet Mr. Kimball in person
(D) Move a venue to another place

174. At 1:17 P.M., why does Mr. Kimball write, "I'm meeting Sylvester Mann at 1:30"?

(A) To reject a suggestion
(B) To approve a request
(C) To describe his schedule tomorrow
(D) To offer to cancel his plans

175. What is suggested about the company picnic?

(A) It will happen in August.
(B) It is held near the company.
(C) It has taken place before.
(D) Only employees may attend.

GO ON TO THE NEXT PAGE →

Questions 176-180 refer to the following letter and e-mail.

Sunfield Golf Resort
1603 Westway Drive
Mesa, AZ 85209

June 23

Lawrence Mercado
294 Hickory Road
Florence, AZ 85143

Dear Mr. Mercado,

Thank you for registering for Sunfield Golf Resort's annual Sun and Fun Tournament on July 17. Your confirmation number is 0638. Please find enclosed your parking pass and name badge. You must wear the name badge at all times while on the resort's grounds to show that you are participating in the tournament.

You should check in at the reception desk in the clubhouse between 7:00 A.M. and 8:30 A.M., and a photo ID will be required. The tournament consists of four categories with the following start times at the first hole: 9:00 A.M. [Semi-Pro], 10:00 A.M. [Advanced], 11:00 A.M. [Intermediate], and noon [Beginner].

There will be tea, coffee, soda, and bottled water available at the reception desk for free. However, you must show your name badge to be served. Food will be available for purchase in our restaurant.

We look forward to seeing you at Sunfield Golf Resort!

Sincerely,

The Sunfield Golf Resort Event Staff

E-Mail

To: Lawrence Mercado <l.mercado@shermansales.com>
From: Nancy Aldridge <nancy@sunfieldgolf.com>
Date: July 6
Subject: Sun and Fun Tournament

Dear Mr. Mercado,

We are excited to welcome our golfers soon for the Sun and Fun Tournament! Your assigned start time is 10:00 A.M. If you are driving to the tournament, please note that you should park in the lot off Avis Street. The one connected to Mooney Street is temporarily closed to make space for the crews working on the expansion of our indoor driving range. To download a map of our site, please click here.

Warmest regards,

Nancy Aldridge

176. What is the purpose of the letter?

(A) To apologize for an error
(B) To confirm registration
(C) To recommend a service
(D) To request funds

177. What will Mr. Mercado be asked to do on July 17 when he arrives?

(A) Show a form of identification
(B) Sign an official document
(C) Choose some group members
(D) Inspect his equipment

178. What is suggested about the reception desk?

(A) Its beverages are for participants only.
(B) It will collect donations for charity.
(C) Its employees can provide parking passes.
(D) It opens daily at 7:00 A.M.

179. What is most likely true about Sunfield Golf Resort?

(A) It has recently changed ownership.
(B) It is holding a competition for the first time.
(C) It provides discounts on events to its members.
(D) It has a building currently under construction.

180. What most likely is Mr. Mercado's skill level in golf?

(A) Beginner
(B) Intermediate
(C) Advanced
(D) Semi-pro

GO ON TO THE NEXT PAGE

Questions 181-185 refer to the following Web pages.

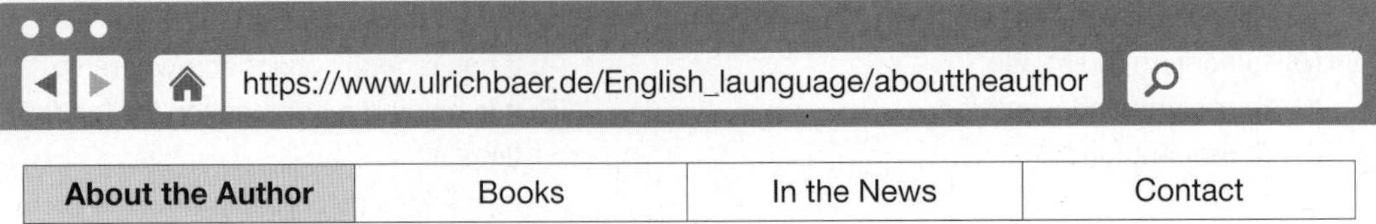

Ulrich Baer was born in Leipzig, Germany, to Sebastian and Ines Baer. His father was in the military, so throughout his childhood he lived in many different parts of the world, moving every couple of years. While at university, one of his friends was planning a trip to Argentina. Mr. Baer had lived there, so he made notes for his friend. They were so useful that he figured he could turn them into a travel guide.

Since that time, Mr. Baer has written eight travel guides for various countries/regions. He also published a collection of historical photos entitled *Through the Lens*, which was highly praised by critics.

Mr. Baer will release his newest travel guide, *Footprints in Asia*, on May 10. It will contain some photos from *Through the Lens* so readers can see how areas have changed. The book will contain maps along with tips about the best times to visit tourist attractions and where to shop for unique souvenirs. It will also feature fifty restaurant reviews for those wanting to try the local cuisine.

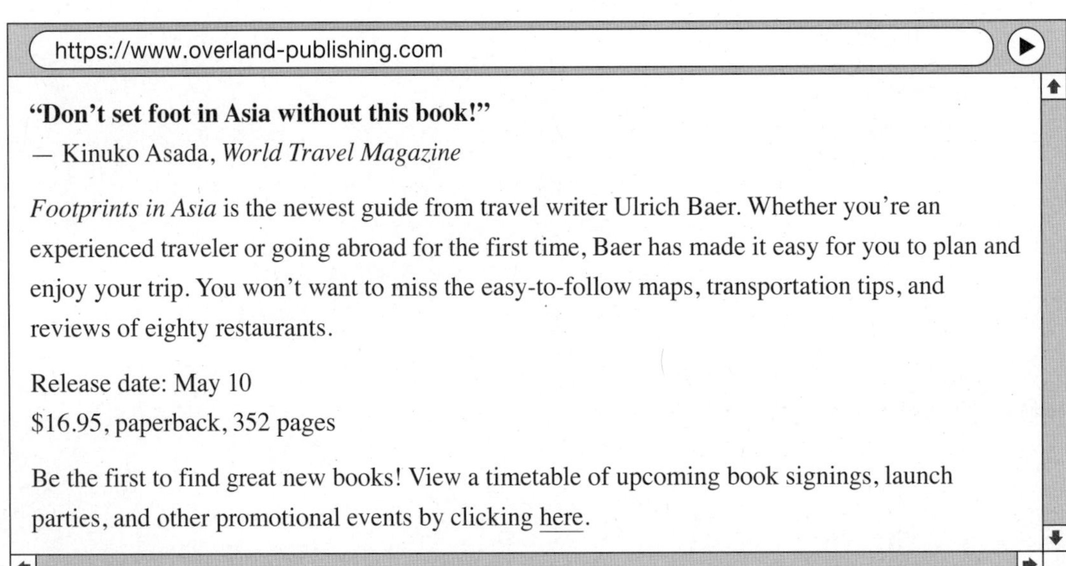
https://www.overland-publishing.com

"Don't set foot in Asia without this book!"
— Kinuko Asada, *World Travel Magazine*

Footprints in Asia is the newest guide from travel writer Ulrich Baer. Whether you're an experienced traveler or going abroad for the first time, Baer has made it easy for you to plan and enjoy your trip. You won't want to miss the easy-to-follow maps, transportation tips, and reviews of eighty restaurants.

Release date: May 10
$16.95, paperback, 352 pages

Be the first to find great new books! View a timetable of upcoming book signings, launch parties, and other promotional events by clicking here.

181. What is true about Mr. Baer?

(A) He moved around a lot when he was young.
(B) He attended a university in Argentina.
(C) He followed the same job as his father.
(D) He wrote fiction in his early career.

182. What is suggested about Mr. Baer's new travel guide?

(A) It received mixed reviews from critics.
(B) It includes historical photos.
(C) It comes with a free souvenir.
(D) It was published in German and English.

183. In the first Web page, the word "figured" in paragraph 1, line 5, is closest in meaning to

(A) appeared
(B) performed
(C) contributed
(D) decided

184. What is true about Overland Publishing?

(A) It is accepting work from new writers.
(B) It has an event schedule online.
(C) It is headquartered in Leipzig.
(D) It publishes *World Travel Magazine*.

185. How did Mr. Baer's latest travel guide change?

(A) It received a new title.
(B) Its publishing date was postponed.
(C) Some maps were featured in it.
(D) More restaurant reviews were added.

GO ON TO THE NEXT PAGE

Questions 186-190 refer to the following report, e-mail, and invoice.

Brandywine Finance
Report on Staff Survey Results
Issues in the Workplace

Employees had the following major workplace concerns as described in September's survey:

1. They have little privacy in open-space office areas. (62% of respondents)
2. The employee lounge is insufficient in size and lacks enough seating capacity. (57% of respondents)
3. Computers are old and break down frequently, thereby causing employees to be less productive at times. (49% of respondents)
4. Employee IDs sometims fail to work, leaving employees locked out of buildings or individual rooms. (27% of respondents)
5. There are not enough recycling bins, so employees must often dispose of recyclable items in trash cans. (15% of respondents)

Employees also complained about high noise levels due to employees talking or listening to music (7%), insufficient break periods (5%), and a drab office interior (3%).

From: jchandler@brandywinefinance.com
To: jasminehoward@brandywinefinance.com
Subject: Report on Staff Survey Results
Date: October 11

Dear Ms. Howard,

Thank you for providing the data in the report on the recent staff survey. I spoke with Luis Guarino in the IT Department, and he assured me he would do his best to maintain the computers better in the future. He emphasized that many machines should be replaced, however. Do we have enough funding for that? Perhaps by replacing a few each month, we can minimize the stress on the budget. What are your thoughts on this matter?

Regarding the fourth concern listed, I recall we had similar problems last year. I was under the impression that this problem had been solved, but I was apparently wrong.

We need to have a meeting about this soon. When are you available?

Sincerely,

Jennifer Chandler

Aaron's Supplies

Customer: Brandywine Finance

Date: October 17

Item Description	Quantity	Unit Price	Total
Comfortable Chair, Black	8	$95.00	$760.00
		Tax	$45.60
		Total	$805.60

Thank you for ordering from us. Your order will be delivered within two business days. If you have any questions, please call us at 1-888-555-9375.

186. What does the report suggest about Brandywine Finance?

(A) It occupies at least two different buildings.
(B) Protecting the environment is a major concern there.
(C) Staff members can park in its employee parking lot.
(D) Many of its employees do not have their own offices.

187. What percentage of respondents were unhappy about loud noises?

(A) 62%
(B) 27%
(C) 15%
(D) 7%

188. What does Ms. Chandler ask Ms. Howard about?

(A) How much money remains in this year's budget
(B) Who she should send the report to
(C) When she has time to discuss some issues
(D) Why problems are not being solved

189. According to Ms. Chandler, what problem happened last year?

(A) ID cards did not work on occasion.
(B) Employee computers broke down.
(C) There was not enough privacy for workers.
(D) Employees worked too much overtime.

190. What concern mentioned in the report most likely resulted in Brandywine Finance's purchase from Aaron's Supplies?

(A) Concern 1
(B) Concern 2
(C) Concern 3
(D) Concern 5

GO ON TO THE NEXT PAGE →

Questions 191-195 refer to the following brochure and e-mails.

The Rosemont Amusement Park provides fun and entertainment for children and adults. Located in the city of Oxford, the park has more than twenty rides, arcades and entertainment areas, a zoo, eating facilities, and souvenir shops.

We have special programs for all visitors to attend.

June 19—Horses and ponies from Jasper Farm will be at the zoo for visitors to pet and to ride on. Members pay $3. Nonmembers pay $5.

June 26—Come to see the elephant show. There will be three shows throughout the day. See what the elephants can do. After the show, go down to the stage to feed the elephants. Members pay $10. Nonmembers pay $20.

Reserve tickets for each event online at our Web site. You can also sign up to become a member of the Rosemont Amusement Park. Membership provides many benefits, including discounts on entrance tickets, food, and souvenirs as well as access to special events. Visit www.rosemontap.com/membership to learn more.

E-Mail

To: rcraig@gladden.com
From: membership@rosemontap.com
Subject: Welcome
Date: June 14

Dear Mr. Craig,

Thank you for becoming a member of the Rosemont Amusement Park. You selected a family membership, so you, your wife, son, and daughter will gain the advantages of membership. Each of you will receive a membership card in the mail within the next three days. You must use it when applying for a discount at the park, or you'll have to pay full price.

The first time you visit the amusement park, stop by the information center to pick up a special gift for you and your family.

Regards,

Tina Southern
Rosemont Amusement Park

TO:	Tina Southern 〈tina_s@rosemontap.com〉
FROM:	Robert Craig 〈rcraig@gladden.com〉
SUBJECT:	Request
DATE:	July 5

Dear Ms. Southern,

When my family and I recently visited your park as members, imagine our surprise when we were informed that my wife, whose card was at home, had to pay the nonmember price to see the elephant show. I paid the extra cost, but I would appreciate a refund. I can pick up the payment the next time I visit the park.

By the way, thank you for the picnic basket we were given. It was a thoughtful gift.

Regards,

Robert Craig

191. What is indicated about the Rosemont Amusement Park?

(A) It charges extra for special programs.
(B) It gives discounts to first-time visitors.
(C) It has plans to build a zoo soon.
(D) It has rides that are mostly for children.

192. What is NOT a benefit of becoming a member at the Rosemont Amusement Park?

(A) A lower price on admission
(B) Access to special events
(C) Discounts on food items
(D) An invitation to a year-end celebration

193. What is true according to the first e-mail?

(A) The price of membership recently increased.
(B) The information center has been closed for repairs.
(C) Membership cards can be picked up at the park.
(D) Everyone in the Craig family is a new member.

194. Why will Mr. Craig's request most likely be rejected?

(A) The application date has already passed.
(B) The park refuses to give any refunds.
(C) A membership card was not presented.
(D) Adults are not eligible for lower prices.

195. What can be inferred about the Craig family?

(A) They reserved tickets for the elephant show online.
(B) They rode on several rides at the amusement park.
(C) They visited the information center on June 26.
(D) They had dinner at the amusement park.

GO ON TO THE NEXT PAGE →

Questions 196-200 refer to the following Web site and e-mails.

http://www.blackforestpark.gov

Black Forest State Park is the biggest local park, yet it gets the fewest visitors in the state. To help potential tourists explore the park, we have created a virtual guide. It will allow visitors to see the best spots in the park and to find out what they can do there. The guide also provides links to local campgrounds, hotels, and restaurants.

To use the virtual guide, first, register on our Web site here. Then, you will have total access to the guide. You will be able to make bookings not only at places inside the park but also at those surrounding it.

Check out the guide when you have time, and let us know what you think. We'll be adding the ability to comment soon, so visitors can see what others think.

Contact us at information@blackforestpark.gov with your questions or comments.

E-Mail

To:	information@blackforestpark.gov
From:	lkeller@miltonhikingclub.org
Subject:	Hiking Trail
Date:	March 28

To Whom It May Concern,

I am impressed with your virtual guide. I have been to the park on numerous occasions, and I was unaware of several places, particularly dining establishments. I will check them out in the future.

I am curious about one thing. I could not locate the hiking trail around Swan Lake. Has the trail been closed due to the inclement winter weather? I'm planning to visit the park on April 4, and that trail is at the top of my list. Please let me know because our group includes twenty-seven people and may need to make some changes.

Sincerely,

Lisa Keller
President, Milton Hiking Club

To:	lkeller@miltonhikingclub.org
From:	information@blackforestpark.gov
Subject:	Re: Hiking Trail
Date:	March 29

Dear Ms. Keller,

Thank you for bringing that oversight to our attention. The necessary information will be added to the guide at once. If you find anything else wrong, please contact me at fchapman@blackforestpark.gov. I'll handle any other issues immediately.

Be advised that there is a new admission fee for groups. The following rates now apply:

Group Size	Fee
10—15	$20
16—25	$30
26—40	$50
41 or more	$70

I hope you have a wonderful time at the park.

Regards,

Fred Chapman
Park Ranger

196. According to the Web site, what is true about Black Forest State Park?

(A) All visitors must complete a form.
(B) Not many people go there.
(C) Park rangers provide tours there.
(D) It is the largest park in the country.

197. What are users of the virtual guide requested to do?

(A) Upload pictures
(B) Send a link to others
(C) Provide feedback
(D) Buy a membership

198. What is suggested about Ms. Keller?

(A) She has volunteered at the park before.
(B) She signed up on the park's Web site.
(C) She recently started a hiking club.
(D) She visits the park on a weekly basis.

199. What is one purpose of the second e-mail?

(A) To confirm a booking
(B) To acknowledge a mistake
(C) To request contact information
(D) To propose a new attraction

200. How much will Ms. Keller's group most likely pay when they visit the park?

(A) $20
(B) $30
(C) $50
(D) $70

ANSWER SHEET

TOEIC 실전 모의고사

응시일자	20 . . .
이름	
맞은 개수	/200

LISTENING (Part I ~ IV)

1	ⓐ ⓑ ⓒ ⓓ	21	ⓐ ⓑ ⓒ	41	ⓐ ⓑ ⓒ ⓓ	61	ⓐ ⓑ ⓒ ⓓ	81	ⓐ ⓑ ⓒ ⓓ
2	ⓐ ⓑ ⓒ ⓓ	22	ⓐ ⓑ ⓒ	42	ⓐ ⓑ ⓒ ⓓ	62	ⓐ ⓑ ⓒ ⓓ	82	ⓐ ⓑ ⓒ ⓓ
3	ⓐ ⓑ ⓒ ⓓ	23	ⓐ ⓑ ⓒ	43	ⓐ ⓑ ⓒ ⓓ	63	ⓐ ⓑ ⓒ ⓓ	83	ⓐ ⓑ ⓒ ⓓ
4	ⓐ ⓑ ⓒ ⓓ	24	ⓐ ⓑ ⓒ	44	ⓐ ⓑ ⓒ ⓓ	64	ⓐ ⓑ ⓒ ⓓ	84	ⓐ ⓑ ⓒ ⓓ
5	ⓐ ⓑ ⓒ ⓓ	25	ⓐ ⓑ ⓒ	45	ⓐ ⓑ ⓒ ⓓ	65	ⓐ ⓑ ⓒ ⓓ	85	ⓐ ⓑ ⓒ ⓓ
6	ⓐ ⓑ ⓒ ⓓ	26	ⓐ ⓑ ⓒ	46	ⓐ ⓑ ⓒ ⓓ	66	ⓐ ⓑ ⓒ ⓓ	86	ⓐ ⓑ ⓒ ⓓ
7	ⓐ ⓑ ⓒ	27	ⓐ ⓑ ⓒ	47	ⓐ ⓑ ⓒ ⓓ	67	ⓐ ⓑ ⓒ ⓓ	87	ⓐ ⓑ ⓒ ⓓ
8	ⓐ ⓑ ⓒ	28	ⓐ ⓑ ⓒ	48	ⓐ ⓑ ⓒ ⓓ	68	ⓐ ⓑ ⓒ ⓓ	88	ⓐ ⓑ ⓒ ⓓ
9	ⓐ ⓑ ⓒ	29	ⓐ ⓑ ⓒ	49	ⓐ ⓑ ⓒ ⓓ	69	ⓐ ⓑ ⓒ ⓓ	89	ⓐ ⓑ ⓒ ⓓ
10	ⓐ ⓑ ⓒ	30	ⓐ ⓑ ⓒ	50	ⓐ ⓑ ⓒ ⓓ	70	ⓐ ⓑ ⓒ ⓓ	90	ⓐ ⓑ ⓒ ⓓ
11	ⓐ ⓑ ⓒ	31	ⓐ ⓑ ⓒ	51	ⓐ ⓑ ⓒ ⓓ	71	ⓐ ⓑ ⓒ ⓓ	91	ⓐ ⓑ ⓒ ⓓ
12	ⓐ ⓑ ⓒ	32	ⓐ ⓑ ⓒ ⓓ	52	ⓐ ⓑ ⓒ ⓓ	72	ⓐ ⓑ ⓒ ⓓ	92	ⓐ ⓑ ⓒ ⓓ
13	ⓐ ⓑ ⓒ	33	ⓐ ⓑ ⓒ ⓓ	53	ⓐ ⓑ ⓒ ⓓ	73	ⓐ ⓑ ⓒ ⓓ	93	ⓐ ⓑ ⓒ ⓓ
14	ⓐ ⓑ ⓒ	34	ⓐ ⓑ ⓒ ⓓ	54	ⓐ ⓑ ⓒ ⓓ	74	ⓐ ⓑ ⓒ ⓓ	94	ⓐ ⓑ ⓒ ⓓ
15	ⓐ ⓑ ⓒ	35	ⓐ ⓑ ⓒ ⓓ	55	ⓐ ⓑ ⓒ ⓓ	75	ⓐ ⓑ ⓒ ⓓ	95	ⓐ ⓑ ⓒ ⓓ
16	ⓐ ⓑ ⓒ	36	ⓐ ⓑ ⓒ ⓓ	56	ⓐ ⓑ ⓒ ⓓ	76	ⓐ ⓑ ⓒ ⓓ	96	ⓐ ⓑ ⓒ ⓓ
17	ⓐ ⓑ ⓒ	37	ⓐ ⓑ ⓒ ⓓ	57	ⓐ ⓑ ⓒ ⓓ	77	ⓐ ⓑ ⓒ ⓓ	97	ⓐ ⓑ ⓒ ⓓ
18	ⓐ ⓑ ⓒ	38	ⓐ ⓑ ⓒ ⓓ	58	ⓐ ⓑ ⓒ ⓓ	78	ⓐ ⓑ ⓒ ⓓ	98	ⓐ ⓑ ⓒ ⓓ
19	ⓐ ⓑ ⓒ	39	ⓐ ⓑ ⓒ ⓓ	59	ⓐ ⓑ ⓒ ⓓ	79	ⓐ ⓑ ⓒ ⓓ	99	ⓐ ⓑ ⓒ ⓓ
20	ⓐ ⓑ ⓒ	40	ⓐ ⓑ ⓒ ⓓ	60	ⓐ ⓑ ⓒ ⓓ	80	ⓐ ⓑ ⓒ ⓓ	100	ⓐ ⓑ ⓒ ⓓ

READING (Part V ~ VII)

101	ⓐ ⓑ ⓒ ⓓ	121	ⓐ ⓑ ⓒ ⓓ	141	ⓐ ⓑ ⓒ ⓓ	161	ⓐ ⓑ ⓒ ⓓ	181	ⓐ ⓑ ⓒ ⓓ
102	ⓐ ⓑ ⓒ ⓓ	122	ⓐ ⓑ ⓒ ⓓ	142	ⓐ ⓑ ⓒ ⓓ	162	ⓐ ⓑ ⓒ ⓓ	182	ⓐ ⓑ ⓒ ⓓ
103	ⓐ ⓑ ⓒ ⓓ	123	ⓐ ⓑ ⓒ ⓓ	143	ⓐ ⓑ ⓒ ⓓ	163	ⓐ ⓑ ⓒ ⓓ	183	ⓐ ⓑ ⓒ ⓓ
104	ⓐ ⓑ ⓒ ⓓ	124	ⓐ ⓑ ⓒ ⓓ	144	ⓐ ⓑ ⓒ ⓓ	164	ⓐ ⓑ ⓒ ⓓ	184	ⓐ ⓑ ⓒ ⓓ
105	ⓐ ⓑ ⓒ ⓓ	125	ⓐ ⓑ ⓒ ⓓ	145	ⓐ ⓑ ⓒ ⓓ	165	ⓐ ⓑ ⓒ ⓓ	185	ⓐ ⓑ ⓒ ⓓ
106	ⓐ ⓑ ⓒ ⓓ	126	ⓐ ⓑ ⓒ ⓓ	146	ⓐ ⓑ ⓒ ⓓ	166	ⓐ ⓑ ⓒ ⓓ	186	ⓐ ⓑ ⓒ ⓓ
107	ⓐ ⓑ ⓒ ⓓ	127	ⓐ ⓑ ⓒ ⓓ	147	ⓐ ⓑ ⓒ ⓓ	167	ⓐ ⓑ ⓒ ⓓ	187	ⓐ ⓑ ⓒ ⓓ
108	ⓐ ⓑ ⓒ ⓓ	128	ⓐ ⓑ ⓒ ⓓ	148	ⓐ ⓑ ⓒ ⓓ	168	ⓐ ⓑ ⓒ ⓓ	188	ⓐ ⓑ ⓒ ⓓ
109	ⓐ ⓑ ⓒ ⓓ	129	ⓐ ⓑ ⓒ ⓓ	149	ⓐ ⓑ ⓒ ⓓ	169	ⓐ ⓑ ⓒ ⓓ	189	ⓐ ⓑ ⓒ ⓓ
110	ⓐ ⓑ ⓒ ⓓ	130	ⓐ ⓑ ⓒ ⓓ	150	ⓐ ⓑ ⓒ ⓓ	170	ⓐ ⓑ ⓒ ⓓ	190	ⓐ ⓑ ⓒ ⓓ
111	ⓐ ⓑ ⓒ ⓓ	131	ⓐ ⓑ ⓒ ⓓ	151	ⓐ ⓑ ⓒ ⓓ	171	ⓐ ⓑ ⓒ ⓓ	191	ⓐ ⓑ ⓒ ⓓ
112	ⓐ ⓑ ⓒ ⓓ	132	ⓐ ⓑ ⓒ ⓓ	152	ⓐ ⓑ ⓒ ⓓ	172	ⓐ ⓑ ⓒ ⓓ	192	ⓐ ⓑ ⓒ ⓓ
113	ⓐ ⓑ ⓒ ⓓ	133	ⓐ ⓑ ⓒ ⓓ	153	ⓐ ⓑ ⓒ ⓓ	173	ⓐ ⓑ ⓒ ⓓ	193	ⓐ ⓑ ⓒ ⓓ
114	ⓐ ⓑ ⓒ ⓓ	134	ⓐ ⓑ ⓒ ⓓ	154	ⓐ ⓑ ⓒ ⓓ	174	ⓐ ⓑ ⓒ ⓓ	194	ⓐ ⓑ ⓒ ⓓ
115	ⓐ ⓑ ⓒ ⓓ	135	ⓐ ⓑ ⓒ ⓓ	155	ⓐ ⓑ ⓒ ⓓ	175	ⓐ ⓑ ⓒ ⓓ	195	ⓐ ⓑ ⓒ ⓓ
116	ⓐ ⓑ ⓒ ⓓ	136	ⓐ ⓑ ⓒ ⓓ	156	ⓐ ⓑ ⓒ ⓓ	176	ⓐ ⓑ ⓒ ⓓ	196	ⓐ ⓑ ⓒ ⓓ
117	ⓐ ⓑ ⓒ ⓓ	137	ⓐ ⓑ ⓒ ⓓ	157	ⓐ ⓑ ⓒ ⓓ	177	ⓐ ⓑ ⓒ ⓓ	197	ⓐ ⓑ ⓒ ⓓ
118	ⓐ ⓑ ⓒ ⓓ	138	ⓐ ⓑ ⓒ ⓓ	158	ⓐ ⓑ ⓒ ⓓ	178	ⓐ ⓑ ⓒ ⓓ	198	ⓐ ⓑ ⓒ ⓓ
119	ⓐ ⓑ ⓒ ⓓ	139	ⓐ ⓑ ⓒ ⓓ	159	ⓐ ⓑ ⓒ ⓓ	179	ⓐ ⓑ ⓒ ⓓ	199	ⓐ ⓑ ⓒ ⓓ
120	ⓐ ⓑ ⓒ ⓓ	140	ⓐ ⓑ ⓒ ⓓ	160	ⓐ ⓑ ⓒ ⓓ	180	ⓐ ⓑ ⓒ ⓓ	200	ⓐ ⓑ ⓒ ⓓ

ANSWER SHEET

TOEIC 실전 모의고사

응시일자	20 . . .
이름	
맞은 개수	/200

LISTENING (Part I ~ IV)

1	ⓐⓑⓒⓓ	21	ⓐⓑⓒ	41	ⓐⓑⓒⓓ	61	ⓐⓑⓒⓓ	81	ⓐⓑⓒⓓ
2	ⓐⓑⓒⓓ	22	ⓐⓑⓒ	42	ⓐⓑⓒⓓ	62	ⓐⓑⓒⓓ	82	ⓐⓑⓒⓓ
3	ⓐⓑⓒⓓ	23	ⓐⓑⓒ	43	ⓐⓑⓒⓓ	63	ⓐⓑⓒⓓ	83	ⓐⓑⓒⓓ
4	ⓐⓑⓒⓓ	24	ⓐⓑⓒ	44	ⓐⓑⓒⓓ	64	ⓐⓑⓒⓓ	84	ⓐⓑⓒⓓ
5	ⓐⓑⓒⓓ	25	ⓐⓑⓒ	45	ⓐⓑⓒⓓ	65	ⓐⓑⓒⓓ	85	ⓐⓑⓒⓓ
6	ⓐⓑⓒⓓ	26	ⓐⓑⓒ	46	ⓐⓑⓒⓓ	66	ⓐⓑⓒⓓ	86	ⓐⓑⓒⓓ
7	ⓐⓑⓒ	27	ⓐⓑⓒ	47	ⓐⓑⓒⓓ	67	ⓐⓑⓒⓓ	87	ⓐⓑⓒⓓ
8	ⓐⓑⓒ	28	ⓐⓑⓒ	48	ⓐⓑⓒⓓ	68	ⓐⓑⓒⓓ	88	ⓐⓑⓒⓓ
9	ⓐⓑⓒ	29	ⓐⓑⓒ	49	ⓐⓑⓒⓓ	69	ⓐⓑⓒⓓ	89	ⓐⓑⓒⓓ
10	ⓐⓑⓒ	30	ⓐⓑⓒ	50	ⓐⓑⓒⓓ	70	ⓐⓑⓒⓓ	90	ⓐⓑⓒⓓ
11	ⓐⓑⓒ	31	ⓐⓑⓒ	51	ⓐⓑⓒⓓ	71	ⓐⓑⓒⓓ	91	ⓐⓑⓒⓓ
12	ⓐⓑⓒ	32	ⓐⓑⓒⓓ	52	ⓐⓑⓒⓓ	72	ⓐⓑⓒⓓ	92	ⓐⓑⓒⓓ
13	ⓐⓑⓒ	33	ⓐⓑⓒⓓ	53	ⓐⓑⓒⓓ	73	ⓐⓑⓒⓓ	93	ⓐⓑⓒⓓ
14	ⓐⓑⓒ	34	ⓐⓑⓒⓓ	54	ⓐⓑⓒⓓ	74	ⓐⓑⓒⓓ	94	ⓐⓑⓒⓓ
15	ⓐⓑⓒ	35	ⓐⓑⓒⓓ	55	ⓐⓑⓒⓓ	75	ⓐⓑⓒⓓ	95	ⓐⓑⓒⓓ
16	ⓐⓑⓒ	36	ⓐⓑⓒⓓ	56	ⓐⓑⓒⓓ	76	ⓐⓑⓒⓓ	96	ⓐⓑⓒⓓ
17	ⓐⓑⓒ	37	ⓐⓑⓒⓓ	57	ⓐⓑⓒⓓ	77	ⓐⓑⓒⓓ	97	ⓐⓑⓒⓓ
18	ⓐⓑⓒ	38	ⓐⓑⓒⓓ	58	ⓐⓑⓒⓓ	78	ⓐⓑⓒⓓ	98	ⓐⓑⓒⓓ
19	ⓐⓑⓒ	39	ⓐⓑⓒⓓ	59	ⓐⓑⓒⓓ	79	ⓐⓑⓒⓓ	99	ⓐⓑⓒⓓ
20	ⓐⓑⓒ	40	ⓐⓑⓒⓓ	60	ⓐⓑⓒⓓ	80	ⓐⓑⓒⓓ	100	ⓐⓑⓒⓓ

READING (Part V ~ VII)

101	ⓐⓑⓒⓓ	121	ⓐⓑⓒⓓ	141	ⓐⓑⓒⓓ	161	ⓐⓑⓒⓓ	181	ⓐⓑⓒⓓ
102	ⓐⓑⓒⓓ	122	ⓐⓑⓒⓓ	142	ⓐⓑⓒⓓ	162	ⓐⓑⓒⓓ	182	ⓐⓑⓒⓓ
103	ⓐⓑⓒⓓ	123	ⓐⓑⓒⓓ	143	ⓐⓑⓒⓓ	163	ⓐⓑⓒⓓ	183	ⓐⓑⓒⓓ
104	ⓐⓑⓒⓓ	124	ⓐⓑⓒⓓ	144	ⓐⓑⓒⓓ	164	ⓐⓑⓒⓓ	184	ⓐⓑⓒⓓ
105	ⓐⓑⓒⓓ	125	ⓐⓑⓒⓓ	145	ⓐⓑⓒⓓ	165	ⓐⓑⓒⓓ	185	ⓐⓑⓒⓓ
106	ⓐⓑⓒⓓ	126	ⓐⓑⓒⓓ	146	ⓐⓑⓒⓓ	166	ⓐⓑⓒⓓ	186	ⓐⓑⓒⓓ
107	ⓐⓑⓒⓓ	127	ⓐⓑⓒⓓ	147	ⓐⓑⓒⓓ	167	ⓐⓑⓒⓓ	187	ⓐⓑⓒⓓ
108	ⓐⓑⓒⓓ	128	ⓐⓑⓒⓓ	148	ⓐⓑⓒⓓ	168	ⓐⓑⓒⓓ	188	ⓐⓑⓒⓓ
109	ⓐⓑⓒⓓ	129	ⓐⓑⓒⓓ	149	ⓐⓑⓒⓓ	169	ⓐⓑⓒⓓ	189	ⓐⓑⓒⓓ
110	ⓐⓑⓒⓓ	130	ⓐⓑⓒⓓ	150	ⓐⓑⓒⓓ	170	ⓐⓑⓒⓓ	190	ⓐⓑⓒⓓ
111	ⓐⓑⓒⓓ	131	ⓐⓑⓒⓓ	151	ⓐⓑⓒⓓ	171	ⓐⓑⓒⓓ	191	ⓐⓑⓒⓓ
112	ⓐⓑⓒⓓ	132	ⓐⓑⓒⓓ	152	ⓐⓑⓒⓓ	172	ⓐⓑⓒⓓ	192	ⓐⓑⓒⓓ
113	ⓐⓑⓒⓓ	133	ⓐⓑⓒⓓ	153	ⓐⓑⓒⓓ	173	ⓐⓑⓒⓓ	193	ⓐⓑⓒⓓ
114	ⓐⓑⓒⓓ	134	ⓐⓑⓒⓓ	154	ⓐⓑⓒⓓ	174	ⓐⓑⓒⓓ	194	ⓐⓑⓒⓓ
115	ⓐⓑⓒⓓ	135	ⓐⓑⓒⓓ	155	ⓐⓑⓒⓓ	175	ⓐⓑⓒⓓ	195	ⓐⓑⓒⓓ
116	ⓐⓑⓒⓓ	136	ⓐⓑⓒⓓ	156	ⓐⓑⓒⓓ	176	ⓐⓑⓒⓓ	196	ⓐⓑⓒⓓ
117	ⓐⓑⓒⓓ	137	ⓐⓑⓒⓓ	157	ⓐⓑⓒⓓ	177	ⓐⓑⓒⓓ	197	ⓐⓑⓒⓓ
118	ⓐⓑⓒⓓ	138	ⓐⓑⓒⓓ	158	ⓐⓑⓒⓓ	178	ⓐⓑⓒⓓ	198	ⓐⓑⓒⓓ
119	ⓐⓑⓒⓓ	139	ⓐⓑⓒⓓ	159	ⓐⓑⓒⓓ	179	ⓐⓑⓒⓓ	199	ⓐⓑⓒⓓ
120	ⓐⓑⓒⓓ	140	ⓐⓑⓒⓓ	160	ⓐⓑⓒⓓ	180	ⓐⓑⓒⓓ	200	ⓐⓑⓒⓓ

ANSWER SHEET

TOEIC 실전 모의고사

응시일자	20 . . .
이름	
맞은 개수	/200

LISTENING (Part I ~ IV)

1	ⓐ ⓑ ⓒ ⓓ	21	ⓐ ⓑ ⓒ	41	ⓐ ⓑ ⓒ ⓓ	61	ⓐ ⓑ ⓒ ⓓ	81	ⓐ ⓑ ⓒ ⓓ
2	ⓐ ⓑ ⓒ ⓓ	22	ⓐ ⓑ ⓒ	42	ⓐ ⓑ ⓒ ⓓ	62	ⓐ ⓑ ⓒ ⓓ	82	ⓐ ⓑ ⓒ ⓓ
3	ⓐ ⓑ ⓒ ⓓ	23	ⓐ ⓑ ⓒ	43	ⓐ ⓑ ⓒ ⓓ	63	ⓐ ⓑ ⓒ ⓓ	83	ⓐ ⓑ ⓒ ⓓ
4	ⓐ ⓑ ⓒ ⓓ	24	ⓐ ⓑ ⓒ	44	ⓐ ⓑ ⓒ ⓓ	64	ⓐ ⓑ ⓒ ⓓ	84	ⓐ ⓑ ⓒ ⓓ
5	ⓐ ⓑ ⓒ ⓓ	25	ⓐ ⓑ ⓒ	45	ⓐ ⓑ ⓒ ⓓ	65	ⓐ ⓑ ⓒ ⓓ	85	ⓐ ⓑ ⓒ ⓓ
6	ⓐ ⓑ ⓒ ⓓ	26	ⓐ ⓑ ⓒ	46	ⓐ ⓑ ⓒ ⓓ	66	ⓐ ⓑ ⓒ ⓓ	86	ⓐ ⓑ ⓒ ⓓ
7	ⓐ ⓑ ⓒ	27	ⓐ ⓑ ⓒ	47	ⓐ ⓑ ⓒ ⓓ	67	ⓐ ⓑ ⓒ ⓓ	87	ⓐ ⓑ ⓒ ⓓ
8	ⓐ ⓑ ⓒ	28	ⓐ ⓑ ⓒ	48	ⓐ ⓑ ⓒ ⓓ	68	ⓐ ⓑ ⓒ ⓓ	88	ⓐ ⓑ ⓒ ⓓ
9	ⓐ ⓑ ⓒ	29	ⓐ ⓑ ⓒ	49	ⓐ ⓑ ⓒ ⓓ	69	ⓐ ⓑ ⓒ ⓓ	89	ⓐ ⓑ ⓒ ⓓ
10	ⓐ ⓑ ⓒ	30	ⓐ ⓑ ⓒ	50	ⓐ ⓑ ⓒ ⓓ	70	ⓐ ⓑ ⓒ ⓓ	90	ⓐ ⓑ ⓒ ⓓ
11	ⓐ ⓑ ⓒ	31	ⓐ ⓑ ⓒ	51	ⓐ ⓑ ⓒ ⓓ	71	ⓐ ⓑ ⓒ ⓓ	91	ⓐ ⓑ ⓒ ⓓ
12	ⓐ ⓑ ⓒ	32	ⓐ ⓑ ⓒ ⓓ	52	ⓐ ⓑ ⓒ ⓓ	72	ⓐ ⓑ ⓒ ⓓ	92	ⓐ ⓑ ⓒ ⓓ
13	ⓐ ⓑ ⓒ	33	ⓐ ⓑ ⓒ ⓓ	53	ⓐ ⓑ ⓒ ⓓ	73	ⓐ ⓑ ⓒ ⓓ	93	ⓐ ⓑ ⓒ ⓓ
14	ⓐ ⓑ ⓒ	34	ⓐ ⓑ ⓒ ⓓ	54	ⓐ ⓑ ⓒ ⓓ	74	ⓐ ⓑ ⓒ ⓓ	94	ⓐ ⓑ ⓒ ⓓ
15	ⓐ ⓑ ⓒ	35	ⓐ ⓑ ⓒ ⓓ	55	ⓐ ⓑ ⓒ ⓓ	75	ⓐ ⓑ ⓒ ⓓ	95	ⓐ ⓑ ⓒ ⓓ
16	ⓐ ⓑ ⓒ	36	ⓐ ⓑ ⓒ ⓓ	56	ⓐ ⓑ ⓒ ⓓ	76	ⓐ ⓑ ⓒ ⓓ	96	ⓐ ⓑ ⓒ ⓓ
17	ⓐ ⓑ ⓒ	37	ⓐ ⓑ ⓒ ⓓ	57	ⓐ ⓑ ⓒ ⓓ	77	ⓐ ⓑ ⓒ ⓓ	97	ⓐ ⓑ ⓒ ⓓ
18	ⓐ ⓑ ⓒ	38	ⓐ ⓑ ⓒ ⓓ	58	ⓐ ⓑ ⓒ ⓓ	78	ⓐ ⓑ ⓒ ⓓ	98	ⓐ ⓑ ⓒ ⓓ
19	ⓐ ⓑ ⓒ	39	ⓐ ⓑ ⓒ ⓓ	59	ⓐ ⓑ ⓒ ⓓ	79	ⓐ ⓑ ⓒ ⓓ	99	ⓐ ⓑ ⓒ ⓓ
20	ⓐ ⓑ ⓒ	40	ⓐ ⓑ ⓒ ⓓ	60	ⓐ ⓑ ⓒ ⓓ	80	ⓐ ⓑ ⓒ ⓓ	100	ⓐ ⓑ ⓒ ⓓ

READING (Part V ~ VII)

101	ⓐ ⓑ ⓒ ⓓ	121	ⓐ ⓑ ⓒ ⓓ	141	ⓐ ⓑ ⓒ ⓓ	161	ⓐ ⓑ ⓒ ⓓ	181	ⓐ ⓑ ⓒ ⓓ
102	ⓐ ⓑ ⓒ ⓓ	122	ⓐ ⓑ ⓒ ⓓ	142	ⓐ ⓑ ⓒ ⓓ	162	ⓐ ⓑ ⓒ ⓓ	182	ⓐ ⓑ ⓒ ⓓ
103	ⓐ ⓑ ⓒ ⓓ	123	ⓐ ⓑ ⓒ ⓓ	143	ⓐ ⓑ ⓒ ⓓ	163	ⓐ ⓑ ⓒ ⓓ	183	ⓐ ⓑ ⓒ ⓓ
104	ⓐ ⓑ ⓒ ⓓ	124	ⓐ ⓑ ⓒ ⓓ	144	ⓐ ⓑ ⓒ ⓓ	164	ⓐ ⓑ ⓒ ⓓ	184	ⓐ ⓑ ⓒ ⓓ
105	ⓐ ⓑ ⓒ ⓓ	125	ⓐ ⓑ ⓒ ⓓ	145	ⓐ ⓑ ⓒ ⓓ	165	ⓐ ⓑ ⓒ ⓓ	185	ⓐ ⓑ ⓒ ⓓ
106	ⓐ ⓑ ⓒ ⓓ	126	ⓐ ⓑ ⓒ ⓓ	146	ⓐ ⓑ ⓒ ⓓ	166	ⓐ ⓑ ⓒ ⓓ	186	ⓐ ⓑ ⓒ ⓓ
107	ⓐ ⓑ ⓒ ⓓ	127	ⓐ ⓑ ⓒ ⓓ	147	ⓐ ⓑ ⓒ ⓓ	167	ⓐ ⓑ ⓒ ⓓ	187	ⓐ ⓑ ⓒ ⓓ
108	ⓐ ⓑ ⓒ ⓓ	128	ⓐ ⓑ ⓒ ⓓ	148	ⓐ ⓑ ⓒ ⓓ	168	ⓐ ⓑ ⓒ ⓓ	188	ⓐ ⓑ ⓒ ⓓ
109	ⓐ ⓑ ⓒ ⓓ	129	ⓐ ⓑ ⓒ ⓓ	149	ⓐ ⓑ ⓒ ⓓ	169	ⓐ ⓑ ⓒ ⓓ	189	ⓐ ⓑ ⓒ ⓓ
110	ⓐ ⓑ ⓒ ⓓ	130	ⓐ ⓑ ⓒ ⓓ	150	ⓐ ⓑ ⓒ ⓓ	170	ⓐ ⓑ ⓒ ⓓ	190	ⓐ ⓑ ⓒ ⓓ
111	ⓐ ⓑ ⓒ ⓓ	131	ⓐ ⓑ ⓒ ⓓ	151	ⓐ ⓑ ⓒ ⓓ	171	ⓐ ⓑ ⓒ ⓓ	191	ⓐ ⓑ ⓒ ⓓ
112	ⓐ ⓑ ⓒ ⓓ	132	ⓐ ⓑ ⓒ ⓓ	152	ⓐ ⓑ ⓒ ⓓ	172	ⓐ ⓑ ⓒ ⓓ	192	ⓐ ⓑ ⓒ ⓓ
113	ⓐ ⓑ ⓒ ⓓ	133	ⓐ ⓑ ⓒ ⓓ	153	ⓐ ⓑ ⓒ ⓓ	173	ⓐ ⓑ ⓒ ⓓ	193	ⓐ ⓑ ⓒ ⓓ
114	ⓐ ⓑ ⓒ ⓓ	134	ⓐ ⓑ ⓒ ⓓ	154	ⓐ ⓑ ⓒ ⓓ	174	ⓐ ⓑ ⓒ ⓓ	194	ⓐ ⓑ ⓒ ⓓ
115	ⓐ ⓑ ⓒ ⓓ	135	ⓐ ⓑ ⓒ ⓓ	155	ⓐ ⓑ ⓒ ⓓ	175	ⓐ ⓑ ⓒ ⓓ	195	ⓐ ⓑ ⓒ ⓓ
116	ⓐ ⓑ ⓒ ⓓ	136	ⓐ ⓑ ⓒ ⓓ	156	ⓐ ⓑ ⓒ ⓓ	176	ⓐ ⓑ ⓒ ⓓ	196	ⓐ ⓑ ⓒ ⓓ
117	ⓐ ⓑ ⓒ ⓓ	137	ⓐ ⓑ ⓒ ⓓ	157	ⓐ ⓑ ⓒ ⓓ	177	ⓐ ⓑ ⓒ ⓓ	197	ⓐ ⓑ ⓒ ⓓ
118	ⓐ ⓑ ⓒ ⓓ	138	ⓐ ⓑ ⓒ ⓓ	158	ⓐ ⓑ ⓒ ⓓ	178	ⓐ ⓑ ⓒ ⓓ	198	ⓐ ⓑ ⓒ ⓓ
119	ⓐ ⓑ ⓒ ⓓ	139	ⓐ ⓑ ⓒ ⓓ	159	ⓐ ⓑ ⓒ ⓓ	179	ⓐ ⓑ ⓒ ⓓ	199	ⓐ ⓑ ⓒ ⓓ
120	ⓐ ⓑ ⓒ ⓓ	140	ⓐ ⓑ ⓒ ⓓ	160	ⓐ ⓑ ⓒ ⓓ	180	ⓐ ⓑ ⓒ ⓓ	200	ⓐ ⓑ ⓒ ⓓ

ANSWER SHEET

TOEIC 실전 모의고사

응시일자	20 . . .
이름	
맞은 개수	/200

LISTENING (Part I ~ IV)

1	ⓐⓑⓒⓓ	21	ⓐⓑⓒ	41	ⓐⓑⓒⓓ	61	ⓐⓑⓒⓓ	81	ⓐⓑⓒⓓ
2	ⓐⓑⓒⓓ	22	ⓐⓑⓒ	42	ⓐⓑⓒⓓ	62	ⓐⓑⓒⓓ	82	ⓐⓑⓒⓓ
3	ⓐⓑⓒⓓ	23	ⓐⓑⓒ	43	ⓐⓑⓒⓓ	63	ⓐⓑⓒⓓ	83	ⓐⓑⓒⓓ
4	ⓐⓑⓒⓓ	24	ⓐⓑⓒ	44	ⓐⓑⓒⓓ	64	ⓐⓑⓒⓓ	84	ⓐⓑⓒⓓ
5	ⓐⓑⓒⓓ	25	ⓐⓑⓒ	45	ⓐⓑⓒⓓ	65	ⓐⓑⓒⓓ	85	ⓐⓑⓒⓓ
6	ⓐⓑⓒⓓ	26	ⓐⓑⓒ	46	ⓐⓑⓒⓓ	66	ⓐⓑⓒⓓ	86	ⓐⓑⓒⓓ
7	ⓐⓑⓒ	27	ⓐⓑⓒ	47	ⓐⓑⓒⓓ	67	ⓐⓑⓒⓓ	87	ⓐⓑⓒⓓ
8	ⓐⓑⓒ	28	ⓐⓑⓒ	48	ⓐⓑⓒⓓ	68	ⓐⓑⓒⓓ	88	ⓐⓑⓒⓓ
9	ⓐⓑⓒ	29	ⓐⓑⓒ	49	ⓐⓑⓒⓓ	69	ⓐⓑⓒⓓ	89	ⓐⓑⓒⓓ
10	ⓐⓑⓒ	30	ⓐⓑⓒ	50	ⓐⓑⓒⓓ	70	ⓐⓑⓒⓓ	90	ⓐⓑⓒⓓ
11	ⓐⓑⓒ	31	ⓐⓑⓒ	51	ⓐⓑⓒⓓ	71	ⓐⓑⓒⓓ	91	ⓐⓑⓒⓓ
12	ⓐⓑⓒ	32	ⓐⓑⓒⓓ	52	ⓐⓑⓒⓓ	72	ⓐⓑⓒⓓ	92	ⓐⓑⓒⓓ
13	ⓐⓑⓒ	33	ⓐⓑⓒⓓ	53	ⓐⓑⓒⓓ	73	ⓐⓑⓒⓓ	93	ⓐⓑⓒⓓ
14	ⓐⓑⓒ	34	ⓐⓑⓒⓓ	54	ⓐⓑⓒⓓ	74	ⓐⓑⓒⓓ	94	ⓐⓑⓒⓓ
15	ⓐⓑⓒ	35	ⓐⓑⓒⓓ	55	ⓐⓑⓒⓓ	75	ⓐⓑⓒⓓ	95	ⓐⓑⓒⓓ
16	ⓐⓑⓒ	36	ⓐⓑⓒⓓ	56	ⓐⓑⓒⓓ	76	ⓐⓑⓒⓓ	96	ⓐⓑⓒⓓ
17	ⓐⓑⓒ	37	ⓐⓑⓒⓓ	57	ⓐⓑⓒⓓ	77	ⓐⓑⓒⓓ	97	ⓐⓑⓒⓓ
18	ⓐⓑⓒ	38	ⓐⓑⓒⓓ	58	ⓐⓑⓒⓓ	78	ⓐⓑⓒⓓ	98	ⓐⓑⓒⓓ
19	ⓐⓑⓒ	39	ⓐⓑⓒⓓ	59	ⓐⓑⓒⓓ	79	ⓐⓑⓒⓓ	99	ⓐⓑⓒⓓ
20	ⓐⓑⓒ	40	ⓐⓑⓒⓓ	60	ⓐⓑⓒⓓ	80	ⓐⓑⓒⓓ	100	ⓐⓑⓒⓓ

READING (Part V ~ VII)

101	ⓐⓑⓒⓓ	121	ⓐⓑⓒⓓ	141	ⓐⓑⓒⓓ	161	ⓐⓑⓒⓓ	181	ⓐⓑⓒⓓ
102	ⓐⓑⓒⓓ	122	ⓐⓑⓒⓓ	142	ⓐⓑⓒⓓ	162	ⓐⓑⓒⓓ	182	ⓐⓑⓒⓓ
103	ⓐⓑⓒⓓ	123	ⓐⓑⓒⓓ	143	ⓐⓑⓒⓓ	163	ⓐⓑⓒⓓ	183	ⓐⓑⓒⓓ
104	ⓐⓑⓒⓓ	124	ⓐⓑⓒⓓ	144	ⓐⓑⓒⓓ	164	ⓐⓑⓒⓓ	184	ⓐⓑⓒⓓ
105	ⓐⓑⓒⓓ	125	ⓐⓑⓒⓓ	145	ⓐⓑⓒⓓ	165	ⓐⓑⓒⓓ	185	ⓐⓑⓒⓓ
106	ⓐⓑⓒⓓ	126	ⓐⓑⓒⓓ	146	ⓐⓑⓒⓓ	166	ⓐⓑⓒⓓ	186	ⓐⓑⓒⓓ
107	ⓐⓑⓒⓓ	127	ⓐⓑⓒⓓ	147	ⓐⓑⓒⓓ	167	ⓐⓑⓒⓓ	187	ⓐⓑⓒⓓ
108	ⓐⓑⓒⓓ	128	ⓐⓑⓒⓓ	148	ⓐⓑⓒⓓ	168	ⓐⓑⓒⓓ	188	ⓐⓑⓒⓓ
109	ⓐⓑⓒⓓ	129	ⓐⓑⓒⓓ	149	ⓐⓑⓒⓓ	169	ⓐⓑⓒⓓ	189	ⓐⓑⓒⓓ
110	ⓐⓑⓒⓓ	130	ⓐⓑⓒⓓ	150	ⓐⓑⓒⓓ	170	ⓐⓑⓒⓓ	190	ⓐⓑⓒⓓ
111	ⓐⓑⓒⓓ	131	ⓐⓑⓒⓓ	151	ⓐⓑⓒⓓ	171	ⓐⓑⓒⓓ	191	ⓐⓑⓒⓓ
112	ⓐⓑⓒⓓ	132	ⓐⓑⓒⓓ	152	ⓐⓑⓒⓓ	172	ⓐⓑⓒⓓ	192	ⓐⓑⓒⓓ
113	ⓐⓑⓒⓓ	133	ⓐⓑⓒⓓ	153	ⓐⓑⓒⓓ	173	ⓐⓑⓒⓓ	193	ⓐⓑⓒⓓ
114	ⓐⓑⓒⓓ	134	ⓐⓑⓒⓓ	154	ⓐⓑⓒⓓ	174	ⓐⓑⓒⓓ	194	ⓐⓑⓒⓓ
115	ⓐⓑⓒⓓ	135	ⓐⓑⓒⓓ	155	ⓐⓑⓒⓓ	175	ⓐⓑⓒⓓ	195	ⓐⓑⓒⓓ
116	ⓐⓑⓒⓓ	136	ⓐⓑⓒⓓ	156	ⓐⓑⓒⓓ	176	ⓐⓑⓒⓓ	196	ⓐⓑⓒⓓ
117	ⓐⓑⓒⓓ	137	ⓐⓑⓒⓓ	157	ⓐⓑⓒⓓ	177	ⓐⓑⓒⓓ	197	ⓐⓑⓒⓓ
118	ⓐⓑⓒⓓ	138	ⓐⓑⓒⓓ	158	ⓐⓑⓒⓓ	178	ⓐⓑⓒⓓ	198	ⓐⓑⓒⓓ
119	ⓐⓑⓒⓓ	139	ⓐⓑⓒⓓ	159	ⓐⓑⓒⓓ	179	ⓐⓑⓒⓓ	199	ⓐⓑⓒⓓ
120	ⓐⓑⓒⓓ	140	ⓐⓑⓒⓓ	160	ⓐⓑⓒⓓ	180	ⓐⓑⓒⓓ	200	ⓐⓑⓒⓓ

삶의 순간순간이
아름다운 마무리이며
새로운 시작이어야 한다.

– 법정 스님

에듀윌 토익 단기완성 850+ LC & RC

발 행 일	2023년 6월 5일 초판
편 저 자	에듀윌 어학연구소
펴 낸 이	김재환
펴 낸 곳	(주)에듀윌
등록번호	제25100-2002-000052호
주 소	08378 서울특별시 구로구 디지털로34길 55 코오롱싸이언스밸리 2차 3층

www.eduwill.net

대표전화 1600-6700

여러분의 작은 소리
에듀윌은 크게 듣겠습니다.

본 교재에 대한 여러분의 목소리를 들려주세요.
공부하시면서 어려웠던 점, 궁금한 점,
칭찬하고 싶은 점, 개선할 점, 어떤 것이라도 좋습니다.

에듀윌은 여러분께서 나누어 주신 의견을
통해 끊임없이 발전하고 있습니다.

에듀윌 토익 단기완성 850+

LC & RC

정답 및 해설

에듀윌 토익 단기완성 850+

정답 및 해설

에듀윌 토익

단기완성 850+

LC & RC

정답 및 해설

LC PART 1

출제 경향 및 전략

본문 p.16

1. 1인 사진
(A) 여자가 프린터를 고치고 있다.
(B) 여자가 재킷을 입는 중이다.
(C) 여자가 서류를 검토 중이다.
(D) 여자가 문서를 복사하고 있다.

어휘 fix ~을 고치다 put on ~을 입다(동작) examine ~을 검사하다 photocopy ~을 복사하다

2. 2인 사진
(A) 그들이 헬멧을 벗고 있다.
(B) 그들이 종이를 접고 있다.
(C) 남자들 중 한 명이 도면에 표시하고 있다.
(D) 남자들 중 한 명이 창유리의 크기를 재고 있다.

어휘 remove ~을 제거하다, ~을 벗다 mark ~에 표시하다 measure ~을 재다 windowpane 창유리

3. 3인 이상 사진
(A) 고객들이 식료품을 고르고 있다.
(B) 고객들이 줄을 서서 기다리고 있다.
(C) 계산원이 현금을 꺼내고 있다.
(D) 계산원이 금전 등록기를 열고 있다.

어휘 pick out 고르다, 선택하다 take out ~을 꺼내다

4. 사물 또는 풍경 사진
(A) 그림들이 벽에 걸려 있다.
(B) 예술작품이 소파에 기대어 있다.
(C) 조명이 벽에 설치되어 있다.
(D) 화분이 테이블에 놓여 있다.

어휘 hang ~이 걸려 있다 prop against ~을 기대 놓다 light fixture 조명

UNIT 01 인물 사진 묘사

CHECK-UP

본문 p.19

1. (C) **2.** (A)

1. 영녀

(A) A toolbox has been left on the ground.
(B) He is putting on knee pads.
(C) He is removing some floor tiles.
(D) Some debris is being cleared from the floor.

(A) 공구함이 바닥 위에 놓여 있다.
(B) 남자가 무릎 보호대를 착용하고 있다. (동작)
(C) 남자가 바닥 타일을 제거하고 있다.
(D) 잔해가 바닥으로부터 치워지고 있다.

어휘 put on ~을 착용하다(동작) knee pad 무릎 보호대 remove ~을 제거하다 debris 잔해 clear 치우다

2. 미남

(A) A customer is handing a worker some cash.
(B) A woman is looking through her purse.
(C) A customer is trying on a patterned blouse.
(D) A man is arranging merchandise on shelves.

(A) 손님이 직원에게 현금을 건네주고 있다.
(B) 여자가 자신의 지갑을 뒤지고 있다.
(C) 손님이 무늬가 있는 블라우스를 착용해 보고 있다.
(D) 남자가 선반에 상품을 정돈하고 있다.

어휘 hand A B A에게 B를 건네다 look through ~을 뒤지다 try on ~을 입어 보다 arrange 정리하다

UNIT 02 사물 및 풍경 사진 묘사

CHECK-UP

본문 p.21

1. (C) **2.** (D)

1. 영녀

(A) Some fishing poles have been left on a deck.
(B) Some boats are sailing in the ocean.
(C) Some chairs have been placed on a dock.
(D) A house overlooks a fishing pier.

(A) 낚싯대 몇 개가 데크에 놓여 있다.

(B) 보트 몇 척이 바다를 항해하고 있다.
(C) 몇몇 의자가 부두에 놓여 있다.
(D) 집 한 채가 낚시 부두를 내려다본다.

어휘 fishing pole 낚싯대 dock 부두, 선창
overlook (건물 등이) ~을 내려다보다

2. 미남

(A) A top drawer has been closed.
(B) A faucet is running water.
(C) There are some cooking utensils on the ground.
(D) There is some fruit on a countertop.

(A) 상단 서랍이 닫혀 있다.
(B) 수도꼭지에서 물이 나오고 있다.
(C) 바닥에 조리도구가 있다.
(D) 조리대 위에 과일이 있다.

어휘 faucet 수도꼭지 cooking utensil 조리도구
countertop 조리대

PRACTICE 고난도 본문 p.23

1. (C) **2.** (D) **3.** (B) **4.** (D) **5.** (C) **6.** (A)

1. 미남

(A) He's loading crates into a vehicle.
(B) He's stocking shelves in a storage room.
(C) Some boxes are stacked in a vehicle.
(D) A car is exiting a parking garage.

(A) 그는 운송용 상자들을 차량에 싣고 있다.
(B) 그는 창고 선반에 물건을 채우고 있다.
(C) 상자들이 차 안에 쌓여 있다.
(D) 차가 주차장을 빠져나가고 있다.

어휘 load ~을 싣다 stock ~을 채우다 stack ~을 쌓다 exit ~을 떠나다 parking garage 주차장

2. 영녀

(A) A watering can has been placed next to a hanger.
(B) The woman is carrying a vase filled with flowers.
(C) There is a clock on top of a shelf.
(D) The woman is watering a plant on a desk.

(A) 옷걸이 옆에 물뿌리개가 놓여 있다.
(B) 여자가 꽃으로 가득 찬 꽃병을 들고 있다.
(C) 선반 꼭대기에 시계가 있다.
(D) 여자가 책상 위에 있는 식물에 물을 주고 있다.

어휘 watering can 물뿌리개 on top of ~의 위에
water ~에 물을 주다

3. 호남

(A) A man is unpacking a suitcase.
(B) A woman is resting her hand on a railing.
(C) They're standing in a doorway.
(D) They're parking bicycles next to a building.

(A) 한 남자가 여행 가방을 풀고 있다.
(B) 한 여자가 손을 난간에 올려놓고 있다.
(C) 그들은 입구에 서 있다.
(D) 그들은 건물 옆에 자전거를 주차하고 있다.

어휘 unpack (여행 가방 등에 든 것을) 꺼내다, (짐을) 풀다 rest (어떤 것에) 받치다[기대다] doorway 입구

4. 미녀

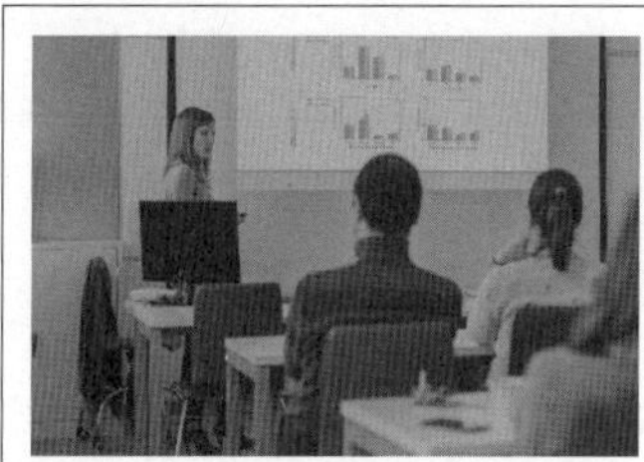

(A) Some people are viewing some artwork.
(B) A woman is drawing a graph on a whiteboard.
(C) The people are seated across from one another.
(D) The audience is facing a screen.

(A) 몇 사람이 예술작품을 보고 있다.
(B) 한 여자가 화이트보드에 그래프를 그리고 있다.
(C) 사람들이 서로를 마주보고 앉아 있다.
(D) 청중이 스크린을 향해 있다.

어휘 view (세심히 살피며) 보다

5. 영녀

(A) Some tables are being wiped down.
(B) Some potted plants are being rearranged.
(C) An outdoor area has been set up for dining.
(D) Some chairs on a patio are occupied.

(A) 몇몇 테이블을 닦고 있다.
(B) 몇몇 화분들이 재배치되고 있다.
(C) 야외에 식사를 위한 공간이 마련되어 있다.
(D) 테라스에 있는 의자에 사람들이 앉아 있다.

어휘 wipe down (젖은 걸레로) 깨끗이 닦다 rearrange 재배치[재배열]하다 be occupied ~이 사용중이다

6. 호남

(A) Some shelves are lined up in a hallway.
(B) Some equipment has been set up on a stage.
(C) Some packages are being unloaded from a cart.
(D) Some items are being removed from storage units.

(A) 선반들이 통로를 따라 늘어서 있다.
(B) 장비가 무대에 설치되어 있다.
(C) 카트에서 꾸러미들을 내리고 있다.
(D) 물건들을 창고에서 꺼내고 있다.

어휘 line up ~을 일렬로 세우다 set up ~을 설치하다 unload (자동차나 선박 등에서 짐을) 내리다 storage unit 창고

PART TEST 1

본문 p.24

1. (A) **2.** (C) **3.** (D) **4.** (B) **5.** (D) **6.** (B)

1. 미남

(A) He's mowing the lawn.
(B) He's kneeling on the grass.
(C) He's pruning a bush.
(D) He's pushing a cart.

(A) 남자가 잔디를 깎고 있다.
(B) 남자가 잔디 위에 무릎을 꿇고 있다.
(C) 남자가 관목의 가지를 치고 있다.
(D) 남자가 카트를 밀고 있다.

어휘 mow (잔디를) 깎다, (풀 등을) 베다 kneel 무릎을 꿇다 prune (나무를) 전지하다, (가지를) 치다

2. 영녀

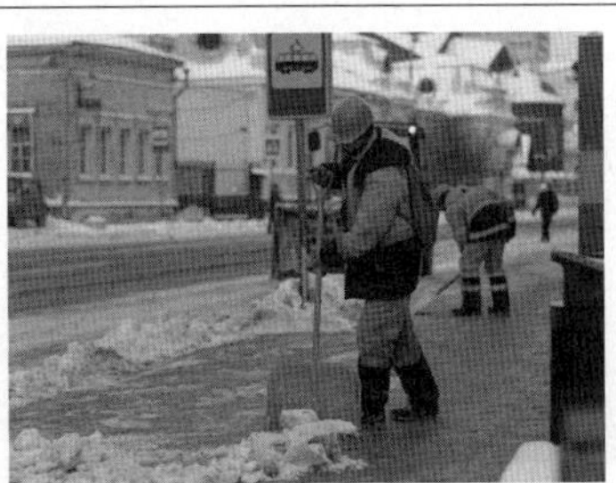

(A) There's a sign posted on a fence.
(B) One of the men is putting on his helmet.
(C) Some snow is being shoveled off a walkway.
(D) The men are sweeping the floor.

(A) 울타리에 표지판이 걸려 있다.
(B) 남자들 중 한 명이 헬멧을 쓰고 있는 중이다.
(C) 보도의 눈을 삽으로 치우고 있다.
(D) 남자들이 바닥을 쓸고 있다.

어휘 post (안내문 등을) 게시하다 shovel 삽질하다, 삽으로 파다 [옮기다 등] sweep 쓸다

3. 호남

(A) The women are facing each other.
(B) One of the women is handing out flyers.
(C) A server is tying an apron.
(D) A server is taking an order.

(A) 여자들이 서로를 향해 있다.
(B) 여자들 중 한 명이 전단지를 나눠주고 있다.
(C) 종업원이 앞치마를 매고 있다. (동작)
(D) 종업원이 주문을 받고 있다.

어휘 hand out ~을 나눠주다 tie 묶다 take an order 주문을 받다

4. 미녀

(A) They're seated in a line.
(B) A man is pointing at a board.
(C) They're examining some documents.
(D) A woman is gesturing towards a chalkboard.

(A) 그들은 일렬로 앉아 있다.
(B) 한 남자가 보드를 가리키고 있다.
(C) 그들은 서류를 검토하고 있다.
(D) 한 여자가 칠판을 향해 손짓하고 있다.

어휘 point at ~을 가리키다 examine ~을 검토하다

5. 미남

(A) She's opening a drawer.
(B) She's fixing an office equipment.
(C) She's emptying a trash bin.
(D) She's refilling a copy machine with paper.

(A) 여자가 서랍을 열고 있다.
(B) 여자가 사무기기를 고치고 있다.
(C) 여자가 쓰레기통을 비우고 있다.
(D) 여자가 복사기에 종이를 채워 넣고 있다.

어휘 fix ~을 고치다 empty ~을 비우다 refill A with B A를 B로 다시 채우다

6. 영녀

(A) Some stairs are being cleaned.
(B) Some chairs are arranged in a circle.
(C) A pathway is being repaired.
(D) A fence is being installed alongside a building.

(A) 계단이 청소되고 있다.
(B) 의자들이 원형으로 배치되어 있다.
(C) 보도가 보수되고 있다.
(D) 건물 옆에 담장이 설치되고 있다.

어휘 in a circle 원형으로 pathway 보도, 인도

PART TEST 2

본문 p.27

1. (B) **2.** (C) **3.** (A) **4.** (C) **5.** (D) **6.** (B)

1. 미남

(A) He's reaching into a shopping basket.
(B) He's holding a refrigerator door open.
(C) He's putting some groceries in a cart.
(D) He's carrying a jacket over his arm.

(A) 남자가 장바구니 안으로 손을 뻗고 있다.
(B) 남자가 냉장고 문을 열고 있다.
(C) 남자가 식료품을 카트에 담고 있다.
(D) 남자가 팔에 재킷을 걸치고 있다.

어휘 reach into ~안으로 손을 넣다 is holding a door open 문을 연 채로 잡고 있다

2. 영녀

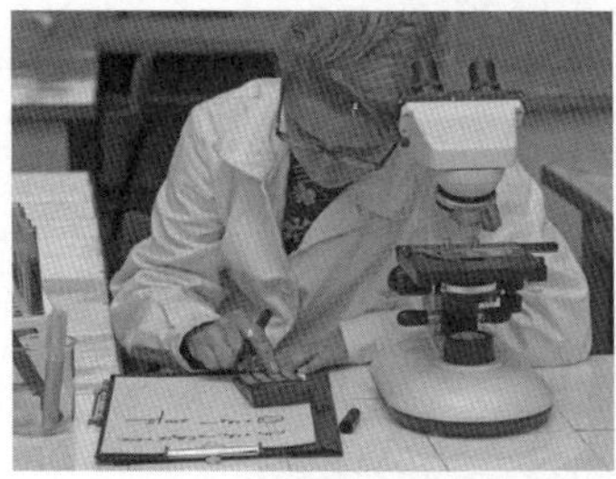

(A) The woman is picking up a test tube.
(B) The woman is adjusting a microscope.
(C) The woman is using a calculator.
(D) The woman is writing on a notepad.

(A) 여자가 시험관을 집어 들고 있다.
(B) 여자가 현미경을 조정하고 있다.
(C) 여자가 계산기를 사용하고 있다.
(D) 여자가 메모장에 글을 쓰고 있다.

어휘 pick up ~을 집다[들어 올리다] adjust (약간) 조정[조절]하다, (매무새 등을) 바로잡다[정돈하다]

3. 호남

(A) The man is vacuuming the floor.
(B) They are putting away some cleaning tools.
(C) One of the women is sweeping a walkway.
(D) One of the women is crouching under a desk.

(A) 남자가 바닥을 진공청소기로 청소하고 있다.
(B) 그들은 청소 도구들을 치우고 있다.
(C) 여자 중 한 명이 보도를 쓸고 있다.
(D) 여자들 중 한 명이 책상 아래에 웅크리고 있다.

어휘 vacuum 진공청소기로 청소하다 put away ~을 치우다 sweep ~을 쓸다 crouch 웅크리다

4. 미녀

(A) Some display areas are being restocked.
(B) A woman is loading some furniture onto a cart.
(C) Some boxes are stacked in a warehouse.
(D) A man is handing some papers to a woman.

(A) 진열장에 물품들이 다시 채워지고 있다.
(B) 여자가 가구를 카트에 싣고 있다.
(C) 상자들이 창고에 쌓여 있다.
(D) 남자가 여자에게 서류를 건네주고 있다.

어휘 restock ~을 다시 채우다 load A onto B A를 B 위에 싣다 warehouse 창고 hand A to B A를 B에게 건네다

5. 미남

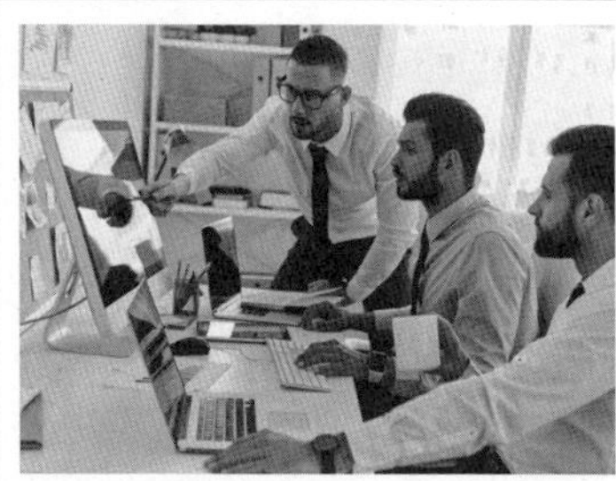

(A) Some of the men are putting on ties.
(B) They're looking at posts on a bulletin board.
(C) A man is organizing documents in a folder.
(D) One of the men are pointing at a monitor.

(A) 남자들 중 몇 명이 넥타이를 매고 있는 중이다.
(B) 그들은 게시판의 게시물을 보고 있다.
(C) 한 남자가 폴더에 있는 문서들을 정리하고 있다.
(D) 남자들 중 한 명이 모니터를 가리키고 있다.

어휘 put on ~을 입다[신다, 착용하다] organize 정리하다 point at ~을 가리키다

6. 🎧 미녀

(A) A rug is being removed from the floor.
(B) Some potted plants are hanging from a ceiling.
(C) Some artwork has been propped up on a shelf.
(D) A blanket is hanging on a table.

(A) 바닥에서 양탄자를 치우고 있다.
(B) 화분 몇 개가 천장에 매달려 있다.
(C) 예술품들이 선반 위에 받쳐져 있다.
(D) 담요가 탁자 위에 걸려 있다.

어휘 remove A from B A를 B에서 제거하다 potted plant 화분 artwork 미술품 prop up ~을 받쳐 넘어지지 않게 하다

 PART 2

UNIT 01 Who/What/Which 의문문

CHECK-UP 본문 p.35

1. (A) **2.** (A) **3.** (B) **4.** (A) **5.** (C) **6.** (A)

1. 🎧 미남/영녀

Who's going to select a candidate for the position?
(A) The marketing team.
(B) That option would be best.
(C) I have her résumé here.

누가 그 자리의 후보를 뽑을 거죠?
(A) 마케팅 팀이요.
(B) 그 옵션이 가장 좋겠군요.
(C) 여기 그녀의 이력서를 가지고 있어요.

2. 🎧 미남/영녀

What was the total charge for the car rental?
(A) I'd have to look at the receipt.
(B) It looks like a compact vehicle.
(C) Yes, for any amount you'd like.

자동차 렌탈 비용이 총 얼마였죠?
(A) 영수증을 봐야 할 것 같아요.
(B) 소형 자동차 같네요.
(C) 네, 얼마든지요.

3. 🎧 미남/영녀

Which floor is Chetwood Financial Services located on?
(A) The financial report will be done this week.
(B) They've already closed for the day.
(C) The department budget for February.

Chetwood Financial Services는 어느 층에 있죠?
(A) 재무 보고서는 이번 주에 끝날 거예요.
(B) 거기는 오늘 벌써 문 닫았어요.
(C) 2월 부서 예산입니다.

4. 🎧 미녀/호남

Who needs a copy of the lease contract?
(A) Marty does.
(B) Yes, I already signed up.
(C) At least $5,000.

누가 이 임대계약서가 필요하죠?
(A) Marty요.

(B) 네, 제가 벌써 서명했어요.
(C) 적어도 5,000달러요.

어휘 sign up (서류 등에) 서명하다, 가입하다, 계약하다

5. 미녀/호남

What kind of restaurants do you usually go to?
(A) Mark made the reservation instead.
(B) Mainly on weekends or holidays.
(C) I'm a big fan of Thai cuisine.

보통 어떤 종류의 식당에 가시나요?
(A) Mark가 대신 예약했어요.
(B) 주로 주말이나 휴일에요.
(C) 저는 태국 요리를 정말 좋아해요.

어휘 make a reservation 예약하다

6. 미녀/호남

Which building did Margaret move her office to?
(A) The tall one on the corner.
(B) Thanks, I appreciate that.
(C) Show the parking pass at the gate.

Margaret은 사무실을 어느 건물로 옮겼나요?
(A) 모퉁이에 있는 높은 건물로요.
(B) 고마워요, 그래 주시면 고맙죠.
(C) 입구에서 주차권을 보여 주세요.

UNIT 02 When/Where 의문문

CHECK-UP 본문 p.37

1. (B) **2.** (B) **3.** (C) **4.** (B) **5.** (C) **6.**(A)

1. 미남/영녀

Where did these pineapples come from?
(A) It's in aisle nine.
(B) From a supplier in Florida.
(C) Here's a cart you can use.

이 파인애플은 어디에서 온 거죠?
(A) 9번 통로에 있어요.
(B) 플로리다에 있는 공급업체요.
(C) 이 카트를 쓰시면 돼요.

2. 미남/영녀

When are they going to decide who to hire?
(A) Lift it up a little higher.
(B) Quite a few résumés have come in.
(C) The department managers.

그들은 누구를 고용할지 언제 결정할까요?
(A) 조금 위로 올려주세요.
(B) 이력서가 상당히 많이 들어왔어요.
(C) 부서장들이요.

해설 (B)는 이력서가 상당히 많이 들어와서 누구를 채용할지 검토하는 데 시간이 걸릴 것이라는 간접적인 답변이다.

3. 미남/영녀

Where did you first learn about the job opening?
(A) No, I didn't apply.
(B) I'm going to open a business account.
(C) I subscribe to a weekly career magazine.

거기 일자리 난 걸 언제 처음 알았어요?
(A) 아뇨, 전 지원하지 않았어요.
(B) 사업자 계정을 열 겁니다.
(C) 저는 주간 커리어 잡지를 구독해요.

해설 커리어 잡지를 통해 그 일자리에 대한 채용 공고가 난 것을 알게 되었다는 간접적인 답변이다.

어휘 subscribe to ~을 구독하다

4. 미녀/호남

When do you need the blueprints for the lobby renovation?
(A) No, the printer is broken right now.
(B) By early afternoon, please.
(C) That's not as expensive as we thought.

로비 보수를 위한 청사진이 언제 필요한가요?
(A) 아뇨, 프린터가 지금 고장 났어요.
(B) 이른 오후까지 부탁드려요.
(C) 생각한 것만큼 비싸지 않네요.

어휘 blueprint 청사진 broken 고장난

5. 미녀/호남

Where is the engineering team?
(A) At the end of this quarter.
(B) More than 20 people.
(C) They're at a training session.

엔지니어링 팀은 어디에 있죠?
(A) 이번 분기 말에요.
(B) 20명 이상이요.
(C) 그들은 교육에 참석 중이에요.

6. 미녀/호남

When will construction on this road finish?
(A) In the spring.
(B) The back entrance of this building.
(C) I'll take the elevator.

이 도로의 공사는 언제 끝날까요?
(A) 봄에요.
(B) 이 건물의 후문이요.
(C) 전 엘리베이터를 탈게요.

UNIT 03 How/Why 의문문

CHECK-UP 본문 p.39

1. (C) **2.** (A) **3.** (C) **4.** (A) **5.** (B) **6.** (A)

1. 미남/영녀

How many tickets do we need for tomorrow's concert?
(A) We're meeting at two o'clock sharp.
(B) The theater's on William Street.
(C) I'll buy mine at the door.

내일 콘서트에 표가 몇 장이나 필요하죠?
(A) 정각 2시에 만날 거예요.
(B) 극장은 William Street에 있어요.
(C) 제 것은 현장에서 살게요.

어휘 sharp (몇 시) 정각에

2. 미남/영녀

How are the Web site updates coming along?
(A) I've been tied up with the other accounts.
(B) That date works for me.
(C) I was stuck in a traffic jam.

웹 사이트 업데이트는 어떻게 되어가나요?
(A) 다른 거래처 때문에 바빴어요.
(B) 그날 괜찮습니다.
(C) 교통체증에 걸렸어요.

어휘 tied up with ~으로 바쁜 account 거래처, 고객

3. 미남/영녀

How did your presentation for Raymond Financial Group go this morning?
(A) Our main client.
(B) That was a nice present.
(C) It went very well.

오늘 아침 Raymond Financial Group 프레젠테이션은 잘됐어요?
(A) 우리 주요 고객입니다.
(B) 좋은 선물이었어요.
(C) 아주 잘됐어요.

4. 미녀/호남

Why did our company decide to offer a free newsletter?
(A) To expand our customer base.
(B) That sounds like a great idea.
(C) The other side of town.

우리 회사는 왜 무료 뉴스레터를 제공하기로 결정한 거죠?
(A) 고객층을 넓히기 위해서입니다.
(B) 좋은 생각 같네요.
(C) 도시의 그쪽 반대편이요.

어휘 customer base 고객 기반

5. 미녀/호남

Why isn't Ms. Watts available to meet the client?
(A) She's a regular customer.
(B) Because she's on a business trip this week.
(C) Tomorrow would be good.

Ms. Watts는 왜 고객을 만날 수가 없는 거죠?
(A) 그녀는 단골입니다.
(B) 그녀는 이번 주에 출장이라서 그래요.
(C) 내일 괜찮을 거예요.

어휘 regular customer 단골

6. 미녀/호남

Why did our sales targets increase this month?
(A) Check with the manager.
(B) No, I'm taking time off at the end of the month.
(C) I'm working on their performance reviews.

왜 이번 달 매출 목표가 증가했죠?
(A) 매니저에게 확인해 보세요.
(B) 아뇨, 저는 이번 달 말에 휴가를 써요.
(C) 저는 그들의 업무 평가를 작성하고 있습니다.

어휘 sales target 판매 목표(액) performance review 업무 평가

UNIT 04 Yes/No 의문문

CHECK-UP 본문 p.41

1. (A) **2.** (A) **3.** (C) **4.** (C) **5.** (A) **6.** (B)

1. 미남/영녀

Does the shop open on Saturdays?
(A) Yes. At 11:00.
(B) Close to the train station
(C) The fund-raiser's on Friday.

그 가게는 토요일에 문을 여나요?
(A) 네. 11시에요.

(B) 기차역 가까이에요.
(C) 그 모금 행사는 금요일이에요.

2. 미남/영녀

Will Dr. Miller be late today?
(A) No, you shouldn't have to wait long.
(B) I haven't seen them lately.
(C) Sure, I'm free now.

Dr. Miller는 오늘 늦나요?
(A) 아뇨, 오래 기다리시지 않아도 돼요.
(B) 그들을 요즘 못 봤어요.
(C) 그럼요, 전 지금 한가해요.

3. 미남/영녀

Aren't there locker rooms at this library?
(A) You have to return the books by May 3.
(B) The door is unlocked.
(C) Yes, they're on the second floor.

이 도서관에 로커룸이 없나요?
(A) 책들을 5월 3일까지 반납하셔야 합니다.
(B) 문은 열려 있어요.
(C) 아뇨, 2층에 있어요.

4. 미녀/호남

Hasn't anyone called you back for the second interview yet?
(A) Here's the phone number.
(B) Yes, we had several positions open.
(C) I'm still waiting.

아직 두 번째 면접에 대해 전화 못 받았어요?
(A) 전화 번호 여기 있습니다.
(B) 네, 공석이 몇 개 있었습니다.
(C) 아직 기다리고 있는 중이에요.

5. 미녀/호남

This shipment will arrive by this Friday, won't it?
(A) Definitely.
(B) I'll sign for the delivery.
(C) It won't fit in my car.

이 배송품이 금요일까지 도착하겠죠, 그렇지 않나요?
(A) 그럼요.
(B) 제가 운송장에 서명할게요.
(C) 그건 제 차에 맞지 않을 거예요.

6. 미녀/호남

Should I bring anything to the trade fair?
(A) Probably in the maintenance room.
(B) Do we have enough handouts?
(C) That sounds like a fair price.

무역 박람회에 뭘 가져가야 하나요?
(A) 아마도 관리실 안일 거예요.
(B) 유인물이 충분한가요?
(C) 적절한 가격으로 보입니다.

어휘 maintenance room 관리실

UNIT 05 제안/요청 및 선택 의문문

CHECK-UP 본문 p.43

1. (C) **2.** (C) **3.** (B) **4.** (A) **5.** (A) **6.** (B)

1. 미남/영녀

Could you call Ms. Thomson and let her know we're in the hotel lobby?
(A) Sorry, it's under repair.
(B) I ordered a room service.
(C) Yes, of course.

Ms. Thomson에게 전화해서 우리가 호텔 로비에 있다고 알려줄래요?
(A) 죄송합니다만, 수리 중입니다.
(B) 저는 룸서비스를 주문했어요.
(C) 네, 물론이지요.

2. 미남/영녀

Could I take a look at some sample floral arrangements?
(A) It's a third floor apartment.
(B) No. I believe Edward is doing that.
(C) Certainly, I have them right here.

꽃꽂이 샘플을 좀 볼 수 있을까요?
(A) 그건 3층 아파트입니다.
(B) 아뇨. Edward가 그걸 하고 있을 거예요.
(C) 물론이죠. 여기 있습니다.

어휘 floral 꽃으로 만든, 꽃 장식의

3. 미남/영녀

Should I make the dinner reservation for Thursday or Friday?
(A) The bistro across the street.
(B) Friday is better.
(C) I enjoyed the pasta salad.

저녁 예약을 목요일로 해야 하나요, 금요일로 해야 하나요?
(A) 길 건너 식당이에요.
(B) 금요일이 나아요.
(C) 저는 파스타 샐러드를 맛있게 먹었어요.

4. 🎧 미녀/호남

Would you prefer a train in the morning or the afternoon?
(A) I'd better leave early.
(B) Because of the traffic jam.
(C) Every morning at ten o'clock.

아침 기차가 좋으세요, 오후 기차가 좋으세요?
(A) 일찍 떠나는 게 낫겠어요.
(B) 교통체증 때문에요.
(C) 매일 아침 10시요.

5. 🎧 미녀/호남

Why don't we provide more samples of the tile patterns for our clients?
(A) There are plenty in the binders.
(B) Because it's out of stock.
(C) I like the striped blanket.

우리 고객들에게 타일 패턴 샘플을 더 제공하는 건 어때요?
(A) 바인더에 충분히 들어 있어요.
(B) 그것의 재고가 없기 때문이에요.
(C) 저는 줄무늬 담요를 좋아해요.

6. 🎧 미녀/호남

Would you like to make a reservation for this Friday?
(A) The flight was cancelled.
(B) Does 8 P.M. work?
(C) Next week's train schedule.

이번 주 금요일로 예약하시겠어요?
(A) 비행기가 취소됐어요.
(B) 오후 8시 가능할까요?
(C) 다음 주 기차 스케줄입니다.

UNIT 06 평서문

CHECK-UP 본문 p.44

1. (A) **2.** (C) **3.** (C) **4.** (B) **5.** (B) **6.** (A)

1. 🎧 미남/영녀

Your expense report seems a bit short.
(A) I didn't spend much this quarter.
(B) I'm leaving shortly.
(C) Maybe one and a half meters?

지출 보고서가 좀 짧아 보이네요.
(A) 이번 분기에 돈을 많이 안 썼거든요.
(B) 곧 떠납니다.
(C) 1.5미터 정도요?

2. 🎧 미남/영녀

I'd like to attend the tech conference next month.
(A) There was a problem with the projector.
(B) The speech starts at noon.
(C) Registration closed yesterday.

다음 달 기술 컨퍼런스에 참석하고 싶어요.
(A) 프로젝터에 문제가 있었어요.
(B) 연설은 정오에 시작합니다.
(C) 등록은 어제 마감됐어요.

3. 🎧 미남/영녀

I had a chance to look over the proposal this morning.
(A) We're under budget.
(B) I'm doing well, thanks.
(C) What did you think of it?

오늘 아침에 제안을 검토할 기회가 있었어요.
(A) 우린 예산이 부족해요.
(B) 전 잘 지내요, 감사합니다.
(C) 어떻게 생각하세요?

4. 🎧 미녀/호남

The market on Maple Street is closed for a week.
(A) Please order more tablecloths.
(B) Is there another one nearby?
(C) That's market price.

Maple Street의 시장이 일주일 동안 문을 닫아요.
(A) 식탁보를 더 주문해 주세요.
(B) 근처에 다른 곳이 있나요?
(C) 그것은 시장 가격입니다.

5. 🎧 미녀/호남

This agreement needs a signature before it's sent out.
(A) I received it.
(B) OK, I'll do that now.
(C) A roofing contractor.

이 계약서는 발송 전에 서명이 필요해요.
(A) 제가 그걸 받았어요.
(B) 네, 지금 할게요.
(C) 지붕 시공업자예요.

어휘 send out ~을 보내다, 발송하다

6. 🎧 미녀/호남

That film has received excellent reviews.
(A) Why don't we go see it?
(B) The department director.
(C) I'd like a room with a view of the sea.

그 영화는 좋은 평을 받았어요.
(A) 보러 가지 않을래요?
(B) 부서장입니다.
(C) 바다 전망이 있는 방을 원해요.

PRACTICE 고난도 본문 p.45

1. (C)	**2.** (C)	**3.** (A)	**4.** (B)	**5.** (A)	**6.** (B)
7. (C)	**8.** (C)	**9.** (A)	**10.** (A)	**11.** (B)	**12.** (A)
13. (A)	**14.** (C)	**15.** (C)	**16.** (C)	**17.** (B)	**18.** (A)
19. (C)	**20.** (B)	**21.** (B)	**22.** (A)	**23.** (C)	**24.** (C)
25. (B)	**26.** (A)	**27.** (C)	**28.** (C)	**29.** (B)	**30.** (C)

1. 🎧 미남/영녀

When can I move these supplies into the storage room?
(A) The warehouse on Lancaster Avenue.
(B) It's a new supplier.
(C) We'll need to clear some space.

제가 이 용품들을 언제 창고로 옮기면 될까요?
(A) Lancaster Avenue에 있는 창고요.
(B) 새로운 공급업체입니다.
(C) 공간을 좀 치워야 할 거예요.

어휘 supplies 비품, 용품, 저장품 supplier 공급업자

2. 🎧 영녀/미남

Where did you go after luncheon yesterday?
(A) Of course I'd be willing to do that.
(B) I'm afraid I just ate.
(C) I had a dentist's appointment.

어제 점심 이후에 어디에 갔었나요?
(A) 물론 그렇게 하겠습니다.
(B) 방금 먹었는데 어쩌죠.
(C) 치과 예약이 있었어요.

3. 🎧 호남/미녀

Who's giving the first part of the sales pitch?
(A) I'm handling the presentation on my own.
(B) It's for a prospective client.
(C) That would be really helpful.

구매 권유 피치에서 누가 첫 번째 부분을 담당하죠?
(A) 저 혼자 발표를 합니다.
(B) 잠재 고객을 위한 거예요.
(C) 무척 도움이 될 거예요.

어휘 on my own 혼자서 prospective client 잠재 고객

4. 🎧 미녀/호남

How did Ms. Carter enjoy her stay at our hotel?
(A) No, five days and four nights.
(B) She didn't check out yet.
(C) Until the end of the month.

Ms. Carter는 저희 호텔 투숙에 만족해했나요?
(A) 아뇨, 4박 5일입니다.
(B) 그녀는 아직 퇴실하지 않았어요.
(C) 이달 말까지요.

5. 🎧 미남/영녀

What's the status of our grant application?
(A) It should be approved early next week.
(B) An interest-free loan.
(C) To my work e-mail address.

우리의 보조금 신청 현황은 어떤가요?
(A) 다음 주 초에 승인될 거예요.
(B) 무이자 대출입니다.
(C) 제 회사 이메일로요.

어휘 grant (정부나 단체에서 주는) 보조금

6. 🎧 영녀/미남

Why are the lights out in the hallway?
(A) He just went out for lunch.
(B) Because they're doing some maintenance work.
(C) We should've turned left.

복도의 등이 왜 나갔죠?
(A) 그는 방금 점심 먹으러 나갔어요.
(B) 그들이 보수 작업을 하고 있어서요.
(C) 우리는 좌회전했어야 해요.

7. 🎧 호남/미녀

Which photograph should we use for the article?
(A) It's a pretty town with a picturesque lake.
(B) For several women's magazines.
(C) The third one on the right.

그 기사에 어떤 사진을 써야 하죠?
(A) 그림 같은 호수가 있는 예쁜 마을이에요.
(B) 몇몇 여성 잡지에요.
(C) 오른쪽에서 세 번째 거요.

8. 미녀/호남

Who's attending Rohan's retirement party?
(A) This calls for celebration.
(B) 3 o'clock sharp.
(C) It should be noted on the guest list.

누가 Rohan의 은퇴 기념 파티에 참석할 건가요?
(A) 이거 축하해야겠는데요.
(B) 3시 정각에요.
(C) 그건 손님 명단에 언급되어 있을 거예요.

어휘 sharp 정확히 (= on the dot)

9. 미남/영녀

Who was in the break room last?
(A) I noticed that it was messy, too.
(B) I think the brake is broken.
(C) It won't last long.

누가 마지막으로 휴게실에 있었나요?
(A) 저도 지저분하다고 느꼈어요.
(B) 브레이크가 고장 난 것 같아요.
(C) 그건 오래가지 않을 거예요.

10. 영녀/미남

What's the best way to get to Roxbury Convention Center?
(A) I'd take the bus.
(B) That one is way better.
(C) 10 people from the sales department.

Roxbury Convention Center로 가는 가장 좋은 방법이 무엇인가요?
(A) 저라면 버스를 타겠어요.
(B) 그게 훨씬 나아요.
(C) 영업부에서 10명이요.

11. 호남/미녀

How did the sales presentation go yesterday?
(A) At the City Convention Center.
(B) Greenwood Motor Company is now one of our clients.
(C) I thought it was on sale.

어제 판매 프레젠테이션은 어떻게 됐나요?
(A) City Convention Center에서요.
(B) Greenwood Motor Company는 이제 저희 고객 중 하나입니다.
(C) 할인하는 줄 알았어요.

해설 발표가 성공적이어서 Greenwood Motor Company와의 판매 계약이 성사되었다는 의미이다.

12. 미녀/호남

When are you moving to your new office?
(A) As early as February.
(B) This equipment is not mobile.
(C) On the second floor.

언제 새 사무실로 옮기세요?
(A) 빠르면 2월에요.
(B) 이 장비는 이동식이 아니에요.
(C) 2층이요.

13. 미남/영녀

When is the library construction starting?
(A) We're a bit behind schedule.
(B) A well-known author.
(C) To construct a bridge.

도서관 공사는 언제 시작하죠?
(A) 일정이 좀 늦어졌어요.
(B) 잘 알려진 작가요.
(C) 다리를 건설하기 위해서요.

14. 영녀/미남

Where's the main entrance to the library?
(A) The entrance fee is $10.
(B) On top of the bookcase.
(C) There's a pretty long line over there.

도서관 정문이 어디죠?
(A) 입장료는 10달러입니다.
(B) 책장 맨 위에요.
(C) 저기 엄청 긴 줄이 있어요.

어휘 on top of ~의 위에

15. 호남/미녀

Why was the shipment late?
(A) I was charged a late fee.
(B) Could you sign for me?
(C) Traffic was really bad this morning.

왜 배송이 늦었죠?
(A) 저는 연체료를 부과받았어요.
(B) 저 대신 서명해 주시겠어요?
(C) 오늘 아침에 도로가 엄청 막혔어요.

어휘 late fee 연체료

16. 미녀/호남

Does the company pay for employee travel?
(A) The fee is $200.
(B) It's a week-long business trip.
(C) Only for work-related expenses.

회사에서 직원 여행 경비를 지불하나요?
(A) 요금은 200달러입니다.
(B) 일주일 간의 출장입니다.
(C) 업무 관련 비용에 한해서요.

17. 미남/영녀

Sales of our cold-brew iced coffee rose by fifteen percent last month.
(A) It's very chilly outside.
(B) I didn't know it was so popular.
(C) Close the coffee shop an hour earlier.

콜드브루 아이스 커피 판매 실적이 지난달에 15% 증가했어요.
(A) 밖이 아주 추워요.
(B) 그게 그렇게 인기가 많은지 몰랐어요.
(C) 커피숍을 한 시간 일찍 닫으세요.

18. 영녀/미남

Has the job ad for the accountant position been posted?
(A) Not yet, but by noon.
(B) Sharon's a great candidate.
(C) I like the account management software.

회계직 채용 공고 올렸나요?
(A) 아직이요, 하지만 정오까지는 될 거예요.
(B) Sharon은 좋은 후보예요.
(C) 계정 관리 소프트웨어가 마음에 들어요.

어휘 accountant 회계원, 회계사

19. 호남/미녀

Are we ready to begin production on the summer clothing line?
(A) Many people are in line.
(B) It comes in various sizes.
(C) Sure, the designs are almost finalized.

여름 의류 제품에 대한 생산을 시작할 준비가 되었나요?
(A) 많은 사람들이 줄을 서 있어요.
(B) 그것은 다양한 사이즈로 나옵니다.
(C) 네, 디자인은 거의 마무리되었습니다.

20. 미녀/호남

Don't you want to buy the rocking chair?
(A) Yes, the living room furniture's new.
(B) We already have one.
(C) We charge cancellation fees.

그 흔들의자를 사고 싶지 않으세요?
(A) 네, 그 거실 가구는 새거예요.
(B) 이미 있어요.
(C) 저희는 취소 수수료를 부과합니다.

어휘 cancellation fee 취소 수수료

21. 미남/영녀

You haven't always worn glasses, have you?
(A) Two glasses of juice, please.
(B) No, only since last month.
(C) The brake pads are very worn.

당신이 항상 안경을 쓴 것은 아니죠, 그렇죠?
(A) 주스 두 잔 주세요.
(B) 네, 지난달부터 쓰기 시작했어요.
(C) 브레이크 패드가 심하게 마모되었습니다.

어휘 worn 해진, 닳은

22. 영녀/미남

Can you show me how to fill out this registration form?
(A) I'm about to join a video conference call.
(B) At the management seminar.
(C) That position has been filled.

이 등록 양식을 어떻게 작성하는지 보여 주시겠어요?
(A) 지금 바로 화상 회의에 참여해야 해서요.
(B) 경영 세미나에서요.
(C) 그 자리는 채워졌어요.

23. 호남/미녀

Isn't Priscilla coming to this meeting?
(A) Sure, we've met before.
(B) In the conference room down the hall.
(C) Yes, she'll be here soon.

Priscilla는 이 회의에 오지 않나요?
(A) 물론이죠, 우리는 전에 만난 적 있어요.
(B) 복도 끝에 있는 회의실에서요.
(C) 아뇨, 곧 올 거예요.

24. 미녀/호남

Do you have this winter coat in a smaller size?
(A) It's so cold inside.
(B) A large number of orders.
(C) Oh, I'm not a sales associate.

이 겨울 코트는 좀 더 작은 사이즈가 있나요?
(A) 안이 너무 추워요.
(B) 주문이 많습니다.
(C) 아, 저는 영업 사원이 아닙니다.

어휘 sales associate 영업 사원

25. 🎧 미남/영녀

Would you mind forwarding me a summary of the results of your research?
(A) We'll visit Belgium this summer.
(B) I don't think I have your e-mail address.
(C) Sure, I'll remind her later.

연구 결과 요약한 걸 제게 전달해 주시겠어요?
(A) 올여름에 벨기에를 방문할 거예요.
(B) 제게 당신의 이메일 주소가 없는 것 같아요.
(C) 물론이요. 나중에 그녀에게 상기시킬게요.

26. 🎧 영녀/미남

I'd like to schedule an appointment for next week.
(A) How about Thursday at ten?
(A) Director of international sales.
(C) No, it's a week-long business trip.

다음 주로 약속을 잡고 싶습니다.
(A) 목요일 10시는 어떠세요?
(A) 해외 영업 이사입니다.
(C) 아뇨, 일주일 출장입니다.

27. 🎧 호남/미녀

Could you change the location of the board meeting?
(A) I have difficulty locating this book.
(B) The board meets once a month.
(C) Lewis books the conference rooms.

이사회 회의 장소를 변경해 주실 수 있나요?
(A) 이 책을 찾기가 어려워요.
(B) 이사회는 한 달에 한 번 열립니다.
(C) Lewis가 회의실을 예약합니다.

28. 🎧 미녀/호남

Do you want to take a morning or afternoon flight to Toronto?
(A) The shuttle is on its way.
(B) A round-trip ticket.
(C) Which one's less expensive?

당신은 토론토행 오전 비행기를 타고 싶나요, 오후 비행기를 타고 싶나요?
(A) 셔틀이 오고 있어요.
(B) 왕복표요.
(C) 어느 것이 덜 비싼가요?

29. 🎧 미남/영녀

I didn't see you at the company picnic yesterday.
(A) I'll prepare some sandwiches.
(B) Oh, there was an urgent meeting.
(C) Every spring.

어제 회사 야유회에서 당신을 못 봤어요.
(A) 제가 샌드위치를 좀 준비할게요.
(B) 아, 급한 회의가 있었어요.
(C) 매년 봄이요.

30. 🎧 영녀/미남

We're behind schedule, aren't we?
(A) Yes, it's behind the building.
(B) Thanks for your extra work.
(C) No, everything's right on time.

우리 예정보다 늦었죠, 그렇지 않나요?
(A) 네, 건물 뒤에 있어요.
(B) 당신의 추가 근무에 감사드립니다.
(C) 아뇨, 모든 게 제시간에 되고 있어요.

어휘 behind schedule 예정보다 늦은

PART TEST

본문 p.46

1. (C)	**2.** (B)	**3.** (A)	**4.** (C)	**5.** (B)	**6.** (A)
7. (A)	**8.** (B)	**9.** (A)	**10.** (C)	**11.** (A)	**12.** (A)
13. (C)	**14.** (C)	**15.** (A)	**16.** (B)	**17.** (C)	**18.** (A)
19. (B)	**20.** (C)	**21.** (A)	**22.** (C)	**23.** (B)	**24.** (C)
25. (B)					

1. 🎧 미남/영녀

Where do you park when you go to Jackson Stadium?
(A) I like spending time at the park.
(B) The restroom is just around the corner.
(C) It's easier to just take the subway.

Jackson Stadium으로 갈 때 어디에 주차하시나요?
(A) 저는 공원에서 시간 보내는 걸 좋아해요.
(B) 화장실은 길모퉁이를 돈 곳에 있습니다.
(C) 그냥 지하철을 타는 게 더 쉬워요.

2. 🎧 영녀/미남

Who's going to interview candidates for the position?
(A) For two weeks.
(B) Is the position not filled yet?
(C) My office is just next door.

누가 그 자리의 지원자들을 면접 볼 건가요?
(A) 2주 동안이요.
(B) 그 자리가 아직 충원되지 않았나요?
(C) 제 사무실은 바로 옆방이에요.

3. 호남/미녀

> Can you help me clean the break room?
> **(A) Sure, I have time right after lunch.**
> (B) The other one's broken.
> (C) I put it in the storage room.

휴게실 청소 좀 도와주시겠어요?
(A) 네, 점심 먹고 바로 시간이 있어요.
(B) 다른 하나는 고장났어요.
(C) 보관실에 뒀어요.

4. 미녀/호남

> Does the entrée have meat in it?
> (A) No, I'll meet them tomorrow.
> (B) The back entrance is over there.
> **(C) The chef can use a substitute.**

이 음식에 고기가 들어가나요?
(A) 아니요, 내일 그들을 만나요.
(B) 뒷문은 저쪽에 있습니다.
(C) 주방장이 다른 재료로 대체할 수 있습니다.
해설 음식에 고기가 들어가는데 주방장에게 요구해서 다른 재료로 대체할 수 있다는 우회 답변이다.

5. 미남/영녀

> Would you prefer I send the report electronically or by mail?
> (A) To the marketing team.
> **(B) I'll print it out myself.**
> (C) Only if you have to.

보고서를 이메일로 보낼까요, 우편으로 보낼까요?
(A) 마케팅팀에요.
(B) 제가 직접 출력해 볼게요.
(C) 당신이 해야만 한다면요.
해설 이메일로(electronically) 보내면 받아서 직접 출력하겠다는 의미이다.

6. 영녀/미남

> I need the phone number for the sales team.
> **(A) I left it on your desk.**
> (B) My degree is in mechanical engineering.
> (C) A large number of orders.

영업팀 전화번호가 필요해요.
(A) 당신 책상 위에 놓아두었어요.
(B) 저의 학위는 기계공학입니다.
(C) 주문이 많습니다.

7. 호남/미녀

> Don't you want to look at the draft before the meeting?
> **(A) My computer is down at the moment.**
> (B) They already left.
> (C) I reserved the meeting room.

회의 전에 초안을 보고 싶지 않으세요?
(A) 제 컴퓨터가 지금 다운되어 있어요.
(B) 그들은 이미 떠났어요.
(C) 저는 회의실을 예약했습니다.

8. 미녀/호남

> Are you printing out the lease contract?
> (A) The computer login information.
> **(B) No, the printer is broken right now.**
> (C) That's my least favorite place.

임대 계약서를 출력하고 있나요?
(A) 컴퓨터 로그인 정보요.
(B) 아니요, 지금 프린터가 고장 났어요.
(C) 그곳은 제가 가장 싫어하는 장소입니다.

9. 미남/영녀

> What do you plan to discuss with Mr. Allen?
> **(A) We're going over the training schedule.**
> (B) Yes, I just finished the floor plan.
> (C) Tomorrow would work for him.

Mr. Allen과 무엇을 의논할 계획입니까?
(A) 우리는 교육 일정을 검토할 거예요.
(B) 네, 방금 도면을 완성했어요.
(C) 내일은 그가 시간이 될 거예요.

10. 영녀/미남

> Why wasn't Brian's proposal approved?
> (A) Would you like to pose next to the sign?
> (B) Yes, I double checked it.
> **(C) Because we don't have enough funding.**

왜 Brian의 제안이 승인되지 않았나요?
(A) 간판 옆에서 포즈를 취해 보시겠어요?
(B) 네, 제가 다시 확인했어요.
(C) 자금이 충분하지 않기 때문입니다.

11. 호남/미녀

> Did you book a campsite?
> **(A) Yes, I have the confirmation number right here.**
> (B) No, the one near the station.
> (C) The book is out of stock now.

캠핑장을 예약했나요?
(A) 네, 여기 확인 번호가 있습니다.
(B) 아니요, 역 근처에 있는 거요.
(C) 그 책은 지금 품절입니다.

12. 미녀/호남

Do I register for the conference online or in person?
(A) You can register online.
(B) No, I'll be at a seminar.
(C) Yes, a small fee.

회의는 온라인으로 신청하나요, 아니면 직접 신청하나요?
(A) 온라인으로 등록할 수 있습니다.
(B) 아뇨, 세미나에 참석할 거예요.
(C) 네, 수수료가 조금 있어요.

13. 미남/영녀

When is Thomas going to the airport?
(A) Use Gate 22.
(B) By bus, I think.
(C) Right after the team meeting.

Thomas는 언제 공항에 가나요?
(A) 22번 게이트를 이용하세요.
(B) 제 생각에는 버스로요.
(C) 팀 미팅 직후에요.

14. 영녀/미남

Where did you buy that handmade soap?
(A) There may be a discount.
(B) Just last week.
(C) At the farmer's market.

그 수제 비누는 어디서 샀어요?
(A) 할인이 있을 수도 있습니다.
(B) 바로 지난주에요.
(C) 농산물 장터에서요.

15. 호남/미녀

This model is selling well, isn't it?
(A) We spend a fortune on advertising.
(B) It's a marketing position.
(C) Sure, I'll stop by the store.

이 모델은 잘 팔리고 있어요, 그렇지 않나요?
(A) 우리는 광고에 많은 돈을 씁니다.
(B) 그것은 마케팅 직책입니다.
(C) 그럼요, 가게에 들를게요.

어휘 fortune 거금 stop by ~에 들르다

16. 미녀/호남

I can help set up the stage if you'd like.
(A) Yes, it was a great performance.
(B) Thanks, but you don't have to do that.
(C) A new assistant manager.

원하시면 제가 무대 설치를 도와드릴 수 있어요.
(A) 네, 정말 좋은 공연이었어요.
(B) 고마워요, 하지만 그럴 필요는 없어요.
(C) 신임 대리입니다.

17. 미남/영녀

Why was the delivery late?
(A) Gillian signed the delivery receipt.
(B) At least 5 hours.
(C) Did you see all the traffic?

왜 배송이 늦었죠?
(A) Gillian이 배달 영수증에 서명했어요.
(B) 적어도 5시간이요.
(C) 차 막히는 거 보셨어요?

18. 영녀/미남

You're leaving to Taiwan soon, aren't you?
(A) The conference was canceled.
(B) Just leave it to me.
(C) No, Friday doesn't work.

당신은 곧 대만으로 떠나죠, 그렇지 않나요?
(A) 그 컨퍼런스는 취소되었습니다.
(B) 그냥 저한테 맡겨 주세요.
(C) 아니요, 금요일은 안 돼요.
해설 대만에서 열리는 컨퍼런스가 취소되었다는 의미이다.

19. 호남/미녀

Ms. Hill will be a great division executive.
(A) The personnel department.
(B) She does hold the company's sales record.
(C) No, I can't remember the exact date.

Ms. Hill은 훌륭한 본부장이 될 거예요.
(A) 인사부입니다.
(B) 그녀는 회사의 매출 기록을 보유하고 있습니다.
(C) 아니요, 정확한 날짜는 기억이 안 나요.

20. 미녀/호남

When did that hotel open?
(A) I'm sorry, but we're fully booked.
(B) The price includes accommodation.
(C) There was an article in the paper last week.

그 호텔이 언제 오픈했죠?
(A) 죄송하지만, 예약이 다 찼습니다.
(B) 숙박료가 포함된 가격입니다.
(C) 지난주에 신문에 기사가 났었어요.

해설 (C) 지난주의 신문에서 호텔 오픈 기사를 읽었다는 우회 답변이다.

21. 미남/영녀

This contract was reviewed by our legal team, wasn't it?
(A) Betty left her comments on some issues.
(B) Yes, it has an excellent view.
(C) I'll contact my doctor.

이 계약서는 우리 법무팀에서 검토한 거죠, 그렇지 않나요?
(A) Betty가 몇 가지 문제에 대해 의견을 남겼습니다.
(B) 네, 전망이 아주 좋아요.
(C) 의사에게 연락해 볼게요.

해설 법무팀의 Betty가 계약서를 검토하고 나서 그에 대한 몇 가지 의견을 남겼다는 우회 답변이다.

22. 영녀/미남

Which dates would you like to book the conference room for?
(A) The department budget for March.
(B) Yes, we close at 6 o'clock.
(C) From the sixth to the eighth, please.

어느 날짜로 회의실을 예약하고 싶으세요?
(A) 3월의 부서 예산입니다.
(B) 네, 6시에 문을 닫습니다.
(C) 6일부터 8일까지 부탁합니다.

23. 호남/미녀

How many new employees are you training today?
(A) The gym on the third floor.
(B) Jason developed an online instruction module instead.
(C) She approved it.

오늘 신입 사원 몇 명을 교육시키나요?
(A) 3층 체육관이요.
(B) Jason이 대신 온라인 교육 모듈을 개발했어요.
(C) 그녀가 승인했어요.

해설 사람들이 한 장소에 모여서 받는 교육을 온라인 교육 모듈로 대체했다는 우회 답변이다.

24. 미녀/호남

Why hasn't Paul updated the database?
(A) Just about two weeks, I think.
(B) Yes, there's a sale on electronics tomorrow.
(C) Didn't you hear that the computer servers are down?

왜 Paul이 데이터베이스를 업데이트하지 않았죠?
(A) 제 생각에는 2주 정도요.
(B) 네, 내일 전자제품 세일이 있어요.
(C) 컴퓨터 서버가 다운되었다는 소식 못 들었어요?

25. 미남/영녀

I can give you a discount if you increase your order to 50 chairs.
(A) At the new furniture store.
(B) I'm not authorized to make that decision.
(C) This place looks great.

의자 주문량을 50개로 늘리면 할인해 드릴 수 있습니다.
(A) 새로 생긴 가구점에서요.
(B) 저는 그런 결정을 내릴 권한이 없습니다.
(C) 여기 정말 좋아 보이네요.

LC PART 3

출제 경향 및 전략

본문 p.51

Example

여 Kaysville 아쿠아리움에 방문해 주신 걸 감사드립니다. 무엇을 도와드릴까요?

남 성인 두 명 입장권을 사고 싶어요.

여 일반 표는 $22입니다. 그런데, 시즌권을 단돈 $75로 구매하실 수 있으세요. 그걸로 1년 동안 원하시는 만큼 저희 아쿠아리움을 이용하실 수 있습니다.

남 흠… 저희가 이 지역에 살아서 아마 자주 방문할 것 같아요. 그걸로 해야겠네요.

여 좋아요! 이 신청서만 작성해주시면 됩니다.

32. 대화는 어디에서 일어나고 있는가?
(A) 영화관에서
(B) 수족관에서
(C) 미술관에서
(D) 경기장에서

33. 남자는 무엇을 살 것 같은가?
(A) 단체 입장권
(B) 반나절 입장권
(C) 시즌 입장권
(D) 학생 입장권

34. 여자는 남자에게 무엇을 하라고 요청하는가?
(A) 서식 작성하기
(B) 다른 지점에 전화하기
(C) 신분증 보여주기
(D) 전화 걸기

UNIT 01 화자의 직업 및 대화 장소

CHECK-UP

본문 p.53

1. (C) **2.** (D)

1. 미남/영녀
Question 1 refers to the following conversation.

M Betty, I just heard at the staff meeting our company won the bid to build the bridge over Rivanna River.

W It's great news. That's the biggest construction project we've had in a while.

M Exactly. Do you happen to know when construction will begin?

W We have to wait until the contract is officially signed. It will be a while before we actually get started.

남 Betty, **방금 직원 회의에서 우리 회사가 Rivanna River 다리 건설 입찰을 따냈다고 들었어요.**

여 정말 기쁜 소식이에요. 근래에 한 것 중 가장 큰 건설 프로젝트예요.

남 맞아요. 혹시 공사가 언제 시작될지 알고 있나요?

여 공식적으로 계약서에 서명할 때까지 기다려야 해요. 시작하려면 한참 걸릴 거예요.

어휘 win a bid 입찰을 따내다 happen to do 혹시 ~하다

1. 화자들은 어느 산업에 종사하는가?
(A) 출판
(B) 운송
(C) 건축
(D) 금융

2. 호남/미녀
Question 2 refers to the following conversation.

M Hello. Lake Park Apartments management office. How can I help you?

W Hi. I'm Helen Thomson. I live in Unit 325B. I'm a new tenant here.

M Are you enjoying your new apartment?

W Yes, I love it. However, I lost my key card for the main entrance. Do you happen to have an extra one?

M No, we don't, but we can get that reissued. It'll take a few days.

W Thank you. How much is it for reissuing that?

M This is your first reissue, so there's no extra charge for that.

남 안녕하세요. **Lake Park Apartments 관리실입니다.** 무엇을 도와드릴까요?

여 안녕하세요. 저는 Helen Thompson인데, 325B에 살아요. 이번에 새로 입주했어요.

남 아파트는 마음에 드세요?

여 네, 마음에 들어요. 그런데 현관문 카드키를 잃어버렸어요. 혹시 여분이 있나요?

남 아뇨, 하지만 재발급해드릴 수 있습니다. 이삼 일 걸릴 거예요.

여 감사합니다. 재발급하는 데 얼마죠?

남 이번이 처음 재발급하는 거니까 추가 요금은 없습니다.

어휘 management office 관리사무소 tenant 세입자 reissue 재발행하다

2. 남자는 누구일 것 같은가?
(A) 인테리어 디자이너

(B) 부동산 중개인
(C) 안전 점검원
(D) 아파트 관리인

UNIT 02 대화 목적 및 주제

CHECK-UP 본문 p.55

1. (B) **2.** (A)

1. 영녀/미남
Question 1 refers to the following conversation.

W Hello, Mr. Lewis? This is Karen Miller calling from Siemens Technologies. I reviewed your application for the mechanical engineer position and would like to interview you.
M Oh, I'm so pleased to hear that.
W Good. I'm wondering if Thursday at 10 A.M. works for you.
M Actually, I have a dentist appointment that morning. Do you mind if I call you back after I reschedule it?

여 안녕하세요, Mr. Lewis. Siemens Technologies의 Karen Miller예요. 기계 엔지니어 직에 지원하신 지원서 살펴봤는데, **면접을 잡고 싶습니다**.
남 아, 감사합니다.
여 네, 목요일 오전 11시 어떠세요?
남 사실 그날 아침에는 치과 예약이 있어서 제가 다시 스케줄을 잡고 전화 드려도 될까요?

어휘 review 검토하다 application 지원서

1. 전화의 목적은 무엇인가?
(A) 주문을 하기 위해
(B) 면접 일정을 잡기 위해
(C) 계약을 확정하기 위해
(D) 약속을 취소하기 위해

2. 호남/미녀
Question 2 refers to the following conversation.

M The lights in my office just went out.
W The power seems to be out in the whole building. I just called the maintenance office and they said it would take at least one hour until the power is restored.
M Oh, I have a meeting with a client in 10 minutes.
W Why don't you have a meeting at the coffee shop across the street?
M That's a good idea.

남 방금 제 사무실 전등이 나갔어요.
여 **건물 전체가 전원이 나간 것 같아요.** 방금 관리실에 전화해 봤는데, 전원이 복구되는 데 적어도 한 시간은 걸릴 거래요.
남 이런, 10분 뒤에 고객과 회의가 있는데.
여 길 건너 커피숍에서 회의하는 건 어때요?
남 그거 좋은 생각이네요.

어휘 go out 불이 나가다 restore 복구하다, (이전의 상황 · 감정으로) 회복시키다

2. 어떤 문제가 논의되고 있는가?
(A) 정전
(B) 도로 폐쇄
(C) 악천후
(D) 고장난 차량

UNIT 03 요청, 제안

CHECK-UP 본문 p.57

1. (A) **2.** (C)

1. 미남/영녀
Question 1 refers to the following conversation.

M Hello. This is Marcus from Special Edge Marketing. I just sent you an e-mail with the design for your new advertising campaign. Did you get a chance to look at it?
W Hi, Marcus. I was just about to call you. I wanted to tell you that we have a new slogan.
M That's not a problem. Can you send it to me before the end of the day? Then I can finalize everything by tomorrow.
W Definitely! After you're finished, please update the contract to reflect the changes.

남 안녕하세요. Special Edge Marketing의 Marcus입니다. 방금 당신의 새로운 광고 캠페인을 위한 디자인을 이메일로 보내드렸습니다. 혹시 보셨나요?
여 안녕하세요, Marcus. 막 전화하려던 참이었는데. 새로운 슬로건이 생겼다는 걸 말씀드리고 싶었어요.
남 그건 문제되지 않습니다. 오늘까지 저에게 보내주실 수 있나요? 그러면 내일까지 모든 것을 마무리할 수 있어요.
여 물론입니다! 작업이 끝나면 **변경사항들을 반영하여 계약서를 업데이트해 주세요**.

어휘 be about to do 막 ~하려 하다
reflect the changes 변경사항을 반영하다

1. 여자는 남자에게 무엇을 할 것을 요청하는가?
(A) 계약서 수정하기
(B) 지급 완료하기
(C) 마감일 연장하기

(D) 상사의 승인 얻기

2. 호남/미녀

Question 2 refers to the following conversation.

M Cindy, have you analyzed the results from the customer satisfaction questionnaire?

W I did, and it seems like customers are satisfied with our service, but they wish we offered more discounts. Compared to other stores, we hardly ever have sales.

M Wow. I actually watched a video about this recently. It said that frequent sales can get more people in the door to your business.

W In that case, why don't we start a rewards program? That way, people will be tempted to come in more often to receive discounts.

남 Cindy, 고객 만족도 설문지 결과 분석해 보셨나요?

여 네, 고객들은 우리 서비스에 만족하는 것 같지만, 우리가 더 할인해 주기를 바라는 것 같아요. 다른 매장과 비교하면, 저희는 거의 세일을 하지 않아요.

남 와, 제가 얼마 전에 이에 관한 영상을 봤어요. 잦은 할인이 더 많은 고객의 방문을 유도한다고 합니다.

여 그렇다면 **보상 프로그램을 시작하는 게 어떨까요**? 그렇게 하면, 사람들은 할인을 받으려 더 자주 오고 싶어 할 거예요.

어휘 questionnaire 설문지 compared to ~와 비교했을 때 tempt 유혹하다, 유도하다 (be tempted to do 유혹에 이끌려 ~하다)

2. 여자는 무엇을 할 것을 제안하는가?

(A) 시장 조사하기

(B) 더 많은 직원 채용하기

(C) 보상 프로그램 제공하기

(D) 컨설턴트 찾기

UNIT 04 문제, 걱정

CHECK-UP 본문 p.59

1. (B) **2.** (C)

1. 영녀/미남

Question 1 refers to the following conversation.

W Kevin, have you ordered the mugs for our guests yet? Our gallery's grand opening is just around the corner.

M I called the Lolly Ceramics yesterday but unfortunately, the style we picked out is sold out. They said they aren't sure when they'll have more available.

W Well, we need the gifts here by the 2nd of July. We can't afford to wait.

M OK, I'll search the Internet to see if any other suppliers have a similar style right away.

여 Kevin, 손님들에게 줄 머그잔 주문했어요? 우리 갤러리의 개장이 얼마 남지 않았습니다.

남 어제 Lolly Ceramics에 전화했는데 **아쉽게도 저희가 고른 스타일은 매진되었습니다**. 언제 재고를 확보할 수 있을지 확신할 수 없다고 했어요.

여 음, 우리는 7월 2일까지 선물이 필요해요. 기다릴 여유가 없어요.

남 네, 지금 바로 인터넷에서 비슷한 스타일의 공급업체가 있는지 찾아볼게요.

어휘 just around the corner ~이 코앞으로 다가와 pick out 고르다 be[have] sold out 매진되다 supplier 공급자

1. 남자는 어떤 문제를 언급하는가?

(A) 마감일을 놓쳤다.

(B) 상품의 재고가 없다.

(C) 주문품이 배송되지 않았다.

(D) 일부 직원을 활용할 수 없다.

2. 호남/미녀

Question 2 refers to the following conversation.

M I appreciate the invitation to your place of business. Like I wrote in my e-mail, I'm searching for a landscaping company to help modernize some of the properties I'm selling.

W No problem. My company is well-known for providing the most up-to-date landscaping possible.

M That sounds wonderful. I'm a little concerned about the price, though. Do you have different options depending on the budget?

W Of course. I'm sure we can find something within your price range. I'll show you a slideshow of some of our work and you can decide what you want done.

남 당신의 사업장에 초대해 주셔서 감사합니다. 제가 이메일에 썼듯이, 저는 제가 팔고 있는 부동산 중 일부를 현대화하는 데 도움을 줄 조경 회사를 찾고 있습니다.

여 문제 없습니다. 우리 회사는 가능한 가장 최신식 조경을 제공하는 것으로 잘 알려져 있습니다.

남 멋지군요. **그래도 가격이 좀 걱정되네요.** 예산에 따라 선택할 수 있는 여러 옵션이 있나요?

여 물론이죠. 당신의 가격대에 맞는 것을 찾을 수 있을 거라고 확신해요. 제가 저희 작업의 슬라이드 쇼를 보여 드릴 테니 무엇을 할지 결정하시면 됩니다.

어휘 place of business 사업장 search for ~을 찾다 up-to-date 최신의 depending on ~에 따라

2. 남자는 무엇에 대해 걱정한다고 말하는가?
(A) 위치
(B) 가능한 날짜
(C) 가격
(D) 크기

UNIT 05 특정 시간

CHECK-UP 본문 p.61

1. (C) **2.** (D)

1. 미남/영녀
Question 1 refers to the following conversation.

M Hello, and thank you for calling Carol's, the customized gift-making shop. What can I do for you?
W I'm calling to order 150 pens with my company's logo. It's our fifth year of being in business, so we're having a small anniversary party. Would it be possible to have them in three weeks?
M Sure. That won't be a problem. And since you plan to order over 100 items, I can give you a 10% discount.
W That's wonderful! How can I pay for my purchase? Do I have to visit the shop or can I provide my credit card details online?

남 안녕하세요, 맞춤형 선물 가게인 Carol's에 전화 주셔서 감사합니다. 뭘 도와 드릴까요?
여 저희 회사 로고가 들어간 펜 150개를 주문하려고 전화 드렸습니다. **창립 5주년을 맞아 기념 파티를 작게 할 거예요. 3주 후에 물건을 받을 수 있을까요?**
남 물론이죠. 그건 문제가 안 됩니다. 그리고 100개 이상 주문하실 예정이니 10% 할인해드릴 수 있습니다.
여 훌륭하네요! 구매 대금은 어떻게 지불하나요? 매장을 방문해야 하나요, 아니면 온라인으로 신용카드 정보를 제공하면 되나요?

어휘 customized 개개인의 요구에 맞춘

1. 여자에 따르면 3주 후에 무슨 일이 발생할 것인가?
(A) 재고 조사
(B) 연간 재고 정리 세일
(C) 기념 파티
(D) 개업

2. 미녀/호남
Question 2 refers to the following conversation.

W You've reached the Allendale Community Center. What can I do for you?
M Hello, I'm looking to start a bird-watching club.
W Sure. To start your own club, you can come to the center and fill out some paperwork.
M Perfect. I'll come by later today. Can I reserve a space at the center?
W Sure, but since you're starting a new club, you might not have a lot of initial members.
M I understand. Also, does the community center have AV equipment? I want to project some pictures of birds on a screen.
W Yes. You can borrow our AV equipment free of charge.

여 Allendale 주민 센터입니다. 뭘 도와 드릴까요?
남 안녕하세요, 조류 관찰 동아리를 시작하려고 하는데요.
여 물론이죠. 동아리를 시작하려면 **센터에 오셔서 서류를 작성하시면 됩니다.**
남 **좋습니다. 오늘 오후에 들를게요.** 센터에 공간을 예약할 수 있나요?
여 물론이죠, 하지만 동아리를 새로 시작하기 때문에 초기 회원이 많지 않을 수도 있어요.
남 이해합니다. 그리고 주민 센터에 시청각 장비가 있나요? 스크린에 새들의 사진을 투사하고 싶어서요.
여 네. 저희 시청각 장비를 무료로 대여하실 수 있습니다.

어휘 fill out (서류 등을) 작성하다 come by 들르다
free of charge 무료로

2. 남자는 오늘 오후에 무엇을 할 것이라고 말하는가?
(A) 발표하기
(B) 온라인 설문조사 작성하기
(C) 차량 예약하기
(D) 주민 센터 방문하기

UNIT 06 다음에 할 일

CHECK-UP 본문 p.63

1. (D) **2.** (B)

1. 미남/영녀
Question 1 refers to the following conversation.

M Hey, Eleanor. I want you to attend the annual book publishing conference in New York. It will be a great chance for you to connect with other publishers.
W That's wonderful! I appreciate the opportunity. Do you mind if we push back the deadline for our latest children's book project? If I'm away for the conference, I won't be able to work on it.
M That's a good point. Let's move the deadline

back one week so you have enough time to work on the project. I'll send out an e-mail notice to the rest of the staff.

남 안녕하세요, Eleanor. 당신이 뉴욕에서 열리는 연례 출판 콘퍼런스에 방문하셨으면 좋겠어요. 당신이 다른 출판사들과 교류할 수 있는 좋은 기회가 될 거예요.

여 그거 멋지네요! 이 기회에 감사해요. 우리가 가장 최근에 진행 중이던 아동용 책 프로젝트의 마감을 좀 미루어 주실 수 있나요? 제가 콘퍼런스에 간다면, 저는 그것에 대한 작업을 하지 못할 거예요.

남 좋은 지적이네요. 당신에게 일할 수 있는 충분한 시간이 주어질 수 있도록 마감을 한 주 늦추도록 하죠. **다른 직원들에게 이메일로 알림 사항을 보내겠습니다.**

어휘 push back the deadline 마감일을 미루다 (=move the deadline back) send out 발송하다

1. 남자는 다음에 무엇을 할 것 같은가?
(A) 전화하기
(B) 회의 준비하기
(C) 점심 먹으러 가기
(D) 공지 사항 전달하기

2. 미녀/호남
Question 2 refers to the following conversation.

W Good morning, Jeremy. The final blueprints for our sorting robot and driverless forklift are ready. We'll be able to show them to our clients from Redhawk Logistics at today's meeting.

M Actually, none of the conference rooms are available. I forgot to book one for today's meeting...

W I see. I'll speak with the other department heads to see if we can take one of their slots. The clients have a tight schedule and we need to have the meeting today.

M Thanks a bunch. I think the marketing and human resource departments reserved the conference room.

W OK.

여 좋은 아침이에요, Jeremy. 선별 로봇과 무인 지게차의 최종 설계도가 준비되어 있습니다. 오늘 회의에서 Redhawk Logistics 고객들에게 보여줄 수 있을 거예요.

남 사실, 어떤 회의실도 이용할 수 없습니다. 오늘 회의를 할 회의실을 예약하는 것을 잊어버렸어요…

여 그렇군요. **다른 부서장들과 상의해서 그들이 예약한 시간 중 한 자리를 차지할 수 있는지 알아볼게요.** 고객들의 일정이 빠듯해서 오늘 회의를 해야 해요.

남 감사합니다. 마케팅 부서와 인사 부서가 회의실을 예약한 것 같아요.

여 네.

어휘 sort 분류하다 driverless 운전자가 없는 forklift 지게차 slot 자리[시간/틈] have a tight schedule 일정이 빡빡하다 reserve 예약하다

2. 여자는 다음에 무엇을 할 것 같은가?
(A) 장비 조사
(B) 동료와 대화
(C) 고객 픽업
(D) 시연 일정 다시 잡기

PRACTICE UNIT 01~06 본문 p.64

1. (C)	**2.** (A)	**3.** (B)	**4.** (B)	**5.** (A)	**6.** (C)
7. (A)	**8.** (C)	**9.** (D)	**10.** (A)	**11.** (B)	**12.** (B)
13. (D)	**14.** (D)	**15.** (B)	**16.** (C)	**17.** (C)	**18.** (B)
19. (B)	**20.** (C)	**21.** (D)	**22.** (C)	**23.** (A)	**24.** (A)

1-3. 영녀/미남
Questions 1-3 refer to the following conversation.

W Good morning. [1]Do you know when you and your crew will be finished with the renovations to our library?

M I can't say for sure. The project is running behind schedule. [2]We're waiting for wooden frames to arrive before we can install new windows in the reading room.

W That's too bad. Our temporary facility across the street is quite small, so our library staff is eager to return to the building as soon as possible.

M I understand. [3]I'll call the supplier to see if they can make a rush delivery of the frames by the end of the week.

여 좋은 아침입니다. [1]**당신과 당신의 인부들이 우리 도서관의 수리를 언제 마치게 될까요?**

남 확실히 말씀드릴 수는 없어요. 프로젝트가 예정보다 늦게 진행되고 있어요. 열람실에 새 창문을 설치하기 전에 [2]**나무 창틀이 도착하기를 기다리고 있거든요.**

여 안 좋은 소식이네요. 길 건너편에 있는 임시 시설이 너무 작아서 도서관 직원들은 가능한 한 빨리 건물로 돌아가고 싶어 하거든요.

남 이해합니다. [3]**공급업체에 전화해서** 이번 주말까지 창틀을 서둘러 납품할 수 있는지 알아보겠습니다.

어휘 run behind schedule 일정에 뒤처지다 be eager to do (간절히) ~하고 싶어 하다 make a rush delivery ~을 서둘러 배송하다

1. 남자는 누구일 것 같은가?
(A) 마케팅 컨설턴트

PART 3

(B) 뉴스 리포터
(C) 건설 관리자
(D) 웹 개발자

2. 남자는 어떤 문제를 언급하는가?
(A) 일부 자재가 없다.
(B) 프로젝트 비용이 너무 비싸다.
(C) 날씨가 안 좋다.
(D) 인부가 그만뒀다.

3. 남자는 다음에 무엇을 할 것인가?
(A) 이메일 보내기
(B) 전화하기
(C) 보고서 작성하기
(D) 관공서 방문하기

4-6. 영녀/미남
Questions 4-6 refer to the following conversation.

W Hi. [4]I'm here with my documentary crew. I'm putting together a series on innovative designs in contemporary medical facilities. I'm here to get footage of your hospital.

M Oh, right. [5]An agent from your film studio e-mailed me this morning to say you were coming.

W Can you please direct me to the newly renovated intensive care unit?

M Sure. [6]I can also introduce you to our Assistant Director. He was in charge of designing the East Wing.

여 안녕하세요. [4]**저흰 다큐멘터리 제작진입니다.** 현대 의료 시설의 혁신적인 디자인에 관한 시리즈를 만들고 있습니다. 병원 영상을 찍고자 왔습니다.

남 아, 맞아요. [5]**오늘 아침에 당신의 영화 스튜디오의 에이전트가 당신이 온다는 이메일을 보냈습니다.**

여 새로 개조된 중환자실로 안내해 주시겠습니까?

남 물론입니다. [6]**저희 부원장님도 소개해 드릴 수 있습니다.** 그분이 동관 디자인을 담당했습니다.

어휘 put together (이것저것을 모아) 만들다 footage (특정한 사건을 담은) 장면[화면, 영상] direct ~에게 길을 안내하다

4. 여자는 누구일 것 같은가?
(A) 내과의사
(B) 영화감독
(C) 건축가
(D) 실내 디자이너

5. 남자는 오늘 아침 무슨 일이 일어났다고 말하는가?
(A) 이메일 메시지를 받았다.
(B) 문제를 발견했다.
(C) 도급업자를 만났다.
(D) 직장에 늦었다.

6. 남자는 무엇을 할 것을 제안하는가?
(A) 면접
(B) 보고서 제출
(C) 대화 주선
(D) 데이터 공유

7-9. 호남/미녀
Question 7-9 refer to the following conversation.

M Thanks for meeting with me today, Lydia. I'd like to discuss your products' performance in the Backpackers' Online Marketplace.

W Sure, Mike. The marketplace has been a great way for me to distribute [7]my apparel to backpackers worldwide.

M Your Shoe Hop boots are among our best-selling items. [8]Customers praise their durability. Customers describe using your boots on rough terrain and in extreme weather, with the boots showing minimal signs of wear and tear.

W I'm glad. [9]I've been getting rubber from a different company recently. I'm pleased with the results and plan to continue working with them.

남 오늘 만나줘서 고마워요, Lydia. Backpackers' Online Marketplace에서 판매되는 귀사 제품의 성능에 대해 논의하고 싶어요.

여 물론이죠, Mike. Backpackers' Online Marketplace는 제가 전 세계 [7]**배낭 여행객들에게 저희 의류를** 배포할 수 있는 좋은 시장이었습니다.

남 귀사의 Shoe Hop 부츠는 저희 회사에서 가장 잘 팔리는 상품 중 하나입니다. [8]**고객들이 내구성이 아주 좋다고 칭찬해요.** 험한 지형과 험악한 기후에서도 부츠의 마모나 손상이 매우 미미하다고 합니다.

여 다행이에요. [9]**최근에 다른 회사에서 고무를 받고 있거든요. 결과가 만족스러워서 그들과 계속 거래할 계획입니다.**

어휘 marketplace 시장, 장터 apparel 의류, 의복 durability 내구성 terrain 지형, 지역 wear and tear 마모

7. 여자의 회사는 무엇을 파는가?
(A) 하이킹 장비
(B) 모바일 앱
(C) 건강 식품
(D) 아동복

8. 남자는 어떤 점을 강조하는가?
(A) 웹사이트가 바뀌었다.
(B) 고객이 만족해하지 않는다.
(C) 제품이 믿을 만하다.
(D) 가격이 올랐다.

9. 여자는 무엇에 대해 만족해하는가?

(A) 광고 캠페인
(B) 배송 서비스
(C) 숙련된 직원
(D) 새로운 공급자

10-12. 미녀/호남
Questions 10-12 refer to the following conversation.

W [10]Welcome to the Brighton Senior Center. Are you here to visit a family member?
M Actually, [11]I'm here because I heard there's an opening for a lifeguard position.
W That's right. Do you have previous experience working as a lifeguard for senior citizens?
M I worked at Sunny Side Beach over in Roslindale for more than three years. The population there was mostly elderly.
W I see. Well, the application process is pretty simple. [12]But first, I can show you around the pool and the rest of the building to give you a clearer idea of what the position requires.
M Thanks, that sounds great.

여 [10]**Brighton Senior Center에 오신 것을 환영합니다.** 가족을 방문하러 오셨습니까?
남 실은, [11]**안전요원 자리가 비어 있다고 해서 왔습니다.**
여 맞아요. 전에 노인 안전요원으로 일한 경험이 있습니까?
남 저는 Roslindale에 있는 Sunny Side Beach에서 3년 이상 일했습니다. 거기 있는 대부분이 노인들이었습니다.
여 알겠습니다. 지원 절차는 매우 간단합니다. [12]**하지만 먼저 수영장과 건물의 다른 부분들을 보여드리면서 이 자리가 무엇을 필요로 하는지 더 명확한 정보를 제공해 드릴게요.**
남 감사합니다. 좋습니다.

어휘 opening 공석 elderly 연세가 드신 give you a clearer idea of ~을 좀더 잘 이해하게 하다

10. 여자는 어디에서 일하는가?
(A) 은퇴자 커뮤니티에서
(B) 대학에서
(C) 채용업체에서
(D) 병원에서

11. 남자의 방문 목적은 무엇인가?
(A) 그는 친척을 만나고 있다.
(B) 그는 일자리에 관해 문의하고 있다.
(C) 그는 상품을 배송하고 있다.
(D) 그는 지불을 하고 있다.

12. 남자는 다음에 무엇을 할 것 같은가?
(A) 짧은 영상을 본다
(B) 시설을 둘러본다
(C) 신청서를 작성한다
(D) 이메일을 쓴다

13-15. 미남/영녀
Questions 13-15 refer to the following conversation.

M Good morning. [13]I'm wondering if you could repair my custom-designed business suit. There's a tear along the right shoulder line, and some frayed ends inside the pocket.
W I see… Yes, I can fix this, but it will take time to make sure I get the stitching right. How soon do you need it?
M [14]I'll be traveling to a business conference in Sao Paulo next weekend. I'd like to take the item with me if possible.
W It shouldn't be a problem. [15]Just fill out this order form with any special instructions and leave the suit in the basket along the back wall.

남 좋은 아침입니다. [13]**주문 제작한 양복을 수선해 주실 수 있는지 궁금합니다.** 오른쪽 어깨선을 따라 터진 데가 있고, 주머니 안쪽에 해어진 부분이 있습니다.
여 알겠습니다… 네, 고칠 수는 있지만 제대로 꿰매려면 시간이 걸릴 것 같습니다. 얼마나 빨리 필요하세요?
남 [14]**저는 다음 주말에 상파울루에서 열리는 비즈니스 회의에 출장을 갈 예정입니다.** 가능하다면 거기에 이 양복을 가져가고 싶어요.
여 문제 없습니다. [15]**이 주문서에 특이사항을 기입하고** 양복은 뒷벽을 따라 놓여 있는 바구니에 넣어 두세요.

어휘 tear 찢어진 데; 찢다 fray (천이) 해어지다, (천을) 해어지게 하다

13. 여자는 누구인가?
(A) 옷가게 점원
(B) 식료품점 직원
(C) 여행사 직원
(D) 재단사

14. 남자는 다음 주에 무슨 일이 일어날 것이라고 말하는가?
(A) 그는 휴가를 쓸 것이다.
(B) 그는 회의를 열 것이다.
(C) 그는 계약을 체결할 것이다.
(D) 그는 행사에 참석할 것이다.

15. 남자는 다음에 무엇을 할 것 같은가?
(A) 대금 지불
(B) 양식 작성
(C) 영수증 수령
(D) 후기 작성

16-18. 영녀/미남
Questions 16-18 refer to the following conversation.

W Greetings, Mr. Valdez, and thank you for coming out to Willow Country Club to meet with me today. I hope our businesses can develop a long-lasting partnership.

M Me, too. I hear there have been some recent changes at your club.

W Yes. [16]Our membership population has doubled over the last six months. Now, we simply don't have enough kitchen staff members to meet our clientele's needs.

M Well, my company's award-winning chefs are among the best in the county. [17]We could come up with new high-end menu items to impress your members and their guests.

W That would be great. [18]I could announce the partnership by launching a televised ad campaign, to our mutual benefit.

여 안녕하세요, Mr. Valdez. 오늘 Willow Country Club에 나와 주셔서 감사합니다. 저는 우리 사업이 오래 지속되는 파트너십으로 발전하기를 바랍니다.

남 저도요. 클럽에 최근 몇 가지 변화가 있었다고 들었습니다.

여 네. [16]**지난 6개월 동안 회원 수가 두 배로 늘었습니다.** 이제는 주방 직원이 부족해서 고객의 요구를 충족시킬 수가 없는 상황이에요.

남 음, 저희 회사의 수상 경력이 있는 요리사들은 카운티에서 가장 뛰어난 요리사들이라고 할 수 있습니다. [17]**새로운 고급 메뉴로 클럽 회원들과 동반 고객들에게 감동을 선사할 수 있을 거예요.**

여 좋습니다. [18]**텔레비전 광고를 통해 우리의 파트너십을 발표하면 어떨까 싶습니다.** 서로에게 이익이 되도록 말이죠.

어휘 long-lasting 오래 지속되는 membership population 회원 수 award-winning 수상을 한 come up with ~을 만들어내다, ~을 생각해내다 televised ad campaign 텔레비전 광고 캠페인

16. 여자에 따르면, 최근 그녀의 회사에 무슨 일이 발생했는가?
(A) 투자자를 발굴했다.
(B) 직원들이 급여 인상을 요구했다.
(C) 고객층이 늘었다.
(D) 위치가 변경되었다.

17. 남자의 회사는 무엇을 할 수 있는가?
(A) 종업원 공급
(B) 식당 마련
(C) 양질의 식사 마련
(D) 음식 배달

18. 여자는 파트너십 발표를 위해 무엇을 할 수 있을 거라고 말하는가?
(A) 특별 행사 계획
(B) 광고 제작
(C) 소셜미디어 캠페인 시작
(D) 신문 광고 게재

19-21. 호남/미녀
Questions 19-21 refer to the following conversation.

M Hi, and welcome to Speedsters Athletic Club. How can I help you?

W [19]I've belonged to this gym for a while, but I've never signed up for individual training sessions before. Can you tell me about them?

M Sure. Here—[20]you just need to fill out this document listing your exercise goals and available time slots. Then we'll match you up with a personal trainer who's a perfect fit for your needs.

W Exciting! Is it possible to meet any of the trainers beforehand? I have some specific questions about training programs.

M Yes. [21]Steve, one of our most popular trainers, is right over here. I'll introduce you.

W Thanks. Lead the way!

남 안녕하세요, Speedsters Athletic Club에 오신 것을 환영합니다. 무엇을 도와드릴까요?

여 [19]**이 체육관에 가입한 지 꽤 됐지만,** 개인 트레이닝을 신청한 적은 한 번도 없었어요. 개인 트레이닝에 대해 설명 좀 해 주시겠어요?

남 물론입니다. 먼저 [20]**여기 서류에 트레이닝 목표와 가능한 시간을 작성해 주세요.** 그러면 고객님의 필요에 딱 맞는 개인 트레이너를 연결해 드리겠습니다.

여 좋습니다! 혹시 어느 분이든 트레이너 중 한 분을 미리 만나볼 수 있을까요? 트레이닝 프로그램에 대해 몇 가지 구체적으로 물어보고 싶은 게 있어서요.

남 네. [21]**가장 인기 있는 트레이너 중 한 명인 Steve가 지금 나와 있어요.** 제가 소개해 드릴게요.

여 감사합니다. 먼저 가시죠!

어휘 sign up for ~에 등록하다/가입하다 fill out (양식을) 작성하다 match A up with B 서로 어울리는 상대(A와 B)를 연결해 주다 a perfect fit for ~에 딱 맞는 사람 lead the way 앞장서다

19. 대화는 어디에서 일어나고 있는 것 같은가?
(A) 사무실 건물에서
(B) 피트니스 센터에서
(C) 스키 리조트에서
(D) 스포츠 용품점에서

20. 남자는 여자에게 무엇을 주는가?
(A) 전화번호
(B) 영수증
(C) 양식
(D) 웹사이트 링크

21. 여자는 다음에 무엇을 할 것 같은가?
(A) 전화한다
(B) 대기실에 간다

(C) 구직 신청서를 제출한다
(D) 직원과 이야기한다

22-24. 호남/미녀
Questions 22-24 refer to the following conversation.

M Hey, Karina. Sorry I'm late. It's been a stressful morning.

W What happened?

M I stopped for gas on the way to work. [22]When I got back in my car, it wouldn't start. A stranger helped me get the engine going, but now it's making loud clunking noises.

W Hmm... [23]do you know Stevenson's Auto Body on 71st street? The owner is really knowledgeable. I bet he can fix your car.

M Thanks, I'll ask him. But first, [24]I'll try to find the invoice from the last time I got the car repaired so I can show it to him. This is a recurring issue.

남 안녕하세요, Karina. 늦어서 죄송해요. 아침부터 골치가 아프네요.

여 무슨 일인데요?

남 출근길에 주유소에 들렀거든요. [22]**주유를 끝내고 시동을 거는데 시동이 안 걸려요.** 어떤 분이 도와줘서 시동이 걸리기는 했지만 엔진이 덜컹거리는 소리를 내요.

여 흠... [23]**71번가에 있는 Stevenson's Auto Body 아세요? 거기 사장님이 모르는 게 없어요. 그분이라면 분명 고칠 수 있을 거예요.**

남 고마워요. 그분에게 물어볼게요. 근데, 저번 수리할 때 받았던 [24]**청구서부터 찾아봐야겠어요.** 그분에게 그걸 보여줘야겠어요. 이게 벌써 한두 번이 아니거든요.

어휘 on the way to work 출근하는 길에 get the engine going 엔진이 작동하게 만들다 knowledgeable 박식한 get the car repaired (카센터에서) 차를 수리 받다 recurring 되풀이하여 발생하는 (recur 되풀이되다, 다시 일어나다 recurrent 되풀이되는, 재발되는)

22. 남자는 무슨 문제를 언급하는가?
(A) 다쳤다.
(B) 타이어가 펑크 났다.
(C) 엔진이 고장났다.
(D) 연료 탱크가 새고 있다.

23. 여자는 무엇을 하라고 제안하는가?
(A) 특정 수리점에 가 보는 것
(B) 품질보증 정보를 확인해 보는 것
(C) 새 보험에 가입하는 것
(D) 환불을 요청하는 것

24. 남자는 무엇을 찾아볼 것이라고 말하는가?
(A) 청구서
(B) 설명서
(C) 명함
(D) 경찰 보고서

UNIT 07 의도 파악

Example 본문 p.66

1. (A) **2.** (C) **3.** (D)

남 Heather, 다음 주 주말에 열리는 셰필드 여름 페스티벌 계획을 하나도 안 짰네요. 페스티벌이 좋은 홍보 기회가 될 거예요.

여 분명 많은 사람들이 올 거예요.

남 맞아요. 우리의 소다 캔 제품을 무료로 나눠주면 어떨까 해요. 한정판 캔에 페스티벌 로고를 찍어서 말이죠.

여 그렇게 하려면 2주가 걸릴 거예요.

남 그렇겠네요. 어쨌든 될 수 있는 다른 방법을 생각해 봐야겠어요.

어휘 take place 발생하다, 일어나다 publicity 홍보 give out 나눠주다 get A printed with B A에 B를 새기다 stand out 돋보이다

1. 다음 주말에 무슨 행사가 벌어질 것인가?
(A) 음악 페스티벌
(B) 자선 모금 행사
(C) 기념 파티
(D) 회사 야유회

2. 화자들의 회사는 무엇을 생산하는가?
(A) 운동 용품
(B) 옷
(C) 음료
(D) 야외용 가구

3. 여자는 왜 "그렇게 하려면 2주가 걸릴 거예요"라고 말하는가?
(A) 실수에 대해 사과하기 위해
(B) 마감일 연장을 제안하기 위해
(C) 서비스에 대해 불만을 표하기 위해
(D) 방안에 대한 우려를 표하기 위해

PRACTICE 고난도 본문 p.67

1. (C) **2.** (D) **3.** (B) **4.** (D) **5.** (D) **6.** (A)
7. (D) **8.** (A) **9.** (D) **10.** (C) **11.** (A) **12.** (B)

1-3. 영녀/미남
Questions 1-3 refer to the following conversation.

W Hello, Daniel. [1]This is Sabrina from Arch Publishing. We were highly impressed with your résumé and interview, so we wish to offer you a position at our Los Angeles branch.

M Thank you so much! It's great to hear that. [2]But

PART 3

I think I need some time to think about moving all the way to Los Angeles before I make a decision.

W Actually, we're looking to hire as soon as possible.

M Ah, I see.

W Working for our company has a lot of perks. As I'm sure you know, [3]the company provides both a housing and transportation stipend for all workers. A huge chunk of your expenses would already be covered by the company.

여 안녕하세요, Daniel. [1]**Arch Publishing의 Sabrina입니다.** 당신의 이력서와 면접이 인상적이어서, 저희 로스앤젤레스 지점에서 근무하실 것을 제안하고 싶어요.

남 정말로 감사합니다! 정말 좋은 소식이에요. [2]**하지만 결정을 내리기 전에 로스앤젤레스로 이사하는 것에 대해 생각할 시간이 좀 필요할 것 같아요.**

여 사실, 최대한 빠른 시일 내로 채용하려고 해요.

남 아, 그렇군요.

여 저희 회사에 근무하게 되면 이점이 많아요. 아시다시피, [3]**회사에선 전 직원에게 주택 수당과 교통 수당을 지급하고 있어요.** 지출의 상당 부분을 이미 회사에서 지불하는 셈이지요.

어휘 look to do ~하고자 하다 perk (급료 이외의) 특전 stipend 봉급, 급료

1. 여자는 어떤 회사에서 근무하는가?
(A) 마케팅 회사
(B) 여행사
(C) 출판사
(D) 법률 사무소

2. 여자가 "최대한 빠른 시일 내로 채용하려고 해요"라고 말할 때 무엇을 의미하는가?
(A) 그녀가 곧 퇴직할 것이다.
(B) 일정이 변경될 것이다.
(C) 추가 자금이 필요하다.
(D) 남자가 빠른 결정을 내려야 한다.

3. 여자에 따르면, 회사는 무엇을 제공하는가?
(A) 무료 식사
(B) 교통 수당
(C) 법인카드
(D) 직원 할인

4-6. 미남/영녀

Questions 4-6 refer to the following conversation.

M Hey, Elois. [4]How are the designs for the new swimsuit line coming along? I was hoping to begin production soon.

W Not great, actually. We finalized the patterns, but we can't decide on what colors to use. We don't know if we should go with bright colors or more neutral tones. [5]I'm a little annoyed because we can't reach a decision.

M So what are you going to do? Summer is coming in a few months.

W I was hoping you could give us some advice since you stay up to date with trends.

남 안녕하세요, Elois. [4]**새로운 수영복 디자인은 어떻게 돼 가고 있나요?** 곧 생산을 시작하는 것을 바라고 있었어요.

여 사실, 잘 안 되고 있어요. 무늬는 결정했는데, 어떤 색깔을 쓸지 정하지 못하고 있어요. 밝은 색깔로 할지, 아니면 뉴트럴톤으로 할지 잘 모르겠어요. [5]**결정을 내리지 못해 좀 짜증이 나네요.**

남 그래서 어떻게 할 거예요? 몇 달 후면 여름이에요.

여 당신이 유행을 잘 따르니 저에게 조언을 좀 해주길 바라고 있었어요.

어휘 How are ~ coming along? ~은 어떻게 되어가고 있죠? go with ~으로 하다 reach a decision 결정을 내리다 stay up to date with trends 최신 트렌드를 놓치지 않다

4. 화자들은 어떤 산업에서 일하고 있을 것 같은가?
(A) 가구
(B) 건강
(C) 화장품
(D) 의류

5. 여자는 무엇에 대해 짜증스러워하는가?
(A) 몇몇 재료의 질이 낮다.
(B) 몇몇 장비들이 고장 났다.
(C) 몇몇 디자인들의 사용이 불가하다.
(D) 몇몇 결정들이 내려지지 않았다.

6. 남자는 왜 "몇 달 후면 여름이에요"라고 말하는가?
(A) 시급함을 강조하기 위해
(B) 여자에게 마감을 상기시키기 위해
(C) 일정 오류를 고치기 위해
(D) 휴가에 대한 열망을 드러내기 위해

7-9. 미녀/호남

Questions 7-9 refer to the following conversation.

W Ben, our game testers are reporting slow load times and [7]faulty mechanics for the new Mars Hunters computer game.

M That's bad news. Our developers will need to fix the problems soon if we want to stay on track for a November release date.

W The project has already been a long haul. We might want to offer extra incentives to anyone who is willing to work overtime this month.

M Good idea. [9]I'll go speak with the human resource manager. Hopefully she can come up with a special offer for our workers.

여 Ben, 우리 게임 테스터들이 새로운 Mars Hunters 컴퓨터 게임의 느린 로딩 시간과 [7]**기술적 결함**을 보고하고 있습니다.

남 안 좋은 소식이군요. 11월 출시일에 맞추려면 개발자들이 곧 문제를 해결해야 할 텐데요.

여 그 프로젝트는 이미 오랜 시간이 걸렸습니다. 이번 달에 초과 근무를 할 의향이 있는 사람에게 추가적인 인센티브를 제공해야 할 거예요.

남 좋은 생각입니다. [9]**인사 담당자와 얘기해 보겠습니다.** 그녀가 우리 직원들에게 특별한 제안을 해 주면 좋겠네요.

어휘 mechanics 역학, 기계학, 메커니즘, (제작) 기술, 기법 stay on track 순조롭게 진행하다 haul (특정 상황에서 이동하는) 거리[여정/길] may[might] want to do~ ~해야 할 거예요 (wouldn't want to do~ ~하지 말아야 할 거예요) come up with ~을 마련하다, ~을 생각해내다

7. 여자는 어떤 문제를 언급하는가?
(A) 판매가 부진하다.
(B) 배송이 늦는다.
(C) 데이터가 사라졌다.
(D) 제품에 결함이 있다.

8. 여자가 "그 프로젝트는 이미 오랜 시간이 걸렸습니다"라고 말할 때 무엇을 의미하는가?
(A) 직원들이 열심히 일해 왔다.
(B) 회사가 새로운 사람들을 고용했다.
(C) 그 프로젝트는 중단되어야 한다.
(D) 그 게임은 상급자들을 위한 것이다.

9. 남자는 다음에 무엇을 할 것인가?
(A) 온라인 조사
(B) 공식 불만 작성
(C) 이메일 발송
(D) 회의

10-12. 미녀/호남
Questions 10-12 refer to the following conversation.

W Hey, Allen. I know we were supposed to look over [10]the blueprints for the new library, but I'm way too busy today.

M Why are you so busy?

W Well, I'm in charge of designing the new bridge for Kline River, but a materials shortage messed up my original plan. Plus, I have the monthly meeting with the company executives. Do you mind looking at the blueprints tomorrow?

M [11]It will only be a few minutes. I've narrowed everything down to two designs, so we just have to decide which one will suit the new library the best.

W Ahh, OK. I think I can find time around 5:30. [12]But I have to leave right after work because I need to pick up dinner for my family.

여 안녕하세요, Allen. 우리가 [10]**새 도서관 설계도를** 검토하기로 한 건 알지만, 오늘은 너무 바빠요.

남 왜 그렇게 바쁘세요?

여 음, 저는 클라인 강의 새 다리를 설계하는 일을 맡고 있지만, 재료 부족으로 인해 원래 계획이 엉망이 됐어요. 게다가, 저는 회사 임원들과 월간 회의가 있어요. 내일 청사진을 보면 안 될까요?

남 [11]**몇 분이면 됩니다.** 제가 모든 것을 두 가지 디자인으로 압축했어요. 그래서 어떤 것이 새 도서관에 가장 적합할지 결정하기만 하면 됩니다.

여 아, 알겠어요. 5시 30분쯤 시간을 낼 수 있을 것 같아요. [12]**하지만 저는 가족들을 위해 저녁을 픽업해 가야 해서 퇴근 후에 바로 떠나야 해요.**

어휘 be supposed to do ~하기로 되어 있다 mess up ~을 망치다 narrow something down (to something) (선택 가능한 수효를) (~까지) 좁히다[줄이다] suit ~에 맞다

10. 화자들은 어느 분야에서 일하는가?
(A) 제조업
(B) 금융
(C) 건축
(D) 농업

11. 남자는 왜 "제가 모든 것을 두 가지 디자인으로 압축했어요"라고 말하는가?
(A) 여자에게 회의가 오래 걸리지 않을 것이라는 것을 확신시키기 위해
(B) 여자에게 허가를 구하기 위해
(C) 설계도들에 대한 놀라움을 보여주기 위해
(D) 계획에 대한 실망감을 표현하기 위해

12. 여자는 퇴근 후에 무엇을 할 것이라고 하는가?
(A) 기념일 만찬에 참석하기
(B) 집에 가져갈 식사 픽업하기
(C) 예약된 진료 받으러 가기
(D) 휴가 계획 세우기

UNIT 08 3인 대화

Example 본문 p.68

1. (D) **2.** (C) **3.** (B)

남 Ms. Washington, 다행히도 팔이 다 나으신 것 같군요. 다음 방문 때 물리치료를 시작하도록 하겠습니다.

여1 아, 하지만 물리치료 예약도 오늘인 줄 알았어요.

남 정말 죄송합니다. 예약을 잡을 때 실수가 있었던 것이 분명합니다. 엑스레이 촬영만 예약되어 있습니다.

여1 아, 그렇군요.

남 리슬로프 씨, Ms. Washington의 물리치료 예약을 잡아 주시겠어요?

여2 그럼요. 하지만 먼저 연락처를 업데이트해야 해요. 저희는

보통 예약 알림을 보내드리는데, 고객님의 휴대폰 번호가 파일에 없는 것 같습니다. 이 연락처 양식을 작성해 주시겠습니까?

여1 그럼요.

1. 화자들은 어디에 있을 것 같은가?
(A) 주민 센터
(B) 헬스클럽
(C) 법무 법인
(D) 병원

2. 남자는 왜 사과하는가?
(A) 일부 장비가 작동하지 않는다.
(B) 동료가 늦게 도착했다.
(C) 예약 오류가 발생했다.
(D) 청구서가 잘못되었다.

3. Ms. Washington은 다음에 무엇을 할 것인가?
(A) 예약을 한다
(B) 양식을 작성한다
(C) 약국에 들른다
(D) 보험회사에 연락한다

PRACTICE 고난도 본문 p.69

1. (C)	**2.** (A)	**3.** (D)	**4.** (C)	**5.** (B)	**6.**(B)
7. (C)	**8.** (A)	**9.** (D)	**10.** (D)	**11.** (A)	**12.**(B)

1-3. 영녀/미녀/미남

Questions 1-3 refer to the following conversation with three speakers.

W1 [1]Jolene, I've really been enjoying the annual interior design conference.

W2 Me too! I hope our company will attract more customers after this. Hey, let's take a look at this booth about sustainable furniture.

M Hello! My name is Jerry Harvest, and [2]I'm head of the sales team at Brothers Furniture. I'm happy to answer any questions you have.

W2 What makes your company different from others?

M We custom-make each piece of furniture specifically to meet the needs of our clients. [3]I'll be giving a talk in the main hall later today about the ordering process.

W1 I have an investor meeting at two, but Jolene, you should go.

W2 That sounds great.

여1 [1]**Jolene, 저는 연례 인테리어 디자인 컨퍼런스를 정말 즐기고 있습니다.**

여2 **저도요! 앞으로 우리 회사가 더 많은 고객을 유치했으면 좋겠어요.** 여기, 이 지속 가능한 가구에 대한 부스를 살펴봅시다.

남 안녕하세요! 저는 Jerry Harvest라고 합니다. [2]**저는 Brothers Furniture의 영업팀장입니다.** 어떤 질문이든 기꺼이 대답해 드리겠습니다.

여2 귀사가 다른 가구와 다른 점은 무엇입니까?

남 우리는 고객의 요구를 충족시키기 위해 가구 하나하나를 맞춤 제작합니다. [3]**오늘 오후에 메인 홀에서 주문 과정에 대해 강연할 예정입니다.**

여1 전 2시에 투자자 회의가 있지만, Jolene, **당신은 참석해 보세요.**

여2 그거 좋겠네요.

어휘 sustainable 지속 가능한 ordering process 주문 절차

1. 여자들은 어디에서 일하는가?
(A) 화학공장에서
(B) 건축회사에서
(C) 인테리어 디자인 회사에서
(D) 컨퍼런스 센터에서

2. 남자의 직업은 무엇인가?
(A) 영업직원
(B) 건물 관리자
(C) 소프트웨어 기술자
(D) 식당 요리사

3. Jolene은 오후에 무엇을 할 계획인가?
(A) 부동산 방문
(B) 시연
(C) 사무실 복귀
(D) 발표 참관

4-6. 미남/영녀/미녀

Questions 4-6 refer to the following conversation with three speakers.

M Hi, Florence and Nicki. [4]I recently heard that our design for the additional storehouse at the local factory has been approved. Florence, any updates for the next step?

W1 Yes, we conducted a preliminary survey with the surrounding residents, and [5]it turns out they're very concerned about the noise during building construction.

M Nicki, how about we set up a meeting at the town hall to discuss these issues with residents?

W2 I already wanted to schedule a meeting for April ninth, [6]but the town hall was booked for then. Luckily, the recreation center offered to provide a venue for free.

남 안녕하세요, Florence와 Nicki. [4]**지역 공장의 추가 보관**

창고를 위한 우리의 설계가 승인되었다고 최근에 들었어요. Florence, 다음 단계에 대한 최신 정보가 있나요?

여1 네, 인근 주민들을 상대로 사전조사를 했는데, [5]**건물 공사 중 발생하는 소음에 대한 우려가 매우 큰 걸로 나왔습니다.**

남 Nicki, 마을 회관에서 주민들과 이 문제를 논의할 수 있도록 간담회를 여는 건 어떨까요?

여2 이미 4월 9일로 회의 일정을 잡고 싶었지만, [6]**그 날짜에는 이미 마을 회관이 예약돼 있었어요.** 다행히도 문화 회관에서 장소를 무료로 제공하겠다고 했습니다.

어휘 preliminary 예비의 surrounding 인근의, 주위의 it turns out that... ~한 것으로 드러나다/밝혀지다 set up a meeting 회의를 잡다 town hall 시청, 시회 의사당, 읍사무소 schedule a meeting 회의 일정을 잡다

4. 공장 근처에 무엇이 건설되는가?
(A) 주차장
(B) 주유소
(C) 보관 시설
(D) 쓰레기장

5. 주민들이 가장 걱정하는 것은 무엇인가?
(A) 안전
(B) 소음
(C) 기금
(D) 교통량

6. 새 회의 장소가 선정된 이유는 무엇인가?
(A) 공간이 더 제공된다.
(B) 원래 장소가 예약되어 있다.
(C) 찾아가기 더 편리하다.
(D) 주민들이 새 장소를 더 선호했다.

7-9. 미남/영녀/호남
Questions 7-9 refer to the following conversation with three speakers.

M1 [7]Hello, P.J.'s Electronics Factory. This is Raymond Daniels. How may I help you?

W Hello, Mr. Daniels. I'm Linda Patterson. [8]I e-mailed you to ask if it was possible for my students to tour your facilities.

M1 Oh, Ms. Patterson! Right. I've been waiting for your call. Actually, my secretary Kevin is in charge of that. I'll transfer you to him. He'll be able to set everything up for you.

W Thank you!

M2 Hello, Ms. Patterson. This is Mr. Daniels' secretary, Kevin. Would your class be able to visit the factory on September 15? That's about a month from now.

W Yes, that would be perfect. But I'm a bit worried about the safety of my students. [9]Are there any guidelines I should know about?

M2 Absolutely. I'll send those to you in an e-mail.

남1 [7]**안녕하세요, P.J. Electronics Factory입니다.** 이쪽은 Raymond Daniels입니다. 어떻게 도와드릴까요?

여 안녕하세요, Mr. Daniels. 저는 Linda Patterson입니다. [8]**제 학생들이 귀하의 시설을 견학하는 것이 가능한지 물어보려고 메일을 보냈었습니다.**

남1 오, Ms. Patterson! 맞아요. 전화 기다리고 있었어요. 사실 제 비서 Kevin이 그 일을 담당하고 있어요. 전화 바꿔 드릴게요. 그가 모든 것을 준비해 드릴 수 있을 거예요.

여 감사합니다!

남2 안녕하세요, Ms. Patterson. Mr. Daniels의 비서 Kevin입니다. 선생님 반이 9월 15일에 공장을 방문할 수 있나요? 지금부터 한 달 정도 후에요.

여 네, 아주 좋습니다. 하지만 제 학생들의 안전이 조금 걱정돼요. [9]**제가 알아야 할 가이드라인이 있나요?**

남2 **물론이죠. 제가 그것들을 이메일로 보내드리겠습니다.**

어휘 tour 순회하다, 관광하다, 견학하다 transfer 전화를 다른 사람에게 돌려주다 set up 준비하다, 마련하다

7. 남자들은 어느 산업에서 일할 것 같은가?
(A) 접객업
(B) 매체
(C) 전자
(D) 건축

8. 전화의 목적은 무엇인가?
(A) 견학에 대해 문의하기 위해
(B) 주문을 하기 위해
(C) 인터뷰를 잡기 위해
(D) 상품을 반품하기 위해

9. 여자에게 무엇이 보내질 것인가?
(A) 보증서
(B) 약도
(C) 계약서 사본
(D) 안전 지침서

10-12. 미녀/미남/호남
Questions 10-12 refer to the following conversation with three speakers.

W Hello. [10]I got an e-mail advertisement for this Crystal Clear 2000 television, but I don't see any of the televisions on the shelves.

M1 Let me check the computer to see if we have more in the back... Looks like we're all sold out. I'll get my manager to help you. Mr. Dowell? Could you come here please? The customer here is looking for the Crystal Clear 2000.

M2 Hi. So sorry about that. That television has been on sale for a few days, so many people came to the store to buy it. [11]That's why we're completely out of stock.

W Is there any way I could still buy it?

M2 Sure. If you pay now, we can ship the television to your preferred address. [12]I can even offer you free express shipping for your trouble.

여 안녕하세요. [10]**제가 이 크리스탈 클리어 2000 텔레비전에 대한 광고 메일을 받았는데, 해당 텔레비전이 진열대에 없네요.**

남1 안쪽에 재고가 있는지 컴퓨터를 확인해볼게요… 완판된 걸로 보여요. 제 매니저에게 손님을 도와드리라고 할게요. Mr. Dowell? 이쪽으로 와주실래요? 손님이 클리스탈 클리어 2000을 찾고 계세요.

남2 안녕하세요. 정말 죄송하게 되었습니다. 저 텔레비전이 며칠간 세일 중이라, 많은 사람이 와서 구매해 갔어요. [11]**그래서 아예 품절 상태에요.**

여 아직 구매할 방법이 있을까요?

남2 물론이죠. 지금 금액을 지불하시면, 원하시는 주소로 텔레비전을 배송해 드릴 수 있어요. [12]**괜한 발품을 파셨으니 배상하는 의미에서 무료 속달 배송을 제공해 드릴게요.**

어휘 be sold out 다 팔리다 on sale 할인하는 out of stock 재고가 없는

10. 화자들은 어떤 제품을 논의하고 있는가?
(A) 가구
(B) 사무용품
(C) 주방용품
(D) 가전제품

11. 여자는 어떤 문제를 언급하는가?
(A) 제품의 재고가 없다.
(B) 판매 가격이 명시되어 있지 않다.
(C) 제품이 파손되었다.
(D) 명세서가 잘못되었다.

12. 매니저가 여자에게 무엇을 제공하는가?
(A) 품질 보증서
(B) 속달 배송
(C) 가게 회원권
(D) 전액 환불

UNIT 09 그래픽

Example 본문 p.70

1. (C) **2.** (B) **3.** (D)

여 저기요, Marcus. 다음 주에 신입 사원들이 오리엔테이션을 받으러 오는데, 환영 점심 메뉴를 정해야 해요. 이 요리들 중에 어떤 게 제일 나아 보여요?

남 음. 저번에 신입사원 교육이 있었을 때 스테이크와 감자를 시켰는데, 다들 좋아했어요.

여 기억나요. 올해는 예산이 조금 줄어들어서 뭔가 다른 것을 시켜야 할 것 같아요.

남 음, 그럼 파스타는 어때요?

여 좋은 생각인 것 같아요. 치킨과 카레도 괜찮은 것 같은데, 식당이 여기서 좀 멀어요.

남 네, 그리고 식당에 예약 전화하기 전에, 오리엔테이션 일정을 정확하게 준비해야 하니 지금 바로 시작하는 게 좋을 것 같아요.

1. 화자들은 무엇을 준비하고 있나?
(A) 은퇴 만찬
(B) 주 박람회
(C) 오리엔테이션
(D) 고객 방문

2. 시각 자료를 보시오. 화자들은 1인당 얼마를 쓸 것 같은가?
(A) 7달러
(B) 10달러
(C) 11달러
(D) 16달러

3. 화자들은 다음에 무엇을 할 것인가?
(A) 상사에게 말하기
(B) 고객에게 설문 조사 요청
(C) 예약하기
(D) 일정 준비

PRACTICE 고난도 본문 p.71

1. (C)	**2.** (D)	**3.** (C)	**4.** (A)	**5.** (D)	**6.** (D)
7. (A)	**8.** (C)	**9.** (D)	**10.** (B)	**11.** (B)	**12.** (C)
13. (A)	**14.** (D)	**15.** (A)	**16.** (A)	**17.** (D)	**18.** (A)

1-3. 영녀/미남
Questions 1-3 refer to the following conversation and catalogue page.

W Thank you for calling Pristine Plates. How can I help you?

M I came across your company's catalogue and was considering ordering some dishes for the grand re-opening of my restaurant. [1]I'm interested in the circular ones with the polka dots around the edge.

W No problem. But just so you know, [2]our shipping prices are going to increase soon.

M Oh, really?

W Starting next week, the price of shipping will increase based on the weight of your order. Since you're ordering for a restaurant, the shipping price could be much higher.

M That's a good point. How much for 100 of those plates? [3]My re-opening isn't until

September, but I think I should order them now.

여 Pristine Plates에 전화해 주셔서 감사합니다. 무엇을 도와드릴까요?

남 귀사의 카탈로그를 접하고서 저희 레스토랑의 대대적 재개장을 위해 접시 주문을 고려중이었어요. [1]**가장자리에 물방울무늬가 있는 원형 제품에 관심이 있습니다.**

여 문제없습니다. 하지만 참고로 말하자면, [2]**저희 배송비가 곧 인상될 예정입니다.**

남 오, 정말인가요?

여 다음 주부터 주문하신 무게에 따라 배송비가 인상됩니다. 식당에 쓰려고 주문하신다면 배송비가 훨씬 높아질 수도 있어요.

남 좋은 지적이네요. 접시 100장의 가격은 얼마인가요? [3]**재개장은 9월이나 되어야 하지만,** 지금 주문해야 할 것 같네요.

어휘 come across ~을 우연히 발견하다
based on ~을 바탕으로

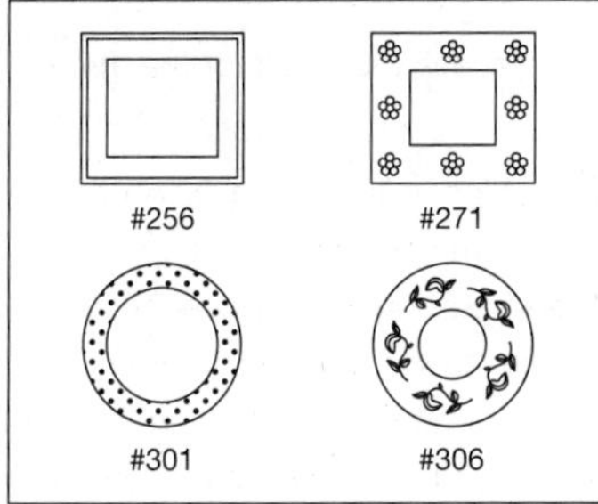

1. 시각 자료를 보시오. 남자는 어떤 접시 무늬에 관심 있는가?
(A) 무늬 #256
(B) 무늬 #271
(C) 무늬 #301
(D) 무늬 #306

2. 여자는 어떤 문제를 언급하는가?
(A) 몇몇 제품들은 재고가 없다.
(B) 카탈로그가 최신이 아니다.
(C) 몇몇 제품들은 한정판이다.
(D) 배송료가 인상될 것이다.

3. 남자에 따르면, 9월에 무슨 일이 일어날 것인가?
(A) 새 직원이 합류할 것이다.
(B) 신제품이 출시될 것이다.
(C) 식당이 재개장을 맞이할 것이다.
(D) 쇼핑몰이 시내에 개장할 것이다.

4-6. 영녀/미남

Questions 4-6 refer to the following conversation and event space layout.

W Hi! Welcome to Jan's Tavern.

M Hello. I made a reservation for Julian, party of two, for 7 p.m. [4]But I'm late because of the icy road conditions on the highway.

W No problem. There are plenty of tables available. We've got local jazz musicians performing tonight. Do you want to be near the stage?

M Actually, that might be too loud for us. [5]My business partner and I are here to talk about launching our start-up, so we need to be able to hear each other.

W I'll put you away from the bar, too, then. [6]Is near the bathroom okay?

M Sure!

여 안녕하세요! Jan's Tavern에 오신 것을 환영합니다.

남 안녕하세요. 저녁 7시에 Julian으로 일행 2명 예약했습니다. [4]**하지만 고속도로의 빙판길 때문에 늦었어요.**

여 괜찮습니다. 이용 가능한 테이블이 많이 있습니다. 오늘 밤에는 지역 재즈 음악가들이 공연을 합니다. 무대 근처 자리 어떠세요?

남 사실, 그 자리는 우리에게 너무 시끄러울 수 있을 것 같네요. [5]**제 사업 파트너와 스타트업 창업에 대해 이야기를 나누러 왔습니다.** 그래서 서로의 의견을 들을 수 있어야 하거든요.

여 그럼, 바에서도 멀리 떨어진 자리로 해 드리겠습니다. [6]**화장실 근처도 괜찮으세요?**

남 물론입니다!

어휘 make a reservation for ~의 이름으로 예약하다 plenty of 많은 put ~ away from ~를 ~로부터 떨어뜨려 놓다

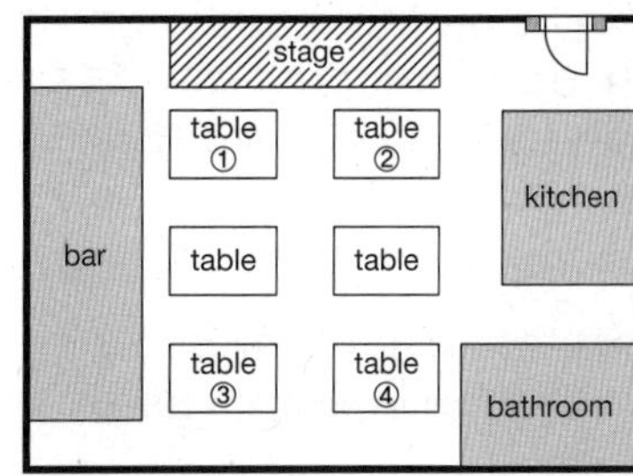

4. 남자에 따르면, 무엇이 지연을 야기했는가?
(A) 길이 미끄럽다.
(B) 주차가 불가능하다.
(C) 러시아워 교통 체증이 심하다.
(D) 가게 위치가 바뀌었다.

5. 남자는 왜 사업 파트너를 만나는가?
(A) 잠정적 합병을 논의하기 위해
(B) 채용 후보에 대해 이야기하기 위해
(C) 상품 매출을 분석하기 위해
(D) 개업을 준비하기 위해

6. 시각 자료를 보시오. 남자는 어디에 앉을 것인가?
(A) 테이블 1
(B) 테이블 2

(C) 테이블 3

(D) 테이블 4

7-9. 🎧 미녀/호남

Questions 7-9 refer to the following conversation and team directory.

> **W** Alan, thanks for taking over during practice today. [7]You did a great job of leading the drills while I had to step out for a family emergency.
>
> **M** I was only imitating your leadership style. Still, I don't think the team is playing with enough energy right now.
>
> **W** You're right. It's been a long season, and [8]our players are exhausted.
>
> **M** What should we do?
>
> **W** I think the team will need a morale boost during our upcoming road trip to the West Coast. Since you're in charge of scheduling, [9]could you find us some fancy hotel options for Friday's game in Phoenix?
>
> **M** I'll get right on it.

여 Alan, 오늘 연습 중에 저를 대신해 주셔서 감사합니다. [7]**제가 집안일 때문에 자리를 비운 동안 훈련을 잘 이끌어 주셨습니다.**

남 저는 단지 당신의 리더십 스타일을 따라했을 뿐입니다. 그래도 지금 팀이 경기하는 데 있어서 많이 지쳐 보입니다.

여 맞아요. 시즌이 길었으니, [8]**지칠 만도 하지요.**

남 어떻게 해야 할까요?

여 이번에 West Coast로 가는 여정에서 팀의 사기 진작이 필요할 것 같습니다. 당신이 일정을 담당하고 있으니, [9]**금요일 Phoenix에서 열리는 경기를 위한 멋진 호텔 옵션을 찾아주실 수 있나요?**

남 바로 찾아볼게요.

어휘 take over ~을 대신 맡다, ~을 인계받다 drill 반복 연습, 훈련 step out 자리를 뜨다, 나가다 morale boost 사기 진작 get right on ~에 바로 착수하다

Directory

- Inez Garcia: Basketball Coach
- Amala Kalil: Player
- Suki Tanoko: Equipment Manager
- Jennifer Snell: Marketing Coordinator

7. 시각 자료를 보시오. 여자는 누구인가?

(A) Inez Garcia

(B) Amala Kalil

(C) Suki Tanoko

(D) Jennifer Snell

8. 화자들은 무슨 문제를 논의하는가?

(A) 경기가 연기되었다.

(B) 팬들이 화가 났다.

(C) 선수들이 지쳐 있다.

(D) 팀이 팔렸다.

9. 남자는 다음에 무엇을 할 것 같은가?

(A) 광고 게시

(B) 새 유니폼 구매

(C) 비행기 표 업그레이드

(D) 숙소 알아보기

10-12. 🎧 미녀/호남

Questions 10-12 refer to the following conversation and brochure.

> **W** Good morning. Are there any units available for rent in your building?
>
> **M** Let me check. When are you looking to move in?
>
> **W** As soon as possible. [10]My husband and I are going to have a baby at the end of the year, and our current place is too small for the three of us.
>
> **M** Congratulations! It looks like we have two open units: a two-bedroom apartment on the third floor, and a three-bedroom unit on the fifth floor. [11]Personally, I recommend the bigger unit, since it has a huge window looking out on the ocean. Here's a brochure listing the prices.
>
> **W** [12]I don't think we can afford the bigger one. Can I take a look at the unit now?

여 안녕하세요. 건물에 임대 나온 아파트 있나요?

남 확인해 볼게요. 언제 이사할 예정인가요?

여 가능한 한 빨리요. [10]**연말에 아이가 태어날 예정인데,** 현재 살고 있는 집이 셋이 살기에는 너무 작거든요.

남 축하합니다! 두 채가 있어요. 3층에 침실 2개짜리 아파트와 5층에 침실 3개짜리 아파트가 있어요. [11]**개인적으로, 둘 중에 더 큰 아파트를 추천하는데, 바다를 내다보는 큰 창문이 있어요.** 여기 가격이 나와 있는 책자가 있습니다.

여 [12]**더 큰 것은 여유가 안 될 것 같아요.** 지금 아파트를 볼 수 있을까요?

어휘 available for rent 임대 가능한 look to ~하고자 하다

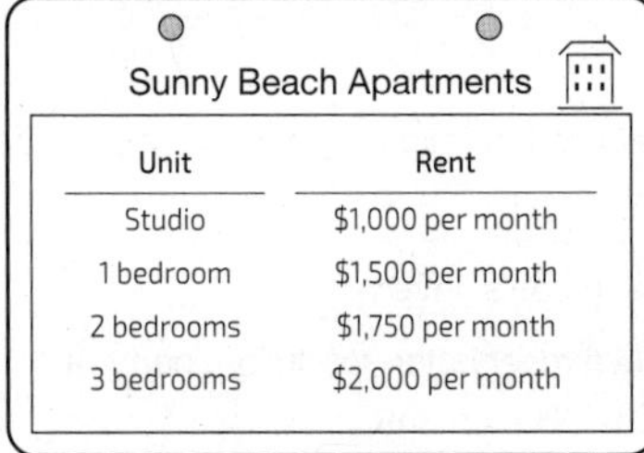

Sunny Beach Apartments

Unit	Rent
Studio	$1,000 per month
1 bedroom	$1,500 per month
2 bedrooms	$1,750 per month
3 bedrooms	$2,000 per month

10. 여자는 왜 이사하려 하는가?
(A) 새 직장을 얻었다.
(B) 임신했다.
(C) 현재 건물이 안전하지 않다.
(D) 임대료가 너무 비싸다.

11. 남자는 더 큰 아파트의 어떤 점을 좋아하는가?
(A) 인테리어 디자인
(B) 풍경
(C) 현대적 가전제품
(D) 커다란 욕실

12. 시각 자료를 보시오. 여자가 임차하고자 하는 아파트의 가격은 얼마인가?
(A) 월 1,000달러
(B) 월 1,500달러
(C) 월 1,750달러
(D) 월 2,000달러

13-15. 영녀/미남
Questions 13-15 refer to the following conversation and schedule.

W [13]Thank you for attending today's lecture series on eco-friendly developments in industrial cleaning. Can I have your name?

M Hi, I'm Gerald. Do you have a schedule listing today's presenters?

W Sure, here you go.

M Thanks... [14]Uh-oh. I have to make a call to a client overseas during Leopold Fritz's talk. That's bad timing.

W I'm sorry to hear it. Also, please note that Kate Marrone's talk may be moved to the afternoon. [15]She's currently experiencing travel delays due to the extreme weather that's been hitting the region this week.

여 [13]**오늘 산업용 청소 분야의 친환경 발전에 대한 강좌 시리즈에 참석해 주셔서 감사합니다.** 성함이 어떻게 되시죠?

남 안녕하세요, 저는 Gerald입니다. 오늘 발표자 명단이 포함된 일정표 있나요?

여 네, 여기 있습니다.

남 감사합니다… [14]**오, 이런, Leopold Fritz의 강연 시간에 해외 고객에게 전화를 해야겠네요.** 타이밍이 안 좋네요.

여 유감입니다. 또한 Kate Marrone의 연설이 오후로 옮겨질 수도 있다는 점을 알려드립니다. 이번 주 이 지역을 강타하고 있는 [15]**악천후 때문에 여행이 지연되고 있거든요.**

어휘 eco-friendly 환경 친화적인 list 목록에 언급하다/포함시키다, 목록을 작성하다 hit 강타하다

Schedule

Emilio Lopez	9 am
Kate Marrone	11 am
Yeonsu Lee	2 pm
Leopold Fritz	4 pm

13. 어떤 행사가 일어나고 있는가?
(A) 비즈니스 세미나
(B) 영화 축제
(C) 시상식
(D) 자선 모금 행사

14. 시각 자료를 보시오. 남자는 고객에게 언제 전화를 할 것인가?
(A) 오전 9시
(B) 오전 11시
(C) 오후 2시
(D) 오후 4시

15. 여자는 어떤 문제를 언급하는가?
(A) 강사가 늦을 것이다.
(B) 회의실이 닫혔다.
(C) 음식공급자가 배달을 하지 않았다.
(D) 청중이 너무 적다.

16-18. 미남/영녀
Questions 16-18 refer to the following conversation and information board.

M Welcome to Saffron Air. How can I help you?

W [16]I'm scheduled to fly to New York on Flight 156 later, but I'm in a rush. Are there any earlier departures?

M Hmm... There's a flight leaving in 30 minutes that goes to New Jersey, which is a short taxi ride away from New York. You'll need to hurry, though. [17]I'll contact transportation security and tell them to put you at the front of the line.

W Wow, that's a huge help.

M [18]I'll just need your current flight information so I can access your records.

남 Saffron Air에 오신 것을 환영합니다. 무엇을 도와드릴까요?

여 [16]**저는 이따가 뉴욕행 156편을 타기로 되어 있는데,** 제가 지금 무척 급합니다. 좀 더 일찍 출발하는 것이 있습니까?

남 음… 30분 후에 뉴저지로 가는 비행기가 있습니다. 뉴저지는 뉴욕에서 택시로 조금만 가면 돼요. 그래도 서둘러야 할 겁니다. [17]**제가 교통 경비원에게 연락해서 당신을 맨 앞줄로 안내하도록 요청하겠습니다.**

여 와, 정말 큰 도움이 되네요.

남 기록에 접근할 수 있도록 [18]**고객님의 현재 항공편 정보가 필요합니다.**

어휘 be in a rush 무척 급하다 a huge help 크나큰 도움

Flight #	Departing From	Arriving At
156	Detroit	New York City
205	Atlanta	Miami
310	Honolulu	Los Angeles
644	San Francisco	Seattle

16. 시각 자료를 보시오. 여자는 어디에서 출발하는가?
(A) 디트로이트(Detroit)
(B) 애틀랜타(Atlanta)
(C) 호놀룰루(Honolulu)
(D) 샌프란시스코(San Francisco)

17. 남자는 여자를 어떻게 도울 것인가?
(A) 환불을 제공한다
(B) 추가 가방을 부쳐준다
(C) 1등석 자리를 준다
(D) 공항 경비에게 말해준다

18. 여자는 다음에 남자에게 무엇을 줄 것 같은가?
(A) 그녀의 항공권
(B) 그녀의 신용카드
(C) 그녀의 할인권
(D) 그녀의 이메일 주소

PART TEST

본문 p.74

1. (A)	**2.** (B)	**3.** (A)	**4.** (D)	**5.** (D)	**6.** (C)
7. (A)	**8.** (B)	**9.** (B)	**10.** (B)	**11.** (B)	**12.** (A)
13. (C)	**14.** (C)	**15.** (A)	**16.** (B)	**17.** (C)	**18.** (B)
19. (A)	**20.** (B)	**21.** (A)	**22.** (C)	**23.** (B)	**24.** (B)
25. (B)	**26.** (D)	**27.** (B)	**28.** (D)	**29.** (A)	**30.** (A)
31. (A)	**32.** (C)	**33.** (C)	**34.** (B)	**35.** (B)	**36.** (C)
37. (B)	**38.** (D)	**39.** (C)			

1-3. 미남/영녀
Questions 1-3 refer to the following conversation.

M Hey, Lizzie. Did you hear about the new company policy?

W [1]I heard that each of us can now choose when our workday starts.

M Right! Personally, I'm leaning toward starting at 10 a.m. to avoid rush hour traffic.

W I bet many people will want that slot. [2]You should put in your request soon. Our team has a limit on the number of people for each slot.

M Good call. Oh, there goes Pedro from Accounting. [3]I'm going to ask if he wants to continue carpooling with me.

남 안녕, Lizzie. 회사의 새로운 정책에 대해 들었어요?

여 [1]**이제 각자의 근무 시작 시간을 선택할 수 있다고 들었어요.**

남 맞아요! 개인적으로는 러시아워를 피하기 위해 10시에 시작하고 싶어요.

여 그 시간대를 원하는 사람들이 많을 거예요. [2]**요청서 제출을 서둘러야 할 거예요.** 우리 팀은 시간대별로 인원수의 제약이 있어요.

남 알려줘서 고마워요. 오, 마침 회계팀의 Pedro가 저기 가네요. [3]**저랑 계속 카풀링을 할 건지 물어봐야겠어요.**

어휘 lean toward 마음이 ~쪽으로 기울다
put in a request 요청서를 제출하다

1. 회사는 어떤 변화를 만들고 있는가?
(A) 유연근무 시간을 제공한다.
(B) 새로운 지점을 연다.
(C) 할인된 음식을 제공한다.
(D) 여행 경비를 환급해 준다.

2. 여자는 무엇을 할 것을 제안하는가?
(A) 경영진에 우려 사안을 보고하는 것
(B) 선호 사항을 빨리 제출하는 것
(C) 상품을 조사하는 것
(D) 면접에 참석하는 것

3. 남자는 다음에 무엇을 할 것 같은가?
(A) 동료와 이야기
(B) 고객에게 전화
(C) 환불 요청
(D) 교육 세션 실시

4-6. 영녀/미남
Questions 4-6 refer to the following conversation.

W Humberto, have you noticed that [4]our figs are taking a long time to ripen this year?

M Yeah, I think it's because of all the storms we've had this summer. [5]Maybe we should install some southern-facing white walls around the fig trees to make sure they're getting maximum sunlight.

W Good idea. [6]I'll get the contractor who built our greenhouse to do it for us. He always charges fair prices.

여 Humberto, 올해는 [4]**우리 무화과가** 익는 데 시간이 오래 걸리는 거 같지 않아요?

남 네, 이번 여름 폭풍 때문인 것 같아요. 무화과나무 주변에 [5]**흰 남향 벽을 설치해서** 햇빛을 최대한 받도록 해야 할 것 같습니다.

여 좋은 생각입니다. [6]**우리 온실을 지은 건설업자에게 부탁해 볼게요.** 그는 항상 공정한 가격을 청구합니다.

어휘 fig 무화과 ripen 익다, 숙성하다

4. 화자들은 어떤 사업체를 가지고 있을 것 같은가?
(A) 편의점
(B) 조경회사
(C) 철물점
(D) 농장

5. 남자는 무엇을 할 것을 제안하는가?
(A) 더 많은 땅을 구매
(B) 새로운 상품 제공
(C) 더 많은 식물 추가
(D) 새로운 건축물 설치

6. 여자는 무엇을 할 것이라고 말하는가?
(A) 재고 확인
(B) 재료 구매
(C) 전문 업자 고용
(D) 계약 갱신

7-9. 미녀/호남
Questions 7-9 refer to the following conversation.

W Good afternoon. [7]I just saw your post about the office space on Brooklane Avenue. Are there any other businesses in the building?
M You'd be on the same floor as two other small businesses. [8]There's a shared kitchen. If you want access to it, that would increase the rental price by $100 per month.
W Okay. When can you show me the place?
M How about tomorrow evening? [9]Just make sure to bring your driver's license so we can do a background check in case you want to get the application process started right away.

여 안녕하세요. [7]**방금 Brooklane Avenue에 있는 사무실 공간에 대한 당신의 게시물을 보았습니다.** 건물 안에 다른 사업체가 있나요?
남 다른 두 중소기업과 같은 층에 있을 겁니다. [8]**같이 쓰는 부엌이 있어요. 만약 부엌을 사용하고자 하신다면, 매달 임대료에 100달러 추가됩니다.**
여 알겠습니다. 언제 그 장소를 보여줄 수 있죠?
남 내일 저녁 어떠세요? 바로 신청을 하고 싶으실 수 있으니까 신분 확인을 위해 [9]**운전면허증을 꼭 지참하시기 바랍니다.**

어휘 rental price 임대료 get ~ started right away ~을 바로 시작하다

7. 여자는 왜 전화하는가?
(A) 부동산 항목에 대해 논의하기 위해
(B) 호텔 방을 예약하기 위해
(C) 신청서 상태를 확인하기 위해
(D) 지불을 하기 위해

어휘 listing 목록, 목록상의 항목

8. 남자에 따르면 무엇이 가격에 영향을 미치나?
(A) 주차 공간 수
(B) 공유실 사용
(C) 고객의 양
(D) 광고 유무

9. 남자는 내일 저녁 무엇을 가져올 것을 권하는가?
(A) 추천서
(B) 신분증
(C) 선금[계약금]
(D) 수입 증명서

10-12. 호남/미녀
Questions 10-12 refer to the following conversation.

M Hi, I'm trying to purchase a train pass, [10]but the automated kiosk isn't working. Can you please help me?
W I'll call in a maintenance worker. It should be back up and running soon.
M Ugh… [11]This is frustrating. I have an important meeting in 30 minutes, and there's no way I'll make it on time.
W Since you're in a hurry, [12]I would recommend downloading the Subway Rider mobile app. You can put in your credit card information and access the platform that way.
M I'll do that.

남 안녕하세요, 기차표를 구매하려고 하는데 [10]**자동 키오스크가 작동하지 않습니다.** 저 좀 도와주시겠어요?
여 정비사를 부르겠습니다. 곧 다시 복구될 거예요.
남 아… [11]**답답하네요. 30분 후에 중요한 회의가 있는데, 제시간에 갈 수가 없겠는데요.**
여 급하시니까 [12]**Subway Rider 모바일 앱을 다운로드하는 것을 추천합니다.** 신용카드 정보를 입력하고 저쪽 플랫폼으로 들어가시면 됩니다.
남 그렇게 하겠습니다.

어휘 train pass 기차표 call in ~를 전화해서 부르다 be back up and running 다시 작동하다 There's no way ~ ~할 방도가 없다 make it on time 제시간에 도착하다

10. 남자는 왜 도움을 필요로 하는가?
(A) 사무실이 이사했다.
(B) 기계가 고장났다.
(C) 열차 노선이 변경되었다.
(D) 물건이 사라졌다.

11. 남자는 왜 기분이 안 좋은가?
(A) 너무 많은 돈을 지불해서
(B) 약속에 늦어서
(C) 잘못된 정보를 받아서
(D) 대기 줄이 길어서

12. 남자는 다음에 무엇을 할 것 같은가?
(A) 앱 사용
(B) 택시 잡기
(C) 매니저에게 전화
(D) 버스 타기

13-15. 미남/영녀/호남

Questions 13-15 refer to the following conversation with three speakers.

M1 Table 2 just made a request about allergens. Is it possible to [13]make the penne dish without risking any exposure to shellfish?

W It's possible, but the timing is bad. The dinner party in the back room just placed their orders, and [14]there are a lot of off-menu requests.

M2 I can take care of it, Gerald. I just finished making the tiramisu for Table 6.

M1 Thanks. You know, [15]maybe we should think about adding some specifically allergen-free dishes to the menu. These requests seem to be getting more common nowadays.

남1 2번 테이블에서 알레르기 때문에 요청을 하셨습니다. 조개를 전혀 사용하지 않고 [13]**펜네 요리를 만들 수** 있을까요?

여 가능은 한데, 타이밍이 안 좋습니다. 뒤쪽 방의 회식 손님들이 방금 주문을 했는데, [14]**메뉴에 없는 요청이 많아요.**

남2 제가 맡을게요, Gerald. 6번 테이블용 티라미수를 막 끝냈거든요.

남1 고마워요. 그래서 말인데, [15]**알레르겐이 없는 음식을 메뉴에 추가하는 것도 생각해봐야 할 것 같아요.** 이러한 요청들이 요즘 점점 더 보편화되고 있는 것 같아요.

어휘 allergen 알레르기 유발 항원, 알레르겐 risk ~의 위험을 무릅쓰다, ~을 위태롭게 하다 place an order 주문하다 off-menu 메뉴에는 없는 take care of ~을 맡아 처리하다 allergen-free 알레르겐이 없는, 알레르기 유발 항원이 없는

13. 화자들은 어디에서 일하고 있을 것 같은가?
(A) 콘서트 홀
(B) 식료품점
(C) 식당
(D) 배달회사

14. 여자는 무엇을 하고 있는가?
(A) 장비 청소
(B) 공급업체와 대화
(C) 특별한 주문 준비
(D) 신규 직원 교육

15. Gerald는 무엇을 할 것을 제안하는가?
(A) 제공하는 메뉴를 확대하는 것
(B) 재고를 다시 채우는 것
(C) 마케팅 캠페인을 시작하는 것
(D) 두 번째 지점을 여는 것

16-18. 미녀/호남

Questions 16-18 refer to the following conversation.

W Is everyone almost ready to film [16]tonight's episode of *Kids' Trivia Show*? We're supposed to start in 20 minutes.

M Yes. The stage crew is just finishing up, and all of our cameras are ready.

W Where are the contestants? [17]They still haven't been given instructions about the rules. That could be a big problem.

M Don't worry. I asked [18]our temp, José Carrasco, to prep them backstage.

W Ah, that's good news. I've been impressed with José's work for us, so I trust him. You know, we should think about giving him a permanent position on the team.

여 [16]**오늘밤 Kids' Trivia Show** 촬영 준비가 거의 다 됐나요? 20분 후에 시작합니다.

남 네. 이제 막 무대 스태프들이 마무리 작업을 하고 있고, 모든 카메라가 준비되어 있습니다.

여 참가자들은 어디에 있나요? [17]**그들은 아직 규칙에 대한 지시를 받지 못했어요. 그러면 큰 문제가 될 수 있습니다.**

남 걱정 마세요. [18]**임시 직원인 José Carrasco가** 무대 뒤에서 그들을 준비시키고 있습니다.

여 오, 잘됐군요. José가 하는 일들에 매번 감동을 받고 있어서 신뢰가 갑니다. 아무래도 그를 우리 팀의 정규직원으로 고용하는 걸 고려해 봐야겠어요.

어휘 be supposed to do ~하기로 되어 있다 contestant 참가자 instructions 지시, 지침

16. 화자들은 무엇에 대해 준비하고 있는가?
(A) 표준화된 시험
(B) 게임쇼
(C) 스포츠 행사
(D) 공개 강연

17. 여자는 어떤 문제를 언급하는가?
(A) 일부 광고가 잘못되었다.
(B) 스크립트에 문제가 있다.
(C) 참가자들이 준비가 안 되어 있다.
(D) 카메라가 망가졌다.

18. José Carrasco는 누구인가?
(A) 엔지니어
(B) 임시직원
(C) 매니저
(D) 시나리오 작가

19-21. 영녀/미남

Questions 19-21 refer to the following conversation.

W Ahmed, I just finished reading through [19]your recommendation to add a company gym on the first floor of our building. You make a strong case. Thanks for your work on this.

M No problem. I think it could really improve staff morale.

W Speaking of boosting people's spirits: A lot of folks are sad about [20]Jim Harlow's upcoming retirement. I'd like to have a party to celebrate his achievements at the company.

M That's a great idea. We could get Frank's Restaurant and Grille to cater the event.

W Actually, I would be happy to prepare some homemade dishes. Then, we could use our budget to hire a performer.

여 Ahmed, 방금 [19]**우리 건물 일층에 회사 체육관을 추가해 달라는 제안**을 검토해 봤어요. **무척 일리 있습니다. 고생 많으셨어요.**

남 아닙니다. 체육관이 생기면 직원들의 사기를 많이 진작시킬 수 있을 거라고 생각합니다.

여 직원 사기 진작에 관해 말이 나와서 그런데, 직원들이 [20]**Jim Harlow의 다가오는 퇴직에** 대해 많이들 슬퍼하고 있어요. 회사에서의 그의 업적을 축하해 주는 파티를 열고 싶어요.

남 좋은 생각이네요. Frank's Restaurant and Grille에 행사 음식 준비를 맡기면 되겠어요.

여 사실, 집에서 만든 요리를 준비하고 싶어요. 그러면 예산으로 공연자를 고용할 수 있을 것 같아요.

어휘 read through ~을 꼼꼼히 읽다 make a strong case 충분한 근거가 있는 주장을 하다 cater (행사에) 음식을 공급하다

19. 여자는 남자에게 무엇에 대해 감사하는가?

(A) 제안서를 제출한 것

(B) 판매를 성사시킨 것

(C) 판매업자를 추천한 것

(D) 회의를 이끈 것

20. 모임은 왜 계획될 것인가?

(A) 회사가 매출 기록을 달성했다.

(B) 직원이 퇴직한다.

(C) 매니저가 생일을 맞이한다.

(D) 일부 직원들이 휴식을 필요로 한다.

21. 여자가 "집에서 만든 요리를 준비하고 싶어요"라고 말할 때 무엇을 의도하는가?

(A) 음식공급업체는 불필요한 비용이다.

(B) 식당에 대한 평이 안 좋다.

(C) 회사가 음식공급에 대한 비용 지불을 거부할 것이다.

(D) 모든 사람들이 각자 음식을 마련해 가져와야 한다.

22-24. 영녀/미남

Questions 22-24 refer to the following conversation.

W The rumor at headquarters is that fewer people are signing up for [22]gym memberships. How bad is the situation?

M This was a rough quarter. Membership dropped by 11%. [23]I would suggest offering reduced annual fees as a way to attract new sign-ups.

W I see. What's your projection for next quarter? I'm particularly curious about the Burbank Street facility that opened last month.

M That location gets a lot of foot traffic, so [24]enrollment should remain the same there for the foreseeable future.

여 본사에서 [22]**체육관 회원** 가입자 수가 줄고 있다는 얘기가 돌더군요. 상황이 얼마나 심각한가요?

남 힘든 분기였습니다. 회원 수가 11% 감소했어요. 신규 가입 유치를 위한 방법으로 [23]**연회비를 줄이는 것을 제안하고 싶습니다.**

여 알겠습니다. 다음 분기의 예상치는 얼마입니까? 특히 지난달에 오픈한 Burbank Street 시설이 궁금하군요.

남 그 지역은 유동 인구가 많기 때문에, 당분간 [24]**등록자 수는 동일하게 유지될 거예요.**

어휘 headquarters 본사 sign up for ~에 가입하다/등록하다 annual fee 연회비 sign-up 가입, 등록 projection 예상, 예측 foot traffic 유동 인구 규모 for[in] the foreseeable future 가까운 미래에

22. 화자들은 어디에서 일하는가?

(A) 은행에서

(B) 스포츠 용품점에서

(C) 헬스클럽에서

(D) 카드사에서

23. 남자는 무엇을 할 것을 추천하는가?

(A) 오픈 시간 변경

(B) 가격 인하

(C) 새로운 광고 제작

(D) 미사용 장비 판매

24. 남자는 무엇을 예측하는가?

(A) 회사가 급여를 줄일 것이다.

(B) 새로운 시설은 회원 수를 유지할 것이다.

(C) 한 지점의 임대료가 오를 것이다.

(D) 소비자들이 긍정적인 후기를 올릴 것이다.

25-27. 영녀/미남/미녀

Questions 25-27 refer to the following conversation with three speakers.

W1 The R&D team just reported that they're having trouble [25] accessing the cloud platform while working in the conference room. Could somebody help them out?

M I can do it. I wonder why that's happening, though.

W1 [26] We recently updated the operating system on the computer in that room. But apparently the teams haven't been trained on how to use the new operating system.

W2 I have some experience creating user guides. [27] I could write one up and post it on the conference room wall for anyone who needs assistance in the future.

W1 That would be great. Thanks, Mei Ling.

여1 R&D 팀에서 회의실에서 일하는 동안 [25] **클라우드 플랫폼에 접속하는** 데 문제가 있다고 방금 연락왔습니다. 그들을 도와줄 수 있는 분 있나요?

남 제가 할 수 있어요. 그런데 왜 그런 일이 일어나는지 궁금하네요.

여1 [26] **우리가 최근에 그 방에 있는 컴퓨터의 운영체제를 업데이트 했어요.** 하지만 팀들이 새로운 운영 체제를 사용하는 방법에 대해 교육을 받지 않은 것 같습니다.

여2 제가 사용자 가이드를 작성한 경험이 있습니다. 앞으로 도움이 필요한 사람들을 위해 [27] **가이드를 작성해서** 회의실 벽에 게시해 볼게요.

여1 좋습니다. 고마워요, Mei Ling.

어휘 have trouble -ing ~하는 데 어려움을 겪다 help ~ out ~을 도와주다 write ~ up ~을 작성하다

25. 화자들은 어느 분야에서 일할 것 같은가?
(A) 마케팅
(B) 정보 기술
(C) 연구조사
(D) 인사

26. 최근 무슨 일이 발생했나?
(A) 신규 직원들이 채용되었다.
(B) 부서가 이동되었다.
(C) 회사 건물이 보수되었다.
(D) 컴퓨터가 업데이트되었다.

27. Mei Ling은 무엇 하기를 제안하는가?
(A) 구인 공고 게시
(B) 설명서[매뉴얼] 작성
(C) 고객들에게 전화
(D) 회의 개최

28-30. 호남/미녀

Questions 28-30 refer to the following conversation.

M Hey, Midori. Can I ask your thoughts on something?

W Sure. What's up?

M [28] I've been offered a minor role in a romantic comedy, but the pay is much lower than I would expect for this kind of part. It's barely enough to cover travel expenses. On the other hand, taking it could help me gain some traction in the industry.

W When I was just starting out, I took some really bad roles. You know, my cousin is a lawyer, and he often helps me out by looking at my contracts before I sign them. [30] I could share his e-mail address with you. I'm sure he'd be happy to offer advice.

남 안녕하세요, Midori. 당신의 생각을 물어봐도 될까요?

여 물론입니다. 무슨 일이에요?

남 [28] **저는 로맨틱 코미디에서 단역을 제안 받았지만,** 출연료는 제가 이런 종류의 배역에 대해 기대했던 것보다 훨씬 낮습니다. 여행 경비를 겨우 충당할 정도예요. 한편으로는, 그 제안을 받아들이면 제가 업계에서 어느 정도의 관심을 얻는 데 도움이 될 수 있어요.

여 제가 갓 일을 시작했을 때, 정말 안 좋은 역을 맡았어요. 아시다시피, 제 사촌이 변호사인데, 제가 계약하기 전에 계약서를 검토해 줘서 도움이 되고 있어요. [30] **그의 이메일 주소를 알려드릴 수 있어요.** 그가 기꺼이 조언을 해 줄 거예요.

어휘 barely 간신히, 가까스로, 빠듯하게 start out 시작하다

28. 남자는 누구인가?
(A) 음악가
(B) 사진사
(C) 영화 평론가
(D) 배우

29. 남자가 "그 제안을 받아들이면 제가 업계에서 어느 정도의 관심을 얻는 데 도움이 될 수 있어요."라고 말할 때 무엇을 의미하는가?
(A) 그는 경험이 많지 않다.
(B) 아직 학위를 따기 위해 공부하고 있다.
(C) 그의 에이전트로부터 안 좋은 조언을 받았다.
(D) 업종을 전환하고자 한다.

30. 여자는 무엇을 할 것이라고 말하는가?
(A) 연락처 제공
(B) 행사 참석
(C) 추천서 작성
(D) 계약서 검토

31-33. 미남/영녀

Questions 31-33 refer to the following conversation and product list.

> **M** Hi there. Enjoying the game?
>
> **W** Yes, it's a good one! So, I work at Caldwell Assisted Living Facility in town, and we're currently on a special outing to the local ballpark with some of our senior citizens. We have enough in our budget to [31] get them souvenirs, but I'm not sure what to get.
>
> **M** [32] These caps are always popular. The size is adjustable.
>
> **W** Great! I'll take ten of them.
>
> **M** Okay. [33] I'll throw in a free tote bag for you. I'm a big supporter of what you all do over at Caldwell.

남 안녕하세요. 경기는 재미있으신가요?

여 네, 재밌어요! 음, 저는 마을에 있는 Caldwell 보조 생활 시설에서 일하고 있는데, 오늘 특별히 노인들을 모시고 지역 야구장으로 야유회를 나왔어요. [31] **그분들께 기념품을 사줄** 만한 예산이 있는데, 무엇을 사야 할지 모르겠네요.

남 [32] **이 모자들은 항상 인기가 많아요. 사이즈 조절이 가능합니다.**

여 좋습니다! 열 개 살게요.

남 네. [33] **토트백을 무료로 드릴게요.** 저는 Caldwell에서 하는 일을 열렬히 지지한답니다.

어휘 outing 야유회 ballpark 야구장 souvenir 기념품 throw in ~을 덤으로 주다

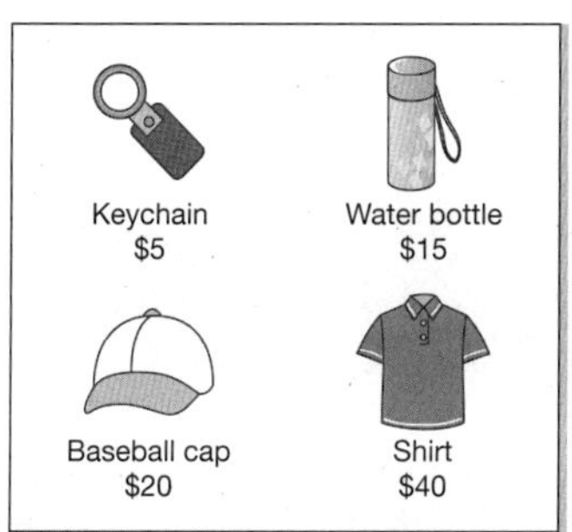

31. 여자는 누구에게 선물을 줄 것인가?
(A) 시설 거주자들
(B) 상위 관리자
(C) 가족 구성원
(D) 사업 파트너

32. 시각 자료를 보시오. 남자가 추천하는 물건은 얼마인가?
(A) 5달러
(B) 15달러
(C) 20달러
(D) 40달러

33. 남자는 무엇을 할 것이라고 말하는가?
(A) 매니저에게 연락
(B) 재고 조사
(C) 물품 추가 제공
(D) 지불 계획 제공

34-36. 미남/영녀

Questions 34-36 refer to the following conversation and pricing list.

> **M** I'm getting excited for the farmer's market in Scantonville this weekend. [34] I think our apples are going to be a big hit.
>
> **W** Me too. We still have to decide on how to package them. Last week, in Mapleton, we tried to sell in large portions, and revenue was lower than I expected.
>
> **M** I noticed that too. [35] Let's go with the small baskets this time. They're visually appealing and a manageable size.
>
> **W** Okay. I'll take care of gathering up all our product. [36] Do you mind driving the van on Saturday? I want to go down early in my own car and get a sense of the event space layout.

남 이번 주말에 Scantonville에서 열리는 농산물 시장이 기대됩니다. [34] **우리 사과가 대박 날 것 같아요.**

여 저도요. 하지만 그것들을 어떻게 포장할지 결정해야 해요. 지난주, Mapleton에서 많은 양으로 포장해서 팔려고 해 봤지만, 수익은 제가 예상했던 것보다 낮았습니다.

남 저도 그렇게 생각했어요. [35] **이번에는 작은 바구니로 하죠.** 그게 시각적으로 매력적이고 다루기 쉬운 크기입니다.

여 네. 제가 저희 상품을 모두 모을게요. [36] **혹시 토요일에 밴을 운전할 수 있겠어요?** 저는 제 차를 타고 일찍 행사장에 가서 배치를 파악하고 싶습니다.

어휘 a big hit 대박 in large portions 많은 양으로 manageable 관리할 수 있는, 다루기 쉬운 gather up ~을 주워 모으다 get a sense of ~을 파악하다

Sales prices	
Plastic bag (4)	$3
Small basket (6)	$4
Large basket (9)	$6
Bucket (12)	$8

34. 화자들은 무엇을 파는가?
(A) 커피 원두
(B) 과일
(C) 견과
(D) 유제품

PART 3

35. 시각 자료를 보시오. 화자들은 판매 가격을 얼마로 할 것인가?
(A) 3달러
(B) 4달러
(C) 6달러
(D) 8달러

36. 여자는 무엇에 대한 도움을 원하는가?
(A) 트럭에 상품을 싣는 것
(B) 부스를 설치하는 것
(C) 상품을 운송하는 것
(D) 행사를 광고하는 것

37-39. 미녀/호남

Questions 37-39 refer to the following conversation and chart.

W So, Reynaldo, we're going to [37]release the new installment of the Underwater Diver video game series in just a few weeks.

M That's great. I can't wait to hear what gamers think of it. How are the beta tests going?

W According to our testers, the graphics on the level with the coral look amazing. [38]But there are still some issues with the level where players search for treasure in a sunken pirate ship. Apparently, there are glitches in the gameplay.

M We can get one of the freelancers to work on that, but the project is getting expensive. Can we afford it?

W [39]I can talk to management and see if they're willing to expand the budget.

여 Reynaldo, 우리는 몇 주 후면 Underwater Diver 비디오 게임 시리즈의 새로운 에피소드를 [37]**출시할** 거예요.

남 잘됐네요. 게이머들이 그것에 대해 어떻게 생각할지 빨리 듣고 싶어요. 베타 테스트는 어떻게 진행되고 있습니까?

여 테스터들에 따르면, 산호가 있는 레벨의 그래픽은 정말 멋져 보인다고 합니다. [38]**하지만 플레이어들이 침몰한 해적선에서 보물을 찾는 레벨에는 여전히 몇 가지 문제가 있습니다.** 분명히, 게임 방식에 결함이 있습니다.

남 프리랜서 중 한 명을 고용해서 그 일을 하게 할 수 있지만, 프로젝트 비용이 점점 더 올라가네요. 그럴 만한 자금 여유가 있을까요?

여 [39]**경영진과 상의해서 예산을 확대할 의향이 있는지 확인해 보겠습니다.**

어휘 I can't wait to do ~하고 싶어서 참을 수 없다 sunken 침몰한 glitch 작은 문제[결함] gameplay (컴퓨터 게임의) 스토리[게임 방식]

Underwater Diver 

Level Name	Level Number
Coral Adventure	1
Swimming with Whales	2
Deep Ocean	3
Buried Treasure	4

37. 화자들은 주로 무엇에 대해 논의하고 있는가?
(A) 연구 프로젝트
(B) 제품 출시
(C) 광고 캠페인
(D) 공급자 변경

38. 시각 자료를 보시오. 어떤 레벨에 문제가 있나?
(A) Coral Adventure (산호 모험)
(B) Swimming with Whales (고래와 헤엄)
(C) Deep Ocean (깊은 바다)
(D) Buried Treasure (묻혀 있는 보물)

39. 여자는 무엇을 하기를 제안하는가?
(A) 영업팀에 연락
(B) 행사 연기
(C) 더 많은 자금 요청
(D) 구인 공고 작성

LC PART 4

출제 경향 및 전략

본문 p.81

Example

여러분 모두가 저희 희귀 도서 모음집 투어에 함께 할 수 있어서 기쁩니다. 여기 존스타운 도서관에서는, 우리는 과거의 문학을 보존하는 것의 가치를 믿습니다. 그것이 우리가 특별한 주의와 취급을 필요로 하는 독특한 책들을 소장하고 있는 이유입니다. 모든 재료가 매우 민감하기 때문에 여기에 있는 어느 것도 만지면 안 됩니다. 먼저, 지하 1층에 있는 중세 기록 보관소를 살펴보도록 하겠습니다. 저를 따라오시죠.

UNIT 01 회의 발췌

CHECK-UP 본문 p.83

1. (A) **2.** (A) **3.** (D) **4.** (C) **5.** (A) **6.** (C)

1-3. 호남

Questions 1-3 refer to the following excerpt from a meeting.

M-Au Hi, everyone. I've got something exciting to share with you. Our company will be moving in a new direction, and it's going to affect [1]all current and future investors, like you all. You may have heard that we've had great success with our new line of luxury vehicles. [2]Now, the company has decided to develop its own line of electric cars. This is an attempt to be more environmentally friendly and appeal to younger consumers. You may be concerned that our existing customers may not be happy with the change, but you'll probably change your mind if you look at this. [3]Here are the results of our recent survey showing more than 90% of our customers are interested in electric cars.

안녕하세요, 여러분. 여러분과 나눌 신나는 이야기가 있습니다. 저희 회사가 새로운 방향으로 움직일 것이고, [1]**여러분과 같은, 현재와 미래의 모든 투자자에게** 영향을 미칠 것입니다. 새로운 고급 차량 제품으로 저희가 큰 성공을 거뒀다는 것을 아마 들어 보셨을 겁니다. [2]**이제, 저희 회사는 독자적인 전기차 제품을 개발하기로 결정하였습니다.** 이것은 더욱 환경친화적인 기업이 되어 더 젊은 고객들의 마음을 끌기 위한 시도입니다. 기존의 고객들이 이런 변화에 흡족해하지 않을 거라 걱정하실 수도 있습니다만, 이걸 보면 아마도 마음이 바뀌실 겁니다. [3]**여기 최근 설문조사 결과를 보시면 저희 고객의 90% 이상이 전기차에 관심을 갖고 있습니다.**

어휘 have great success with ~에 큰 성공을 거두다

1. 청자들은 누구일 것 같은가?

(A) 투자자들

(B) 마케팅 전문가들

(C) 임원들

(D) 제품 디자이너들

2. 화자에 따르면, 회사는 무엇을 바꿀 것인가?

(A) 만드는 차의 종류

(B) 본사의 위치

(C) 카탈로그 제작 출판사

(D) 고객의 피드백을 얻는 방법

3. 화자는 왜 "이걸 보면 아마도 마음이 바뀌실 겁니다"라고 말하는가?

(A) 실수를 정정하기 위해

(B) 의문을 제기하기 위해

(C) 제안을 거절하기 위해

(D) 안심시키기 위해

4-6. 영녀

Questions 4-6 refer to the following excerpt from a meeting.

W-Br I'm happy everyone made it to today's meeting. I'm thrilled with the way [4]our new software came out. Everyone did their part to make its launch a success. I also read through your responses to [5]the employee questionnaire I handed out last week. Thank you for taking the time to complete them. A lot of you suggested increasing our social media presence. I think that's a great idea, but we do have a limited hiring budget. [6]If anyone is interested in working overtime to help with the company's social media, please let me know at the end of the meeting.

모두가 오늘 회의에 참석하여서 기쁩니다. [4]**우리의 새로운 소프트웨어** 결과물에 대해 아주 흥분됩니다. 성공적 출시를 위해 모두가 각자의 역할을 다해 주었습니다. 저는 또한 지난주에 나눠 준 [5]**직원 설문지에** 대한 여러분의 답변들을 읽었습니다. **그것을 작성하기 위해 시간을 내어 주셔서 감사합니다.** 많은 분들이 저희의 소셜 미디어 영향력을 늘리는 것을 추천하였습니다. 좋은 견해라 생각합니다, 하지만 고용 예산은 한정돼 있습니다. [6]**만약 회사의 소셜 미디어를 돕기 위해 초과 근무할 의향이 있다면** 회의가 끝날 때 저에게 말씀해 주세요.

어휘 be thrilled with ~에 몹시 흥분되다 read through ~을 꼼꼼히 읽다

4. 청자들은 어떤 산업에서 일하는가?

(A) 광고

(B) 건설

(C) 소프트웨어

(D) 운송

5. 화자는 청자에게 무엇에 대해 감사하는가?

(A) 설문지를 작성한 것

(B) 영업 목표를 달성한 것

(C) 계약을 확정한 것

(D) 새로운 기기를 만든 것

6. 화자는 왜 "고용 예산은 한정돼 있습니다"라고 말하는가?

(A) 청자들에게 더 많은 판매를 하도록 장려하기 위해
(B) 청자들에게 손실에 대해 상기시키기 위해
(C) 청자들에게 그녀가 더 이상 직원을 고용하지 않는다고 말하기 위해
(D) 청자들에게 새로운 소프트웨어를 사라고 권하기 위해

UNIT 02 전화 메시지

CHECK-UP 본문 p.85

1. (D) **2.** (B) **3.** (A) **4.** (B) **5.** (B) **6.** (D)

1-3. 미남
Questions 1-3 refer to the following telephone message.

M-Am How's it going, Bruce? I just got off a phone call with a candidate for the marketing specialist position. She wants to interview this week, but I know you're quite busy. [1]Do you think you could free up your schedule for just an hour to join in on the interview? [2]She's the first candidate who's trilingual. She speaks English, Spanish, and French! I want to have the chance to interview her before she chooses another company. [3]I just sent you an e-mail with her available dates and times. Let me know if any of them works for you.

어떻게 지내요, Bruce? 방금 마케팅 전문가 자리에 지원하는 사람과 전화 통화를 했어요. 그녀는 이번 주에 면접을 보고 싶어 하지만, 전 당신이 무척 바쁘다는 것을 알아요. 면접에 참여할 수 있도록 [1]**딱 한 시간만 스케줄을 비워주실 수 있나요?** [2]**그녀는 3개 국어를 구사하는 첫 번째 후보자입니다.** 그녀는 영어, 스페인어, 그리고 프랑스어를 해요! 그녀가 다른 회사를 선택하기 전에 면접을 볼 기회를 갖고 싶어요. [3]**제가 방금 그녀가 면접 가능한 날짜와 시간이 적힌 이메일을 보내드렸어요.** 그중에 언제가 가능한지 알려주세요.

1. 화자는 왜 전화하고 있는가?
(A) 실수를 바로잡기 위해
(B) 다가오는 여행을 계획하기 위해
(C) 조언을 구하기 위해
(D) 일정 변경을 요청하기 위해

2. 화자는 채용 후보자에 대해 뭐라고 말하는가?
(A) 그녀는 좋은 추천서를 가지고 있다.
(B) 그녀는 여러 가지 언어를 구사한다.
(C) 그녀는 다른 곳에서 일하기로 했다.
(D) 그녀는 그 지역에 살지 않는다.

3. 화자는 이메일에 무엇을 보냈는가?
(A) 일정
(B) 비용 견적
(C) 계약서
(D) 이력서

4-6. 호남
Questions 4-6 refer to the following recorded message.

M-Au You've reached the voicemail of Henry Raynor. [4]I am currently taking my annual summer vacation and will return to the office on Monday, August 3rd. If you are interested in participating in the photography contest announced in [5]our January issue, please visit our Web site. [6]There you can complete a form to enter the contest as well as find out the details about the judging criteria. For other matters, please leave a message after the tone. Thank you.

Henry Raynor의 음성 메일입니다. [4]**저는 현재 여름휴가를 보내고 있으며** 8월 3일 월요일에 사무실로 복귀합니다. [5]**1월호**에 발표된 사진 공모전에 참여하고 싶으시다면 저희 웹사이트를 방문해 주십시오. [6]**거기에서 심사 기준에 대한 세부 사항뿐만 아니라 대회에 참가할 수 있는 양식을 작성할 수 있습니다.** 다른 용건이 있으시면 삐 소리가 난 후 메시지를 남겨 주시기 바랍니다. 감사합니다.

어휘 judging criteria 심사 기준

4. 화자는 현재 왜 전화를 받을 수 없는가?
(A) 그는 업계 행사에 참석하고 있다.
(B) 그는 휴가 중이다.
(C) 그의 팀이 교육을 받는 중이다.
(D) 그의 사무실 장비가 고장이 났다.

5. 화자는 어떤 일에 종사하고 있을 것 같은가?
(A) 컴퓨터 소프트웨어 배급사
(B) 잡지사
(C) 전자제품 제조업체
(D) 녹음 스튜디오

6. 화자에 따르면, 웹사이트에서는 무엇을 찾을 수 있는가?
(A) 직업 설명
(B) 행사 달력
(C) 사진 갤러리
(D) 지원 양식

UNIT 03 안내방송 및 공지

CHECK-UP 본문 p.87

1. (B) **2.** (A) **3.** (A) **4.** (D) **5.** (C) **6.** (B)

1-3. 영녀
Questions 1-3 refer to the following announcement.

W-Br Attention patrons. The library will close an hour early this evening. We'll be using this time to [1]update the layout of the bookshelves, making it easier for you to find what you're looking for. To learn more about how the stacks will look after the work is complete, [2]you can ask a staff member before leaving. And for those of you planning to participate in [3]tomorrow morning's book club meeting, don't worry. The gathering will still take place as scheduled. Thank you.

고객 여러분께 안내 말씀 드립니다. 도서관은 오늘 저녁에 한 시간 일찍 문을 닫을 것입니다. 이 시간을 사용하여 원하는 항목을 쉽게 찾을 수 있도록 [1]**책장의 배치를 새롭게 바꿉니다.** 작업이 완료된 후 서고가 어떻게 변화될지 자세히 알아보려면 나가시기 전에 [2]**직원에게 문의하십시오.** 그리고 [3]**내일 아침 북클럽 모임에** 참석할 예정이신 분들은 걱정하지 마세요. 모임은 여전히 예정대로 진행됩니다. 감사합니다.

어휘 patron 고객 the stacks (도서관의) 서가[서고] gathering 모임 as scheduled 예정대로

1. 화자는 오늘 저녁 무엇이 일어날 것이라고 하는가?
(A) 새 책들이 추가될 것이다.
(B) 책장들이 다시 배치될 것이다.
(C) 온라인 카탈로그가 업데이트될 것이다.
(D) 안내 데스크가 옮겨질 것이다.

2. 화자에 따르면, 청자들은 추가 정보를 어떻게 얻을 수 있는가?
(A) 사서에게 말함으로써
(B) 웹사이트를 확인함으로써
(C) 유인물을 통해서
(D) 안내 데스크에 전화함으로써

3. 내일 무엇이 일어나는가?
(A) 집단 토론
(B) 책 사인회
(C) 학술 강연
(D) 영화 상영

4-6. 영녀
Questions 4-6 refer to the following announcement.

W-Br I have a couple of announcements before we get started with [4]this month's farmer's market. Joe from Joe's Pickles is under the weather, so [5]he won't be able to make it this weekend. If customers ask for his booth, please let them know that he will be back next month. Also, most of the booths have been set up already, but I want you all to walk down the aisles to make sure everything is running smoothly. Remember that, as volunteers, you're often the first person customers see or talk to at the farmer's market, so [6]greet people warmly and with a smile.

[4]**이번 달 농산물 직판장을** 열기 전에 몇 가지 공지 사항들이 있습니다. Joe's Pickles의 Joe가 몸이 안 좋아, [5]**이번 주말에 참여할 수 없을 것입니다.** 만약 고객들이 그의 부스에 관해 묻는다면, 그가 다음 달에 참여한다는 것을 알려주세요. 또한, 대부분의 부스들이 벌써 준비되었지만, 여러분 모두 통로들을 걸으며 모든 것이 순조롭게 진행되고 있는지를 확인해 주시기 바랍니다. 자원봉사자로서, 여러분이 고객이 가장 먼저 보거나 말하는 사람이라는 것을 기억해주세요, 그래서 [6]**사람들에게 따듯하게, 그리고 미소로 인사를 건네야 합니다.**

어휘 under the weather 몸이 좀 안 좋은 set up 설치하다 run smoothly 순조롭게 진행되다

4. 공지는 어디에서 이루어지고 있는 것 같은가?
(A) 미용실에서
(B) 식료품점에서
(C) 컨벤션 센터에서
(D) 농산물 직판장에서

5. Joe's Pickles에 대해 무엇이 언급되는가?
(A) 할인행사를 한다.
(B) 현금만 받는다.
(C) 참가하지 않는다.
(D) 파산했다.

6. 화자는 청자들이 무엇을 할 것을 권하는가?
(A) 일찍 오는 것
(B) 사람들에게 친절하게 인사하는 것
(C) 초과 근무를 하는 것
(D) 도움을 요청하는 것

UNIT 04 TV/라디오 방송 및 팟캐스트

CHECK-UP 본문 p.89

1. (C) **2.** (B) **3.** (D) **4.** (D) **5.** (C) **6.** (D)

1-3. 영녀
Questions 1-3 refer to the following broadcast.

W-Br In other news, tomorrow marks the final day of our town's Theater Festival, which has been taking place in the town park. The festival is sponsored by [1]Discover Works, a company that funds outdoor theater performances and highlights the work of lesser-known playwrights. Anyone who plans to attend tomorrow's shows may want to arrive early, because [2]an early-bird discount is available for those who show up before 11 a.m. The Theater Festival is only one of many festivities hosted in the park this summer. [3]You can visit the town park Web site to see the full series of activities that are offered.

다음 뉴스입니다. 내일은 마을 공원에서 열리고 있는 우리 마을 연극제의 마지막 날입니다. 이 축제는 [1]**야외 연극 공연에 자금을 지원하고 덜 알려진 극작가들의 작품을 조명하는 회사인 Discover Works에** 의해 후원됩니다. 내일 공연에 참석할 분은 일찍 도착하시기 바랍니다. [2]**오전 11시 이전에 도착하는 관람객은 조조할인을 이용할 수 있기 때문입니다.** 연극제는 올 여름 공원에서 열리는 많은 축제들 중 하나일 뿐입니다. [3]**마을 공원 웹사이트를 방문하시면 제공되는 일련의 활동들을 확인해 보실 수 있습니다.**

어휘 in other news 다른 소식으로 A mark B A(연도, 달, 주 등)는 B(기념일 등의 이벤트)에 해당하다 highlight (특히 사람들이 더 많은 관심을 기울이도록) 강조하다 lesser-known 별로 유명하지 않은 playwright 극작가 may want to do ~해야 한다 (should의 의

PART 4

미) show up 나타나다, 도착하다

1. Discover Works는 무엇에 자금을 대는가?
(A) 공원 보수
(B) 음악 그룹
(C) 무대 공연
(D) 단편 영화

2. 화자에 따르면, 청자들은 왜 일찍 도착해야 하는가?
(A) 좋은 자리를 맡기 위해서
(B) 돈을 절약하기 위해서
(C) 공연자들을 만나기 위해서
(D) 교통 체증을 피하기 위해서

3. 마을 공원 웹사이트에서는 무엇을 이용할 수 있는가?
(A) 토론 게시판
(B) 일련의 영상
(C) 회원 가입 정보
(D) 행사 목록

4-6. 미남
Questions 4-6 refer to the following podcast.

M-Am Welcome to Space Cadets, a podcast for those who love studying [4]planets, stars, and everything in between. I've got an exciting guest coming on today. Her name is Kiran Buttar, and [5]she has just designed a new rocket propulsion system that will get humans closer to exploring Mars than ever before. Aspiring engineers will be particularly interested in this interview. The first fifteen minutes are available for free, [6]but the rest of the interview is reserved for those with annual memberships. So if you're not a member, subscribe today!

[4]**행성, 별, 그리고 그 사이의 모든 것을** 연구하는 것을 좋아하는 사람들을 위한 팟캐스트인 Space Cadets에 오신 것을 환영합니다. 오늘은 흥미로운 손님을 모십니다. 그녀의 이름은 Kiran Buttar이고, 그녀는 인간이 그 어느 때보다 화성을 탐험하는 데 더 가까이 다가갈 수 있는 [5]**새로운 로켓 추진 시스템을 얼마 전에 설계했습니다.** 엔지니어 지망생들은 이 인터뷰에 특히 관심을 가질 것입니다. 처음 15분은 무료로 이용할 수 있지만, [6]**나머지 인터뷰는 연간 회원권을 가진 분들만 이용 가능합니다.** 그러니 회원이 아니라면 오늘 구독하세요!

어휘 cadet 생도, (경찰·군대의) 간부[사관] 후보생 propulsion 추진, 추진력 aspiring 장차 ~이 되려는 reserve (어떤 권한 등을) 갖다[보유하다], (자리 등을) 따로 잡아[남겨] 두다

4. 팟캐스트는 주로 무엇에 관한 것인가?
(A) 화학
(B) 비디오 게임
(C) 여행
(D) 천문학

5. Kiran Buttar는 최근 무엇을 했는가?
(A) 공공 모금 행사를 주최했다.
(B) 사업을 시작했다.
(C) 혁신적 기술을 창조했다.
(D) 장학금을 탔다.

6. 화자에 따르면, 청자들은 왜 연간 회원에 가입해야 하는가?
(A) 비공개 행사에 대해 알아보기 위해
(B) 대본을 다운로드 받기 위해
(C) 다른 회원들을 만나기 위해
(D) 전체 회차를 이용하기 위해

UNIT 05 광고

CHECK-UP

본문 p.91

1. (A) **2.** (B) **3.** (C) **4.** (C) **5.** (B) **6.** (B)

1-3. 미남
Questions 1-3 refer to the following advertisement.

M-Am If you've spotted moths, termites, or any other [1]unwanted insects inside your home, you might have a pest problem. Bug-Finder Pest Control is here to help. We offer an initial consultation at no cost to you. During that appointment, we'll complete [2]a thorough sweep of your home and come up with a treatment plan. Also, for a limited time, [3]you can receive a 10% discount if you enter the word "MOSQUITO" when you book your first appointment online.

만약 여러분이 집 안에서 나방, 흰개미 또는 다른 [1]**원치 않는 곤충들을** 발견했다면, 여러분은 해충 문제가 있을 수 있습니다. Bug-Finder Pest Control이 도와드리겠습니다. 무료 초기 상담을 제공합니다. 상담 기간 동안, [2]**여러분의 집을 샅샅이 훑어보고** 퇴치 계획을 세울 것입니다. 또한 한정된 기간 동안 온라인으로 첫 예약 시 [3]**'MOSQUITO'라는 단어를 입력하면 10% 할인을 받을 수 있습니다.**

어휘 spot ~을 발견하다 moth 나방 unwanted 원치 않는, 반갑지 않은 at no cost 무료로 sweep 훑음 come up with (계획을) 마련하다

1. 무엇이 광고되고 있는가?
(A) 해충 구제업자
(B) 집안 청소 도우미
(C) 반려동물 돌봄 서비스
(D) 인테리어 디자이너

2. 무엇이 무료로 제공되는가?
(A) 청소 제품
(B) 주택 검사
(C) 한 시간 분량의 작업
(D) 회원 카드

3. 청자들은 어떻게 할인을 받을 수 있는가?
(A) 친구를 추천함으로써

(B) 소셜 미디어 포스트를 게시함으로써
(C) 프로모션 코드를 사용함으로써
(D) 여러 예약을 잡음으로써

4-6. 영녀

Questions 4-6 refer to the following advertisement.

W-Br If you're looking for a one-of-a-kind experience, come visit us at Walter's Coffee Factory. [4]Every tour begins with a special lecture about our beans by our resident coffee expert, Joe Walters. After that, our staff will guide you to the factory floor and show you around. [5]At the very end, everyone will receive a discount coupon to purchase our amazing coffee beans at the gift shop. Due to safety regulations, [6]children under 10 years old are not allowed to participate in the tour, so please keep that in mind when making your plans.

만약 당신이 세상에 단 하나뿐인 경험을 찾고 있다면, 저희 Walter's Coffee Factory에 방문하세요. [4]**모든 견학은** 전속 커피 전문가인 Joe Walters가 진행하는 저희 커피콩에 관한 **특별 강연으로 시작합니다.** 그 후에, 저희 직원들이 여러분을 작업 현장으로 모시고 그곳을 안내해 드릴 겁니다. [5]**맨 마지막엔, 모든 분이** 선물 가게에서 저희의 놀라운 커피콩을 구매하실 수 있게 **할인 쿠폰을 받을 겁니다.** 안전 수칙 관계로 [6]**10살 미만 어린이들은 견학에 참가할 수 없으니,** 계획을 세우실 때 참고해 주시기 바랍니다.

어휘 one-of-a-kind 독특한[유례를 찾기 힘든] show someone around ~를 데리고 여기저기 둘러보다 safety regulation 안전 규정 children under 10 years old 10세 미만의 어린이 keep something in mind ~을 명심하다

4. 견학은 어떻게 시작되는가?
(A) 다과가 제공된다.
(B) 영상을 보여준다.
(C) 강연이 주어진다.
(D) 보호 장구를 나누어 준다.

5. 참가자들은 견학 끝에 어떤 종류의 선물을 받는가?
(A) 포스터
(B) 할인 쿠폰
(C) 커피 한 봉지
(D) 엽서

6. 화자는 청자에게 무엇에 대해 경고하는가?
(A) 건강상의 위험
(B) 나이 제한
(C) 휴무 가능성
(D) 한정된 주차 공간

UNIT 06 연설, 소개, 견학/관광 안내

CHECK-UP 본문 p.93

1. (A) **2.** (C) **3.** (C) **4.** (B) **5.** (C) **6.** (C)

1-3. 영녀

Questions 1-3 refer to the following tour information.

W-Br Thank you for coming down to Daisy Marie's [1]All-Natural Dairy Farm. I'm excited to introduce you to this four-acre plot of land which is home to the best organic dairy products on Earth. Here, in the field, you can see our herd of cows grazing peacefully in the afternoon sun. This is a lucky day for you visitors, because [2]you'll get the chance to hand-feed these amazing creatures their favorite snack – oats! [3]Now, I'm handing out a pamphlet on the best ways to handle dairy cows, to ensure you develop a happy relationship with these loveable animals.

Daisy Marie의 [1]**All-Natural Dairy Farm**에 와주셔서 감사합니다. 저는 여러분을 이 4에이커의 대지에 모시게 되어 기쁩니다. 이 땅은 **지구상 최고의 유기농 유제품의 본고장입니다.** 이곳, 들판에서, 여러분은 오후의 태양 아래 평화롭게 풀을 뜯고 있는 소떼를 볼 수 있습니다. 오늘 여러분은 무척 운이 좋습니다. 왜냐면 [2]**이 놀라운 생명체들에게 그들이 가장 좋아하는 간식인 귀리를 직접 손으로 줄 기회를 얻게 될 것이니까요!** 이제, 저는 여러분이 이 사랑스러운 동물들과 행복한 관계를 맺을 수 있도록, 젖소를 다루는 가장 좋은 방법이 적힌 [3]**팸플릿을 나눠드리겠습니다.**

어휘 plot (특정 용도의) 작은 땅 조각, 터, 대지 be home to ~의 본거지[본고장]이다 dairy product 낙농 제품, 유제품 oat 귀리

1. 농장에서는 무엇이 생산되는가?
(A) 유기농 우유
(B) 솜
(C) 소고기 육포
(D) 신선한 과일

2. 청자들은 무엇을 할 기회를 가질 것인가?
(A) 동물들과 함께 산책
(B) 제품 시식
(C) 동물들에게 먹이 제공
(D) 주인들과의 만남

3. 청자들은 무엇을 받게 될 것인가?
(A) 비디오 링크
(B) 과자용 소스
(C) 전단
(D) 솔

4-6. 호남

Questions 4-6 refer to the following speech.

M-Au Hi, everyone! Thanks for coming to the grand opening of Elephant World, [4]a theme park featuring rides and games for people of all ages. I know you're excited to get inside. Before opening the gates, I want to let you know about a special promotion. We're trying to encourage a social atmosphere, [5]so we're offering tickets at half-price for anyone who comes in a group of six or more. It's perfect for a birthday party or your next social gathering. We also have a major event coming up: [6]this Friday, there will be a performance by famous singing group The Fluffy Bears. Don't miss it!

안녕하세요, 여러분! 모든 연령대의 사람들을 위한 놀이기구와 게임으로 가득한 [4]**테마 파크**, Elephant World의 개막식에 와주셔서 감사합니다. 어서 안으로 들어가고 싶어 하시는 거 압니다. 문을 열기 전에 특별 프로모션에 대해 알려드리고 싶습니다. 사교적인 분위기를 증진하기 위해 [5]**6인 이상 단체로 오시는 분들은 누구나 반값에 입장권을 드리고 있습니다.** 생일 파티나 사교 모임으로 딱이지요. 또한 가지 중요한 행사가 기다리고 있습니다. [6]**이번 주 금요일, 유명한 가수 그룹 The Fluffy Bears의 공연이 있습니다.** 놓치지 마세요!

어휘 feature ~을 특징으로 하다 at half-price 반값에

4. 화자는 어떤 곳에 대해 말하고 있는가?
(A) 미술관
(B) 놀이공원
(C) 애완 동물원
(D) 경기장

5. 화자는 어떤 특별한 할인을 언급하는가?
(A) 무료 식사
(B) 친구를 위한 할인권
(C) 많은 인원의 단체 할인
(D) 연간 회원권

6. 금요일에 무엇이 일어날 것인가?
(A) 미술 워크숍
(B) 가이드 동반 투어
(C) 라이브 콘서트
(D) 영화 상영

PRACTICE 고난도(의도 파악, 그래픽)

본문 p.94

1. (D)	**2.** (B)	**3.** (A)	**4.** (C)	**5.** (A)	**6.** (A)
7. (B)	**8.** (D)	**9.** (A)	**10.** (D)	**11.** (A)	**12.** (A)
13. (D)	**14.** (A)	**15.** (D)			

1-3. 미남

Questions 1-3 refer to the following telephone message.

M-Am Hi, I'm calling about [1]the pickup truck you dropped off at Sotheby's this afternoon. We looked it over, and it turns out your radiator is leaking coolant. We can do some patchwork now, but you're going to need to get the radiator replaced, which will be a major job. If you want to do it with us, let me know and [2]I'll suggest some possible times for next week. In the meantime, [3]Benny will be working late this evening, so you can pick the vehicle up anytime before 8 p.m.

안녕하세요, [1]**오늘 오후에 Sotheby's에 맡기신 픽업 트럭** 때문에 전화드렸습니다. 저희가 살펴봤는데 라디에이터에서 냉각수가 새고 있는 것으로 드러났습니다. 지금은 임시로 땜질을 할 수 있지만 결국에는 라디에이터를 교체하셔야 합니다. 그건 큰 작업입니다. 저희에게 맡기실 거면, 말씀해 주시면 [2]**다음 주에 가능한 시간을 알려드리겠습니다.** 어쨌거나, [3]**Benny가 오늘 저녁 늦게까지 근무할 예정이니** 오후 8시 전에는 언제든지 차량을 픽업할 수 있습니다.

어휘 drop something off somewhere 물건을 어떤 장소에 가져가서 놓고 떠나다 look over ~을 살펴보다 leak ~이 새다 patchwork 여러 조각[부분]들로 이뤄진 것 (여기에서는 새고 있는 부분들을 임시방편으로 땜하는 작업을 의미) patch 조각, 덧대다 major 주요한, 중대한, 심각한

1. 화자는 어디에서 일하고 있는 것 같은가?
(A) 세차장
(B) 이사 업체
(C) 렌터카 업체
(D) 자동차 수리 센터

2. 남자가 "그건 큰 작업입니다"라고 말할 때 무엇을 의미하는가?
(A) 선금을 지급해야 한다.
(B) 작업하는 데 시간이 걸릴 것이다.
(C) 더 많은 사람을 고용해야 한다.
(D) 곧 휴가를 떠날 것이다.

3. 화자는 오늘 저녁에 대해 뭐라고 말하는가?
(A) 직원이 머물러 있을 것이다.
(B) 부품이 도착할 것이다.
(C) 영업이 종료될 것이다.
(D) 지불 시스템이 업데이트될 것이다.

4-6. 호남

Questions 4-6 refer to the following talk.

M-Au Hello, customer support center. As you're probably aware, a recent news report about environmental damage caused by the plastic utensils manufacturing industry has many people upset. [4]You can expect to receive a lot of calls from angry consumers today. Please assure them that [5]our company's products do not contain any of the toxic chemicals on this document I'm handing out now. We've radically changed our production process over the last five years. To help you, I'm also providing a list of talking points to emphasize during challenging calls. [6]Please look it over and feel free to ask questions.

안녕하세요, 고객 지원 센터 여러분. 여러분도 알고 있겠지만, 플라스틱 식기 제조 산업에 의한 환경 피해에 대한 최근의 뉴스 보도는 많은 사람들을 화나게 했습니다. [4]**여러분은 오늘 화가 난 소비자들로부터 많은 전화를 받을 것으로 예상합니다.** [5]**우리 회사 제품에는 제가 지금 배포하는 서류에 적힌 독성 화학물질이 전혀 포함되어 있지 않다**는 것을 소비자에게 확실히 해 주시기 바랍니다. 지난 5년간 우리는 생산 공정을 근본적으로 변화시켰습니다. 여러분을 돕기 위

해, 대처하기 어려운 상담 전화에서 강조해야 할 요점들을 정리해 보았습니다. [6]**검토해 보시고** 언제든지 질문해 주세요.

어휘 utensil 식기 assure ~에게 확신시키다 contain 포함하다 hand out 나눠주다 radically 급진적으로 talking points 할 말의 요점들

4. 담화의 목적은 무엇인가?
(A) 청자들에게 소송에 대해 말해 주기 위해
(B) 새 환불 정책에 대해 발표하기 위해
(C) 청자들이 불만에 대처하도록 준비시키기 위해
(D) 팀의 확대를 제안하기 위해

5. 화자가 "우리는 생산 공정을 근본적으로 변화시켰습니다"라고 말할 때 무엇을 의미하는가?
(A) 회사는 한때 위험한 화학물질을 사용했었다.
(B) 제품이 더 큰 마진으로 팔리고 있다.
(C) 생산성이 급격히 향상되었다.
(D) 뉴스 보도가 잘못되었다.

6. 청자들은 무엇을 하도록 요청받는가?
(A) 유인물 읽기
(B) 잠시 휴식 취하기
(C) 보고서 작성하기
(D) 이메일에 답장하기

7-9. 미남

Questions 7-9 refer to the following talk and design plan.

M-Am I'm Raja Abdul from WMTH. I'm here reporting on [7]the construction of a series of walking paths, which are being funded by the city. Together, the paths extend 5 miles, stretching from Alpha Hospital to Lake Capra. [8]The project was launched after a recent study showed that Coolidge City is less pedestrian-friendly than others in the region. [9]Work has already been completed between Alpha Hospital and the Market District. Meanwhile, the areas surrounding Lake Capra are expected to be finished by the end of the month.

WMTH의 Raja Abdul입니다. 시에서 자금을 지원하는 [7]**일련의 산책로 건설에 대해** 보고드리겠습니다. 이 길들은 Alpha 병원에서 Capra 호수까지 5마일에 걸쳐 뻗어 있습니다. 이 프로젝트는 Coolidge City가 이 지역의 다른 도시들보다 덜 보행자 친화적이라는 [8]**최근 연구 결과가 나온 후에 시작되었습니다.** [9]**Alpha 병원과 시장 구역 사이의 작업은 이미 완료되었습니다.** 한편, Capra 호수 주변 지역들은 이달 말에 완공될 것으로 예상됩니다.

어휘 walking path 산책로 fund 자금[기금]을 대다 stretch (어떤 지역에 걸쳐) 뻗어 있다

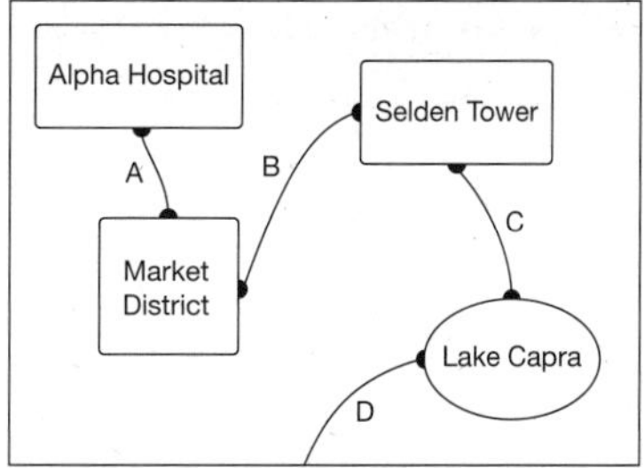

7. 화자는 무슨 프로젝트에 대해 주로 이야기하고 있는가?
(A) 시청 건물
(B) 인도
(C) 강변 공원
(D) 경기장

8. 그 프로젝트는 왜 시작되었는가?
(A) 회사가 그에 대한 비용 지불을 제시했다.
(B) 납세자들에 의해 결정되었다.
(C) 시장이 그것의 필요성을 언급했다.
(D) 조사 보고서에 의해 촉발되었다.

9. 시각 자료를 보시오. 화자에 따르면, 프로젝트의 어느 구역이 완성되었는가?
(A) A 구역
(B) B 구역
(C) C 구역
(D) D 구역

10-12. 영녀

Questions 10-12 refer to the following telephone message and table.

W-Br Hi. Thanks for inquiring about staying at La Vida Tropica Hotel. Unfortunately, our facilities don't contain any three-bedroom units. However, we do have some units [10]with two large bedrooms that also offer stunning views of the ocean. [11]Our hotel caters mainly to young families, so I think it would be a perfect spot for your vacation. If you'd like to book a room through me, I'll be available until the end of the day. [12]I'm out of the office tomorrow, but you can also call the front desk at 555-0196.

안녕하세요. La Vida Tropica Hotel 숙박에 대해 문의해 주셔서 감사합니다. 안타깝게도 저희 시설에는 침실 3개짜리 객실이 없습니다. 하지만, [10]**멋진 바다 전망을 제공하는 두 개의 큰 침실이 있는 객실들이 있습니다.** [11]**저희 호텔은 주로 젊은 가족들을 위한 곳이기 때문에** 손님께서 휴가를 보내기에 완벽한 장소가 될 것 같습니다. 저를 통해 방을 예약하실 거라면, 오늘 중으로 연락 주시기 바랍니다. [12]**내일은 제가 호텔에 없으며,** 555-0196번으로 프런트로 전화하셔도 됩니다.

어휘 inquire about ~에 대해 문의하다 stunning 굉장히 아름다운[멋진], 깜짝 놀랄 unit 객실

Unit Features	Unit Type			
	A	B	C	D
Two bedrooms	✓			✓
Ocean view		✓		✓
Massage chair	✓		✓	

10. 시각 자료를 보시오. 화자는 어느 객실을 언급하는가?
(A) Type A
(B) Type B
(C) Type C
(D) Type D

11. 화자는 호텔의 어떤 점을 강조하는가?
(A) 가족 친화적인 분위기
(B) 낮은 가격
(C) 고품질의 음식
(D) 청결도

12. 내일 무엇이 일어날 것인가?
(A) 화자가 하루 휴가를 낼 것이다.
(B) 호텔이 문을 닫을 것이다.
(C) 화자가 고객을 방문할 것이다.
(D) 호텔 예약이 다 찰 것이다.

13-15. 영녀
Questions 13-15 refer to the following excerpt from a meeting and map.

W-Br Hello, everyone. I called this meeting to talk about expanding our customer base in various regions of the country. Word of mouth has gotten [13]our medicinal products a long way in our home state, but on the other side of the country, sales are lagging. Take a look at this map. [14]You'll see that sales were lowest in the Northeast last quarter, where we generated only 2% of the company's total revenue. [15]Now, our marketing team plans to launch a new digital promotional campaign at the end of the year. That should help to improve brand awareness with younger generations in the regions where sales are struggling.

안녕하세요, 여러분. 저는 전국의 다양한 지역에서 고객층을 넓히는 것에 대해 이야기하기 위해 이 회의를 소집했습니다. [13]**우리 의약품은** 우리 주에서는 입소문을 타고 성장했지만, 다른 주에서는 판매가 저조한 상황입니다. 이 지도를 보겠습니다. [14]**지난 분기 매출액이 북동부 지역에서 가장 낮았음을 알 수 있는데,** 이 지역에서는 전체 매출액의 2%밖에 창출하지 못했습니다. [15]**이제 우리 마케팅팀은 연말에 새로운 디지털 홍보 캠페인을 시작할 계획입니다.** 그것은 매출이 고전하고 있는 지역에서 젊은 세대들에게 브랜드 인지도를 향상시키는 데 도움이 될 것입니다.

어휘 call a meeting 회의를 소집하다 word of mouth 입소문 medicinal product 의약품 lag 뒤에 처지다, 뒤떨어지다

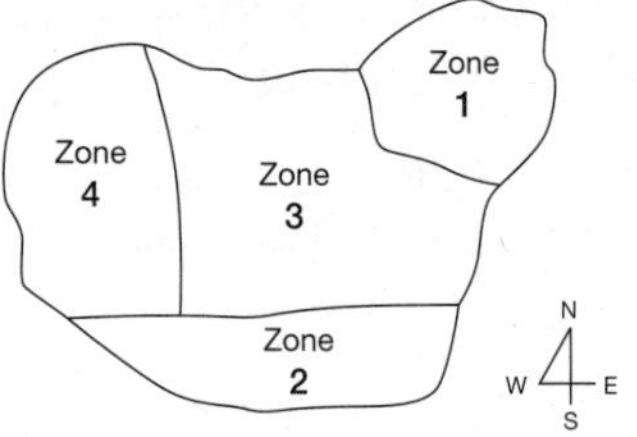

13. 화자의 회사는 무엇을 파는가?
(A) 문구
(B) 미용 제품
(C) 자동차 부품
(D) 의약품

14. 시각 자료를 보시오. 지난 분기 어느 지역이 가장 저조한 매출을 거뒀나?
(A) Zone 1
(B) Zone 2
(C) Zone 3
(D) Zone 4

15. 화자에 따르면, 연말에 무엇이 시작(출시)될 것인가?
(A) 연구 조사 프로젝트
(B) 디지털 가전제품
(C) 새로운 제품 라인
(D) 온라인 광고

PART TEST

본문 p.96

1. (C)	**2.** (D)	**3.** (A)	**4.** (B)	**5.** (C)	**6.** (D)
7. (D)	**8.** (B)	**9.** (D)	**10.** (A)	**11.** (D)	**12.** (A)
13. (B)	**14.** (D)	**15.** (C)	**16.** (B)	**17.** (B)	**18.** (A)
19. (B)	**20.** (D)	**21.** (C)	**22.** (B)	**23.** (C)	**24.** (A)
25. (C)	**26.** (D)	**27.** (B)	**28.** (B)	**29.** (C)	**30.** (C)

1-3. 미남
Questions 1-3 refer to the following talk.

M-Am On the screens in front of you, you'll see the reservation software [1]you'll be using to book rooms when customers call the front desk. The first time you log in, you'll be asked to create [2]a password. Please write it down for today, as you'll be logging in and out frequently. But eventually, you'll need to memorize it. [3]We've just upgraded the system, so it's a lot more user-friendly than it used to be.

여러분이 마주하신 화면에, [1]**고객이 프런트 데스크에 전화를 걸 때 객실 예약에 사용할** 예약 소프트웨어가 보일 겁니다. 처음 로그인할 때 [2]**암호를** 만들라는 메시지가 뜰 겁니다. 오늘 로그인과 로그아웃이 잦으실 테니 일단 **오늘 하루는 그것을 적어 두세요**. 하지만 결국에는 그것을 외워둬야 합니다. [3]**갓 시스템을 업그레이드했기 때문에** 예전보다 훨씬 더 사용자 친화적입니다.

1. 청자들은 어떤 직무로 고용되었는가?
(A) 여행 가이드
(B) 객실 관리 직원
(C) 응접원[접수원]
(D) 슈퍼마켓 점원

2. 청자들은 무엇을 적어 두도록 요청받는가?
(A) 선호하는 근무일
(B) 유니폼 사이즈
(C) 연락처
(D) 비밀번호

3. 화자는 시스템에 대해 뭐라고 말하는가?
(A) 최근 업데이트되었다.
(B) 관리자 전용이다.
(C) 재시작하려면 시간이 꽤 걸린다.
(D) 그다지 자주 사용되지 않는다.

4-6. 호남
Questions 4-6 refer to the following telephone message.

M-Au Hi, [4]this is Robert Jensen from the marketing department. When I arrived at my office this morning … um … number 203, [5]my overhead lights wouldn't turn on. They were fine yesterday, so I'm not sure what the problem is. I'll be working in the conference room temporarily, so that's where you can find me if you have any questions. [6]But please note that I'll only be on site until 2 P.M., as I'm leaving then to catch the express train to Dover. Thank you.

안녕하세요, [4]**저는 마케팅 부서의 Robert Jensen입니다.** 제가 오늘 아침 사무실에 도착했을 때… 음… 203호인데, [5]**제 머리 위의 전등이 켜지지 않았어요.** 어제는 괜찮았는데, 무슨 문제인지 잘 모르겠어요. 제가 회의실에서 임시로 일을 할 테니, 질문이 있으시면 거기에서 저를 찾으시면 됩니다. [6]**하지만 저는 오후 2시까지만 회사에 있다가 도버행 급행열차를 타기 위해 나갈 예정입니다.** 감사합니다.

어휘 overhead 머리 위의 on site 현장에

4. 화자는 무슨 부서에서 일하는가?
(A) 구매
(B) 마케팅
(C) 데이터 관리
(D) 제품 개발

5. 화자는 무슨 문제를 언급하는가?
(A) 그는 초과 근무를 해야 했다.
(B) 회의실이 잠겨 있다.
(C) 전등이 나갔다.
(D) 파일이 일시적으로 손실되었다.

6. 화자는 오후 2시에 어디로 갈 것 같은가?
(A) 백화점
(B) 강의실
(C) 은행
(D) 기차역

7-9. 영녀
Questions 7-9 refer to the following excerpt from a meeting.

W-Br Our advertising campaign on social media has been a major success. We have several large orders from shop owners for [7]our handmade jewelry. We don't have enough merchandise in stock, [8]so everyone will be working overtime to get these items made. I know you were planning on starting our new line of necklaces this week, but those won't go on the Web site until April. [9]In hindsight, we shouldn't have offered express shipping, especially since we have no maximum order size. We'll adjust this policy to prevent issues in the future.

우리의 소셜 미디어 광고 캠페인이 큰 성공을 거두었습니다. 가게 주인들로부터 몇 가지 큰 건의 [7]**수제 보석** 주문을 받았습니다. 재고가 충분하지 않기 때문에 [8]**모두 이 제품들을 만들기 위해 초과 근무를 할 것입니다.** 이번 주에 새로운 목걸이 제품을 시작할 계획이었던 것은 알지만, 그것들은 4월이 되어서야 웹사이트에 올라갈 것입니다. [9]**돌이켜보면**, 최대 주문 수량 제한을 두지 않은 상태였기에 **속달 배송을 제공하지 말았어야 했습니다.** 향후 문제가 발생하지 않도록 이 정책을 조정하겠습니다.

어휘 have something in stock ~의 재고가 있다 work overtime 초과 근무하다 plan on doing ~할 계획이다 in hindsight 돌아보면, 돌이켜보건대 express shipping 급송

7. 화자의 회사는 무엇을 파는가?
(A) 페인트
(B) 도자기
(C) 가구
(D) 보석류

8. 화자가 "그것들은 4월이 되어서야 웹사이트에 올라갈 것입니다"라고 말할 때 무엇을 의미하는가?
(A) 여자는 기술적인 문제를 겪고 있다.
(B) 여자는 다른 일이 더 중요하다고 여긴다.
(C) 여자는 일정상의 오류를 발견했다.
(D) 여자는 지연에 대해 사과하기를 원한다.

9. 화자는 회사가 무슨 실수를 했다고 생각하는가?
(A) 가격을 너무 낮게 매겼다.
(B) 광고에 너무 많은 돈을 썼다.
(C) 믿을 수 없는 공급업체로 변경했다.
(D) 속달 배송 옵션을 제공했다.

10-12. 미남
Questions 10-12 refer to the following announcement.

M-Am Hello, passengers. Unfortunately, we're coming into bad weather, with a storm just on the horizon. There will be choppy waves and some heavy winds [10]on the top deck for the next twenty minutes or so. [11]I encourage everyone to take a break from their mobile devices to avoid getting seasick. Those of you who are standing may also want to look for a seat. [12]One of our attendants, Malia, will now provide updated estimates on our arrival times at each stop.

승객 여러분, 안녕하세요. 안타깝게도, 기상악화로 곧 폭풍이 몰려옵니다. 앞으로 20분 정도는 파도가 거칠고 [10]**꼭대기 갑판에** 바람이 강하게 불 것입니다. [11]**뱃멀미를 할 수도 있으니 모두 모바일 기기 사용을 중단하고 휴식을 취할 것을 권장합니다.** 서 계신 분들도 착석해 주실 것을 부탁드립니다. [12]**이제 저희 직원 Malia가 각 도착지의 변경된 도착 시간을 알려드릴 것입니다.**

어휘 choppy 작은 파도가 거칠게 일렁이는 get seasick 뱃멀미를 하다 may want to do ~해야 한다

10. 공지는 어디에서 하고 있는 것 같은가?
(A) 연락선에서
(B) 기차에서
(C) 비행기에서
(D) 버스에서

11. 청자들은 무엇을 하도록 권유되는가?
(A) 먹는 것을 삼가는 것
(B) 안전벨트 착용
(C) 다른 층으로 이동
(D) 핸드폰 사용 중지

12. 다음에 무엇이 일어날 것 같은가?
(A) 더 많은 정보가 주어질 것이다.
(B) 경로가 변경될 것이다.
(C) 더 많은 승객을 태울 것이다.
(D) 화물이 집하될 것이다.

13-15. 미녀
Questions 13-15 refer to the following advertisement.

W-Am Are you ready to explore the history and culture of Europe? Leave the planning to our experts and enjoy an all-inclusive [13]bus tour from Graystone. We'll show you the top attractions in amazing cities such as Rome, Milan, and Paris. And if you have a large group, [14]you can customize the itinerary to include only the sites you're interested in. Take advantage of our special offer [15]in March. Book any trip to receive a complimentary T-shirt with the Graystone logo.

유럽의 역사와 문화를 탐험할 준비가 되었습니까? 계획은 전문가에게 맡기고 Graystone의 패키지 [13]**버스 투어를** 즐기십시오. 로마, 밀라노, 파리와 같은 놀라운 도시들의 최고의 명소들을 보여드리겠습니다. 또한 일행이 많은 경우 여러분이 관심 있는 장소만 포함하도록 [14]**여행 일정을 고객에 맞춰 변경할 수 있습니다.** [15]**3월** 특가 상품을 이용해 보세요. 예약하시는 모든 고객께는 Graystone 로고가 새겨진 **무료 티셔츠**를 드립니다.

어휘 all-inclusive 여행에 필요한 모든 통상 경비가 포함돼 있는 attraction 관광명소 take advantage of (기회, 이득, 혜택 등을) 이용하다 special offer 특별 할인 complimentary 무료의

13. 무엇이 광고되고 있는가?
(A) 콘서트홀
(B) 여행사
(C) 호텔
(D) 항공사

14. 화자는 업체의 어떤 혜택을 언급하는가?
(A) 취소 시 전액 환불을 제공한다.
(B) 막바지의 요청을 수용할 수 있다.
(C) 환경 친화적인 재료를 사용한다.
(D) 고객 맞춤형 옵션을 제공한다.

15. 3월에 무엇이 제공될 것인가?
(A) 음식 이용권
(B) 단체 할인
(C) 무료 의복
(D) 보험

16-18. 영녀
Questions 16-18 refer to the following talk.

W-Br Now that everyone is here, [16]I'm ready to begin this hike through the beautiful Clarion National Park. [17]Unfortunately, due to some fallen trees from the storm a few days ago, the Haven Trail is closed. This was supposed to be part of our hike today, so I'm sorry about that. Before we leave, don't forget that there is a water fountain here in case anyone needs to [18]fill up their water bottle.

이제 모두 모였으니, [16]**아름다운 Clarion National Park를 관통하는 이 하이킹을 시작해 보도록 하겠습니다.** [17]**안타깝게도,** 며칠 전 폭풍으로 쓰러진 나무들 때문에, Haven Trail은 **폐쇄되었습니다.** 이곳은 원래 오늘 우리의 하이킹 코스의 일부였는데, 유감입니다. 떠나기 전에, 이곳에 분수가 있으니 [18]**물병에 물을 채우실** 분은 잊지 마시기 바랍니다.

어휘 be supposed to do ~하기로 되어 있다 in case 만약 ~할 경우를 위해 fill up ~을 가득 채우다

16. 화자는 누구일 것 같은가?
(A) 피트니스 강사
(B) 공원[산림] 관리원
(C) 버스 운전기사
(D) 연구 과학자

17. 화자는 무엇에 대해 사과하는가?
(A) 요금 인상
(B) 뜻밖의 폐쇄
(C) 출발 지연
(D) 인쇄 오류

18. 청자 중 일부는 다음에 무엇을 할 것인가?
(A) 용기 채우기
(B) 시연 보기
(C) 간식 고르기
(D) 명찰 착용

19-21. 호남
Questions 19-21 refer to the following excerpt from a meeting.

M-Au Good morning, everyone. I'd like to take this opportunity to introduce [19]our latest addition to the team, Mr. Terrance Hickman. Since graduating from the prestigious Edsel University, he has built an impressive career background in a short time. He will be helping you with [20]reviewing contracts to ensure they are in compliance with the law. Although he'll receive training from me, [21]he may also have a lot of questions for the rest of you about our process. I know that you all have busy schedules and it's difficult to be interrupted, but when you started here you all had the same opportunity.

좋은 아침입니다. 이 자리를 빌려 [19]**팀에 새로 합류한 Mr. Terrance Hickman을** 소개합니다. 그는 명문 Edsel University를 졸업한 이후, 짧은 시간에 인상적인 경력을 쌓았습니다. 그는 여러분을 도와 계약이 [20]**법에 어긋나는 부분은 없는지 검토할** 것입니다. 그는 저로부터 교육을 받겠지만, 우리의 절차에 대해 [21]**여러분께 물어볼 게 많을 것입니다.** 여러분 모두가 바쁜 일정으로 인해 짬을 내기 어렵다는 것을 알지만, 여러분이 여기에 왔을 때 여러분도 같은 기회를 누렸습니다.

어휘 addition 추가된 구성원[것] in compliance with ~에 따라, ~에 응하여 interrupt 방해하다

19. Terrance Hickman은 누구인가?
(A) 잠재적 투자자
(B) 새로운 직원
(C) 대학 교수
(D) 이사회 임원

20. 청자들은 어느 부서 소속일 것 같은가?
(A) 그래픽 디자인
(B) 기술 지원
(C) 광고
(D) 법무

21. 화자는 왜 "여러분도 같은 기회를 누렸습니다"라고 말하는가?
(A) 마감일에 대해 경고를 주기 위해
(B) 최고 직원들을 인정해 주기 위해
(C) 청자들이 도움을 주도록 장려하기 위해
(D) 오해를 설명하기 위해

22-24. 미녀
Questions 22-24 refer to the following telephone message.

W-Am Hi, this is Evelyn Owens from Edgewood Financial. I've been showing [22]the blueprints you made for our new headquarters building, and everyone loves them. As I mentioned a few weeks ago, we may add an extension out the back instead of having additional parking. It depends on approval from the board to increase the budget. [23]I know you've been waiting to find out whether more work is needed on this project. Well, the board meeting is tomorrow. If you need to get a hold of me today, please note that you should call my mobile phone. I won't be in the office because [24]I'm going to a conference this afternoon.

안녕하세요, Edgewood Financial의 Evelyn Owens입니다. [22]**당신이 새 본사 건물을 위해 만든 청사진을** 보여줬는데 모두가 좋아합니다. 제가 몇 주 전에 언급했듯이, 우리는 주차장을 추가하는 대신 뒤쪽 건물을 연장할 수 있습니다. 예산을 늘리는 것은 이사회의 승인에 달려 있습니다. [23]**이 프로젝트에 추가 작업이 더 필요한지에 대한 결정을 기다리고 있었다는 것을 알고 있습니다.** 이사회가 내일 열립니다. 오늘 저에게 연락하실 일이 있다면 제 휴대폰으로 전화 부탁드립니다. [24]**저는 오늘 오후에 콘퍼런스에 가야 해서** 사무실에 없을 것입니다.

어휘 headquarters 본사 extension 연장 get a hold of ~와 연락하다, ~와 (전화로) 통화하다

22. 화자는 누구에게 전화하고 있는 것 같은가?
(A) 통역가
(B) 건축가
(C) 회계사
(D) 재정 고문

23. 화자가 "이사회가 내일 열립니다"라고 말할 때 무엇을 의미하는가?
(A) 그녀가 원했던 방을 예약할 수 없다.
(B) 청자와의 약속 일정을 다시 잡아야 한다.
(C) 곧 정보를 얻게 될 것이다.
(D) 청자가 발표를 해 주기를 원한다.

24. 화자는 오늘 오후에 무엇을 할 계획인가?
(A) 회의 참석
(B) 동료 교육
(C) 계약서 서명
(D) 가족 구성원 방문

25-27. 🎧 미남

Questions 25-27 refer to the following speech and report.

> **M-Am** Good afternoon. I'm Salvador Carlson, the head of research and development at Crenshaw Industries, and I'd like to thank you for your attendance [25]here at this press conference. [26]In February, we acquired our competitor, Renzelli Enterprises. Members of that team as well as ours have been working to create an efficient battery-powered bike. Well, the design we created will hit the market later this year, and our testing has had amazing results so far. In fact, I was the rider for one of the tests and traveled [27]one hundred twenty-one miles, breaking an industry record.

안녕하세요. 저는 Crenshaw Industries의 연구개발 책임자인 Salvador Carlson입니다. [25]**이 기자회견에** 참석해 주셔서 감사합니다. [26]**2월에 경쟁사인 Renzelli Enterprises를 인수했습니다.** 우리 팀뿐만 아니라 그 팀의 구성원들도 효율적인 배터리 구동 자전거를 만들기 위해 노력해 왔습니다. 우리가 만든 디자인은 올해 후반기에 시장에 출시될 예정이며, 지금까지 실시한 테스트들은 놀라운 결과를 낳았습니다. 사실, 그 테스트들 중 한 번은 제가 직접 자전거를 탔으며, [27]**121마일을 이동해 업계 기록을 깼습니다.**

어휘 acquire 인수하다 battery-powered 배터리(전지)로 움직이는 hit the market 출시하다 break a record 기록을 깨다

Test Results	
Test #	**Distance**
1	95 miles
2	121 miles
3	103 miles
4	99 miles

25. 청자들은 어디에 있는가?

(A) 직원 오리엔테이션
(B) 취업 면접
(C) 기자회견
(D) 시상식 연회

26. 화자에 따르면, 2월에 무엇이 일어났는가?

(A) 발명 특허가 승인되었다.
(B) 안전 보고서가 발표되었다.
(C) 부서장이 변경되었다.
(D) 기업 인수가 마무리되었다.

27. 시각 자료를 보시오. 화자는 어떤 테스트에 참여했는가?

(A) Test 1
(B) Test 2
(C) Test 3
(D) Test 4

28-30. 🎧 미녀

Questions 28-30 refer to the following excerpt from a meeting and map.

> **W-Am** Let's get this meeting started. This morning, [28]I had a conference call with all of the managers of our department store's branches. Fortunately, operations are running smoothly at most places. [29]However, our branch in Flanigan is temporarily closed because of damage from last night's storm. Actually, a lot of buildings and roads in that district were damaged. Therefore, some of the shipments intended for that branch will be redirected here. [30]We need to make space in the main section of our storage facility for those deliveries. Annabelle, could your team handle that?

회의를 시작하겠습니다. 오늘 아침, [28]**저는 우리 백화점의 모든 지점장들과 전화 회의를 했습니다.** 다행히 대부분의 지점에서 운영이 원활하게 진행되고 있습니다. [29]**하지만, 어젯밤 폭풍으로 인한 피해 때문에 Flanigan에 있는 지점은 일시적으로 문을 닫았습니다.** 사실 그 지역의 많은 건물과 도로가 피해를 입었습니다. 따라서 해당 지점으로 가야 할 일부 배송물이 여기로 도착하게 됩니다. [30]**창고 시설의 메인 섹션에 그 배송물들을 보관할 공간을 마련해야 합니다. Annabelle, 당신 팀이 처리할 수 있나요?**

어휘 get something started ~을 시작하다 conference call (3인 이상이) 전화로 하는 회의 operation 운영 run smoothly 순조롭게 진행되다 redirect (다른 주소·방향으로) 다시 보내다

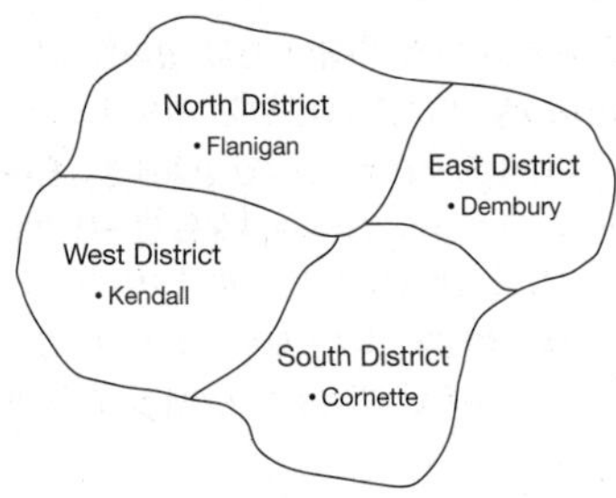

28. 화자는 아침에 누구와 통화했는가?

(A) 시설 회사 직원들
(B) 백화점 관리자들
(C) 응급 구조자들
(D) 공장 감독들

29. 시각 자료를 보시오. 어느 지역이 폭풍 피해를 입었는가?

(A) 동부 지역
(B) 서부 지역
(C) 북부 지역
(D) 남부 지역

30. 화자는 Annabelle의 팀에 무엇을 하라고 요청하는가?

(A) 서류 검토
(B) 고객들에게 전화
(C) 공간 정리
(D) 차량 수리

RC PART 5

UNIT 01 명사

PRACTICE 본문 p.106

1. (C) **2.** (B) **3.** (B) **4.** (B) **5.** (C) **6.** (D)
7. (C) **8.** (B) **9.** (C) **10.** (D) **11.** (B) **12.** (B)
13. (D) **14.** (D) **15.** (A) **16.** (D) **17.** (C) **18.** (D)
19. (A) **20.** (B)

1. (C)

해석 회사 소식지에 따르면 부사장님이 이번 주 목요일에 회사의 진행 상황에 대한 토론회를 열 예정이다.

해설 빈칸 앞에 관사 a가 있으므로 명사인 (C) discussion이 정답이다.

어휘 newsletter 소식지, 뉴스레터 firm 회사 progress 진행, 진척

2. (B)

해석 조립 라인 근처에서 안전 수칙 위반이 발생하면 관리자와 이야기하세요.

해설 빈칸 앞에 명사가 있고, 뒤에 동사가 있으므로 빈칸은 safety와 함께 복합 명사를 이루는 명사가 올 수 있다. 따라서 (B) violations가 정답이다.

어휘 supervisor 관리자, 감독관 safety 안전 violation 위반 occur 일어나다, 발생하다 assembly line (공장의) 조립 라인

3. (B)

해석 변호사들은 협의된 계약을 주의 깊게 검토하여 어떤 문제가 있는지 확인한다.

해설 문장의 주어는 The lawyers, 동사는 review이고, 빈칸은 review의 목적어이자 negotiated의 수식을 받는 명사 자리이다. 따라서 (B) agreements가 정답이다.

어휘 review 검토하다 negotiated 협의된 agreement 협정, 계약

4. (B)

해석 Irene Krakow는 내일 아침에 그녀가 다니는 헬스장의 트레이너를 만날 계획이다.

해설 빈칸은 관사 a의 수식을 받으며 동사 meet의 목적어가 되는 명사 자리이다. 따라서 관사의 수식을 받을 수 있는 명사인 (B) trainer가 정답이다. (D) training은 관사 a의 수식을 받을 수 없으며 문맥적으로도 의미가 맞지 않으므로 오답이다.

어휘 intend 작정하다, 생각하다 gym 헬스장, 체육관

5. (C)

해석 은행 직원들 사이에서는 경영진이 제시한 계약 제안을 받아들이기를 주저하는 분위기가 있다.

해설 there is 뒤에는 단수 명사가 나와야 하므로 (C) hesitation이 정답이다.

어휘 hesitation 주저, 망설임 teller 은행 창구 직원 contract 계약(서) put forth 제시하다

6. (D)

해석 Mr. Cromwell은 Maxell 프로젝트를 성공적으로 마친 뒤 과제의 선택권이 주어졌다.

해설 빈칸 앞에 전치사가 있으므로 전치사의 목적어가 되는 명사나 동명사가 올 수 있다. 따라서 assigning과 assignments가 정답이 될 수 있다. 동명사는 뒤에 목적어가 와야 하는데, 목적어가 없으므로 명사인 (D) assignments가 정답이다.

어휘 choice 선택(권) complete 끝마치다

7. (C)

해석 Dover Sporting Goods는 지역 내 몇 개의 야구팀들과 장기적인 제휴 관계를 맺고 있다.

해설 빈칸은 관사 a와 형용사 long-term의 수식을 받는 명사 자리이다. 선택지 중에서 명사는 affiliate(계열사)와 affiliation(제휴, 가맹)이 있는데, 의미상 적절한 (C) affiliation이 정답이다.

어휘 sporting goods 스포츠 용품 long-term 장기적인 affiliation 제휴

8. (B)

해석 예상되는 폭설로 인해 여행객들은 산 속에 있는 도로를 피하라는 권고를 받게 될 것이다.

해설 빈칸은 문장의 주어이자 권고를 받는 대상이다. 따라서 명사인 Travel과 Travelers 중에 사람 명사인 (B) Travelers가 정답이다.

어휘 advise 충고하다, 권고하다 avoid 피하다 on account of ~ 때문에 expected 예상되는 heavy snowfall 폭설

9. (C)

해석 대표이사의 결정에 따라 전 직원에게 추가로 하루의 유급 휴가가 주어졌다.

해설 빈칸 앞뒤로 전치사가 있으므로 전치사의 목적어가 되는 명사인 (C) accordance가 정답이다.

어휘 in accordance with ~에 따라서 extra 추가의 paid leave 유급 휴가

10. (D)

해석 휴가철에는 온라인으로 이루어진 모든 호텔 예약은 전혀 환불되지 않을 것이다.

해설 빈칸은 명사 hotel과 복수 명사를 형성하여 문장의 주어가 되며 한정사 all의 수식을 받고 있다. all은 복수 명사 또는 불가산명사를 수식하므로 선택지 중에서 복수 명사인 (D) bookings가 정답이다.

어휘 make a booking 예약하다 completely 완전히, 전혀 nonrefundable 환불되지 않는

11. (B)

해석 Mr. Hightower는 자신의 교량 디자인이 시장에 의해 선정

되었다는 사실에 만족감을 나타냈다.

해설 빈칸은 동사 expressed의 목적어이므로 명사인 (B) satisfaction이 정답이다.

어휘 express 표현하다, 나타내다 select 선정하다 mayor 시장

12. (B)

해석 Mr. Burbank는 회사에서 확보한 신규 고객들을 처리하기 위해 컨설턴트들로 이루어진 그룹을 조직할 것이다.

해설 앞에 전치사 of가 있으므로 전치사의 목적어가 되는 명사 자리이다. consultant와 consultants가 정답 후보가 되는데, group은 여럿으로 이루어진 집단이므로 복수 명사인 (B) consultants가 정답이다.

어휘 establish 설립하다 handle 다루다, 처리하다 obtain 얻다, 확보하다

13. (D)

해석 지난 3일 동안의 피아니스트 Judy Watson의 공연은 관객들로부터 널리 찬사를 받았다.

해설 빈칸 앞에 소유격인 Judy Watson's가 있으므로 빈칸은 명사 자리이며, performance와 performances가 정답 후보가 된다. 문장의 동사가 복수 동사인 have이므로 복수 명사인 (D) performances가 정답이다.

어휘 performance 공연 widely 널리 praise 칭찬하다 audience 관객

14. (D)

해석 피에몬트에서, 일부 신축 건물의 양식은 고대 로마에서 사용되었던 것과 닮았다.

해설 관사 the의 수식을 받고 있으므로 명사 자리이다. 명사인 stylist와 style 중에서 의미상 전치사구인 of some new buildings의 수식을 받을 수 있는 것은 (D) style이다.

어휘 resemble 닮다 ancient 고대의

15. (A)

해석 정부의 권고에 따르면, 가정에서는 에너지 효율이 좋은 단열재를 사용해야 한다.

해설 According to는 전치사이고, According to부터 빈칸까지는 절이 아닌 구의 형태이므로, 동사 형태인 (B), (D)와 to부정사인 (C)를 소거할 수 있다. government와 함께 복합 명사를 이루는 (A) recommendations가 정답이다.

어휘 according to ~에 따르면 recommendation 권고, 추천 energy-efficient 에너지 효율적인 insulation material 단열재

16. (D)

해석 30년 동안 계속해서 Weyland Aerospace에 고용되었음에도 불구하고 Dan Jenkins는 다른 회사에서 일하기 위해 사직했다.

해설 빈칸 앞에 형용사가 있고 뒤에 전치사구가 있으므로 빈칸은 형용사와 전치사구의 수식을 받는 명사 자리이다. employee와 employment 중에서 의미상 적절한 (D) employment가 정답이다.

어휘 continual 계속적인, 거듭되는 resign 사직하다, 사임하다

17. (C)

해석 직원들은 출장 경비가 아무리 적더라도 보고해야 한다.

해설 빈칸 앞에 한정사 any가 있으므로 명사인 (C) expenses가 정답이다.

어휘 be supposed to do ~해야 한다 report 보고하다, 알리다 business trip 출장

18. (D)

해석 Mr. Klein은 남미 시장 진출 방법에 관한 제안을 해 달라는 요청을 받았다.

해설 동사 make의 목적어가 되며 관사 a의 수식을 받는 명사 자리이므로 proposer와 proposal이 정답 후보가 되는데, 문맥상 (D) proposal이 정답이다.

어휘 make a proposal 제안하다 regarding ~에 관해 enter 들어가다, 진입하다

19. (A)

해석 상점들은 앞으로 두 달 동안 신제품의 유통이 제한될 것이라는 통보를 받았다.

해설 빈칸은 명사절의 주어 자리이며 전치사구의 수식을 받고 있으므로 명사인 (A) distribution이 정답이다. 동명사인 distributing은 바로 뒤에 전치사 없이 목적어가 나와야 하므로 오답이다.

어휘 inform 통보하다, 알리다 distribution 유통, 배부 product line 제품군 limit 제한하다

20. (B)

해석 Dr. Audrey는 항상 자신의 과학자들에게 그들이 실험에 필요로 하는 재료들을 주고 싶어 한다.

해설 〈동사(give)+간접목적어(her scientists)+직접목적어〉의 문장 구조이며, 빈칸 뒤에 관계절이 이어지고 있으므로 빈칸에는 관계대명사 that의 선행사가 되는 명사가 와야 한다. materials와 materialization 중에서 의미상 적절한 (B) materials가 정답이다.

어휘 be eager to do ~을 하고 싶어 하다 experiment 실험

UNIT 02 대명사

PRACTICE 본문 p.109

1. (C) **2.** (B) **3.** (B) **4.** (D) **5.** (B) **6.** (A)
7. (A) **8.** (B) **9.** (C) **10.** (C)

1. (C)

해석 Mr. Toole은 내일 비행기를 타고 멤피스로 가는데, 그곳에서 잠재 고객을 만나야 하기 때문이다.

해설 빈칸은 부사절의 주어 자리이므로 주격 인칭대명사인 (C) she가 정답이다.

어휘 potential 잠재적인 client 고객

2. (B)

해석 로봇 공학 분야의 직업에 관심이 있는 사람은 누구나 그 자리에 지원하는 것을 환영한다.

해설 빈칸 뒤에 관계사 who가 있고 단수 동사 is가 이어지므로 anyone who의 구조라는 것을 알 수 있다. 따라서 (B) Anyone이 정답이다.

어휘 career 직업, 경력 robotics 로봇 공학 apply for ~에 지원하다

3. (B)

해석 직원 회의는 의무이므로, 모든 사람은 겹치는 약속을 취소하고 내일 회의에 참석해야 한다.

해설 빈칸 뒤에 동사구 must cancel이 있으므로 빈칸에는 주어가 와야 한다. 따라서 주어가 될 수 있는 (B) everybody가 정답이다.

어휘 staff 직원 mandatory 의무적인 conflicting 상충되는, 충돌하는

4. (D)

해석 Jules Desmond는 소설책의 한 부분을 읽은 후, 직접 1부, 1부 사인을 해줄 것이다.

해설 주어(Jules Desmond), 동사(will autograph), 목적어(copies)가 갖추어진 완벽한 문장이다. 이럴 때는 강조용법으로 쓰인 재귀대명사가 빈칸에 들어갈 수 있으므로 (D) himself가 정답이다.

어휘 section 부분 novel 소설 autograph 사인을 해주다; 사인 copy 1부, 사본

5. (B)

해석 테이블 위에 놓여 있는 교육 매뉴얼 대신 방 뒤쪽에 있는 매뉴얼을 이용해 주세요.

해설 빈칸에는 복수 명사인 the training manuals를 대신하는 단어가 와야 하므로 지시대명사인 (B) those가 정답이다. 빈칸과 sitting 사이에는 〈관계대명사+be동사〉인 that[which] are가 생략되어 있다고 볼 수 있다.

어휘 training 교육 manual 매뉴얼, 안내서

6. (A)

해석 프로젝트가 완료될 때마다 여러분의 관리자에게 연락해서 새로운 임무를 받으세요.

해설 빈칸은 명사 manager를 수식하고 있으므로 소유격 인칭대명사인 (A) your가 정답이다.

어휘 complete 완료된; 완료하다 assignment 과제, 임무

7. (A)

해석 타이어가 2년밖에 되지 않았지만, Ms. Vernon은 그것들을 새로운 것으로 교체하기로 결정했다.

해설 빈칸은 to replace의 목적어 자리이므로 tires를 의미하는 목적격 인칭대명사인 (A) them이 정답이다.

어휘 replace 교체하다, 바꾸다

8. (B)

해석 엔지니어 자리에 지원한 최고의 지원자는 Rita Kraus였고, 우리는 그 사람에게 일자리를 제안해야 한다.

해설 주어는 The best -------이고 who ~ position은 주어를 수식하는 관계절이다. 따라서 형용사 best의 수식을 받을 수 있고 관계절의 선행사 역할을 할 수 있는 부정대명사인 (B) one이 정답이다. 나머지 선택지들은 형용사의 수식을 받을 수 없고, 문법적으로도 맞지 않다.

어휘 apply for ~에 지원하다 engineering 공학, 엔지니어링 offer 제안하다, 주다

9. (C)

해석 우리가 탔던 관광버스는 빨간색으로 칠해져 있어서 차가 가득 찬 주차장에서도 우리 차를 쉽게 찾을 수 있었다.

해설 빈칸은 to locate의 목적어 자리이므로 us, ours, ourselves 등이 빈칸에 올 수 있다. 빈칸은 문맥상 the tour bus를 의미하므로 '우리의 것', 즉, '우리가 탔던 버스'를 의미하는 소유대명사인 (C) ours가 정답이다.

어휘 locate 정확한 위치를 찾아내다

10. (C)

해석 Ms. Atkins는 노고와 헌신 덕분에 자기 자신을 매우 유능한 컴퓨터 프로그래머로 변모시켰다.

해설 동사 turned의 목적어는 문장의 주어인 Ms. Atkins와 동일하므로 재귀대명사인 (C) herself가 정답이다.

어휘 turn A into B A를 B로 바꾸다 highly 매우 competent 유능한 thanks to ~ 덕분에 dedication 헌신

UNIT 03 형용사와 한정사

PRACTICE 본문 p.111

1. (D)	**2.** (A)	**3.** (C)	**4.** (C)	**5.** (A)	**6.** (B)
7. (C)	**8.** (A)	**9.** (A)	**10.** (B)		

1. (D)

해석 Ms. Howell은 오늘날 기술의 최신 발전에 대해서도 포괄적인 이해를 하고 있다.

해설 빈칸은 명사 developments를 수식하는 형용사 자리이며, 앞에 최상급을 만드는 관사 the가 있으므로 (D) latest가 정답이다.

어휘 comprehensive 포괄적인

2. (A)

해석 워크숍에 참석한 후, 모든 사람은 실험실에서 몇 가지 실습 교육을 받아야 한다.

해설 빈칸은 person과 함께 주어를 형성하므로 단수 명사를 수식하는 한정사인 (A) every가 정답이다. which는 의문문에서 한정사로 쓰일 수 있고, many는 복수 명사를 수식하므로 오답이다.

어휘 hands-on 직접 해보는, 실습의 lab 실험실

3. (C)

해석 모든 중요한 사항들이 다루어질 수 있도록 회의 전에 의제를 만드는 것이 좋다.

해설 빈칸은 주격 보어가 되는 형용사가 들어갈 자리이므로 (C) beneficial이 정답이다. 보기에 형용사와 분사가 함께 있을 경우 형용사가 우선하기 때문에 benefiting은 오답이다.

어휘 agenda 의제 cover 다루다, 포함시키다

4. (C)

해석 Destiny Media는 목표를 달성하기 위해 기꺼이 열심히 일할 야심찬 지원자들만을 채용한다.

해설 빈칸에는 동사 hires의 목적어인 applicants를 수식하는 형용사 또는 applicants와 함께 복합 명사를 이루는 명사가 올 수 있다. 따라서 형용사인 (C) ambitious가 정답이다. 명사 ambition은 applicants와 함께 쓰일 수 없으므로 오답이다.

어휘 ambitious 야심찬 applicant 지원자 willing 기꺼이 하는 achieve 성취하다 goal 목표

5. (A)

해석 물품이 고객에게 시기 적절하게 배송되는 것이 중요하다.

해설 앞에 관사 a가 있고 뒤에 명사 manner가 있으므로 빈칸에는 명사를 수식하는 형용사 또는 manner와 함께 복합 명사를 형성하는 명사가 올 수 있다. time과 times는 복합 명사를 형성할 수 없고, 형용사인 (A) timely가 정답이다. in a timely manner라는 숙어 표현을 외워 둘 필요가 있다.

어휘 vital 중요한, 필수적인 item 물품 ship 발송하다, 배송하다 in a timely manner 시기적절하게

6. (B)

해석 모든 기사들은 근무일에는 실험실에서 안전 장비를 착용해야 한다.

해설 빈칸은 주어인 technicians를 수식할 수 있어야 하므로 복수 명사를 수식하는 한정사인 (B) All이 정답이다. each는 단수 명사를 수식하고, none은 〈none of 복수 명사〉의 형태로 쓰이므로 오답이다. either는 side와 같은 단어를 수식할 수 있지만 이처럼 숫자가 명확하지 않은 복수형 명사는 수식할 수 없으므로 오답이다.

어휘 technician 기사, 기술자 be required to do ~하도록 요구되다 safety gear 안전 장비 laboratory 실험실 workday 근무일, 평일

7. (C)

해석 참석자들은 댄스 공연이 축제에서 가장 인상적인 부분이었다고 말했다.

해설 빈칸 앞에 한정사 most가 있고 뒤에 명사 part가 있으므로, 한정사의 수식을 받으면서 명사를 수식하는 형용사가 와야 한다. 따라서 (C) impressive가 정답이다.

어휘 performance 공연

8. (A)

해석 Horace Powers는 승진한 후 자신의 가족과 함께 며칠 동안 휴가를 가질 계획이다.

해설 복수 명사인 days를 수식하는 (A) several이 정답이다.

어휘 get promoted 승진하다 intend 의도하다, 작정하다 take a vacation 휴가를 내다

9. (A)

해석 Ms. Cunningham은 지난 몇 년 동안 여러 개의 광범위한 프로젝트를 했다.

해설 빈칸은 명사 projects를 수식하는 형용사 자리이거나 projects와 함께 복합 명사를 형성하는 명사 자리이다. 따라서 형용사인 (A) extensive가 정답이다. 형용사가 있으므로 분사인 extending은 오답이다.

어휘 multiple 많은, 다수의 extensive 광범위한, 폭넓은

10. (B)

해석 Luxor Furniture는 하루의 대부분을 앉아 있는 사람들을 위해 편안한 사무용 의자를 디자인한다.

해설 명사 office chairs를 수식하는 형용사 (B) comfortable이 정답이다. 형용사가 있으므로 분사인 (C) comforting은 오답이다.

어휘 individual 사람, 개인 remain seated 앉아 있다

UNIT 04 부사

PRACTICE 본문 p.113

1. (D)	**2.** (D)	**3.** (B)	**4.** (D)	**5.** (B)	**6.** (D)
7. (C)	**8.** (D)	**9.** (D)	**10.** (A)		

1. (D)

해석 웹사이트에 대한 개선은 IT 부서의 책임자에 의해 직접 이루어졌다.

해설 빈칸이 be동사와 분사 사이에 있으므로 부사 자리이다. 따라서 (D) personally가 정답이다.

어휘 make improvements 개선하다, 개량하다 personally 개인적으로, 직접 director 관리자, 이사

2. (D)

해석 관객들은 그 영화의 매우 사실적인 특수 효과에 깊은 인상을 받았다.

해설 빈칸은 형용사 realistic 앞에 있으므로 형용사를 수식하는 부사 자리이다. 따라서 (D) highly가 정답이다.

어휘 audience 관객, 청중 be impressed by ~에 깊은 인상을 받다 highly 매우 realistic 사실적인, 현실적인 special effect 특수 효과 film 영화

3. (B)

해석 그 표지판은 그 방이 허가 받지 않은 사람들에게는 분명히 출입 금지라는 것을 나타낸다.

해설 빈칸은 be동사의 뒤, 그리고 형용사구인 off limits 앞에 있으므로 부사 자리이다. 따라서 (B) clearly가 정답이다.

어휘 sign 표지판, 간판 indicate 나타내다, 가리키다 clearly 분명히, 명백히 off limits 출입 금지의 unauthorized 허가 받지 않은, 권한이 없는 personnel 인원

4. (D)

해석 사무실 관리자인 Mr. Olson은 직원들에게 특별 행사를 위해 제시간에 오라고 거듭 지시했다.

해설 Mr. Olson은 주어, instructed는 동사, the office manager는 주어를 수식하는 동격의 명사구이다. 빈칸은 동사 앞에 있으므로 부사인 (D) repeatedly가 정답이다.

어휘 repeatedly 거듭, 반복해서 instruct 지시하다 on time 시간을 어기지 않고, 제때에

5. (B)

해석 배가 오전 7시 정각에 출발하기 때문에 투어 참가자들은 시간을 어기지 않아야 한다.

해설 동사 departs를 뒤에서 수식하는 부사인 (B) promptly가 정답이다.

어휘 on time 시간을 어기지 않고, 정각에 depart 출발하다 promptly 정확히 제시간에

6. (D)

해석 Julie Sharpe는 Meridian 사에서 근무를 시작한 이후로 그녀의 업적에 대해 자주 인정을 받았다.

해설 조동사 has와 과거분사 received 사이에 빈칸이 있으므로 부사 자리이다. 따라서 (D) regularly가 정답이다.

어휘 regularly 정기적으로, 자주 recognition 인정, 인식 accomplishment 업적, 성취

7. (C)

해석 웨이터는 식사를 하는 손님들에게 그들이 음식점에서 식사를 즐겼는지 정중하게 물었다.

해설 빈칸은 명사 diners 뒤에 있지만, 의미상 동사 asked를 수식하고 있다. 따라서 부사인 (C) politely가 정답이다.

어휘 diner 식사 손님; 작은 식당 politely 정중히

8. (D)

해석 고객 서비스 담당자들은 모든 민원을 보다 신속하게 해결하라는 지시를 받았다.

해설 〈동사(solve)+명사(all complaints)+부사〉의 문장 구조이므로 (D) promptly가 정답이다.

어휘 customer service representative 고객 서비스 담당자 instruct 지시하다 solve 풀다, 해결하다 complaint 불만, 민원

9. (D)

해석 창고 관리자는 새로운 배송품을 위한 공간을 마련하기 위해 서둘러 전자 기기 상자들을 치웠다.

해설 The warehouse supervisor는 주어, had는 동사, the boxes of electronics는 목적어, 그리고 과거분사 removed는 목적격 보어가 된다. 빈칸은 동사의 뒤, 그리고 분사의 앞에 있으므로 부사 자리이다. 따라서 (D) hastily가 정답이다.

어휘 warehouse 창고 supervisor 관리자, 감독관 electronics 전자 기기 remove 없애다, 제거하다 make space for ~을 위한 장소를 마련하다 shipment 배송(품)

10. (A)

해석 카운티 박람회 추첨의 당첨자는 오늘 저녁 무작위로 선정된 번호로 결정됩니다.

해설 〈관사(a)+분사(selected)+명사(number)〉의 구조에서 형용사 역할을 하는 분사 앞에 올 수 있는 것은 부사밖에 없다. 따라서 (A) randomly가 정답이다.

어휘 raffle 추첨 fair 박람회 randomly 무작위로

UNIT 05 동사, 수 일치, 태, 시제

PRACTICE 본문 p.116

1. (D)	**2.** (D)	**3.** (C)	**4.** (C)	**5.** (A)	**6.** (D)
7. (A)	**8.** (C)	**9.** (D)	**10.** (D)	**11.** (A)	**12.** (C)
13. (A)	**14.** (C)	**15.** (A)	**16.** (B)	**17.** (C)	**18.** (B)
19. (B)	**20.** (B)				

1. (D)

해석 Danzig Office Supplies는 국내 구매자들에 의한 대량 구매 시 현금 결제를 선호한다.

해설 빈칸은 동사 자리이고, 주어인 Danzig Office Supplies는 회사명이므로 형태는 복수형이지만 단수 취급한다. 따라서 단수 동사인 (D) prefers가 정답이다.

어휘 prefer 선호하다, 좋아하다 cash 현금 payment 지불, 결제 domestic 국내의

2. (D)

해석 많은 기술 회사들은 사람들이 대학을 졸업한 후 봄에 신입 사원들을 채용한다.

해설 빈칸은 복수 명사인 Many technology companies를 주어로 하는 동사 자리이므로 복수 동사인 (D) hire가 정답이다.

어휘 technology 기술 hire 채용하다 graduate from ~을 졸업하다

3. (C)

해석 Daylight Media는 인터넷으로 뉴스 프로그램을 방송할 것이며 텔레비전 방송도 고려할 것이다.

해설 주어인 Daylight Media는 단수 명사인데 등위 접속사 and 뒤의 동사가 단수 동사인 considers가 아니라 동사원형인 consider이므로, 빈칸에 들어가는 첫 번째 동사와 consider는 모두 조동사에 연결되어 동사원형으로 제시된다는 것을 파악할 수 있다. 따라서 (C) will broadcast가 정답이다.

어휘 broadcast 방송하다 consider 고려하다 as well 또한, ~도

4. (C)
해석 Eagle Builders가 제출한 입찰 서류는 시 정부에 의해 작성된 요건들을 충족시킨다.

해설 The bid는 주어이고 과거분사구인 submitted by Eagle Builders의 수식을 받고 있다. 따라서 빈칸은 동사 자리이므로 분사 (B)와 to부정사 (D)를 소거할 수 있다. 주어는 단수 명사이므로 단수 동사인 (C) fulfills가 정답이다.

어휘 bid 입찰(가) submit 제출하다 fulfill 충족하다 requirement 요건, 필요 조건 list 리스트를 작성하다

5. (A)
해석 그 프로젝트에 대한 작업은 David Simpson이 일을 마치는 즉시 완료될 것이다.

해설 as 이하는 시간 부사절로서, 시간 부사절에서는 미래 시제 대신 현재 시제를 쓰므로 (A) finishes가 정답이다.

어휘 complete 완료하다, 끝마치다

6. (D)
해석 Mr. Reynolds는 해외 기업들과 몇 건의 계약을 성사시킨 것으로 여겨진다.

해설 빈칸은 명사절의 동사 자리이므로 동사 형태가 아닌 분사 (A)와 to부정사 (B)를 소거할 수 있다. 빈칸 뒤에 목적어인 several contracts가 있으므로 능동태인 (D) has negotiated가 정답이다.

어휘 negotiate 협상하다, 성사시키다 contract 계약(서) corporation 기업, 회사

7. (A)
해석 그 가게의 영업 시간은 계절에 따라 일년 내내 다르다.

해설 주어는 복수 명사인 hours이므로 복수 동사인 (A) differ가 정답이다. 바로 앞의 단수 명사 operation을 보고 differs를 고르지 않도록 주의해야 한다.

어휘 operation 운영 differ 다르다 throughout the year 일년 내내 depending on ~에 따라

8. (C)
해석 Star Technology의 소프트웨어는 회사가 그것을 구매한 직후에 다운로드되었다.

해설 빈칸은 The software from Star Technology를 주어로 하는 동사 자리로서 뒤에 목적어가 없으므로 수동태인 (C) was downloaded가 정답이다.

어휘 immediately after 직후에 purchase 구매하다

9. (D)
해석 계약서의 조항들이 마음에 든다면 계약서에 서명하세요.

해설 빈칸에서 the contract까지는 주절이고, if ~ to you는 부사절이다. 절에는 주어와 동사가 있어야 하는데, 주절에는 주어와 동사가 모두 보이지 않는다. 명령문은 주어 없이 동사원형만으로 절을 형성할 수 있으므로 동사원형인 (D) Sign이 정답이다.

어휘 contract 계약(서) term (계약서의) 조항 agreeable 받아들일 수 있는, 마음에 드는

10. (D)
해석 Ms. Alderson은 퇴임하는 최고경영자의 연설회에 모든 정규직 직원들이 참석할 것을 제안했다.

해설 빈칸은 명사절의 동사 자리로서, 문장의 동사가 제안, 주장, 요구, 명령을 의미하는 proposed이므로 빈칸에는 〈should+동사원형〉인 should be가 오는데, 이때 should는 생략될 수 있으므로 (D) be가 정답이다.

어휘 propose 제안하다 full-time 상근의, 정규직의 employee 직원 present 참석한 outgoing 물러나는, 퇴임하는

11. (A)
해석 오리엔테이션 무대가 준비되는 동안 수령하신 보험 서류를 작성해 주세요.

해설 접속사 while은 '~하는 동안'이라는 의미로서 어떤 일이 다른 일과 동시에 일어나는 상황을 나타낼 때 쓰인다. 따라서 과거 시제 및 현재완료 시제인 (B), (D)는 오답이다. 주절이 명령문으로서 현재 일어나는 일을 나타내고 있으므로 수동태 현재진행 시제인 (A) is being이 정답이다.

어휘 complete 완성하다, 작성하다 insurance 보험 paperwork 서류 (작업) stage 무대 set up 준비하다, 설치하다

12. (C)
해석 사무실 관리자는 신입 사원들을 수용하기 위해 더 많은 책상과 의자를 주문할 것이다.

해설 빈칸은 문장의 동사 자리이므로 동사 형태가 아닌 (B)와 (D)를 소거할 수 있고, 뒤에 목적어(more desks and chairs)가 있으므로 수동태인 (A)도 소거할 수 있다. 따라서 능동태인 (C) will be ordering이 정답이다.

어휘 accommodate 수용하다

13. (A)
해석 강한 직업 윤리를 가진 지원자들은 면접관들에게 확신을 주어 그들을 채용하게 만들 수 있다.

해설 빈칸은 동사 자리로서 앞에 조동사 can이 있으므로 동사원형인 (A) convince가 정답이다. 빈칸 뒤에 목적어인 interviewers가 있으므로 수동태인 (C)는 오답이다.

어휘 applicant 지원자 work ethic 직업 윤리 convince 확신시키다, 설득하다

14. (C)
해석 Ms. Parker에 의해 검토되기 전까지는 지방 당국에 보조금 요청서를 제출하지 마십시오.

해설 빈칸 뒤에 목적어가 없으므로 능동태인 (A), (B)를 소거할 수 있다. 접속사 until은 시간 부사절을 이끄는데, 시간과 조건의 부사절에서는 미래 시제 대신 현재 시제가 쓰이므로 (C) is reviewed가 정답이다.

어휘 submit 제출하다 grant 보조금 authority 당국, 정부 review 검토하다

15. (A)

해석 외국 제조업체들이 주문한 컴퓨터 칩의 수가 30% 감소했다.

해설 주어는 The number이고, of computer ~ manufacturers의 수식을 받고 있다. 주어가 단수 명사이므로 (A)와 (C)가 정답 후보가 되는데, 뒤에 목적어가 없으므로 수동태인 (A) has been reduced가 정답이다. 의미상으로도 외국 업체들이 컴퓨터 칩을 주문한 특정 시점부터 지금까지 30%가 줄어든 상황이므로 현재완료 시제가 적절하다. 주어가 복수 명사인 computer chips가 아니라는 점에 주의해야 한다.

어휘 manufacturer 제조업자, 제조업체 reduce 줄이다

16. (B)

해석 회사의 선임 과학자인 Dr. Morelli는 의학 연구원들로 이루어진 큰 팀을 감독한다.

해설 Dr. Morelli는 주어, the company's head scientist는 주어를 수식하는 동격어구, 그리고 빈칸은 목적어를 취하는 동사 자리이다. 따라서 (B) supervises가 정답이다.

어휘 supervise 감독하다 researcher 연구원

17. (C)

해석 예상 참석자들 중 몇 명이 일정이 맞지 않아 회의에 참석할 수 없어서 회의가 취소되었다.

해설 빈칸은 주절의 동사 자리이고 뒤에 목적어가 없으므로 수동태가 와야 한다. 따라서 (C) was canceled가 정답이다.

어휘 expected 예상되는 attendee 참석자 due to ~로 인해 conflicting schedule 중복되는 일정

18. (B)

해석 사용 설명서는 기기를 설치하는 정확한 방법을 설명하고 있으므로 반드시 그것을 확인하세요.

해설 부사절을 이끄는 접속사 because 뒤에 주어와 동사가 없으므로 빈칸에는 주어와 동사가 들어가야 한다. 주절의 단수 명사인 the user's manual은 단수 대명사 it으로 표현할 수 있기 때문에 동사는 단수 동사인 explains가 되므로 (B) it explains가 정답이다.

어휘 be sure to 반드시 ~하다 user's manual 사용 설명서 precise 정확한 method 방법 install 설치하다 appliance 기기

19. (B)

해석 Caldwell International은 이달 말까지 직원 7명을 싱가포르 지사로 전근시킬 것이다.

해설 미래의 시점을 나타내는 부사구인 By the end of this month가 있으므로 미래완료 시제인 (B) will have transferred가 정답이다.

어휘 transfer 전근시키다, 이동하다 branch 지사, 지점

20. (B)

해석 고객에게 지급되는 환불은 매장 지배인에 의해 처리되었을 때 유효한 것으로 간주된다.

해설 빈칸은 접속사 when이 이끄는 부사절 내에 있다. 부사절에 주어와 동사가 보이지 않는데, 선택지는 동사의 활용형으로만 구성되어 있고 빈칸 뒤에 목적어 없이 행위의 주체를 나타내는 전치사구가 있으므로 〈주어+be동사〉가 생략된 수동태라는 것을 알 수 있다. 따라서 (B) processed가 정답이다. 이 문장에서는 refunds를 가리키는 대명사 주어 they와 be동사 are가 생략되었다.

어휘 give a refund 환불해 주다 consider 여기다, 생각하다 valid 유효한 process 처리하다

UNIT 06 to부정사와 동명사

PRACTICE 본문 p.119

1. (D)	**2.** (A)	**3.** (B)	**4.** (B)	**5.** (C)	**6.** (A)
7. (D)	**8.** (D)	**9.** (A)	**10.** (B)		

1. (D)

해석 Ken Richards는 연구개발부 내에 꾸려지고 있는 신생 팀을 이끌 가장 유력한 후보다.

해설 주어는 Ken Richards, 동사는 is, 보어는 the top candidate이고, 빈칸부터 문장의 끝까지는 candidate를 수식하고 있다. 따라서 명사를 수식하는 형용사적 용법으로 쓰인 to부정사인 (D) to lead가 정답이다.

어휘 candidate 후보자 lead 이끌다, 인솔하다 form 구성하다, 형성하다 R&D 연구 개발(= research and development)

2. (A)

해석 7월에 Alps Airlines는 아시아 전역의 도시들로 취항하는 자사의 신규 노선을 홍보하기 시작할 것이다.

해설 빈칸 앞에 동사 start가 있고, 빈칸 뒤에 its newest routes가 있으므로, 빈칸에는 동사 start의 목적어가 되면서 동시에 its newest routes를 목적어로 취할 수 있는 to부정사나 동명사가 오는 것이 적절하다. 따라서 (A) promoting이 정답이다.

어휘 promote 홍보하다 route 노선, 경로

3. (B)

해석 그 회사의 최고 경영자는 직원들이 승진을 신청하는 것을 1년에 두 번 허용할 계획이다.

해설 동사 permit은 〈permit+목적어+to부정사〉의 형태로 쓰이므로, to apply와 applying 중에서 to부정사인 (B) to apply가 정답이다.

어휘 permit 허용하다 apply for ~에 지원하다 promotion 승진 twice 두 번

4. (B)

해석 Mr. Solomon은 수익성 때문에 오클랜드 지점을 폐쇄하는 것은 실수라고 생각한다고 말했다.

해설 빈칸에는 동사 considers의 목적어가 되며, 동시에 the Auckland branch를 목적어로 취하는 동명사 (B) closing이 들어가는 것이 적절하다. consider는 동명사를 목적어로 취하는 대표적인 동사이다.

어휘 state 말하다 consider 생각하다, 고려하다 branch 지점,

PART 5

지사 due to ~ 때문에 profitability 수익성

5. (C)

해석 보다 빠른 배송 시간을 보장하기 위해 그 회사는 지역의 택배사인 Mercury Delivery를 독점적으로 이용하고 있다.
(A) ~에도 불구하고 (B) ~하자마자 (C) ~하기 위해 (D) ~에 관해서는

해설 빈칸 뒤에 주어 없이 동사 guarantee가 있으므로 전치사인 In spite of와 접속사인 As soon as를 소거할 수 있다. In order to는 뒤에 동사가 오지만, With regard to는 뒤에 명사가 오므로 (C) In order to가 정답이다.

어휘 guarantee 보장하다 exclusively 독점적으로, 전용으로 courier 택배회사, 배달원

6. (A)

해석 우리의 모스크바행 비행기를 타려면 앞으로 20분 내에 공항에 도착해야 한다.

해설 〈be+to부정사〉는 예정, 의무, 가능, 의도 등의 의미를 나타낸다. 따라서 to부정사인 (A) to make가 정답이다. 다른 선택지들은 문법적으로 맞지 않다.

어휘 make a flight 비행하다

7. (D)

해석 경영진은 사무실에 에어컨을 새로 설치한 이후로 생산성이 상당히 향상되었다는 것을 알아차렸다.

해설 빈칸에는 a new air conditioner를 목적어로 취할 수 있는 품사가 와야 하므로 동명사인 (D) installing이 정답이다. since는 이처럼 접속사뿐만 아니라 전치사로도 쓰일 수 있다.

어휘 since ~ 이후로 install 설치하다 management 경영(진) notice 알아차리다 significant 상당한, 큰 improvement 향상, 개선 productivity 생산성

8. (D)

해석 Mr. Edwards는 전문 건축가를 이용하여 회사의 새로운 연구 센터가 될 곳을 설계했다.

해설 문장의 주어는 Mr. Edwards, 동사는 utilized, 목적어는 a professional architect이므로 동사 형태인 (A), (B), (C)를 소거할 수 있다. 빈칸은 관계대명사 what을 목적어로 취할 수 있는 부사적 용법의 to부정사인 (D) to design이 정답이다.

어휘 utilize 이용하다, 활용하다 architect 건축가

9. (A)

해석 마케팅 팀의 목표는 온라인에 광고를 더 많이 하는 한편 팀의 지출을 줄이는 것이다.

해설 등위 접속사 yet은 to부정사인 to advertise와 빈칸을 연결하는 역할을 하고 있으므로 빈칸에도 to부정사가 나와야 한다. 선택지에 to부정사가 없으므로 to advertise의 to에 연결되는 부정사인 (A) reduce를 정답으로 고를 수 있다.

어휘 goal 목표 advertise online 온라인으로 광고하다 yet 그러나, 하지만 reduce 줄이다 expenditure 지출

10. (B)

해석 지난 5년 동안, Amanda Watson의 신분은 매장의 바닥을 청소하는 것에서 매장을 소유하는 것으로 바뀌었다.

해설 〈go from A to B〉의 문장 구조로서 A와 B의 품사가 동일해야 한다. A에 해당하는 sweeping이 동명사이므로 빈칸에도 동명사인 (B) owning이 와야 한다.

어휘 sweep (바닥을) 쓸다 own 소유하다, 가지다

UNIT 07 분사

PRACTICE 본문 p.121

1. (A) **2.** (C) **3.** (A) **4.** (B) **5.** (C) **6.** (B)
7. (B) **8.** (D) **9.** (D) **10.** (B)

1. (A)

해석 Ms. Long은 팀장이 제출한 수정된 경과 보고서를 검토했다.

해설 빈칸은 progress report를 수식하는 분사가 올 수 있다. 사물인 report는 스스로 수정할 수 있는 것이 아니라 수정되는 대상이므로 과거분사인 (A) revised가 정답이다.

어휘 revise 수정하다 progress 진척, 진행 submit 제출하다

2. (C)

해석 전문 회계원들의 사용이 확장 중인 업체들에게 적극 권장된다.

해설 명사 expansion은 businesses와 함께 복합 명사를 이루지 못하므로 (A), (B)를 소거한다. 빈칸 뒤의 businesses(업체들)를 수식할 수 있는 것은 형용사나 분사이므로 expanding과 expanded가 가능한데, 이미 확장한 업체가 아니라 확장 중인 업체가 전문 회계원을 사용한다는 문맥이 어울리므로 (C) expanding이 정답이다.

어휘 accountant 회계원, 회계사 highly 매우 recommend 추천하다

3. (A)

해석 연기된 회의는 상호간에 편리한 시간으로 일정이 재조정되어야 한다.

해설 문장의 동사는 should be rescheduled이므로 동사 형태인 (B)와 (C)를 소거할 수 있다. Postponing을 빈칸에 넣으면 meetings를 목적어로 취하는 동명사가 되어 '회의를 연기하는 것'이라는 의미가 되므로 뒤에 이어지는 내용과 맞지 않는다. '연기된 회의'라는 의미가 되어야 하므로 과거분사인 (A) Postponed가 정답이다.

어휘 postpone 연기하다 reschedule 일정을 다시 잡다 mutually 상호간에 convenient 편리한

4. (B)

해석 제품에 불만이 있는 고객은 누구나 구매 후 7일 이내에 그것을 반품할 권리가 있다.

해설 주어는 Any customer, 동사는 is이고 빈칸부터 product까지 주어를 수식한다. 따라서 동사 형태인 (A), (C)를 소거할 수 있다. 고객은 제품을 능동적으로 불만족시키는 것이 아니라 제품으로

인해 수동적으로 불만족을 당하는 사람이므로 과거분사인 (B) displeased가 정답이다.

어휘 displeased 화난, 불만스러운 be entitled to ~할 자격이 있다 purchase 구매

5. (C)

해석 Eric Murphy는 여행보다는 휴식을 선호했기 때문에 휴가 기간 내내 자신의 집에 머물렀다.

해설 빈칸 앞에 주어가 없으므로 동사 형태인 (A), (B), (D)를 소거할 수 있다. 빈칸은 접속사와 주어가 생략된 분사구문으로서 분사가 들어갈 수 있으므로 (C) preferring이 정답이다. 풀어 쓰면 because[since] he preferred가 된다.

어휘 remain 남다, 계속 ~이다 entire 전체의, 모든 prefer 좋아하다, 선호하다 rest 휴식

6. (B)

해석 Mr. Roberts는 청중들과 나누고 싶은 몇 가지 준비된 발언이 있다.

해설 빈칸 앞에 동사 has가 있으므로 동사 형태인 (D)를 소거할 수 있고, 의미상 remarks와 복합 명사를 형성하지 못하므로 명사인 (C)도 소거할 수 있다. '준비하는 발언'이 아니라 '준비된 발언'이 의미상 적절하므로 과거분사인 (B) prepared가 정답이다.

어휘 remark 발언; 발언하다 share with ~와 공유하다, 나누다 audience 청중, 관객

7. (B)

해석 전기톱을 제대로 사용하려면 사용 설명서에 포함된 설명을 읽어야 합니다.

해설 빈칸부터 manual까지는 the instructions를 수식한다. 따라서 명사를 뒤에서 수식할 수 있는 분사 형태인 (B) included가 정답이다. 빈칸 앞에 〈관계사+be동사〉인 which[that] are가 생략된 형태라고 볼 수 있다. 빈칸 뒤에 목적어가 없으므로 to부정사인 (D)는 오답이다.

어휘 electric saw 전기톱 properly 제대로 instruction 설명, 지시 include 포함하다 manual 사용 설명서, 매뉴얼

8. (D)

해석 곧 있을 회계 워크숍에 참석하기를 희망하는 모든 직원은 Ms. Taylor와 이야기해야 합니다.

해설 주어는 Any employees, 동사는 must speak이고, 빈칸부터 accounting까지는 주어를 수식하고 있다. 따라서 명사를 뒤에서 수식할 수 있는 분사가 올 수 있다. hoped와 hoping 중에서, 사람인 employees는 능동적으로 희망할 수 있으므로 현재분사인 (D) hoping이 정답이다.

어휘 upcoming 다가오는, 곧 있을 accounting 회계

9. (D)

해석 새로운 키오스크들은 줄을 서는 데 소비되는 시간을 크게 줄일 것으로 기대된다.

해설 spend는 '돈/시간 등을 쓰다'라는 뜻의 타동사이다. 이 문장에서는 spend의 목적어에 해당하는 the amount of time이 spend의 수식을 받아 '쓰인 시간'이라는 수동의 의미가 되므로 과거분사인 spent가 정답이다.

어휘 kiosk 키오스크, (주문용) 단말기 expect 기대하다, 예상하다 significantly 상당히 reduce 줄이다

10. (B)

해석 이번주 토요일을 시작으로 Hamilton 백화점은 매장 내 모든 제품을 할인 판매한다.

해설 'Starting/Beginning+시간'은 주로 문두에서 '(언제)를 시작으로'라는 뜻의 관용적 분사구로 쓰이며, 일의 시작 시점을 강조하는 부사구 역할을 한다.

어휘 discount 할인 item 물품, 품목

UNIT 08 전치사

PRACTICE 본문 p.124

1. (A)	**2.** (C)	**3.** (D)	**4.** (A)	**5.** (A)	**6.** (B)
7. (D)	**8.** (B)	**9.** (A)	**10.** (B)	**11.** (A)	**12.** (A)
13. (D)	**14.** (B)	**15.** (C)	**16.** (B)	**17.** (A)	**18.** (A)
19. (C)	**20.** (B)				

1. (A)

해석 모든 인턴사원들은 오리엔테이션 행사를 위해 월요일 오전 7시 30분까지 도착해야 합니다.

(A) ~을 위해, ~에 (B) ~와 함께 (C) ~로서 (D) ~ 위에

어휘 orientation 오리엔테이션 event 행사

2. (C)

해석 Blaine Toys가 온라인으로 판매한 제품의 모든 반품은 배송 후 2주 이내에 이루어져야 한다.

(A) ~ 전에 (B) ~에 대한, ~의 위에 (C) ~의 (D) ~부터

어휘 make a return 반납하다, 반품하다

3. (D)

해석 Melissa Standish는 회사의 회계사로 근무할 뿐만 아니라 사무실장으로도 고용되어 있다.

(A) 결과적으로 (B) ~로 인해 (C) ~에 관해서는 (D) ~일 뿐만 아니라

어휘 serve 근무하다 firm 회사 accountant 회계사, 회계원

4. (A)

해석 카운티 박람회에서 매번 공연이 끝난 후에 자원봉사자로 구성된 팀이 극장 전체를 청소한다.

(A) ~ 후에 (B) ~을 통해 (C) ~ 둘레에 (D) ~ 이내에

어휘 performance 공연 county (행정 구역) 카운티 fair 박람회 volunteer 자원봉사자 entire 전체의 theater 극장

5. (A)

해석 뉴스 속보를 정확하게 보도함으로써, Melinda Carter는 언론인으로서의 자신의 명성을 높일 수 있었다.

(A) ~을 함으로써 (B) ~의 위에 (C) ~와 함께 (D) ~에 대해

PART 5

어휘 breaking news 뉴스 속보 accurately 정확하게 reputation 명성

6. (B)
해석 Hudson Mining은 3개월 전에 금을 발견한 이후로 주식 가치가 두 배로 뛰었다.
(A) ~ 전에 (B) ~ 이후로 (C) ~하지 않는 한 (D) 그러므로
어휘 value 가치 stock 주식 double 두 배가 되다

7. (D)
해석 Hardaway Textiles 영업부에 있는 많은 사람들 중에서 Ms. Montague가 가장 생산성이 좋다.
(A) ~ 안으로 (B) ~ 위에 (C) ~을 위해 (D) ~ 중에
어휘 salesforce 판매 인력, 판매부 productive 생산적인

8. (B)
해석 업계의 몇몇 전문가들의 조언으로 Mr. Harrison은 자기 자신의 사업을 시작할 수 있었다.
(A) ~을 위해 (B) ~을 가지고 (C) ~을 따라 (D) ~ 위에
어휘 expert 전문가 industry 산업, 업계

9. (A)
해석 유럽에서 살고 싶다는 열망 때문에, Ms. Hooper는 그녀의 회사의 밀라노 사무실로 전근을 자원했다.
(A) ~ 때문에 (B) ~ 동안 (C) 결과적으로 (D) ~도
어휘 volunteer 자원하다, 지원하다 transfer 전근

10. (B)
해석 Mr. Abernathy는 자신의 교육 수준을 발전시키는 것에 대한 관심 때문에 평일 밤에 대학원을 다닐 것이다.
(A) ~을 위해 (B) ~ 때문에 (C) ~ 이후로 (D) ~에 관해
어휘 graduate school 대학원 weeknight 평일 밤 further 발전시키다

11. (A)
해석 정부 규정에 따르면, 모든 사람은 부지 내에서 항상 안전모를 착용해야 한다.
(A) ~에 따르면 (B) ~ 대신에 (C) 그 결과로 (D) 하지만
어휘 regulation 규정 hard hat 안전모 on the premises 부지 내에서, 구내에서 at all times 항상

12. (A)
해석 Mr. Dearborn은 바쁜 휴가철을 앞두고 그의 자리에서 물러났다.
(A) ~에 앞서, 먼저 (B) ~을 제외하고 (C) ~에 따라서 (D) ~ 대신에
어휘 resign 사임하다, 물러나다

13. (D)
해석 면접이 예정된 5명의 사람들은 78명의 지원자들 중에서 선정되었다.
(A) ~와 함께 (B) ~을 위해 (C) 밖으로 (D) ~으로부터, ~ 중에서
어휘 individual 사람, 개인 scheduled 예정된 select 선정하다 pool 이용 가능 인력

14. (B)
해석 Nelson Technology는 직원들과 그들의 가족들에게 지역 문화 행사의 티켓을 제공하는 전통을 가지고 있다.
해설 provide A with B(A에게 B를 제공하다) 형태의 구문이므로 (B) with가 정답이다.
어휘 tradition 전통 provide 주다, 제공하다 local 지역의

15. (C)
해석 Paladin Shoes는 신제품 운동화의 인기로 인해 해당 운동화의 생산을 늘렸다.
(A) 모든 것 (B) 아마도 (C) ~로 인해 (D) 총
어휘 popularity 인기 sneakers 고무창 운동화

16. (B)
해석 Kathy Ibsen은 앞으로 몇 달 안에 자신의 부서에서 차장으로 임명될 것으로 기대하고 있다.
(A) ~ 이후로 (B) ~ 내에 (C) 대략 (D) ~에
어휘 expect 기대하다, 예상하다 name 지명하다

17. (A)
해석 모든 사람들은 사무실을 떠나기 전에 업무 공간을 청소하고 컴퓨터를 꺼야 한다.
(A) ~ 전에 (B) ~까지 (C) ~ 위에 (D) ~을 넘어
어휘 workspace 업무 공간 turn off 끄다 depart 떠나다

18. (A)
해석 Marconi Textiles는 면과 실크를 비롯한 다양한 직물로 여성용 의류를 제조한다.
(A) ~을 포함하여 (B) 그 동안에 (C) ~하자마자 (D) 도처에
어휘 manufacture 제조하다 a variety of 다양한 fabric 직물 cotton 면

19. (C)
해석 성과급에 관한 결정은 월말까지 내려질 예정이다.
(A) ~와 함께 (B) ~ 중에 (C) ~에 관한 (D) ~에
어휘 make a decision 결정을 내리다 performance bonus 성과급

20. (B)
해석 Mr. Flint는 임시직 직원을 고용하는 대신 자신의 팀원들에게 3월에 초과 근무를 요청했다.
(A) 명백히 (B) ~하기보다는, ~ 대신에 (C) ~에 따르면 (D) ~ 위에
어휘 take on 고용하다 temporary 임시의 staff 직원 work overtime 야근하다

UNIT 09 접속사

PRACTICE 본문 p.128

1. (B)	**2.** (A)	**3.** (B)	**4.** (D)	**5.** (C)	**6.** (A)
7. (A)	**8.** (B)	**9.** (D)	**10.** (C)	**11.** (B)	**12.** (A)
13. (B)	**14.** (D)	**15.** (D)	**16.** (B)	**17.** (A)	**18.** (A)
19. (B)	**20.** (B)				

1. (B)
해석 직원들은 궂은 날씨에는 재택 근무를 하거나 대중교통을 이용해 출근하는 것을 고려해야 한다.
(A) 그리고 (C) ~이기 때문에, ~한 이후로 (D) ~이라면
해설 빈칸 앞에 동명사를 목적어로 취하는 동사 consider가 있고, 뒤에 동명사 working과 taking이 접속사 or로 연결되어 있으므로 〈either A or B〉의 구조라는 것을 알 수 있다. 따라서 상관 접속사인 (B) either가 정답이다.
어휘 inclement weather 악천후, 궂은 날씨 work from home 재택 근무를 하다 public transportation 대중교통

2. (A)
해석 Jasmine Cartier는 자신의 발표 기술을 연마해서 지금은 훌륭한 대중 연설가이다.
(A) 그리고 (B) ~을 위해 (C) 하지만 (D) 또는
해설 주어는 Jasmine Cartier이고, worked와 is라는 두 개의 동사가 주어에 연결된 문장 형태이다. 따라서 절과 절을 연결할 수 있는 등위 접속사가 와야 한다. and와 or가 정답 후보가 되는데, 문맥상 (A) and가 정답이다.
어휘 work on ~에 노력을 기울이다 presentation 발표 accomplished 기량이 뛰어난

3. (B)
해석 Mr. Hamilton은 7월의 절반을 휴가로 보냈음에도 불구하고, 그의 팀에서 가장 많은 수치의 판매량을 기록했다.
(A) ~하기 위해서 (B) 비록 ~이지만 (C) 더욱이 (D) ~에도 불구하고
해설 빈칸 뒤에 주어(Mr. Hamilton)와 동사(spent)가 있으므로 접속사가 아닌 (C)와 (D)를 소거할 수 있다. 휴가를 보내서 결과적으로 업무 시간이 많지 않았다는 부사절의 내용과 최고의 매출을 기록했다는 주절의 내용이 상충되므로 양보의 부사절 접속사인 (B) Although가 적절하다.
어휘 on vacation 휴가로 sales 판매량, 매출액

4. (D)
해석 대출 시스템이 전산화된 이후로 더 많은 도서관 책들이 제때에 반납되고 있다.
(A) ~ 주위에 (B) 명백히 (C) 그래서 (D) ~한 이후로; ~이기 때문에
해설 빈칸은 두 개의 절을 연결하고 있으므로 접속사가 와야 한다. 따라서 so와 since가 정답 후보가 된다. 빈칸이 있는 부사절이 '~한 이후로'라는 의미이므로 시간을 나타내는 부사절 접속사인 (D) since가 정답이다.
어휘 on time 제시간에, 제때 checkout (도서) 대출 computerize 전산화하다

5. (C)
해석 Emerson 사는 신제품을 출시할 때마다 그 제품을 대대적으로 광고한다.
(A) ~이므로 (B) ~ 동안 (C) ~할 때마다 (D) 그러한
해설 빈칸 뒤에 주어(Emerson Inc.), 동사(releases)가 있으므로 빈칸은 접속사 자리이다. 따라서 Because와 Whenever가 정답 후보가 되는데, 문맥상 제품을 출시하면 언제나 대대적으로 광고한다는 의미가 자연스러우므로 (C) Whenever가 정답이다.
어휘 release 출시하다 market 광고하다 heavily 아주 많이, 심하게

6. (A)
해석 특가 혜택을 받을 수 있도록 Aubrey's Bookstore에서 회원 가입을 하는 것을 기억하세요.
(A) 그래서, 그 결과로 (B) ~을 위해 (C) 또는 (D) 여전히
해설 빈칸 뒤에 주어(you)와 동사(can be)가 있으므로 접속사가 들어가야 한다. 따라서 접속사가 아닌 (B)와 (D)를 소거한다. 빈칸 앞의 절과 뒤의 절은 의미상 인과 관계를 형성하므로 (A) so가 정답이다.
어휘 sign up for ~을 신청하다 membership 회원 (자격) be eligible for ~할 자격이 있다 special offer 특가품, 특가 판매

7. (A)
해석 유명 요리사인 Andrew Hutchins는 신선한 재료가 사용될 때 요리가 훨씬 더 맛이 좋다고 말한다.
(A) ~할 때 (B) ~에도 불구하고 (C) ~을 위해 (D) 어떻게
해설 빈칸은 명사절 내에서 부사절을 이끄는 역할을 하고 있다. 따라서 부사절 접속사인 (A) when이 정답이다.
어휘 famed 저명한 chef 요리사 state 말하다 ingredient 재료 taste 맛이 나다

8. (B)
해석 이사회는 캐나다의 사업 환경이 그곳에 새로운 시설을 개장하기에 이상적인지 여부를 결정해야 한다.
(A) 주위에 (B) ~인지 아닌지 (C) 반면에 (D) 비록 ~이지만
해설 빈칸에는 동사 determine의 목적어가 되는 명사절을 이끄는 접속사가 들어가야 하므로 명사절 접속사 (B) whether가 정답이다.
어휘 board of directors 이사회 climate 기후; 분위기, 풍조 ideal 이상적인 facility 시설

9. (D)
해석 Ms. Grayson은 그녀가 속한 단체의 다른 회원들이 비행기를 타고 그곳에 가기로 선택했음에도 불구하고 세인트루이스에 있는 세미나에 차를 몰고 갔다.
(A) ~에도 불구하고 (B) ~와 같은 (C) ~뿐만 아니라 (D) ~에도 불구하고
해설 빈칸은 앞의 절과 뒤의 절을 연결하고 있으므로 접속사가 들어가야 한다. 따라서 (D) even though가 정답이다. 다른 선택지들

PART 5

은 전치사이다.

어휘 drive 운전하다 fly 비행기를 타다

10. (C)

해석 고객이 빠른 배송을 명시하지 않는 한, 모든 주문품은 주문을 받은 후 하루 후에 우편으로 발송됩니다.
(A) ~라는 것을 제외하면 (B) ~이므로 (C) ~하지 않는 한 (D) ~조차

해설 빈칸은 접속사 자리이며, 빈칸이 있는 부사절은 의미상 조건을 나타내므로 (C) Unless가 정답이다.

어휘 specify 명시하다, 명확히 말하다 express delivery 속달, 빠른 배송 order 주문(품) mail 우편으로 보내다

11. (B)

해석 Kevin Watts는 상당한 임금 인상을 받았기 때문에 Nottingham Securities에 남기로 결정했다.
(A) 그 결과로 (B) ~이기 때문에 (C) ~뿐만 아니라 (D) 혹은

해설 빈칸 앞뒤로 주어와 동사가 갖추어진 절이 있고, 두 절이 의미상 인과 관계를 형성하므로 접속사인 (B) because가 정답이다.

어휘 substantial 상당한 pay raise 임금 인상

12. (A)

해석 Jupiter Groceries의 최초 구매자들은 무료 배송을 받거나 추가 비용 없이 샘플 음식 플래터를 요청할 수 있다.

해설 조동사 can 뒤에 receive와 request라는 두 개의 동사가 병렬 연결되어 있으므로, 빈칸에는 두 개의 동사구를 대등하게 연결하는 등위 접속사가 들어가야 한다. 따라서 or와 so가 정답 후보가 된다. 두 개의 절이 문맥상 취사 선택의 의미를 가지고 있으므로 (A) or가 정답이다.

어휘 platter (음식을 차려내는) 접시 extra cost 추가 비용

13. (B)

해석 Ms. Harrison은 Dubois Bank의 일자리를 수락하기 전에 리스본에 있는 학교에서 금융을 공부했다.
(A) 어떻게 (B) ~ 전에 (C) 어느 것 (D) 꽤, 차라리

해설 빈칸 뒤에 완전한 절이 이어지므로 빈칸은 접속사 자리이다. 따라서 (B) Before가 정답이다. 다른 선택지들은 부사 또는 대명사나 한정사로 쓰이므로 오답이다.

어휘 accept 받아들이다, 수락하다 position 일자리, 직위 finance 금융, 재무

14. (D)

해석 Raymond Mercer는 자신의 식당을 운영하고 있기 때문에, 매일 재료를 조달할 책임이 있다.
(A) 마치 ~인 것처럼 (B) 게다가 (C) ~라는 것 (D) ~이므로

해설 빈칸 뒤에 절이 이어지므로 빈칸은 접속사 자리이고, 두 개의 절이 의미상 인과 관계를 형성하므로 (D) Now that이 정답이다.

어휘 run 운영하다, 경영하다 acquire 획득하다, 취득하다 ingredient 재료

15. (D)

해석 연례 주주총회 장소가 정해지면 발표가 있을 것이다.
(A) ~하기 위하여 (B) ~의 일자로 (C) 대신에 (D) 일단 ~하면

해설 빈칸은 접속사 자리이므로 In order that과 Once가 정답 후보가 된다. 문맥상 시간 순서를 나타내므로 '일단 ~하면'이라는 의미의 (D) Once가 정답이다.

어휘 location 장소 annual 연례의 shareholder 주주 determine 결정하다 make an announcement 발표하다

16. (B)

해석 금리가 상승하고 있기 때문에, 신규 주택에 대한 담보 대출을 받는 사람들이 감소하고 있다.
(A) ~라는 것을 제외하면 (B) ~이므로 (C) 하지만 (D) 왜

해설 빈칸은 접속사 자리이고 의미상 두 개의 절이 인과 관계를 형성하므로 (B) Since가 정답이다.

어휘 interest rate 이자율 mortgage 주택 담보 대출

17. (A)

해석 퇴근 때까지 Stella Reynolds와 Jeffery Harper는 그 누구도 Edmund 프로젝트에 대한 제안서를 제출하지 않았다.

해설 〈neither A nor B〉의 문장 구조이므로 (A) nor가 정답이다.

어휘 submit 제출하다 proposal 제안(서)

18. (A)

해석 당사의 기사가 수리 방법을 알려드릴 수 있도록 새 기기의 오작동에 대해 정확하게 설명해 주십시오.
(A) ~하도록 (B) ~한 이후로; ~이기 때문에 (D) 만약 ~라면

해설 빈칸은 접속사 자리이며, 앞뒤 절이 의미상 인과 관계를 이루므로 (A) so that이 정답이다.

어휘 malfunction 오작동, 고장 precisely 정확하게 device 기기, 장치 technician 기술자, 기사

19. (B)

해석 Harris Manufacturing은 멤피스에 있는 자사 고객에게 제품을 배달했지만, 비용 전액 지불은 2주가 지나고 나서야 이루어졌다.
(A) ~하기 위하여 (B) ~인데 반하여 (C) 그렇게 함으로써 (D) 아마

해설 빈칸 뒤에 주어, 동사가 있는 완전한 문장이 있으므로 빈칸은 접속사 자리이고, 따라서 (B) While이 정답이다. (A)는 전치사, (C)와 (D)는 부사이므로 오답이다.

어휘 client 고객 make a payment 지불하다 full payment 완납

20. (B)

해석 누구나 회의 중에 발언하는 것은 환영하지만, 발언들이 긍정적으로 기여할 수 있는 경우에만 그렇다.
(A) ~할 때 (B) ~해야만, ~하는 경우에 한해 (C) 그렇기는 하지만 (D) ~보다는

해설 빈칸은 접속사가 들어갈 자리이고, 의미상 빈칸이 속한 절은 조건을 나타내므로 (B) only if가 정답이다.

어휘 positive 긍정적인 contribute 기여하다

UNIT 10 관계사

PRACTICE 본문 p.131

1. (C) **2.** (C) **3.** (B) **4.** (C) **5.** (B) **6.** (C)
7. (D) **8.** (A) **9.** (A) **10.** (B)

1. (C)

해석 Mr. Cross는 누구든지 이번 달에 신규 고객을 가장 많이 모집하는 사람은 현금 보너스를 받을 것이라고 말했다.

해설 빈칸은 명사절의 주어 자리이므로 주격 관계사가 올 수 있다. '~하는 사람은 누구든지'라는 의미이므로 주어 역할을 할 수 있는 복합관계사인 (C) whoever가 정답이다.

어휘 state 말하다, 진술하다 recruit 모집하다 cash 현금

2. (C)

해석 Nantucket Construction은 Peter Carroll이 소유하고 있는데, 그는 어릴 적부터 그 지역에서 살고 있다.

해설 빈칸은 주어 자리이며 선행사가 사람인 Peter Carroll이므로 사람을 나타내는 주격 관계대명사 (C) who가 정답이다.

어휘 own 소유하다 childhood 어린 시절

3. (B)

해석 제시간에 물품을 배달하는 물류 회사는 전국 대부분 지역에서 수요가 많다.

해설 빈칸 앞에 주어인 Logistics companies가 있고 뒤에 동사 deliver가 있으므로 빈칸은 Logistics companies를 선행사로 하는 주격 관계사가 들어갈 수 있다. 따라서 (B) that이 정답이다.

어휘 logistics 물류 goods 물품, 상품 on time 제시간에, 제때 be in high demand 수요가 많다

4. (C)

해석 Jessica Yeltsin은 지역의 노숙 문제를 끝내기 위해 그녀가 이용하려고 시도했던 자선 재단을 설립했다.

해설 빈칸 뒤에 주어(she), 동사구(attempted to use)가 있는데 use의 목적어가 보이지 않으므로 빈칸은 a charitable foundation을 선행사로 하는 목적격 관계사가 들어가야 한다. 따라서 (C) that이 정답이다. (B) what은 선행사를 포함하는 관계사여서 선행사인 a charitable foundation이 없어야 하므로 오답이다.

어휘 establish 설립하다 charitable 자선의 foundation 재단 attempt 시도하다 homeless 홈리스의, 노숙의 crisis 위기

5. (B)

해석 1월에 신규 투자를 하는 Jacobson Financial의 고객들은 무료 상담을 받을 자격이 있다.

해설 빈칸은 주어인 clients와 동사 make 사이에 있으므로 clients를 선행사로 하는 주격 관계대명사 (B) who가 적절하다.

어휘 make an investment 투자하다 eligible for ~할 자격이 있는 consultation 상담

6. (C)

해석 학회는 Piedmont Hotel에서 열릴 텐데, 그곳에는 대규모 인원을 지원할 수 있는 현대적인 시설이 있다.

해설 빈칸 앞뒤로 두 개의 절이 나열되었으므로 빈칸에는 접속사나 접속사 역할을 하는 품사가 들어가야 한다. 접속사 except는 문맥상 맞지 않고, Piedmont Hotel이라는 장소를 선행사로 하는 관계부사 (C) where가 정답이다.

어휘 conference 회의, 학회 facility 시설 capable of ~할 수 있는

7. (D)

해석 정부는 건물 붕괴에 대한 조사를 지시했는데, 그 원인을 규명하는 데는 다소 시간이 걸릴 것이다.

해설 빈칸은 사물인 building collapse를 선행사로 하는 주격 관계사가 들어갈 수 있다. 따라서 (D) which가 정답이다. 이처럼 콤마 뒤의 〈명사/대명사+전치사+관계대명사〉의 문장 구조는 앞에 나온 절의 내용을 부연하며, 접속사가 있는 문장으로 바꾸면 'and the cause of it ~'이 된다.

어휘 investigation 조사 collapse 붕괴 cause 원인, 이유 require 필요로 하다

8. (A)

해석 Ms. Matthews는 Ryan Varnum을 고용하기로 결정했는데, 회사법 분야에서 그의 전문성은 잘 알려져 있었다.

해설 빈칸 앞뒤의 Ryan Varnum과 expertise는 'Ryan Varnum의 전문성'이라는 소유 관계가 성립되므로 소유격 관계대명사인 (A) whose가 정답이다.

어휘 expertise 전문성 field 분야 corporate 기업의

9. (A)

해석 오리엔테이션 연사는 Hollmann International에서 성공하기 위해서는 무엇이 필요한지 설명했다.

해설 빈칸에는 동사 explained의 목적어이자 명사절 내의 동사 takes의 목적어가 되는 관계사가 와야 한다. 빈칸 앞에 선행사가 없으므로 선행사를 포함하는 관계사인 (A) what이 정답이다.

10. (B)

해석 Mr. Acuna는 교육 과정을 가르치는데, 교육 과정에서 참가자들은 회사의 컴퓨터 시스템 사용법을 배운다.

해설 빈칸 뒤에 절이 이어지므로 (C)와 (D)를 소거할 수 있다. 빈칸 뒤에 주어인 participants가 있으므로 주격 관계사인 (A) who도 소거할 수 있다. 이 문장은 "Mr. Acuna teaches a training course. Participants learn to use the firm's computer system in it."이라는 두 개의 문장에서 〈전치사+대명사〉인 in it을 〈전치사+관계사〉인 in which로 바꿔 하나의 문장으로 만든 것이다. 따라서 (B) in which가 정답이다. 이 문장의 in which는 관계부사 where로 바꿔 쓸 수 있다는 것도 알아 두자.

어휘 participant 참가자 firm 회사

UNIT 11 고득점 획득을 위한 명사 어휘

PRACTICE 본문 p.134

1. (D)	**2.** (D)	**3.** (A)	**4.** (A)	**5.** (D)	**6.** (B)
7. (A)	**8.** (A)	**9.** (B)	**10.** (D)	**11.** (B)	**12.** (C)
13. (A)	**14.** (D)	**15.** (A)	**16.** (A)	**17.** (B)	**18.** (C)
19. (B)	**20.** (B)				

1. (D)
해석 몇몇 지역 회사들은 직원들이 사무실에 물리적으로 실재하는 것을 선호하기 때문에 재택 근무를 허용하지 않는다.
(A) 모습; 출현 (B) 방법 (C) 업무 (D) 존재, 있음
해설 재택 근무는 사무실이 아닌 집에서 일하는 것이고, 회사가 재택 근무를 반대한다는 것은 직원들이 사무실에 있기를 원한다는 의미이므로 '존재, 있음'이라는 의미의 (D) presence가 정답이다.
어휘 permit 허용하다 telecommuting 재택 근무 physical 물리적인

2. (D)
해석 오랜 고객들로 이루어진 평가단이 슈퍼마켓의 최신 제품들에 대한 평가를 담당했다.
(A) 시스템 (B) 버전, 판 (C) 설문 조사 (D) 패널, 평가단
어휘 long-term 장기의 rate 평가하다

3. (A)
해석 그 회사가 보유한 차량에 가장 최근에 추가된 것은 Cobra Motors에서 만든 SUV이다.
(A) 추가 (B) 장치 (C) 물체; 목적 (D) 프로그램
해설 '회사가 보유한 모든 차량에 최근에 -------은 SUV 차량'이라는 의미이므로 '추가된 것'이라는 의미의 (A) addition이 정답이다. addition은 회사에 새로 합류한 사원 등을 가리킬 때도 쓰이는 표현이다.
어휘 fleet 한 기관이 소유한 모든 보유 차량 vehicle 차량

4. (A)
해석 직원 휴게실을 재단장하는 것은 현 시점에서는 우선순위가 낮은 것으로 여겨진다.
(A) 우선순위 (B) 모험적 사업, 벤처 기업 (C) 시도 (D) 결과
어휘 redecorate 재단장하다 lounge 휴게실, 라운지 consider 고려하다, 여기다

5. (D)
해석 Mr. Peterson은 잔디 깎는 기계의 내구성 덕분에 그것을 산 이후로 한 번도 수리할 필요가 없었다.
(A) 측정 (B) 다양성 (C) 고려 (D) 내구성
어휘 lawnmower 잔디 깎는 기계 once 한 번 thanks to ~ 덕분에

6. (B)
해석 관심 있는 고객들은 필요한 모든 수리를 포함하는 3년 보증에 가입할 수 있다.
(A) 서비스 (B) 보증(서) (C) 예산 (D) 약속
어휘 interested 관심 있는 acquire 얻다, 취득하다 cover 다루다, 포함시키다

7. (A)
해석 Edmund Blair는 영국에서 1년간 공부할 수 있도록 허용하는 장학금의 수혜자로 선정되었다.
(A) 받는 사람, 수취인 (B) 보상 (C) 지원자 (D) 참석자
어휘 name 지명하다, 이름을 말하다 scholarship 장학금 allow 허락하다

8. (A)
해석 Adelaide Park는 회사 모임이나 자선 기금 모금 행사와 같은 행사를 주기적으로 여는 장소다.
(A) 장소 (B) 항구 (C) 판, 호 (D) 경우
어휘 regular 정기적인, 주기적인 get-together 모임 charity 자선 fundraiser 기금 모금 행사

9. (B)
해석 그 건축가의 스타일의 주목할 만한 면은 몇 가지 특징들에 있어 자연 환경에 대한 의존이다.
(A) 디자인 (B) 측면, 양상 (C) 안도 (D) 전통
어휘 notable 주목할 만한, 두드러진 architect 건축가 reliance 의존 feature 특징, 특색

10. (D)
해석 채용 과정에서 어떤 문제라도 있으면 Ms. Bradley와 즉시 상의해야 합니다.
(A) 가능성 (B) 잘못, 단점 (C) 싼 물건 (D) 문제, 이슈
어휘 process 과정 consult 상의하다, 상담하다 at once 즉시

11. (B)
해석 한 금융 전문가는 Douglas Aerospace가 지난 몇 년간 채무를 졌기 때문에 회사의 수익성에 의문을 제기했다.
(A) 재발 (B) 수익성 (C) 발행; 문제 (D) 수락
어휘 financial 재무의 expert 전문가 be in debt 빚을 지다

12. (C)
해석 위반된 법이 없는지 확인하기 위해 다음 주에 정부 감사가 실시될 것이다.
(A) 방법 (B) 목적 (C) 감사 (D) 조사관
어휘 conduct 수행하다 confirm 확인하다, 확정하다 break a law 법을 위반하다

13. (A)
해석 Devlin 사에서 근무하는 한 가지 이점은 회사가 직원들이 재택 근무를 하는 것을 허용한다는 것이다.
(A) 이점, 혜택 (B) 변화 (C) 영향, 충격 (D) 상기시키는 것
어휘 work from home 재택 근무를 하다

14. (D)
해석 가이드 부족으로 인해 추후 공지가 있을 때까지 회사의 모든 투어가 중단된다.
(A) 인식, 자각 (B) 리셉션, 접수 (C) 공급 (D) 공고, 안내문
어휘 suspend 중단하다, 유예하다 due to ~로 인해 lack 부족 until further notice 추후 공지가 있을 때까지

15. (A)
해석 모든 고객은 주문 후 5분 이내에 주문 확인 이메일을 받게 됩니다.
(A) 확인, 확정 (B) 평가 (C) 기여 (D) 접수처
어휘 place an order 주문하다

16. (A)
해석 Mr. Hamilton은 그가 Chamberlain Group에 제출한 보조금 요청서에 몇 가지 수정을 해달라는 요청을 받았다.
(A) 수정 (B) 결정 (C) 사양 (D) 생산
어휘 make revisions to ~을 수정하다 several 몇 개의 grant 보조금 submit 제출하다

17. (B)
해석 전국적으로 발생하고 있는 배송 문제로 인해 매장의 재고 수준이 감소했다.
(A) 인원, 직원들 (B) 재고 (C) 경영 (D) 교체
어휘 level 수준 decrease 감소하다 on account of ~ 때문에 shipping 배송 nationwide 전국적으로

18. (C)
해석 부사장은 새로운 광고 캠페인에 대한 작업을 완료하는 데 필요한 대략적인 추정 시간을 요구했다.
(A) 설득 (B) 필요, 요건 (C) 추정; 견적 (D) 전략
어휘 vice president 부사장, 부회장 rough 대략적인 advertising campaign 광고 캠페인

19. (B)
해석 Ms. Scott은 항공사에 연락해서 금요일에 베를린행 심야 항공편 좌석이 있는지 문의했다.
(A) 보장, 확언 (B) 이용 가능성 (C) 애플리케이션; 지원 (D) 등장
어휘 contact 연락하다 airline 항공사 inquire 문의하다

20. (B)
해석 Denice Burns가 주도하는 기금 모금 계획은 두 달 동안 계속될 것이며 100만 달러를 모금해야 한다.
(A) 리그, 연합 (B) (새로운) 계획 (C) 긴급한 일 (D) 상징
어휘 fundraising 기금 모금 last 계속되다, 지속되다 raise (자금을) 모으다

UNIT 12 고득점 획득을 위한 형용사 어휘

PRACTICE 본문 p.138

1. (C)	**2.** (A)	**3.** (C)	**4.** (B)	**5.** (C)	**6.** (A)
7. (B)	**8.** (C)	**9.** (C)	**10.** (B)	**11.** (D)	**12.** (A)
13. (C)	**14.** (A)	**15.** (C)	**16.** (A)	**17.** (C)	**18.** (B)
19. (B)	**20.** (D)				

1. (C)
해석 〈Hampton Times〉의 Jessica Roth 기자는 Emerson Howell 주지사와 단독 인터뷰를 가졌다.
(A) 간헐적인 (B) 번갈아 생기는 (C) 독점적인, 단독의 (D) 피할 수 없는, 필수의
어휘 state 주 governor 주지사

2. (A)
해석 새로운 마케팅 소프트웨어에 대한 교육 프로그램은 의무적인 것은 아니지만, 직원들은 그것을 수강하는 것이 권고된다.
(A) 의무적인 (B) 노출된 (C) 연습된 (D) 교체된
어휘 be advised to do ~하는 것이 권고되다

3. (C)
해석 모든 고객 불만 사항은 매장 담당자들에 의해 신속한 방식으로 처리되어야 한다.
(A) 상대적인 (B) 가까운 (C) 즉각적인 (D) 다양한
어휘 complaint 불만, 민원 handle 처리하다, 다루다 manner 방식; 태도 representative 담당자

4. (B)
해석 Milton Technology의 인턴 사원들은 그들이 받는 멘토링과 병행할 수 있는 일상적인 업무를 배정받는다.
(A) 서로 겨루는 (B) 일상적인 (C) 능숙한 (D) 접근할 수 있는
어휘 assign 배정하다, 할당하다 task 과제 go along (활동을) 계속하다

5. (C)
해석 최고경영자는 연말에 실시된 고객 설문 조사의 고무적인 결과에 만족했다.
(A) 실용적인 (B) 외딴, 먼 (C) 안심시키는 (D) 외부의
어휘 survey 설문 조사 conduct 실시하다

6. (A)
해석 여름에 가장 기대되는 영화 중 하나는 Martin Lincoln이 감독한 스릴러다.
(A) 기대하던, 대망의 (B) 제안된 (C) 혁명적인 (D) 수정된
어휘 highly anticipated 몹시 기대되는 direct 감독하다

7. (B)
해석 그가 가진 방대한 연락처 목록 덕분에, Mr. Rumsfeld는 자신의 회사에 몇 명의 새로운 고객을 확보할 수 있었다.
(A) 풍부한 (B) 방대한, 광범위한 (C) 반박된 (D) 자격이 있는

어휘 thanks to ~ 덕분에 secure 확보하다, 입수하다

8. (C)

해석 Ms. Cartwright는 자신의 최근의 성과에 대한 보상으로 상당한 급여 인상을 요청했다.
(A) 자신 있는 (B) 비싼 (C) 상당한 (D) 이로운

어휘 reward 보상 performance 성과, 실적

9. (C)

해석 사무실 관리자의 주된 임무는 직원들 사이의 문제를 해결하면서 그들을 감독하는 일이 될 것이다.
(A) 자격이 있는 (B) 상대적인 (C) 주요한 (D) 유연한

어휘 supervise 감독하다 resolve 해결하다 issue 문제

10. (B)

해석 Mr. Dunlop의 담당 정비사는 그에게 그의 트럭의 오일 교환 주기가 지났다는 것을 알렸다.
(A) 걱정하는 (B) 기한이 지난 (C) 보고된 (D) 분명한

어휘 mechanic 정비공 inform 알리다, 통보하다

11. (D)

해석 시의 몇몇 지역은 금융 지구와 가까운데도 불구하고 여전히 저렴한 주택이 있다.
(A) 가능한 (B) 시기적절한 (C) 통합된 (D) 저렴한, 입수 가능한

어휘 several 몇몇의, 여러 housing 주택 despite ~에도 불구하고 financial 재무의, 금융의 district 지구, 지역

12. (A)

해석 엔지니어가 되려면 1년에 두 번 있는 자격 시험에 합격해야 한다.
(A) 자격을 주는 (B) 반복되는 (C) 기량이 뛰어난 (D) 다양한

어휘 engineer 엔지니어, 기사 twice 두 번

13. (C)

해석 Verducci Consulting의 직원들은 그들의 연간 성과에 따라 점진적인 임금 인상을 받는다.
(A) 혹독한 (B) 진보한, 선진의 (C) 서서히 증가하는 (D) 결정적인

어휘 raise (임금) 인상 depending upon ~에 따라 annual 연례의, 연간의 performance 성과, 실적

14. (A)

해석 Jackson Auction House는 잠재 구매자들에게 그들이 입찰하는 물품에 대해 경쟁력 있는 액수를 제안할 것을 요청한다.
(A) 경쟁력 있는 (B) 느긋한 (C) 선진의 (D) 매일의

어휘 auction 경매 potential 잠재적인 make an offer 제안하다, 제의하다 bid on ~에 입찰하다

15. (C)

해석 유급 휴가를 받을 자격이 있는 사람들은 상사로부터 서면 허가를 받아야 한다.
(A) 노출된 (B) 허용된 (C) 자격이 있는 (D) 분류된

어휘 paid 유급의 time off 휴가, 휴식 permission 허가 supervisor 상사, 관리자

16. (A)

해석 프로그래머는 자신의 컴퓨터에 소프트웨어를 다운로드하려고 할 때 잦은 문제를 겪었다.
(A) 잦은 (B) 너그러운 (C) 대안이 되는 (D) 필수적인

어휘 encounter 맞닥뜨리다, 접하다

17. (C)

해석 대부분의 평가자들은 Meridian Motors에서 제조한 신형 세단의 우수한 성능을 언급한다.
(A) 절대적인 (B) 통합된 (C) 우수한 (D) 신중한

어휘 evaluator 평가자 mention 말하다, 언급하다 performance 성능 manufacture 제조하다

18. (B)

해석 시내의 몇몇 도로들이 곧 있을 도시를 관통하는 가두 퍼레이드를 대비하여 폐쇄되었다.
(A) 보고된 (B) 다가오는, 곧 있을 (C) 임시의 (D) 확인된

어휘 downtown 시내의 in preparation for ~에 대한 준비로

19. (B)

해석 그 기기는 수 년간의 잦은 사용에도 불구하고 여전히 작동한다.
(A) 특정한 (B) 작동하는, 기능하는 (C) 분명한, 명백한 (D) 진취적인

어휘 appliance 기기 remain 계속 ~이다 heavy usage 잦은 사용

20. (D)

해석 Bakersfield의 신제품 화장품들은 몇몇 이용자들이 알레르기 반응을 겪는 바람에 생산이 중단되었다.
(A) 홍보하다 (B) 수출하다 (C) 확신하다 (D) 단종하다

어휘 line (상품의) 종류, 제품군 cosmetics 화장품 on account of ~ 때문에 suffer 겪다 allergic reaction 알레르기 반응

UNIT 13 고득점 획득을 위한 부사 어휘

PRACTICE 본문 p.142

1. (A)	**2.** (C)	**3.** (C)	**4.** (B)	**5.** (C)	**6.** (D)
7. (C)	**8.** (B)	**9.** (B)	**10.** (A)	**11.** (B)	**12.** (A)
13. (A)	**14.** (C)	**15.** (D)	**16.** (B)	**17.** (C)	**18.** (B)
19. (D)	**20.** (B)				

1. (A)

해석 Mary Hartford는 총회 개최일을 건너뛰고, 대신에 둘째 날에 참석할 계획이다.
(A) 대신에 (B) 다양하게 (C) 문자 그대로 (D) 비슷하게

어휘 skip 건너뛰다, 거르다 conference 총회, 학회

2. (C)
해석 직원들은 비용의 상환을 요구하는 모든 서류를 온라인으로 제출해야 한다.
(A) 다행히도 (B) 우아하게 (C) 온라인으로 (D) 노골적으로
어휘 submit 제출하다 reimbursement 상환 expenditure 지출, 비용

3. (C)
해석 Mr. Burns는 처음에는 낮은 연봉을 제안 받았지만, 그가 거절하자 회사는 액수를 늘렸다.
(A) 쾌적하게 (B) 완전히 (C) 처음에 (D) 특히
어휘 offer 제안하다 reject 거절하다

4. (B)
해석 Denton Office Supplies는 모든 온라인 주문을 신속하게 포장하고 배송한다.
(A) 진지하게 (B) 신속히 (C) 거의 ~ 아닌 (D) 정말로
어휘 make sure 확실히 하다, 반드시 ~하다 package 포장하다; 소포

5. (C)
해석 이사회는 만장일치로 Reid Harmon에게 Watergate Industries의 사장직을 제안하기로 표결했다.
(A) 엄청나게 (B) 아마도 (C) 만장일치로 (D) 정기적으로
어휘 board of directors 이사회 vote 투표하다

6. (D)
해석 주방에 기기를 설치하려고 시도하기 전에 사용 설명서를 꼼꼼히 읽어보세요.
(A) 행복하게 (B) 거의 (C) 정당하게 (D) 철저히, 꼼꼼히
어휘 instructions 사용 설명서, 지침 prior to ~하기 전에 attempt 시도하다 install 설치하다 appliance 기기

7. (C)
해석 Perkins Electronics는 신임 사장의 지시에 의해 멕시코의 공장을 갑자기 폐쇄했다.
(A) 설득력 있게 (B) 우연히 (C) 갑자기, 예상외로 (D) 오히려, 차라리
어휘 factory 공장 order 지시, 명령

8. (B)
해석 현재 〈Daily Times〉를 구독하고 있는 사람들만 특별 할인 혜택을 받을 수 있다.
(A) 정확히 (B) 현재, 지금 (C) 단지 (D) 공교롭게도
어휘 individual 사람, 개인 subscribe to ~을 구독하다 be eligible for ~을 할 자격이 있다

9. (B)
해석 Ms. Galbraith는 새로운 문서 정리 시스템을 시행하여 사무실의 효율을 크게 향상시켰다.
(A) 언제나, 지금까지 (B) 상당히 (C) 곧 (D) 정확히
어휘 improve 향상시키다, 개선하다 efficiency 효율 implement 시행하다 file 문서를 정리하다

10. (A)
해석 Mr. Edwards는 밤 늦게 비행기를 타는 일이 거의 없지만, 오늘 아침까지 도쿄에 도착해야 했다.
(A) 좀처럼 ~하지 않는 (B) 그때는 (C) 하지만 (D) 누구

11. (B)
해석 도서관의 단골 이용자들과 방문객들 모두 이번 주 금요일 저녁에 있을 Janet Evans의 신작 소설 낭독회에 초대됩니다.
(A) 그 사이에 (B) 모두, 똑같이 (C) 꽤 (D) 정말로
어휘 regular 정기의, 보통의 patron (도서관) 이용자

12. (A)
해석 Mr. Orbison은 어제는 고객과 함께 카페에서 점심을 먹었지만, 대부분 회사 구내식당에서 식사를 한다.
(A) 대부분 (B) 오직 (C) 힘차게 (D) 재빨리
어휘 while ~인데 반하여 cafeteria 구내식당

13. (A)
해석 Otto von Steuben 셰프가 운영하는 레스토랑은 다른 곳에서는 찾을 수 없는 요리들을 제공한다.
(A) 다른 곳에서 (B) 저 너머에 (C) 주위에 (D) 대략
어휘 dish 요리; 접시 available 이용할 수 있는, 구할 수 있는

14. (C)
해석 Nano Technologies는 외부 자금을 확보했기 때문에 자사의 새로운 설비에서 일할 추가적인 직원들을 빠르게 고용하고 있다.
(A) 지나치게 (B) 드물게 (C) 신속하게, 빠르게 (D) 독특하게
어휘 since ~ 때문에; ~ 이후로 secure 확보하다 funding 자금(지원) facility 시설

15. (D)
해석 12월에는 휴가가 승인되지 않을 것이니, 그에 맞춰 휴가 계획을 세우십시오.
(A) 제대로 (B) 깨끗이 (C) 확실히 (D) 그에 맞춰
어휘 time off 휴가 grant 승인하다

16. (B)
해석 항상 뉴포트에서 근무하고 있음에도 불구하고, Ken Dayton은 자신이 결국 해외로 전근을 가게 될 것이라고 우려했다.
(A) 빈번히 (B) 결국 (C) 거의 (D) 명백히
어휘 concerned 걱정하는, 염려하는 transfer 전근시키다 abroad 해외로

17. (C)
해석 소포는 이틀 전에 우리 창고를 떠났고 곧 귀하의 사무실로 배송될 것입니다.
(A) 최근에 (B) 공평하게 (C) 곧 (D) 전에
어휘 package 소포, 꾸러미 warehouse 창고

PART 5

18. (B)
해석 지역 공영 주차장은 표면이 재포장되는 동안 일시적으로 폐쇄되었다.
(A) 마침내 (B) 일시적으로 (C) 조심스럽게 (D) 아슬아슬하게
어휘 community 지역사회 while ~하는 동안 surface 표면 repave 재포장하다

19. (D)
해석 예산을 확인한 후, Ms. Jenkins는 직원 모임을 위한 충분한 돈이 정말로 남아 있다는 것을 알아냈다.
(A) 둘 다 ~가 아닌 (B) 그 외의 (C) 더 많은 (D) 정말로
어휘 budget 예산 determine 알아내다; 결정하다 gathering 모임

20. (B)
해석 신청 절차가 원활히 진행될 수 있도록 사전에 여러분의 모든 서류를 준비하십시오.
(A) 자유롭게 (B) 사전에, 미리 (C) 이딘가에 (D) 마찬가시로
어휘 ensure 확실하게 하다, 보장하다 application 신청(서) process 절차, 과정 smoothly 원활히

UNIT 14 고득점 획득을 위한 동사 어휘

PRACTICE 본문 p.146

1. (C)	**2.** (D)	**3.** (B)	**4.** (B)	**5.** (C)	**6.** (D)
7. (B)	**8.** (C)	**9.** (D)	**10.** (C)	**11.** (A)	**12.** (B)
13. (A)	**14.** (C)	**15.** (B)	**16.** (A)	**17.** (A)	**18.** (D)
19. (B)	**20.** (A)				

1. (C)
해석 Mr. Washington은 직원들이 회의에 늦게 도착하는 것을 허용하지 않는 엄격한 방침을 시행한다.
(A) 방해하다 (B) 최소화하다 (C) 시행하다 (D) 드러내다
어휘 strict 엄격한 policy 정책, 방침 allow 허용하다

2. (D)
해석 모든 사람들이 공평하게 대접을 받을 수 있도록 하기 위해 규칙은 모든 사람에게 동등하게 적용되어야 한다.
(A) 협상하다 (B) 임명하다 (C) 통합하다 (D) 확실히 하다, 보장하다
어휘 individual 사람, 개인 treat 대하다, 취급하다 fairly 공평하게 apply 적용하다 equally 똑같이, 균등하게

3. (B)
해석 세미나 날짜는 회사 야유회와 겹치지 않도록 변경될 것이다.
(A) 협력하다 (B) 동시에 일어나다 (C) 보고하다 (D) 할당하다
어휘 date 날짜 company picnic 회사 야유회

4. (B)
해석 Greg's Shopping Club은 100달러 이상의 모든 구매에 대해 배송비를 면제해 줍니다.
(A) 치우다 (B) 포기하다, 적용하지 않다 (C) 탐험하다 (D) 자동화하다
어휘 shipping 배송 fee 요금 purchase 구매; 구매하다

5. (C)
해석 주문하시는 각각의 의류의 사이즈와 색상을 반드시 명기하세요.
(A) 균형을 잡다 (B) 곱하다 (C) 명시하다, 명기하다 (D) 화해시키다
어휘 article 물품, 물건

6. (D)
해석 할인 쿠폰은 뒷면에 기재된 만료일 이전에 상품과 교환해야 합니다.
(A) 묘사하다 (B) 결심하다 (C) 다가가다 (D) (상품과) 교환하다
어휘 prior to ~ 이전에 expiration 만료, 만기 list 기입하다, 기재하다

7. (B)
해석 늦어도 금요일 오후까지 회사 인트라넷 시스템에서 여러분의 사용자 이름을 인증하십시오.
(A) 변형시키다 (B) 인증하다 (C) 발전시키다 (D) 수입하다
어휘 username 사용자 이름 no later than 늦어도 ~까지

8. (C)
해석 그 자리에 지원하는 사람들은 반드시 종합 건강 검진을 받아야 한다.
(A) 승인하다 (B) 검사하다 (C) 겪다, 받다 (D) 시도하다
어휘 apply for ~에 지원하다 complete 완전한, 철저한 physical checkup 건강 검진

9. (D)
해석 수준 높은 교육을 받았음에도 불구하고, Mr. Bevers는 임원의 직책을 맡는 데 필요한 리더십 기술이 부족하다.
(A) 대체하다 (B) 드러내다 (C) 묘사하다 (D) 부족하다
어휘 highly 고도로, 매우 take on ~을 맡다 executive 중역의

10. (C)
해석 Ms. Jansen은 집에 휴대전화를 두고 왔음에도 불구하고 부하 직원에게 가까스로 연락을 취할 수 있었다.
(A) 실패하다 (B) 고려하다 (C) 간신히 해내다 (D) 계획하다, 예상하다
어휘 contact 연락하다 assistant 조수, 비서

11. (A)
해석 그 시설은 이용하기도 용이한 최첨단 운동 설비를 특징으로 한다.
(A) 특징으로 하다 (B) 제거하다 (C) 보고하다 (D) 방해하다
어휘 facility 시설 state-of-the-art 최첨단의 workout 운동 equipment 시설, 설비

12. (B)

해석 박물관 투어의 회원들은 언제든지 가이드에게 질문을 할 수 있다.

(A) 반대하다 (B) 향하게 하다 (C) 허락하다 (D) 우선 순위를 매기다

어휘 at any time 언제든지

13. (A)

해석 Brian Harper는 자신의 회계 자격증을 받는 데 필요한 서류들을 제출했다.

(A) 제출하다 (B) 초대하다 (C) 제안하다 (D) 문의하다

어휘 accounting 회계 license 자격증

14. (C)

해석 사용 설명서는 장비를 사용하기 위해 사람들이 취해야 하는 필요한 단계들을 요약하고 있다.

(A) 고려하다 (B) 제출하다 (C) 개요를 서술하다, 요점을 말하다 (D) 시도하다

어휘 user's manual 사용 설명서 utilize 이용하다, 활용하다 equipment 장비

15. (B)

해석 해외 출장을 가는 직원은 상사에게 이야기해서 법인 카드를 받을 수 있다.

(A) 승진시키다 (B) 얻다 (C) 적용하다 (D) 남다

어휘 company credit card 법인 카드 supervisor 상사, 감독관

16. (A)

해석 공장을 방문하는 모든 사람은 현지 직원들의 어떠한 지시에도 따라야 한다.

(A) 따르다 (B) 결론을 내리다 (C) 나타나다 (D) 연습하다

어휘 instructions 지시 provide 주다, 제공하다

17. (A)

해석 그 항공사는 기내 반입 수하물에 대한 자사의 규정을 명확히 하겠다고 밝혔다.

(A) 분명히 하다 (B) 방해하다 (C) 폭로하다 (D) 참가하다

어휘 state 말하다, 공표하다 regulation 규정 regarding ~에 관한 carry-on 기내 반입의 baggage 수하물

18. (D)

해석 신임 최고경영자인 Deborah Burgess는 토론토 시설에서의 정리 해고 가능성에 대한 우려를 해결하기 위해 노력하겠다고 약속했다.

(A) 제공하다 (B) 개편하다 (C) 광고하다 (D) 다루다, 처리하다

어휘 concern 염려, 우려 layoff 정리 해고

19. (B)

해석 고객은 배송 도중 물품이 손상되었을 때 그의 손실에 대한 보상을 승인 받았다.

(A) 강화하다 (B) 인정하다, 승인하다 (C) 여기다 (D) 탐지하다

어휘 compensation 보상, 배상 loss 손실 shipment 배송, 배송품

20. (A)

해석 Fairmont Cab은 자사의 기사들이 자신과 승객들이 보험 혜택을 받을 수 있는 종합 보험에 가입하도록 하는 새로운 정책을 시행했다.

(A) 시행하다 (B) 관련시키다 (C) 지시하다 (D) 운반하다

어휘 policy 정책, 방침 require 필요로 하다, 요구하다 comprehensive insurance 종합 보험 cover 보험에 들다 passenger 승객

PRACTICE 고난도 본문 p.148

1. (A)	**2.** (A)	**3.** (D)	**4.** (A)	**5.** (B)	**6.** (B)
7. (A)	**8.** (C)	**9.** (C)	**10.** (A)	**11.** (B)	**12.** (A)
13. (B)	**14.** (B)	**15.** (C)	**16.** (C)	**17.** (C)	**18.** (B)
19. (B)	**20.** (B)	**21.** (B)	**22.** (C)	**23.** (D)	**24.** (D)
25. (D)	**26.** (D)	**27.** (B)	**28.** (C)	**29.** (C)	**30.** (C)

1. (A)

해석 잡지의 최종본이 제시간에 인쇄되도록 하기 위해, 기자들은 6월 8일 이전에 자신들의 글에 모든 수정을 해야 한다.

(A) 수정 사항 (B) 에세이 (C) 권고 (D) 제안서

어휘 ensure 확실히 하다, 보장하다 draft 원고, 초안 print 인쇄하다 on time 제시간에, 제때에 reporter 기자 make a revision 수정하다 text 글, 본문 prior to ~ 이전에

2. (A)

해석 농업 전문가들은 식물들이 잘 자랄 수 있는 기회를 가질 수 있도록 가능한 한 가장 안정적인 환경을 제공할 것을 권고한다.

해설 빈칸은 명사 environment를 수식하며 관사 the의 수식을 받으므로 형용사 또는 복합 명사를 이루는 명사가 올 수 있다. 그러므로 the의 수식을 받는 최상급 형태의 형용사인 (A) most stable이 정답이다. 분사는 형용사에 우선하지 못하므로 stabilizing은 오답이고, 명사 stability는 environment와 복합 명사를 이루지 못하므로 역시 오답이다.

어휘 agriculture 농업 expert 전문가 recommend 추천하다 provide 제공하다, 주다 stable 안정적인 plant 식물 thrive 잘 자라다, 번창하다

3. (D)

해석 Mr. Kamal은 접수되는 이력서들을 검토해서 어떤 이력서가 관리직에 필요한 자격 요건을 반영하는지 알아낼 것이다.

해설 빈칸 앞뒤로 determine과 reflect라는 두 개의 동사가 있으므로, 빈칸에는 determine의 목적어이자 reflect의 주어가 될 수 있는 문장 성분이 필요하다. now that과 even though는 접속사이므로 소거할 수 있고, some such와 which ones 중에서 이 같은 조건을 충족하는 (D) which ones가 정답이다.

어휘 incoming 들어오는, 도착하는 résumé 이력서

determine 알아내다, 결정하다 reflect 반영하다 qualifications 자격 요건

4. (A)

해석 조사 결과, 창고에서의 지연은 라벨이 잘못 부착된 몇 개의 상자 때문인 것으로 확인되었다.

해설 빈칸에는 한정사 a few와 함께 명사 boxes를 수식하는 수식어구가 필요하다. 분사인 mislabeled와 mislabeling이 정답이 될 수 있는데, boxes는 스스로 동작을 할 수 없으므로 과거분사인 (A) mislabeled가 정답이다.

어휘 investigation 조사 delay 지연 warehouse 창고 cause 야기시키다 mislabel 라벨을 잘못 붙이다

5. (B)

해석 Nelson Recruitment는 입사 지원자들이 리크루터와 협력하여 분명한 취업 목표를 만들어야 한다고 주장한다.

해설 선택지가 동일한 단어의 다른 품사들로 구성된 자리 문제이다. 빈칸 앞에 명사절의 주어인 job applicants가 있는데 동사가 보이지 않으므로 빈칸에는 동사가 들어가야 한다. 따라서 cooperating과 cooperation을 소거할 수 있다. 동사 insist는 제안, 주장, 요구, 명령을 의미하는 동사이므로 that절에서 〈should+동사원형〉으로 쓰이는데, should는 보통은 생략되므로 동사원형인 (B) cooperate가 정답이다.

어휘 applicant 지원자 cooperate 협력하다 recruiter 리크루터, 헤드헌터 employment 취업, 고용

6. (B)

해석 Ms. Maddock이 선호하는 행사 장소는 넉넉한 주차 공간과 최첨단 음향 시스템을 가진 곳이다.

해설 빈칸에는 소유격인 Ms. Maddock's의 수식을 받는 명사가 올 수 있다. 따라서 복수 명사인 preferences와 단수 명사인 preference가 정답 후보가 된다. 문장의 동사는 복수 동사인 include이므로 (B) preferences가 정답이다.

어휘 preference 선호(도) venue 장소 ample 충분한 state-of-the-art 최첨단의

7. (A)

해석 Newton Footwear의 매출은 프로 운동선수들이 등장하는 광고 캠페인이 시작된 직후에 온라인과 매장에서 증가했다.

해설 선택지가 동일한 단어의 다른 품사들로 구성된 자리 문제이다. 빈칸을 제외해도 문법적으로 완벽하므로 빈칸에는 부사가 들어가야 한다. 따라서 부사 (A) promptly가 정답이다. promptly after는 '~의 직후에'라는 의미이다.

어휘 promptly 즉시, 지체 없이 launch 개시, 시작 feature 특징으로 삼다 athlete 운동 선수

8. (C)

해석 위험 수준을 정확하게 분석하지 못한 실패로부터 발생하는 손실은 투자 회사의 책임이 될 수 있다.

(A) 어디쯤에 (B) 따로 (C) ~에서 비롯되는 (D) ~에 따라

해설 문장의 주어는 Any losses, 동사구는 may be이고, 빈칸부터 risk까지는 주어를 수식하는 어구이다. 명사 수식 어구를 이끌 수 있는 것은 전치사이므로 전치사가 아닌 whereabouts와 apart를 소거할 수 있다. resulting from과 in compliance with 중에서 문맥상 적절한 (C) resulting from이 정답이다.

어휘 loss 손실, 손해 failure 실패 analyze 분석하다 risk 위험 investment 투자 firm 회사

9. (C)

해석 세탁 세제의 효과에 대해 불만이 있는 사람은 신속히 고객 서비스 담당자에게 연결될 것이다.

해설 빈칸은 전치사구인 with ~ detergent의 수식을 받는 주어 자리이다. 대명사가 주어가 될 수 있으므로 (C) Anyone이 정답이다. Whoever는 뒤에 바로 동사가 나와야 하므로 오답이다.

어휘 complaint 불만, 민원 regarding ~에 관한 effectiveness 효과(성) laundry 세탁 detergent 세제 promptly 즉시 direct 보내다, 향하다

10. (A)

해석 Mr. Conway는 그날 오전 음향 기기에 기술적인 어려움이 있었음에도 불구하고 제시간에 기조 연설을 시작할 수 있었다.

(A) 비록 ~이지만 (B) ~뿐만 아니라 (C) ~ 덕분에 (D) ~하는 동안

해설 빈칸은 앞뒤의 절을 연결하고 있으므로 접속사가 올 수 있다. even though와 while 중에서 문맥상 적절한 (A) even though가 정답이다.

어휘 keynote address 기조 연설 on time 제시간에, 제때에 technical 기술적인 equipment 장비, 장치

11. (B)

해석 지방자치단체 소유 토지에 건립되는 기반 시설 공사는 논란의 소지가 많은 특성상 어제 공개 토론회에서 활발한 논의를 야기시켰다.

(A) 저항하는 (B) 활기찬 (C) 썩기 쉬운 (D) 현재의

어휘 controversial 논란의 nature 성격, 특성 infrastructure 기반 시설 municipal 지방자치제의, 시의 provoke 유발하다 forum 토론회, 포럼

12. (A)

해석 교육 시간의 목표가 이미 달성되었기 때문에, 우리는 남은 시간을 좀 더 격식이 없는 팀 단합 활동에 써도 될 것 같다.

(A) ~이므로 (B) ~까지 (C) ~할 때마다 (D) ~하지 않는 한

해설 앞의 절과 뒤의 절의 내용이 인과 관계를 형성하므로 이유를 나타내는 접속사인 (A) Since가 정답이다.

어휘 training 교육 meet an objective 목표를 달성하다 session (교육) 시간 casual 격식이 없는, 캐주얼한 team building 팀 단합 activity 활동

13. (B)

해석 Larkin Appliances의 모든 세탁기에 대한 평생 보증은 놀라운 일이 아닌데, 이 회사의 제품은 내구성으로 유명하기 때문이다.

(A) 수정 (B) 내구성 (C) 근접성 (D) 성과

어휘 lifetime 평생의 warranty (품질) 보증

14. (B)

해석 버스 요금이 얼마나 많이 인상될 것인가는 평균 승객 수와 예상 연료비 지출에 달려 있다.

해설 주어는 How ~ increase이고 depends on이 동사이다. 〈how+형용사/부사〉는 '얼마나 ~한/하게'라는 뜻으로 쓰일 수 있는데, 이 문장에서는 동사 increase를 수식하는 부사가 필요하므로 (B) substantially가 정답이다.

어휘 substantially 상당히, 많이 passenger 승객 fuel 연료 expenditure 지출

15. (C)

해석 모든 예산 결정은 연례 음악 축제의 주최자인 Tony Calderon에 의해 사전에 승인되어야 한다.

해설 빈칸 앞에 관사 the가 있고 뒤에 전치사구가 있으므로 빈칸에는 명사가 나와야 한다. organization과 organizer가 정답 후보가 되는데, 빈칸은 Tony Calderon과 동격이므로 사람 명사인 (C) organizer가 정답이다.

어휘 budget 예산 approve 승인하다 organizer 주최자, 조직인 annual 연례의 in advance 사전에

16. (C)

해석 건축 허가를 여러 번 거부당하자 그 건설사는 빈 부지를 고급 아파트 타워로 개발하는 것을 포기할 수밖에 없었다.

해설 주어는 Multiple ~ permit이고 동사는 forced이다. 동사 force는 〈force A to부정사〉의 형태로 쓰여 'A로 하여금 어쩔 수 없이 ~하도록 만들다'라는 의미를 형성하므로 to부정사인 (C) to abandon이 정답이다.

어휘 multiple 여러, 다수의 rejection 거절 permit 허가 abandon 포기하다 vacant plot 공터 luxury 고급의

17. (C)

해석 이번 주 토요일로 예상되는 악천후를 고려하여, 국제음식축제의 행사 기획자들은 행사를 연기했다.

(A) ~의 방법으로 (B) 그 이후로 (C) ~을 고려하여, ~에 비추어 볼 때 (D) ~라는 것을 고려하면

해설 의미상으로는 (D)도 가능할 것 같지만 접속사 that 뒤에는 절이 나와야 하므로 오답이다.

어휘 severe 혹독한 predict 예측하다 planner 기획자 postpone 연기하다

18. (B)

해석 Elkview Engineering은 대단히 뛰어난 명성을 확립했기 때문에 마케팅과 광고에 더 이상 자금을 배정할 필요가 없다.

해설 〈such a/an 형용사+명사〉와 〈so 형용사 a/an 명사〉는 '매우 ~한 ~'라는 뜻으로 쓰이는 구문이다.

어휘 establish 확립하다, 쌓다 reputation 명성, 평판 allocate 배정하다 fund 자금

19. (B)

해석 제품개발팀의 모든 사람들은 우리의 것이 전국 디자인 공모전에 제출된 가장 인상적인 시제품이라는 것에 동의한다.

해설 빈칸은 동사 agrees의 목적어가 되는 명사절의 주어 자리이다. 빈칸 뒤의 동사가 is이므로 '우리의 것'이라는 의미의 소유대명사인 (B) ours가 정답이다. we와 ourselves는 복수이므로 is와 함께 쓰일 수 없다.

어휘 impressive 인상적인 prototype 시제품 submit 제출하다 competition 대회, 시합

20. (B)

해석 해외 송금 요청서가 오후 3시까지 제출된다면 Henley Bank는 당일에 거래를 마무리 지을 것이다.

(A) ~까지 (B) 만약 ~라면 (C) ~ 하자마자 (D) 꼭 ~처럼

해설 뒤에 주어와 동사가 갖추어진 절이 오므로 빈칸에는 접속사가 와야 한다. 따라서 Provided와 As soon as가 정답 후보가 된다. 앞 절의 의미가 조건을 나타내므로 (B) Provided가 정답이다. provided는 '만약 ~라면'이라는 뜻의 접속사로 쓰인다는 점에 주의해야 한다.

어휘 transfer 이동, 이체 submit 제출하다 finalize 마무리 짓다 transaction 거래

21. (B)

해석 Lapointe Bank가 제시한 매력적인 금리 때문에 고객들은 새로운 계좌를 개설하고 잉여 자금을 그 계좌로 옮기게 되었다.

해설 주어는 단수 명사인 The attractive interest rate이고 과거분사구인 offered by Lapointe Bank의 수식을 받고 있다. 따라서 동사의 복수 형태인 (A), (D)를 소거할 수 있다. 빈칸 뒤에 목적어인 customers가 있으므로 능동태인 (B) has motivated가 정답이다.

어휘 attractive 매력적인 interest rate 금리, 이율 motivate 동기를 부여하다 account 계좌 surplus 잉여의, 과잉의

22. (C)

해석 VT Logistics는 Camden Couriers가 지속적으로 배송 마감일을 지키지 못해 계약을 해지할 계획이다.

(A) 격렬하게 (B) 꾸준히 (C) 지속적으로 (D) 잠정적으로

어휘 logistics 물류 terminate 종료하다, 끝내다 contract 계약 courier 택배 회사 meet the deadline 마감에 맞추다

23. (D)

해석 부서장은 내년에 대면 미팅을 통해 고객과의 관계를 개선하기 위해 출장 경비에 더 많은 지출을 할 것으로 예상한다.

해설 동사 anticipate는 to부정사가 아닌 동명사를 목적어로 취하는 특징을 가지고 있다. 정답은 (D) spending.

어휘 department head 부서장 anticipate 예상하다 client 고객 face-to-face 마주보는, 대면의

24. (D)

해석 대다수의 일등석 여행자들은 경유하느라 추가로 시간을 쓰기보다는 직항편에 대해 추가 비용을 지불할 의향이 있다.

(A) 사실은 (B) ~의 결과로 (C) ~의 경우에는 (D) ~보다는

어휘 the majority of 대다수의 extra 추가의; 추가로 direct flight 직항편 항공기 additional 추가적인 deal with ~을 처리하다 layover 경유

25. (D)

해석 Murillo Incorporated의 해외 확장 계획에는 해외 조세 규정 관련 업무 경험이 있는 직원들을 보유한 회계 법인을 고용하는 것이 포함된다.

해설 빈칸 뒤의 employees는 빈칸 앞의 선행사인 accounting firm에 소속되어 있으므로 소유격 관계대명사 (D) whose가 정답이다. what은 관계대명사로 쓰일 때 선행사가 없어야 하고, 빈칸 뒤에 주어나 목적어가 빠진 상태가 아니므로 관계대명사 which도 적절하지 않다.

어휘 overseas 해외의 expansion 확장 involve 포함하다, 수반하다 accounting firm 회계 법인 regulation 규정

26. (D)

해석 자동화를 가능하게 하기 위한 더 많은 장비 구입은 생산 시설에서 필요한 인력의 규모를 감소시켰다.
(A) 모이다 (B) 간주하다 (C) 조사하다 (D) 감소시키다

어휘 purchase 구입 equipment 장비 enable ~을 가능하게 하다 automation 자동화 workforce 인력 manufacturing 생산, 제조 facility 시설

27. (B)

해석 무급 병가에 대한 새로운 방침은 자세한 사항이 회사 웹사이트에 게시되는 즉시 시행될 것이다.

해설 빈칸 뒤에 절이 이어지므로 빈칸에는 접속사가 와야 한다. 문맥상 (B) after가 정답이다. immediately after는 '~한 직후에'라는 의미로 쓰인다는 것을 알아 두자.

어휘 policy 방침, 정책 unpaid 무급의 medical leave 병가 go into effect 시행되다, 발효되다 immediately 즉시 details 세부 사항 post 게시하다

28. (C)

해석 사용자 정보를 검토한 결과 직원의 약 45%가 이메일에 공지된 데이터베이스에 접속했던 것으로 드러났다.
(A) 계산하다 (B) 소개하다 (C) 접속하다 (D) 질문하다

어휘 review 검토 reveal 드러내다, 밝히다 approximately 약, 대략

29. (C)

해석 관리자들은 아무리 바쁘더라도 시간을 내서 팀원들의 관심사를 들어야 한다.

해설 빈칸 뒤에 형용사 busy가 있고, 〈주어+동사〉인 they may be가 이어지므로 '아무리 ~일지라도, 비록 ~라 할지라도'의 의미로 쓰이는 〈however+형용사+주어+동사〉 구문이라는 것을 알 수 있다. 따라서 (C) however가 정답이다.

어휘 supervisor 관리자, 감독관 concern 우려, 관심사

30. (C)

해석 Mr. Zhang이 자신의 분기 판매 할당량에 도달하는 것을 놓치지 않았다면, 그는 승진 대상자로 고려되었을지도 모른다.

해설 콤마 뒤의 절에 과거 사실에 대한 불확실한 추측을 나타내는 〈might have 과거분사〉 구문이 쓰였으므로 가정법 과거완료 문장이라는 것을 알 수 있다. 따라서 가정법 문장을 만드는 (C) Had가 정답이다. 이 문장을 바꿔 쓰면 'If Mr. Zhang had not missed ~'가 된다.

어휘 miss 놓치다 sales 판매, 매출 quota 할당량 quarter 분기 consider 고려하다 promotion 승진

PART TEST

본문 p.151

1. (C)	**2.** (D)	**3.** (C)	**4.** (D)	**5.** (C)	**6.** (C)
7. (A)	**8.** (C)	**9.** (A)	**10.** (D)	**11.** (A)	**12.** (B)
13. (C)	**14.** (C)	**15.** (A)	**16.** (A)	**17.** (B)	**18.** (B)
19. (C)	**20.** (D)	**21.** (A)	**22.** (C)	**23.** (B)	**24.** (C)
25. (B)	**26.** (D)	**27.** (A)	**28.** (A)	**29.** (D)	**30.** (A)

1. (C)

해석 Mr. Cross는 그의 요리사가 두 명 모두 제시간에 식당에 도착하지 않았기 때문에 주방에서 도왔다.

해설 빈칸은 부사절의 주어 자리로서 문맥상 nobody와 neither가 가능한데, 전치사구인 of his chefs의 수식을 받을 수 있는 것은 (C) neither이다.

어휘 assist 돕다 since ~이기 때문에 on time 제시간에

2. (D)

해석 금융 전문가들에 따르면, 제조업체들이 올해 기록적인 이익을 낼 것으로 예상된다.

해설 빈칸은 동사 make의 목적어이자 record의 수식을 받는 명사 자리이다. 명사인 profitability와 profits 중에서 의미상 make의 목적어가 될 수 있는 것은 (D) profits이다. record는 이처럼 명사가 아니라 형용사로 쓰일 수 있다는 것을 주의해야 한다.

어휘 financial 재무의, 금융의 expert 전문가 manufacturing 제조(업) record 기록적인

3. (C)

해석 자동화된 시스템은 공장 근로자들이 그들이 맡은 업무에서 생산성을 발휘할 수 있도록 만들 것으로 기대된다.

해설 〈동사(make)+목적어(the factory workers)+목적격 보어〉의 문장 구조이므로 빈칸에는 목적격 보어가 되는 명사 또는 형용사가 올 수 있다. '공장 근로자들을 ~한 상태로 만들다'라는 의미이므로, '~한'에 해당하는 형용사인 (C) productive가 정답이다.

어휘 expect 기대하다, 예상하다 productive 생산적인

4. (D)

해석 Dayton Tech의 연구개발팀은 제조상의 문제점에 대한 해결책을 찾을 수 있는 두 번째 기회가 주어졌다.

해설 빈칸은 동사 자리로서, 동사 give는 능동태로는 〈give+간접 목적어+직접 목적어〉 또는 〈give+직접 목적어+to 대상〉의 형태로 쓰인다. a second chance는 직접 목적어인데, 그 뒤에 대상이 아니라 부사적 용법의 to부정사가 나오므로 능동태인 (A), (B), (C)는 모두 오답이다. 문장이 수동태로 전환되면서 간접 목적어인 The R&D team at Dayton Tech가 주어가 되었다는 것을 알 수 있으므로 수동태인 (D) has been given이 정답이다.

어휘 R&D 연구개발(= research and development) solution 해결책 manufacturing 제조, 생산

5. (C)

해석 배송 도중 여러 개의 물품이 파손되었을 때 고객은 손실에 대해 상당한 보상을 받았다.

(A) 승인하다 (B) 감사하다 (C) 보상하다 (D) 보상하다

해설 compensate와 reward는 우리말로는 모두 '보상하다'이지만, compensate는 손해를 입혔을 때 그것을 벌충하기 위해 보상하는 것이고, reward는 포상 차원에서 보상을 한다는 의미 차이가 있다.

어휘 fairly 꽤, 상당히 loss 손실 item 물품 delivery 배달, 배송

6. (C)

해석 팀의 멤버 두 명 모두 자신들의 아이디어가 즉시 실행되어야 한다고 느꼈다.

해설 선택지 중에서 복수 명사를 수식할 수 있는 것은 한정사인 (C) Both 뿐이다. (A)와 (B)는 단수 명사를 수식하고, (D)는 neither A nor B의 형태로 쓰이거나 바로 뒤에 단수 명사가 온다.

어휘 implement 시행하다 at once 즉시

7. (A)

해석 연설 내내 배경 소음이 계속되었고, 일부 청중들은 어떤 소리도 들을 수 없는 어려움을 겪었다.

(A) ~ 내내 (B) 주위에 (C) ~에 (D) ~ 이후로

어휘 background 배경의 noise 소음, 잡음 speech 연설 audience member 청중

8. (C)

해석 Mr. Greg는 3월이 봄에 출시되는 신제품들을 광고하기에 적절한 시기라고 생각한다.

해설 빈칸은 an appropriate time을 수식하면서 the new line을 목적어로 취한다. 따라서 형용사적 용법의 to부정사인 (C) to advertise가 정답이다. 명사절의 동사는 is이므로 동사 형태인 (D)는 오답이다.

어휘 appropriate 적절한 line 제품군

9. (A)

해석 언뜻 보기에, 건물의 디자인은 효율적이고 가용 공간을 잘 활용하는 것처럼 보인다.

해설 빈칸에는 문장의 보어가 들어가야 하므로 명사나 형용사가 올 수 있다. 따라서 형용사인 (A) efficient가 정답이다. 명사인 efficiency, efficiencies는 '디자인=효율성'이라는 관계가 성립되지 않으므로 오답이다.

어휘 at first glance 언뜻 보기에 make good use of ~을 잘 활용하다 available 이용 가능한 space 공간

10. (D)

해석 Harrison Shipbuilding은 지난 분기에 수주가 증가한 반면 경쟁사인 Baden 사는 기록적인 손실을 보고했다.

(A) ~ 덕분에 (B) ~에도 불구하고 (C) 결과적으로 (D) ~인 반면에

해설 빈칸 앞뒤의 절이 서로 상반된 내용이므로 역접의 접속사인 (D) whereas가 정답이다. (A)와 (B)는 전치사, (C)는 부사이므로 오답이다.

어휘 quarter 분기 record 기록적인 loss 손실

11. (A)

해석 Stanton Bank에서 인증 과정은 거주 증명서와 사진이 있는 두 가지 종류의 신분증을 필요로 한다.

(A) 인증, 검증 (B) 철회 (C) 도입, 시행 (D) 조정

어휘 process 과정 proof 증명(서) residency 거주 form 종류, 유형 identification 신분증

12. (B)

해석 대부분의 애널리스트들이 꼽았던 Edward Hope의 가장 큰 업적은 회사를 파산에서 구해낸 것이다.

해설 〈consider+목적어+목적격 보어(to be)〉 구조이다. 빈칸에는 be의 보어 역할을 하면서 his company를 목적어로 취하는 동명사 (B) getting이 들어가야 적절하다.

어휘 analyst 분석가, 애널리스트 accomplishment 업적, 성과 bankruptcy 부도, 파산

13. (C)

해석 Spruce Corporation은 리치먼드에서 저가 주택을 개발하기 위해 Magpie 사와 함께 일하기로 합의했다.

(A) 반영, 반향 (B) 공제, 추론 (C) 연대, 공동 (D) 축적

해설 선택지가 서로 다른 명사들로 이루어져 있으므로 'in ~ with'의 형태로 쓰이는 명사를 찾아야 한다. 따라서 in conjunction with (~와 함께, ~와 연대하여)의 형태로 쓰일 수 있는 (C) conjunction이 정답이다.

어휘 low-cost 저가의 housing 주택, 집

14. (C)

해석 모든 직원들은 가능한 한 많은 것을 배우기 위해 세미나에서 주의를 기울여야 한다.

(A) 임의의 (B) 충동적인 (C) 주의 깊은 (D) 협력적인

15. (A)

해석 Dr. Hatfield는 아침부터 쉬지 않고 일하던 사람들에게 휴식을 취하라고 지시했다.

해설 빈칸은 동사 instructed의 목적어이자 주격 관계사 who의 선행사가 된다. 따라서 those who(~하는 사람들)의 형태로 쓰이는 (A) those가 정답이다.

어휘 instruct 지시하다 nonstop 휴식 없이 take a break 휴식을 취하다

16. (A)

해석 그 세미나는 선택적인 것으로 여겨졌지만, 경리부에서는 거의 모든 사람들이 세미나에 등록했다.
(A) 선택적인 (B) 결론이 난 (C) 진보적인 (D) 책임 있는

어휘 while ~인 반면에 register for ~에 등록하다

17. (B)

해석 Failsafe의 최고위급 관리자 중 한 명인 Ms. Jacobs는 지역 대학교에서 리더십에 관한 수업을 가르치고 있다.

해설 빈칸 뒤에 목적어인 a class가 있으므로 능동태가 와야 하고, 주어가 단수 명사인 Ms. Jacobs이므로 단수 동사가 와야 한다. 따라서 (B) teaches가 정답이다.

어휘 manager 관리자

18. (B)

해석 기계 장치는 제대로 작동되어 오작동이 일어나지 않도록 해야 한다.
(A) 공평하게; 상당히 (B) 제대로 (C) 확실히 (D) 창조적으로

어휘 machinery 기계류, 기계 장치 operate 작동하다, 운전하다 suffer 겪다, 당하다 malfunction 오작동, 기능 장애

19. (C)

해석 Ms. Oxford는 제조 공정의 결함을 찾기 위해 무작위로 추출한 품목들을 면밀히 검사한다.
(A) 집중하다 (B) 구매하다 (C) 검사하다 (D) 개발하다

어휘 closely 면밀히, 빈틈없이 random 무작위의 in an effort to ~하기 위한 노력으로 flaw 결점, 결함 manufacturing 제조, 생산

20. (D)

해석 그 잡지의 새로운 사진 작가가 포착한 이미지들은 시각적으로 꽤 매력적이다.

해설 빈칸은 주격 보어 자리이자 부사 visually의 수식을 받고 있으므로 형용사인 (D) appealing이 정답이다.

어휘 capture 포착하다 quite 꽤, 상당히 visually 시각적으로 appealing 매력적인

21. (A)

해석 혹시 있을지 모를 부상을 방지하기 위해 안전 장비를 제대로 착용하는 것을 기억하십시오.

해설 please로 시작하는 문장이므로 명령문이라는 것을 알 수 있다. 따라서 동사원형인 (A) remember가 정답이다.

어휘 put on 착용하다 gear 장비 properly 제대로, 적절히 potential 잠재적인 injury 부상

22. (C)

해석 Mr. Hollander는 적절한 절차가 지켜지고 있는지 확인할 책임이 있는 사람이다.

해설 빈칸 앞의 형용사 responsible을 보았다면 함께 쓰이는 전치사 for를 바로 떠올릴 수 있어야 한다. 정답은 (C) for.

어휘 confirm 확인하다, 확실히 하다 proper 적절한, 제대로 된 procedure 절차, 과정

23. (B)

해석 설계 결함의 발견으로 인해 공사가 중단되었을 때 교량은 단지 부분적으로 완공된 상태였다.

해설 빈칸은 형용사 complete를 수식하고 있으므로 부사인 (B) partially가 정답이다.

어휘 halt 중단시키다 flaw 결함

24. (C)

해석 자선단체에 대한 Megan Reyna의 주된 기여는 몇몇 부유한 기부자들을 모집한 것이었다.
(A) 상여금 (B) 지지 (C) 기여 (D) 변이, 변화

어휘 major 주된, 주요한 charity 자선단체 recruit 모집하다 donor 기부자

25. (B)

해석 물품은 수취인에 의해 서명된 경우 Grossman Shipping에 의해 배송된 것으로 간주됩니다.

해설 빈칸 뒤에 행위의 주체를 나타내는 전치사 by가 있으므로 수동태 형태가 와야 한다. 따라서 앞에 to be가 생략된 (B) delivered가 정답이다. 문장의 동사는 is이므로 동사 형태인 (D)는 오답이다.

어휘 item 물품 consider 여기다, 간주하다 recipient 수취인, 수령인

26. (D)

해석 Jeremy Tyler의 다음 프로젝트는 마케팅부의 두 명의 부서원과의 협업이 될 것이다.

해설 빈칸 앞에 관사 a가 있으므로 단수 명사가 와야 한다. 사람 명사인 collaborator와 사물 명사인 collaboration 중에서 '프로젝트=협업'의 관계가 적절하므로 (D) collaboration이 정답이다.

어휘 collaboration 협업

27. (A)

해석 Focal 사의 주요 고객들은 물론 모든 정규직 직원들은 12월 29일에 열리는 기념 행사에 초대된다.
(A) ~뿐만 아니라, ~은 물론 (B) 그 사이에 (C) ~하도록 (D) ~하기 위해

해설 빈칸 뒤에 its major clients라는 구가 이어지므로 빈칸은 전치사 자리이다. 따라서 전치사인 (A) as well as가 정답이다.

어휘 full-time 정규직의, 상근의 celebration 기념행사

28. (A)

해석 우리는 축제가 성공적으로 개최되도록 하기 위해 필요한 모든 것을 하라는 지시를 받았다.

해설 빈칸은 동사 do의 목적어가 되는데, 뒤에 주어가 없는 불완전

한 절이 이어지고 있으므로 복합관계사인 (A) whatever가 정답이다. 다른 선택지들은 선행사가 필요하므로 오답이다.

어휘 instruct 지시하다 ensure 확실히 하다, 보장하다

29. (D)

해석 영업부는 북미 영업에 집중할 수 있도록 최소 6명의 부서 직원을 투입할 계획이다.

해설 앞에 전치사 on이 있고 뒤에 목적어인 six members가 있으므로 전치사의 목적어가 되는 동명사 (D) committing이 정답이다.

어휘 commit ~ to do ~하는 데 ~을 사용하기로 결정하다
at least 적어도

30. (A)

해석 Mr. Davis는 자신이 Leeway's의 임원직을 제안 받아야 한다고 굳게 믿고 있다.

해설 빈칸은 명사절의 주어 자리이므로 주격 인칭대명사인 (A) he가 정답이다.

어휘 executive 중역의, 임원의

출제 경향 및 전략

본문 p.156

수신: Blacktail Logistics 전 직원
〈stafflist@blacktaillogistics.com〉
발신: Alfred Orozco
〈a.orozco@blacktaillogistics.com〉
날짜: 11월 12일
제목: 성과 평가

Blacktail Logistics 직원 여러분:
다음 주 내내, 관리자들은 모든 직원들을 대상으로 성과 평가를 실시할 것입니다. 우리는 여러분이 자신의 역할을 이해하고 있는지 확실히 하기 위해 [131]**종종** 이 일을 합니다. [132]**또한** 우리는 여러분이 자신의 최고 수준에서 일할 수 있도록 지원을 잘 받고 있는지 확인하고 싶습니다. 여러분은 직속 상사와 만나서 본인의 장점과 [133]**개선**이 필요한 부분에 대해 논의하게 될 것입니다. 평가 후에 여러분은 의견 카드를 작성하는 기회를 갖게 됩니다. 이 카드는 인사부에 직접 제출할 수 있으며, 의견은 익명으로 유지됩니다. [134]**그러니, 여러분의 솔직한 의견을 공유해 주세요.** 여러분의 관리자가 여러분의 평가가 예약된 시간을 알려줄 것입니다.

여러분의 협조에 감사드립니다.

Alfred Orozco
Blacktail Logistics 실장

131. (A)

해설 빈칸 앞은 주어(We), 동사(carry out), 목적어(this task)가 갖추어진 완벽한 문장이므로 빈칸에는 부사가 올 수 있다. 따라서 carry out을 수식하는 부사인 (A) occasionally가 정답이다.

132. (D)

(A) 대조적으로 (B) 그 결과 (C) 그러나 (D) 또한, 게다가

133. (B)

(A) 숙련 (B) 개선 (C) 배열 (D) 허가

134. (A)

(A) 그러니, 여러분의 솔직한 의견을 공유해 주세요.
(B) 우리는 당신이 새로운 역할에서 뛰어난 활약을 할 것으로 생각합니다.
(C) 다행히도 리더십 기술은 시간이 흐르면서 개발될 수 있습니다.
(D) 정책 갱신 사항은 항상 온라인에 즉시 게시됩니다.

UNIT 01 문법

본문 p.158

1. (C)

Ms. Lampron,

Victoria City Bookstore의 회원이 되어 주셔서 감사합니다. [1]**귀하의** 회원 가입은 소기업들을 지원하는 데 도움이 되고, 종이 책들이 계속 출간되도록 해 줍니다. 우리 매장은 규모는 크지 않지만, 다양한 종류의 책들을 구비하고 있으며, 현재 우리 매장

PART 6

선반에 진열되어 있지 않은 대부분의 책들에 대해 빠른 배송을 제공합니다.

어휘 membership 회원권, 회원 자격 ensure 보장하다, 확실히 하다 in print 출판 중인 storefront 가게 앞 modest 수수한 a wide array of 다수의 title 서적, 출판물 shelf 선반

2. (A)

Hogan Insurance의 연례 만찬이 12월 17일 금요일 오후 7시에 열리게 됩니다. Hogan Insurance의 모든 직원과 그들의 가족이 초대되오니 경영실로 회신을 부탁드립니다. 회사에서 최고의 성과를 거둔 직원들에게는 만찬이 끝날 때 [2]**표창이 주어지게 될 것입니다.** 여러분 모두를 그곳에서 볼 수 있기를 바랍니다!

어휘 annual 연례의 banquet 연회, 만찬 take place 열리다, 발생하다 RSVP 회답 주시기 바랍니다 administrative office 경영실, 행정실 perform 수행하다 recognize 인정하다, 표창하다

3. (D)

직원 공지 IT 팀이 소프트웨어를 업데이트할 예정이므로 금요일에 퇴근하기 전에 컴퓨터를 끄지 마세요. 우리는 시스템의 보안을 보장하기 위해 매달 소프트웨어 업데이트를 [3]**수행합니다.** 질문이 있으면 IT 관리자인 Sean Hendrix에게 내선 18번으로 문의하십시오.

어휘 turn off 끄다 leave work 퇴근하다 be scheduled to do ~하기로 되어 있다 update 업데이트하다 ensure 보장하다, 반드시 ~이게 하다 security 보안 direct 향하게 하다 extension 내선 번호

PRACTICE 본문 p.159

1. (B) **2.** (A) **3.** (B) **4.** (D)

1-4 기사

이탈리아 나폴리—Romulus Construction은 나폴리 지역에서 매우 존경받는 회사이다. [1]**이 회사는** 토지를 취득하고 개발한 다음 나폴리와 주변 지역에 완성된 주택을 판매한다. 이 주택들은 저렴한 가격[2]**뿐만 아니라** 시공의 품질로도 알려져 있다. Romulus Construction은 해안을 따라 넓게 펼쳐진 부지를 인수[3]**할 계획이라고** 얼마 전에 발표했다. "우리는 그곳에 개인용 주택들을 건설하면서, 자연 환경의 아름다움도 유지할 것입니다."라고 Romulus의 Ernesto Humbert 최고경영자가 말했다. "[4]**우리가 짓는 주택이 구매자들 사이에서 인기가 있을 것으로 봅니다.** 우리는 앞으로 몇 주 이내에 더 많은 세부 정보를 공개할 것입니다." 회사는 가까운 장래에 더 많은 토지를 매입하기를 희망한다고 덧붙였다.

어휘 highly 매우 acquire 취득하다, 얻다 complete 완성된, 완전한 unit 한 개, 구성 단위 affordability 감당할 수 있는 비용 a stretch of 넓게 펼쳐진 along ~을 따라 residence 주택 release 공개하다, 발표하다 add 더하다, 덧붙이다 in the near future 가까운 미래에

1. (B)

해설 앞선 문장의 단수 사물 주어인 Romulus Construction을 대신하는 주격 인칭대명사가 들어가야 하므로 (B) It이 정답이다.

2. (A)

(A) ~뿐만 아니라 (B) ~을 제외하고 (C) ~하기 위하여 (D) 그동안

해설 선택지가 전치사와 부사 등으로 구성되어 있는데, 빈칸 뒤에 구가 나오므로 전치사인 as well as와 except for가 정답 후보가 된다. 문맥상 except for는 답이 될 수 없고 (A) as well as가 정답이다.

3. (B)

해설 빈칸 앞의 it은 명사절의 주어이고 빈칸에는 동사가 들어가야 한다. 주어가 단수이므로 복수 동사인 plan, have been planned 등을 소거할 수 있다. 뒤에 목적어가 되는 명사적 용법의 to 부정사가 나오므로 능동태인 (B) is planning이 정답이다.

4. (D)

(A) 건설되고 있는 건물들은 거의 완성되었습니다.
(B) 토지 구입 결정은 신속히 내려져야 합니다.
(C) 한 가족이 이미 새 집으로 입주했습니다.
(D) 우리가 짓는 주택이 구매자들 사이에서 인기가 있을 것으로 봅니다.

어휘 make a decision 결정하다

UNIT 02 품사

본문 p.160

1. (D)

귀하의 〈World Travel Magazine〉 구독은 8월 31일에 만료될 예정입니다. 이 간행물을 계속해서 [1]**받으시려면** 아래 링크를 따라가서 가능한 한 빨리 온라인 양식을 작성해 주십시오. 그렇게 하면, 귀하는 전세계 최고의 휴가지에 대한 우리의 유용한 기사를 하나도 놓치지 않을 수 있을 것입니다

어휘 subscription 구독 be due to ~할 예정이다 expire 만료되다 issue 호, 발행물 publication 간행물, 출판물 complete 작성하다, 완성하다 form 양식 miss 놓치다 article 기사 destination 목적지, 도착지

2. (B)

브랜치버그 시는 록웰 북부 지역에 새로운 아파트 단지 건설을 승인했다. 건물은 침실이 하나 있는 마흔 다섯 가구와 건물 내 세탁 시설을 포함하게 될 것이다. 그 목적은 유명 [2]**관광지**인 Skye Amusement Park의 직원들뿐만 아니라 고속버스 노선을 이용하는 통근자들에게 저렴한 주택을 공급하는 것이다.

어휘 approve 승인하다 apartment complex 아파트 단지 neighborhood 지역, 인근 contain 포함하다, 들어 있다 unit 가구, 호 on-site 건물 내의, 현장의 laundry 세탁 facility 시설 aim 목적 supply 공급하다 affordable 저렴한 attraction 관광지, 명소 commuter 통근자 route 노선

3. (A)

> Sampson Foods의 연구개발팀은 자사의 건강 간식 제품들을 위한 새로운 포장 절차를 개발했다. 물품들은 이제 밀봉된 환경을 유지하기 위해 비닐 포장이 한 겹 더 추가될 것이다. 그 같은 변화는 오랜 보관 기간 동안에도 식품의 질감과 맛에 있어 보다 일관되고 [3]**예측 가능한** 결과를 제공할 것으로 기대된다.

어휘 R&D 연구 개발 packing 포장 procedure 절차 line 제품군 healthy 건강에 좋은 snack 간식 package 포장하다 additional 추가의 layer 층 plastic 비닐, 플라스틱 maintain 유지하다 airtight 밀봉의, 밀폐의 consistent 일관된, 꾸준한 predictable 예측 가능한 texture 질감 storage 보관, 저장 period 기간

PRACTICE

본문 p.161

1. (D) **2.** (D) **3.** (A) **4.** (C)

1-4 회람

> 수신: 간부 직원들
> 발신: Helen Schnell
> 제목: 옥스포드 공장 소식
> 날짜: 8월 10일
>
> 3개월 동안, 우리는 옥스포드에 있는 신규 공장에서 충원되어야 할 자리에 대해 대대적으로 광고를 했습니다. [1]**저는 그 자리의 절반이 충원되었다는 것을 알리게 되어 기쁩니다.** 우리는 현재 일정보다 앞서 있으며, 8월 말까지 모든 자리에 직원을 완전히 충원해야 합니다. 우리는 또한 경력 직원들로 공장을 [2]**충원하는** 것에 관심이 있습니다. 옥스포드로 전근을 하는 것에 관심이 있는 사람은 누구나 [3]**제게** 연락 주십시오. 채용 과정에서 현 직원들에게 우선권이 주어질 것입니다. 우리는 다음 주에 현장을 시찰하게 됩니다. 현장을 직접 보시려면 이 이메일에 회신하세요. 그러면 제가 필요한 [4]**준비**를 하겠습니다.

어휘 plant 공장 update 최신 소식 heavily 아주 많이 fill a position 자리를 채우다 staff 직원을 제공하다 transfer 이동하다, 전근하다 preference 우선권, 선호 conduct (특정 활동을) 하다 tour 견학, 투어 site 현장, 장소 in person 직접 arrangement 준비, 마련

1. (D)

(A) 지금 시설 설계에 대한 입찰이 접수되고 있습니다.
(B) 우리는 부정적인 평가를 받은 후 그곳을 폐쇄하기로 결정했습니다.
(C) 오늘 오후에 우리 사장님께서 중요한 발표를 하실 겁니다.
(D) 저는 그 자리의 절반이 충원되었다는 것을 알리게 되어 기쁩니다.

어휘 bid 입찰 facility 시설 close down 폐쇄하다 negative 부정적인 review 후기 make an announcement 발표하다

2. (D)

(A) 대체하다 (B) 설계하다 (C) 채용하다 (D) 충원하다

3. (A)

해설 동사 contact의 목적어가 되는 목적격 인칭대명사 (A) me가 정답이다.

4. (C)

해설 관사 the와 형용사 necessary의 수식을 받는 명사 (C) arrangements가 정답이다.

UNIT 03 어휘

본문 p.162

1. (D)

> 국립역사박물관은 방문객들에게 오래 전 사람들의 삶을 엿볼 수 있는 멋진 기회를 제공합니다. 우리 전시회는 의류, 도자기, 미술품 등을 선보입니다. 입장료는 1인당 7달러 50센트에 불과합니다. 박물관은 104번이나 1288번 버스를 이용해 대중교통으로 쉽게 [1]**접근할** 수 있습니다. 보다 많은 정보를 얻으려면 저희 웹 사이트인 www.nationalhm.org를 방문하십시오.

어휘 fascinating 매혹적인 glimpse 흘끗 보기, 짧은 경험 exhibit 전시(회) feature 특별히 포함하다 pottery 도자기 admission 입장(료) public transportation 대중교통

2. (C)

> Ms. Burnett,
>
> 귀하께서 신청하신 Arlington Bank 소상공인 대출이 승인되었음을 알려드리게 되어 기쁩니다. 대출금은 영업일로 5일 이내에 귀하의 기업 계좌로 입금될 것입니다. 귀하의 기록을 위해 동봉된 대출 [2]**계약서**를 보관해 주십시오. 질문이나 염려되는 점이 있으면 언제든지 저희 고객 서비스 팀에 연락 주십시오.

어휘 pleased 기쁜, 즐거운 inform 알리다, 통지하다 application 신청(서) small business 소기업 loan 대출 fund 돈, 자금 credit 입금하다 account 계정, 계좌 retain 보유하다, 유지하다 enclose 동봉하다 record 기록 concern 걱정, 염려 feel free to 마음대로 ~하다 contact 연락하다

3. (A)

> Salisbury Suites 세입자 공지
>
> 복도 조명의 배선을 바꾸기 위해 1월 19일에 전기 기사가 이곳을 방문하도록 일정을 잡았습니다. 작업이 진행되는 동안 건물에 전기가 들어오지 않을 것입니다. 오전 9시에 전기가 끊겼다가 늦어도 오후 2시까지는 [3]**복구될** 것입니다. 이로 인해 발생할 수 있는 불편에 대해 사과드립니다.

어휘 tenant 세입자 schedule 일정을 잡다 electrician 전기 기사 site 장소, 현장 corridor 복도 rewire 다시 배선하다 while ~하는 동안 take place 일어나다, 열리다 electricity 전기 shut off 차단하다 no later than 늦어도 ~까지는 apologize for ~에 대해 사과하다 inconvenience 불편

PRACTICE 본문 p.163

1. (A) **2.** (C) **3.** (B) **4.** (A)

1-4 기사

하트퍼드 (5월 19일)—하트퍼드에 기반을 두고 있는 자선단체인 Peterson House가 7월 1일에 연례 모금 행사가 있을 것이라고 공지했다. Peterson House는 2001년에 [1]**설립되었으며**, 하트퍼드 지역의 어린이들에게 음식, 의복, 그리고 교육 용품을 제공하는 데 초점을 맞춰 왔다.
Peterson House의 이사장인 Jenny Blair는 "우리는 처음으로 입찰식 경매를 열 것입니다. 우리는 이것이 우리에게 제공하는 기회에 [2]**들떠 있습니다.**"라고 말했다.
Ms. Blair는 자선단체가 몇 번의 지연 끝에 [3]**마침내** 새 사무실 건설을 완료했다고 덧붙였다. [4]**공사는 올봄에 악천후에 의해 상당한 영향을 받았다.** 그녀는 또한 자선단체가 여름과 가을을 위한 몇 가지 큰 계획들을 가지고 있으며 나중에 그것들에 대해 논의할 것이라고 말했다.

어휘 based 본사를 둔 charity 자선단체 annual 연례의 fundraiser 모금 행사 supplies 물품, 공급품 silent auction 입찰식 경매 present 제시하다 state 말하다 at a later date 나중에

1. (A)
(A) 설립하다 (B) 기부하다 (C) 호소하다 (D) 건설하다

2. (C)
해설 뒤에 목적어가 없으므로 be동사와 함께 수동태를 형성하는 (C) are excited가 정답이다.

3. (B)
(A) 항상 (B) 마침내 (C) 그 대신에 (D) 특별히

4. (A)
(A) 공사는 올봄에 악천후에 의해 상당한 영향을 받았다.
(B) 그녀는 경매에서 백만 달러를 모을 것으로 기대하고 있다.
(C) Ms. Blair는 2001년부터 자선단체에서 일하고 있다.
(D) 자선단체는 지역에서 받은 지원에 만족하고 있다.

어휘 affect 영향을 미치다 raise (자금을) 모으다 locally 지역에서

UNIT 04 접속 부사

본문 p.164

1. (B)

안녕하세요, Ashley.
다음 주 신입사원 연수 워크숍을 맡겠다고 자원해 주셔서 감사합니다. 우리 지점과 우드데일 지점에서 직원들이 올 거라는 걸 방금 알았어요. 이로써 전체 참석자는 13명에서 25명으로 늘어났습니다. [1]**따라서**, 우리는 워크숍을 대회의실로 옮길 예정인데, 그곳이 더 크기 때문입니다. 궁금한 것이 있으면 저에게 알려주세요.

어휘 volunteer 자원하다 lead 이끌다 training 교육 branch 지점, 지사 bring (결과를) 이르게 하다 total 도합 main 주요한, 주된 conference room 회의실

2. (B)

Brisbane Hotel은 8월 8일 목요일에 중앙 로비의 엘리베이터들을 교체합니다. 고객님들께서는 객실로 가기 위해 프런트 데스크 바로 우측에 위치한 계단을 이용해 주시기 바랍니다. [2]**그렇지 않으면**, 고객님들께서는 제이콥스 스트리트 출입구 근처에 있는 엘리베이터들을 이용하실 수 있습니다. 양해해 주셔서 감사합니다.

어휘 replace 교체하다, 대체하다 stairwell 계단통 locate 위치하다 directly 곧장, 곧바로 entrance 출입구 patience 인내

3. (D)

Mr. Bradley,
저는 Blake Patterson을 팀장 승진자로 추천하고 싶습니다. Mr. Patterson은 회사에서 5년간 근무해 왔으며, 우리 부서 내에서 매우 존경을 받고 있습니다. 그는 뛰어난 서면 의사소통 능력을 가지고 있습니다. [3]**마찬가지로**, 그는 대화에서도 자신을 잘 표현할 수 있습니다. 저는 Mr. Patterson이 이 역할에서 잘해 나갈 것이라고 믿습니다.

어휘 recommend 추천하다 promotion 승진 communication 의사소통 express 표현하다 thrive 번창하다, 성공하다

PRACTICE 본문 p.165

1. (A) **2.** (D) **3.** (C) **4.** (A)

1-4 이메일

수신: Carl Lambert 〈carl_lambert@safehold.com〉
발신: Harold Beemer 〈hbeemer@safehold.com〉
날짜: 10월 3일
제목: 일정 수립

Mr. Lambert,

이것은 다음 주 일정과 관련된 것입니다. [1]**유감스럽게도** 저는 다음 주 월요일에 근무를 할 수 없습니다. 제 상사인 Brenda Malone은 지난주에 10월 10일 월요일로 요청한 저의 휴가 신청을 승인해 주셨습니다. 제가 그날 다른 지역에 사시는 부모님을 [2]**찾아뵙기** 때문입니다. 저는 이번 주 금요일에 출발해서 월

요일 밤에 돌아옵니다. Ms. Malone이 이 내용을 당신에게 알리지 않았을 것으로 생각합니다.
[3]**제가 화요일에 근무 일정이 없다는 것을 알았습니다.** 월요일에 저 대신 근무를 해줄 사람이 있으면 그 사람과 기꺼이 교대 근무를 바꾸도록 하겠습니다.
우리가 이 상황을 어떻게 조정할 수 있는지 알려주세요. 언제든지 당신을 만나서 우리가 [4]**선택할 수 있는 방안들**을 논의할 수 있습니다.
Harold Beemer

어휘 in regard to ~에 관한 supervisor 상사, 감독관 approve 승인하다 time off 휴가 out of town 시외의 depart 출발하다, 떠나다 assume 추정하다, 생각하다 inform A of B A에게 B를 알리다 matter 문제, 건 shift 교대 근무 rectify 바로잡다, 조정하다

1. (A)
(A) 유감스럽게도, 불행히도 (B) 진심으로 (C) 분명히 (D) 아마

2. (D)
해설 이메일을 보낸 날짜는 10월 3일이고, 예정된 휴가일은 10월 10일이므로 빈칸에는 미래 시제의 동사가 와야 한다. 따라서 (D) will be visiting이 정답이다.

3. (C)
(A) 당신을 위해 이곳에서 근무하게 되어 즐거웠습니다.
(B) 제 상황을 이해해 주셔서 감사합니다.
(C) 제가 화요일에 근무 일정이 없다는 것을 알았습니다.
(D) 이번이 저의 올해 첫 휴가였습니다.
어휘 notice 알아차리다

4. (A)
(A) 선택권 (B) 선택 (C) 상황 (D) 기기

UNIT 05 문맥에 맞는 문장 고르기 본문 p.166

1. (C)

Hilltop Rentals는 자사의 렌터카 보유 대수를 늘리기 위한 신규 투자 자금을 조달했다. Hilltop Rentals의 대변인은 80대의 소형 고연비 차량을 구입할 것이라고 말했다. [1]**회사는 10대의 이삿짐 트럭도 구입할 것이다.** 그 같은 변화는 보다 넓은 선택권이 필요하다는 고객의 의견에 따른 것이다. 렌탈 선택권에 관한 자세한 내용은 www.hilltop-rentals.com에서 확인할 수 있다.

(A) 그것들은 주차 시간에 따라 가격이 다르다.
(B) 직원들은 더 나은 근무 시간에 만족한다.
(C) 회사는 10대의 이삿짐 트럭도 구입할 것이다.
(D) 그는 임대 비용에 대해 몇 차례의 불만을 접수했다.
어휘 procure 입수하다, 조달하다 fund 자금 expand 확대하다, 확장하다 fleet 모든 보유 차량 spokesperson 대변인 fuel-efficient 연비가 좋은 in response to ~에 응하여 feedback 의견, 피드백 indicate 나타내다 vary 서로 다르다 moving van 이삿짐 트럭 block 막다, 차단하다

2. (A)

Ms. Milton,
복사기 중 한 대를 5층 직원 휴게실에서 3층 사무실로 옮기는 것을 제안하고 싶습니다. 이것은 시간을 절약하는 데 도움이 될 텐데, 많은 직원들이 단지 문서를 복사하기 위해 여러 층의 계단을 올라가야 하기 때문입니다. [2]**또한, 우리는 일부 공간을 비울 수 있습니다.** 그로 인해 제가 많은 불만을 가지고 있었던, 휴게실이 너무 붐비는 문제를 해결하게 될 것입니다.
Keisha

(A) 또한, 우리는 일부 공간을 비울 수 있습니다.
(B) 가장 좋은 평가를 받은 기계들은 일반적으로 더 비쌉니다.
(C) 많은 사람들은 사용 설명서가 혼란스럽다고 생각합니다.
(D) 우리는 양면 인쇄를 통해 종이를 절약할 수 있습니다.
어휘 propose 제안하다 lounge 휴게실 save 절약하다 flight 계단, 층계 crowded 붐비는 numerous 무수히 많은 complaint 불만 in addition 또한, 게다가 free up 개방하다, 자유롭게 하다 instruction manual 사용 설명서

PRACTICE 본문 p.167

1. (B) **2.** (B) **3.** (D) **4.** (A)

1-4 광고

Daniels Landscaping
Daniels Landscaping은 20년 이상 부동산을 [1]**관리해** 왔습니다. 우리는 여러분의 집이나 사업장이 최대한 좋게 보이도록 만들기 위해 다양한 조경 서비스를 제공합니다. 서비스에는 잔디 깎기, 덤불 다듬기, 나무와 꽃 심기, 그리고 마당에 물 주기 등이 포함됩니다. [2]**게다가,** 우리는 야외 구역을 돌보는 것과 관련된 기타 서비스들을 제공할 수 있습니다.
우리의 조경사들은 각각 수 년간의 경력이 있으며, 모두 뛰어난 자질을 갖추고 있습니다. [3]**그들은 또한 효율적이고 즐겁게 근무합니다.** Daniels Landscaping의 가격은 따라올 수 없습니다. 우리의 작업은 여러분을 만족시킬 것을 [4]**보장하며,** 그렇지 않을 경우 환불을 받게 되실 겁니다. 더 많은 정보를 원하시면 555-9845로 전화하세요.

어휘 landscaping 조경 property 부동산, 재산 decade 10년 a variety of 다양한 trim 다듬다 bush 덤불 water 물을 주다 yard 마당 outdoor 야외의, 실외의 qualified 자격이 있는 beat 이기다

1. (B)
해설 뒤에 기간을 나타내는 for 전치사구가 있으므로 현재완료진행 시제를 만드는 (B) has been taking이 정답이다.

PART 6

2. (B)

(A) 하지만 (B) 게다가 (C) 그 결과로 (D) 예를 들어

3. (D)

(A) 다행히도, 우리에게는 작업자들로 구성된 큰 팀이 있습니다.
(B) 저희 웹사이트를 확인하는 것을 잊지 마세요.
(C) 저희에게 관심을 가져 주셔서 감사합니다.
(D) 그들은 또한 효율적이고 즐겁게 근무합니다.

어휘 check out 확인하다, 보다 efficiently 효율적으로 cheerfully 즐겁게

4. (A)

(A) 보장된 (B) 분명한 (C) 약속된 (D) 놀란

PART TEST

본문 p.168

131. (B) **132.** (D) **133.** (A) **134.** (D) **135.** (A) **136.** (D) **137.** (C) **138.** (D) **139.** (A) **140.** (C) **141.** (B) **142.** (C) **143.** (B) **144.** (D) **145.** (C) **146.** (C)

131-134 광고

〈International Business News Report〉는 비즈니스에 관한 최고의 소식통입니다. 전 세계의 모든 최신 소식을 알아보시고 비즈니스 세계의 다양한 [131] **트렌드**를 숙지하세요. 저희 기자들은 업계에서 최고의 명성을 가진 사람들입니다. 그들은 [132] **매일** 기사를 쓰고 새로운 정보가 입수될 때마다 최신 소식을 제공합니다. 구독하시려면 저희 웹사이트 www.ibnr.com/subscriptions를 방문하세요. 웹사이트에 가입하시면 당사의 [133] **전체** 기사 자료실을 이용하실 수 있으며, 다양한 분야의 최고의 사람들과 온라인 채팅에 참여할 수 있습니다. 무엇을 기다리세요? [134] **오늘 구독하시고 비즈니스에 대해 보다 많은 것을 배우기 시작하세요.**

어휘 source 원천, 근원 be aware of ~을 알다 industry 업계, 산업 article 기사 update 최신 정보 subscribe 구독하다 access 접근, 이용 archive 자료실, 기록 보관소 field 분야

131. (B)

(A) 매력 (B) 트렌드, 동향 (C) 구독 (D) 버전, 판

132. (D)

(A) 상대적으로, 비교적 (B) 진지하게, 심각하게 (C) 점진적으로 (D) 매일

133. (A)

해설 빈칸 뒤의 명사 archives를 수식하는 형용사 (A) complete가 정답이다.

134. (D)

(A) 저희 잡지를 계속 애용해 주셔서 감사드립니다.
(B) 저희가 진행하고 있는 특별 세일에 대해 말씀드리겠습니다.
(C) 귀하의 첫 번째 호는 월요일 아침까지 우편으로 도착할 것입니다.
(D) 오늘 구독하시고 비즈니스에 대해 보다 많은 것을 배우기 시작하세요.

어휘 appreciate 감사하다, 고마워하다 continued 지속적인 dedication 호감, 헌신 issue (신문, 잡지 등의) 호

135-138 광고

First Avenue Mechanics

여러분 차의 엔진이 이상한 소음을 내나요? 여러분의 차가 더 잘 달리기를 원하시나요? [135] **그렇다면 여러분의 차를 좀 더 자세히 들여다볼 때입니다.** 여러분의 차량을 First Avenue Mechanics로 가져오십시오. 인가를 받은 우리 정비사들이 여러분의 차가 금방 [136] **부드럽게** 달릴 수 있도록 해드릴 것입니다. 또한 여러분 차체의 크고 작은 문제들도 모두 수리해 드릴 수 있습니다. 예약을 하실 필요가 없습니다. 저희는 24시간 영업합니다. 그러니 1번가 85번지로 오셔서 여러분의 차량을 놓고 가시기만 하면 됩니다. [137] **대부분의** 경우 우리는 당일에 차를 수리합니다. 당사의 [138] **종합적인** 요금표를 보시려면 당사의 웹사이트인 www.firstavenuemechanics.com을 방문하세요.

어휘 mechanic 정비공 licensed 면허가 있는, 인가된 minor 경미한, 사소한 major 주요한 make an appointment 예약하다 twenty-four hours a day 하루 종일 fix 고치다 comprehensive 종합적인

135. (A)

(A) 그렇다면 여러분의 차를 좀 더 자세히 들여다볼 때입니다.
(B) 각 차량은 아주 세심하게 검사됩니다.
(C) 우리의 신차들은 합리적인 가격으로 제공됩니다.
(D) 일부 부품은 특별히 주문해야 할 수도 있습니다.

어휘 inspect 검사하다 with care 주의 깊게 reasonable 합리적인

136. (D)

(A) 명백히 (B) 꽤 (C) 편리하게 (D) 부드럽게

137. (C)

해설 명사 cases를 수식하는 형용사인 (C) most가 정답이다. every는 단수 명사를 수식하고 much는 불가산 명사를 수식하므로 오답이고, 빈칸 앞에 their가 가리키는 어휘가 보이지 않으므로 their도 오답이다.

138. (D)

해설 명사 price list를 수식하는 형용사인 (D) comprehensive가 정답이다. 선택지에 형용사와 분사가 함께 있으면 형용사가 우선하므로 분사 형태의 comprehended와 comprehending은 오답이다.

139-142 웹사이트

Nantucket Seafood: 배달 방침

Nantucket Seafood는 전국에 48시간 이내 배송이 가능합니다. [139]**모든 주문품은 드라이아이스로 포장되어 빠른 우편으로 배송됩니다.** 낸터킷에 있는 우리 공장에서 3시간 이내에 거주하시는 분들은 당일 퀵서비스 배송을 선택하실 수 있습니다. 가격은 소포의 무게와 이동 거리에 [141]**따라** 다릅니다. 주문 당시 저희가 통지를 받지 않는 한, 모든 배송은 수취인에 의해 서명되어야 합니다. 악천후 및 기타 부득이한 문제로 인해 지연된 배송에 대해 당사는 [142]**책임을 지지** 않습니다. 자세한 내용은 고객 서비스 담당자에게 연락하세요.

어휘 seafood 해산물 policy 방침, 정책 ship 배송하다 opt 선택하다, 고르다 courier 배달원 vary 다르다 recipient 수취인 notify 통보하다, 알리다 place an order 주문하다 unavoidable 피할 수 없는 contact 연락하다

139. (A)

(A) 모든 주문품은 드라이아이스로 포장되어 빠른 우편으로 배송됩니다.
(B) 앞으로 몇 주 안에 더 많은 해산물 선택권을 이용할 수 있을 것입니다.
(C) 우리의 가격은 전국 최저가라는 것을 보장합니다.
(D) 그것은 여러분의 주문품이 이미 도착했어야 한다는 것을 의미합니다.

어휘 order 주문(품) pack 포장하다, 싸다 express mail 빠른 우편 guarantee 보장하다

140. (C)

해설 빈칸 앞에 사람 선행사인 individuals가 있고 뒤에 동사가 있으므로, 사람을 나타내는 주격 관계사인 (C) who가 정답이다.

141. (B)

(A) 고려하다 (B) 의존하다, 좌우되다 (C) 기다리다 (D) 보고하다

해설 빈칸 뒤의 전치사 upon과 함께 쓰이며 의미상 적절한 (B) depending이 정답이다.

142. (C)

해설 빈칸 앞에 be동사 are가 있으므로 빈칸에는 보어 역할을 하며 전치사 for와 연결되는 형용사가 필요하다. 따라서 (C) responsible이 정답이다. responsive는 '즉각 반응하는'이라는 의미로 문맥상 맞지 않으므로 오답이다.

143-146 이메일

수신: Alexandria Houston
발신: Winston Pierce
제목: 벽지
날짜: 7월 5일

Ms. Houston,

귀사에서 저희 매장에 제공해 주신 벽지는 아주 잘 판매되고 있습니다. 제 고객들은 그 디자인들을 좋아하며, 벽지가 고객들의 집안에서 보이는 모습에 [143]**만족합니다.** [144]**고객들은 가격을 낮게 책정하는 것도 아주 마음에 들어 합니다.** 그렇기 때문에 저는 벽지를 매달 주기적으로 [145]**배송** 받기를 원합니다.

저는 또한 디자인의 숫자를 늘리고 싶습니다. 현재, 저는 가용한 귀사의 디자인 중 7가지를 보유하고 있습니다만, 15가지가 더 좋을 것 같습니다. 귀사의 가장 인기 있는 디자인 샘플 몇 개를 보내 주시겠습니까? [146]**일단** 제가 디자인을 봐야 어떤 것들을 취급해야 할지 결정할 수 있을 것입니다.

Winston Pierce
Pierce Home Furnishings

어휘 wallpaper 벽지 as such 그 결과, 그렇기 때문에 set up 준비하다, 설립하다 shipment 배송(품) currently 현재, 지금 available 이용 가능한 carry (상품을) 취급하다

143. (B)

해설 빈칸 뒤에 목적어 없이 전치사구가 이어지므로 수동태가 적절하다. 따라서 (B) are pleased가 정답이다.

144. (D)

(A) 제 매장은 최근에 새로운 코너를 추가했습니다.
(B) 고객들이 온라인으로 물품을 구입하려고 합니다.
(C) 많은 사람들이 제가 벽지를 발라 주기를 원합니다.
(D) 고객들은 가격을 낮게 책정하는 것도 아주 마음에 들어 합니다.

어휘 department (상점의) 매장, 코너 charge 부과하다

145. (C)

해설 빈칸 앞에 동사 like와 형용사 regular가 있으므로, 형용사의 수식을 받으면서 동사의 목적어가 되는 명사가 올 수 있다. 앞에 관사 a가 있으므로 단수 명사인 (C) shipment가 정답이다.

146. (C)

(A) 여전히 (B) ~하기 전에 (C) 일단 ~하고 나면 (D) 하지만

RC PART 7

출제 경향 및 전략

본문 p.174

164-167 이메일

수신: Allison Holder
발신: Clarissa Simpson
날짜: 3월 16일
제목: 중요 메시지

Allison,

[164]**11월 1일자로, 우리 회사는 정규직과 파트타임 직원 누구에게도 더 이상 건강 보험을 제공하지 않을 것입니다. 대신에, 직원들은 자기 자신의 개인 건강 보험에 가입할 수 있도록 약간의 급여 인상을 받게 될 것입니다.**
우리가 현재 이곳 Newport Technology에서 하는 것과 같은 단체 보험을 운영하는 비용이 최근에 너무 많이 증가해서 [165]**우리가 적자를 보고 있습니다.** 따라서 이사회는 비용 절감 조치로 이러한 변경을 하기로 결정했습니다. 우리는 직원들이 자신과 가족에게 가장 적합한 보험사를 선택할 수 있도록 상담 서비스를 제공할 계획입니다.
[166]**David Schuler가 전환을 담당할 것입니다. 그는 11월 1일까지 당신에게 매주 최신 소식을 제공할 것입니다.** 우리는 6월에 이번 변경 사항과 관련된 것을 발표할 예정이므로, 그 무렵에 직원들로부터 많은 질문을 받을 것으로 예상합니다.

Clarissa Simpson
Newport Technology

어휘 as of ~일자로 no longer 더 이상 ~ 않다 health insurance 건강 보험 enable ~할 수 있게 하다 acquire 얻다, 취득하다 policy 보험 증권 currently 현재, 지금 board of directors 이사회 therefore 그러므로, 따라서 measure 방책, 방법 assist 돕다 select 선택하다 provider 제공자, 공급자 transition 전환, 이행 update 최신 정보 make an announcement 발표하다 regarding ~에 관해 anticipate 예상하다, 예측하다

164. 이메일의 목적은 무엇인가?
(A) 정보를 제공하려고
(B) 도움을 요청하려고
(C) 회의 일정을 잡으려고
(D) 조언을 청하려고

165. Newport Technology에 대해 암시된 것은 무엇인가?
(A) 여름에 새로운 직원들을 채용할 계획이다.
(B) 의료 업계에 속해 있다.
(C) 다른 나라에 지사들이 있다.
(D) 현재 이익을 내고 있지 못하다.

166. Ms. Simpson에 따르면 Mr. Schuler는 무엇을 할 것인가?
(A) 직원들의 급여 인상을 결정하기
(B) 이사회와 협력하기
(C) Ms. Holder에게 최신 소식을 제공하기
(D) 직원들을 위한 새로운 보험사 찾기

167. 세 번째 단락 첫 번째 줄의 어휘 'transition'과 의미상 가장 가까운 것은?
(A) 발달
(B) 접근
(C) 변화
(D) 수정

UNIT 01 주제/목적

본문 p.176

대표 유형 맛보기

Mr. Douglas,

귀하께서 정기 검진을 위해 저희를 방문하신 지 6개월 이상의 시간이 지났습니다. 여기를 클릭하시어 치아 세척 및 충치 검사 예약을 하실 수 있습니다. 저희는 5명의 치과 의사를 직원으로 보유하고 있으며, 그들 모두는 귀하를 도울 준비가 되어 있습니다. 선호하시는 특정 치과 의사가 있는 경우 예약하실 때 그 점을 말씀하실 수 있습니다.

Tina Gooden
White Teeth Clinic

어휘 routine 정기적인 checkup 건강 검진 make an appointment 예약하다 cavity 충치 dentist 치과 의사 staff 직원 prefer 선호하다 indicate 나타내다

Q. 이메일의 주된 목적은 무엇인가?
(A) 새로운 곳을 추천하려고
(B) 상기시켜 주려고
(C) 새로운 서비스를 홍보하려고
(D) 예약을 확인하려고

어휘 recommend 추천하다 location 지점 provide 주다, 제공하다 reminder 상기시키는 것 promote 홍보하다 confirm 확정하다 booking 예약

PRACTICE

본문 p.177

1. (D) **2.** (B) **3.** (C)

1-3 보도 자료

즉시 배포 요망

[1]**Porterhouse Manufacturing이 제품 시연을 실시할 예정**

Porterhouse Manufacturing은 세계 최고의 첨단 기계 제조사 중 하나이다. 오늘 회사는 자사의 엔지니어들이 얼마 전 개발을 완료했으며 겨울에 시판할 예정인 [1]**기계에 대한 제품 시연회를 열 것이라고 발표했다.** 행사는 10월 3일 월요일 오후 3시에 애틀랜타에 있는 본사에서 열릴 것이다. 시연되는 제품은 회사가 개발한 최신 자동차 엔진이다. 이 엔진은 현재 이용 가능한

다른 어떤 엔진보다 35% 더 효율적이기 때문에, 자동차 산업에 혁명을 일으킬 것이다.
행사에 직접 참석하는 것에 관심이 있는 기자와 아나운서는 사전에 등록해야 한다. [2]**등록하려면 정규 업무 시간 중에 회사의 홍보 직원인 Gregory Frye에게 555-2871로 연락해야 한다.** 팟캐스트와 블로그를 운영하며 자동차 기술에 관심이 있는 사람들도 초대된다. [3]**프로젝트의 수석 엔지니어인 Jeremy Smith는 시연 후에 질문에 답할 것이다.** 참석자들은 사진과 동영상 촬영이 허용될 것이다.

어휘 release 공개, 발표 conduct 하다, 수행하다 demonstration 시연 leading 선도적인 advanced 진보된 machinery 기계류 intend 의도하다, 계획하다 headquarters 본사 be set to do ~하도록 예정되어 있다 revolutionize 혁명을 일으키다 efficient 효율적인 broadcaster 아나운서, 방송 출연자 register 등록하다 in advance 사전에, 미리 public relations 홍보 business hours 영업 시간 as well 또한, ~도

1. 보도 자료의 목적은 무엇인가?
(A) 투자자들에게 제품 출시를 알리려고
(B) 회사의 업데이트된 서비스를 공개하려고
(C) 회사의 제품을 구매하는 방법에 대한 세부 정보를 제공하려고
(D) 제품 시연에 대한 정보를 제공하려고

어휘 details 세부 사항 acquire 얻다, 입수하다

2. 사람들은 어떻게 행사에 등록할 수 있는가?
(A) 기술에 대해 알리는 블로그를 방문함으로써
(B) Porterhouse Manufacturing 직원에게 전화함으로써
(C) Porterhouse Manufacturing 웹페이지에 등록함으로써
(D) 행사를 취재할 기자와 이야기함으로써

패러프레이즈 contact → calling

어휘 report 보고하다, 알리다 technology 기술

3. 다가오는 행사에 대해 시사된 것은 무엇인가?
(A) 참석하려면 요금 지불을 필요로 한다.
(B) 주말에 열릴 것이다.
(C) 참석자들은 질문이 허용될 것이다.
(D) 참석자들에게 동영상이 상영될 것이다.

어휘 upcoming 다가오는, 곧 있을 payment 지불 fee 요금 take place 열리다, 일어나다

UNIT 02 NOT/True

본문 p.178

대표 유형 맛보기

그린브라이어 글쓰기 워크숍, 첫 번째 모임
오후 1시~3시
그린브라이어 공립도서관
4월 11일

전문가처럼 글을 쓰고 싶으세요? 굉장한 이야깃거리가 있지만 그것을 말로 표현하는 방법을 모르시나요? **그렇다면 Allison Herbst가 주관하는 워크숍이 당신에게 안성맞춤입니다. Ms. Herbst는 10권 이상의 소설을 출간했고** 또한 그린브라이어 공립 대학에서 교편을 잡고 있습니다.
등록을 하고 전체 시리즈의 모든 일정을 보려면 www.greenbrierlibrary.org를 방문하십시오. 모든 워크숍은 무료이지만 사전 등록이 필수입니다. Ms. Herbst는 워크숍이 끝난 후에 질문에 답할 것입니다.

어휘 put into words 말로 나타내다 host 주관하다, 주최하다 publish 출간하다, 펴내다 register 등록하다 complete 완전한, 모든 advance 사전의 conclude 끝나다, 마치다

Q. 워크숍에 대해 나타난 것은 무엇인가?
(A) 사람들은 참석하려면 돈을 내야 한다.
(B) 온라인상에서 열릴 것이다.
(C) 작가가 주관할 것이다.
(D) 대학교가 주최하고 있다.

어휘 take place 일어나다, 열리다 lead 이끌다

PRACTICE 본문 p.179

1. (A) **2.** (D) **3.** (D)

1-3 안내문

Silverwood Botanical Garden 이용권

[2]**Silverwood Botanical Garden은 주 전체에서 규모가 가장 큽니다.** 200에이커 이상의 면적을 차지하고 있는 정원에 대표적인 것들로는 남동부에 자생하는 나무, 꽃, 식물뿐만 아니라 열대종을 비롯한 매우 다양한 외래종들이 있습니다. [1]**정원의 방문객들은 숲이 우거진 지역을 통과하는 하이킹을 즐길 수 있고,** 다섯 개의 연못가에서 소풍을 즐길 수 있고, 지역에 서식하는 야생 동물 중 일부를 보는 것을 즐길 수 있습니다.
Silverwood Botanical Garden 이용권은 1년에 50달러에 불과하며 4인 가족 전체가 이용할 수 있습니다. [3]**무료 주차뿐만 아니라 정원을 매일 입장하는 것도 허용됩니다.** 여러분이 내시는 돈은 우리가 정원의 식물들을 유지하고 새로운 식물들을 입수하는 것을 가능케 할 것입니다.
이용권은 매표소나 www.silverwoodbg.org에서 온라인으로 구입할 수 있습니다. 매표소 근처 상점에서 판매하는 음식이나 다른 상품에 대한 특별 할인은 불가능하다는 것을 유념해 주세요.

어휘 botanical garden 식물원 pass 통행증 state (행정 구역) 주 cover 걸치다, 포함시키다 feature 특징으로 하다 native to ~에 고유한, ~의 토종인 a wide variety of 매우 다양한 species (생물의) 종 tropics 열대 wooded 나무가 우거진 picnic 소풍을 하다 pond 연못 wildlife 야생 동물 inhabit 서식하다 contribution 기여, 기부금 maintain 유지하다 acquire 얻다 note 유념하다 available 이용할 수 있는

1. 어떤 활동이 안내문에 언급되어 있는가?
(A) 하이킹
(B) 수영
(C) 사냥
(D) 캠핑

PART 7

2. Silverwood Botanical Garden에 대해 나타난 것은 무엇인가?
(A) 그 지역의 식물들만 보유하고 있다.
(B) 오로지 회원들의 기부에 의존한다.
(C) 손님들이 연못에서 낚시를 하는 것을 허용한다.
(D) 근처의 다른 식물원들보다 크다.

어휘 rely on ~에 의존하다 solely 오로지 donation 기부 go fishing 낚시하다 nearby 근처의

3. Silverwood Botanical Garden 이용권의 혜택은 무엇인가?
(A) 저렴한 음식 가격
(B) 가이드를 동반하는 식물원 투어
(C) 기념품에 대한 할인
(D) 무료 주차

패러프레이즈 free → complimentary

어휘 benefit 혜택, 이익 guided 가이드의 안내를 받는 souvenir 기념품 complimentary 무료의

UNIT 03 추론/암시

본문 p.180

대표 유형 맛보기

Emily Hudson (오후 2:24)
David, 9월분 예산 보고서는 어제까지였어요. 하지만 저는 아직 당신의 보고서를 기다리고 있어요.
David Weber (오후 2:25)
죄송합니다. 헬싱키 출장 여행에서 방금 돌아왔거든요. 지금 보고서 작업 중입니다.
Emily Hudson (오후 2:26)
당신이 해외 출장 중이었는지 몰랐네요. 출장이 성공적이었으면 좋겠어요. 당신의 부서는 예산을 초과한 것 같나요?
David Weber (오후 2:27)
퇴근 전까지 알려 드리겠습니다.
Emily Hudson (오후 2:28)
고마워요. **금요일까지 제 최종 보고서를 끝내야 하는데, 당신의 수치를 받아야 그럴 수 있거든요.**

어휘 budget 예산 submit 제출하다

Q. Ms. Hudson에 대해 유추할 수 있는 것은 무엇인가?
(A) 그녀는 헬싱키로 출장을 갈 것이다.
(B) 그녀는 Mr. Weber가 출장 중이었다는 것을 알았다.
(C) 그녀는 아직 자신의 보고서를 완성하지 못했다.
(D) 그녀는 금요일에 자신의 상사를 만날 것이다.

어휘 complete 완성하다

PRACTICE 본문 p.181

1. (A) **2.** (B) **3.** (D)

1-3 온라인 채팅

Bill Hagler (오후 2:03)
여러분, 안녕하세요. 건물에 대한 작업은 어떻게 진행되고 있나요? 우리는 제시간에 끝나는 건가요? [2]**정말이지 3월 1일에 문을 열 수 있으면 좋겠어요.**
Susan Denton (오후 2:06)
모든 것이 좋아 보여요, Bill. [1]**주방은 거의 모든 것이 설치되었어요.** 테이블과 의자는 내일 도착할 겁니다. 우리는 그것들을 설치하는 걸 도와줄 누군가가 필요할 거예요.
Dallas Blair (오후 2:08)
Chris와 제가 그 일을 할 수 있어요, Susan. 제가 몇 시에 그곳에 가면 되는지만 알려주세요.
Susan Denton (오후 2:09)
고마워요, Dallas. 당신이 쉬는 날에도 기꺼이 일을 해주시겠다니 정말 감사해요.
Dallas Blair (오후 2:10)
아, 우리의 바로 옆에 있는 가게 주인과 제가 이야기를 나눴습니다. 그분은 앞으로 두어 달 안에 그만두실 계획이라고 말씀하시더군요.
Bill Hagler (오후 2:11)
[3]**그분의 가게를 임대할 수 있을까요?**
Dallas Blair (오후 2:12)
그분은 그렇게 말씀하셨어요. [3]**우리가 아마도 그걸 확인해봐야 할 것 같아요.** 두 장소를 연결하는 것이 가능할 수도 있습니다. [1]**그러면 공간이 더 넓어져 식당을 확장할 수 있을 거예요.**
Susan Denton (오후 2:13)
[3]**제가 부동산 중개인에게 연락해 볼게요.**
Bill Hagler (오후 2:14)
좋아요, Susan.

어휘 property 부동산, 건물 on time 제시간에 install 설치하다 appreciate 감사하다 day off 쉬는 날, 비번일 next to ~의 옆에 retire 폐업하다, 은퇴하다 available 이용 가능한 rent 임대 connect 연결하다 expand 확장하다 real estate agent 부동산 중개인

1. 메시지 작성자들은 어디에서 근무하겠는가?
(A) 음식점
(B) 부동산 중개소
(C) 슈퍼마켓
(D) 제과점

2. Mr. Hagler는 무엇에 대해 걱정하는가?
(A) 일부 장비의 설치 비용을 지불하는 것
(B) 특정 일자까지 시설을 오픈하는 것
(C) 테이블들을 설치할 의향이 있는 직원을 찾는 것
(D) 옆집 가게 주인과 잘 지내는 것

어휘 pay for ~에 대한 대금을 지불하다 installation 설치 equipment 장비 establishment 시설 certain 특정한 get along with ~와 잘 지내다 shopkeeper 가게 주인 next door 옆집에

3. 오후 2시 13분에, Ms. Denton이 "제가 부동산 중개인에게 연

락해 볼게요"라고 쓰는 이유는 무엇인가?
(A) 그녀가 월세를 낮추는 것에 대해 물어볼 것이라고 말하기 위해
(B) 그녀가 임대 계약서에 서명할 수 있음을 나타내기 위해
(C) 그녀가 새 아파트를 찾을 필요가 있다고 말하기 위해
(D) 이용 가능한 부동산을 확인하겠다고 제안하기 위해

어휘 lower 낮추다 indicate 나타내다, 표시하다 agreement 계약(서) state 말하다

UNIT 04 세부 사항

본문 p.182

대표 유형 맛보기

Stamford Daily

6월 28일—**스탬퍼드 시는 벨뷰 드라이브 86번지에 위치한 집이 역사적인 건축물이라고 선포했다. 현재 Mark Whitman이 소유하고 있는 그 집은 1772년에 건설되었다.** 그곳은 그때부터 Whitman 가문에서 조상 대대로 내려오는 집이다. Thomas Whittaker 시장은 그 집이 현재 보호되고 있으며 철거될 수 없다고 말했다. **Mr. Whitman은 더 이상 그 집에 살고 있지 않지만 그곳을 새로 단장할 계획이며, 식민지 시대의 삶에 대해 배우고 싶은 사람들을 위한 투어를 제공할 것이다.** Mr. Whitman에 따르면, 많은 가구들이 집이 지어질 당시부터 있던 것이라고 한다.

어휘 declare 선언하다, 언명하다 structure 구조물, 건축물 currently 현재, 지금 own 소유하다 ancestral 조상의, 대대로 내려오는 tear down 허물다, 철거하다 intend 의도하다 refurbish 재단장하다 colonial 식민지의 furnishing 가구, 세간

Q. Mr. Whitman은 벨뷰 드라이브에 있는 집으로 무엇을 할 계획인가?
(A) 자신이 들어가서 살 수 있도록 보수하기
(B) 스탬퍼드 시에 매각하기
(C) 사람들이 방문하여 볼 수 있도록 하기
(D) 가구 박물관으로 탈바꿈하기

어휘 renovate 보수하다, 수리하다 transform 변형시키다, 탈바꿈하다

PRACTICE

본문 p.183

1. (A) **2.** (D) **3.** (A)

1-3 이메일

수신: Dearborn Finance 전 직원
발신: Jefferson Grant 최고경영자
날짜: 7월 27일
제목: David Stillman

Dearborn Finance 전 직원 여러분께,

David Stillman이 이곳 Dearborn Finance의 본인의 직책에서 물러난다는 것을 제게 알려왔다는 사실을 여러분에게 알리게 되어 유감스럽습니다. [3B, 3C] **Mr. Stillman은 우리 회사의 수석 연구원으로 12년 이상 근무해 왔습니다.** [2] **그는 연로하신 부모님을 돌볼 수 있도록 자신의 고향 근처에서 일자리를 잡기로 결정했습니다.** David에게 그가 이곳에 있었던 시간을 여러분이 얼마나 소중하게 여겼는지 꼭 알려주시고 행운을 빌어주세요. [1] **David의 사임으로 인해, 우리는 가능한 한 빨리 그의 자리를 채워야 합니다. 연구 직무에 관심이 있는 사람은 누구나 Susan Westmoreland에게 susan@dearbornfinance.com으로 이메일을 보내세요.** 여러분이 그 자리에 적합한 이유를 반드시 설명해 주시고 이력서 사본 한 통도 첨부하세요.
[3D] **David은 자신의 후임자를 교육하는 것을 돕기로 동의했기 때문에, 우리는 그가 그 후로 몇 주 동안 새로운 직원과 함께 일할 수 있도록 앞으로 3주 이내에 그 자리를 채울 수 있기를 희망합니다.**

Jefferson Grant
최고경영자
Dearborn Finance

어휘 regret 유감스럽게 생각하다 inform 알리다 step down 물러나다, 사직하다 chief 최고의 care for ~을 돌보다 elderly 연로한 value 중시하다, 높이 평가하다 departure 사임, 출발 be qualified for ~에 자격이 있다 attach 첨부하다 copy 사본, 1통 résumé 이력서 as well 또한, ~도 replacement 후임자

1. 이메일의 한 가지 목적은 무엇인가?
(A) 일자리 기회를 알리기 위해
(B) 자원봉사자들을 요청하기 위해
(C) 회사 야유회 일정을 잡기 위해
(D) 회사 구조의 변화를 설명하기 위해

어휘 volunteer 자원봉사자 schedule 일정을 잡다 outing 야유회

2. Mr. Stillman은 무엇을 하고 있는가?
(A) 회사의 본사로 전근하기
(B) 학위를 취득하기 위해 학교로 돌아가기
(C) 그의 가족과 시간을 보내기 위해 은퇴하기
(D) 다른 일자리를 갖기 위해 사임하기

어휘 degree 학위 resign 사임하다

3. Mr. Stillman에 대해 언급되지 않은 것은 무엇인가?
(A) 3주 후에 Dearborn Finance를 떠날 것이다.
(B) 회사의 선임 연구원이다.
(C) Dearborn Finance에서 10년 넘게 근무했다.
(D) 그는 기꺼이 다른 직원을 교육할 것이다.

어휘 decade 10년

UNIT 05 문장 삽입

본문 p.184

대표 유형 맛보기

펜사콜라 (4월 19일)—간밤에 Atlantic Shipping이 깜짝 놀랄 만한 발표를 했다. **회사는 Kevin Davenport 사장이 즉시 사임할 것이라고 말했다.** Mr. Davenport는 불과 3월에 Atlantic에서 근무하기 시작했기 때문에 그의 갑작스러운 사임 결정은 모두를 놀라게 했다. <u>그가 떠나는 이유에 대해서는 아무런 발표도 없었다.</u> 회사의 대변인인 Melissa Samuels는 정

식으로 그를 대체할 사람을 찾을 때까지 회사의 운영 담당 부사장인 Bradley Wellman이 임시로 사장직을 맡을 것이라고 말했다. 그녀는 회사가 새로운 리더를 언제 맞을 것으로 예상하는지에 대한 일정을 제시하지 않았다.

어휘 make an announcement 발표하다 step down 사임하다, 물러나다 immediately 즉시 spokesperson 대변인 vice president 부사장 operation 운영 interim 임시의 permanent 정규직의 replacement 후임자 timeline 시각표

Q. [1], [2], [3], [4]로 표시된 위치 중 다음 문장이 들어가기에 가장 적절한 곳은?
"그가 떠나는 이유에 대해서는 아무런 발표도 없었다."
(A) [1]
(B) [2]
(C) [3]
(D) [4]

PRACTICE 본문 p.185

1. (D) **2.** (A) **3.** (C)

1-3 기사

노퍽 (9월 4일)—[1] **새로운 음식점이 얼마 전 노퍽에 문을 열었고, 그곳은 빠르게 시에서 가장 유명한 음식점 중 하나가 되고 있다.** 업소의 이름은 Kirk's Diner이다. Stephanie Kirk가 주인인 이 음식점은 이탈리아와 스페인 음식을 전문으로 한다.
음식점에서 제공되는 거의 모든 식재료는 지역 농부들로부터 오는데, Ms. Kirk는 이 점을 매우 자랑스러워한다. "노퍽 지역은 훌륭한 식재료를 많이 생산하는데, 저는 제 식당이 그것을 우리 고객들에게 제공할 수 있어서 기쁩니다."라고 그녀는 말했다.
[2] **Ms. Kirk는 업주일 뿐만 아니라 수석 요리사이기도 하다.** [3] **그녀는 이탈리아의 밀라노 요리학교에서 요리를 공부했다. 그 후 그녀는 유럽의 런던, 파리, 그리고 아테네에서 요리사로 일했다.** 그녀는 해외에서 20년 이상을 보냈다. 그녀는 작년에 고향인 노퍽의 집으로 돌아왔는데, 노퍽에서는 Italian Delights에서 일했다. 이제 그녀는 자신의 음식점을 가지고 있다. 테이블의 오랜 대기로 미루어 볼 때, 그곳은 성공적인 음식점이 될 것이다.

어휘 rapidly 빠르게 eatery 식당 establishment 시설, 업소 specialize in ~을 전문으로 하다 serve 제공하다 chef 요리사, 주방장 culinary arts 요리법

1. 기사의 목적은 무엇인가?
(A) 식당의 음식을 논평하기 위해
(B) 업체의 개업을 서술하기 위해
(C) 신제품을 홍보하기 위해
(D) 식당을 소개하기 위해

패러프레이즈 restaurant → dining establishment

어휘 review 논평하다 meal 음식 describe 서술하다 grand opening 개업(식) promote 홍보하다 dining 식사

2. Ms. Kirk에 대해 언급된 것은 무엇인가?
(A) 식당의 주인이다.
(B) 이탈리아어와 스페인어를 구사한다.
(C) 노퍽에 농장을 가지고 있다.
(D) 런던에서 요리를 공부했다.

3. [1], [2], [3], [4]로 표시된 위치 중 다음 문장이 들어가기에 가장 적절한 곳은?
"그녀는 해외에서 20년 이상을 보냈다."
(A) [1]
(B) [2]
(C) [3]
(D) [4]

UNIT 06 동의어 찾기

본문 p.186

대표 유형 맛보기

Lux Warehouse의 온라인 쇼핑 클럽 회원이 되기 위해 등록해 주셔서 감사합니다. 우리의 모든 회원들은 모든 구매에 대해 자동으로 10% 할인을 받을 뿐만 아니라 무료로 빠른 배송도 받을 수 있습니다. 모든 특전의 목록을 보시려면 여기를 클릭하십시오. 매주 일요일 밤에는 회원 전용 특가 상품을 받으실 수 있으니 이메일을 확인하시기 바랍니다. 회원들은 또한 신제품을 **평가해** 달라는 요청을 종종 받게 되며, 고객 만족도 설문 조사를 해달라는 요청을 받을 수도 있습니다. 우리는 단골 고객들께서 우리의 서비스에 만족하시는 것을 보장하고 싶습니다.

어휘 register 등록하다 automatic 자동적인 purchase 구매; 구매하다 as well as ~뿐만 아니라, ~ 또한 express shipping 빠른 배송 complete 완전한 benefit 혜택, 특전 special offer 특가 판매 frequently 빈번히, 자주 grade 등급을 매기다, 평가하다 complete 작성하다 survey 설문 조사 ensure 보장하다, 반드시 ~이게 하다 loyal customer 단골 고객

Q. 일곱 번째 줄의 어휘 "grade"와 의미상 가장 가까운 것은?
(A) 구매하다
(B) 시식하다
(C) 평가하다
(D) 고려하다

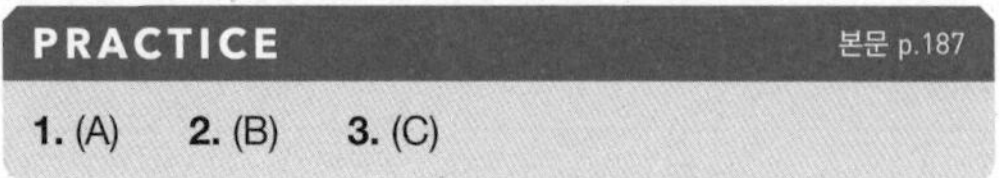

1-3 광고

CHAMBERLIN MARKETING

많은 소기업들은 그들이 팔고자 하는 뛰어난 제품과 서비스를 보유하고 있습니다. 그러나 소기업주들은 이러한 상품과 서비스를 마케팅할 시간도 능력도 없습니다. 다행히 Chamberlin Marketing이 그들의 모든 필요성을 [1] **처리할** 수 있습니다. Chamberlin Marketing은 35년 동안 영업을 해왔습니다. 그 기간 동안 우리는 500개 이상의 소기업에 도움을 제공해 왔

습니다. [2]**우리는 기업들이 지역적으로, 전국적으로, 그리고 국제적으로 자신들을 마케팅하는 것을 지원해 왔습니다. 우리 직원들은 수많은 시장에 경험을 가지고 있으며, 그들 모두는 적어도 하나의 외국어에 익숙합니다.**
[3]**1시간 상담을 원하시면 정규 근무 시간 중에 555-0271로 저희에게 전화를 주십시오. 귀사에 대해 말씀해 주시면 우리가 무료로 예비 마케팅 계획을 마련해 드리겠습니다.** 우리의 서비스를 이용할 의무는 없습니다. 하지만 이용하신다면 후회하지 않으실 겁니다.

어휘 outstanding 뛰어난 market 마케팅하다 handle 처리하다 be in business 사업을 하다 provide 제공하다, 주다 assistance 도움, 조력 numerous 수많은 consultation 상담 business hours 근무 시간, 영업 시간 come up with ~을 마련하다, 내놓다 preliminary 예비의 obligation 의무 regret 후회하다

1. 첫 번째 단락 세 번째 줄의 어휘 "handle"과 의미상 가장 가까운 것은?
(A) 처리하다, 돌보다
(B) ~에 대해 생각하다
(C) 촉진하다, 홍보하다
(D) 드러내다

2. Chamberlin Marketing에 대해 나타난 것은 무엇인가?
(A) 온라인 제품 마케팅에 초점을 맞춘다.
(B) 외국에서 제품을 홍보할 수 있다.
(C) 지난 10년 사이에 설립되었다.
(D) 500명 이상의 직원을 두고 있다.
패러프레이즈 internationally → in foreign countries
어휘 focus on ~에 초점을 맞추다 establish 설립하다 decade 10년

3. Chamberlin Marketing은 소기업주들에게 무엇을 제공하고 있는가?
(A) 웹페이지 제작 할인
(B) 요금 할인
(C) 무료 상담
(D) 현금 환불
패러프레이즈 at no cost → free
어휘 reduced 할인된 rate 요금 cash 현금 refund 환불

UNIT 07 이중 지문

본문 p.188

대표 유형 맛보기

1-5 기사, 라벨

Calico Crackers, 라벨을 바꿀 예정

로스앤젤레스 (9월 5일)—인기 있는 통밀 스낵인 Calico Crackers가 제품 라벨을 바꾼다는 계획을 발표했다. 이제 포장지에서 어떤 종류의 치즈가 각각의 Calico Crackers의 풍미와 가장 잘 어울리는지와 같은 페어링 제안을 제공하게 될 것이다. [1]**회사의 목표는 고객들로 하여금 크래커만 먹는 대신 다른 음식들과 함께 맛보도록 하는 것이다.**
[2]**이 조치는 Crispy Dreams가 Calico Crackers를 제치고 시장에서 선도적인 크래커 스낵으로 등극한 후,** Calico Crackers가 시장 점유율을 회복하기 위한 일환으로 기획된 것이다. 치열한 경쟁은 Calico Crackers의 관계자들로 하여금 제품을 홍보할 새로운 방법을 찾도록 [3]**만들었다.**
"Calico Crackers는 여러분이 활동할 때 아주 좋은 간식입니다."라고 회사 대변인인 Jocelyn Watkins가 말했다. "하지만 여러분은 집에 있을 때 우리 크래커로 보다 정교한 레시피와 음식 조합을 만들 수 있습니다. [4-1]**9월 25일 이후에 우리가 만드는 모든 라벨에는 이러한 추가적인 아이디어가 포함될 것이며,** 우리의 SNS 플랫폼에서 우리 고객들이 직접 만든 것에 대한 이야기를 듣고 싶습니다."

어휘 label 라벨, 표 whole wheat 통밀 packaging 포장(재) pair (둘씩) 짝을 짓다 variety 종류 go with ~와 어울리다 flavor 맛, 풍미 intend 의도하다 regain 되찾다, 회복하다 market share 시장 점유율 overtake 추월하다 prompt 촉발하다 promote 홍보하다 on the go 쉴 새 없이 활동하여 spokesperson 대변인 elaborate 정교한 combination 조합 social media 소셜 미디어, SNS

CALICO CRACKERS
허브와 마늘 맛

100g
캐나다 토론토에서 포장
[4-2]**페어링 제안: 이 크래커를 크림치즈와 함께, 또는 햇볕에 말린 토마토를 얹어서 드셔 보시는 게 어때요?**
[5]**Calico Crackers로 만들 수 있는 더 많은 요리의 단계별 동영상 레시피를 찾으려면 www.calicocrackers.com을 방문하세요!**

어휘 garlic 마늘 package 포장하다; 포장 top 위에 놓다 step-by-step 단계적인

1. 기사에 따르면, Calico Crackers는 고객을 위해 무엇을 하기를 희망하는가?
(A) 고객들의 구매품에서 포장재의 양을 감소시키기
(B) 알레르기가 있는 사람들이 성분을 쉽게 확인할 수 있도록 하기
(C) 고객들이 새로운 음식과 함께 제품을 맛보도록 영감을 주기
(D) 고객들이 어떤 크래커 맛을 좋아할지 빨리 결정하기
어휘 reduce 줄이다, 감소시키다 amount 분량 purchase 구매(품) ingredient 재료, 성분 inspire 영감을 주다, 고무시키다

2. 기사는 Crispy Dreams에 대해 무엇을 암시하는가?
(A) 최근에 스낵을 생산하기 시작했다.
(B) Calico Crackers보다 더 많은 상품을 판매한다.
(C) 현재 로스앤젤레스에 본사를 두고 있다.
(D) 시장에서 가장 저렴한 브랜드이다.
어휘 goods 상품, 제품 currently 현재, 지금 be based in ~에 기반을 두다, 본사를 두다

3. 기사에서 두 번째 단락 두 번째 줄의 단어 "prompted"와 의미상 가장 가까운 것은?
(A) 돕다
(B) 유발하다
(C) 서두르다
(D) 상기시키다

4. 포장의 라벨에 대해 암시된 것은 무엇인가?
(A) 새로운 식품 공장에서 만들어졌다.
(B) 무게가 잘못 기재되었다.
(C) 새로 출시된 제품을 위한 것이다.
(D) 9월 25일 이후에 인쇄되었다.

어휘 weight 무게 list 기입하다, 기재하다 incorrectly 틀리게, 부정확하게 release 출시하다

5. 라벨에 따르면, 고객들은 웹사이트에서 무엇을 할 수 있는가?
(A) 새로운 크래커 맛을 제안하기
(B) 제품 레시피 후기를 작성하기
(C) 교육용 동영상을 보기
(D) 쿠폰을 다운로드 하기

어휘 instructional 교육용의

PRACTICE

본문 p.190

1. (C) **2.** (A) **3.** (D) **4.** (B) **5.** (B)

1-5 이메일, 보고서

수신: information@jasperrealty.com
발신: samjackson@hoffmanassociates.com
날짜: 8월 18일
제목: 사무실 공간

관계자 귀하,

제 회사는 링컨에 작은 지사를 열 계획을 가지고 있습니다. 제 동료 중 한 명이 저더러 귀하의 중개업소에 연락해서 괜찮은 사무실을 찾는 과정을 도와달라고 해 보라고 제안하더군요.
지사에서는 10명의 직원이 근무하게 될 겁니다. [5-1] **그 공간에는 최소 6개의 개별 사무실과 나머지 직원들을 [1] 수용할 수 있는 개방된 업무 공간이 필요합니다. 건물은 버스 정류장에서 두어 블록 이내에 있어야 하는데, 많은 직원들이 그런 방식으로 통근하기 때문입니다. 고객들이 주차할 수 있는 주차장이 있다면 이상적이겠지만, 필수는 아닙니다. 지역의 식당과 커피숍과 가까이 있는 것도 이상적일 것입니다.**
제 기준에 맞는 가용한 부동산들을 알려주시기 바랍니다. [2] **그리고 공과금이 한 달 기준으로 대략 얼마가 들지도 알고 싶습니다.** 우리는 두 달 안에 사무실을 열고 싶기 때문에, 빨리 장소를 찾아야 합니다. 2년의 임대 계약도 할 수 있습니다.

Sam Jackson
Hoffman Associates

어휘 To Whom It May Concern (편지의 수신인을 모를 때) 관계자 귀하 firm 회사 branch office 지사 colleague 동료 agency 소개소, 대리점 acceptable 괜찮은, 받아들일 수 있는 minimum 최소, 최저 individual 개별의, 개개의 workspace 업무 공간 accommodate 수용하다 commute 통근하다 ideal 이상적인 property 부동산 fit 맞다, 적합하다 criteria 기준 roughly 대략 utility 공공요금, 공과금 on a monthly basis 월 단위로 lease 임대차 계약

Hoffman Associates를 위한 가능한 사무실 공간
Alice Moreno 작성

Rhubarb Avenue 88번지
[3-B] **4개의 개별 사무실**과 6명을 위한 넓은 개방된 공간. 지하에 무료 주차. [3-C] **버스 정류장 바로 앞.**

[5-2] **Catfish Lane 192번지**
7개의 개별 사무실과 5명을 위한 하나의 개방된 공간. 태양열 발전에 의해 제공되는 전기. 버스 정류장과 기차역에서 한 블록 거리.

Hamilton Boulevard 27번지
[4-B] **12명을 위한 두 개의 개방된 공간.** [4-A] **개별 사무실 없음.** 같은 건물에 위치한 어린이집. [4-C] **버스 정류장에서 네 블록 거리.** [4-D] **근처에 공영 주차장.**

Maple Street 64번지
신축 건물. 12개의 개별 사무실. [3-A] **지하에 위치한 식당들.** 해안가의 멋진 전망. 버스 정류장 근처.

어휘 basement 지하(실) electricity 전기 solar power 태양광 발전 daycare center 어린이집 nearby 근처에 brand-new 신형의 seafront 해안가

1. 이메일에서 두 번째 단락 두 번째 줄의 "accommodate"와 의미상 가장 가까운 것은?
(A) 위치를 찾아내다
(B) 승인하다
(C) ~에 맞다, ~에 적합하다
(D) 만족시키다

2. Mr. Jackson이 요청하는 것은 무엇인가?
(A) 공과금 금액
(B) 계약서 견본
(C) 지역의 지도
(D) 사무실 소유자들의 전화번호

3. 사무실 공간에 대해 제공되지 않는 정보는 무엇인가?
(A) 인근의 시설
(B) 개별 사무실의 숫자
(C) 대중교통의 위치
(D) 월세

어휘 public transportation 대중교통 rent 임대료

4. 보고서에 따르면 Hamilton Boulevard에 위치한 사무실 공간에 대한 설명으로 옳은 것은 무엇인가?
(A) 12개의 개별 사무실이 있다.

(B) 12명을 위한 충분한 공간이 있다.
(C) 버스 정류장에서 가깝다.
(D) 근처에 주차장이 없다.

5. Mr. Jackson이 가장 관심을 가질 만한 사무실 공간은 무엇이겠는가?
(A) Rhubarb Avenue 88번지
(B) Catfish Lane 192번지
(C) Hamilton Boulevard 27번지
(D) Maple Street 64번지

해설 연계 문제로서, 첫 번째 지문에서 제시된 요구 조건을 충족하는 사무실 공간을 두 번째 지문에서 찾아야 한다. (A)와 (C)는 개별 사무실의 숫자가 충분하지 않거나 없기 때문에 오답이고 (D)는 개방된 업무 공간이 없으므로 오답이다. (B)는 개별 사무실과 개방된 업무 공간, 그리고 대중교통에서 가깝기 때문에 정답이다. (B)에는 주차장이 없지만, 첫 번째 지문에서 주차장 시설은 필수 요소는 아니라고 했으므로 Mr. Jackson이 언급한 조건을 충족하는 것은 (B)이다.

UNIT 08 삼중 지문

본문 p.192

대표 유형 맛보기
1-5 웹페이지, 양식, 이메일

국제 생명공학자 협회 (IABE)
제15차 연례 총회

[5-3] **장소: 그리스, 아테네, Bayside Hotel**
날짜: 9월 22-25일
주제: 생명공학의 새로운 트렌드
다음에 나오는 중요 날짜에 유념해 주십시오:
* 제안서 제출 - 3월 1일
* [2] **제안서 수락 - 5월 1일**
* 전체 논문 제출 - 6월 30일
모든 제안서는 400단어에서 500단어 사이여야 하며 당사 웹사이트인 www.iabe.org/proposals에서 온라인으로 제출되어야 합니다. 제안서 작성 방법은 웹사이트의 지침을 따르십시오.
총회 등록은 6월 1일부터 시작됩니다. [1] **비용에는 총회 티셔츠, 다과, 오찬, 모든 회의 참석, 그리고 모든 논문의 사본 한 부가 포함됩니다.** www.iabe.org/registration에서 등록하세요.
[3-2] **참석자 - 6월 20일 이전에 조기 등록 시 500달러**
참석자 - 6월 20일 이후 등록 시 600달러
발표자 - 400달러
학생 - 300달러

어휘 association 협회 biomedical 생물 의학의 annual 연례의 conference 총회, 학회 note 주목하다 proposal 제안(서) submission 제출 acceptance 수용, 수락 regarding ~에 관한 registration 등록 refreshments 다과, 간식 session (교육) 시간

https://www.iabe.org/registration
국제 생명공학자 협회
제15차 연례 총회 등록
[3-1, 5-2] **이름: Susanna Madsen**
회사: Klein Pharmaceuticals
관심 분야: 의약품 개발
전화번호: 805-555-8573
이메일: smadsen@klein.com
[3-1] **등록비: 500달러**

어휘 pharmaceutical 제약의, 약학의

[5-1] **수신: Susanna Madsen**
[5-1] **발신: Sunshine Hotel**
날짜: 8월 14일
[4] **제목: 회신: 질문**

Ms. Madsen,

저희는 다음 달에 귀하를 이곳에서 손님으로 맞는 것을 고대하고 있습니다. [4] **귀하의 질문에 답하자면,** 호텔은 바다에서 도보로 5분 거리에 있습니다. 귀하는 호텔 근처에서 쇼핑을 하고 음식을 먹을 수 있는 온갖 종류의 장소를 찾을 수 있을 것입니다. [5-1] **저희는 또한 귀하께서 참석하시는 총회장의 바로 길 건너편에 위치해 있습니다.** 그러므로 귀하는 그곳에 쉽게 걸어서 가실 수 있습니다. 다른 질문이 있으면 저에게 알려주세요.

[4] **Ioannis Papadopoulos**
고객 서비스 담당자
Sunshine Hotel

어휘 therefore 그러므로, 따라서 with ease 쉽게

1. 웹페이지에 따르면, 총회에 대해 사실인 것은 무엇인가?
(A) 그 기간 동안 점심 행사가 열릴 것이다.
(B) IABE 회원들에게만 개방된다.
(C) 몇몇 사람들은 무료로 참석할 수 있다.
(D) 일주일 동안 계속될 것이다.

패러프레이즈 luncheon → lunch event

어휘 for free 무료로

2. 사람들은 언제 그들의 제안서가 수락되었는지 여부에 대한 통지를 받겠는가?
(A) 3월 1일
(B) 5월 1일
(C) 6월 1일
(D) 6월 30일

3. Ms. Madsen에 대해 암시된 것은 무엇인가?
(A) 그녀는 IABE의 회원이 아니다.
(B) 그녀의 총회 참석은 이번이 두 번째이다.
(C) 그녀는 6월 20일 전에 총회에 등록했다.
(D) 그녀는 총회에서 논문을 발표할 것이다.

어휘 sign up for ~에 등록하다 present 소개하다

PART 7

4. Mr. Papadopoulos가 이메일을 보낸 이유는 무엇인가?
(A) 객실 예약을 확인하려고
(B) 특별 할인을 제공하려고
(C) 몇 가지 문의에 응답하려고
(D) 예약 날짜를 변경하려고

어휘 confirm 확인하다, 확정하다 reservation 예약 respond to ~에 답하다 booking 예약

5. Sunshine Hotel에 대해 나타난 것은 무엇인가?
(A) Bayside Hotel에서 가까운 곳에 위치해 있다.
(B) 최근에 보수 공사를 받았다.
(C) 총회 참석자들에게 할인을 제공한다.
(D) 9월에는 빈방이 없다.

어휘 close to ~에 가까운 recently 최근에 undergo 겪다, 받다 renovation 수리, 보수 vacancy 빈방

PRACTICE

본문 p.194

1. (D) **2.** (B) **3.** (D) **4.** (C) **5.** (D)

1-5 웹페이지, 이메일, 이메일

[1]**Boston Tours는 33년 이상 보스턴 시와 그 주변 지역의 투어를 제공해 온 경험이 있습니다.** 모든 투어는 그 지역 출신으로 보스턴에서 가장 가볼 만한 유명한 장소들을 아주 잘 알고 있는 가이드가 인솔하게 됩니다. 우리는 사람들이 선택할 수 있는 4개의 투어를 제공합니다.

1번 패키지 상품 보스턴 시내와 수족관을 방문하는 반나절 투어
- 일 인당 50달러

2번 패키지 상품 시내 쇼핑을 중점으로 하는 보스턴 반나절 투어
- 일 인당 40달러

3번 패키지 상품 하버드, MIT, 수족관, 비컨 힐을 방문하는 보스턴과 케임브리지 1일 투어
- 일 인당 80달러

[3-2]**4번 패키지 상품 미국 독립전쟁과 관련된 유적지 방문을 포함하는 보스턴 및 그 주변 지역의 1일 투어**
- 일 인당 100달러

더 많은 정보를 원하시거나 예약을 하시려면 information@bostontours.com으로 이메일을 보내세요.

어휘 surrounding 주위의, 인근의 native 현지인, 토착민 familiarity 익숙함 notable 유명한, 주목할 만한 package 패키지 상품 aquarium 수족관 downtown 시내에 the American Revolution 미국 독립전쟁

수신: information@bostontours.com
발신: Marcus Cartwright
⟨marcus_c@prometheus.com⟩
날짜: 6월 11일
제목: 투어

안녕하세요.

[2]**저는 올 여름에 뉴잉글랜드로 가족 여행을 계획 중인데,** 전에 귀사의 서비스를 이용한 적이 있는 친구가 귀사를 추천해 주었습니다. 친구의 말로는 귀사의 가이드들이 지식이 풍부하고, 자기가 갔던 투어가 재미있고 교육적이었다고 하더군요. [4-1]**우리는 6월 28일부터 7월 1일까지 보스턴 지역에 있을 것입니다. 저는 우리가 그곳에 도착한 첫날에 투어를 하고 싶습니다. 하지만 그날 가능한 자리가 없다면 다음 날도 괜찮습니다.** 우리 가족은 5명입니다. 제 아내와 세 아이들이 저와 동행할 것입니다. [3-1]**아이들이 역사를 좋아하기 때문에 우리의 선호에 맞는 투어가 있었으면 좋겠습니다.**

Marcus Cartwright

어휘 recommend 추천하다 knowledgeable 아는 것이 많은 entertaining 재미있는 accompany 동행하다 accommodate (의견을) 수용하다, 담다

[5]**수신: Marcus Cartwright**
⟨marcus_c@prometheus.com⟩
발신: Cynthia Potter ⟨cynthia@bostontours.com⟩
날짜: 6월 15일
제목: 회신: 투어

Mr. Cartwright,

Boston Tours에 연락 주셔서 감사합니다. 귀하의 자녀의 관심사에 딱 맞는 1일 투어가 있습니다. [4-2]**하지만 아쉽게도 귀하께서 보스턴에 머무르는 첫째 날의 투어는 이미 예약이 꽉 찼습니다. 하지만 둘째 날 투어에는 아직 5개의 빈자리가 있습니다.** 예약을 확정하려면 각각의 티켓 금액의 절반에 해당하는, 환불이 되지 않는 보증금을 지불하셔야 합니다. [5]**자녀가 몇 살이죠?** 저희의 소아 요금을 이용할 자격이 있을지도 모르는데, 그것은 정가의 절반입니다. 투어 예약을 원하시는지 여부를 알려주시면 저희가 결제 준비를 해드리겠습니다.

Cynthia Potter
Boston Tours

어휘 contact 연락하다 fully booked 예약이 꽉 찬 opening 빈자리 confirm 확정하다, 확인하다 reservation 예약 nonrefundable 환불되지 않는 deposit 보증금 be eligible for ~할 자격이 있다 rate 요금 regular price 정가 arrangement 준비

1. 웹페이지는 Boston Tours에 대해 무엇을 나타내는가?
(A) 외국어를 할 수 있는 가이드들을 고용한다.
(B) 최근에 보스턴의 투어를 제공하기 시작했다.
(C) 현금과 신용카드 결제를 모두 받는다.
(D) 30년 이상 사업을 해왔다.

어휘 hire 고용하다 cash 현금 payment 결제, 비용 지불 be in business 사업을 하다 decade 10년

2. Mr. Cartwright에 대해 나타난 것은 무엇인가?
(A) 보스턴 지역에서 자랐다.
(B) 가족과 함께 여행할 것이다.
(C) 보스턴을 처음으로 방문한다.
(D) 보스턴에서 일주일을 보낼 것이다.

3. Mr. Cartwright는 어떤 패키지 상품을 선택하겠는가?
(A) 1번 패키지 상품
(B) 2번 패키지 상품
(C) 3번 패키지 상품
(D) 4번 패키지 상품

해설 연계 문제로서, Cartwright, package 등을 키워드로 지문을 검색한다. 두 번째 지문에서 Mr. Cartwright는 자신의 아이들이 역사를 좋아하며 그에 맞는 투어를 요청했는데, 첫 번째 지문에서 역사와 관련된 패키지 상품은 Package 4이므로 (D)가 정답이다.

4. Mr. Cartwright는 언제 투어를 하겠는가?
(A) 6월 15일
(B) 6월 28일
(C) 6월 29일
(D) 7월 1일

해설 연계 문제로서, 숫자에 집중하며 Cartwright, go on a tour 등의 키워드로 지문을 검색한다. 두 번째 지문에서 Mr. Cartwright는 6월 28일에 투어를 가고 싶다고 했으나 그날 자리가 없으면 그 다음 날인 6월 29일도 괜찮다고 했다. 세 번째 지문에서 Mr. Cartwright의 보스턴 체류 둘째 날에 투어 자리가 있다는 정보를 확인할 수 있으므로 Mr. Cartwright는 6월 29일에 투어를 할 것이다.

5. Ms. Potter는 Mr. Cartwright에게 무엇을 요청하는가?
(A) 그의 신용카드 정보
(B) 그의 가족들의 이름
(C) 그를 픽업해야 하는 장소
(D) 그의 아이들의 나이

어휘 pick up 차에 태우다, 픽업하다

PART TEST

본문 p.196

147. (B) **148.** (A) **149.** (C) **150.** (C) **151.** (D) **152.** (C)
153. (B) **154.** (D) **155.** (A) **156.** (B) **157.** (D) **158.** (C)
159. (D) **160.** (A) **161.** (A) **162.** (A) **163.** (D) **164.** (A)
165. (C) **166.** (B) **167.** (A) **168.** (A) **169.** (B)

147-148 공지

[147] 애즈베리 로드 주차장 소식

올봄 들어 최근에 악천후로 인해 애즈베리 로드 주차장 보수 공사가 상당히 지연되고 있습니다. [148] 작업은 5월 1일까지 완료될 것으로 예상되었습니다. 그러나 눈이 내리는 날씨 동안에는 건설 인부들이 현장에 접근할 수 없었습니다. 게다가, 일부 구조적인 문제들이 엔지니어들에 의해 확인되어 작업이 더욱 더 지연되었습니다. **[147, 148] 그 결과, 공사는 이제 8월 15일까지 완료될 예정입니다.** 궁금한 점이 있는 사람은 Vanderbilt Construction의 Russell Mayer에게 802-555-9361로 언제든지 연락주십시오.

어휘 update 최신 정보 recent 최근의 cause 야기하다 renovation 보수, 수리 significantly 상당히 delay 지연시키다 crew 작업반 access 접근하다 site 현장, 부지 furthermore 게다가, 더구나 structural 구조적인 issue 문제, 쟁점 identify 확인하다 further 더, 더 나아가 as a result 그 결과, 결과적으로

147. 공지의 목적은 무엇인가?
(A) 최근의 기상 상태에 대해 알리기 위해
(B) 일부 계획의 변경을 설명하기 위해
(C) 마감일을 놓친 것을 사과하기 위해
(D) 해야 하는 작업에 대한 세부 정보를 제공하기 위해

어휘 apologize for ~에 대해 사과하다 miss a deadline 기한을 놓치다 details 세부 사항

148. 애즈베리 로드 주차장 프로젝트에 대해 나타난 것은 무엇인가?
(A) 제때에 끝나지 않을 것이다.
(B) 주차장의 규모를 확장할 것이다.
(C) 5월에 완료될 것이다.
(D) 예산을 초과할 것으로 예상된다.

어휘 on time 제때에 expand 확장하다, 확대하다 budget 예산

149-151 양식

구매 요청 양식

직원 이름: Kenneth Dumont 요청 일자: 11월 11일
[151] 부서: IT 이메일: kdumont@dmr.com

품목	판매자	수량
Syntax 4000 디지털 카메라	MTR Technology	1
Xtreme 1000G 노트북 컴퓨터	CompuServe	1
[149] 4TB 외장 하드 드라이브	CompuServe	**2**
Steady Sound 헤드폰	Techno Sound	1

- **[150] 이 양식을 제출할 때 해당 품목을 구매할 수 있는 기타 관련 정보를 첨부하십시오. 그것에는 해당 품목을 구입할 수 있는 웹페이지 주소와 품목의 캡처 이미지를 포함합니다.**
- **[151] 직속 상사의 서명 없이는 어떠한 요청도 승인되지 않습니다.**
- 구입한 물품은 업무용이어야만 하며 개인적인 용도로 쓰일 수 없습니다.

직원 서명: *Kenneth Dumont*
[151] 부서장 서명: *Leslie Wheeler*

어휘 item 품목 vendor 판매자 quantity 수량 laptop 노트북 컴퓨터 submit 제출하다 attach 첨부하다 relevant 적절한 enable ~할 수 있게 하다 capture 캡처하다 approve 승인하다 signature 서명 immediate supervisor 직속 상사

149. Mr. Dumont가 두 개 이상을 요청하는 품목은 무엇인가?
(A) 디지털 카메라
(B) 노트북 컴퓨터
(C) 외장 하드 드라이브
(D) 헤드폰

150. Mr. Dumont는 양식과 함께 무엇을 제출했겠는가?
(A) 현금 지불
(B) 영수증
(C) 품목의 이미지
(D) 신용카드 번호

어휘 along with ~와 함께 receipt 영수증

151. Ms. Wheeler는 누구이겠는가?
(A) MRT Technology의 직원
(B) Mr. Dumont의 고객
(C) 구매 부서의 직원
(D) IT 부서의 관리자

패러프레이즈 Department Head → Department supervisor

152-155 기사

Brentwood News
2월 26일
[152] **미국 최대의 자동차 제조사 중 하나인 Grant Autos가 브렌트우드에 생산 시설을 열 것이다.** 시설은 Roth Textiles가 한때 있었던 곳이 될 것이다. 기존 건물들은 철거 작업이 진행 중이며, 그 자리에 세 개의 새로운 제조 센터가 건립될 예정이다. 첫 번째 센터는 18개월 이내에 운영될 것이고, 나머지 두 곳은 완공되기까지 최대 2년이 걸릴 것이다.
[153] **Grant Autos의 수석 부사장인 Jefferson Trent**는 이렇게 말했다. "[152] **우리는 세 개의 시설이 모두 가동되면 하루 최대 300대의 차량을 생산하기를 희망합니다. 우리는 브렌트우드에 대규모 투자를 하고 있으며, 이 투자가 [154] 결실을 맺을 것으로 기대하고 있습니다.**"
[155] **Grant Autos는 단지에서 일할 2,500명 이상의 정규직 직원을 고용할 것이다. 그들 중 대부분은 생산 라인에서 근무할 것이다. 하지만, 향후 2년 동안 회사는 디자이너, 엔지니어, 임원 및 그 밖의 사람들도 구할 예정이다.**

어휘 manufacturer 제조업체 facility 시설 located 위치한 existing 기존의 be in the process of ~하는 중이다 demolish 철거하다 erect 세우다, 짓다 operational 가동 중인 vice president 부사장 state 분명히 말하다 investment 투자 pay off 기대했던 성과를 거두다 complex 단지, 종합 빌딩 executive 임원, 이사

152. 기사의 목적은 무엇인가?
(A) 사업 합병을 알리려고
(B) 브렌트우드의 문제를 설명하려고
(C) 공장 개장을 발표하려고
(D) 몇몇 Grant Autos 차량을 홍보하려고

해설 생산 시설의 개장을 알리고 있으므로 (C)가 정답이다.

패러프레이즈 manufacturing facility → factory

어휘 report 보고하다, 알리다 merger 합병 describe 설명하다, 묘사하다 promote 홍보하다

153. Mr. Trent는 누구인가?
(A) 공장장
(B) Grant Autos 임원
(C) 자동차 제조사 대변인
(D) 브렌트우드의 정부 관리

패러프레이즈 vice president → executive

어휘 spokesperson 대변인

154. 두 번째 단락 여섯 번째 줄의 어구 "pay off"와 의미상 가장 가까운 것은?
(A) 변상하다
(B) 발전시키다
(C) 회수하다
(D) 성공하다

155. 기사에 따르면 Grant Autos는 무엇을 할 것인가?
(A) 다양한 근로자를 채용하기
(B) 기존 시설을 보수하기
(C) 시에 대출을 요청하기
(D) 새로운 차량 종류를 설계하기

패러프레이즈 employees → workers

어휘 a variety of 다양한 renovate 보수하다 existing 기존의 loan 대출 line (상품의) 종류

156-159 이메일

수신: Tim Chapman
〈timchapman@chapmandesigns.com〉
발신: Dustin Peters
〈d_peters@beaumontconsulting.com〉
제목: 디자인 결정
날짜: 8월 19일

[156] **Mr. Chapman,**

[156] **저희 사무실의 새로운 인테리어 디자인을 위해 저희에게 제시해 주신 다섯 가지 선택권에 대해 귀하와 귀하의 팀에게 감사드리고 싶습니다. [157] 그리고, 인내심을 가지고 저희의 답변을 기다려 주신 점에 감사드립니다.** 그런 일이 생겨서 정말 죄송합니다. 의사 결정 과정에 참여한 몇몇 사람들이 휴가 중이었고 이번 주에야 사무실로 돌아왔답니다. 아무튼 저희는 결정을 내렸고 당신이 이달 말 이전에 프로젝트를 시작하실 수 있기를 바랍니다.
[158] **우리는 '미래 지향적 디자인'이라는 제목의 세 번째 선택권으로 가기로 결정했습니다. 우리는 이 디자인의 독특한 외관이 마음에 들고, 우리 회사의 이미지와 잘 어울릴 거라고 생각합니다.** 그리고 많은 개방된 공간이 있어서 사무실을 실제보다 넓어 보이게 합니다.
[159] **우리는 작업이 시작되기 전에 설계상 몇 가지 측면에 대해 논의해야 합니다. 당신과 당신의 팀이 이번 주에 저희를 직접 만나기 위해 이곳에 오실 수 있는지 궁금합니다.** 그렇게 하면 우리가 디자인을 자세히 검토할 수 있는 기회가 생길 것입니다. 그럴 시간이 있는지 알려주세요.

Dustin Peters

어휘 option 선택권, 옵션 present 제시하다, 주다 in addition 또한, 게다가 appreciate 감사하다, 고마워하다 involve 관련시키다 entitle 제목을 붙이다 unique 독특한 appearance 외관, 겉모양 go with ~와 어울리다 in reality 실제로는 aspect 양상, 측면 available 시간이 있는 in person 직접

156. Mr. Chapman은 누구이겠는가?
(A) 재무 컨설턴트
(B) 인테리어 디자이너
(C) 부동산 중개인
(D) 주택 건축가

어휘 property 부동산, 재산 residential 주택의, 주거의

157. Mr. Peters가 Mr. Chapman에게 사과하는 이유는 무엇인가?
(A) 전에 보낸 이메일에서 실수를 했다.
(B) 예정된 회의에 참석하는 것을 잊었다.
(C) 제때에 대금을 지불하지 못했다.
(D) 오랫동안 답변하지 않았다.

어휘 previous 전의, 이전의 submit 내다

158. '미래 지향적 디자인'에 대해 시사된 것은 무엇인가?
(A) 회사의 모든 사람들에게 인기가 있었다.
(B) 시행하는 데 짧은 시간이 걸릴 것이다.
(C) 회사가 가진 이미지와 일치한다.
(D) 회사의 예산 내에서 행해질 수 있다.

어휘 favor 찬성하다, 호의를 보이다 implement 시행하다 match 맞다, 일치하다 budget 예산

159. [1], [2], [3], [4]로 표시된 위치 중 다음 문장이 들어가기에 가장 적절한 곳은?
"그렇게 하면 우리가 디자인을 자세히 검토할 수 있는 기회가 생길 것입니다."
(A) [1]
(B) [2]
(C) [3]
(D) [4]

어휘 go over 검토하다 in detail 상세히, 자세히

160-164 광고, 이메일

Sanderson Home Improvement

[160] **Sanderson Home Improvement는 스터브릿지 지역의 주택 소유자들을 12년 넘게 도와드리고 있습니다.** 우리는 정기적으로, 그리고 일회성으로 다양한 서비스를 제공합니다.

우리가 제공하는 서비스 중 일부는 다음과 같습니다:
- 에어컨 설치 및 유지 보수
- 지붕 설치 및 수리
- 굴뚝 청소
- 수영장 건설
- 주택 확장 및 수리

연락처 정보

일반 정보: Cody Wilde, cwilde@sandersonhomes.com
[161] **에어컨: Julius Clover,** jclover@sandersonhomes.com
지붕 및 굴뚝: Eric Blaine, eblaine@sandersonhomes.com
[163-2] **수영장: Carla Crow,** ccrow@sandersonhomes.com
주택 보수: Douglas Montana, dmontana@sandersonhomes.com

어휘 improvement 개선, 향상 a wide variety of 매우 다양한 on a regular basis 정기적으로 installation 설치 maintenance 유지 보수 chimney 굴뚝 expansion 확장 general 일반적인 renovation 보수, 개조

[163-1] **수신: Carla Crow** 〈ccrow@sandersonhomes.com〉
[162, 163-1] **발신: Alyson Roswell** 〈a_roswell@moderntimes.com〉
날짜: 4월 11일
제목: 내일

안녕하세요, Carla.

[162, 164] **죄송하지만 내일 Jack Haley의 작업반 방문은 연기해야 할 것 같아요.** 제가 시외로 출장을 가야 하거든요. 저는 오늘 밤에 출발하는데 내일 늦게나 되어서야 돌아올 겁니다. 그래서 내일은 집에 작업자들을 들여보낼 사람이 없을 거예요. 그 점은 대단히 죄송합니다.
[164] **프로젝트가 완료될 때까지 이틀밖에 남지 않았다는 것을 알고 있습니다. 오늘 아침에 Mr. Haley가 그렇게 말씀하시더군요.** 주의 나머지 기간 동안에는 제가 집에 있을 거니까 작업반은 주말까지는 다 끝낼 수 있을 것 같아요.
작업이 완료되면 최종 비용 지불을 하겠습니다.

Alyson Roswell

어휘 work crew 작업반 take a trip 여행하다, 출장을 가다 out of town 시외로

160. Sanderson Home Improvement에 대해 암시된 것은 무엇인가?
(A) 스터브리지에 위치해 있다.
(B) 고객들에게 할인을 제공한다.
(C) 굴뚝 설계 서비스를 제공한다.
(D) 가정에 난방기를 설치한다.

어휘 quality 양질의 install 설치하다

161. 광고에 따르면 냉방 시스템에 관해 누구에게 연락해야 하는가?
(A) Julius Clover
(B) Douglas Montana
(C) Cody Wilde
(D) Eric Blaine

패러프레이즈 Air Conditioning → cooling systems

PART 7

162. Ms. Roswell의 이메일의 주된 목적은 무엇인가?

(A) 어떤 작업을 연기하려고

(B) 회의를 예약하려고

(C) 지불을 하려고

(D) 취업 기회를 논의하려고

패러프레이즈 delay → postpone

어휘 arrange 마련하다, 처리하다

163. Ms. Roswell이 자신의 주택에서 하고 있는 것은 무엇이겠는가?

(A) 에어컨 설치

(B) 굴뚝 청소

(C) 주택 확장

(D) 수영장 건설

해설 연계 문제로서, Ms. Roswell은 두 번째 지문의 발신인이며 Carla Crow에게 이메일을 보내고 있다. 첫 번째 지문에서 Carla Crow는 수영장을 공사할 때 연락해야 할 담당자이므로 (D)가 정답이다.

164. Mr. Haley는 누구이겠는가?

(A) 공사 감독관

(B) 지붕 설치업자

(C) Sanderson Home Improvement의 사장

(D) Sanderson Home Improvement의 고객

어휘 supervisor 감독관, 관리자

165-169 이메일, 청구서, 회람

수신: Preston Peterson
〈ppeterson@tristatemedia.com〉

발신: Curtis Harrier
〈curtis_harrier@vanguardautos.com〉

날짜: 10월 11일

제목: 메모

[165] **첨부파일: @comments**

Mr. Peterson,

저와 저희 팀은 Vanguard Auto의 최신 차량을 위해 Tristate Media의 당신의 팀이 만들어 주신 동영상의 최초 버전을 보았습니다. 우리는 당신의 작업물에 깊은 인상을 받았습니다. 동영상은 특히 오프로드 상황에서 Stallion이 얼마나 잘 작동하는지를 분명히 보여줍니다. [165] **동영상 내에서 당신이 처리해 주었으면 하는 문제들이 몇 가지 있습니다.**

* 10초: 화면 하단에 회사의 이름과 로고를 큰 글씨로 넣어 주세요.

* [166] **25초: 차량 내부 사진들이 선명하지 않습니다. 시청자들이 내부가 얼마나 편안한지 볼 수 있기를 원합니다. 그 부분을 다시 촬영해 주실 수 있나요?**

* 1분: 오프로드 장면에 먼지가 너무 많습니다. 먼지 때문에 차를 보기가 힘듭니다.

첨부된 문서에 이러한 문제점들을 보다 자세히 설명했습니다. 저는 10월 19일까지 동영상의 최종 버전을 볼 수 있기를 기대하고 있습니다. 우리는 전국의 모든 판매상들과 몇몇 주요 고객들에게 그것을 보낼 것입니다. 제가 제안한 변경 사항과 관련하여 궁금한 점이 있으시면 연락 주시기 바랍니다.

[168-2] **Curtis Harrier**

미디어 부서

Vanguard Autos

어휘 attachment 첨부 파일 initial 초기의, 최초의 handle 처리하다, 감당하다 off-road 포장 도로에서 벗어난 issue 사안, 문제 address 처리하다, 다루다 print 활자 shot 사진, 한 장면

Vanguard Autos

청구서 5433

청구 일자: 11월 15일

배송 일자: 11월 19일

[169-2] **청구 주소지:**

Silverado Ranch

버팔로 레인 45번지

빌링스, 몬태나

수량	품목 번호	제품 사양	단가	합계
[167, 169-2] **5**	57231	**Stallion SUV**	$53,000	$265,000

세금	$10,600
합계	$275,600

어휘 invoice 청구서, 송장 bill 청구서를 보내다 quantity 수량 description 설명, 제품 사양 unit price 단가

회람

수신: 전 직원

발신: 영업 담당 부사장 Christina Wilson

날짜: 11월 20일

회신: 축하합니다

Stallion의 최신 홍보 동영상 제작에 애써 주신 모든 분들께 감사드립니다. 우리의 전국 판매상들은 그 동영상을 매우 좋아하며, 우리가 동영상을 보낸 고객들도 마찬가지입니다. [168-1] **저는 동영상을 완성하기 위해 애써 주신 Mr. Harrier에게 특히 감사드리고 싶습니다.**

Stallion의 공식적인 판매는 12월 1일 이후이지만, [169-1] **우리는 이미 몇 대를 판매했습니다. 그것들은 어제 장기 고객에게 배송되었습니다. 구매를 하신 Ben Freeman**은 동영상이 시운전조차 하지 않고 차량을 구매하도록 만들 만큼 중요한 역할을 했다고 우리에게 말씀하셨습니다. 우리는 곧 Stallion을 위한 몇 가지 광고 제작이 필요할 것이기 때문에, 12월에 여러분들의 활약을 기대하겠습니다.

어휘 recent 최근의 informational 정보를 제공하는 officially 공식적으로 go on sale 판매되다 unit 한 개[단위] instrumental 중요한 test-drive 시운전하다 commercial 광고

165. 이메일에 첨부된 것은 무엇인가?

(A) 청구서

(B) 신차에 대한 설명
(C) 동영상 제작물에 대한 평가
(D) 영수증 사본

어휘 review 평가, 검토 copy 사본, 1부 receipt 영수증

166. Mr. Harrier는 왜 25초에 나오는 장면을 다시 찍기를 원하는가?
(A) 차량이 너무 빨리 이동한다.
(B) 동영상 속 이미지가 불분명하다.
(C) 장면에 먼지가 너무 많다.
(D) 회사 로고가 나오지 않는다.

패러프레이즈 shots → image

어휘 unclear 불분명한 scene 장면 appear 나타나다

167. 청구서에는 Stallion에 대해 무엇이 나타나 있는가?
(A) 구매자는 5대를 주문했다.
(B) 할인이 제공되었다.
(C) 배송비가 있었다.
(D) 그것들은 12월 15일에 배송되었다.

어휘 purchaser 구매자 fee 비용, 요금

168. Ms. Wilson은 구체적으로 누구를 칭찬하는가?
(A) 미디어 부서의 직원
(B) 장기 고객
(C) 동영상 제작자
(D) 전국 판매원

해설 연계 문제로서, 마지막 지문에서 특히 Mr. Harrier에게 감사하다고 했는데, 첫 번째 지문에서 Curtis Harrier는 Media Department의 직원이라는 것을 확인할 수 있으므로 (A)가 정답이다.

169. Mr. Freeman은 어디에서 근무하겠는가?
(A) Vanguard Autos
(B) Silverado Ranch
(C) Tristate Media
(D) 시승 센터

해설 연계 문제로서, 마지막 지문에서 Stallion 몇 대가 Ben Freeman이라는 장기 고객에게 배송되었다는 단서를 찾을 수 있는데, 두 번째 지문에서 배송지가 Silverado Ranch라는 단서를 찾을 수 있으므로 (B)가 정답이다.

실전 모의고사

본문 p.206

LISTENING TEST

1. (D)	**2.** (A)	**3.** (C)	**4.** (B)	**5.** (A)
6. (B)	**7.** (A)	**8.** (A)	**9.** (A)	**10.** (B)
11. (C)	**12.** (C)	**13.** (B)	**14.** (B)	**15.** (B)
16. (B)	**17.** (A)	**18.** (C)	19 (B)	**20.** (C)
21. (B)	**22.** (A)	**23.** (B)	**24.** (A)	**25.** (B)
26. (C)	**27.** (B)	**28.** (C)	**29.** (A)	**30.** (B)
31. (A)	**32.** (C)	**33.** (D)	**34.** (C)	**35.** (C)
36. (C)	**37.** (B)	**38.** (A)	**39.** (B)	**40.** (B)
41. (B)	**42.** (A)	**43.** (D)	**44.** (B)	**45.** (B)
46. (C)	**47.** (C)	**48.** (A)	**49.** (A)	**50.** (D)
51. (B)	**52.** (B)	**53.** (B)	**54.** (D)	**55.** (C)
56. (D)	**57.** (C)	**58.** (A)	**59.** (A)	**60.** (C)
61. (A)	**62.** (D)	**63.** (C)	**64.** (C)	**65.** (A)
66. (D)	**67.** (C)	**68.** (B)	**69.** (B)	**70.** (C)
71. (B)	**72.** (D)	**73.** (D)	**74.** (A)	**75.** (C)
76. (A)	**77.** (A)	**78.** (D)	**79.** (C)	**80.** (C)
81. (D)	**82.** (A)	**83.** (B)	**84.** (D)	**85.** (B)
86. (C)	**87.** (A)	**88.** (B)	**89.** (B)	**90.** (A)
91. (C)	**92.** (C)	**93.** (B)	**94.** (B)	**95.** (C)
96. (A)	**97.** (B)	**98.** (C)	**99.** (C)	**100.** (D)

READING TEST

101. (A)	**102.** (D)	**103.** (C)	**104.** (B)	**105.** (C)
106. (D)	**107.** (B)	**108.** (A)	**109.** (A)	**110.** (C)
111. (D)	**112.** (B)	**113.** (D)	**114.** (A)	**115.** (C)
116. (B)	**117.** (A)	**118.** (C)	**119.** (A)	**120.** (B)
121. (D)	**122.** (B)	**123.** (C)	**124.** (C)	**125.** (A)
126. (D)	**127.** (A)	**128.** (D)	**129.** (B)	**130.** (A)
131. (D)	**132.** (B)	**133.** (A)	**134.** (C)	**135.** (C)
136. (C)	**137.** (A)	**138.** (D)	**139.** (D)	**140.** (A)
141. (C)	**142.** (D)	**143.** (D)	**144.** (C)	**145.** (C)
146. (B)	**147.** (C)	**148.** (B)	**149.** (C)	**150.** (A)
151. (C)	**152.** (D)	**153.** (B)	**154.** (A)	**155.** (C)
156. (A)	**157.** (A)	**158.** (D)	**159.** (C)	**160.** (D)
161. (C)	**162.** (A)	**163.** (C)	**164.** (A)	**165.** (D)
166. (D)	**167.** (D)	**168.** (B)	**169.** (C)	**170.** (B)
171. (B)	**172.** (B)	**173.** (C)	**174.** (A)	**175.** (C)
176. (B)	**177.** (A)	**178.** (A)	**179.** (D)	**180.** (C)
181. (A)	**182.** (B)	**183.** (D)	**184.** (B)	**185.** (D)
186. (D)	**187.** (D)	**188.** (C)	**189.** (A)	**190.** (B)
191. (A)	**192.** (D)	**193.** (D)	**194.** (C)	**195.** (C)
196. (B)	**197.** (C)	**198.** (B)	**199.** (B)	**200.** (C)

1. 🎧 미녀

(A) She's writing some notes on a pad of paper.
(B) She's rolling up her sleeves.
(C) Some cartons have been stacked on the floor.
(D) Ceramic pots have been arranged on shelves.

(A) 여자가 종이 위에 필기하고 있다.
(B) 여자가 소매를 걷어 올리고 있다.
(C) 상자들이 바닥에 쌓여 있다.
(D) 도자기들이 선반에 놓여 있다.

2. 🎧 미남

(A) They're lifting a sofa.
(B) They're moving some chairs.
(C) They're assembling some furniture.
(D) They're walking through a doorway.

(A) 그들은 소파를 들고 있다.
(B) 그들은 의자를 옮기고 있다.
(C) 그들은 가구를 조립하고 있다.
(D) 그들은 걸어서 출입구를 통과하고 있다.

3. 🎧 영녀

(A) She's examining a price tag.
(B) She's removing her sunglasses.
(C) She's reaching for a vegetable on a shelf.
(D) She's pushing a cart filled with items.

(A) 여자가 가격표를 살펴보고 있다.
(B) 여자가 선글라스를 벗고 있다.
(C) 여자가 선반에 있는 야채를 향해 손을 뻗고 있다.
(D) 여자가 물건이 가득 담긴 카트를 밀고 있다.

4. 🎧 호남

(A) The woman is drinking from a cup.
(B) The man is pointing at a menu.
(C) Some food is being served at a table.
(D) Flowers have been stitched on a tablecloth.

(A) 여자가 컵에 든 물을 마시고 있다.
(B) 남자가 메뉴를 가리키고 있다.
(C) 식탁에 음식이 서빙되고 있다.
(D) 식탁보에 꽃무늬가 수놓아져 있다.

5. 🎧 미녀

(A) One of the men is giving a presentation.
(B) One of the men is putting on a jacket.
(C) One of the women is adjusting a computer monitor.
(D) One of the women is putting away her laptop.

(A) 남자들 중 한 명이 발표를 하고 있다.
(B) 남자들 중 한 명이 재킷을 입고 있다. (동작)
(C) 여자들 중 한 명이 컴퓨터 모니터 위치를 조정하고 있다.
(D) 여자들 중 한 명이 노트북을 치우고 있다.

6. 🎧 미남

(A) Kitchen towels have been placed on a countertop.
(B) Some lamps are hanging from the ceiling.
(C) A cupboard door has been left open.
(D) Some cooking utensils are being arranged on a table.

(A) 주방용 수건들이 조리대 위에 놓여 있다.
(B) 램프 몇 개가 천장에 매달려 있다.
(C) 찬장 문이 열려 있다.
(D) 식탁 위 요리 도구들이 정리되고 있다.

7. 🎧 미남/영녀

Have the company vehicles in the parking lot been cleaned?
(A) No, not yet.
(B) I just parked it on the street.
(C) I put it in the recycling bin.

주차장에 있는 회사 차량들은 세차가 된 건가요?
(A) 아니오, 아직요.
(B) 그냥 길에 주차했어요.
(C) 그건 재활용품 수거함에 넣었어요.

8. 🎧 영녀/미남

How much will the budget increase next year?
(A) About 10 percent.
(B) Sorry, I must have dropped it.
(C) At the end of this quarter.

내년도 예산은 얼마나 증액될까요?
(A) 10퍼센트 정도요.
(B) 미안해요, 제가 떨어뜨렸나 봐요.
(C) 이번 분기 말에요.

9. 🎧 호남/미녀

You're going to have a meeting with Mr. Woodman before you leave, aren't you?
(A) Yes, right after lunch.
(B) I'd better take the bus.
(C) Three months' parental leave.

가시기 전에 Mr. Woodman과 회의를 하실 거죠?
(A) 네, 점심 먹고 바로요.
(B) 버스를 타는 게 낫겠어요.
(C) 삼 개월 간의 육아 휴직이요.

10. 미녀/호남

Aren't you going to schedule an eye doctor appointment?
(A) These glasses are not expensive.
(B) I already scheduled one.
(C) The new manager was appointed today.

안과 예약을 하지 않으실 건가요?
(A) 이 안경은 비싸지 않아요.
(B) 이미 예약했어요.
(C) 신임 관리자는 오늘 임명되었어요.

11. 미남/영녀

I'm going to try to fix this copy machine.
(A) Double-sided copies.
(B) Light fixtures for the lobby.
(C) Are you sure it can be repaired?

제가 이 복사기를 고쳐 보려고 합니다.
(A) 양면 복사요,
(B) 로비에 설치할 조명 기구요.
(C) 수리가 가능한 게 확실한가요?

12. 영녀/미남

What should we do with these brochures?
(A) Sure, I have time this afternoon.
(B) It's close to the seashore.
(C) Let me leave them at the front desk.

이 안내 책자들을 어떻게 해야 할까요?
(A) 물론이죠. 오늘 오후에 시간이 있습니다.
(B) 그건 해안에 가까이 있어요.
(C) 제가 프런트 데스크에 놓아둘게요.

13. 호남/미녀

Has the policy meeting been rescheduled?
(A) The staffing policy.
(B) Yes, it's happening next Monday instead.
(C) The entire management team.

정책 회의 일정이 변경되었나요?
(A) 직원 채용 정책입니다.
(B) 네, 대신 다음 주 월요일에 열릴 겁니다.
(C) 운영팀 전체요.

어휘 staffing 직원 채용 (staff 직원, 직원을 제공하다)

14. 미녀/호남

Why don't we stop by the warehouse on our way to the workshop?
(A) The store on Oak Street.
(B) Sure, we have time for that.
(C) The topic has just changed.

워크숍에 가는 길에 창고에 잠깐 들르는 게 어때요?
(A) 오크 스트리트에 있는 상점이요.
(B) 네, 그렇게 할 시간이 있어요.
(C) 주제가 방금 바뀌었습니다.

어휘 on our way to ~로 가는 길에

15. 미남/영녀

Have you tried our famous salmon dish?
(A) I'm afraid I can't make it on time.
(B) Yes, it was delicious.
(C) We need a table for six.

저희의 유명한 연어 요리를 드셔 보셨나요?
(A) 제시간에 도착할 수 없을 것 같네요.
(B) 네, 맛있었어요.
(C) 우리는 6인용 테이블이 필요합니다.

어휘 make it (어떤 곳에 간신히) 시간 맞춰 가다

16. 영녀/미남

Who's the opening act at tonight's concert?
(A) It's too crowded here.
(B) Sandra booked tickets.
(C) There're several job openings on our design team.

오늘밤 콘서트의 오프닝 공연자는 누구인가요?
(A) 이곳은 너무 붐비네요.
(B) Sandra가 표를 예매했어요.
(C) 우리 디자인팀에는 몇 개의 공석이 있습니다.

어휘 act 음악 그룹

해설 Sandra가 표를 예매했으니 오프닝 공연자에 대해서는 Sandra가 알 것이라는 의미이다.

17. 호남/미녀

When do the software demonstrations start?
(A) The schedule was e-mailed to everyone.
(B) A lot of attractive features.
(C) In the conference room, I think.

소프트웨어 시연은 언제 시작하나요?
(A) 일정은 모든 사람에게 이메일로 발송됐습니다.
(B) 많은 매력적인 기능들이요.
(C) 제 생각에는 회의실에서요.

해설 일정이 모든 사람에게 이메일로 발송되었으니 이메일을 확인해 보라는 의미이다.

18. 미녀/호남

The health inspector will be visiting the restaurant soon.
(A) Take this to table three.

(B) I'm fine, thanks for asking.
(C) We're all set.

위생 검사관이 곧 식당에 방문할 거예요.
(A) 이걸 3번 테이블로 가져가세요.
(B) 괜찮아요. 물어봐 줘서 고마워요.
(C) 저희는 모두 준비됐어요.

19. 미남/영녀

Did you find a good welding specialist?
(A) I have some wedding invitation templates.
(B) Yes, he starts next week.
(C) The list of special guests.

실력이 좋은 용접공을 찾으셨나요?
(A) 제게 청첩장 견본이 몇 개 있어요.
(B) 네, 그분은 다음 주에 일을 시작합니다.
(C) 특별 초청 손님 명단이요.

어휘 welding specialist 용접 전문가 (welder 용접공)

20. 영녀/미남

How was the tile pattern for the rest room chosen?
(A) The service was good.
(B) I like this checkered shirt.
(C) I wasn't involved.

화장실 타일 무늬는 어떻게 선정되었나요?
(A) 서비스가 좋았어요.
(B) 이 체크무늬 셔츠가 마음에 듭니다.
(C) 저는 관여하지 않았습니다.

21. 호남/미녀

When are we ordering office supplies for new employees?
(A) In front of the storage closet.
(B) Next week on Tuesday.
(C) They're training now.

신입 사원들에게 줄 사무용품은 언제 주문할 건가요?
(A) 수납장 앞에요.
(B) 다음 주 화요일이요.
(C) 그들은 지금 교육을 받고 있습니다.

어휘 office supplies 사무용품 train 교육[훈련]시키다, 교육[훈련]받다

22. 미녀/호남

The garden lights are going to be solar-powered, right?
(A) We are still in the planning stages.
(B) Yes, this plant grows best in the shade.
(C) $250 per year.

정원 조명은 태양 에너지로 작동될 거죠?
(A) 아직은 기획 단계에 있습니다.
(B) 네, 이 식물은 그늘에서 가장 잘 자랍니다.
(C) 연간 250달러요.

어휘 solar-powered 태양열 동력의

23. 미남/영녀

Where can I buy a charger for this camera?
(A) This has excellent resolution.
(B) I can order one for you.
(C) Around 2:30.

이 카메라의 충전기는 어디서 살 수 있나요?
(A) 이건 해상도가 뛰어납니다.
(B) 제가 하나 주문해 드릴 수 있어요.
(C) 2시 30분경에요.

24. 영녀/미남

Do I need to reserve a conference room?
(A) Yes, Jeff will show you how.
(B) I booked the trip already.
(C) There's room for improvement.

제가 회의실을 예약해야 하나요?
(A) 네. Jeff가 방법을 알려줄 겁니다.
(B) 제가 벌써 여행을 예약했어요.
(C) 개선할 필요가 있어요.

25. 호남/미녀

When's the new department director supposed to start?
(A) Yes, for a summer vacation.
(B) Mr. Anderson is not retiring until May.
(C) No, he should be in the office.

신임 부서장이 언제 근무를 시작하죠?
(A) 네, 여름휴가를 위해서요.
(B) Mr. Anderson이 5월이나 되어야 퇴직해요.
(C) 아니오, 그는 사무실에 있을 거예요.

해설 현재 부서장인 Mr. Anderson이 5월이나 되어야 퇴직을 하게 되므로 신임 부서장이 일을 시작하는 것은 빨라야 5월일 것이라는 간접 답변이다.

26. 미녀/호남

Should I finish designing these fliers now, or can it wait until tomorrow?
(A) I'm flying to San Francisco.
(B) In the waiting room.
(C) Tomorrow's fine.

이 전단지 디자인을 지금 끝내야 하나요, 아니면 내일까지 해도 되나요?

(A) 저는 샌프란시스코로 비행기를 타고 갑니다.
(B) 대기실에서요.
(C) 내일 해도 돼요.

27. 미남/영녀

This laptop is becoming quite slow.
(A) Attendance was low.
(B) When did you last check for viruses?
(C) No, you shouldn't have to wait long.

이 노트북 속도가 너무 느려지고 있어요.
(A) 참석률이 낮았어요.
(B) 마지막으로 바이러스 검사를 한 게 언제예요?
(C) 아뇨, 오래 기다릴 필요 없어요.

28. 영녀/미남

How much will the repairs cost?
(A) In about three days.
(B) I'd like you to do this in pairs.
(C) Everything is covered under the warranty plan.

수리비가 얼마나 나올까요?
(A) 3일 정도 후예요.
(B) 여러분이 짝을 지어 이걸 해주시면 좋겠습니다.
(C) 모든 것은 보험으로 보장됩니다.

29. 호남/미녀

Why don't you check the prices at a different hardware store?
(A) Do you know of a good one?
(B) She's a software engineer.
(C) You can check in after 10 o'clock.

다른 철물점에서는 얼마인지 가격을 확인해 보는 게 어때요?
(A) 괜찮은 데 아세요?
(B) 그녀는 소프트웨어 엔지니어예요.
(C) 10시 이후에 입실하실 수 있습니다.

30. 미녀/호남

Can you give me a tour of the property on Abbey Street this afternoon?
(A) It has a large backyard.
(B) Sorry, I won't have time until Friday.
(C) Over 20 people.

오늘 오후에 저에게 애비 스트리트에 있는 부동산을 보여주실 수 있나요?
(A) 넓은 뒷마당이 있어요.
(B) 미안하지만 금요일까지는 시간이 안 돼요.
(C) 20명이 넘어요.

31. 미남/영녀

Who's scheduled to do the product demonstration tomorrow?
(A) We are waiting for confirmation.
(B) At the Wilson Hotel.
(C) Let me show you a few more.

누가 내일 제품 시연을 할 예정인가요?
(A) 우리는 승인을 기다리는 중이에요.
(B) Wilson 호텔에서요.
(C) 제가 몇 개 더 보여 드릴게요.

32-34. 영녀/미남
Questions 32-34 refer to the following conversation.

W Hassan, [32] I've finished restocking the power tools. Ted said that you wanted to talk to me about an issue we're having in the paint section.

M That's right. [33] The paint-mixing machine has broken down. So, we can't mix any custom paints for customers at the moment.

W Hmm ... I wonder if it's something easy to fix. [34] I'll take a look at the user manual to see if I can figure out the problem.

여 Hassan, [32] **제가 전동 공구를 다시 채워놨어요. Ted가 그러는데 페인트 코너에 문제가 있어서 저를 찾으셨다고요?**

남 맞아요. [33] **페인트 혼합기가 망가졌어요.** 그래서 지금 주문 제작용 혼합 페인트를 만들 수가 없어요.

여 음... 쉽게 고칠 수 있는 건지 모르겠네요. [34] **일단 사용 설명서를 보고 문제가 뭔지 알아볼게요.**

어휘 restock (재고품을) 다시 채우다 power tool 전동 공구 section 구획, 부분 break down 망가지다 at the moment 현재, 지금 fix 고치다 take a look at ~을 한번 보다

32. 화자들은 어디에 있겠는가?
(A) 배송 회사
(B) 국립공원
(C) 철물점
(D) 청소 용역 업체

33. 남자에 따르면 문제를 야기한 것은 무엇인가?
(A) 직원 부족
(B) 일정 충돌
(C) 안 좋은 후기
(D) 고장 난 장비

34. 여자는 자신이 무엇을 할 거라고 말하는가?
(A) 문서를 출력하기
(B) 전문가를 고용하기
(C) 사용설명서를 확인하기
(D) 결제를 처리하기

35-37. 영녀/미남

Questions 35-37 refer to the following conversation.

W [35]I've reviewed your design for Ms. Osborne's living room, and I think you've done a great job. I love the unique style!

M Thank you. She had a clear vision for that room, so I tried to follow it.

W There's just one adjustment needed, though. [36]We can't use the wood panels you selected because they've been discontinued by the manufacturer.

M I hadn't realized that. They're a major feature of my design.

W Well, you might be able to achieve the same look with wallpaper. [37]Check out the photos of the room that Yuki did for Mr. Harris. Then you can see what I mean.

여 [35]**당신이 작업한 Ms. Osborne의 거실 디자인을 검토해 봤는데 일을 아주 잘 하신 것 같아요.** 독창적인 스타일이 마음에 듭니다!

남 고맙습니다. 그분이 원하는 거실 모습이 뚜렷했기 때문에 그걸 따르려고 노력했답니다.

여 그런데 한 가지 조정할 게 있어요 [36]**당신이 선택한 목재 패널이 제조사에 의해 단종돼서 사용할 수가 없어요.**

남 그건 몰랐네요. 그게 제 디자인에서 주요한 특징인데요.

여 음, 벽지를 통해서 그와 동일한 모습을 연출할 수도 있을 거예요. [37]**Yuki가 Mr. Harris를 위해 작업한 방의 사진을 확인해 보세요.** 그러면 제가 무슨 말을 하는지 이해하실 거예요.

어휘 review 검토하다 unique 독특한, 개성적인 adjustment 조정, 수정 panel 판, 판자 discontinue (생산을) 중단하다 major 주요한, 주된 feature 특징 wallpaper 벽지

35. 남자는 누구이겠는가?

(A) 건물주

(B) 미술 강사

(C) 인테리어 디자이너

(D) 기자

36. 여자는 무엇을 걱정하는가?

(A) 늘어난 비용

(B) 안전 문제

(C) 이용할 수 없는 재료

(D) 지키지 못한 마감

37. 여자는 무엇을 할 것을 제안하는가?

(A) 연수를 받는 것

(B) 몇 가지 이미지를 보는 것

(C) 제조업체에 연락하는 것

(D) 급히 주문을 하는 것

38-40. 호남/미남/미녀

Questions 38-40 refer to the following conversation with three speakers.

M1 I'm glad we were both able to visit this site in person.

M2 Me, too. I hope it'll be suitable for our car dealership.

M1 Well, [38]the real estate agent said that it is in an excellent location. Oh, here she is now. Hi, Cindy.

W Good morning. So, what's your first impression?

M2 It's a great neighborhood. [39]But we need a lot of space to display our vehicles. I'm worried about the small size.

M1 Right. We'll need extra room for customer parking as well.

W You know, there's a grassy area on the east side that could be paved. [40]Let me show you the property line on the map.

남1 우리가 이곳을 직접 올 수 있게 되어서 기뻐요.

남2 저도요. 여기가 우리 자동차 대리점에 적합한 장소면 좋겠어요,

남1 음, [38]**공인중개사의 말로는 이곳의 입지가 아주 훌륭하다고 하네요. 아, 저기 오시네요, 안녕하세요, Cindy.**

여 안녕하세요. 그래서, 첫인상이 어떠세요?

남2 동네가 아주 좋습니다. [39]**하지만 우리 자동차를 전시할 아주 큰 공간이 필요해요. 크기가 작아서 걱정이 되네요.**

남1 맞아요. 고객 주차를 위한 추가적인 공간도 필요할 거예요.

여 음, 동쪽에 바닥 포장이 가능한 녹지 공간이 있어요. [40]**지도상에서 대지 경계선을 보여 드릴게요.**

어휘 site 장소, 부지 in person 직접 dealership (자동차) 대리점 real estate agent 부동산 중개인 location 입지, 위치

38. 남자들은 누구를 만나고 있는가?

(A) 공인중개사

(B) 정비공

(C) 안전 검사원

(D) 회계원

39. 남자들은 무엇에 대해 우려하고 있는가?

(A) 입지를 찾기가 어렵다.

(B) 장소가 충분히 크지 않다.

(C) 양식에 정보가 누락되어 있다.

(D) 주차 요금이 너무 높다.

40. 화자들은 다음에 무엇을 하겠는가?

(A) 건물에 들어가기

(B) 문서를 보기

(C) 다른 장소로 가기

(D) 치수 재기

41-43. 미녀/호남

Questions 41-43 refer to the following conversation.

W Good morning. This is Pamela at Lubbock Sales. [41] You were supposed to deliver some boxes today, but I'm wondering if you can do it tomorrow instead. They're carrying out emergency repairs on our road, so it's difficult to access our entrance.

M Don't you need the items urgently?

W We can wait another day. [42] They're containers for moving our office items, and we aren't quite ready to start packing anyway.

M I see. [43] Then, let me call our driver, Milton, to see if he can do it.

여 안녕하세요. Lubbock Sales의 Pamela입니다. [41] **오늘 상자 몇 개를 배송해 주시기로 되어 있는데, 대신 내일 배송해 주실 수 있는지 궁금합니다.** 저희 도로에 긴급 수리를 하고 있기 때문에 입구로 들어오기가 어렵거든요.

남 그 물건들이 당장 필요하신 거 아닌가요?

여 하루 늦어도 돼요. [42] **저희 사무실 비품을 이사하는 데 쓰일 용기들인데, 어쨌든 짐을 쌀 준비가 안 되어 있거든요.**

남 알겠습니다. [43] **그러면 저희 운전기사인 Milton에게 전화해서 그렇게 할 수 있는지 알아볼게요.**

어휘 carry out ~을 수행하다 pack 짐을 싸다

41. 여자가 전화하는 이유는 무엇인가?
(A) 할인을 요청하기 위해
(B) 배송 일정을 다시 정하기 위해
(C) 비용을 지불하기 위해
(D) 반품에 대해 문의하기 위해

42. 여자가 물건들을 주문한 이유는 무엇인가?
(A) 여자는 몇몇 물품을 옮길 계획이다.
(B) 여자는 어떤 기계 장치들을 고쳐야 한다.
(C) 여자는 직원들에게 선물을 나눠줄 것이다.
(D) 여자는 자신의 사무실을 재단장하고 있다.

43. 남자가 다음에 할 일은 무엇인가?
(A) 운전해서 여자의 업체로 가기
(B) 회사의 웹사이트를 업데이트하기
(C) 여자의 관리자와 이야기하기
(D) 직원이 시간이 되는지 확인하기

44-46. 미남/영녀

Questions 44-46 refer to the following conversation.

M Good morning, [44] Chapman Health Center.

W Hi, I have a doctor's appointment on Thursday at ten, but I need to reschedule it.

M I can help you with that. Could you please tell me your name?

W It's Bonnie Phillips. [45] I'm supposed to have my annual checkup, but now I need to fly to Sacramento for a work conference.

M Are you available next Wednesday at nine o'clock?

W Yes. Thanks.

M Okay. Let's see ... [46] your insurance policy expires in November, right?

W [46] I'll have to check. Just a moment.

남 안녕하세요, [44] **Chapman Health Center입니다.**

여 안녕하세요. 목요일 10시에 진료 예약이 있는데요, 일정을 조정해야 해서요.

남 제가 도와드리겠습니다. 성함을 말씀해 주시겠어요?

여 Bonnie Phillips예요. [45] **매년 하는 건강 검진을 받기로 되어 있는데, 업무 회의를 위해 비행기를 타고 Sacramento에 가야 하거든요.**

남 수요일 아홉 시에 시간이 되시나요?

여 네. 감사합니다.

남 알겠습니다. [46] **좀 볼게요... 보험이 11월 중에 만료되는데, 맞나요?**

여 [46] **확인해 볼게요. 잠시만요.**

어휘 doctor's appointment 병원 예약 reschedule 일정을 변경하다 be supposed to do ~하기로 되어 있다 annual 연례의, 매년의 checkup 건강 진단 insurance policy 보험 증권 expire 만료되다, 만기가 되다

44. 남자가 근무하는 곳은 어디인가?
(A) 컴퓨터 수리점
(B) 병원
(C) 은행
(D) 인력 소개소

45. 여자가 변경을 하려는 이유는 무엇인가?
(A) 자동차에 문제가 있다.
(B) 출장을 떠날 것이다.
(C) 수업을 진행해야 한다.
(D) 몸이 좋지 않다.

46. 여자가 다음에 할 일은 무엇이겠는가?
(A) 정식으로 민원을 제기하기
(B) 새로운 연락처 정보를 제공하기
(C) 만기 날짜를 확인하기
(D) 다른 지점에 전화하기

47-49. 미남/영녀

Questions 47-49 refer to the following conversation.

M Christina, most of the feedback on the customer comment cards is positive. [47] However, there were quite a few complaints about our menu being so limited.

W I didn't realize that was an issue.

M [47] Well, I thought maybe we could add a better

variety of main dishes.

W Hmm ... All of our cooks would have to learn how to make those, and the training period is already quite long.

M Then how about just adding more desserts? [49]Steven makes all of them, so the change wouldn't affect others. I'm sure he could handle it, as he's worked in the industry for a long time.

남 Christina, 고객 의견 카드에 적힌 대부분의 의견은 긍정적이에요. [47]**하지만 우리 메뉴가 너무 제한적이라는 불만도 꽤 있었어요.**

여 그게 문제인지 몰랐어요.

남 [47]**음, 우리가 주요리를 좀 더 다양하게 추가할 수 있을 것 같아요.**

여 흠... 모든 요리사가 그것들을 어떻게 만드는지 배워야 하겠고, 교육 기간이 이미 상당히 길어요.

남 그러면 디저트를 좀 더 추가하는 건 어때요? [49]**Steven이 디저트를 모두 만드니까 다른 사람들에게는 영향을 미치지 않을 거예요. 그는 그 업계에서 오래 일해 왔으니까 분명히 그 일을 처리할 수 있을 거예요.**

어휘 comment 의견, 논평 quite a few 상당수의 limited 제한된 a variety of 다양한 main dish 주요리 affect 영향을 주다 handle 다루다, 처리하다

47. 화자들이 근무하는 곳은 어디이겠는가?
(A) 농장에서
(B) 창고에서
(C) 카페에서
(D) 가정용 기기 상점에서

48. 여자가 "교육 기간이 이미 상당히 길어요"라고 말하는 이유는 무엇인가?
(A) 제안을 거절하려고
(B) 남자를 안심시키려고
(C) 도움을 주려고
(D) 일정 변경을 제안하려고

49. 남자는 Steven에 대해 무엇을 말하는가?
(A) 경험이 많다.
(B) 근무 조건에 불만이 있다.
(C) 공급자를 추천할 수 있다.
(D) 업무량에 어려움을 겪을지도 모른다.

50-52. 미남/미녀/호남
Questions 50-52 refer to the following conversation with three speakers.

M1 Good afternoon. [50]Do you have a pass to our gym?

W Not yet. I'd like to know more about your classes.

M1 Of course. My colleague can tell you more. [51]Joseph, could you please explain our system for group exercise classes?

M2 Sure. [51]You can sign up online and attend up to five per week. These are included in your membership fees.

W That's great. Also, I heard that you give discounts to Wesley Sales employees. [52]I just began working there last month. Am I eligible?

남1 안녕하세요. [50]**저희 헬스클럽 출입증을 가지고 계신가요?**

여 아직요. 이곳 수업에 대해 좀 더 많은 것을 알고 싶습니다.

남1 물론이죠. 제 동료가 더 많은 것을 말씀 드릴 수 있을 겁니다. [51]**Joseph, 단체 운동 수업에 대한 우리 시스템을 설명해 주시겠어요?**

남2 네. [51]**온라인으로 등록하실 수 있고, 일주일에 5번까지 참가하실 수 있어요.** 모두 회비에 포함되어 있답니다.

여 아주 좋네요. 그리고 Wesley Sales 직원들에게 할인을 해주신다고 들었거든요. [52]**저는 지난달부터 거기서 일을 시작했는데요.** 제가 자격이 되나요?

어휘 pass 통행권, 출입증 gym 헬스클럽, 체육관 colleague 동료 sign up 등록하다 membership fee 회비 eligible 자격이 있는

50. 화자들이 있는 곳은 어디인가?
(A) 영화관
(B) 도서관
(C) 식당
(D) 헬스클럽

51. Joseph은 여자에게 무엇에 대한 정보를 전달하고 있는가?
(A) 직원들을 만나는 것
(B) 단체 수업에 참가하는 것
(C) 계정에 접속하는 것
(D) 시설을 돌아보는 것

52. 여자는 자신이 지난달에 무엇을 했다고 말하는가?
(A) 다른 도시로 이사했다.
(B) 새로운 일을 시작했다.
(C) 증명서를 받았다.
(D) 온라인으로 공부를 시작했다.

53-55. 호남/미녀
Questions 53-55 refer to the following conversation.

M [53]Demand for our software programs is still growing, Danielle. We need to expand our team of programmers, but we're having a lot of problems filling the positions.

W [54]You know, if we want to remain competitive, we need to increase the annual salary we offer to the staff. That would help to retain good workers as well as attract the top talent for new workers.

M That sounds like a good idea, but would our current situation support that change?

W I believe so, since our sales have been strong. [55]I'll look over our budget categories to see what's possible.

남 [53]**우리 소프트웨어 프로그램에 대한 수요가 계속해서 증가하고 있어요**, Danielle. 프로그래머 팀을 확장할 필요가 있는데, 그 자리들을 채우는 데 문제가 많네요.

여 [54]**있잖아요, 우리가 계속해서 경쟁력을 유지하려면 직원들 연봉을 높일 필요가 있어요.** 그렇게 하면 좋은 직원들을 유지하고 유능한 사람들을 영입하는 데 도움이 될 겁니다.

남 좋은 생각 같은데, 우리의 현재 상황이 그런 변화를 뒷받침할 수 있을까요?

여 우리 매출이 좋기 때문에 그럴 수 있을 거예요. [55]**예산 카테고리를 살펴보고 무엇이 가능할지 알아볼게요.**

어휘 demand 수요 expand 확장하다 competitive 경쟁력 있는 annual salary 연봉 retain 유지하다, 보유하다 talent 재능 있는 사람; 재주 look over 살펴보다, 훑어보다 budget 예산

53. 화자들이 근무하는 업종은 무엇이겠는가?
(A) 광고
(B) 기술
(C) 에너지
(D) 제약

54. 화자들은 어떤 변화를 논의하고 있는가?
(A) 다른 곳으로 이전하는 것
(B) 기계를 구입하는 것
(C) 운영 시간을 연장하는 것
(D) 직원들의 급여를 인상하는 것

55. 여자는 무엇을 하겠다고 제안하는가?
(A) 세일 상품 준비
(B) 전문가에게 연락
(C) 재무 데이터 검토
(D) 직원들로부터 의견 수렴

56-58. 미남/영녀
Questions 56-58 refer to the following conversation.

M Hi, I'm calling because I just got my bill for September and there's an issue. [56]I've been charged twice my normal amount.

W I'm sorry about that, sir. [57]Our Internet company strives to ensure accuracy. Could you please tell me your account number?

M Yes, it's 47801. [58]I moved to a new home on the fifteenth of last month, and it looks like I've been charged the full fee at both places.

W I see. Please wait while I look into this further.

남 안녕하세요, 제가 9월 고지서를 받았는데 문제가 있어서 연락드렸습니다. [56]**평소 요금의 두 배가 부과되었어요.**

여 죄송합니다, 고객님. [57]**저희 인터넷 회사는 정확성을 보장하기 위해 노력하고 있습니다.** 고객님의 계정 번호를 알려주시겠어요?

남 네, 47801입니다. [58]**제가 지난달 15일에 새집으로 이사를 했는데,** 양쪽 모두에서 요금 전액이 부과된 것 같습니다.

여 그렇군요. 제가 좀 더 알아보는 동안 기다려 주십시오.

어휘 bill 청구서, 고지서 charge 부과하다, 청구하다 ensure 보장하다, 확실히 하다 accuracy 정확도 account 계정; 계좌

56. 남자는 어떤 문제에 대해 전화를 하고 있는가?
(A) 비밀번호를 잊어버렸다.
(B) 몇 가지 부정확한 정보를 제공했다.
(C) 가장 최근의 고지서를 잃어버렸다.
(D) 과다 청구를 받았다.

57. 여자가 근무하는 곳은 어디인가?
(A) 배송 업체
(B) 이사 업체
(C) 인터넷 공급 업체
(D) 회계 사무실

58. 남자는 지난달에 무엇을 했는가?
(A) 새로운 주소로 이사했다.
(B) 서비스 패키지 상품을 상향 조정했다.
(C) 자신의 사업을 시작했다.
(D) 여자의 회사를 방문했다.

59-61. 영녀/미남
Questions 59-61 refer to the following conversation.

W Good morning, Andrew. [59][60]I want to talk to you about the software developer position that my team is currently interviewing candidates for.

M Sure. What's up?

W So far, none of the applicants we've seen have had sufficient experience in web development. I think we need to expand the applicant pool. Can HR increase the salary listed in the job posting?

M I'll need to discuss it with my team members. How soon do you need a response?

W Well, the project manager has already moved up our deadline.

M Understood. I'll e-mail you as soon as a decision is reached.

여 안녕하세요, Andrew. [59][60]**저희 팀이 지금 면접 보고 있는 소프트웨어 개발자 자리에 대해 이야기할 것이 있어서요.**

남 물론이죠. 무슨 일인데요?

여 지금까지 우리가 본 지원자들 중에 아무도 웹 개발에 충분한 경력을 가지고 있지 않았어요. 지원자의 인력 풀을 늘려야 할 것 같아요. 인사 쪽에서 구인 공고에 적힌 급여를 올려 줄 수 있나요?

남 저희 팀원들과 이 문제를 논의해야 할 것 같습니다. 얼마나 빨리 답변을 드려야 할까요?

여 음, 프로젝트 관리자가 이미 마감일을 앞당겼어요.

남 알겠습니다. 결정이 나는 대로 이메일을 보내 드릴게요.

어휘 currently 현재, 지금 so far 지금까지 applicant 지원자 sufficient 충분한 expand 늘리다, 확장하다 pool 풀, 이용 가능 인력 job posting 구인 공고 move up 앞당기다 reach a decision 결정을 내리다

59. 화자들은 무엇에 대해 논의하고 있는가?
(A) 채용
(B) 제품 출시
(C) 회사 이전
(D) 연간 행사

60. 여자는 어느 부서에 근무하고 있을 것 같은가?
(A) 재무
(B) 마케팅
(C) 정보 기술
(D) 운영 관리

61. 여자가 "프로젝트 관리자가 이미 마감일을 앞당겼어요"라고 말하는 이유는 무엇인가?
(A) 급하다는 것을 보여주기 위해
(B) 감사를 표하기 위해
(C) 타협을 제안하기 위해
(D) 혼란스러움을 나타내기 위해

62-64. 미녀/호남
Questions 62-64 refer to the following conversation and diagram.

W Phoenix Appliances. How can I help you?

M Hi, [62]last week I ordered a toaster oven for the break room at my law firm ... uh ... model D-670. We already have an issue. It was order 49522.

W Alright. What seems to be the problem?

M When I was using it this morning, [63]the door panel suddenly cracked.

W I'm sorry for the inconvenience. Unfortunately, that model is currently out of stock, but it can be repaired at one of our centers. The e-mail address we have on file is tedfletcher@wagner.com. Is that the best way to reach you?

M Yes, it is.

W Okay. [64]I'll e-mail you the addresses of the repair centers nearest to you.

여 Phoenix Appliances입니다. 무엇을 도와드릴까요?

남 안녕하세요, [62]**제가 지난주에 저희 법률사무소의 휴게실에서 사용할 오븐 토스터기를 주문했는데요**, 어, D-670 모델이요. 벌써 문제가 생겼네요. 주문 번호는 49522였습니다.

여 알겠습니다. 무슨 문제인 것으로 보이세요?

남 제가 오늘 아침에 그걸 사용하고 있었는데, [63]**갑자기 문에 금이 갔습니다.**

여 불편을 끼쳐 드려 죄송합니다. 공교롭게도 그 모델은 현재 재고가 없지만, 저희 센터 중 한 곳에서 수리될 수 있습니다. 저희 파일상의 이메일 주소가 tedfletcher@wagner.com이네요. 여기로 연락드릴까요?

남 네, 그렇게 해 주세요.

여 알겠습니다. [64]**이메일로 가장 근처에 있는 수리 센터의 주소를 보내 드리겠습니다.**

어휘 appliances 가전제품 break room 휴게실 panel 틀, 판자 crack 금이 가다 inconvenience 불편 out of stock 재고가 없는 reach 연락하다

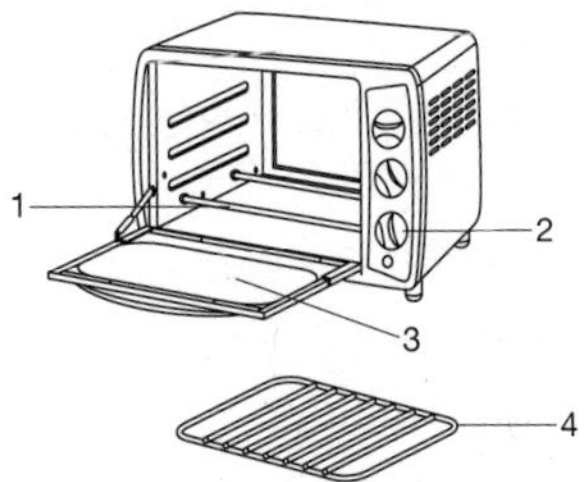

62. 남자는 어디에서 근무하는가?
(A) 연구소
(B) 식당
(C) 백화점
(D) 법률 사무소

63. 시각 자료를 보시오. 어느 부분이 파손되었는가?
(A) Part 1
(B) Part 2
(C) Part 3
(D) Part 4

64. 여자는 다음에 무엇을 하겠는가?
(A) 제품 사용 설명서 찾기
(B) 대체 부품 주문하기
(C) 지점들의 목록 보내기
(D) 물품이 있는지 여부 확인하기

65-67. 미녀/호남
Questions 65-67 refer to the following conversation and catalog.

W [65]I've just spoken to a representative from Tahoka Manufacturing. They plan to begin sending our shipments on the first Monday of every month instead of every Friday.

M When does that start?

W Next month. We'd have to place larger orders and figure out where to store the items.

M I think it's still worth buying their wool rugs for our shop. Their products are excellent.

W I agree. [66]I like that they only use high-quality wool. And didn't they just release some new designs?

M Yes. I've got the new catalog here. [67]I like this wavy design. How about getting that?

W Sure. It's nice that it's available in both blue and gray.

여 [65]**방금 Tahoka Manufacturing의 담당자와 이야기를 나눴어요. 그 회사는 매월 첫 번째 금요일 대신에 첫 번째 월요일에 우리 물품의 발송을 시작할 계획이더라고요.**

남 그게 언제 시작하는 거죠?

여 다음 달이요. 그리고 더 대량의 물품을 발주해야 하는 데다가 그 물품들을 어디에 보관할지도 알아봐야 해요.

남 그래도 그 회사의 모직 러그를 구입하는 것은 여전히 가치가 있다고 생각해요. 그 회사의 제품은 뛰어나잖아요.

여 저도 같은 생각이에요. [66]**그 회사가 품질이 좋은 양모만을 사용하는 점이 마음에 들어요.** 그리고 그 회사가 얼마 전에 새로운 디자인 몇 개를 출시하지 않았나요?

남 네. 여기 새 카탈로그가 있어요. [67]**이 물결 무늬 디자인이 마음에 드네요. 그것을 구입하는 게 어때요?**

여 **좋아요.** 파란색과 회색 두 가지 모두로 구입할 수 있는 점이 좋네요.

어휘 representative 담당자 shipment 배송(품) place an order 주문하다 figure out 알아내다 store 보관하다 item 물품, 품목 rug 러그, 깔개 release 출시하다 wavy 물결치는

New Arrivals!	
Circles: code G33 Colors: blue, green	Stripe: code H18 Colors: brown, blue
Waves: code N29 Colors: blue, gray	Stars: code P77 Colors: red, gray

65. Tahoka Manufacturing은 무엇을 바꿀 것인가?
(A) 배송 일정
(B) 보증 기간
(C) 사무실 위치
(D) 보관 수수료

66. 여자가 Tahoka Manufacturing에 대해 좋아하는 점은 무엇인가?
(A) 배달 속도
(B) 다양한 무늬들
(C) 직원의 친절함
(D) 재료의 품질

67. 시각 자료를 보시오. 화자들이 주문하기로 동의하는 디자인은 무엇인가?
(A) G33
(B) H18
(C) N29
(D) P77

68-70. 미남/영녀
Questions 68-70 refer to the following conversation and schedule.

M [68]Did you hear about Victor's promotion?

W Yes, I'm glad he was offered the team leader role. He'll do a great job.

M I agree. I'd like to have a small party this Friday to celebrate.

W You know, Libby from HR just told me that she's participating in a dance show this Friday.

M Oh, really? Where's that?

W It's at the Murphy Center. Let's see ... here's the schedule on the Web site. [69]Her group goes on at 7:30.

M Hmm ... [70]but it costs twenty-five dollars per person to get in. That's quite a lot.

W We might be able to use some company funds, since it'll be a team-building event.

남 [68]**Victor의 승진 소식을 들었어요?**

여 네. 그가 팀장직을 제안 받아서 기쁘네요. 그는 잘해낼 거예요.

남 저도 같은 생각이에요. 이번 금요일에 조촐한 축하 파티를 가질까 해요.

여 있잖아요, 인사팀의 Libby가 그러는데, 그녀가 이번 주 금요일에 댄스 쇼에 참가한대요.

남 아, 정말요? 어디서요?

여 Murphy Center요. 어디 보자... 여기 웹사이트에 일정이 나오네요. [69]**그녀가 속한 그룹은 7시 30분에 나와요.**

남 음, [70]**그런데 입장료가 인당 25달러예요. 너무 비싼데요.**

여 팀 단합을 위한 행사가 될 테니, 회삿돈을 쓸 수도 있을 것 같아요.

어휘 promotion 승진 HR 인사(= human resources) cost 비용이 들다 fund 자금 team building 팀워크 형성

Performance Schedule	
7:00 P.M.	Tango Treats
7:30 P.M.	Marlana Music
8:00 P.M.	BC Dance Troupe
8:30 P.M.	The Chapmans

68. 남자가 파티를 열기를 원하는 이유는 무엇인가?
(A) 한 팀이 프로젝트를 완료했다.
(B) 동료 한 명이 승진했다.
(C) 회사가 수상 후보로 추천되었다.
(D) 판매 목표를 초과했다.

69. 시각 자료를 보시오. Libby는 어떤 팀의 멤버인가?
(A) Tango Treats
(B) Marlana Music
(C) BC Dance Troupe
(D) The Chapmans

70. 남자는 어떤 문제점을 언급하는가?
(A) 장소가 먼 지역에 있다.
(B) 교통편을 이용할 수 없다.
(C) 입장료가 비싸다.
(D) 일부 팀원이 불참할 것이다.

71-73. 미남
Questions 71-73 refer to the following advertisement.

M Whether you're planning a wedding reception, a corporate function, or anything in between, it can be hard to find the perfect venue. At King's Convention Center, we're here to help. [71]Equipped with the latest technology and luxury furniture, our site is sure to satisfy all of your attendees. [72]King's Convention Center is famous for having a unique building design, featuring high ceilings and stain glass windows that make you feel like you're in a royal court. [73]For reservations, simply go to our Web site. We hope to see you soon!

남 여러분이 결혼식 피로연을 계획하시건, 기업 행사를 계획하시건, 그것이 무엇이든 완벽한 장소를 찾는 것은 어려울 수 있습니다. 이곳 King's Convention Center가 도움을 드리겠습니다. [71]**최신 기술과 고급 가구가 갖추어진 저희 공간은 분명 여러분의 모든 참석자들을 만족시켜 드릴 것입니다.** [72]**King's Convention Center는 독특한 건물 디자인으로 유명한데,** 여러분이 마치 왕실에 있는 것과 같은 기분을 느끼게 해드릴 높은 층고의 천장과 스테인 글라스 창문이 특징적입니다. [73]**예약을 하려면 저희 웹사이트로 가시면 됩니다.** 여러분을 조만간 뵙기를 바랍니다!

어휘 wedding reception 결혼 피로연 corporate 기업의 function 행사 in between 중간의, 사이에 venue 장소 equip (장비를) 갖추다 attendee 참석자 feature 특징으로 하다 ceiling 천장 royal court 궁궐 simply 단지, 그저

71. 어떤 종류의 업체가 광고되고 있는가?
(A) 출장 뷔페 서비스
(B) 행사 장소
(C) 임대 주택
(D) 영화관

72. 화자는 업체가 무엇으로 가장 유명하다고 말하는가?
(A) 재능 있는 직원들
(B) 편리한 위치
(C) 오랜 역사
(D) 독창적인 건축 양식

73. 청자들은 웹사이트에서 무엇을 할 수 있는가?
(A) 사진 보기
(B) 후기 읽기
(C) 할인 코드 찾기
(D) 예약하기

74-76. 호남
Questions 74-76 refer to the following podcast.

M Welcome back to the Entrepreneurial Ventures podcast. [74]Today, my topic is digital self-promotion. When is the right time to start a new viral marketing campaign, and how can you do so effectively in the modern world? To answer these questions and more, I'll be introducing a special guest: Amara Dambe. The founder of the famous tech start-up, Financing Together, [75]Ms. Dambe is known for her ability to get into the mentalities of consumers when they're using virtual spaces. I think you'll enjoy this episode. But before getting started, [76]I'm going to briefly talk about a new service that I'm offering for a small monthly fee.

남 Entrepreneurial Ventures 팟캐스트에 다시 오신 것을 환영합니다. [74]**오늘 저의 주제는 디지털 자기 홍보입니다.** 새로운 바이럴 마케팅 캠페인을 시작하기에 적절한 시기는 언제이고, 현대 세계에서 어떻게 효과적으로 그렇게 할 수 있을까요? 이러한 질문 등에 답변하기 위해 특별 초대 손님인 Amara Dambe를 소개하겠습니다. 유명 기술 스타트업인 Financing Together의 설립자인 [75]**Ms. Dambe는 소비자들이 가상공간을 이용할 때 그들의 생각 속으로 들어가는 능력으로 잘 알려져 있습니다.** 여러분이 이번 편을 재미있게 보실 거라고 생각합니다. 하지만 시작하기 전에, [76]**제가 매달 소액의 요금으로 제공하고 있는 새로운 서비스에 대해 간략하게 이야기하려고 합니다.**

어휘 promotion 홍보 founder 설립자 start-up 스타트업 get into ~로 들어가다 mentality 심리, 사고방식 virtual space 가상공간 episode (방송의) 회 briefly 짧게, 간략히

74. 이 팟캐스트 회차는 무엇에 관한 것인가?
(A) 온라인 광고
(B) 컴퓨터 프로그래밍
(C) 창업
(D) 해외 확장

75. 화자는 Ms. Dambe가 무엇을 잘한다고 말하는가?
(A) 기술적인 문제들을 해결하는 것
(B) 자금을 유치하는 것
(C) 소비자들을 이해하는 것
(D) 공급업체들과 협상하는 것

76. 화자는 다음에 무엇을 논의하겠는가?
(A) 구독 서비스
(B) 연구 프로젝트
(C) 청취자의 질문
(D) 뉴스 보고

77-79. 미녀
Questions 77-79 refer to the following excerpt from a meeting.

W [77]Next Monday, we'll have the first in a series of seminars about reducing stress in the workplace. Our first guest lecturer will help you learn to use meditative breathing exercises to calm your body and mind. [78]I was inspired to launch this series when I read a recent news story about the effects of physical and mental health on employee productivity. As part of the initiative, we've also started installing mood-enhancing lighting throughout the building. [79]I'm distributing a pamphlet that talks about the scientific reason for the change.

여 [77]**다음 주 월요일에, 직장 내에서 스트레스를 줄이는 것에 관한 일련의 세미나 중 첫 번째 세미나를 갖게 됩니다.** 우리의 첫 번째 초청 강사는 여러분이 몸과 마음을 진정시키기 위해 명상 호흡 운동법을 사용하는 것을 배울 수 있도록 도울 것입니다. [78]**저는 최근에 신체적, 정신적 건강이 직원 생산성에 미치는 영향에 대한 뉴스 기사를 읽고 이 시리즈를 시작할 영감을 얻었습니다.** 계획의 일환으로, 우리는 건물 전체에 분위기를 개선하는 조명도 설치하기 시작했습니다. [79]**제가 그 같은 변화의 과학적인 이유를 담은 팸플릿을 나누어 드리겠습니다.**

어휘 workplace 직장 lecturer 강사, 강연자 meditative 명상의 breathing 호흡 inspire 영감을 주다 launch 시작하다 productivity 생산성 initiative (진취적인) 계획 enhance 향상시키다 distribute 나누어주다, 배포하다

77. 다음 주 월요일에 무슨 일이 일어나겠는가?
(A) 발표가 있을 것이다.
(B) 제품을 구입할 것이다.
(C) 새로운 지점이 개장할 것이다.
(D) 사무 공간이 다시 디자인될 것이다.

78. 무엇이 연사에게 영감을 주었는가?
(A) 광고
(B) 유명한 도서
(C) 직원 제안
(D) 언론 보도

79. 청자들은 새로운 조명의 이점을 어떤 방법으로 알아낼 수 있는가?
(A) 이메일을 읽음으로써
(B) 웹사이트를 방문함으로써
(C) 유인물을 봄으로써
(D) 동영상을 시청함으로써

80-82. 영녀
Questions 80-82 refer to the following recorded message.

W Good afternoon. [80]You've reached the Blandensville County Power Company. Please note that a telephone pole was recently knocked down near McArthur Avenue as a result of a traffic accident. A team of responders is on site. We thank you for your patience. [82]If you'd like to receive updates about the electric grid in your area, press 1 to sign up for our automatic texting service.

여 안녕하세요, [80]**Blandensville County Power Company에 전화 주셨습니다.** 교통사고로 인해 맥아더 애비뉴 근처에 있는 전신주 하나가 쓰러졌다는 사실을 양지해 주십시오. 긴급복구팀이 현장에 나가 있습니다. 참고 기다려 주시면 감사하겠습니다. [82]**지금 계신 지역의 전력망에 대한 최신 소식을 받고 싶으시다면 1번을 눌러서 저희의 문자 자동 안내 시스템에 등록해 주십시오.**

어휘 reach 연락하다 note 유념하다 telephone pole 전신주 knock down 쓰러뜨리다 as a result of ~의 결과로 responder 응급상황 대기 직원 update 최신 정보 electric grid 전력망 sign up for ~을 신청하다 text 문자 메시지를 보내다

80. 청자는 어떤 종류의 업체에 전화하고 있는가?
(A) 케이블 제공업체
(B) 컨설팅 회사
(C) 전력 회사
(D) 자동차 제조업체

81. 화자가 "참고 기다려 주시면 감사하겠습니다"라고 말할 때 의미하는 것은 무엇인가?
(A) 긴급복구팀원들이 미숙하다.
(B) 회사가 곧 문을 닫는다.
(C) 많은 사람들이 불만을 터뜨리고 있다.
(D) 수리가 아직 끝나지 않았다.

82. 청자가 계속해서 최신 소식을 받을 수 있는 방법은 무엇인가?
(A) 자동 발송 이메일을 받음으로써
(B) 나중에 다시 전화함으로써
(C) 경고 문자를 받음으로써
(D) 웹사이트를 확인함으로써

83-85. 미녀
Questions 83-85 refer to the following excerpt from a meeting.

W The City Council will now discuss the issue of street maintenance. [83]A group of citizens submitted a petition to repair and repave a number of the town's streets. In particular, Main Street has been reported as a dangerous area due to the presence of potholes in various locations. While the motion has been approved, [84]Chairperson John Daly has raised a concern that the requested work will be obtrusively loud for Main Street residents. [85]To compensate these residents, the city will reimburse up to a one week stay at the nearby Comfort Plus Inn for those who live within a 50-meter radius of the work site.

여 시의회는 이제 도로 정비 문제를 논의할 것입니다. [83]**일단의 시민들이 다수의 시내 도로를 보수하고 재포장해 달라는 청원을 올렸습니다.** 특히 메인 스트리트는 여러 군데 움푹 패인 곳이 있기

때문에 위험한 지역으로 신고되었습니다. 발의가 승인되었지만, [84]**John Daly 의장은 요청된 작업이 메인 스트리트 주민들의 신경이 거슬릴 정도로 소음을 유발할 것이라는 우려를 나타냈습니다.** [85]**이 같은 주민들에 대한 보상 차원에서 시에서는 작업 반경 50미터 이내에 거주하는 사람들을 근처에 있는 Comfort Plus Inn에서 일주일 동안 투숙할 수 있도록 할 것입니다.**

어휘 submit 제출하다 petition 청원서, 진정서, 탄원서 in particular 특히 pothole 도로의 파인 곳 motion 발의 obtrusively 역력히, 눈에 거슬리게 radius 반경

83. 시민들은 왜 불만을 제기했는가?
(A) 노상 주차장을 이용할 수 없다.
(B) 도로가 파손되었다.
(C) 도로 청소를 너무 뜸하게 한다.
(D) 주차장이 너무 비싸다.

84. John Daly는 무엇에 대해 염려하는가?
(A) 높은 세금
(B) 환경 파괴
(C) 증가한 교통량
(D) 공사 소음

85. 일부 주민들은 무엇을 받게 되는가?
(A) 주차권
(B) 호텔 예약 요금
(C) 행사 티켓
(D) 교통 서비스

86-88. 미남
Questions 86-88 refer to the following speech.

M Hi! [86]Welcome to today's seminar about the future of publishers in our increasingly paperless society. I'm Jean Couturier, and I've been working in the publishing industry for over thirty years. [87]Before I get started, I want to thank those of you who submitted anonymous inquiries through my website. Those questions helped me design my slides for today's presentation. [88]I also want to express my gratitude for my assistant, Melanie Grichuk, who worked hard to make this event happen. There's Melanie in the back corner—let's give her a round of applause.

남 안녕하세요. [86]**점점 더 종이의 사용이 불필요해지는 우리 사회에서 출판사의 미래에 관한 오늘 세미나에 오신 것을 환영합니다.** 저는 Jean Couturier이고, 출판업계에서 30년 이상 근무하고 있습니다. [86]**시작하기 전에 제 웹사이트를 통해 익명으로 질문을 제출해 주신 분들께 감사를 드리고 싶습니다.** 그 질문들이 제가 오늘 발표를 위한 슬라이드를 만드는 데 도움이 되었습니다. [88]**그리고 저를 도와주고 있는 Melanie Grichuk에게도 감사를 드리고 싶은데, 그녀는 이 행사를 위해 노고를 아끼지 않았습니다. 저기 뒤쪽 구석에 Melanie가 있네요.** 그녀에게 힘찬 박수를 부탁드립니다.

어휘 publisher 출판사 increasingly 점점 더 submit 내다, 제출하다 anonymous 익명의 inquiry 질문, 문의 presentation 발표 gratitude 감사 assistant 조수, 비서 give a round of applause 박수를 치다

86. 세미나의 주제는 무엇인가?
(A) 제조
(B) 배송
(C) 출판
(D) 언론

87. 화자가 몇몇 청자들에게 감사하는 이유는 무엇인가?
(A) 그들이 질문을 해 주었다.
(B) 그들은 자신들의 경험을 공유했다.
(C) 그들은 예전 강연에 참석했다.
(D) 그들은 슬라이드에 대한 의견을 주었다.

88. 화자는 왜 강연장의 뒤쪽을 언급하는가?
(A) 그곳에서 간식을 얻을 수 있다.
(B) 직원이 그곳에 앉아 있다.
(C) 정보가 담긴 자료가 그곳에 있다.
(D) 그곳에서 책이 판매 중이다.

89-91. 영녀
Questions 89-91 refer to the following telephone message.

W Hi, [89]Matteo. I hope your university talk goes well tonight. Everything's fine here at Vezia Bistro while you're away, but I want to follow up on the instructions you left behind. I know you wanted to offer chicken marsala as our weekly special, but some of the supplies for that dish are running low. Fettuccini alfredo has always been a hit with our regulars. Also, I've got good news. [91]An influential blogger visited the restaurant last night and wrote up some major praise for us on his site this morning.

여 안녕하세요, [89]**Matteo. 오늘 밤 있을 당신의 대학교 강연이 잘 되었으면 좋겠어요.** 당신이 없는 동안 이곳 Vezia Bistro는 잘 돌아가고 있는데, 당신이 남기고 간 지시에 대한 후속 보고를 하고 싶어요. 당신이 우리의 주간 특선 요리로 치킨 마살라를 내놓기를 원했던 것은 알고 있는데, 그 요리에 들어가는 재료 몇 가지가 얼마 안 남았어요. 페투치니 알프레도는 우리 단골손님들에게 항상 인기가 있어요. 그리고 좋은 소식이 있어요. [91]**영향력이 있는 블로거가 어젯밤에 식당을 방문했는데, 오늘 아침 자기 웹사이트에 우리 식당에 대한 굉장한 칭찬을 썼답니다.**

어휘 follow up on ~에 대한 후속 조치를 하다 instruction 지시 leave behind 남기다 supplies 물품 run low 모자라게 되다, 고갈되다 regular 단골손님

89. Matteo가 자신의 업체에 있지 않은 이유는 무엇인가?
(A) 공급업체를 만나고 있다.
(B) 강연을 하고 있다.
(C) 취업 면접장에 있다.
(D) 부동산을 보고 있다.

90. 화자가 "페투치니 알프레도는 우리 단골손님들에게 항상 인기가 있어요"라고 말하는 이유는 무엇인가?

(A) 제안을 하려고

(B) 칭찬을 하려고

(C) 문제점을 보여주려고

(D) 성과를 축하하려고

91. 화자가 식당에 대해 공유하는 좋은 소식은 무엇인가?

(A) 1년에 한 번 주어지는 상을 받았다.

(B) 고객들이 밀려들었다,

(C) 온라인에서 주목을 받았다.

(D) 텔레비전 프로그램에 나왔다.

92-94. 호남

Questions 92-94 refer to the following excerpt from a meeting.

M Hello everyone. [92]We've got a busy week ahead, with the new Delillo models of beds and shelving units arriving soon, and all of our dining sets on sale. There should be plenty of customers streaming in. Now, with Enrico having moved on to another company, we're short-staffed until we find his replacement. But don't worry: I have experience in sales, even though most of you haven't seen it. I also need to mention that the back room is starting to get disorganized. [94]I want everyone to spend a few minutes straightening it after lunch today.

남 안녕하세요, 여러분. [92]**우리는 바쁜 한 주를 앞두고 있는데, 최신 Delillo 침대와 선반 세트가 곧 입고될 것이고, 우리의 모든 식탁과 의자 세트가 세일에 들어가기 때문입니다.** 분명히 많은 고객들이 밀려들 것입니다. 현재 Enrico가 다른 회사로 옮겼기 때문에 우리는 그의 후임자를 찾을 때까지는 일손이 부족합니다. 하지만 걱정 마세요. 여러분 대다수는 본 적이 없겠지만, 저도 판매를 해본 경험이 있습니다. 그리고 뒷방이 어지러워지기 시작했다는 것을 언급하고 싶네요. [94]**오늘 점심식사 후에 모든 사람들이 몇 분간 시간을 내어 그곳을 정리해 주시기 바랍니다.**

어휘 shelving unit 선반 dining set 식탁과 의자 세트 stream in 계속해서 들어오다 short-staffed 인력이 부족한 replacement 후임자, 대체할 사람 disorganized 어수선한, 무질서한 straighten 똑바르게 하다

92. 화자가 근무하는 업종은 무엇이겠는가?

(A) 철물점

(B) 건설회사

(C) 가구점

(D) 배달업체

93. 화자가 "저도 판매를 해 본 경험이 있습니다"라고 말할 때 암시하는 것은 무엇인가?

(A) 그가 몇몇 직원들에게 멘토 역할을 할 것이다.

(B) 그가 몇 차례 교대 근무를 할 것이다.

(C) 그는 곧 지원자들을 면접할 것이다.

(D) 그는 초과 근무 수당을 지급할 것이다.

94. 화자는 청자들이 무엇을 할 것으로 기대하는가?

(A) 매장 배치 재조정

(B) 어떤 구역의 청소

(C) 오찬 준비

(D) 채용 행사 기획

95-97. 미남

Questions 95-97 refer to the following telephone message and map.

M Hi, my name is Phil, [95]and I'm supposed to pick you up in front of Old House Theater by the box office in a few minutes. The problem is, there's a major accident on Wright Avenue. [96]I'm wondering if you're willing to go out the back exit of the theater and meet me there instead so we can avoid a major delay. [97]All you need to do is text "YES" to this number to agree to the change.

남 안녕하세요, 제 이름은 Phil이고, [95]**몇 분 후에 Old House Theater의 매표소 옆에서 당신을 차에 태우기로 되어 있습니다.** 문제는 Wright Avenue에 큰 교통사고가 났다는 거예요. [96]**대신에 극장의 후문으로 나오셔서 거기서 저를 만나실 수 있는지 알고 싶습니다.** 그렇게 하면 시간이 크게 지체되는 것을 피할 수 있거든요. [97]**이 변경 사항에 동의하신다면 이 번호에 "네"라고 문자를 보내주시기만 하면 됩니다.**

어휘 be supposed to do ~하기로 되어 있다 pick up (차에) 태우다 box office 매표소

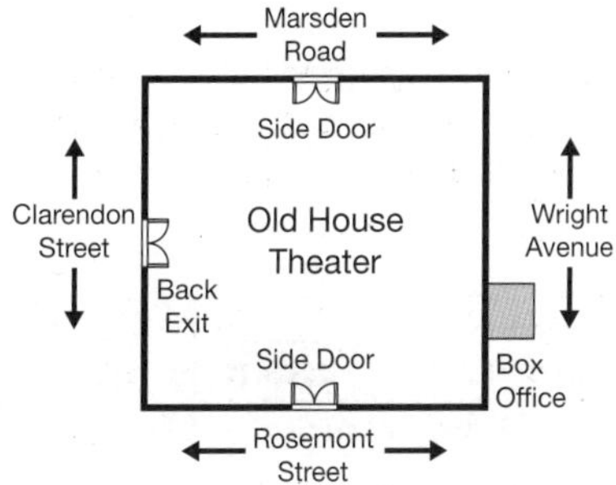

95. 화자는 누구이겠는가?

(A) 버스 운전사

(B) 투어 가이드

(C) 승차 공유 서비스 운전자

(D) 기차 차장

96. 시각 자료를 보시오. 화자는 어디서 만나기를 원하는가?

(A) Clarendon Street에서

(B) Wright Avenue에서

(C) Rosemont Street에서

(D) Marsden Road에서

97. 청자는 변경 사항을 어떻게 확정할 수 있는가?

(A) 회사에 전화해서

(B) 메시지를 보내서

(C) 앱을 이용해서
(D) 밖에 서 있음으로써

98-100. 미녀

Questions 98-100 refer to the following talk and schedule.

W [98]Greetings, people of Innersville, and thanks for coming out to the opening of our brand-new bus station in the heart of downtown. This facility will drastically improve travel conditions throughout the region. [99]Right now, there are limited resources in terms of public transportation in the area. To compensate, these private bus lines offer comfortable rides at very affordable prices. We are excited to welcome Kiwi Bird Bus Travel and Clockwork Bus Company to the area for the first time. [100]The first departure, from Clockwork Bus Company, leaves in 30 minutes, so check the schedule and happy travels!

여 [98]**안녕하세요, Innersville 주민 여러분.** 시내 중심부에 있는 우리의 새로운 버스 터미널의 개장에 와 주셔서 감사합니다. 이 시설은 이 지역 전체에 걸쳐 교통 여건의 괄목할 만한 개선을 가져오게 될 것입니다. [99]**현재 이 지역은 대중교통 측면에서 자원이 한정되어 있습니다.** 이를 보완하기 위해, 이 사설 버스 노선은 매우 저렴한 가격에 편안한 승차를 제공합니다. 우리는 우리 지역에 처음으로 Kiwi Bird Bus Travel과 Clockwork Bus Company를 기쁜 마음으로 환영합니다. [100]**Clockwork Bus Company에서 제공하는 첫차는 30분 후에 출발하니** 일정을 확인하시고, 즐거운 여행이 되시기 바랍니다.

어휘 greetings 안녕하세요 brand-new 최신의 in the heart of ~의 한가운데에 downtown 시내, 도심지 drastically 대폭 limited 제한된 in terms of ~의 관점에서 public transportation 대중교통 affordable 저렴한

Innersville Bus Station	
Terminal A	Fulton Bus Lines
Terminal B	Kiwi Bird Bus Travel
Terminal C	Speedy Friends Buses
Terminal D	Clockwork Bus Company

98. 담화의 청자는 누구인가?
(A) 여행사 직원
(B) 직원
(C) 시민
(D) 투자자

99. 화자에 의하면 시설이 필요했던 이유는 무엇인가?
(A) 정부에서 자동차 교통량을 줄이기를 원한다.
(B) 오래된 버스 정류장의 상태가 안 좋았다.
(C) 시는 대중교통 시설이 부족하다.
(D) 지역 공항이 최근에 폐쇄되었다.

100. 시각 자료를 보시오. 첫 번째로 출발할 터미널은 어디인가?
(A) Terminal A
(B) Terminal B
(C) Terminal C
(D) Terminal D

---

101. (A)
해석 그 컨설팅 회사는 다음 주에 자사의 신입 사원들을 대상으로 연수회를 열 계획이다.
(A) (특정한 활동을 위한) 시간 (B) 방법 (C) 접근법 (D) 길, 방법
해설 training session(연수회), informational session(설명회) 등의 형태로 자주 쓰이는 (A) session이 정답이다.
어휘 intend 의도하다, 작정하다 hold 열다, 개최하다

102. (D)
해석 유럽에서 오는 주문품은 아마 늦어도 내일 저녁까지는 도착할 것이다.
(A) 상당히, 꽤 (B) 혹독하게 (C) 정확하게 (D) 아마
어휘 no later than 늦어도 ~까지

103. (C)
해석 Ms. Patterson은 댈러스에서 열리는 마케팅 세미나에 참석하고 싶다는 소망을 상사에게 밝혔다.
(A) 묻다 (B) 제출하다 (C) 표현하다 (D) 주의를 환기시키다
어휘 attend 참석하다 supervisor 상사, 관리자

104. (B)
해석 Sylvester Deli에서 엄선한 육류는 도시 내의 다른 상점들보다 더 뛰어나다.
해설 빈칸은 형용사 보어 자리로서 뒤에 than이 있으므로 형용사의 비교급인 (B) greater가 정답이다.
어휘 selection 선택(된 것들)

105. (C)
해석 유감스럽게도 Mr. Carpenter가 연구개발부에서 사임한다는 소식을 알립니다.
해설 빈칸 앞에 한정사가 있으므로, 한정사의 수식을 받는 명사인 (C) resignation이 정답이다.
어휘 regret 유감스럽게 생각하다, 후회하다 resign 사임하다 R&D Department 연구개발부

106. (D)
해석 물류 학회에 참석한 거의 모든 사람은 업계에 직접적으로 관련되어 있다.
해설 빈칸 뒤에 단수 명사가 있으므로 단수 명사를 수식할 수 있는 (D) every가 정답이다. almost는 부사이므로 명사를 수식할 수 없고, all과 those는 복수 명사를 수식하므로 오답이다.
어휘 nearly 거의 attendee 참석자 logistics 물류 conference 학회, 총회 directly 직접적으로 be involved in ~에 관련되다 industry 산업, 업계

107. (B)

해석 고객과의 모든 거래는 서면으로, 그리고 전산으로 기록된다.

해설 앞에 be 동사가 있고 뒤에 목적어 없이 전치사구가 이어지므로, be동사와 함께 수동태를 이루는 과거분사 (B) recorded가 정답이다.

어휘 transaction 거래 client 고객 record 기록하다 electronically 전자적으로, 컴퓨터로

108. (A)

해석 Mr. Anderson은 이달 예산을 논의할 목적으로 직원 회의의 일정을 잡았다.

(A) 목적 (B) 견해, 시야 (C) 의견 (D) 약속

해설 for the purpose of(~의 목적으로)의 형태로 쓰이는 (A) purpose가 정답이다.

어휘 schedule 일정을 잡다 staff (전체) 직원 for the purpose of ~의 목적으로, ~을 위해 budget 예산

109. (A)

해석 세미나 참석자들은 도착하자마자 그룹으로 나뉘어 역할극 활동을 할 것이다.

해설 빈칸은 주절의 주어 자리이므로 주격 인칭대명사인 (A) they가 정답이다.

어휘 divide 나누다, 나뉘다 activity 활동

110. (C)

해석 새로운 규정이 얼마 전에 제정되었기 때문에 정부 조사가 반드시 실시되어야 한다.

(A) 하지만 (B) ~에도 불구하고 (C) 왜냐하면 (D) ~하자마자

해설 선택지가 접속사, 전치사, 부사 등으로 이루어져 있다. 빈칸 뒤로 완전한 절이 이어지므로 문장과 문장을 연결하는 접속 부사인 (A)와 전치사인 (B)를 소거한다. 주절과 부사절의 내용이 인과 관계를 이루므로 (C) because가 정답이 된다.

어휘 government 정부 inspection 검사, 점검 conduct (특정 활동을) 하다 regulation 규정 enact 제정하다

111. (D)

해석 새로운 법은 결과적으로 금융 산업에 대한 외국인들의 투자 증가로 이어졌다.

(A) 공급 (B) 방법 (C) 소유 (D) 투자

어휘 result in ~한 결과를 낳다 financial 금융의

112. (B)

해석 가장 최근에 입사한 관리자 중 한 명인 Mr. Jackson이 식당에서 야간 교대 근무를 선호한다는 것은 잘 알려져 있다.

해설 빈칸은 that절의 동사 자리인데, that절의 주어는 단수 명사인 Mr. Jackson이므로 단수 동사인 (B) prefers가 정답이다. 빈칸 뒤의 to부정사가 목적어 역할을 하므로 수동태인 (C)와 (D)는 오답이다.

어휘 prefer 좋아하다, 선호하다 shift 교대 근무

113. (D)

해석 Ms. Chamberlain은 마드리드로 출장을 가는 동안 대략 1주일 동안 자리에 없을 것이다.

(A) ~ 이내에 (B) ~에 (C) ~ 동안 (D) ~ 동안

해설 뒤에 one week라는 기간이 있으므로 기간을 나타내는 전치사 (D) for가 정답이다. 전치사 for는 이처럼 숫자 앞에 쓰이지만, during은 the winter(겨울)와 같이 특정한 기간 앞에 쓰이는 것이 차이점이다.

어휘 absent 부재 중인 roughly 대략, 거의 on business 업무로

114. (A)

해석 엔지니어는 배관 균열의 정확한 위치를 알아내야 한다.

해설 빈칸 앞에 관사와 형용사 precise가 있으므로 형용사의 수식을 받는 명사 자리이다. 따라서 (A) location이 정답이다.

어휘 determine 알아내다, 정하다 precise 정확한 location 위치, 장소 locate 정확한 위치를 찾아내다 crack (갈라진) 금

115. (C)

해석 Ms. Lopez는 이사회로부터 신제품에 대한 질문을 받았을 때 그것을 사려 깊게 묘사했다.

(A) 엄청나게 (B) 확실히 (C) 세심하게, 사려 깊게 (D) 궁극적으로, 결국

어휘 describe 묘사하다 board of directors 이사회

116. (B)

해석 다음 달에 근로 계약이 만료되는 파트타임 직원들은 이번 주 목요일까지 Ms. Matisse와 이야기를 해야 한다.

해설 문장의 주어는 Those part-timers, 동사는 should speak이고, 빈칸부터 month까지는 주어를 수식하는 관계대명사절이다. 선행사인 part-timers가 사람이므로 사물을 가리키는 (A) which와 부사인 (C) when을 소거한다. 선행사 part-timers와 work contracts는 소유 관계가 성립하므로 소유격 관계대명사 (B) whose가 정답이다.

어휘 part-timer 파트타임 직원, 아르바이트생 contract 계약(서) expire 만료되다

117. (A)

해석 외국 지사로 전근하는 임원들은 보다 높은 연봉을 받지만 자신의 주거를 책임져야 한다.

(A) 하지만 (B) ~한 이후로 (C) 또한, 마찬가지로 (D) ~하기 위하여

해설 문장의 주어는 Executives, 동사는 receive와 are이며, who transfer to foreign branches는 주어를 수식하는 관계절이다. 빈칸에는 동사와 동사를 대등하게 연결하는 등위 접속사가 적절하므로 (A) but이 정답이다.

어휘 executive 임원, 이사 transfer 옮기다, 이동하다 branch 지점, 지사 housing 주택

118. (C)

해석 각각의 볼트는 선반이 함께 고정될 수 있도록 단단히 고정되어야 한다.

해설 빈칸은 동사 뒤에 있으며 빈칸 뒤로는 to부정사구가 이어지므로 동사를 수식하는 부사 자리이다. 따라서 (C) tightly가 정답이다.

어휘 attach 부착하다, 붙이다 tightly 단단히, 꽉 ensure 확실히 하다, 보장하다 shelf 선반

119. (A)

해석 지방 당국의 허가 없이는 화물을 선박에서 하역할 수 없다.
(A) ~ 없이 B) ~ 사이에 (C) ~ 대신에 (D) ~을 제외하고

어휘 cargo 화물 unload 하역하다 permission 허가 authorities 당국

120. (B)

해석 현재 아무런 자금을 구할 수 없기 때문에, 다리는 부분적으로만 건설되었다.

해설 빈칸은 수동태를 이루는 be동사 is와 과거분사 constructed 사이에 있으므로 부사 자리이다. 따라서 (B) partially가 정답이다.

어휘 since ~이므로 funding 자금 (지원) currently 현재, 지금 available 구할 수 있는, 이용 가능한

121. (D)

해석 영업팀의 최신 정보에 따르면, 새로운 화장품은 예상했던 것보다 더 잘 팔리고 있다고 한다.
(A) 왜냐하면 (B) 결과적으로 (C) ~에도 불구하고 (D) ~에 따르면

해설 빈칸 뒤에 구가 이어지므로 빈칸에는 전치사가 적절하다. (C)와 (D) 중에서 문맥상 적절한 (D) According to가 정답이다.

어휘 sales 판매의 cosmetics 화장품 line (상품의) 종류 anticipate 예상하다, 기대하다

122. (B)

해석 컴퓨터 산업의 국내 고용은 지난 4개월 동안 증가하고 있다.

해설 빈칸 앞에 형용사, 빈칸 뒤에 전치사구가 이어지므로 빈칸은 형용사의 수식을 받는 명사 자리이다. 따라서 (A)를 소거할 수 있다. 명사인 (B), (C), (D) 중에서 의미상 가장 적절한 것은 (B) employment이다.

어휘 domestic 국내의 employment 고용, 채용

123. (C)

해석 정식 요청을 고려한 후, 경영진은 마침내 자사 직원들에게 추가적인 유급 휴가를 제공하기로 합의했다.

해설 빈칸은 주어인 management와 동사 agreed 사이에 있으므로 동사를 수식하는 부사 자리이다. 따라서 (C) eventually가 정답이다.

어휘 consider 고려하다 formal 공식적인, 정식의 management 경영(진) provide 제공하다, 주다 extra 추가의, 여분의 paid vacation 유급 휴가

124. (C)

해석 업계 전문가들은 공급망의 문제로 인해 향후 몇 달 동안 수출이 감소할 것으로 보고 있다.

해설 빈칸은 exports를 주어로 하는 명사절의 동사 자리로서 미래의 시점을 나타내는 부사구인 in the coming months가 있으므로 미래 시제인 (C) will decline이 정답이다.

어휘 expert 전문가 export 수출 decline 감소하다 in the coming months 앞으로 몇 달 동안 due to ~로 인해 issue 문제 supply chain 공급망

125. (A)

해석 지역 농부들은 비교적 선선한 여름 날씨에도 불구하고 놀라울 정도로 높은 수확량을 기록했다고 알려 왔다.
(A) 놀랍게도 (B) 명령조로 (C) 해마다 (D) 점점

어휘 report 보고하다, 알리다 crop 곡물 yield 수확량 relatively 상대적으로, 비교적

126. (D)

해석 소비자들이 제품에 열광했다는 것을 보여 주는 시장 조사에도 불구하고, Gladden Technology는 제품의 생산을 중단했다.
(A) 감명을 받은 (B) 환상적인 (C) 단호한 (D) 열광적인

해설 (A) impressed는 with, by 등의 전치사와 함께 쓰인다.

어휘 indicate 보여 주다, 나타내다 halt 중단하다

127. (A)

해석 Skylar Electronics는 더 많은 컴퓨터를 현지에서 제조하되 그것들을 유럽 국가에 유통시킬 계획이다.

해설 빈칸은 등위 접속사 yet에 의해 to manufacture와 대등하게 연결되어 있으므로, to가 생략된 부정사 (A) distribute가 정답이다.

어휘 manufacture 제조하다, 생산하다 locally 국지적으로 yet 그러나 distribute 유통하다

128. (D)

해석 콘서트 참석자들은 두 밴드의 공연에 만족했다.
(A) 유지되는 (B) 예상되는 (C) 감탄한 (D) 만족한

어휘 attendee 참석자, 참가자 performance 공연

129. (B)

해석 Mr. Gibson은 유지보수 요청 양식을 정리하기 위해 문서를 보관할 지정된 폴더를 만들었다.

해설 빈칸 앞에 관사, 빈칸 뒤에 명사가 있으므로 빈칸에는 명사를 수식하는 형용사가 올 수 있다. 분사인 designated와 designating이 형용사 역할을 할 수 있는데, '지정하는 폴더'가 아닌 '지정된 폴더'가 문맥상 적절하므로 (B) designated가 정답이다.

어휘 organize 정리하다 maintenance 유지, 보수 form 양식 designated 지정된 store 보관하다, 저장하다

130. (A)

해석 Ms. Sulla는 자신의 월별 전기 요금 고지서를 받았을 때, 전력 사용량이 지난달보다 감소했다는 것을 알아차렸다.
(A) 알아차리다 (B) 흘끗 보다 (C) 나타나다 (D) 반복하다

어휘 electric bill 전기 요금 고지서 usage 사용, 이용 decline 감소하다 previous 이전의

131-134 공지

모든 고객 여러분께,

Marigold Bakery의 켄싱턴 지점이 3월 31일자로 문을 닫는다는 것을 [131]**알리게 되어** 유감입니다. 저희는 더 이상 그곳의 우리 고객님들께 페이스트리, 케이크, 그리고 [132]**다른** 품목들을 제공할 수 없을 것입니다. 베이커리가 입주해 있는 건물이 수리될 예정이라 이 문제에 있어서 저희는 선택의 여지가 없습니다. [133]**근처에 다른 지점이 세 곳 있다는 것을 양지해 주시기 바랍니다.** 그 지점들은 메이필드, 웨스트사이드, 그리고 헤이우드에 있습니다. 여러분은 또한 온라인으로 주문해서 물품을 무료로 배송 받을 수 있습니다. 지난 17년 동안 여러분의 [134]**지속적인** 성원에 다시 한번 감사드립니다.

어휘 regret 후회하다, 유감스럽게 생각하다 inform 알리다, 통보하다 branch 지점, 지사 as of ~일자로 provide 제공하다, 주다 renovate 수리하다, 보수하다 matter 문제 continual 끊임없는

131. (D)
해설 빈칸 앞의 동사 regret은 to부정사와 동명사를 모두 목적어로 취할 수 있으므로, 부사적 용법으로 쓰인 to부정사인 (D) to inform이 정답이다. 문장의 동사는 regret이므로 동사 형태인 다른 선택지들은 오답이다.

132. (B)
해설 빈칸 뒤에 복수 명사인 items가 있으므로 단수 명사를 수식하는 another와 every를 소거할 수 있다. 문맥상 pastries와 cakes를 제외한 '다른' 품목을 의미하므로 (B) other가 정답이 된다.

133. (A)
(A) 근처에 다른 지점이 세 곳 있다는 것을 양지해 주시기 바랍니다.
(B) 우리는 더 많은 손님들이 안에서 식사를 하실 수 있도록 매장을 확장하기로 결정했습니다.
(C) 켄싱턴에서 사업을 하는 비용이 크게 증가했습니다.
(D) 식재료 공급 사업을 영위하는 것이 더 이상 가능하지 않습니다.
해설 빈칸 뒤의 문장에 Mayfield, Westside, Haywood라는 세 개의 지명이 나오므로 그에 관해 언급한 (A)가 정답이다.
어휘 be aware that ~라는 것을 알다 location 위치, 장소 nearby 근처의 expand 확장하다 dine 식사하다 do business 장사하다, 사업하다

134. (C)
해설 빈칸 앞에 한정사 your가 있고 뒤에 명사 support가 있으므로, 빈칸에는 명사를 수식하는 형용사 또는 support와 복합 명사를 이루는 명사가 올 수 있다. 따라서 형용사인 (C) continual이 정답이다.

135-138 회람

수신: 전 직원
발신: Eric Horner
날짜: 2월 11일
제목: 헬스장 회원권

경영진이 정규직 직원들의 헬스장 회원권 비용을 지원하기로 합의했다는 사실을 알리게 되어 기쁩니다. 이 특전은 1월 직원 만족도 조사에서 많은 여러분들에 의해 [135]**요청되었던** 것입니다. 3월 1일부터 직원들은 Westfield Gym의 무료 회원이 될 수 있는 쿠폰을 받을 수 있습니다. 규칙적으로 운동할 [136]**의향이 있는** 분들만 신청해 주시기 바랍니다. 쿠폰은 반 년 동안 유효한 회원권입니다. [137]**기간**이 만료되면 추가 쿠폰을 요청하실 수 있습니다. 쿠폰에는 개인 트레이너와 함께 운동하는 것은 포함되지 않습니다. [138]**그 비용은 여러분이 직접 지불하셔야 합니다.**

어휘 gym 헬스장, 체육관 membership 회원 (자격) sponsor 후원하다 full-time 정규직의, 풀타임의 perk (급여 이외의) 특전 survey 설문조사 voucher 쿠폰, 할인권 work out 운동하다 regularly 주기적으로, 규칙적으로 additional 추가의

135. (C)
해설 빈칸은 문장의 동사 자리로서 뒤에 목적어 없이 전치사구가 이어지므로 수동태가 들어가야 한다. 회람을 보낸 날짜가 2월 11일인데 1월에 있었던 설문조사를 언급하고 있으므로 수동태 과거 시제인 (C) was requested가 정답이다.

136. (C)
(A) 예상하다 (B) 나타나다 (C) 의도하다, 작정하다 (D) 승인하다

137. (A)
(A) 기간 (B) 쿠폰, 할인권 (C) 교육 (D) 투어, 견학

138. (D)
(A) 우리는 여러분 모두가 이곳의 시설을 이용해 주시기를 바랍니다.
(B) 여러분의 성원에 감사드립니다.
(C) 여러분 각자에게 쿠폰이 발송되었습니다.
(D) 그 비용은 여러분이 직접 지불하셔야 합니다.
어휘 facility 시설

139-142 공지

또 다시 연말 시상식 후보자를 추천할 때가 됐습니다. 올해는 두 개의 상이 [139]**수여될 것입니다.**
첫 번째는 올해의 직원상입니다. 두 번째는 올해의 신입사원상입니다. 모든 후보 추천은 11월 30일까지 Maryanne Carter에게 해주십시오. 여러분이 추천하는 사람이 상을 받아야 하는 [140]**이유**를 설명하는 간단한 글을 포함시켜 주십시오.
수상자는 12월 29일 우리의 연례 모임에서 발표될 것입니다. [141]**올해 행사는 Hillsdale Restaurant에서 열릴 것입니다.**
각각의 수상자는 [142]**상금**과 기타 부상을 받게 될 것입니다.

어휘 submit 제출하다 nomination 지명, 추천 award 상 present 주다, 수여하다 newcomer 신참, 새로 온 사람 brief 짧은, 간략한 statement 성명, 진술 annual 연례의 get-together 모임 cash 현금

139. (D)
해설 빈칸 뒤에 목적어가 없으므로 빈칸에는 수동태가 들어가야 하

며, 연말 시상식은 앞으로 일어날 일이므로 수동태 미래 시제인 (D) will be presented가 정답이다.

140. (A)

해설 자신이 추천한 사람이 상을 받아야 하는 '이유'를 설명하는 진술이므로 (A) why가 정답이다.

141. (C)

(A) 우리 사장님이신 Mr. Anderson이 행사를 주최했습니다.
(B) 우리는 작년 파티에 거의 완벽한 참석률을 보였습니다.
(C) 올해 행사는 Hillsdale Restaurant에서 열릴 것입니다.
(D) 모든 수상자에게 초대장이 발송될 것입니다.

어휘 host 주최하다 attendance 참석 invitation 초대(장)

142. (D)

(A) 급여 (B) 트로피 (C) 메달 (D) 보상(금)

143-146 안내문

Madison Electronics에서 가전제품을 구입해 주셔서 감사합니다. 우리는 제품의 품질에 [143]**자부심**을 가지고 있습니다. 가지고 계신 기기에 어떤 문제가 있을 경우 1-888-555-8473으로 연락 주십시오. 우리의 무료 상담 전화는 24시간 열려 있습니다. 우리 고객 서비스 담당자들은 언제라도 여러분을 돕기 위해 [144]**대기하고 있습니다.**

여러분의 기기에는 2년간 완전한 품질 보증이 딸려 나옵니다. 그러나 인가 받지 않은 사람이 기기를 수리할 경우 보증은 [145]**더 이상** 유효하지 **않을 것입니다.**

자세한 내용은 당사 웹사이트인 www.madisonelectronics.com을 방문하십시오. [146]**info@madisonelectronics.com으로 저희에게 이메일을 보내실 수도 있습니다.**

어휘 purchase 구입하다 appliance 가전제품, 기기 toll-free 무료의 hotline (고객) 상담 전화 customer service representative 고객 서비스 담당자 assist 돕다 come with ~이 딸려 나오다 warranty 보증 unauthorized 인가 받지 않은 work on ~을 수리하다, 작업하다 no longer 더 이상 ~하지 않다 in effect 유효한

143. (D)

해설 빈칸 앞에 동사 take, 빈칸 뒤에 전치사가 있으므로 빈칸은 동사의 목적어인 명사 자리이다. 따라서 (D) pride가 정답이다.

144. (C)

해설 주어인 customer service representatives는 현재 하루 24시간 대기하며 근무를 하고 있으므로 현재 진행 시제인 (C) are standing by가 정답이다.

145. (C)

해설 인가 받지 않은 사람이 제품을 수리할 경우 보증은 더 이상 유효하지 않다는 것이 문맥상 자연스러우므로 (C) no longer가 정답이다.

146. (B)

(A) 환불은 구매 후 10일 이내에 요청되어야 합니다.
(B) info@madisonelectronics.com으로 저희에게 이메일을 보내실 수도 있습니다.
(C) 영수증을 꼭 보관해 주세요.
(D) 원래 포장된 상태로 물품을 보내셔야 합니다.

147-148 공지

시의 모든 인명 구조원들은 주목해 주세요
[147]**4월 30일부터 휴대폰 문자 메시지로 여러분의 업무 스케줄이 전송될 것입니다.** 스케줄은 매주 일요일에 늦어도 저녁 6시 이전에 도착할 것입니다. 스케줄이 겹치거나 문제가 있는 경우 1시간 이내에 메시지에 응답해 주십시오. 악천후의 경우, 수영장이나 해수욕장이 폐쇄된다는 것을 알리는 문자 메시지가 언제든지 발송될 수 있습니다.
[148]**현재 보관 중인 여러분의 전화번호가 정확한지 확인하기 위해 도시공원여가부 사무실의 Wendy Sullivan에게 연락해 주세요.**

어휘 lifeguard 인명 구조원 text message 문자 메시지 no later than 늦어도 ~까지 scheduling conflict 일정 충돌, 겹치는 일정 issue 문제 respond to ~에 응답하다 in case of ~의 경우 inclement weather 악천후 indicate 보여 주다, 나타내다 make sure 확실히 하다 currently 현재, 지금 on file 기록되어, 보관되어 accurate 정확한

147. 인명 구조원들이 문자 메시지로 통보 받게 될 한 가지는 무엇인가?

(A) 초과 근무 기회
(B) 직원 회의
(C) 스케줄
(D) 정부 감사

어휘 overtime 초과 근무, 야근 inspection 검사, 감사

148. 인명 구조원들은 왜 사무실에 연락해야 하는가?

(A) 휴가를 요청하려고
(B) 어떤 정보를 확인하려고
(C) 날씨 상태에 대해 문의하려고
(D) 도움을 요청하려고

패러프레이즈 make sure → confirm / phone number → information

어휘 time off work 휴가, 휴일 confirm 확정하다 inquire about ~에 대해 문의하다 assistance 도움

149-150 기사

Bradenton Times

10월 11일—지역 사업가인 Harold Grimes가 브래든턴에 또 다른 사업체를 설립할 계획이라고 조금 전에 발표했다. [149]**Ms. Grime는 두 개의 슈퍼마켓뿐만 아니라 시내에 네 개의 음식점을 소유하고 있다.** 그러나 그의 새로운 사업은 식품 업종에 속하지 않을 것이다. 대신에, 그는 병원을 개업할 것이다. Grimes Medical Care는 브래든턴 도서관 맞은편 이스턴 드

라이브 67번지에 위치할 것이다. Mr. Grimes 자신은 의학적인 배경이 없지만, [150]**그는 시민들을 위한 질 좋고 저렴한 의료 서비스를 보유할 필요를 언급했다.** 병원은 5명의 상근 의사를 고용할 것이며, 첨단 의료 장비를 갖출 것이다.Mr. Grimes는 병원이 11월에 문을 열 것으로 기대한다고 말했다. 관심 있는 사람들은 539-9573으로 전화를 걸어 의사들의 전공 분야와 예약에 관한 보다 많은 정보를 얻을 수 있다.

어휘 intend 의도하다, 계획하다 establish 설립하다 business 사업(체) own 소유하다 a couple of 둘의, 두 개의 venture (모험적) 사업 be located 위치하다 while ~에 반하여, ~인데도 background 배경, 경력 state 분명히 말하다 quality 양질의 affordable 저렴한 medical care 의료 서비스 full-time 전임의 state-of-the-art 첨단의 equipment 장비 specialty 전문, 전공 make a reservation 예약하다

149. Ms. Grimes에 대해 나타난 것은 무엇인가?
(A) 그는 대학에서 의학을 공부했다.
(B) 그는 병원의 의사들을 몇 명 교체할 것이다.
(C) 그는 여러 개의 사업체를 가지고 있다.
(D) 그는 지역 정치에 관여하고 있다.

해설 슈퍼마켓과 음식점을 소유하고 있다고 했으므로 (C)가 정답이다. 의사를 채용한다고 했을 뿐 교체한다는 언급은 없었으므로 (B)는 오답이다.

패러프레이즈 restaurants, supermarkets → business establishments

어휘 medicine 의학 be involved in ~에 관여하다 politics 정치(학)

150. Grimes Medical Care가 개장하는 이유는 무엇인가?
(A) 지역 주민들에게 양질의 의료 서비스를 제공하기 위해
(B) 폐원하는 병원을 대신하기 위해
(C) 전문화된 수술 선택권을 제공하기 위해
(D) 브래든턴 주민들의 요청을 이행하기 위해

패러프레이즈 quality, affordable medical care → good health care

어휘 replace 대신하다, 대체하다 specialized 전문화된 surgical 수술의, 외과의 option 선택권, 옵션 fulfill 이행하다, 다하다

151-154 기사

토론토 (4월 23일)—유럽 시장으로 진입하기 위한 노력의 일환으로 캐나다의 전자제품 생산업체인 Galleon 사는 여러 나라의 시장을 조사하기 위해 Baldrick과 계약을 체결했다.
[154]**Baldrick은 영국 런던에 본사를 둔 컨설팅 회사로, 마드리드, 로마, 파리를 비롯한 여러 유럽 주요 도시에 사무실을 두고 있다.** <u>이 회사는 아시아와 북미에도 지사를 두고 있다.</u> **"[151]우리는 유럽 사람들이 무엇을 원하는지 이해하고 있다고 느낍니다." 라고 최고경영자인 Ian Smythe가 말했다. "우리는 유럽에서 성공하기 위한 많은 다른 북미 기업들의 노력을 지원해 왔으며, Galleon도 도울 수 있다고 확신합니다."**
[152]**Baldrick은 30년 이상 사업을 해왔으며** 영국에서 가장 큰 가족 소유의 컨설팅 회사이다.
"한 시장에서 다른 시장으로 전환하는 것은 쉽지 않습니다."라고 Mr. Smythe가 말했다. "[153]**예를 들어, 미국의 소비자들은 그들의 전자 기기에서 특정 기능을 기대할 수 있지만, 유럽 소비자들은 그런 것들에 전혀 관심이 없습니다.** 우리는 Galleon이 성공하기 위해 자사의 제품을 조정할 수 있는 방법을 알아낼 것입니다."
Galleon은 올해 12월까지 Baldrick으로부터 보고서를 받을 것으로 예상하고 있다. 자료를 분석하고 나면, 내년에는 수출용으로 맞춤 제작된 제품을 생산하기 위한 노력을 시작할 것이다.

어휘 in an effort to ~하기 위한 노력의 일환으로 break into 진입하다, 침입하다 agreement 동의(서) be headquartered in ~에 본사가 있다 major 주요한, 주된 numerous 많은 positive 긍정적인 as well 또한 be in business 사업하다 decade 10년 switch 전환하다, 바꾸다 function 기능 electronic device 전자 기기 identify 알아내다, 확인하다 adapt 조정하다, 맞추다 anticipate 기대하다, 예측하다 analyze 분석하다 tailor-made 맞춤의

151. Baldrick은 Galleon 사를 어떻게 돕고 있는가?
(A) 생산 동향을 분석함으로써
(B) 새로운 직원을 채용함으로써
(C) 소비자 선호를 파악함으로써
(D) 컴퓨터 데이터베이스를 개선함으로써

어휘 trend 경향, 트렌드 recruit 모집하다, 채용하다 determine 밝혀내다; 결정하다 preference 선호

152. 기사에서 Baldrick에 대해 언급하는 것은 무엇인가?
(A) 본사가 토론토에 있다.
(B) 전기 제품을 제조한다.
(C) 다른 회사의 소유이다.
(D) 설립된 지 30년이 넘었다.

패러프레이즈 three decades → thirty years

어휘 manufactures 제조하다 electric appliance 전기 기기

153. Mr. Smythe에 따르면, 소비자들은 어떤 점에서 서로 다른가?
(A) 그들이 구입하는 브랜드가 무엇인지
(B) 그들이 기기에서 원하는 기능이 무엇인지
(C) 그들이 필요로 하는 설명서의 세부 내용이 무엇인지
(D) 그들이 지불하고자 하는 가격이 어느 정도인지

어휘 brand name 상표명 instructions 사용 설명서

154. [1], [2], [3], [4]로 표시된 위치 중 다음 문장이 들어가기에 가장 적절한 곳은?
"이 회사는 아시아와 북미에도 지사를 두고 있다."
(A) [1]
(B) [2]
(C) [3]
(D) [4]

해설 주어진 문장의 대명사 it이 가리키는 것은 Baldrick으로서 유럽 각지에 사무실을 두고 있다는 문장이 나온 다음인 [1]에 들어가는 것이 가장 적절하다.

155-156 문자 메시지

> Jeff Daniels (오전 10:14)
> 안녕하세요, Samantha. [155] **어제 우리가 만났던 Madison Technology의 대표자 이름을 기억해요?**
> Samantha West (오전 10:15)
> 물론이죠. 그 여자분의 이름은 Cecily Peters예요. 왜 묻는 거죠?
> Jeff Daniels (오전 10:16)
> Mr. Anderson은 제가 그분과 또 다른 회의 일정을 잡기를 원하세요.
> Samantha West (오전 10:17)
> [156] **그분의 전화번호가 필요하세요?**
> Jeff Daniels (오전 10:18)
> 그러면 좋겠어요.
> Samantha West (오전 10:19)
> 끊지 말고 잠시 기다리세요. 어딘가에 제가 갖고 있어요.

어휘 representative 대표(자) schedule a meeting 회의 일정을 잡다 hold on (전화를 끊지 않고) 기다리다

155. 글쓴이들에 대해 암시된 것은 무엇인가?
(A) 그들은 Madison Technology에서 일한다.
(B) 그들은 Mr. Anderson에게 보고서를 제출해야 한다.
(C) 그들은 전날 함께 회의에 참석했다.
(D) 그들은 Ms. Peters에게 제품 시연을 할 것이다.

해설 지문의 that we met yesterday에서 문자 메시지를 주고받는 Jeff Daniels와 Samantha West가 전날 함께 Cecily Peters를 만났다는 것을 추론할 수 있으므로 (C)가 정답이다.

패러프레이즈 yesterday → the previous day

어휘 submit 제출하다 attend a meeting 회의에 참석하다 previous 이전의 give a demonstration 시연하다

156. 오전 10시 18분에 Mr. Daniels가 "그러면 좋겠어요"라고 쓸 때 그는 무엇을 의미하겠는가?
(A) 그는 어떤 사람의 연락처 정보를 원한다.
(B) 그는 오늘 중에 Ms. West를 만나고 싶어 한다.
(C) 그는 Ms. West가 회의 일정을 잡을 것이어서 기쁘다.
(D) 그는 새 전화기를 사고 싶어 한다.

패러프레이즈 phone number → contact information

어휘 contact 연락 be eager to ~을 하고 싶어 하다

157-159 광고

> Graham's Custom Shoes
>
> Graham's Custom Shoes는 당신의 인생에서 특별한 누군가를 위한 이상적인 선물입니다. [157] **우리 신발은 다양한 색상의 부드러운 가죽으로 만들어집니다.** 신발의 치수는 각각의 고객의 사이즈에 딱 맞게 정해집니다. 신발은 적어도 3년은 유지된다는 것을 보장합니다. [158, 159] **우리 신발은 맞춤 제작되기 때문에 고객들은 매장을 직접 방문하거나, 우리에게 온라인으로 정확한 발 치수를 보내주셔야 합니다.** 발의 크기는 개인마다 조금씩 다르기 때문에 양발을 각각 확인해 주십시오. 이용 가능한 스타일에 대해 더 알고 싶으시다면, 로체스터 로드 58번지를 방문하거나 www.grahamscustomshoes.com을 방문하세요. 저희 신발을 한 번만 체험해 보시면 다시는 다른 곳에서 신발을 구입하지 않게 될 것입니다.

어휘 custom 주문 제작한, 맞춤의 ideal 이상적인 leather 가죽 a variety of 다양한 guarantee 보장하다 last 지속되다, 계속되다 in person 직접 precise 정확한 measurement 치수 once 한 번

157. 광고에 있는 품목들에 대해 나타난 것은 무엇인가?
(A) 동일한 종류의 재료로 만들어진다.
(B) 모두 같은 가격이다.
(C) 만들어지는 데 약 2주가 걸린다.
(D) 우편으로 해외 주소에 보낼 수 있다.

어휘 type 종류 material 재료 mail 우편으로 보내다

158. 광고는 몇몇 고객들에게 무엇을 할 것을 추천하는가?
(A) 보다 많은 정보를 요구하기
(B) 원하는 스타일의 사진을 제출하기
(C) 제품 보증에 관해 묻기
(D) 정확한 정보를 제공하기

패러프레이즈 precise → accurate

어휘 call for 요구하다 guarantee 보증, 보장 accurate 정확한

159. [1], [2], [3], [4]로 표시된 위치 중 다음 문장이 들어가기에 가장 적절한 곳은?
"발의 크기는 개인마다 조금씩 다르기 때문에 양발을 각각 확인해 주십시오."
(A) [1]
(B) [2]
(C) [3]
(D) [4]

160-163 편지

> 3월 11일
>
> Patrick Peterson
> 머서 애비뉴 546번지
> 새크라멘토, 캘리포니아 94258
>
> Mr. Peterson,
>
> 귀하는 Daniel's Green Grocer의 장기 고객으로서, [161] **저희가 다양한 국내외 식품을 판매한다는 것을 알고 계실 겁니다.** 또한 저희에게는 조제 식품 판매점과 베이커리가 있으며, 그곳에서 많은 음식을 만들고 있다는 사실도 알고 계실 겁니다. [160] **저희가 만드는 음식에 대한 귀하의 조언을 듣고 싶습니다. 그렇기 때문에 저희는 귀하께서 시식자가 될 수 있는 기회를 드리고자 합니다.**
>
> 여러분의 지정된 주말에 이곳에 오시기만 하면 됩니다. 다섯 가지에서 열 가지의 서로 다른 음식 샘플이 귀하께 시식용으로 제공될 것입니다. 귀하께서 [162] **시식하게** 될 음식에는 제빵류, 페이스트리, 치즈, 육류, 그리고 라자냐와 지티와 같은 조리 식품이 포함될 것입니다. 그런 다음 간단한 설문조사를 작성하시어 각

품목에 대한 솔직한 의견을 제공해 주십시오. 전체 과정은 10분이 걸릴 것입니다.

이 기회를 신청하시려면 앞으로 2주 이내에 언제든지 Daniel's에 들러 Marjorie Benson 점장과 말씀을 나누세요. [163] **도움을 주신 대가로 댁으로 가져가실 수 있는 무료 시식용 음식뿐만 아니라 10달러 상당의 매장 쿠폰을 받게 되십니다.**

곧 긍정적인 답변을 받을 수 있기를 희망합니다.

Eric Quinn
Daniel's Green Grocer 사장

어휘 grocer 식료품 상인 be aware that ~을 알고 있다 a variety of 다양한 domestic 국내의 deli 조제 식품 판매점 bakery 베이커리, 제과점 input 조언 regarding ~에 관한 extend 베풀다; 확대하다 taster 시식자 show up 나타나다 designated 지정된 sample 샘플; 시식하다 baked goods 제빵류 frank 솔직한 complete 작성하다 survey 설문조사 drop by 잠시 들르다 in return for ~에 대한 대가로

160. 편지의 목적은 무엇인가?
(A) 특가 판매를 알리려고
(B) 몇 가지 신제품을 광고하려고
(C) 채용 기회를 논의하려고
(D) 활동 참가를 요청하려고

161. Daniel's Green Grocer에 대해 나타난 것은 무엇인가?
(A) 시내에 여러 개의 지점이 있다.
(B) 시에서 가장 큰 식료품점이다.
(C) 다른 나라의 음식을 판매한다.
(D) 곧 새로운 제과점을 세울 것이다.

패러프레이즈 international foods → food from other countries

어휘 multiple 다수의, 복수의 branch 지점, 지사

162. 세 번째 단락 두 번째 줄의 어휘 'sampling'과 의미상 가장 가까운 것은?
(A) 맛보다
(B) 제공하다
(C) 참석하다
(D) 보고하다

163. Mr. Peterson은 Daniel's Green Grocer로부터 무엇을 받을 수 있는가?
(A) 빠른 배송 서비스
(B) 월간 쿠폰
(C) 무료 음식
(D) 쇼핑 클럽 회원권

어휘 express 속달의 coupon 쿠폰, 우대권 membership 회원 (자격)

164-165 웹페이지

Axle 렌터카 멤버십

Allen Darcy, Axle 렌터카 회원 전용 클럽에 오신 것을 환영합니다. 귀하의 회원 가입 신청이 접수되었고, 이제 모든 종류의 특가 상품을 이용할 자격이 있습니다.

[164] **귀하의 계정 번호는 75234ADP23입니다. 저희에게 예약하실 때, 그리고 차량을 인수하거나 반납하실 때마다 이 번호를 사용하셔야 합니다.** 또한 저희 스마트폰용 모바일 앱을 다운로드하는 것을 추천 드립니다. 그렇게 하면 어디에 계시든 항상 계정에 로그인하실 수 있습니다.

[165] **매주, 저희는 이 클럽의 회원들만을 위한 특가 행사를 열 것입니다.** 해당 주의 특가는 매주 일요일 자정에 바뀝니다. 여기를 클릭하여 이메일로 그 내용들을 받아보는 것을 선택하실 수 있습니다. 회원권을 더 많이 이용할수록 더 많은 포인트를 적립하실 수 있습니다. 그렇게 되면 훨씬 더 많은 할인을 받을 자격을 갖출 수 있습니다.

어휘 rental car 렌터카 membership 회원 (자격) application 신청(서) be eligible for ~할 자격이 있다 special deal 특가 상품 account 계정; 계좌 make a booking 예약하다 drop off 가져다 놓다, 맡기다 log in to ~에 접속하다 accrue 획득하다, 생기다 enable 가능하게 하다 qualify 자격을 얻다

164. Mr. Darcy는 차량을 받을 때 무엇을 해야 하는가?
(A) 자신의 계정 번호 제시하기
(B) 유효한 운전면허증을 보여 주기
(C) 신용카드로 결제하기
(D) 자신이 보험에 가입되어 있다는 것을 증명하기

어휘 present 제시하다 valid 유효한 driver's license 운전면허증 prove 증명하다 insurance 보험

165. Axle 렌터카의 회원 전용 클럽에 대해 나타난 것은 무엇인가?
(A) 회원들이 차량을 무료로 빌릴 수 있게 해준다.
(B) 장기 고객들에게만 개방되어 있다.
(C) 연회비를 지불해야 한다.
(D) 매주 여러 개의 특가를 제공한다.

패러프레이즈 special offers → deals

어휘 for free 무료로 annual 연례의, 연간의 deal 싸게 사는 물건

166-168 기사

Haverford Construction, 신축 아파트 단지 건설 예정

서드베리(11월 12일)—서드베리의 시장실은 어젯밤 시 외곽에 있는 넓은 부지를 Haverford Construction에 매각했다고 발표했다. [166] **이 부지는 14에이커에 달하며, 시의 동부인 달링턴 산 근처의 32번 고속도로 옆에 위치해 있다.** Haverford의 대변인은 회사가 그 부지를 최소 7개의 건물을 포함하는 아파트 단지로 개발할 계획이라고 말했다. 회사는 내년 초쯤에 새로운 단지의 디자인을 발표할 것으로 예상한다. 시장실의 한 소식통에 따르면, 그 토지에 다른 입찰자는 한 명뿐이었다. 그것은 그 토지를 농사에 이용하기를 원하는 개인이었다. 그러나 시는 새로운 주택이 절실히 필요한 입장이다. 몇몇 회사들이 시 근처에 시설을 건설할 계획을 발표함에 따라, [167] **지역 인구는 곧 크게 증가할 것으로 예상된다.** 따라서 더 많은 주택을 [168] **확보하는** 것이 시장실에 있어 가장 중요하다.

어휘 apartment complex 아파트 단지 mayor 시장 plot 부지, 구역 on the outskirts of ~의 외곽에 alongside ~ 옆에, 나란히 spokesperson 대변인 contain 포함하다 no fewer than 최소한 release 발표하다, 공개하다 source 자료의 출처 bidder 입찰자 desperate 절실한, 필사적인 facility 시설 population 인구 secure 확보하다 be of the utmost importance 아주 중요하다

166. 취득된 토지는 어디에 위치해 있는가?
(A) 달링턴 산 위에
(B) 시장 집무실 건너편에
(C) 농장 근처에
(D) 서드베리의 동쪽에

어휘 acquire 얻다, 인수하다 farm 농장

167. 기사에 따르면, 서드베리에 주택이 필요한 이유는 무엇인가?
(A) 시내의 많은 집들이 상태가 좋지 않다.
(B) 최근에 일부 아파트 단지들이 소실되었다.
(C) 그 지역의 집값이 너무 가파르게 오르고 있다.
(D) 가까운 장래에 많은 사람들이 그곳으로 이사할 것이다.

어휘 burn down 전소하다, 소실되다 recently 최근에

168. 열두 번째 줄의 어휘 "securing"과 의미상 가장 가까운 것은?
(A) 보존하다
(B) 획득하다
(C) 검사하다
(D) 보호하다

169-171 안내문

E-Z 세탁소

[169]**E-Z 세탁소는 이제 고객님들이 저희 세탁기와 건조기를 이용하기 위해 더 이상 동전을 휴대할 필요가 없음을 알려드리게 되어 자랑스럽게 생각합니다. 대신, 고객님들은 카드를 구매해서 그 안에 돈을 충전할 수 있습니다. 그런 다음, 이 카드들은 기계를 작동시키는 데 사용될 수 있습니다.**

저희의 새 시스템을 이용하려면 다음과 같이 하시면 됩니다:
1. 매장 뒤편에 있는 기계 중 하나로 가세요. 카드에 넣을 금액을 선택한 후 필요한 현금을 넣으세요.
2. 그러면 현금 포인트가 적힌 카드를 받게 될 겁니다.
3. [170]**세탁물을 세탁기나 건조기에 넣고 원하는 설정을 선택하세요.**
4. **카드를 투입구에 넣고 "사용" 버튼을 누르세요.** 기계가 작동하기 시작할 것이며 카드에서 요금이 빠져나갈 것입니다.

[171]**기계를 이용하여 사용하지 않는 카드에 남아 있는 돈을 환불받을 수 있습니다.**

어휘 laundry 세탁소, 세탁물 no longer 더 이상 ~하지 않는 carry 가지고 다니다, 휴대하다 washer 세탁기 dryer 건조기 instead 그 대신에 operate 작동시키다 select 선택하다 cash 현금 credit (현금처럼 쓸 수 있는) 포인트 insert 넣다, 삽입하다 slot 투입구, 기계의 가느다란 구멍 deduct 차감하다, 공제하다 refund 환불

169. 안내문의 목적은 무엇인가?
(A) 실수에 대해 사과하려고
(B) 설문조사 결과를 설명하려고
(C) 새로운 서비스를 알리려고
(D) 지점의 개장을 홍보하려고

어휘 apologize for ~을 사과하다 survey 설문조사 promote 홍보하다

170. 자신의 의류에 맞는 기능을 선택한 후 해야 할 일은 무엇인가?
(A) 돈을 투입구에 넣기
(B) 카드를 삽입하기
(C) 직원과 이야기하기
(D) 세탁 세제를 첨가하기

해설 카드를 투입구에 넣고 사용 버튼을 누르라고 했으므로 (B)가 정답이다. (A)는 카드를 받기 위해 해야 하는 행동이므로 오답이다.

패러프레이즈 select the setting → choosing the cycle

어휘 cycle (세탁기, 건조기 등의) 기능 add 더하다, 추가하다 detergent 세제

171. 카드에 대해 나타난 것은 무엇인가?
(A) 한 번만 사용할 수 있다.
(B) 사용자들은 카드에서 돈을 돌려받을 수 있다.
(C) 기한 만료일이 있다.
(D) 카드에 돈을 넣는 데 신용카드를 사용할 수 있다.

패러프레이즈 receive a refund → get their money back

어휘 expiration 만료, 만기

172-175 온라인 채팅

Dieter Kimball (오후 1:12)
여러분 안녕하세요. 제가 방금 사무실로 돌아왔는데 누군가가 제 책상 위에 서류철을 몇 개 놔뒀네요. 누구죠?
Sally Beecher (오후 1:15)
George와 제가 그랬어요, [172]**Mr. Kimball. 몇 가지 지출에 대해 승인이 필요해서요.** 아시다시피, 회사 야유회가 곧 다가오는데, 저희가 야유회를 준비하라고 뽑혔거든요.
[173]**George White** (오후 1:16)
오늘 모든 것을 보실 시간이 있나요? [173, 174]**저희가 5분 후에 사무실로 찾아뵐 수 있어요.**
Dieter Kimball (오후 1:17)
<u>저는 1시 30분에 Sylvester Mann을 만나기로 했어요.</u>
George White (오후 1:18)
그게 시간이 얼마나 걸릴지 아시나요?
Dieter Kimball (오후 1:19)
예측하기 어려워요. 우리는 검토할 것이 많거든요. 제게 준 서류철에 제가 알아야 할 것이 있나요?
Sally Beecher (오후 1:20)
유일한 문제점은 우리가 예산을 약간 초과할 거라는 점이에요. [175]**평소보다 더 많은 사람들이 가족과 함께 참석하겠다는 의사를 밝혔거든요.** 그래서 평소보다 더 많은 음식과 다른 물품들을 구매해야 했어요.
George White (오후 1:21)

그게 우리의 주된 관심사이지만, 논의했으면 하는 다른 몇 가지 사소한 문제들도 있습니다.
Dieter Kimball (오후 1:22)
4시 30분에 제 사무실에 들르세요. 그때 모든 것을 검토할 수 있겠네요.

어휘 notice 알아차리다 folder 서류철, 폴더 approval 승인 expenditure 지출 organize 준비하다, 조직하다 go over 검토하다 issue 문제 exceed 초과하다 budget 예산 commit 의사를 밝히다, 약속하다 supplies 물품 primary 주된, 주요한 concern 관심사, 걱정 minor 사소한

172. Mr. Kimball은 누구이겠는가?
(A) 취업 지원자
(B) 관리자
(C) 행사 기획자
(D) 고객

해설 Dieter Kimball은 Sally Beecher와 George White가 작성한 지출건에 대해 승인을 해주는 사람이라는 것을 추론할 수 있으므로 (B)가 정답이다.

173. Mr. White는 무엇을 하고 싶어 하는가?
(A) 행사 날짜 변경하기
(B) 추가 자금을 받기
(C) Mr. Kimball을 직접 만나기
(D) 행사 장소를 다른 곳으로 옮기기

어휘 extra 추가의 funding 자금 (제공) in person 직접 venue (행사) 장소

174. 오후 1시 17분에 Mr. Kimball이 "저는 1시 30분에 Sylvester Mann을 만나기로 했어요."라고 쓰는 이유는 무엇인가?
(A) 제안을 거부하기 위해
(B) 요청을 승인하기 위해
(C) 내일 그의 일정을 설명하기 위해
(D) 그의 계획을 취소하겠다고 제안하기 위해

해설 자신들이 Mr. Kimball의 사무실로 갈 수 있다는 George White의 제안에 이렇게 답했으므로, 약속이 있으니 사무실에 오지 말라는 뜻으로 말했다는 것을 알 수 있다. 따라서 (A)가 정답이다.

어휘 reject 거절하다 suggestion 제안 describe 묘사하다, 설명하다 offer 제안하다 cancel 취소하다

175. 회사 야유회에 대해 암시된 것은 무엇인가?
(A) 8월에 열릴 것이다.
(B) 회사 근처에서 열린다.
(C) 전에 열린 적이 있다.
(D) 직원들만 참석할 수 있다.

해설 지문의 than usual(평소보다)에서 단서를 찾을 수 있으므로 (C)가 정답이다.

어휘 take place 열리다, 일어나다 employee 직원

176-180 편지, 이메일

Sunfield Golf Resort
웨스트웨이 드라이브 1603번지
메사, 애리조나 85209

6월 23일

Lawrence Mercado
히코리 로드 294번지
플로렌스, 애리조나 85143

Mr. Mercado,

[176]**7월 17일에 열리는 Sunfield Golf Resort의 연례 Sun and Fun 토너먼트에 등록해 주셔서 감사합니다. 귀하의 확인 번호는 0638입니다.** 주차권과 이름표를 동봉합니다. [178]**리조트 구내에 계시는 동안에는 토너먼트에 참가한다는 것을 보여 주기 위해 이름표를 항상 패용하셔야 합니다.**
[177]**귀하는 오전 7시에서 8시 30분 사이에 클럽하우스 내 접수처에서 체크인하셔야 하며, 사진이 들어 있는 신분증이 필요합니다.** 토너먼트는 네 개의 부문으로 구성되며, 첫 번째 홀에서의 시작 시간은 다음과 같습니다: 오전 9시 [세미프로], [180-2]**오전 10시 [상급]**, 오전 11시 [중급], 정오 [초급].
[178]**접수처에서 차, 커피, 탄산음료, 생수를 무료로 이용하실 수 있습니다. 하지만 이용하려면 이름표를 보여주셔야 합니다.** 저희 식당에서는 음식을 구입할 수 있습니다.
Sunfield Golf Resort에서 만나 뵙기를 바라겠습니다!

Sunfield Golf Resort 행사 직원 일동

어휘 register for ~에 등록하다 annual 연례의 confirmation 확인, 확정 enclose 동봉하다 pass 통행증 at all times 항상, 언제나 while ~하는 동안 grounds 구내, 부지 check in 체크인하다 reception desk 접수처 photo ID 사진이 있는 신분증 consist of ~로 이루어지다 category 부문, 카테고리 intermediate 중급의 bottled water 생수 serve (음식물을) 제공하다

수신: Lawrence Mercado
〈l.mercado@shermansales.com〉
발신: Nancy Aldridge 〈nancy@sunfieldgolf.com〉
날짜: 7월 6일
제목: Sun and Fun 토너먼트

Mr. Mercado,

곧 Sun and Fun 토너먼트에 저희 골퍼들을 맞이하게 되어 기쁩니다. [180-1]**귀하의 지정된 시작 시간은 오전 10시입니다.** 운전을 해서 토너먼트로 오신다면, 에이비스 스트리트에서 벗어난 곳에 있는 주차장에 주차하셔야 한다는 점을 유념하시기 바랍니다. [179]**무니 스트리트와 연결된 주차장은 당사의 실내 골프 연습장 확장 공사를 하는 작업자들을 위한 공간을 마련하기 위해 일시적으로 폐쇄되었습니다.** 저희 골프장의 지도를 다운로드하려면 여기를 클릭하십시오.

Nancy Aldridge

어휘 assign 지정하다, 할당하다 note 주의하다, 유념하다 lot 주차장 temporarily 일시적으로, 임시로 make space for ~을 위

해 장소를 비우다 crew 작업반 expansion 확장 indoor 실내의 driving range 골프 연습장 site 장소, 부지

176. 편지의 목적은 무엇인가?
(A) 실수를 사과하려고
(B) 등록을 확인하려고
(C) 서비스를 추천하려고
(D) 기금을 요청하려고

어휘 apologize for ~을 사과하다 registration 등록 fund 기금, 자금

177. Mr. Mercado는 7월 17일에 도착하면 무엇을 하라는 요청을 받게 될 것인가?
(A) 신분증의 한 종류를 보여주기
(B) 공문서에 서명하기
(C) 단체의 구성원을 선택하기
(D) 자신의 장비를 점검하기

패러프레이즈 a photo ID → a form of identification

어휘 form 양식, 종류 identification 신분증(= ID) inspect 검사하다, 점검하다 equipment 장비

178. 접수처에 대해 암시된 것은 무엇인가?
(A) 음료는 참가자들만을 위한 것이다.
(B) 자선 단체를 위한 기부금을 모을 것이다.
(C) 직원들이 주차권을 제공할 수 있다.
(D) 매일 오전 7시에 문을 연다.

어휘 beverage 음료 donation 기부(금) charity 자선 단체

179. Sunfield Golf Resort에 대해 사실인 것은 무엇이겠는가?
(A) 최근에 소유권이 바뀌었다.
(B) 처음으로 대회를 개최한다.
(C) 회원들에게 행사에 대한 할인을 제공한다.
(D) 현재 공사 중인 건물을 보유하고 있다.

어휘 recently 최근에 ownership 소유권 competition 대회 currently 현재, 지금 under construction 공사 중인

180. Mr. Mercado의 골프 실력 수준은 어느 정도이겠는가?
(A) 초급
(B) 중급
(C) 상급
(D) 세미프로

해설 연계 문제로서, 두 번째 지문에서 수신인인 Mr. Mercado에게 지정된 시작 시간이 오전 10시라고 했는데, 첫 번째 지문을 찾아보면 오전 10시는 상급자의 시작 시간이므로 (C) 상급이 정답이다.

181-185 **웹페이지, 웹페이지**

https://www.ulrichbaer.de/English_launguage/abouttheauthor

작가 정보	도서	언론 보도	연락처

Ulrich Baer는 독일 라이프치히에서 Sebastian Baer와 Ines Baer의 사이에서 태어났습니다. 그의 아버지는 군대에 있었고, [181] **그래서 그는 어린 시절 내내 세계 여러 지역에서 살았고, 2년에 한 번씩 이사를 했습니다.** 대학에 다닐 때 그의 친구 중 한 명이 아르헨티나 여행을 계획하고 있었습니다. Mr. Baer는 전에 그곳에 살았었기 때문에 그의 친구를 위해 노트를 만들었습니다. 그것들은 매우 유용해서 그는 그것을 여행 가이드북으로 바꿀 수 있다고 [183] **생각했습니다.**

그 이후로 Mr. Baer는 다양한 국가와 지역을 위한 8권의 여행 가이드북을 썼습니다. [182] **그는 또한 〈Through the Lens〉라는 제목의 역사적인 사진들을 모은 사진첩을 출간했는데,** 그것은 평론가들로부터 높은 평가를 받았습니다.

[185-1] **Mr. Baer는 5월 10일에 그의 최신 여행 가이드북인 〈Footprints in Asia〉를 출간할 것입니다.** [182] **그 책은 〈Through the Lens〉에 있는 사진들을 일부 수록하고 있기 때문에,** 독자들은 어떤 지역들이 어떻게 변했는지 볼 수 있습니다. 책에는 관광지를 방문하기에 가장 좋은 시기와, 독특한 기념품을 사기 위한 쇼핑 장소에 대한 조언과 함께 지도가 포함될 것입니다. [185-1] **그 책은 또한 지역 음식을 맛보고 싶은 사람들을 위한 50개의 음식점 후기를 포함할 것입니다.**

어휘 author 작가, 저자 note 노트, 메모 figure 생각하다, 판단하다 turn A into B A를 B로 바꾸다 guide 안내 책자, 가이드북 collection 모음집 entitled ~라는 제목의 highly 매우 critic 평론가, 비평가 release 출간하다, 출시하다 footprint 발자국 contain 포함하다 along with ~와 함께 tip 조언, 팁 tourist attraction 관광지 unique 독특한 souvenir 기념품 feature 특별히 포함하다 review 후기, 리뷰 cuisine 요리

[184] **https://www.overland-publishing.com**

"이 책 없이 아시아에 발을 들여놓지 마시라!"

— Kinuko Asada, 〈World Travel Magazine〉

[185-2] **〈Footprints in Asia〉는 여행 작가인 Ulrich Baer의 최신 가이드북이다.** 당신이 경험 많은 여행자이든, 처음으로 해외에 가든, Baer는 여러분이 쉽게 여행을 계획하고 즐길 수 있도록 해준다. 알아 보기 쉬운 지도와, 교통편에 관한 조언, 그리고 [185-2] **80개 식당에 대한 후기도 놓치지 말아야 할 것들이다.**

출시일: 5월 10일
16.95달러, 페이퍼백, 352페이지

멋진 신간 도서를 가장 먼저 접하세요! [184] **여기를 클릭해서 앞으로 있을 도서 사인회, 출간 기념 파티, 그리고 기타 판촉 행사의 일정을 확인하세요.**

어휘 set foot 발을 들여놓다 experienced 노련한, 숙련된 miss 놓치다 easy-to-follow 따라하기 쉬운 transportation 교통 timetable 일정표 upcoming 다가오는, 곧 있을 launch 출판, 발표 promotional 홍보의

181. Mr. Baer에 대해 사실인 것은 무엇인가?
(A) 어렸을 때 이사를 많이 다녔다.
(B) 아르헨티나에 있는 대학에 다녔다.
(C) 자신의 아버지와 같은 일을 했다.
(D) 경력 초반부에 소설을 썼다.

어휘 attend 다니다 fiction 소설 career 경력

182. Mr. Baer의 새 여행 가이드북에 대해 암시된 것은 무엇인가?
(A) 평론가들로부터 엇갈린 평가를 받았다.
(B) 역사적인 사진들이 포함되어 있다.
(C) 무료 기념품이 딸려 나온다.
(D) 독일어와 영어로 출간되었다.

어휘 mixed 엇갈리는 come with ~이 딸려 나오다

183. 첫 번째 웹페이지에서, 첫 번째 단락 다섯 번째 줄의 "figured"와 의미상 가장 가까운 것은?
(A) 나타나다
(B) 수행하다
(C) 기여하다
(D) 결정하다

184. Overland Publishing에 대한 사실은 무엇인가?
(A) 신인 작가들의 작품을 접수한다.
(B) 온라인상에 행사 일정이 있다.
(C) 라이프치히에 본사가 있다.
(D) 〈World Travel Magazine〉을 발행한다.

어휘 headquarter 본부를 두다

185. Mr. Baer의 신간 여행 가이드북은 어떻게 바뀌었는가?
(A) 새로운 제목을 받았다.
(B) 출간일이 연기되었다.
(C) 몇 개의 지도가 그 안에 포함되었다.
(D) 더 많은 음식점 후기가 추가되었다.

해설 연계 문제로서, 첫 번째 지문에서는 〈Footprints in Asia〉에 쇼핑 장소에 대한 조언, 지도, 50개의 음식점 후기가 포함된다고 했는데, 두 번째 지문에서는 80개 식당에 대한 후기가 있다고 했으므로 후기의 숫자가 늘었다. 따라서 (D)가 정답이다.

어휘 title 제목 postpone 연기하다 add 더하다, 추가하다

186-190 보고서, 이메일, 청구서

Brandywine Finance
직원 설문조사 결과 보고서
직장 내 문제

직원들은 9월 설문조사에서 나온 바와 같이 다음과 같은 주요 직장 문제를 가지고 있었다:
1. [186]**개방된 사무 구역 내에서 프라이버시가 거의 없다.** (응답자의 62%)
2. [190-2]**직원 휴게실은 규모가 충분하지 않고 좌석이 부족하다.** (응답자의 57%)
3. 컴퓨터가 오래되고 자주 고장이 나서 직원들의 생산성이 떨어지는 경우가 있다. (응답자의 49%)
4. [189-2]**직원 신분증이 가끔 작동하지 않아서 직원들이 건물이나 개인 사무실로 들어가지 못한다.** (응답자의 27%)
5. 재활용함이 부족하여 직원들이 종종 재활용품을 쓰레기통에 버려야 한다. (응답자의 15%)

직원들은 또한 [187]**직원들이 말을 하거나 음악을 들을 때 발생하는 높은 소음 수준(7%)**, 충분치 않은 휴식 시간(5%), 칙칙한 사무실 인테리어(3%) 등에 대해서도 불만을 제기했다.

어휘 survey 설문조사 workplace 직장, 업무 현장 concern 문제, 우려 describe 서술하다, 묘사하다 respondent 응답자 insufficient 불충분한 lack 없다, 부족하다 seating capacity 좌석 수 break down 고장 나다 frequently 자주, 종종 thereby 그것 때문에 productive 생산적인 at times 가끔 ID 신분증 fail ~하지 못하다 lock out of 열쇠가 없어서 ~에 들어가지 못하다 dispose of ~을 처리하다 recyclable item 재활용품 break 휴식 period 시간 drab 칙칙한, 생기 없는

발신: jchandler@brandywinefinance.com
수신: jasminehoward@brandywinefinance.com
제목: 직원 설문조사 결과 보고서
날짜: 10월 11일

[188]**Ms. Howard,**
최근의 직원 설문조사에 대한 보고서 내에 데이터를 제공해 주셔서 감사합니다. IT 부서의 Luis Guarino와 이야기를 나눴는데, 그가 앞으로 컴퓨터를 더 잘 유지 관리하기 위해 최선을 다하겠다고 약속했습니다. 하지만 그는 많은 기계들이 교체되어야 한다는 것을 강조하더군요. 우리가 그렇게 할 충분한 자금이 있나요? 아마도 매달 몇 대씩 교체하는 방법으로 예산에 가해지는 부담을 최소화할 수 있을 겁니다. 이 문제에 대한 당신의 생각은 어떤가요?
[189-1]**리스트에 언급된 네 번째 문제와 관련하여, 우리가 작년에도 비슷한 문제가 있었던 것으로 기억합니다.** 저는 이 문제가 해결되었다고 믿었는데 제가 틀렸던 것이 분명하군요.
[188]**우리는 이 문제에 대해 빨리 회의를 해야 합니다. 언제 시간이 되세요?**
[188]**Jennifer Chandler**

어휘 assure 확언하다, 장담하다 maintain 유지하다 emphasize 강조하다 replace 교체하다, 대체하다 funding 자금 (제공) minimize 최소화하다 budget 예산 matter 문제, 사안 regarding ~에 관하여 list 리스트를 작성하다 recall 회상하다 be under the impression that ~라고 믿다 apparently 분명히, 명백히 available 시간이 있는

Aaron's Supplies
[190-1]**고객: Brandywine Finance**
날짜: 10월 17일

제품 사양	수량	단가	합계
[190-1]**안락 의자**, 검정색	8	95.00달러	760.00달러
		세금	45.60달러
		합계	805.60달러

저희에게서 주문해 주셔서 감사합니다. 주문하신 물품은 영업일 기준으로 2일 이내에 배송됩니다. 문의 사항이 있으시면 1-888-555-9375로 전화 주십시오.

어휘 supplies 물품, 공급품 item 물품 description 묘사, 설명 quantity 수량 unit price 단가 business day 영업일, 평일

186. 보고서에서 Brandywine Finance에 대해 암시된 것은 무엇인가?

(A) 적어도 두 개의 다른 건물에 입주해 있다.
(B) 환경 보호가 회사의 주요 관심사이다.
(C) 직원들은 자사의 직원 주차장에 주차할 수 있다.
(D) 많은 직원들이 개인 전용 사무실을 가지고 있지 않다.

해설 첫 번째 지문의 open-space office areas는 업무 공간이 개방되어 있다는 것을 의미하므로 (D)가 정답이다.

어휘 occupy 차지하다, 점유하다 at least 적어도, 최소한

187. 몇 퍼센트의 응답자가 큰 소음에 대해 불만스러워 했는가?
(A) 62%
(B) 27%
(C) 15%
(D) 7%

패러프레이즈 high noise levels → loud noises

188. Ms. Chandler는 Ms. Howard에게 무엇에 대해 질문하는가?
(A) 올해 예산에 남은 돈이 얼마인지
(B) 자기가 누구에게 보고서를 보내야 하는지
(C) 언제 몇 가지 문제를 논의할 시간이 있는지
(D) 문제가 해결되지 않는 이유가 무엇인지

어휘 budget 예산

189. Ms. Chandler에 따르면, 작년에 무슨 문제가 발생했는가?
(A) 신분증 카드가 가끔 작동하지 않았다.
(B) 직원들의 컴퓨터가 고장났다.
(C) 직원들에게 프라이버시가 충분하지 않았다.
(D) 직원들이 야근을 너무 많이 했다.

해설 연계 문제로서, Chandler로 지문을 검색하면, 두 번째 지문에서 이메일의 발신인인 Jennifer Chandler는 작년에도 네 번째 문제가 있었다고 언급했다. 다른 지문에서 네 번째 문제를 찾아보면, 첫 번째 지문에서 네 번째 문제는 신분증이 작동하지 않는 문제점이라는 것을 확인할 수 있으므로 (A)가 정답이다.

패러프레이즈 sometimes → on occasion

어휘 on occasion 가끔, 때때로 work overtime 야근하다

190. 보고서에서 언급된 어떤 문제가 Brandywine Finance가 Aaron's Supplies로부터 구매하게 만들었겠는가?
(A) 문제 1
(B) 문제 2
(C) 문제 3
(D) 문제 5

해설 연계 문제로서, 세 번째 지문인 청구서를 보면 Brandywine Finance가 안락 의자 8개를 구입했다는 것을 알 수 있다. 첫 번째 지문에서 안락 의자와 관련 있는 문제점을 찾아 보면 직원 휴게실의 좌석 부족(seating capacity)이다. 좌석 부족은 2번 문제이므로 (B)가 정답이다.

어휘 result in 그 결과 ~가 되다

191-195 안내 책자, 이메일, 이메일

Rosemont 놀이공원은 어린이들과 어른들에게 재미와 오락을 제공합니다. 옥스퍼드 시에 위치한 이 공원에는 20개 이상의 놀이기구, 오락실, 동물원, 음식점 시설, 그리고 기념품 상점들이 있습니다.
191 **우리는 모든 방문객들이 참가할 수 있는 특별한 프로그램들을 가지고 있습니다.**
6월 19일— Jasper 농장의 말들과 조랑말들이 방문객들이 쓰다듬고 탈 수 있도록 동물원에 있을 것입니다. 191 **회원 요금은 3달러, 비회원 요금은 5달러.**
195-2 **6월 26일— 코끼리 쇼를 보러 오세요.** 하루 종일 세 번의 공연이 있을 것입니다. 코끼리들이 무엇을 할 수 있는지 보세요. 공연이 끝난 후, 무대로 내려가서 코끼리들에게 먹이를 주세요.
191 **회원 요금은 10달러, 비회원 요금은 20달러.**
저희 웹사이트에서 각 행사의 티켓을 온라인으로 예약하세요. 또한 Rosemont 놀이공원의 회원으로 등록하실 수 있습니다.
192 **회원권으로 특별 행사를 이용할 수 있을 뿐만 아니라 입장권, 음식, 기념품에 대한 할인을 포함한 많은 혜택을 제공합니다.** 보다 자세히 알아보시려면 www.rosemontap.com/membership를 방문하세요.

어휘 amusement park 놀이공원 provide 제공하다, 주다 entertainment 오락, 여흥 ride 놀이기구 arcade 오락실 facility 시설 souvenir 기념품 pet 쓰다듬다, 어루만지다 nonmember 비회원 feed 먹이를 주다 reserve 예약하다 sign up 등록하다 benefit 혜택, 특전 access 접근, 입장

수신: rcraig@gladden.com
발신: membership@rosemontap.com
제목: 환영합니다
날짜: 6월 14일

Mr. Craig,

Rosemont 놀이공원에 회원으로 가입해 주셔서 감사합니다. 193 **가족 멤버십을 선택하셨기 때문에 귀하와 부인, 아드님, 그리고 따님이 멤버십의 혜택을 받게 될 것입니다.** 여러분 각자는 앞으로 3일 이내에 우편으로 회원 카드를 받게 됩니다. 194-1 **놀이공원에서 할인을 신청하실 때 반드시 카드를 이용하셔야 하며, 그렇지 않으면 전액을 지불하셔야 합니다.**
195-3 **놀이공원을 처음 방문하실 때 안내소에 들러서 귀하와 귀하의 가족들을 위한 특별한 선물을 받으세요.**

Tina Southern
Rosemont 놀이공원

어휘 select 고르다, 선택하다 apply for ~을 신청하다 stop by 잠시 들르다 pick up 찾다, 수령하다

수신: Tina Southern ⟨tina_s@rosemontap.com⟩
발신: Robert Craig ⟨rcraig@gladden.com⟩
제목: 요청
날짜: 7월 5일

Ms. Southern,

194-2, 195-1 **저와 제 가족이 최근에 회원 자격으로 귀사의 놀이공원을 방문했을 때, 집에 카드를 두고 온 제 아내가 코끼리 쇼를 보려면 비회원 가격을 지불해야 한다는 말을 들었을 때의 저희의 놀라움을 상상해 보세요. 저는 추가 비용을 지불했지만, 환불해 주시면 감사하겠습니다.** 제가 다음에 공원을 방문할 때 돈을 받으러 갈 수 있습니다.

195-1 **그건 그렇고, 저희가 받은 소풍 바구니는 감사합니다. 사려 깊은 선물이었어요.**

Robert Craig

어휘 inform 알리다, 통지하다 appreciate 감사하다, 고마워하다 refund 환불 thoughtful 사려 깊은

191. Rosemont 놀이공원에 대해 나타난 것은 무엇인가?
(A) 특별 프로그램에 추가 요금을 부과한다.
(B) 최초 방문객들에게 할인을 제공한다.
(C) 곧 동물원을 지을 계획을 가지고 있다.
(D) 주로 어린이들을 위한 놀이기구를 보유하고 있다.

해설 첫 번째 지문에서 말과 코끼리와 관련된 특별 프로그램에는 추가 요금이 있다는 것을 알리고 있으므로 (A)가 정답이다. 첫 번째 지문의 서두에서 놀이기구는 성인들도 이용할 수 있다고 했으므로 (D)는 오답이다.

어휘 charge 부과하다 extra 추가의; 추가되는 것 first-time 처음으로 해 보는 mostly 주로

192. Rosemont 놀이공원의 회원이 되는 것의 이점이 아닌 것은 무엇인가?
(A) 저렴한 입장료
(B) 특별 행사 이용
(C) 음식에 대한 할인
(D) 연말 축하 행사에 초대

어휘 admission 입장(료) access to ~에 대한 이용, ~에의 접근 celebration 축하 (행사)

193. 첫 번째 이메일에 따르면 사실인 것은 무엇인가?
(A) 회원권의 가격이 최근에 올랐다.
(B) 안내소가 수리를 위해 문을 닫았다.
(C) 회원 카드는 공원에서 수령할 수 있다.
(D) Craig 가족의 모든 사람들이 새로운 회원이다.

194. Mr. Craig의 요청이 거절될 가능성이 높은 이유는 무엇인가?
(A) 신청 날짜가 이미 지났다.
(B) 공원 측은 환불을 거부한다.
(C) 회원 카드가 제시되지 않았다.
(D) 성인들은 요금 할인을 받을 자격이 없다.

해설 연계 문제로서, 두 번째 지문에서 놀이공원에서 할인을 신청할 때는 반드시 멤버십 카드를 이용하라고 했는데, 세 번째 지문에서 Robert Craig는 집에 카드를 두고 가서 비회원 가격을 지불했고 그 차액만큼을 환불 받기를 원하고 있다. 회원 카드가 제시되지 않았기 때문에 환불 요청은 거절될 가능성이 크므로 (C)가 정답이다.

어휘 application 신청(서) give a refund 환불해 주다 present 제시하다 be eligible for ~할 자격이 있다

195. Craig 가족에 대해 유추할 수 있는 것은 무엇인가?
(A) 그들은 온라인으로 코끼리 쇼 티켓을 예약했다.
(B) 그들은 놀이공원에서 몇 개의 놀이기구를 탔다.
(C) 그들은 6월 26일에 안내소를 방문했다.
(D) 그들은 놀이공원에서 저녁을 먹었다.

해설 연계 문제로서, 세 번째 지문에서 Robert Craig는 자신의 가족이 놀이공원에 코끼리 쇼를 보러 가서 소풍 바구니를 선물로 받았다고 했는데, 첫 번째 지문에서 코끼리 쇼는 6월 26일에 있다는 정보를 확인할 수 있고, 두 번째 지문에서 신규 회원은 첫 방문 시 놀이공원 안내소에서 선물을 받을 수 있다는 정보를 확인할 수 있다. Craig 가족은 6월 26일에 놀이공원을 처음 방문해서 안내소에서 선물을 받았다는 것을 알 수 있으므로 (C)가 정답이다.

어휘 reserve 예약하다

196-200 웹사이트, 이메일, 이메일

196 **블랙 포레스트 주립 공원은 가장 큰 지역 공원이지만, 주에서 방문객이 가장 적습니다.** 잠재적인 관광객들이 공원을 알아보는 것을 돕기 위해, 우리는 버추얼 가이드를 만들었습니다. 그것은 방문객들이 공원에서 가장 좋은 장소를 볼 수 있도록 하고, 그들이 그곳에서 무엇을 할 수 있는지를 찾을 수 있도록 해줄 것입니다. 가이드는 지역의 캠핑장, 호텔, 식당에 대한 링크도 제공합니다.

198-2 **버추얼 가이드를 이용하시려면 먼저 여기에서 당사 웹사이트에 등록하십시오.** 그렇게 하면 가이드를 제한 없이 이용할 수 있게 됩니다. 공원 내의 장소뿐만 아니라 공원 주변의 장소도 예약할 수 있습니다.

197 **시간이 있을 때 가이드를 확인해 보시고, 여러분의 의견을 우리에게 알려주세요.** 우리는 방문자들이 다른 사람들의 의견을 볼 수 있도록 댓글 기능을 곧 추가할 예정입니다.

질문이나 의견이 있으면 information@blackforestpark.gov로 문의해 주십시오.

어휘 state 주, 국가 yet 그렇지만 potential 잠재적인, 가능성 있는 explore 알아보다, 탐험하다 virtual (컴퓨터를 이용한) 가상의 guide 가이드, 안내원 spot 곳, 장소 campground 캠핑장 register 등록하다 have access to ~에 접근할 수 있다, 출입할 수 있다 comment 의견을 말하다; 의견

수신: information@blackforestpark.gov
발신: lkeller@miltonhikingclub.org
제목: 하이킹 코스
날짜: 3월 28일

관계자 귀하,

198-1 **저는 귀사의 버추얼 가이드에 깊은 인상을 받았습니다.** 저는 공원을 많이 가보았는데 특히 음식점 시설과 같은 몇몇 곳을 모르고 있었습니다. 나중에 그곳들을 확인해 봐야겠네요.
한 가지 궁금한 것이 있습니다. 스완 레이크를 둘러싼 하이킹 코스를 찾을 수가 없더군요. 동계 악천후 때문에 코스가 폐쇄되었나요? 제가 4월 4일에 공원을 방문할 계획인데, 그 하이킹 코스

는 제 일순위이거든요. [200-1] **저희 단체에는 27명이 있는데 변경이 필요할 수도 있으니 알려주십시오.**

Lisa Keller
Milton 하이킹 동호회, 회장

어휘 hiking trail 하이킹 코스 to whom it may concern 담당자 귀하 impressed 감명을 받은 numerous 많은 occasion 경우, 때 be unaware of ~을 알지 못하다 dining establishment 식당 locate 위치를 찾다 inclement 궂은, 좋지 않은

수신: lkeller@miltonhikingclub.org
발신: information@blackforestpark.gov
제목: 회신: 하이킹 코스
날짜: 3월 29일

Ms. Keller,

[199] **우리가 간과하고 있던 것을 알려 주셔서 감사합니다. 필요한 정보는 바로 가이드에 추가될 것입니다.** 다른 틀린 것이 발견되면 fchapman@blackforestpark.gov으로 제게 연락 주십시오. 다른 문제점들도 즉시 처리하겠습니다.
단체에는 새로운 입장료가 부과된다는 것을 알려 드립니다. 이제 다음과 같은 요금이 적용됩니다:

단체 규모	요금
10-15명	20달러
16-25명	30달러
[200-2] **26-40명**	**50달러**
41명 이상	70달러

공원에서 멋진 시간을 보내기를 바라겠습니다.

Fred Chapman
공원 관리인

어휘 bring ~ to one's attention ~에게 ~을 알게 해주다 oversight 간과, 실수 add 추가하다, 더하다 at once 즉시 be advised that ~을 명심하다 admission fee 입장료 rate 요금 apply 적용하다 ranger 공원 관리원

196. 웹사이트에 따르면, 블랙 포레스트 주립 공원에 대해 사실인 것은 무엇인가?
(A) 모든 방문객은 양식을 작성해야 한다.
(B) 그곳에 가는 사람은 그리 많지 않다.
(C) 공원 관리인들은 그곳에서 투어를 제공한다.
(D) 전국에서 가장 큰 공원이다.

197. 버추얼 가이드의 이용자들은 무엇을 하라는 요청을 받는가?
(A) 사진 업로드하기
(B) 다른 사람들에게 링크를 보내기
(C) 의견을 제공하기
(D) 회원권을 구입하기

패러프레이즈 let us know what you think → provide feedback

어휘 upload 업로드하다

198. Ms. Keller에 대해 암시된 것은 무엇인가?
(A) 전에 공원에서 자원봉사를 한 적이 있다.
(B) 공원의 웹사이트에 등록했다.
(C) 최근에 하이킹 동호회를 시작했다.
(D) 매주 공원을 방문한다.

해설 연계 문제로서, Ms. Keller는 첫 번째 이메일의 발신자로 버추얼 가이드에 깊은 인상을 받았다고 말한다. 그리고 첫 번째 지문에는 버추얼 가이드를 이용하려면 웹사이트에 등록해야 한다는 내용이 나온다. 따라서 Lisa Keller는 웹사이트에 등록하고 버추얼 가이드를 체험했다는 것을 유추할 수 있으므로 (B)가 정답이다.

패러프레이즈 register → signed up

어휘 volunteer 자원하다 recently 최근에 on a weekly basis 매주, 주마다

199. 두 번째 이메일의 한 가지 목적은 무엇인가?
(A) 예약을 확인하려고
(B) 실수를 인정하려고
(C) 연락처 정보를 요청하려고
(D) 새로운 관광지를 제안하려고

어휘 confirm 확정하다 booking 예약 acknowledge 인정하다 attraction 관광지

200. Ms. Keller의 일행은 공원을 방문할 때 얼마를 지불하겠는가?
(A) 20달러
(B) 30달러
(C) 50달러
(D) 70달러

해설 연계 문제로서, 두 번째 지문에서 Lisa Keller는 27명이 참여하는 하이킹을 계획하고 있다고 말한다. 그리고 세 번째 지문에서 27명이 속하는 단체 입장료는 50달러이므로, Lisa Keller는 입장료로 50달러를 지불하게 될 것이다. 따라서 (C)가 정답이다.

정답 및 해설

에듀윌 토익 단기완성 850+

정답 및 해설

고객의 꿈, 직원의 꿈, 지역사회의 꿈을 실현한다

펴낸곳 (주)에듀윌 **펴낸이** 김재환 **출판총괄** 오용철
개발책임 이순옥 **개발** 김기상, 박은석, Corey Steiner
주소 서울시 구로구 디지털로34길 55 코오롱싸이언스밸리 2차 3층
대표번호 1600-6700 **등록번호** 제25100-2002-000052호

에듀윌 도서몰 book.eduwill.net
• 부가학습자료 및 정오표: 에듀윌 도서몰 → 도서자료실
• 교재 문의: 에듀윌 도서몰 → 문의하기 → 교재(내용, 출간) / 주문 및 배송

업계 최초 대통령상 3관왕,
정부기관상 19관왕 달성!

2010 대통령상 / 2019 대통령상 / 2019 대통령상

대한민국 브랜드대상 국무총리상

국무총리상

문화체육관광부 장관상

농림축산식품부 장관상

과학기술정보통신부 장관상

여성가족부장관상

서울특별시장상

과학기술부장관상

정보통신부장관상

산업자원부장관상

고용노동부장관상

미래창조과학부장관상

법무부장관상

- 2004
  서울특별시장상 우수벤처기업 대상
- 2006
  부총리 겸 과학기술부장관 표창 국가 과학 기술 발전 유공
- 2007
  정보통신부장관상 디지털콘텐츠 대상
  산업자원부장관 표창 대한민국 e비즈니스대상
- 2010
  대통령 표창 대한민국 IT 이노베이션 대상
- 2013
  고용노동부장관 표창 일자리 창출 공로
- 2014
  미래창조과학부장관 표창 ICT Innovation 대상
- 2015
  법무부장관 표창 사회공헌 유공
- 2017
  여성가족부장관상 사회공헌 유공
  2016 합격자 수 최고 기록 KRI 한국기록원 공식 인증
- 2018
  2017 합격자 수 최고 기록 KRI 한국기록원 공식 인증
- 2019
  대통령 표창 범죄예방대상
  대통령 표창 일자리 창출 유공
  과학기술정보통신부장관상 대한민국 ICT 대상
- 2020
  국무총리상 대한민국 브랜드대상
  2019 합격자 수 최고 기록 KRI 한국기록원 공식 인증
- 2021
  고용노동부장관상 일·생활 균형 우수 기업 공모전 대상
  문화체육관광부장관 표창 근로자휴가지원사업 우수 참여 기업
  농림축산식품부장관상 대한민국 사회공헌 대상
  문화체육관광부장관 표창 여가친화기업 인증 우수 기업
- 2022
  국무총리 표창 일자리 창출 유공
  농림축산식품부장관상 대한민국 ESG 대상